Pearson Education

## AP* Test Prep Series

# AP*ECONOMICS

*to accompany*
**Foundations of Economics
AP* Edition**

**By Robin Bade and Michael Parkin**

**Margaret Pride,** *St. Louis High School*

**Sandra Wright,** *Adlai E. Stevenson High School*

**Mark Rush,** *Editor*
*University of Florida*

PEARSON
Addison
Wesley

Boston  San Francisco  New York
London  Toronto  Sydney  Tokyo  Singapore  Madrid
Mexico City  Munich  Paris  Cape Town  Hong Kong  Montreal

ISBN    0-13-173078-9

2 3 4 5 6 BB 09 08 07

PEARSON

Addison
Wesley

# Table of Contents

# Your AP* Test

## ■ Introduction

We know when you use this workbook, you have one paramount goal: To pass your AP* test. However, after you finish your class, you will realize that much more has occurred. You will understand the language of economics, and you will be able to integrate economic concepts into your everyday experiences. You will make more informed personal decisions, and you will better understand economic issues highlighted in the media. In short, you will see the world in a fresh perspective and new light. It is these facts that make economics so exciting and also a core competency for responsible citizens.

## ■ Your Textbook and Your AP Test Prep Workbook

Each chapter in your textbook is divided into Checkpoints. These Checkpoints are smaller sections that revolve around a key point. These divisions provide a logical and understandable framework for the material you are learning. At the end of each Checkpoint is a page that offers you a Practice Problem to test your understanding of the key ideas of the part, a worked and illustrated solution to the Practice Problem, and a further (parallel) exercise. The Checkpoints enable you to review material when it's fresh in your mind—the most effective and productive time to do so. The Checkpoints guide you through the material in a step-by-step approach that takes the guesswork out of learning.

This AP Test Prep Workbook follows the same Checkpoint divisions. Each chapter in this workbook has a Chapter Summary that summarizes the material using the same Checkpoints. For each Checkpoint the workbook has additional worked and illustrated Practice Problems to help insure your grasp of the material. Following these are Self-Test questions. These questions are designed to help you learn the material to answer the questions you will encounter on your AP test. There are multiple choice, short response and long response questions. There also are true and false questions. While the AP test does not have true and false questions, the questions in your workbook are designed to tackle a definition or calculation that you might see on your AP exam.

In addition to the Checkpoints, each chapter of your textbook also opens with a Chapter Checklist that tells you what you'll be able to do when you've completed the chapter. This AP Test Prep Workbook has an extended Chapter Checklist after the Chapter Summary. These Checklists alert you about what is important and what you should learn as you study the material.

---

\* AP, Pre-AP, Advanced Placement, and Advanced Placement Program are registered trademarks of The College Entrance Examination Board, which was not involved in the production of, and does not endorse, this product.

Make these Checkpoints and the Checklists work for you! To learn economics you have to do economics. The Checklist-Checkpoint system provides you with a structure for doing just that. To make it work for you, start by familiarizing yourself with the Checklist at the opening to each chapter in the textbook: it tells you where you'll be heading. As you progress through the chapter, you'll see that each major section corresponds to one of the Checklist items. After studying each section, be sure to work the Checkpoint in the textbook! That's the time to reinforce what you've just read—while it's still fresh in your mind. The number of tasks varies from two to five and most often is three or four.

After your work the Checkpoint in the text, you face a choice: For more immediate reinforcement, you can immediately switch to the questions (and answers) for the Checkpoint in this workbook. Or you can use this book as a chapter review by working with it only after you have completed the chapter in the textbook. Which procedure will work best for you? That is a question you must answer. Perhaps you can try them both and see which is superior. But, regardless of the answer, remember the most important point: To learn economics you have to do economics!

This workbook contains an additional section that can be of incredible worth, a section called "Your AP Test Hints." You should review this section *very* carefully. It has hints and insights that may prove invaluable on your AP test. In addition, *be sure* to work the problems in the last chapter of this workbook, the "AP Graphing Question" chapter. These problems will increase your skill in using what you have learned to answer questions that are similar to what you will be asked on your AP test.

## ■ How to Use Your AP Test Prep Workbook To Succeed on Your AP Test

No matter whether you choose to use this workbook while you are studying a chapter in the textbook or after you have completed the textbook chapter, there are a few hints we can offer about how to best use this book.

### Chapter in Perspective

This first section is a short summary of the key material. It is designed to focus you quickly and precisely on the core material that you must master. It is an excellent study aid for the night before your AP test. Think of it as notes that serve as a final check of the key concepts you have studied.

### Additional Practice Problems

The practice problems in each checkpoint in the textbook are extremely valuable because they help you do economics in order to grasp what you have just studied. In this workbook are additional Practice Problems to help you do more economics. Although the answer is given to the additional Practice Problem, try to solve it on your own before reading the answer.

Following the additional Practice Problem is the Self Test section. These questions are designed to give you practice and to test skills and techniques you must master to do well on your AP test. Before we describe the parts of the Self Test section, here are some general tips that apply to all parts.

Use a pencil to write your answers. Write your answers in the workbook so you have neat, complete pages from which to study. Draw graphs wherever they are applicable. Some questions will ask explicitly for graphs; others will not but will require a chain of reasoning that involves shifts of curves on a graph. Always draw the graph. Don't try to work through the reasoning in your head — you are much more likely to make mistakes that way. Whenever you draw a graph, even in the margins of this book, label the axes. You might think that you can keep the labels in your head, but you will be confronting many different graphs with many different variables on the axes. Avoid confusion and label. As an added incentive, remember that on your AP exam, you will lose points for unlabelled axes.

Do the Self Test questions as if they were real exam questions, which means do them without looking at the answers. This is the single most important tip we can give you about effectively using this workbook to improve your exam performance. Struggling for the answers to questions that you find difficult is one of the most effective ways to learn. The adage — no pain, no gain — applies well to studying. You will learn the most from right answers you had to struggle for and from your wrong answers and mistakes. Only after you have attempted all the questions should you look at the answers. When you finally do check the answers, be sure to understand where you went wrong and why the right answer is correct.

### True or False

First are a few true or false questions. The AP test does *not* have true or false questions. But we think these questions are a highly effective way to learn important definitions or facts so do not skip them. The answers to the questions (indeed, the answers to all the questions) are given at the end of the chapter. The answer also has a page reference to the textbook. If you missed the question or did not completely understand the answer, definitely turn to the textbook and study the topic so that you will not miss similar questions on your exams.

### Multiple Choice

As we describe below, multiple choice questions are a major important component of your AP test, so pay particular attention to these questions. The answers are given at the end of the chapter. If you had any difficulty with a question, use the textbook page reference in the answer to look up the topic and then study it to remove this potential weakness.

### Short Response and Long Response Questions

The other major component of your AP test will be short response and long response questions. The last two sections of questions in this workbook are designed to ensure that you are well prepared to handle these questions. Most checkpoints have both short response and long response questions, though a few have only one style of question. Although the answer is given at the end of the chapter, as we said above do *not* look at the answer before you attempt to solve the problem. It is much too easy to deceive yourself into thinking you understand the answer when you simply look at the question and then read the answer. Involve yourself in the material by answering the question and then looking at the answer. If you cannot answer the question or if you got the answer wrong, use the reference to the page number in the text to study the material.

These questions are also excellent for use in a study group. If you and several friends are studying, you can use these questions to quiz your understanding. If you have disagreements about the correct answers, use the page references to the text so that you can settle these disagreements and be sure that everyone has a solid grasp of the point!

It is an extremely safe bet that you will be expected to use graphs on at least some of the questions on your AP test. So many of these questions require that you use a graph as part of your answer. In addition, save the last chapter, Chapter 36, until a week or so before the end of your class or before your AP test. The broad questions in this chapter all require that you use a graph to answer them. They serve as the workbook's "final exam" and so should be among the last topics you study.

## ■ Your AP Test

The AP Economics Examinations make use of a variety of question types and graphical analysis to assess the skill level of AP students. The AP examinations reflect the types of assessment that occur at the college level.

The AP Economics Examinations take two hours and 10 minutes to complete. In both the multiple-choice and free-response sections of the exams, you can expect to work with graphs, charts, and tables. Each examination consists of a 70-minute, multiple-choice section and a 60-minute free-response section that may require graphical analysis. The free-response section begins with a mandatory 10-minute reading period that can be used to read each of the questions, sketch graphs, make notes, and plan answers in the green insert. You then have 50 minutes to write the answers in the pink booklet.

The AP Economics Examinations contain these distinct question types:
- Definition or identification questions
- Graph or table questions
- Analysis or cause and effect questions
- Multiple-choice questions

### Multiple Choice

The multiple-choice section of each exam contains 60 questions, with 70 minutes allotted for Section I. The multiple-choice section accounts for 2/3 of your examination grade. As is the case for the multiple choice questions in this workbook, each question has five choices and only one choice is judged correct. The questions are straightforward, and many require analysis and interpretation. Some will require analysis of a graph, chart, or table.

The questions are machine scored and determined by crediting one point for a correct answer and by deducting 1/4 of a point for an incorrect answer. No points are gained or lost for unanswered questions. If you have no idea what the correct answer is, leave the answer blank. But, if you can eliminate two or more of the five choices, you should make an educated guess.

### Free Response

The free-response section begins with a mandatory 10-minute reading period, during which you are encouraged to read the questions, sketch graphs, make notes, and plan answers in the green insert. You then have 50 minutes to write your answers in the pink booklet. There will be three questions, one longer and two shorter.

The free-response questions in Section II of each exam will require you to analyze a given economic situation and use economic principles to explain answers. Using explanatory diagrams that clarify the analysis and clearly explain the reasoning results in the greatest number of points. Sometimes a graph is given as part of the question and your task is to derive the answer from the graph data. Generally, the longer free-response questions require you to interrelate several content areas, while the two shorter free-response questions focus on a specific topic in a given content area.

This section of the exam is 1/3 of the score. The raw score for Section II is composed of the scores from the three questions and then apportioned according to value assigned to each (the larger question is 50 percent of the score and the two smaller questions are each 25 percent of score.)

## ■ Taking Your AP Test

### Multiple Choice Hints

- Remember to sort through the choices. Eliminate quickly those answer choices you know are incorrect. You will feel comfortable with the test format if you have studied the questions in this book.

- You have 70 minutes to answer 60 multiple-choice questions, so don't spend too much time on any one question. You don't need to get every multiple-choice question right to score well on the AP Economics exam.

- Make sure that you first answer all the questions that you know rather than answering the questions in consecutive order. Put a mark in the test booklet next to the questions that you cannot easily answer and return to them later. Often your subconscious will be working on these questions and you will see the answer the second time you look at the question, so make sure to give yourself enough time to return. Remember that questions are random and disconnected so do not carry an assumption from one question to the next.

- Practice all the assignments in this book and accompanying resources. That strategy will build your confidence on test day. With confidence, your mindset, approach, and score should benefit.

## Free Response Hints

- A 10-minute reading period begins the free-response portion of the AP Economics exam. This time gives you an opportunity to read the questions and plan for the answers. You can sketch an answer in the test booklet (this is the page with the question); however, you cannot open your answer book (blank pages for your answer) and write the answer. When planning, pay attention to how the parts of a question might influence or be related to sequential subquestions. This might help you to confirm that you are answering a section completely or heading in the right direction.

- Remember that time might be an issue so allocate your time appropriately for the weighting of the questions asked. You have 25 minutes for the first essay and 12 minutes for each of the remaining two. If you used the 10-minute planning period well, you should have no problem finishing this section.

- Use correct terminology. Learn and use the correct language of economics.

- You may answer the questions in any order, but clearly indicate which question is being addressed. Use the same outline numbers or letters from the question in your answer, and answer them in the same order. The questions are divided into parts such as (a), (b), (c), and (d), with each part calling for a different response. Attempt to answer them all since points are earned independently. If the answer to a later part of a question depends on the answer to an earlier part, you may still be able to receive points for the later part, even if the earlier answer is wrong. If you write nothing for a subsection, you will receive nothing; if you write at least a partial answer, you may well receive partial credit.

- If the question requires you to draw a graph, it is important, if asked, to explain what the graph shows. Label graphs clearly, correctly, and fully. Label the curves and the axes. Changes in curves should be indicated clearly with arrows or clear sequencing, such as showing a change in a supply curve with the first curve labeled $S$ or $S_1$ and the second curve labeled $S'$ or $S_2$. You should also indicate the initial equilibrium and the final equilibrium by clearly labeling the points in the figure and then referring to them in your answer.

- Recall the terms used in your practice questions and exercises. All assertions, such as "the price increased," should explain the reason.

- If there is time, review your answers, always asking whether or not you have answered the question directly.

## ■ AP Economics Correlation Charts

This chart correlates the Advanced Placement Microeconomics topics as outlined by The College Board with the corresponding chapters and section numbers in *Foundations of Economics*, AP Edition. Use this chart to help you quickly find a topic you want to study or review.

| AP Microeconomic Topics | Textbook Chapters and Checkpoints |
|---|---|
| **I. Basic Economic Concepts** | **Chapters 1, 2, 3** |
| A. Scarcity, Choice, and Opportunity Costs | 1.1, 1.2, 3.2, 12.1 |
| B. Production Possibility Curve | 3.1 |
| C. Comparative Advantage, Specialization, and Trade | 3.5, 34.2 |
| D. Circular Flow | 2.2 |
| E. Property Rights and Role of Incentives | 1.2, 9.1 |
| F. Marginal Analysis | 1.2, 3.3 |
| **II. Nature and Functions of Product Markets** | **Chapters 4, 5, 6, 7, 8, 11, 12, 13, 14, 15, 16, 17** |
| A. Supply and Demand | Chapter 4 |
|   1. Market equilibrium | 4.3 |
|   2. Determinants of supply and demand | 4.1, 4.2 |
|   3. Price and quantity controls | Chapter 7 |
|     a. Price ceiling | 7.1 |
|     b. Price floor | 7.2 |
|     c. Production quota | 7.3 |
|   4. Elasticity | Chapter 5 |
|     a. Price elasticity of demand | 5.1 |
|     b. Income and cross-price | 5.3 |
|     c. Price elasticity of supply | 5.2 |
|   5. Consumer surplus, producer surplus, and market efficiency | 6.2, 6.3, 6.4 |
|   6. Tax incidence and deadweight loss | 8.1 |
| B. Theory of Consumer Choice | Chapter 11 |
|   1. Total utility and marginal utility | 11.2 |
|   2. Utility maximization: equalizing marginal utility per dollar | 11.2 |
|   3 Income and substitution effects | This *AP Test Prep Workbook* |
| C. Production and Costs | Chapter 12 |
|   1. Production functions: short and long run | 12.2 |
|   2. Marginal product and diminishing returns | 12.2 |
|   3. Short-run costs | 12.3 |
|   4. Long-run costs and economies of scale | 12.4 |
|   5. Cost minimizing input combination | This *AP Test Prep Workbook* |
| D. Firm Behavior and Market Structure | Chapters 12, 13, 14, 15, 16 |
|   1. Profit | Chapters 12, 13 |
|     a. Accounting versus economic profit | 12.1 |

This chart correlates the Advanced Placement Macroeconomics topics as outlined by The College Board with the corresponding chapters and section numbers in Foundations of Economics, AP Edition. Use this chart to help you quickly find a topic you want to study or review.

| AP Macroeconomic Topics | Textbook Chapters and Checkpoints |
|---|---|
| **I. Basic Economic Concepts** | **Chapters 1, 3, 4, 20, 21, 22** |
|     A. Scarcity, Choice, and Opportunity Cost | 1.1, 1.2 |
|     B. Production Possibilities Curve | 3.1 |
|     C. Comparative Advantage, Specialization, and Exchange | 3.5, 34.2 |
|     D. Demand, Supply, and Market Equilibrium | 4.1, 4.2, 4.3 |
|     E. Macroeconomic Issues: Business Cycle, Unemployment, Inflation, Growth | Chapters 20, 21, 22 |
| **II. Measurement of Economic Performance** | |
|     A. National Income Accounts | Chapter 20 |
|       1. Circular flow | 2.2, 20.1 |
|       2. Gross domestic product | 20.1, 20.2 |
|       3. Components of gross domestic product | 20.1 |
|       4. Real versus nominal gross domestic product | 20.3 |
|     B. Inflation Measurement and Adjustment | Chapters 22, 28 |
|       1. Price indices | 22.1, 22.2 |
|       2. Nominal and real values | 22.3 |
|       3. Costs of inflation | 28.3 |
|     C. Unemployment | Chapter 21 |
|       1. Definition and measurement | 21.1 |
|       2. Types of unemployment | 21.3 |
|       3. Natural rate of unemployment | 21.3, 23.1, 23.2 |
| **III. National Income and Price Determination** | |
|     A. Aggregate Demand | Chapter 29 |
|       1. Determinants of aggregate demand | 29.3, 30.1, 30.2, 30.3, 30.4 |
|       2. Multiplier and crowding-out effects | 24.3, 30.3 |
|     B. Aggregate Supply | Chapter 29 |
|       1. Short-run and long-run analyses | 23.1, 30.1, 30.2, 32.1, 32.2 |
|       2. Sticky versus flexible wages and prices | 32.1, 32.2 |
|       3. Determinants of aggregate supply | 29.2 |
|     C. Macroeconomic Equilibrium | Chapters 21, 23, 29, 32 |
|       1. Real output and price level | 29.4 |
|       2. Short and long run | 32.1, 32.2 |
|       3. Actual versus full-employment output | 21.3, 23.1, 29.4 |
|       4. Economic fluctuations | 29.4 |

## ■ Ending Thoughts

In writing this book, we had the privilege of working with many talented instructors. We worked with and managed contributions from Carl Coates, Bruce L. Damasio, Joy Joyce, Vanessa Lal, Matt Pedlow, and Amy Shrout. Pamela Schmitt deserves special thanks for her accuracy checking. She went well beyond what we expected and vastly improved the quality of the workbook. Finally, the sponsoring editor, Adrienne D'Ambrosio provided guidance and motivation for us. It is fair to say that without her help and insight, this workbook would never have been written.

We have tried to make this AP Workbook as helpful and useful as possible. Undoubtedly we have made some mistakes; mistakes that you may see. If you find any, we, and succeeding generations of students, would be grateful if you could point them out to us. If you have questions, suggestions, or simply comments, please let us know by emailing Mark Rush at MARK.RUSH@CBA.UFL.EDU.

Peggy Pride, Sandra Wright, and Mark Rush

# Chapter 1

## Getting Started

Chapter 1 defines economics, discusses the three major questions of *what, how,* and *for whom,* covers the five core economic ideas that shape how economists think about issues, defines the differences between microeconomics and macroeconomics, and examines methods used by economists to study the economic world.

■ **Define economics and explain the kinds of questions that economist try to answer.**

Economic questions exist because of scarcity, the point that wants exceed the ability of resources to satisfy them. Economics is the social science that studies the choices that individuals, businesses, government, and entire societies make as they cope with scarcity and the incentives that influence these choices. Economics studies how choices wind up determining: *what* goods and services get produced?; *how* are goods and services produced?; and *for whom* are goods and services produced? Economics also studies when choices made in someone's self-interest also serve the social interest. For instance, are the self-interested choices made about globalization and international outsourcing, use of tropical rain forests, and social security also promote the social interest about these issues?

■ **Explain the core ideas that define the economic way of thinking.**

The five ideas that are the core of the economic approach: people make rational choices by comparing benefits and costs; cost is what you must give up to get something; benefit is what you gain when you get something and is measured by what you are willing to give up to get it; a rational choice is made on the margin; and choices respond to incentives. A rational choice uses the available resources to most effectively satisfy the wants of the person making the choice. The opportunity cost of an activity is the highest-valued alternative forgone. The benefit of a good or service is the gain or pleasure it brings and is measured by what someone is willing to give up to get the good or service. Making choices on the margin means comparing all the relevant alternatives systematically and incrementally to determine which is the best choice. A choice on the margin is one that adjusts a plan. The marginal cost is the cost of a one-unit increase in an activity; the marginal benefit is the gain from a one-unit increase in an activity. Rational choices compare the marginal benefit of an activity to its marginal cost. Microeconomics studies choices made by individuals and businesses. Macroeconomics studies the national economy and global economy. Statements about "what is" are positive statements; statements about "what should be" are normative statements. Economists are interested in positive statements about cause and effect but determining causality can be difficult because usually many things change simultaneously. So economists often use the idea of *ceteris paribus,* a Latin term that means "other things equal" and is used to sort out the effect of individual influence. Correlation is the tendency for the values of two variables to move together in a predictable way. Economics can be used by individuals, business, and governments as a policy tool to help them make better decisions.

## EXPANDED CHAPTER CHECKLIST

**When you have completed this chapter, you will be able to:**

**1 Define economics and explain the kinds of questions that economist try to answer.**

- Define economics and explain the meaning of scarcity.
- Discuss the "how," "what," and "for whom" questions and be able to identify which question a particular issue involves.
- Contrast and explain the difference between "self-interest" and "social interest."

**2 Explain the core ideas that define the economic way of thinking.**

- Define rational choice and explain why a rational choice is made on the margin.
- Define opportunity cost.
- Define benefit.
- Define marginal cost and marginal benefit.
- Explain the role of incentives in making rational choices.
- Distinguish between macroeconomics and microeconomics and discuss what subjects each studies.
- Explain the difference between positive and normative statements.
- Define *ceteris paribus* and explain why it is used in economic models.
- Discuss what it means for two variables to be correlated.

## YOUR AP TEST HINTS

### AP Topics

| Topic on your AP test | Corresponding textbook section |
| --- | --- |
| **Basic economic concepts** | |
| Scarcity, Choice, Opportunity Cost | Chapter 1 |
| • Scarcity | Checkpoint 1.1 |
| • Opportunity cost | Checkpoint 1.2 |

### Extra AP material

- Depending on how an economy is structured to answer the "how," "what," and "for whom" questions, it can be classified as a "free market," "command," or "mixed" economy. A free market economy answers these questions using private ownership of capital (so that individuals own the business firms) and markets that are left free of government regulation. A command economy answers the same questions using public ownership of capital (so that the government owns the business firms) and government planners telling businesses what and how they will produce. A mixed economy uses elements of both. Some mixed economies use more free market aspects and others use more command elements.

## CHECKPOINT 1.1

**■ Define economics and explain the kinds of questions that economist try to answer.**

### Quick Review

- *Self-interest* The choices that people make that they think are the best for them.
- *Social interest* The choices that are best for society as a whole.

### Additional Practice Problems 1.1

1. Which of the following headlines deals with *what, how,* and *for whom* questions?:
   a. A new government program is designed to provide high-quality school lunches for children from poorer families.
   b. Intel researchers discover a new chip-making technology.
   c. Regis Hairstyling sets a record for hair-stylings in month of July

2. Which of the following headlines concern social interest and self interest?
   a. A new government program is designed

to provide high-quality school lunches for children from poorer families.

b. Intel researchers discover a new chip-making technology.

c. Regis Hairstyling sets a record for hairstylings in month of July.

## Solutions to Additional Practice Problems 1.1

1a. "More lunches" is a *what* question and "for children from poorer families" is a *for whom* question.

1b. "New chip-making technology" is a *how* question because it deals with how computer chips will be manufactured.

1c. "Record for hairstylings" is a *what* question because it notes that a record number of hairstylings have taken place in July.

2a. The decision to implement a new government program is a decision that is most likely made in the social interest. The self-interest of the government bureaucrat who made the decision might also be involved, particularly if the bureaucrat also will help manage the program.

2b. Intel's decision to research new chip-making technology is made in Intel's self-interest.

2c. Regis's decision to offer hairstylings is made in its self-interest as are the decisions of the people who had their hair styled by Regis.

## ■ AP Self Test 1.1

### True or false

1. Faced with scarcity, we must make choices.

2. The question of *what* refers to what production method should a firm use?

3. The answers to the *what, how* and *for whom* questions depend on the interactions of the choices people, businesses, and governments make.

4. If Sam buys a pizza because she is hungry, her choice is made in the social interest.

5. Because everyone is a member of society, all choices made in self-interest are also in the social interest.

### Multiple choice

1. The characteristic from which all economic problems arise is
   a. political decisions.
   b. providing a minimal standard of living for every person.
   c. how to make a profit.
   d. hunger.
   e. scarcity.

2. Scarcity results from the fact that
   a. people's wants exceed the resources available to satisfy them.
   b. not all goals are desirable.
   c. we cannot answer the major economic questions.
   d. choices made in self-interest are not always in the social interest.
   e. the population keeps growing.

3. To economists, scarcity means that
   a. limited wants cannot be satisfied by the unlimited resources.
   b. a person looking for work is not able to find work.
   c. the number of people without jobs rises when economic times are bad.
   d. there can never be answers to the *what, how* or *for whom* questions.
   e. unlimited wants cannot be satisfied by the limited resources.

4. The question "Should we produce video tapes or DVD discs?" is an example of a ____ question.
   a. what
   b. how
   c. for whom
   d. where
   e. why

5. The question "Should we produce houses using bricks or wood?" is an example of a ____ question.
   a. what
   b. how
   c. for whom
   d. where
   e. why

6. If a decision is made and it is the best choice for society, the decision is said to be
   a. a valid economic choice.
   b. made in self-interest.
   c. made in social interest.
   d. consistent with scarcity.
   e. a want-maximizing choice.

### Short Response Questions

1. If there was no scarcity, would there be a need for economics?
2. What are the three major questions answered by people's economic choices?

### Long Response Questions

1. Will there ever come a time without scarcity?
2. Why is the distinction between choices made in self-interest and choices made in social interest important?

## CHECKPOINT 1.2

■ **Explain the core ideas that define the economic way of thinking.**

### Quick Review

- *Opportunity cost* The opportunity cost of something is the best thing you must give up to get it.
- *Marginal cost* The opportunity cost that arises from a one-unit increase in an activity.
- *Marginal benefit* The benefit that arises from a one-unit increase in an activity.
- *Rational choice* A choice that uses the available resources to most effectively satisfy the wants of the person making the choice.
- *Positive statement* A positive statement tells what is currently understood about the way the world operates. We can test a positive statement.
- *Normative statement* A normative statement tells what ought to be. It depends on values. We cannot test a normative statement.

### Practice Problems 1.2

1. Kate usually plays tennis for two hours a week and her grade on each math test is usually 70 percent. Last week, after playing two hours of tennis, Kate thought long and hard about playing for another hour. She decided to play another hour of tennis and cut her study time by one additional hour. But the grade on last week's math test was 60 percent.
   a. What was Kate's opportunity cost of the third hour of tennis?
   b. Given that Kate made the decision to play the third hour of tennis, what can you conclude about the comparison of her marginal benefit and marginal cost of the second hour of tennis?
   c. Was Kate's decision to play the third hour of tennis rational?

2. Classify each of the following statements as positive or normative:
   a. There is too much poverty in the United States.
   b. An increase in the gas tax will cut pollution.
   c. Cuts to social security in the United States have been too deep.

### Solutions to Additional Practice Problems 1.2

1a. The opportunity cost of the third hour of tennis was the 10 percentage point drop on her math test grade because she cut her studying time by one hour to play an additional hour of tennis. If Kate had not played tennis for the third hour, she would have studied and her grade would not have dropped.

1b. Kate chose to play the third hour of tennis, so the marginal benefit of the third hour of tennis was greater than the marginal cost of the third hour. If the marginal benefit of the third hour of tennis was less than the marginal cost of the third hour, Kate would have chosen to study rather than play tennis.

1c. Even though her grade fell, Kate's choice used the available time to most effectively satisfy her wants because the marginal benefit of the third hour of playing tennis exceeded the marginal cost of the third hour. This was a choice made in her self-interest.

2a. A normative statement because it depends on the speaker's values and cannot be tested.

2b. A positive statement because it can be tested by increasing the gas tax and then measuring the change in pollution.

2c. A normative statement because it depends on the speaker's values (someone else might propose still deeper cuts) and cannot be tested.

## ■ AP Self Test 1.2

**True or false**

1. Instead of attending his microeconomics class for two hours, Jim can play a game of tennis or watch a movie. For Jim the opportunity cost of attending class is forgoing the game of tennis *and* watching the movie.

2. Marginal cost is what you gain when you get one more unit of something.

3. A rational choice involves comparing the marginal benefit of an action to its marginal cost.

4. A change in marginal benefit or a change in marginal cost brings a change in the incentives that we face and leads us to change our actions.

5. The subject of economics divides into two main parts, which are macroeconomics and microeconomics.

6. The statement, "When more people volunteer in their communities, crime rates decrease" is a positive statement.

**Multiple choice**

1. Jamie has enough money to buy either a Mountain Dew, or a Pepsi, or a bag of chips. He chooses to buy the Mountain Dew. The opportunity cost of the Mountain Dew is
   a. the Pepsi and the bag of chips.
   b. the Pepsi or the bag of chips, whichever the highest-valued alternative forgone.
   c. the Mountain Dew.
   d. the Pepsi because it is a drink, as is the Mountain Dew.
   e. zero because he enjoys the Mountain Dew.

2. The benefit of an activity is
   a. purely objective and measured in dollars.
   b. the gain or pleasure that it brings.
   c. the value of its sunk cost.
   d. measured by what must be given up to get one more unit of the activity.
   e. not measurable on the margin.

3. The cost of a one-unit increase in an activity
   a. is the total one-unit cost.
   b. is called the marginal cost.
   c. decreases as you do more of the activity.
   d. is called the marginal benefit/cost.
   e. is called the sunk cost.

4. The marginal benefit of an activity is
   i. the benefit from a one-unit increase in the activity.
   ii. the benefit of a small, unimportant activity.
   iii. measured by what the person is willing to give up to get one additional unit of the activity.
   a. i only.
   b. ii only.
   c. iii only.
   d. i and iii.
   e. ii and iii.

5. If the marginal benefit of the next slice of pizza exceeds the marginal cost, you will
   a. eat the slice of pizza.
   b. not eat the slice of pizza.
   c. be unable to choose between eating or not eating.
   d. eat half the slice.
   e. More information is needed about how much the marginal benefit exceeds the marginal cost to determine if you will or will not eat the slice.

6. Which of the following is a microeconomic issue?
   a. Why has unemployment risen nationwide?
   b. Why has economic growth been rapid in China?
   c. What is the impact on the quantity of Pepsi purchased if consumers' tastes change in favor of non-carbonated drinks?
   d. Why is the average income lower in Africa than in Latin America?
   e. Why did overall production within the United States increase last year?

7. A positive statement
   a. must always be right.
   b. cannot be tested.
   c. can be tested against the facts.
   d. depends on someone's value judgment.
   e. cannot be negative.

8. Which of the following is an example of a normative statement?
   a. If cars become more expensive, fewer people will buy them.
   b. Car prices should be affordable.
   c. If wages increase, firms will fire some workers.
   d. Fewer people die in larger cars than in smaller cars.
   e. Cars emit pollution.

9. The Latin term *ceteris paribus* means
   a. after this, therefore because of this.
   b. other things being equal.
   c. what is correct for the part is not correct for the whole.
   d. on the margin.
   e. when one variable increases, the other variable decreases.

**Short Response Questions**
1. What is a sunk cost?
2. What is benefit and how is it measured?
3. Identify each of the following as either a normative or a positive statement.
   a. The high temperature today was 15 degrees.
   b. It was too cold today.
   c. Government action is needed if the unemployment rate exceeds 6 percent.
   d. The government should decrease its tax on gasoline.

**Long Response Questions**
1. Define "opportunity cost."
2. You have $12 and can buy a pizza, a movie on a DVD, or a package of CD-Rs. You decide to buy the pizza and think that if you hadn't been so hungry, you would have purchased the DVD. What is the opportunity cost of your pizza?
3. What is a marginal cost? A marginal benefit? How do they relate to rational choice?
4. Explain the difference between microeconomics and macroeconomics.

**YOUR AP SELF TEST ANSWERS**

### ■ CHECKPOINT 1.1

**True or false**

1. True;  page 2
2. False; page 3
3. True;  page 4
4. False; page 4
5. False; page 5

**Multiple choice**

1. e; page 2
2. a; page 2
3. e; page 2
4. a; page 3
5. b; page 3
6. c; page 4

**Short Response Questions**

1. If there was no scarcity, then there likely would be no need for economics. Economics studies the choices that people make to cope with scarcity, so if there was no scarcity, then people's choices would not be limited by scarcity; page 3.

2. The questions are "*What* goods and services get produced and in what quantities?", "*How* are goods and services produced?", and "*For whom* are the goods and services produced?" page 3.

**Long Response Questions**

1. There will never be a time without scarcity because human wants are unlimited. For instance, anyone daydreaming about what he or she wants can list a limitless number of goods and services. Clearly it is impossible for this person to ever attain all these wants. Similarly, it will be impossible for society to ever be able to meet everyone's wants. For instance, how many people want to ski on non-crowded, nicely groomed ski runs in Utah on a pleasant day? Because there are a limited number of nicely groomed ski runs in Utah, it is impossible for everyone who

wants to ski there to do so much less to ski there on a non-crowded slope; page 2.

2. In general economists believe that people make choices according to their self-interest. These choices might or might not be in the social interest. Part of what economists study, especially in microeconomics, is when choices made in people's self-interest also further the social interest; page 5.

### ■ CHECKPOINT 1.2

**True or false**

1. False; page 11
2. False; page 12
3. True;  page 13
4. True;  page 13
5. True;  page 14
6. True;  page 15

**Multiple choice**

1. b; page 11
2. b; page 11
3. b; page 12
4. d; page 12
5. a; page 13
6. c; page 14
7. c; page 15
8. b; page 15
9. b;  page 15

**Short Response Questions**

1. A sunk cost is a previously occurred and irreversible cost; page 11.

2. The benefit of something is the gain or pleasure that it brings. Economists measure the benefit of something by what a person is willing to give up to get it; pages 11, 12.

3. a. Positive statement; page 15.
   b. Normative statement; page 15.
   c. Normative statement; page 15.
   d. Normative statement; page 15.

## Long Response Questions

1. The opportunity cost of something is the highest-valued other thing that must be given up. The opportunity cost is only the one single highest-valued alternative forgone, *not* all alternatives forgone; page 11.

2. The opportunity cost of the pizza is the highest-valued alternative forgone, which in this case is the DVD. The opportunity cost is *not* the DVD and the CD-Rs because you would not have been able to purchase both of them with your $12; page 11.

3. Marginal cost is the cost of a one-unit increase in an activity. Marginal benefit is the benefit of a one-unit increase in an activity. A rational choice is made by comparing the marginal cost and marginal benefit. If the marginal benefit of an activity exceeds or equals the marginal cost, the activity is undertaken. On the other hand, if the marginal benefit of an activity falls short of the marginal cost, then the activity is not undertaken; pages 12-13.

4. Microeconomics studies individual units within the economy, such as a consumer, a firm, a market, and so forth. Macroeconomics studies the overall, or aggregate, economy, such as the overall unemployment rate, or overall economic growth rate; page 14.

# Appendix: Making and Using Graphs

## Chapter 1

After you have completed the appendix, you will have thoroughly reviewed the graphs used in your economics course.

### ■ Making and using graphs.

Graphs represent quantities as distances. The vertical axis is the $y$-axis and the horizontal axis is the $x$-axis. A scatter diagram plots a graph of one variable against the value of another variable. A time-series graph measures time along the $x$-axis and the variable (or variables) of interest along the $y$-axis. A cross-section graph shows the values of an economic variable for different groups in the population at a point in time. Graphs can show the relationship between two variables in an economic model. Variables that move in the same direction have a positive, or direct, relationship. Variables that move in the opposite direction have a negative, or inverse, relationship. Some relationships have minimum or maximum points. The slope of a relationship is the change in the value of the variable measured on the $y$-axis divided by the change in the value of the variable measured on the $x$-axis. To graph a relationship among more than two variables, we use the *ceteris paribus* assumption and graph the relationship between two of the variables, holding the other variables constant.

### EXPANDED APPENDIX CHECKLIST

**When you have completed this appendix, you will be able to:**

**1 Interpret a scatter diagram, time-series graph, and cross-section graph.**

- Identify the $x$-axis, the $y$-axis, and the origin in a graph.
- Explain what is plotted in and the differences among a scatter diagram, a time-series diagram, and a cross-section graph.

**2 Interpret the graphs used in economic models.**

- Be able to draw a figure showing a positive (direct) relationship between two variables.

- Be able to draw a figure showing a negative (inverse) relationship between two variables.
- Be able to draw figures showing a maximum and a minimum.
- Be able to draw figures showing two variables that are unrelated.

**3 Define and calculate slope.**

- Present the formula used to calculate the slope of a relationship and use it to calculate slopes.

**4 Graphing relationships among more than two variables.**

- Describe how the *ceteris paribus* assumption is used to allow us to illustrate the relationship among more than two variables.

## YOUR AP TEST HINTS

### Extra AP material

- Your AP test probably will not ask strictly mathematical questions such as in this appendix, but this material will be important in answering some of the questions.

## CHECKPOINT 1

### ■ Making and using graphs.

### Additional Practice Problems

1. You have data on the average monthly rainfall and the monthly expenditure on umbrellas in Seattle, Washington. What sort of graph would be the best to reveal if any relationship exists between these variables?

### ■ FIGURE A1.1

2. In Figure A1.1, draw a straight line showing a positive relationship and another straight line showing a negative relationship.

3. The table above in the next column has the average price of a gallon of gasoline, excluding taxes, for ten years. In Figure A1.2, label the axes and then plot these data. What type of graph are you creating? What is the general trend of gas prices during this decade

| Year | Price (dollars per gallon) |
|------|----------------------------|
| 1994 | 0.79 |
| 1995 | 0.79 |
| 1996 | 0.82 |
| 1997 | 0.80 |
| 1998 | 0.68 |
| 1999 | 0.73 |
| 2000 | 1.09 |
| 2001 | 1.02 |
| 2002 | 0.94 |
| 2003 | 1.13 |

### ■ FIGURE A1.2

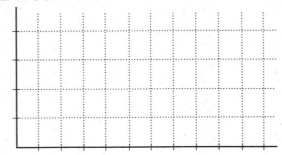

### ■ FIGURE A1.3

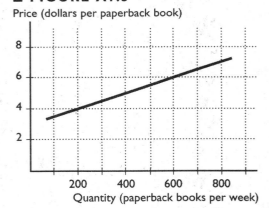

4. Figure A1.3 shows the relationship between the price of a paperback book and the quantity of paperback books a publisher is willing to sell. What is the slope of the line in Figure A1.3?

## Solution to Additional Practice Problems 1

1. A scatter diagram would be the best graph to use. A scatter diagram would plot the monthly value of, say, rainfall along the vertical axis (the *y*-axis) and the monthly value of umbrella expenditure along the horizontal axis (the *x*-axis).

### ■ FIGURE A1.4

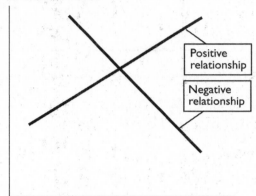

2. Figure A1.4 has two lines, one showing a positive relationship and the other showing a negative relationship. Your figure does not need to have identical lines. The key point your figure needs is that the line for the positive relationship slopes up as you move rightward along it and the line for the negative relationship slopes down as you move rightward along it.

### ■ FIGURE A1.5
Price (dollars per gallon)

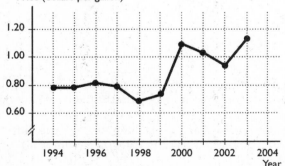

3. Figure A1.5 labels the axes and plots the data in the table. The graph is a time-series graph. The trend is positive because gas prices generally increased during these years.

### ■ FIGURE A1.6
Price (dollars per paperback book)

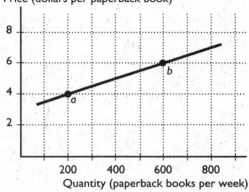

4. The slope of a line is the change the variable measured on the *y*-axis divided by the change in the variable measured on the *x*-axis. To calculate the slope of the line in the figure, use points *a* and *b* in Figure A1.6. Between *a* and *b*, *y* rises by 2, from 4 to 6. And *x* increases by 400, from 200 to 600. The slope equals $2/400 = 0.005$.

## ■ AP Self Test 1

### True or false

1. A point that is above and to the right of another point will have a larger value of the *x*-axis variable and a larger value of the *y*-axis variable.

2. A scatter diagram shows the values of an economic variable for different groups in a population at a point in time.

3. A time-series graph compares values of a variable for different groups at a single point in time.

4. A trend is a measure of the closeness of the points on a graph.

5. A positive relationship is always a linear relationship.

6. A relationship that starts out sloping upward and then slopes downward has a maximum.

7. A graph that shows a horizontal line indicates variables that are unrelated.

8. The slope at a point on a curve is equal to the slope of the straight line that is tangent to the curve at that point.

## Multiple choice

1. Demonstrating how an economic variable changes from one year to the next is best illustrated by a
   a. scatter diagram.
   b. time-series graph.
   c. linear graph.
   d. cross-section graph.
   e. trend-line

2. To show the values of an economic variable for different groups in a population at a point in time, it is best to use a
   a. scatter diagram.
   b. time-series graph.
   c. linear graph.
   d. cross-section graph.
   e. trend diagram.

3. If whenever one variable increases, another variable also increases, these variables are
   a. positively related.
   b. negatively related.
   c. inversely related.
   d. cross-sectionally related.
   e. not related.

4. A graph of the relationship between two variables is a line that slopes down to the right. These two variables are ____ related.
   a. positively
   b. directly
   c. negatively
   d. not
   e. trend-line

5. Two variables are unrelated if their graph is
   i.  a vertical line.
   ii. a 45 degree line.
   iii. a horizontal line.
   a. i only.
   b. ii only
   c. iii only
   d. i and iii.
   e. i, ii, and iii.

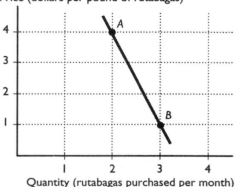

■ **FIGURE A1.7**

Price (dollars per pound of rutabagas)

Quantity (rutabagas purchased per month)

6. In figure A1.7, between points $A$ and $B$, what is the slope of the line?
   a. 4
   b. 1
   c. 3
   d. –3
   e. 0

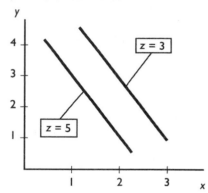

■ **FIGURE A1.8**

7. In Figure A1.8, an increase in z leads to a
   a. movement up along one of the lines showing the relationship between $x$ and $y$.
   b. movement down along one of the lines showing the relationship between $x$ and $y$.
   c. rightward shift of the line showing the relationship between $x$ and $y$.
   d. leftward shift of the line showing the relationship between x and y.
   e. trend change in both $x$ and $y$.

8. In Figure A1.8, *ceteris paribus*, an increase in $x$ is associated with
   a. an increase in $y$.
   b. a decrease in $y$.
   c. an increase in $z$.
   d. a random change in $z$.
   e. no change in either $y$ or $z$.

**Short Response Questions**

| Year | Workers (millions) |
|------|--------------------|
| 1990 | 6.5 |
| 1991 | 6.5 |
| 1992 | 6.6 |
| 1993 | 6.8 |
| 1994 | 7.1 |
| 1995 | 7.4 |
| 1996 | 7.5 |
| 1997 | 7.6 |
| 1998 | 7.8 |
| 1999 | 7.9 |

1. The table above gives the number of people working in restaurants and bars in the United States during the decade of the 1990s. In Figure A1.9, measure time on the horizontal axis and the number of workers on the vertical axis, and then plot these data.

■ **FIGURE A1.9**

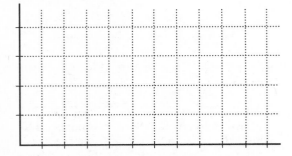

   a. What type of graph are you creating?
   b. Using your figure, what was the trend in the number of people working in restaurants and bars during the 1990s?

| Year | Revenue (billions of dollars) | Workers (millions) |
|------|-------------------------------|--------------------|
| 1990 | 190 | 6.5 |
| 1991 | 194 | 6.5 |
| 1992 | 200 | 6.6 |
| 1993 | 213 | 6.8 |
| 1994 | 222 | 7.1 |
| 1995 | 230 | 7.4 |
| 1996 | 239 | 7.5 |
| 1997 | 254 | 7.6 |
| 1998 | 267 | 7.8 |
| 1999 | 285 | 7.9 |

2. The table above gives the annual revenue for restaurants and bars and the number of people employed in restaurants and bars in the United States during the decade of the 1990s. In Figure A1.10, measure the revenue along the horizontal axis and the number of workers along the vertical axis and plot the data.

   a. What type of graph are you creating?
   b. What relationship do you see in your figure between the revenue and the number of workers?

■ **FIGURE A1.10**

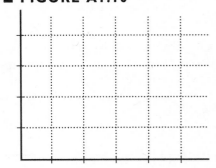

| Price (dollars per sack of cat food) | Quantity (sacks of cat food per month) |
|--------------------------------------|----------------------------------------|
| 1 | 10,000 |
| 2 | 8,000 |
| 3 | 7,000 |
| 4 | 4,000 |

3. The number of sacks of premium cat food that cat lovers will buy depends on the price of a sack of cat food. The relationship is given in the table above. In Figure A1.11,

■ **FIGURE A1.11**

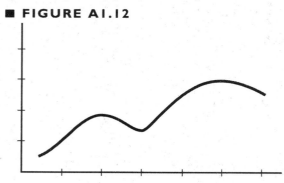

plot this relationship, putting the price on the vertical axis and the quantity on the horizontal axis.

a. If the price of a sack of cat food is $2, how many sacks will be purchased?

b. If the price of a sack of cat food is $3, how many sacks will be purchased?

c. Is the relationship between the price and the quantity positive or negative?

■ **FIGURE A1.12**

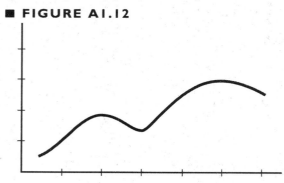

4. In Figure A1.12, label the maximum and minimum points.

5. In Figure A1.13 at the top of the next column, draw a line through point A with a slope of 2. Label the line "1." Draw another line through point A with a slope of –2. Label this line "2."

6. What are the three types of graphs?

7. If two variables are positively related, will the slope of a graph of the two variables be positive or negative? If two variables are

■ **FIGURE A1.13**

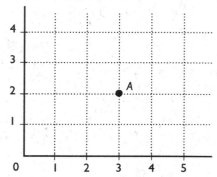

negatively related, will the slope of a graph of the two variables be positive or negative?

8. If a line slopes upward to the right, is its slope positive or negative? If a line slopes downward to the right, is its slope positive or negative?

■ **FIGURE A1.15**

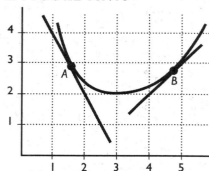

9. In Figure A1.15, what is the slope of the curved line at point A? At point B?

| Price (dollars per compact disc) | Quantity of compact discs purchased, low income | Quantity of compact discs purchased, high income |
|---|---|---|
| 11 | 4 | 5 |
| 12 | 3 | 4 |
| 13 | 1 | 3 |
| 14 | 0 | 2 |

10. Bobby says that he buys fewer compact discs when the price of a compact disc is higher. Bobby also says that he will buy more compact discs after he graduates and his income is higher. The table above shows

**■ FIGURE A1.14**

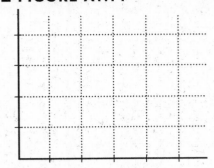

the number of compact discs Bobby buys in a month at different prices when his income is low and when his income is high.

a. In Figure A1.14, put the price on the vertical axis and the quantity purchased on the horizontal axis. Show the relationship between the number of discs purchased and the price when Bobby's income is low.

b. On the same figure draw the relationship between the number of discs purchased and the price when his income is high.

c. Does an increase in Bobby's income cause the relationship between the price of a compact disc and the number purchased to shift rightward or leftward?

# YOUR AP SELF TEST ANSWERS

## ■ CHECKPOINT 1

### True or false

1. True;  page 23
2. False;  page 24
3. False;  page 24
4. False;  page 24
5. False;  page 26
6. True;  page 28
7. True;  page 28
8. True;  page 29

### Multiple choice

1. b; page 24
2. d; page 24
3. a; page 26
4. c; page 27
5. d; page 28
6. d; page 29
7. d; page 30
8. b; page 30

### Short Response Questions

■ **FIGURE A1.16**

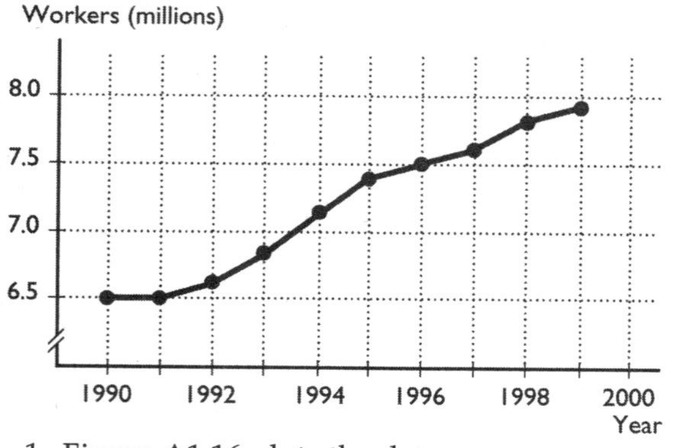

Workers (millions)

1. Figure A1.16 plots the data.
   a. This is a time-series graph;  page 24.
   b. The trend is positive. During the 1990s there is an increase in the number of people working in restaurants and bars;  page 24.

■ **FIGURE A1.17**

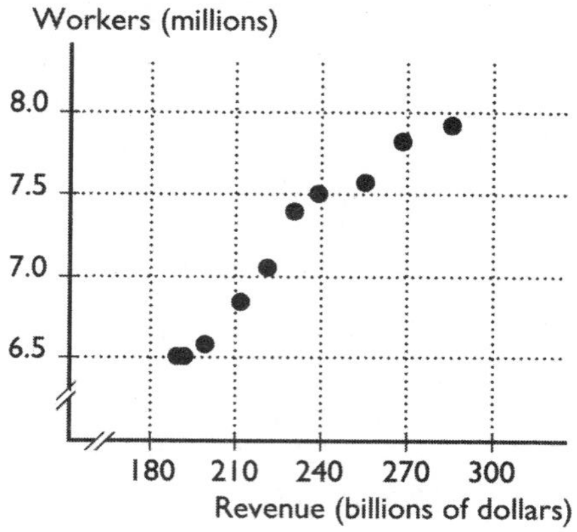

Workers (millions)

Revenue (billions of dollars)

2. Figure A1.17 plots the data.
   a. The figure is a scatter diagram;  page 24.
   b. The relationship between the revenue and the number of workers is positive;  page 26.

■ **FIGURE A1.18**

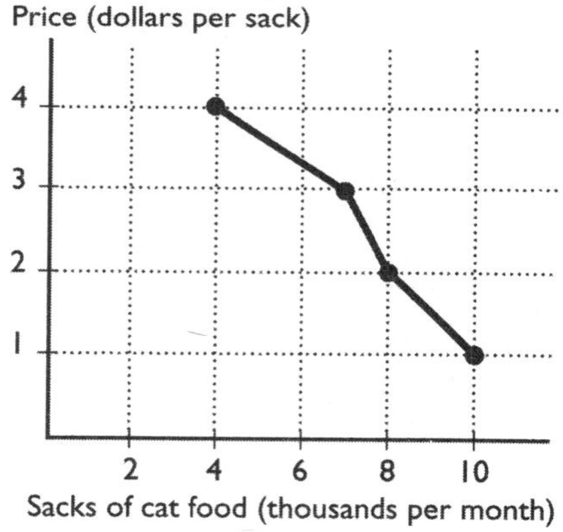

Price (dollars per sack)

Sacks of cat food (thousands per month)

3. Figure A1.18 plots the relationship.
   a. If the price is $2 per sack, 8,000 sacks are purchased;  page 23.
   b. If the price is $3 per sack, 7,000 sacks are purchased;  page 23.
   c. The relationship between the price and quantity of sacks is negative;  page 27.

■ **FIGURE A1.19**

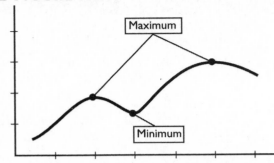

4. Figure A1.19 labels the two maximum points and one minimum point; page 28.

■ **FIGURE A1.20**

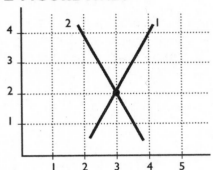

5. Figure A1.20 shows the two lines; page 29.

6. The three types of graphs are scatter diagram, time-series graph, and cross-section graph; page 24.

7. If two variables are positively related, a graph of the relationship will have a positive slope. If two variables are negatively related, a graph of the relationship will have a negative slope; pages 26, 27, 29.

8. If a line slopes upward to the right, its slope is positive. If a line slopes downward to the right, its slope is negative; page 29.

9. The slope of a curved line at a point equals the slope of a straight line that is tangent to the curve at that point. The slope of the curved line at point $A$ is –2 and the slope of the curved line at point $B$ is 1; page 29.

■ **FIGURE A1.21**

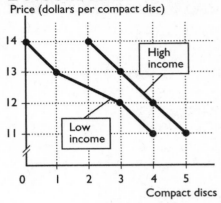

10. a. Figure A1.21 plots the relationship; page 30.

   b. Figure A1.21 plots the relationship; page 30.

   c. An increase in Bobby's income shifts the relationship rightward; page 30.

# Chapter 2

# The U.S. and Global Economies

Chapter 2 introduces fundamental concepts about how households, firms, markets, and government are linked together. A circular flow model is presented to show how goods and services and expenditures flow from and to households, firms, and the government.

■ **Describe what, how, and for whom goods and services are produced in the United States.**

The production of goods and services, the "what" question, is divided into four broad categories defined in terms of the ultimate buyer: individuals (consumption goods and services), businesses (capital goods), governments (government goods and services), and other countries (export goods and services). The "how" of production involves the factors of production: land, labor, capital, and entrepreneurship. Goods and services are sold to those who have income, so the personal distribution of income is one way of showing who ends up with our national output. The functional distribution of income shows how much is paid to the owners of each type of productive resource. The largest share of national income goes to labor, so workers get the largest share of our nation's goods and services.

■ **Use the circular flow model to provide a picture of how households, firms, and government interact.**

The circular flow model shows that households provide factors of production, and firms hire factors of production in factor markets. The circular flow also shows that households purchase goods and services, and firms sell goods and services in goods markets. The decisions made by households and firms (and the government) in these markets determine the answers to the "what," "how," and "for whom" questions. The federal government provides public goods and services, and makes social security and other benefit payments. In the circular flow, the government purchases goods and services in goods markets. It makes transfers to firms and households and also taxes them. The federal government's largest expenditure is Social Security and its largest source of tax revenue is personal income taxes.

■ **Describe what, how, and for whom goods and services are produced in the global economy.**

Countries are divided into advanced economies, the richest 29 countries, and emerging market and developing economies. The advanced economies produce 44 percent of the world's total output, with 18 percent produced in the United States. Two third's of the world's oil reserves and two fifths of the natural gas reserves are in the Middle East. The share of agriculture in the advanced economies is much smaller than in the other countries but the advanced economies still produce one third of the world's food. The advanced economies have much more human capital and physical capital than the developing countries. Inequality of incomes across the entire world has decreased during the past twenty years, primarily because incomes in China and India have grown rapidly.

## EXPANDED CHAPTER CHECKLIST

**When you have completed this chapter, you will be able to:**

**1 Describe what, how, and for whom goods and services are produced in the United States.**

- Define consumption goods and services, investment goods, government goods and services, and exports.
- Discuss the four factors of production.
- Distinguish between the functional and personal distributions of income.

**2 Use the circular flow model to provide a picture of how households, firms, and government interact.**

- Define households, firms, and markets.
- Tell what is bought and sold in goods markets and in factor markets.
- Draw the circular flow between households and firms showing factor markets and goods markets.
- Draw the circular flow model with the government added.
- State the main expenditures and sources of tax revenue for the federal government.
- State the main expenditures and sources of tax revenue for state and local governments.

**3 Describe what, how, and for whom goods and services are produced in the global economy.**

- Distinguish between advanced economies and emerging market and developing economies, and give examples of each.
- Discuss differences and similarities across the different types of economies.
- Explain how and why world inequality of income has changed over the last two decades.

## YOUR AP TEST HINTS

*AP Topics*

| Topic on your AP test | Corresponding textbook section |
|---|---|
| **Measurement of economic performance** | |
| National Income Accounting | Chapter 2 |
| • Factors of production and payments | Checkpoint 2.1 |
| • Circular flow | Checkpoint 2.2 |

*AP Vocabulary*

- On the AP test, the term "capital" can be used to refer to both "human capital" and "physical capital."
- On the AP test, the economy can be specialized in different ways. The term "private economy" refers to an economy comprised of only households and businesses while the term "public economy" refers to the entire economy with households, business, and the government. The term "closed economy" refers to an economy without any international trade and the term "open economy" refers to an economy with international trade.

## CHECKPOINT 2.1

■ **Describe what, how, and for whom goods and services are produced in the United States.**

**Quick Review**

- *Consumption goods and services* Goods and services that are bought by individuals and used to provide personal enjoyment and contribute to a person's standard of living.
- *Capital goods* Goods that are bought by businesses to increase their productive resources.
- *Government goods and services* Goods and services that are bought by governments.

- *Exports* Goods and services produced in the United States and sold in other countries.

## Additional Practice Problems 2.1

1. Tell whether the following goods and services are consumption goods and services, capital goods, government goods and services, or exports.

    a. A taco at Taco Bell purchased for lunch by Shaniq.

    b. An HP printer manufactured in Idaho purchased by Maria in Peru.

    c. A new grill purchased by Taco Bell.

    d. A tour down the Colorado river from Rimrock Adventures purchased by the Miller family.

    e. CamelBak drinking packs purchased by the U.S. Marine Corp.

    f. CamelBak drinking packs purchased by Rimrock Adventures for use by their customers during tours.

    g. A CamelBak drinking pack purchased by Anne for use while mountain biking.

    h. A CamelBak drinking pack purchased by Sebastian, a German racing in the Tour de France.

2. How much labor is there in the United States? What determines the quantity of labor?

## Solutions to Additional Practice Problems 2.1

1a. Shaniq's taco is a consumption good.

1b. Maria's printer is an export good.

1c. The new grill is a capital good.

1d. The tour is a consumption service.

1e. The drinking pack purchased by the Marines is a government good because it is purchased by the government.

1f. The drinking pack purchased by Rimrock Adventures is a capital good because it is purchased by a business.

1g. The drinking pack purchased by Anne is a consumption good.

1h. The drinking pack purchased by Sebastian is an export good.

2. In the United States, in 2005 about 149 million people had jobs or were available for work and they provided about 240 billion hours of labor a year. The quantity of labor depends on the size of the population, the percentage of the population that takes jobs, and on social relationships that influence things such as how many women take paid work. An increase in the proportion of women who have taken paid work has increased the quantity of labor in the United States over the past 50 years.

## ■ AP Self Test 2.1

### True or false

1. Consumption goods and services include a slice of pizza purchased to eat at home.

2. A gold mine is included in the "land" category of productive resources.

3. Michael Dell, the person who founded and manages Dell computers, is an example of an entrepreneur.

4. In the United States, the richest 20 percent of individuals earn approximately 30 percent of total income.

### Multiple choice

1. When the total U.S. production of goods and services is divided into consumption goods and services, capital goods, government goods and services, and export goods and services, the largest component is

    a. consumption goods and services.

    b. capital goods.

    c. government goods and services.

    d. export goods and services.

    e. capital goods and government goods and services tie for the largest component.

2. An example of a capital good is

    a. a fiber optic cable TV system.

    b. an insurance policy.

    c. a hair cut.

    d. an iPod.

    e. a slice of pizza.

3. Goods and services produced in the United States and sold in other countries are called
    a. consumption goods and services.
    b. capital goods.
    c. government goods and services.
    d. export goods and services.
    e. import goods and services.

4. Which of the following correctly lists the categories of productive resources?
    a. machines, buildings, land, and money
    b. hardware, software, land, and money
    c. capital, money, and labor
    d. owners, workers, and consumers.
    e. land, labor, capital, and entrepreneurship

5. Human capital is
    a. solely the innate ability we are born with.
    b. the money humans have saved.
    c. the knowledge humans accumulate through education and experience.
    d. machinery that needs human supervision.
    e. any type of machinery.

6. Wages are paid to ____ and interest is paid to ____.
    a. entrepreneurs; capital
    b. labor; capital
    c. labor; land
    d. entrepreneurs; land
    e. labor; entrepreneurs

7. Dividing the nation's income among the factors of production, the largest percentage is paid to
    a. labor.
    b. land.
    c. capital.
    d. entrepreneurship.
    e. labor and capital, with each receiving about 41 percent of the total income.

## Short Response Questions

1. Is an automobile a consumption good or a capital good?

2. Compare the incomes earned by the poorest and richest 20 percent of individuals.

## CHECKPOINT 2.2

■ **Use the circular flow model to provide a picture of how households, firms, and governments interact.**

### Quick Review

- *Circular flow model* A model of the economy, illustrated in Figure 2.1, that shows the circular flow of expenditures and incomes that result from firms', households', and governments' choices.

■ **FIGURE 2.1**

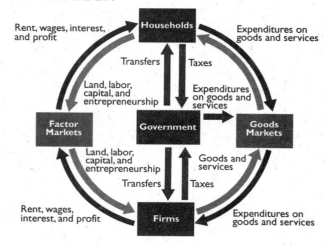

### Additional Practice Problem 2.2

1. Describe where the following money flows fit in the circular flow.
    a. Shaniq pays for a taco at Taco Bell.
    b. Sam receives his monthly Social Security payment.
    c. Jennifer gets a $10,000 end of the year bonus from Bank of America, where she works.
    d. Exxon pays landowners in Texas $20,000 for the oil under their land.
    e. Bill pays property tax of $6,000.

2. In the circular flow, what is the relationship between the flow of expenditures into the goods markets (from households and the government) and the flow of revenues out of the goods markets to firms?

**Solutions to Additional Practice Problems 2.2**

1a. Shaniq's payment is an expenditure on a good that flows from households through the goods market to Taco Bell, a firm.

1b. Sam's check is a transfer payment from the government to households.

1c. Jennifer's payment is wages flowing from a firm, Bank of America, through the factor market to households.

1d. Exxon's payment is rent flowing from a firm, Exxon, through the factor market to households.

1e. Bill's payment is a tax flowing from households to government.

2. The flow of expenditures into the goods markets–the funds that households and the government spend on the goods and services they purchase–equals the flow of revenue out of the goods markets.

### ■ AP Self Test 2.2

**True or false**

1. Firms own the factors of production.

2. A market is any arrangement where buyers and sellers meet face-to-face.

3. Factors of production flow from households to firms through goods markets.

4. Rent, wages, interest, and profit are the payments made by firms to households through factor markets.

5. Social security payments are made by state and local governments.

6. The largest part of the expenditures of state and local government is on education.

**Multiple choice**

1. Within the circular flow model, economists define households as
   a. families with at least 2 children.
   b. families living in their own houses.
   c. individuals or groups living together.
   d. married or engaged couples.
   e. individuals or groups within the same legally defined family.

2. A market is defined as
   a. the physical place where goods are sold.
   b. the physical place where goods and services are sold.
   c. any arrangement that brings buyers and sellers together.
   d. a place where money is exchanged for goods.
   e. another name for a store such as a grocery store.

3. In the circular flow model,
   a. only firms sell in markets.
   b. only households buy from markets.
   c. some firms only sell and some firms only buy.
   d. the money used to buy goods and the goods themselves travel in the same direction.
   e. both firms and households buy or sell in different markets.

4. _____ choose the quantities of goods and services to produce, while _____ choose the quantities of goods and services to buy.
   a. Households; firms
   b. Firms; households and the government
   c. The government; firms
   d. Firms; only households
   e. Households; the government

5. In the circular flow model, the expenditures on goods and services flow in the
   a. same direction as goods and services in all cases.
   b. same direction as goods and services *only if* they both flow through the goods market.
   c. same direction as goods and services *only if* they both flow through the factor market.
   d. opposite direction as goods and services.
   e. same direction as factor markets.

6. Of the following, the largest expenditure category of the federal government is
   a. the purchase of goods and services.
   b. interest on the national debt.
   c. grants to states and local governments.
   d. education.
   e. Social Security.

7. Of the following, the largest source of revenue for the federal government is
   a. personal income taxes.
   b. sales taxes.
   c. corporate income taxes.
   d. property taxes.
   e. lottery revenue.

### Short Response Questions

1. In the circular flow model, what are the sources of expenditures on goods and services?

2. The circular flow reveals that which two groups interact to determine what will be the payments to the factors of production?

3. In 2004, which spent more, the federal government or state and local governments?

### Long Response Questions

1. Ignoring taxes and transfer payments, what funds flow into firms and what funds flow out of them?

2. Is it possible for something to affect households and not firms? To affect firms and not households? Explain your answers.

■ FIGURE 2.2

3. Figure 2.2 ignores the government and shows the flows into and out of households. In this model of the private economy, label the flows and identify who they come from and who they go to.

■ FIGURE 2.3

4. Figure 2.3 ignores the government and shows the flows into and out of firms. In this model of the private economy, label the flows and identify who they come from and who they go to.

■ FIGURE 2.4

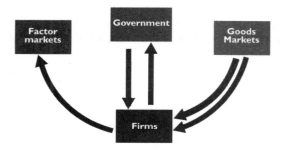

5. Figure 2.4 now includes the government and shows the money flows into and out of firms. In this model of the public economy, label the money flows.

## CHECKPOINT 2.3

■ **Describe what, how, and for whom goods and services are produced in the global economy.**

### Quick Review

- *Advanced economies* The 28 countries (or areas) that have the highest living standards.

- *Emerging markets and Developing economies* Emerging markets are the 28 countries in Europe and Asia that were until the early 1990s part of the Soviet Union or its satellites and are changing the way they organize their economies. Developing economies are the 118 countries in

Africa, the Middle East, Europe, and Central and South America that have not yet achieved a high standard of living for their people.

### Additional Practice Problems 2.3

1. What percentage of the world's population live in developing economies? In places such as China, India, and Africa, what was the average income per day?

2. What percentage of the world's population live in advanced economies? In countries such as the United States, Canada, and Japan, what was the average income per day?

3. How does production within the advanced economies, the emerging market economies, and the developing economies compare?

### Solutions to Additional Practice Problems 2.3

1. The world's population is about 6.5 billion. More than 5 billion of the people live in developing economies. So, approximately 80 percent of the world's population lives in developing economies. Average daily income in China is $14, in India is $8, and in Africa is $6. Because these are the average, many people live on less than these amounts.

2. About 1 billion people, or 15 percent of the world's population live in the 28 advanced economies. The average income per day in the United States was $108, in Canada was $90, and in Japan was $80.

3. Of the world's total production, the advanced economies produce 44 percent (18 percent is produced in the United States). The emerging market economies produce 16 percent of the world's production and the developing economies produce the remainder, 40 percent.

### ■ AP Self Test 2.3

#### True or false

1. About 50 percent of the world's population lives in the advanced economies.

2. Mexico is an emerging market economy.

3. Taken as a group, the 118 developing economy nations produce a larger percentage of total world production than do the 29 advanced economy nations.

4. Income inequality within most nations has increased over the past years.

#### Multiple choice

1. The percentage of the world's population that lives in the advanced economies is
   a. more than 51 percent.
   b. between 41 percent and 50 percent.
   c. between 31 percent and 40 percent.
   d. between 20 percent and 30 percent.
   e. less than 20 percent.

2. Which of following groups of countries are *all* advanced economies?
   a. Australia, Brazil, and the United States
   b. Hong Kong, Japan, France, and the United Kingdom
   c. Italy, the United States, China, and Russia
   d. Singapore, Russia, France, and Chad
   e. Mexico, Canada, Germany, and Egypt

3. The emerging market economies are
   a. the largest grouping including the nations of China and India.
   b. in transition from state-owned production to free markets.
   c. most of the nations of Western Europe.
   d. the nations that are currently agricultural in nature.
   e. the nations with the highest standards of living.

#### Long Response Questions

1. What are the groups the International Monetary Fund uses to classify countries? Describe each group. Which group has the largest number of countries? The largest number of people?

# YOUR AP SELF TEST ANSWERS

## ■ CHECKPOINT 2.1

**True or false**
1. True; page 34
2. True; page 36
3. True; page 39
4. False; page 40

**Multiple choice**
1. a; page 34
2. a; page 34
3. d; page 34
4. e; page 36
5. c; page 37
6. b; page 39
7. a; page 40

**Short Response Questions**
1. An automobile might be either a consumption or a capital good. It is a consumption good if it is purchased by a household. It is a capital good if it is purchased by a business for use within the business; page 34.
2. The richest 20 percent of households earn about 50 percent of the total U.S. income. The poorest 20 percent of individuals have an average income of about $10,000 and earn about 3.4 percent of the total U.S. income; page 40.

## ■ CHECKPOINT 2.2

**True or false**
1. False; page 42
2. False; pages 42-43
3. False; pages 42-43
4. True; pages 42-43
5. False; page 44
6. True; page 47

**Multiple choice**
1. c; page 42
2. c; page 42
3. e; pages 42-43
4. b; pages 42-43
5. d; page 43

6. e; page 46
7. a; page 46

**Short Response Questions**
1. The circular flow identifies two sources of expenditures on goods and services, expenditures by households and expenditures by the government; page 45.
2. Payments to the factors of production are determined by the interaction of households, who own and provide the factors of production, and firms, who employ the factors; page 43.
3. In 2004, the federal government spent $2.4 trillion and state and local governments spent $1.7 trillion. The federal government spent significantly more than state and local governments; page 46.

**Long Response Questions**
1. Funds that flow to firms are households' expenditures and government purchases of goods and services. Funds that flow from firms are payments for rent, wages, interest, and profit (or loss) to households in exchange for the factors of production; pages 43, 45.
2. The circular flow shows that at the macroeconomic level it is impossible for something to influence only firms or only households. An influence that changes households' buying behavior in goods markets affects firms because they sell to households in goods markets; page 43.

## ■ FIGURE 2.5

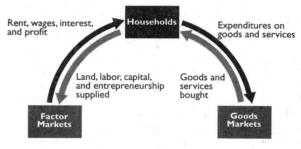

3. Figure 2.5 labels the flows. Rent, wages, interest, and profits (or losses) flow from the labor market while land, labor, capital, and

entrepreneurship flow to the factor market. In addition, expenditures on goods and services flow to the goods market, and goods and services flow from the goods market; page 43.

### ■ FIGURE 2.6

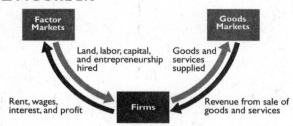

4. Figure 2.6 labels the flows in this model of the private economy. Revenue from the sale of goods and services, which are the expenditures on goods and services, flow to firms from the goods market and payments of rent, wages, interest, and profit (or loss) flow from firms into the factor market. Land, labor, capital, and entrepreneurship flow to firms from the factors markets, and goods and services flow from firms into the goods markets; page 43.

### ■ FIGURE 2.7

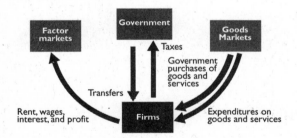

5. Figure 2.7 labels the money flows into and out of firms. The difference between this fig-

ure and Figure 2.6 is the addition of transfers and taxes. So Figure 2.6 examines the private economy only while Figure 2.7 looks at the public economy  page 45.

## ■ CHECKPOINT 2.3

### True or false
1. False;  page 49
2. False;  page 49
3. False;  page 50
4. True;  page 55

### Multiple choice
1. e;  page 49
2. b;  page 49
3. b;  page 49

### Long Response Questions
1. The groups are the advanced economies and the emerging market and developing economies. Advanced economies have the highest standard of living. Emerging market and developing economies have yet to achieve a high standard of living. The emerging market economies are changing their economies from government management and state-ownership of capital to market-based economies similar to that in the United States. There are more nations, 118, and more people, almost 5 billion, in developing economies; page 49.

# The Economic Problem

# Chapter
# 3

Chapter 3 develops an economic model, the production possibilities frontier or *PPF* model. The *PPF* shows how the opportunity cost of a good or service increases as more of the good or service is produced and how societies and individuals gain by specializing according to comparative advantage.

■ **Use the production possibilities frontier to illustrate the economic problem.**

The production possibilities frontier, *PPF*, is the boundary between the combinations of goods and services that can be produced and those that cannot be produced, given the available factors of production and technology. Production points outside the *PPF* are unattainable. Points on and inside the *PPF* are attainable. Production points on the *PPF* are production efficient. Moving along the *PPF* producing more of one good, less of another good is produced—a tradeoff. Moving from inside the *PPF* to a point on the *PPF*, more of some goods and services can be produced without producing less of others—a free lunch.

■ **Calculate opportunity cost.**

Along the *PPF* all choices involve a tradeoff. Along the *PPF*, the opportunity cost of the good on the *x*-axis is equal to the decrease in the good on the *y*-axis divided by the increase in the good on the *x*-axis. As more of a good is produced, its opportunity cost increases, so the *PPF* is bowed outward. The opportunity cost increases because resources are not equally productive in all activities. In the real world, most activities have increasing opportunity cost.

■ **Define efficiency and describe an efficient use of resources.**

Allocative efficiency occurs when we produce the quantities of goods and services that people value most highly. Allocative efficiency requires production efficiency and producing at the highest-valued point on the *PPF*. The marginal benefit curve is downward sloping and the marginal cost curve is upward sloping. Allocative efficiency requires producing where the curves intersect, that is, the quantity that makes the marginal benefit equal the marginal cost.

■ **Explain what makes production possibilities expand.**

Economic growth is the sustained expansion of production possibilities. If more capital is accumulated production possibilities increase and the *PPF* shifts outward. The (opportunity) cost of economic growth is that resources used to increase capital cannot be used to produce current consumption goods and services.

■ **Explain how people gain from specialization and trade.**

A person has a comparative advantage in an activity if he or she can perform the activity at lower opportunity cost than someone else. People can gain from specializing in production according to comparative advantage and then trading with others. An absolute advantage occurs when one person is more productive than another person in several or even all activities. A person can have an absolute advantage in all activities but cannot have a comparative advantage in all activities.

## EXPANDED CHAPTER CHECKLIST

**When you have completed this chapter, you will be able to:**

**1 Use the production possibilities frontier to illustrate the economic problem.**

- Define the production possibilities frontier, *PPF*, and explain the relationship between the *PPF* and the available factors of production and technology.
- State which production points are attainable and which are unattainable.
- Discuss a tradeoff and a free lunch.

**2 Calculate opportunity cost.**

- Measure opportunity cost along the *PPF*.
- Explain why opportunity costs increase and tell how this affects the shape of the *PPF*.

**3 Define efficiency and describe an efficient use of resources.**

- Define production efficiency and allocative efficiency.
- Use a marginal benefit curve and marginal cost curve to find the efficient use of resources.

**4 Explain what makes production possibilities expand.**

- Define economic growth and illustrate it using a *PPF*.
- Explain the opportunity cost of economic growth.

**5 Explain how people gain from specialization and trade.**

- Define comparative advantage and tell its relationship to the gains from trade.
- Determine which of two people has a comparative advantage in the production of a good.
- Define absolute advantage and tell why it is different from comparative advantage.

## YOUR AP TEST HINTS

*AP Topics*

| Topic on your AP test | Corresponding textbook section |
|---|---|
| **Basic economic concepts** | |
| • Production possibility curve | Checkpoint 3.1 |
| • Scarcity, choice, opportunity cost | Checkpoint 3.2 |
| • Marginal analysis | Checkpoint 3.3 |
| • Comparative advantage, specialization, and trade | Checkpoint 3.4 |

*AP Vocabulary*

- On the AP test, the production possibilities frontier, *PPF*, might be called the "production possibility curve" or the "*PPC*."

*Extra AP material*

- If the opportunity cost along the *PPF* is constant, then the *PPF* is a straight line. Conversely, if the *PPF* is a straight line, the opportunity cost of producing another unit of a good is constant. The opportunity cost per unit of good *A* from gaining some of good *A* while losing some of good *B* equals the (loss in *B*) ÷ (gain in *A*).

## CHECKPOINT 3.1

■ **Use the production possibilities frontier to illustrate the economic problem.**

**Quick Review**

- *Production possibilities frontier* The boundary between combinations of goods and services that can be produced and combinations that cannot be produced, given the available factors of production and the state of technology. This is also called the "production possibility curve."
- *Unattainable points* Production points outside the *PPF* are unattainable.

## Additional Practice Problem 3.1

| Possibility | Fish (pounds) | | Fruit (pounds) |
|:---:|:---:|:---:|:---:|
| A | 0.0 | and | 36.0 |
| B | 4.0 | and | 35.0 |
| C | 7.5 | and | 33.0 |
| D | 10.5 | and | 30.0 |
| E | 13.0 | and | 26.0 |
| F | 15.0 | and | 21.0 |
| G | 16.5 | and | 15.0 |
| H | 17.5 | and | 8.0 |
| I | 18.0 | and | 0.0 |

1. The table above shows Crusoe's *PPF*. Can Crusoe gather 21 pounds of fruit and catch 30 pounds of fish? Explain your answer. Suppose that Crusoe discovers another fishing pond with more fish, so that he can catch twice as many fish as before. Now can Crusoe gather 21 pounds of fruit and catch 30 pounds of fish? Explain your answer.

### Solution to Additional Practice Problem 3.1

1. Initially, Crusoe cannot gather 21 pounds of fruit and catch 30 pounds of fish. This production point lies outside his *PPF* and so is unattainable. Once Crusoe discovers the new pond, however, he can gather 21 pounds of fruit and catch 30 pounds of fish. (In Row *F*, double the amount of Crusoe's fish.) The *PPF* depends on the available factors of production and when the factors of production increase, Crusoe's production possibilities change.

## ■ AP Self Test 3.1

### True or false

1. A point outside the production possibility curve is unattainable.

2. If all the factors of production are fully employed, the economy will produce at a point on the production possibility curve.

3. Moving from one point on the *PPF* to another point on the *PPF* illustrates a free lunch.

4. All production points on the *PPF* are production efficient.

### Multiple choice

1. The production possibility curve is a graph showing the
   a. exact point of greatest efficiency for producing goods and services.
   b. tradeoff between free lunches.
   c. maximum combinations of goods and services that can be produced.
   d. minimum combinations of goods and services that can be produced.
   e. resources available for the economy's use.

2. The production possibility curve is a boundary that separates
   a. the combinations of goods that can be produced from the combinations of services.
   b. attainable combinations of goods and services that can be produced from unattainable combinations.
   c. equitable combinations of goods that can be produced from inequitable combinations.
   d. reasonable combinations of goods that can be consumed from unreasonable combinations.
   e. affordable production points from unaffordable points.

3. Points inside the *PPC* are all
   a. unattainable and have fully employed resources.
   b. attainable and have fully employed resources.
   c. unattainable and have some unemployed resources.
   d. attainable and have some unemployed resources.
   e. unaffordable.

4. Points on the *PPF* are all
   a. unattainable and have fully employed resources.
   b. free lunches.
   c. inefficient.
   d. attainable and have some unemployed resources.
   e. production efficient.

5. During a time with high unemployment, a country can increase the production of one good or service
   a. without decreasing the production of something else.
   b. but must decrease the production of something else.
   c. and must increase the production of something else.
   d. by using resources in the production process twice.
   e. but the opportunity cost is infinite.

6. Moving along the production possibility curve itself illustrates
   a. the existence of tradeoffs.
   b. the existence of unemployment of productive resources.
   c. the benefits of free lunches.
   d. how free lunches can be exploited through trade.
   e. how tradeoffs need not occur if the economy is efficient.

### Short Response  Questions

■ **FIGURE 3.1**
Computers (millions per year)

Food (tons per year)

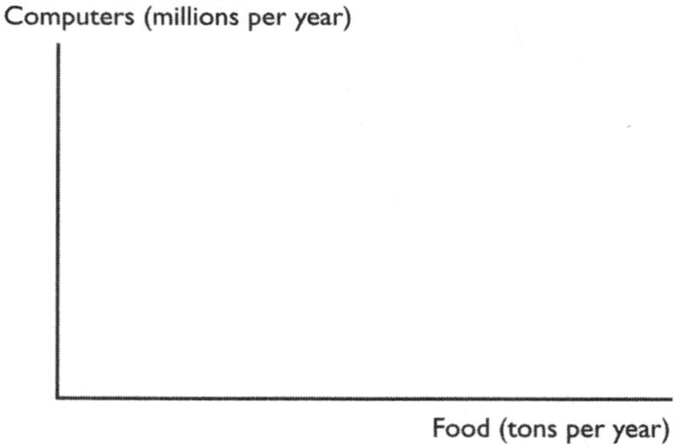

1. In Figure 3.1, draw a production possibilities frontier showing combinations of computers and food. Label the points that are attainable and unattainable. Label the points that have full employment and the points that have unemployment.

2. What is the effect on the production possibility curve if the unemployment rate falls from 8.3 percent to 5.5 percent?

3. What factors limit the amount of production?
4. What points are production efficient? Moving between these points, is there a tradeoff or a free lunch?

### CHECKPOINT 3.2

■ **Calculate opportunity cost.**

**Quick Review**
- *Opportunity cost is a ratio* Along a *PPF*, the opportunity cost of one good equals the quantity of the other good forgone divided by the increase in the good.

**Additional Practice Problem 3.2**

| Possibility | Fish (pounds) | | Fruit (pounds) |
|---|---|---|---|
| A | 0.0 | and | 36.0 |
| B | 4.0 | and | 35.0 |
| C | 7.5 | and | 33.0 |
| D | 10.5 | and | 30.0 |
| E | 13.0 | and | 26.0 |
| F | 15.0 | and | 21.0 |
| G | 16.5 | and | 15.0 |
| H | 17.5 | and | 8.0 |
| I | 18.0 | and | 0.0 |

1. The table above shows Robinson Crusoe's production possibilities. How does Crusoe's opportunity cost of a pound of fish change as he catches more fish?

**Solution to Additional Practice Problem 3.2**

| Move from | Increase in fish (pounds) | Decrease in fruit (pounds) | Opportunity cost of fish (pounds of fruit) |
|---|---|---|---|
| A to B | 4.0 | 1.0 | 0.25 |
| B to C | 3.5 | 2.0 | 0.57 |
| C to D | 3.0 | 3.0 | 1.00 |
| D to E | 2.5 | 4.0 | 1.60 |
| E to F | 2.0 | 5.0 | 2.50 |
| F to G | 1.5 | 6.0 | 4.00 |
| G to H | 1.0 | 7.0 | 7.00 |
| H to I | 0.5 | 8.0 | 16.00 |

1. The table above shows Crusoe's opportunity cost of a pound of fish. His opportunity cost of a pound of fish increases as he catches more fish. As he moves from point *A* to point *B* and

catches his first fish, the opportunity cost is only 0.25 pounds of fruit per pound of fish. But as he moves from point *H* to point *I* and catches only fish, the opportunity cost has increased to 16.0 pounds of fruit per pound of fish.

## ■ AP Self Test 3.2

### True or false

1. Moving from one point on the *PPF* to another point on the *PPF* has no opportunity cost.

2. When moving along the *PPF*, the quantity of CDs increases by 2 and the quantity of DVDs decreases by 1, so the opportunity cost is 2 CDs minus 1 DVD.

3. Increasing opportunity costs are common.

### Multiple choice

1. The opportunity cost of one more slice of pizza in terms of sodas is the
   a. number of pizza slices we have to give up to get one extra soda.
   b. number of sodas we have to give up to get one extra slice of pizza.
   c. total number of sodas that we have divided by the total number of pizza slices that we have.
   d. total number of pizza slices that we have divided by the total number of sodas that we have.
   e. price of pizza minus the price of the soda.

2. Moving between two points on a *PPF*, a country gains 6 automobiles and forgoes 3 trucks. The opportunity cost of 1 automobile is
   a. 3 trucks.
   b. 6 automobiles – 3 trucks.
   c. 2 trucks.
   d. 1/2 of a truck.
   e. 1 automobile.

3. Moving between two points on a *PPF*, a country gains 8 desktop computers and forgoes 4 laptop computers. The opportunity cost of 1 desktop computer is
   a. 4 laptops.
   b. 8 desktops.
   c. 1 desktop.
   d. 2 laptops.
   e. 1/2 of a laptop.

## ■ FIGURE 3.2
Potato chips (millions of bags per day)

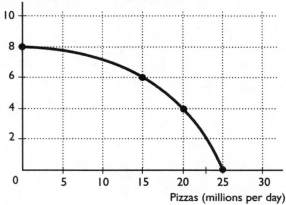

4. In the figure above, the opportunity cost of increasing production of pizza from 15 million to 20 million pizzas per day is
   a. 5 million pizzas.
   b. 2.50 pizzas per bag of chips.
   c. 0.40 of a pizza per bag of chips.
   d. 2.50 bags of chips per pizza.
   e. 0.40 of a bag of chips per pizza.

5. A country produces only cans of soup and pens. If the country produces on its *PPF* and increases the production of cans of soup, the opportunity cost of additional
   a. cans of soup is increasing.
   b. cans of soup is decreasing.
   c. cans of soup remain unchanged.
   d. ink pens is increasing.
   e. More information is needed to determine what happens to the opportunity cost.

6. Moving along a country's *PPF*, a reason opportunity costs increase is that
   a. unemployment decreases as a country produces more and more of one good.
   b. unemployment increases as a country produces more and more of one good.
   c. technology declines as a country produces more and more of one good.
   d. some resources are better suited for producing one good rather than the other.
   e. technology must advance in order to produce more and more of one good.

### Short Response Questions

1. Explain how constant opportunity costs are reflected by the production possibility curve.

### Long Response Questions

| Production point | MP3 players (millions per year) | | DVD players (millions per year) |
|---|---|---|---|
| A | 4.0 | and | 0.0 |
| B | 3.0 | and | 3.0 |
| C | 2.0 | and | 4.0 |
| D | 1.0 | and | 4.7 |
| E | 0.0 | and | 5.0 |

1. The table shows the production possibilities for a nation.
   a. Placing MP3 players on the vertical axis, label the axes in Figure 3.3 and graph the production possibilities frontier.

### ■ FIGURE 3.3

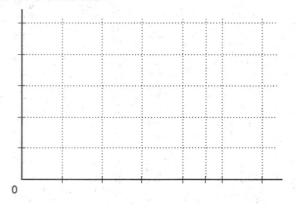

b. What is the opportunity cost per DVD player of moving from point *A* to point *B*?

*B* to *C*? *C* to *D*? *D* to *E*? How does the opportunity cost change as more DVD players are produced?

| Production point | Cans of soda (millions per year) | | Candy bars (millions per year) |
|---|---|---|---|
| A | 8.0 | and | 0.0 |
| B | 6.0 | and | 4.0 |
| C | 4.0 | and | 6.0 |
| D | 2.0 | and | 7.0 |
| E | 0.0 | and | 7.5 |

2. The table above shows the production possibilities for Sweetland.
   a. What is the opportunity cost per candy bar player of moving from point *A* to point *B*? *B* to *C*? *C* to *D*? *D* to *E*?
   b. What is the opportunity cost per can of soda of moving from point *E* to point *D*? *D* to *C*? *C* to *B*? *B* to *A*?
   c. How does the opportunity cost of a candy bar change as more candy bars are produced? How does the opportunity cost of a soda change as more sodas are produced?

3. What is the opportunity cost of increasing the production of a good while moving along a *PPC*? Why does this opportunity cost generally increase?

## CHECKPOINT 3.3

### ■ Define efficiency and describe an efficient use of resources.

*Quick Review*
- *Marginal benefit* The benefit that a person receives from consuming one more unit of a good or service.
- *Marginal cost* The opportunity cost of producing one more unit of a good or service.
- *Allocative efficiency* When we produce the combination of goods and services on the *PPC* that we value most highly.
- *Production efficiency* A situation in which we cannot produce more of one good

without producing less of some other good—production is on the *PPF*.

## Additional Practice Problem 3.3

1. Explain the relationship between production efficiency and allocative efficiency.

## Solution to Additional Practice Problem 3.3

1. Production efficiency is a situation in it is impossible to produce more of one good or service without producing less of some other good or service—production is at a point on the *PPF*. Allocative efficiency is the most highly valued combination of goods and services on the *PPF*.

*All* the combinations of goods on the *PPF* achieve production efficiency. But only one combination is the most highly valued and this point is the allocative efficient production point. The combination that is most highly valued is the combination where the marginal benefit equals the marginal cost.

## ■ AP Self Test 3.3

### True or false

1. All combinations of goods and services on the production possibilities frontier are combinations of allocative efficiency.

2. The marginal benefit of a good increases as more of the good is consumed.

3. Marginal benefit is derived from the production possibilities frontier.

4. A production point can be allocative efficient but not production efficient.

### Multiple choice

1. Allocative efficiency occurs when
   a. the most highly valued goods and services are produced.
   b. all citizens have equal access to goods and services.
   c. the environment is protected at all cost.
   d. goods and services are free.
   e. production takes place at any point on the *PPC*.

2. Production efficiency occurs
   a. anywhere inside or on the production possibility curve.
   b. when the total cost of production is minimized.
   c. at all points on the production possibility curve.
   d. at only one point on the production possibility curve.
   e. at all points inside the production possibility curve.

3. In general, the marginal cost curve
   a. has a positive slope.
   b. has a negative slope.
   c. is horizontal.
   d. is vertical.
   e. is U-shaped.

| Production point | Wheat (millions of bushels per year) | | Corn (millions of bushels per year) |
|---|---|---|---|
| A | 40.0 | and | 120.0 |
| B | 50.0 | and | 80.0 |

4. The table above gives two points on a nation's production possibilities curve. What is the marginal cost of moving from point *A* to point *B*?
   a. zero
   b. 0.25 of a bushel of wheat per bushel of corn
   c. 4 bushels of wheat per bushel of corn
   d. 0.25 of a bushel of corn per bushel of wheat
   e. 4 bushels of corn per bushel of wheat

5. Allocative efficiency is achieved when the marginal benefit of a good
   a. exceeds marginal cost by as much as possible.
   b. exceeds marginal cost but not by as much as possible.
   c. is less than its marginal cost.
   d. equals the marginal cost.
   e. equals zero.

### Short Response Questions

1. Define allocative efficiency in terms of marginal benefit and marginal cost.

**Long Response Questions**

1. In Figure 3.1 you indicated the points in a production possibilities frontier that are unattainable, attainable with full employment, and attainable with unemployment. In that figure, now indicate the points that are production efficient. Can you tell which point is allocatively efficient?

■ **FIGURE 3.4**

Marginal benefit and marginal cost (trucks per tractor)

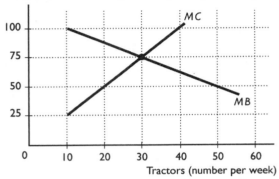

2. An economy produces only trucks and tractors and Figure 3.4 shows the marginal benefit and marginal cost of tractors. How many tractors are produced at the point of allocative efficiency?

3. Along a production possibilities frontier, to produce the first skateboard, 1 pair of roller blades must be forgone. To produce the second skateboard, 2 more pairs of roller blades must be forgone. Is the marginal cost of the second skate board 2 or 3 pairs of roller blades?

| Production point | Cans of soda (millions per year) | | Candy bars (millions per year) |
|---|---|---|---|
| A | 8.0 | and | 0.0 |
| B | 6.0 | and | 4.0 |
| C | 4.0 | and | 6.0 |
| D | 2.0 | and | 7.0 |
| E | 0.0 | and | 7.5 |

4. The table above shows the production possibilities for Sweetland.
   a. The table below shows the marginal benefit schedule for cans of soda. Complete the table by calculating the marginal cost.

| Cans of soda (millions per year) | Marginal benefit (bars per can) | Marginal cost (bars per can) |
|---|---|---|
| 6.0 | 1.50 | ___ |
| 4.0 | 2.50 | ___ |
| 2.0 | 3.50 | ___ |

   b. What is the allocative efficient quantity of cans of soda? Of candy bars?

5. Why does allocative efficiency require producing where marginal benefit equals marginal cost rather than where marginal benefit exceeds marginal cost?

## CHECKPOINT 3.4

■ **Explain what makes production possibilities expand.**

**Quick Review**

- *Opportunity cost of growth* The opportunity cost of economic growth is the current consumption goods and services forgone.

**Additional Practice Problem 3.4**

1. Does economic growth eliminate scarcity?

**Solution to Additional Practice Problem 3.4**

1. Economic growth does not eliminate scarcity. Scarcity exists as long as people's wants exceed what can be produced. Economic growth increases the goods and services that can be produced but people's wants will continue to outstrip the ability to produce. While economic growth means that additional wants can be satisfied, people's wants are infinite and so scarcity will continue to be present even with economic growth.

■ **AP Self Test 3.4**

**True or false**

1. The opportunity cost of economic growth is less consumption goods in the future.

2. Production possibilities per person in the United States have remained constant during the last 30 years.

## Multiple choice

1. To increase its economic growth, a nation should
   a. limit the number of people in college because they produce nothing.
   b. encourage spending on goods and services.
   c. encourage education because that increases the quality of labor.
   d. increase current consumption.
   e. eliminate expenditure on capital goods.

2. Other things being equal, if Mexico devotes more resources to train its population than Spain,
   a. Mexico will be able to eliminate opportunity cost faster than Spain.
   b. Mexico will be able to eliminate scarcity faster than Spain.
   c. Spain will grow faster than Mexico.
   d. Mexico will grow faster than Spain.
   e. Mexico will have more current consumption than Spain.

3. If a nation devotes a larger share of its current production to consumption goods, then
   a. its economic growth will slow down.
   b. the *PPCF* will shift outward.
   c. the *PPC* will shift inward.
   d. some productive factors will become unemployed.
   e. it must produce at a point within its *PPC*.

4. Which of the following statements is (are) correct?
   i. As an economy grows, the opportunity costs of economic growth necessarily decrease.
   ii. Economic growth has no opportunity cost.
   iii. The opportunity cost of economic growth is current consumption forgone.
   a. i only.
   b. ii only.
   c. iii only.
   d. i and iii.
   e. i and ii.

5. When a country's production possibilities frontier shifts outward over time, the country is experiencing
   a. no opportunity cost.
   b. economic growth.
   c. higher unemployment of resources.
   d. a decrease in unemployment of resources.
   e. an end to opportunity cost.

6. The opportunity cost of economic growth is ____ and the benefit of economic growth is ____.
   a. increased current consumption; increased future consumption
   b. increased current consumption; decreased future consumption
   c. decreased current consumption; increased future consumption
   d. decreased current consumption; decreased future consumption.
   e. nothing; increased future consumption.

## Short Response Question

1. What is the effect on the production possibility curve if the work force of a nation becomes more productive over time as the number of vocational school and college graduates rises?

## Long Response Questions

■ **FIGURE 3.5**

Automobiles (millions per year)

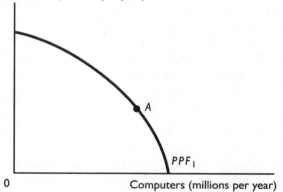

1. In the above figure, illustrate what happens if there is an improvement in the technology used to produce computers but not in the technology used to produce automobiles.

a. Suppose the economy was initially producing at point *A*. After the breakthrough, is it possible for the economy to produce more computers *and* more automobiles?

b. Suppose the economy was initially producing at point *A* but there were improvements in the technology used to produce *both* computers *and* automobiles. In Figure 3.5, show what happens to the production possibility curve.

2. What is the opportunity cost of economic growth?

3. What is the benefit of economic growth?

## CHECKPOINT 3.5

■ **Explain how people gain from specialization and trade.**

### Quick Review

- *Comparative advantage* The ability of a person to perform an activity or produce a good or service at a lower opportunity cost than someone else.

### Additional Practice Problem 3.5

1. Tony and Patty produce scooters and snowboards. The figure shows their production possibilities per day. With these production possibilities, the opportunity cost of a snowboard for Patty is 1/2 a

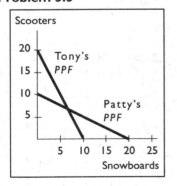

scooter and for Tony is 2 scooters. Patty has a lower opportunity cost and therefore she has the comparative advantage in snowboards. The opportunity cost of a scooter for Patty is 2 snowboards and for Tony is 1/2 of a snowboard. Tony has a lower opportunity cost and so he has the comparative advantage in scooters.

Suppose Patty acquires new equipment for scooter production that lets her produce a maximum of 60 rather than 10 scooters a day. What are her opportunity costs? Should Patty and Tony specialize and trade?

### Solution to Additional Practice Problem 3.5

1. Once Patty can produce 60 scooters a day, her opportunity costs change. Her opportunity cost of a scooter falls to 1/3 of a snowboard per scooter and her opportunity cost of a snowboard rises to 3 scooters per snowboard. With these opportunity costs, the comparative advantages have switched: Patty now has a comparative advantage in scooters and Tony in snowboards. Patty and Tony will still specialize and trade, only Patty will specialize in scooters and Tony in snowboards.

■ **AP Self Test 3.5**

### True or false

1. A person has an absolute advantage in an activity if the person can perform the activity at lower opportunity cost than someone else.

2. To achieve the gains from trade, a producer specializes in the product in which he or she has a comparative advantage and then trades with others.

3. Specialization and trade can make both producers better off even if one of them has an absolute advantage in producing all goods.

### Multiple choice

1. "Comparative advantage" is defined as a situation in which one person can produce
   a. more of all goods than another person.
   b. more of a good than another person.
   c. a good for a lower dollar cost than another person.
   d. a good for a lower opportunity cost than another person.
   e. all goods for lower opportunity costs than another person.

For the next three questions, use the following information: Scott and Cindy both produce only pizza and tacos. In one hour, Scott can produce

20 pizzas or 40 tacos. In one hour, Cindy can produce 30 pizzas or 40 tacos.

2. Scott's opportunity cost of producing 1 taco is
   a. 1/2 of a pizza.
   b. 1 pizza.
   c. 2 pizzas.
   d. 20 pizzas.
   e. 2 tacos

3. Cindy's opportunity cost of producing 1 taco is
   a. 3/4 of a pizza.
   b. 1 pizza.
   c. 30 pizzas.
   d. 40 pizzas.
   e. 1 taco.

4. Based on the data given,
   a. Cindy has a comparative advantage in producing tacos.
   b. Scott has a comparative advantage in producing tacos.
   c. Cindy and Scott have the same comparative advantage when producing tacos.
   d. neither Cindy nor Scott has a comparative advantage when producing tacos.
   e. Cindy and Scott have the same comparative advantage when producing pizzas.

5. In one hour John can produce 20 loaves of bread or 8 cakes. In one hour Phyllis can produce 30 loaves of bread or 15 cakes. Which of the following statements is true?
   a. Phyllis has a comparative advantage when producing bread.
   b. John has a comparative advantage when producing cakes.
   c. Phyllis has an absolute advantage in both goods.
   d. John has an absolute advantage in both goods.
   e. Phyllis has a comparative advantage in producing both cakes and bread.

6. In one hour John can produce 20 loaves of bread or 16 cakes. In one hour Phyllis can produce 30 loaves of bread or 15 cakes. Which of the following statements is true?
   a. Phyllis has a comparative advantage when producing cakes.
   b. John has a comparative advantage when producing cakes.
   c. Phyllis has an absolute advantage in both goods.
   d. John has an absolute advantage in both goods.
   e. Phyllis has a comparative advantage in producing both cakes and bread.

**Short Response Questions**
■ **FIGURE 3.6**

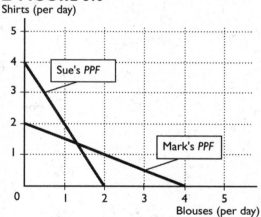

1. Figure 3.6 shows Mark and Sue's *PPF*s.
   a. What is Sue's opportunity cost of producing a shirt? What is Mark's opportunity cost of producing a shirt?
   b. Who has the comparative advantage in producing shirts?
   c. What is Sue's opportunity cost of producing a blouse? What is Mark's opportunity cost of producing a blouse?
   d. Who has the comparative advantage in producing blouses?
   e. Who should specialize in producing blouses and who should specialize in producing shirts?

f. If Mark and Sue specialize according to their comparative advantage, indicate the total production of shirts and blouses by putting a point in Figure 3.4 showing the total production. Label the point *A*.

g. How does point *A* show the gains from trade?

**Long Response Questions**

1. Why should people specialize according to their comparative advantage?

2. To achieve gains from trade, the opportunity costs of the trading partners must diverge. Why?

3. When it comes to trading one good for another, why is comparative advantage crucial and absolute advantage unimportant?

## YOUR AP SELF TEST ANSWERS

### ■ CHECKPOINT 3.1

**True or false**
1. True; page 64
2. True; page 64
3. False; page 65
4. True; pages 64-65

**Multiple choice**
1. c; page 62
2. b; page 64
3. d; page 64
4. e; pages 64-65
5. a; page 65
6. a; page 65

**Short Response Questions**

### ■ FIGURE 3.7
Computers (millions per year)

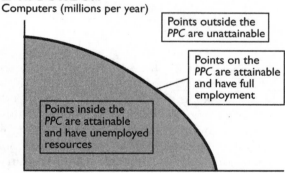

Food (tons per year)

1. Figure 3.7 shows a production possibilities curve between computers and food; pages 63-64.
2. Unemployment means that labor is not fully utilized so the economy is producing inside its *PPC*. As the unemployment rate falls, more workers are employed, and there is a movement closer to the *PPC*; page 64.
3. The factors that limit the amount of our production are the available resources and the state of technology. If any of these factors change, the *PPC* curve shifts; page 62.
4. All points *on* the production possibility curve are production efficient. Moving from one point to another incurs an opportunity cost

so there is tradeoff; pages 64-66

### ■ CHECKPOINT 3.2

**True or false**
1. False; page 68
2. False; page 69
3. True; page 70

**Multiple choice**
1. b; page 68
2. d; page 68
3. e; page 68
4. e; page 69
5. a; page 69
6. d; page 70

**Short Response Questions**

1. Constant opportunity costs mean there is a constant tradeoff between the two goods. As a result, the *PPC* is downward sloping and linear; page 70.

**Long Response Questions**

### ■ FIGURE 3.8
MP3 players (millions per year)

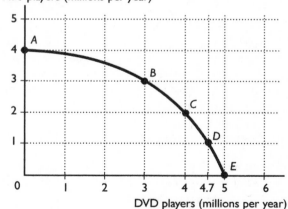

DVD players (millions per year)

1. a. Figure 3.8 illustrates the production possibilities frontier; page 68.
   b. The opportunity cost of moving from point *A* to point *B* to is 0.33 MP3 players per DVD player; from *B* to *C* is 1.00 MP3 player per DVD player; from *C* to *D* is 1.43

MP3 players per DVD player; and, from *D* to *E* is 3.33 MP3 players per DVD player. The opportunity cost increases; page 68

2. a. The opportunity cost of moving from point *A* to point *B* to is 0.5 cans of soda per candy bar; from *B* to *C* is 1.0 can of soda per candy bar; from *C* to *D* is 2.0 cans of soda per candy bar; and, from *D* to *E* is 4.0 cans of soda per candy bar; page 68.

   b. The opportunity cost of moving from point *E* to point *D* to is 0.25 candy bars per can of soda; from *D* to *C* is 0.50 candy bars per can of soda; from *C* to *B* is 1.00 candy bar per can of soda; and, from *B* to *A* is 2.00 candy bars per can of soda; page 68.

   c. As more candy bars are produced, the opportunity cost increases. As more cans of soda are produced, the opportunity cost increases; page 69.

3. The opportunity cost of increasing production of one good is the production of some other good forgone. The opportunity cost generally increases, so that increasingly large amounts of the other good are forgone, because resources are not equally productive in all activities. When initially increasing the production of one good, resources that are well suited for its production are used. When still more of the good is produced, resources that are less well suited must be used. Because the resources are ill suited, more are necessary to increase the production of the first good, and the forgone amount of the other good increases; page 70.

## ■ CHECKPOINT 3.3

**True or false**

1. False; page 73
2. False; pages 73-74
3. False; pages 73-74
4. False; page 72

**Multiple choice**

1. a; page 72
2. c; page 72
3. a; page 75

4. e; pages 68, 75
5. d; page 76

**Short Response Questions**

1. Allocative efficiency is the combination of goods that society most values. In marginal terms, when marginal cost is equal to marginal benefit, allocative efficiency is achieved; page 77.

**Long Response Questions**

■ FIGURE 3.9

Computers (millions per year)

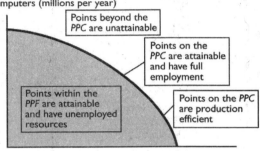

Food (tons per year)

1. Figure 3.9 shows the production possibilities frontier with the production points that are production efficient labeled. Note that these are the points that are attainable with full employment. Although the allocative efficient point will be a point on the *PPC*, it is not possible to determine which it is without additional information about the marginal benefits of the goods; pages 72-73.

■ FIGURE 3.10

Marginal benefit and marginal cost (trucks per tractor)

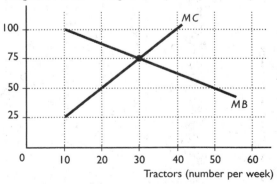

2. Allocative efficiency is the most highly valued combination of goods and services on

the *PPF*. It is the combination where marginal cost equals marginal benefit. In Figure 3.10, allocative efficiency is achieved when 30 tractors a week are produced;  pages 76-77.

3. The marginal cost of the second skate board is 2 pairs roller blades. Marginal cost is the opportunity cost of producing one more unit of a good or service. It is not the cost of all the units produced;  page 75.

| Cans of soda (millions per year) | Marginal benefit (bars per can) | Marginal cost (bars per can) |
|---|---|---|
| 6.0 | 1.50 | 1.50 |
| 4.0 | 2.50 | 0.75 |
| 2.0 | 3.50 | 0.38 |

4. a. The completed table is above. The marginal cost from 2.0 million cans of soda to 4.0 million is 0.50 candy bars per soda and the marginal cost from 4.0 million cans of soda to 6.0 million cans of soda is 1.0 candy bars per soda. So the marginal cost at 4.0 million cans of soda is the average, 0.75 candy bars per can of soda;  pages 68, 75.

   b. Marginal benefit equals marginal cost at 6.0 million cans of soda, so this is the allocatively efficient quantity of soda. The production possibilities table shows that with this quantity of soda, 4.0 million candy bars are produced, so 4.0 million candy bars is the allocatively efficient quantity of candy bars;  pages 76-77.

5. As long as the marginal benefit from an additional good or service exceeds the marginal cost, the unit should be produced because its production benefits society more than it costs society to produce. Producing where marginal benefit equals marginal cost insures that *all* units that have a net benefit for society are produced, so this level of production is the point of allocative efficiency;  page 76.

### ■ CHECKPOINT 3.4

**True or false**
1. False;  pages 79-80
2. False;  page 80

**Multiple choice**
1. c;  page 79
2. d;  pages 79-80
3. a;  page 79
4. d;  page 79
5. b;  page 79
6. c;  pages 79-80

**Short Response Questions**
1. As the work force gains knowledge and work skills, workers can produce more output. The nation's *PPC* curve shifts rightward; page 79.

**Long Response Questions**

**■ FIGURE 3.11**
Automobiles (millions per year)

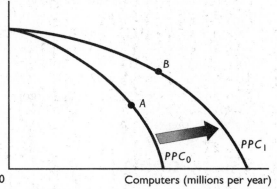

1. Figure 3.11 illustrates the new production possibility curve, *PPC₁*. Because the technological breakthrough did not affect automobile production, the maximum amount of automobiles that can be produced on the vertical axis does not change;  pages 79-80.

   a. Figure 3.11 shows that it is possible for the production of *both* automobiles and computers to increase, as a movement from the initial point *A* to a possible new point *B* illustrates;  page 79.

   b. Figure 3.12 (on the next page) shows that when the technology used to produce both computers and automobiles improves, the *PPC* curve shifts outward to *PPC₂*;  page 79.

■ **FIGURE 3.12**

Automobiles (millions per year)

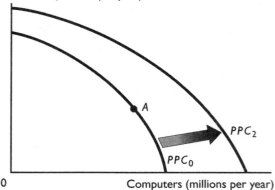

2. Economic growth requires either developing new technologies, accumulating more human capital, or accumulating more capital. All of these avenues require resources, so the opportunity cost of economic growth is the decrease in the current production of goods and services; page 79.

3. The benefit from economic growth is increased consumption per person in the future after the production possibilities have expanded, that is, after the *PPC* has shifted outward; page 79.

■ **CHECKPOINT 3.5**

**True or false**

1. False; pages 81-82
2. True; page 82
3. True; pages 82-83

**Multiple choice**

1. d; page 81
2. a; page 81
3. a; page 81
4. b; pages 81-82
5. c; page 82
6. b; page 82

**Short Response Questions**

1. a. Sue's opportunity cost of a shirt is 1/2 of a blouse because, when moving along her *PPC* to produce 1 more shirt she forgoes 1/2 of a blouse. Mark's opportunity cost of a shirt is 2 blouses; page 81

b. Sue has the comparative advantage in producing shirts because her opportunity cost is lower; page 81.

c. Sue's opportunity cost of a blouse is 2 shirts because, when moving along her *PPC*, to produce 1 more blouse she forgoes 2 shirts. Mark's opportunity cost of a blouse is 1/2 of a shirt; page 81.

d. Mark has the comparative advantage in producing blouses because his opportunity cost is lower; page 81.

e. Mark should specialize in producing blouses and Sue should specialize in producing shirts; page 82.

■ **FIGURE 3.13**

Shirts (per day)

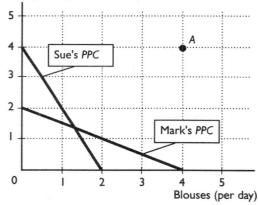

f. Mark produces 4 blouses and Sue produces 4 shirts, so a total of 4 shirts and 4 blouses are produced. Figure 3.13 shows this production as point *A*; pages 82-83.

g. If the total production at point *A* is divided evenly, both Mark and Sue will receive 2 shirts and 2 blouses. When both were producing only for themselves, they could not produce 2 shirts and 2 blouses because this point is beyond both their *PPC*s. By specializing and trading, Mark and Sue can consume at a point outside their *PPC*s; page 83.

**Long Response Questions**

1. A person's comparative advantage is the good that the person can produce at a lower opportunity cost than other people. When this person specializes in the production of the good, it is produced at the lowest cost; page 82.

2. If the trading partners' opportunity costs are the same, there is no incentive for them to trade. For instance, if two people produce either gum or soda and both have the same opportunity cost of 5 gums for 1 soda, neither is willing to buy or sell to the other. Only when opportunity costs diverge will one person be willing to buy (the person with the higher opportunity cost) and the other willing to sell (the person with the lower opportunity cost); page 82.

3. People are willing to trade if they can obtain a good at lower opportunity cost than what it costs them to produce the good. Comparative advantage tells which person has a lower opportunity cost. Even if a person has an absolute advantage in all goods, he or she does not have a comparative advantage in all goods. So comparative advantage determines who produces a product and who buys it; page 82.

# Demand and Supply

# *Chapter*

# 4

## CHAPTER IN PERSPECTIVE

The tools of demand and supply explain how competitive markets work. We use the demand and supply tools to determine the quantities and prices of the goods and services produced and consumed.

■ **Distinguish between quantity demanded and demand and explain what determines demand.**

The quantity demanded is the amount of any good, service, or resource that people are willing and able to buy during a specified period at a specified price. Demand is the relationship between the quantity demanded and the price of a good when all other influences on buying plans remain the same. The law of demand states that other things remaining the same, if the price of a good rises, the quantity demanded of that good decreases; and if the price of a good falls, the quantity demanded of that good increases. A demand curve is a graph of the relationship between the quantity demanded of a good and its price when all other influences on buying plans remain the same. The market demand is the sum of the demands of all the buyers in a market. A change in price leads to a *change in the quantity demanded* and a movement along the demand curve. Factors that *change demand* and shift the demand curve are: prices of related goods; income; expectations; number of buyers; and preferences.

■ **Distinguish between quantity supplied and supply and explain what determines supply.**

The quantity supplied is the amount of any good, service, or resource that people are willing and able to sell during a specified period at a specified price. Supply is the relationship between the quantity supplied and the price of a good when all other influences on selling plans remain the same. The law of supply states that other things remaining the same, if the price of a good rises, the quantity supplied of that good increases; and if the price of a good falls, the quantity supplied of that good decreases. A supply curve is a graph of the relationship between the quantity supplied of a good and its price when all other influences on selling plans remain the same. A change in price leads to a *change in the quantity supplied* and a movement along the supply curve. Factors that *change supply* and shift the supply curve are: prices of related goods; prices of resources and other inputs; expectations; number of sellers; and productivity. If supply increases (decreases), the supply curve shifts rightward (leftward).

■ **Explain how demand and supply determine price and quantity in a market, and explain the effects of changes in demand and supply.**

The equilibrium price and equilibrium quantity occur when the quantity demanded equals the quantity supplied. An increase in demand raises the price and increases the quantity. An increase in supply lowers the price and increases the quantity. An increase in both demand and supply increases the quantity and the price might rise, fall, or not change. An increase in demand and a decrease in supply raises the price and the quantity might increase, decrease, or not change. Changes in demand and supply in the opposite direction to those given above lead to reverse changes in price and quantity.

## EXPANDED CHAPTER CHECKLIST

**When you have completed this chapter, you will be able to:**

**1 Distinguish between quantity demanded and demand and explain what determines demand.**

- Define quantity demanded.
- State and explain the law of demand.
- Define demand, demand schedule, and demand curve.
- Illustrate the law of demand using a demand schedule and a demand curve.
- Define market demand.
- Derive the market demand curve from individual demand curves.
- List the influences on buying plans that change demand.
- Define substitute and complement.
- Define and give an example of a normal good and an inferior good.
- Distinguish between a change in the quantity demanded and a change in demand.

**2 Distinguish between quantity supplied and supply and explain what determines supply.**

- Define quantity supplied.
- State and explain the law of supply.
- Define supply, supply schedule, and supply curve.
- Illustrate the law of supply using a supply schedule and a supply curve.
- Define market supply.
- Derive the market supply curve from individual supply curves.
- List the influences on selling plans that change supply.
- Define substitute in production and complement in production.
- Distinguish between a change in the quantity supplied and a change in supply.

**3 Explain how demand and supply determine the price and quantity in a market and explain the effects of changes in demand and supply.**

- Determine the equilibrium price and quantity in a supply and demand diagram.
- Indicate the amount of a surplus or shortage if the price is not the equilibrium price.
- Illustrate the effects of a change in demand and a change in supply.

## YOUR AP TEST HINTS

*AP Topics*

| Topic on your AP test | Corresponding textbook section |
|---|---|
| **Nature and function of product markets** | |
| Supply and Demand | Chapter 4 |
| • Determinants of demand | Checkpoint 4.1 |
| • Determinants of supply | Checkpoint 4.2 |
| • Market equilibrium | Checkpoint 4.3 |

*AP Vocabulary*

- On the AP test, factors that change demand are often said to be "determinants of demand."
- On the AP test, factors that change supply are often referred to as "determinants of supply."
- When referring to productivity as a factor that changes supply, often the AP test refers to "new technology" being added or developed to production.
- The phrase, "other things remaining the same" is typically expressed on the AP test as "other things constant".
- When both the demand and supply curves shift, the result that you cannot tell if the price or quantity rises, falls or stays the same is expressed on the AP test by saying there is an "indeterminate result."

*Extra AP material*

- Consumer information, both favorable and not, can be a factor that changes demand. For instance, if consumers become aware of health risks from a food, the demand for that type of food decreases and the demand curve shifts leftward.

- The time period available for production can be a factor affecting a change in supply. The longer the time available, the greater the supply, so the supply curve shifts rightward as more time passes.

## CHECKPOINT 4.1

■ **Distinguish between quantity demanded and demand and explain what determines demand.**

### Quick Review

- *Change in the quantity demanded* A change in the quantity of a good that people plan to buy that results from a change in the price of the good.

- *Law of demand* If the price of a good rises, the quantity demanded of that good decreases; and if the price of a good falls, the quantity demanded of that good decreases.

- *Change in demand* A change in the quantity that people plan to buy when any influence on buying plans, other than the price of the good, changes. These other influences include: prices of related goods, income, expectations, number of buyers, and preferences.

### Additional Practice Problems 4.1

1. In the market for scooters, several events occur, one at a time. Explain the influence of each event on the quantity demanded of scooters and on the demand for scooters. Illustrate the effects of each event either by a movement along the demand curve or a shift in the demand curve for scooters and say which event (or events) illustrates the law of demand in action. These events are:

a. The price of a scooter falls.

b. The price of a bicycle falls.

c. Consumers become aware that riding a scooter can lead to injury.

d. Income increases.

e. Scooters become unfashionable and the number of buyers decreases.

2. Suppose that each year Anna, Ben, Carol, and Dana are willing and able to buy scooters as shown in the table.

| Price (dollars per scooter) | Quantity demanded | | | |
|---|---|---|---|---|
| | Anna | Ben | Carol | Dana |
| 100 | 0 | 0 | 0 | 0 |
| 75 | 1 | 0 | 0 | 0 |
| 50 | 2 | 1 | 1 | 0 |
| 25 | 2 | 1 | 2 | 1 |

■ **FIGURE 4.1**

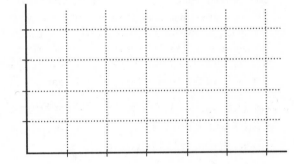

Using the information in the table:

a. Label the axes in Figure 4.1 above.

b. Graph the market demand curve.

### Solutions to Additional Practice Problems 4.1

1a. This problem emphasizes the distinction between a change in the quantity demanded and a change in demand. A fall in the price of a scooter brings an increase in

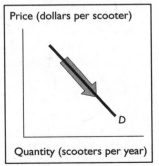

the quantity demanded of scooters, which is

illustrated by a movement down along the demand curve for scooters as shown in the figure. This event illustrates the law of demand in action.

1b. A bicycle is a substitute for a scooter. With the lower price of a bicycle, some people who previously would have bought a scooter will now buy a bicycle instead. So a fall

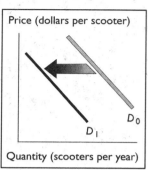

in the price of a bicycle decreases the demand for scooters. The demand curve for scooters shifts leftward as shown in the figure by the shift from demand curve $D_0$ to demand curve $D_1$.

1c. Rising awareness of injury rates changes preferences and makes scooters less desirable. The demand for scooters decreases and the demand curve for the scooters shifts leftward as shown in the figure above.

1d. A scooter is probably a normal good. So, people buy more scooters when their income increases. The demand for scooters increases and the demand curve shifts rightward as illustrated in the figure.

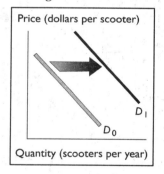

1e. A decrease in the number of buyers decreases the demand for scooters. The demand curve shifts leftward.

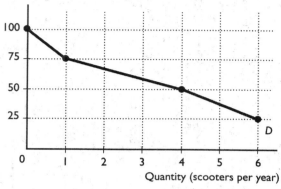

■ **FIGURE 4.2**

Price (dollars per scooter)

2a. Figure 4.2 labels the axes.

2b. The market demand curve is derived by adding the quantities demanded by Anna, Ben, Carol, and Dana at each price. The market demand curve is illustrated in Figure 4.2.

■ **AP Self Test 4.1**

**True or false**

1. The law of demand states that other things constant, if the price of a good rises, the quantity demanded of that good increases.

2. If the quantity of ice cream demanded at each price increases, there is a movement along the demand curve for ice cream.

3. When Sue's income increases, her demand for movies increases. For Sue, movies are a normal good.

4. A rise in the price of a computer increases the demand for computers because a computer is a normal good.

5. If people's incomes fall and all other influences on buying plans remain the same, the demand for computers will decrease and there will be a movement along the demand curve.

**Multiple choice**

1. The "law of demand" indicates that if the University of Maine increases the tuition, all other things remaining the same,
    a. the demand for classes will decrease at the University of Maine.
    b. the demand for classes will increase at the University of Maine.
    c. the quantity of classes demanded will increase at the University of Maine.
    d. the quantity of classes demanded will decrease at the University of Maine.
    e. both the demand for and the quantity of classes demanded will decrease at the University of Maine.

2. Other things remaining the same, the quantity of a good or service demanded will increase if the price of the good or service
    a. rises.
    b. falls.
    c. does not change.
    d. rises or does not change.
    e. rises or falls.

3. Teenagers demand more soda than other age groups. If the number of teenagers increases, everything else remaining the same,
    a. market demand for soda increases.
    b. market demand for soda decreases.
    c. market demand for soda does not change.
    d. there is a movement along the market demand curve for soda.
    e. None of the above answers is correct because the effect on the demand depends whether the supply curve shifts.

4. One reason the demand for laptop computers might increase is a
    a. fall in the price of a laptop computers.
    b. fall in the price of a desktop computer.
    c. a change in preferences as laptops have become more portable, with faster processors and larger hard drives.
    d. poor quality performance record for laptop computers.
    e. a decrease in income if laptops are a normal good.

5. The number of buyers of sport utility vehicles, SUVs, decreases sharply. So
    a. the demand curve for SUVs shifts leftward.
    b. the demand curve for SUVs shifts rightward.
    c. there is neither a shift nor a movement along the demand curve for SUVs.
    d. there is a movement down along the demand curve for SUVs.
    e. the supply curve for SUVs shifts rightward.

■ **FIGURE 4.3**

Price (dollars per pizza)

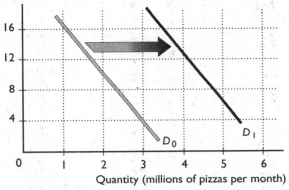

6. The shift of the demand curve for pizza illustrated in Figure 4.3 could be the result of
    a. a rise in income if pizza is a normal good.
    b. a fall in the price of fried chicken, a substitute for pizza.
    c. consumers coming to believe that pizza is unhealthy.
    d. the belief that pizza will fall in price next month.
    e. a fall in the price of a pizza.

7. The shift of the demand curve for pizza illustrated in Figure 4.3 could be the result of
    a. a rise in income if pizza is an inferior good.
    b. a fall in the price of soda, a complement for pizza.
    c. a decrease in the number of people who like pizza.
    d. a rise in the price of a pizza.
    e. a rise in the price of the cheese used to produce the pizza.

8. When moving along a demand curve, which of the following changes?
   a. the consumers' incomes
   b. the prices of other goods
   c. the number of buyers
   d. the price of the good
   e. the consumers' preferences

9. If the price of a CD falls,
   i. the demand curve for CDs shifts rightward.
   ii. the demand curve for CDs will not shift.
   iii. there is a movement along the demand curve for CDs.
   a. i only.
   b. ii only.
   c. iii only.
   d. ii and iii.
   e. i and iii.

10. Pizza and tacos are substitutes and the price of a pizza increases. Which of the following correctly indicates what happens?
   a. The demand for pizzas decreases and the demand for tacos increases.
   b. The demand for both goods decreases.
   c. The quantity of tacos demanded increases and the quantity of pizza demanded decreases.
   d. The quantity of pizza demanded decreases and the demand for tacos increases.
   e. The demand for each decreases because both are normal goods.

## Short Response Questions

| Price (dollars per bundle of cotton candy) | Quantity (bundles of cotton candy per month) |
| --- | --- |
| 1 | 10,000 |
| 2 | 8,000 |
| 3 | 7,000 |
| 4 | 4,000 |

1. The demand schedule for cotton candy is given in the following table. In Figure 4.4, draw the demand curve. Label the axes.
   a. If the price of cotton candy is $2 a bundle, what is the quantity demanded?

■ **FIGURE 4.4**

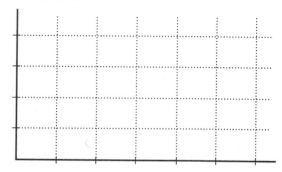

   b. If the price of cotton candy is $3 a bundle, what is the quantity demanded?
   c. Does the demand curve you drew slope upward or downward?

■ **FIGURE 4.5**

Price (dollars per pound of butter)

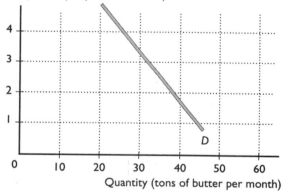

Quantity (tons of butter per month)

2. Butter is a normal good and margarine is substitute for butter. Figure 4.5 shows the demand curve for butter.
   a. In Figure 4.5, show how the demand curve shifts if incomes rise. Label this demand curve $D_1$.
   b. In Figure 4.5, show how the demand curve shifts if margarine falls in price. Label this demand curve $D_2$.
   c. If the price of butter falls from $4 a pound to $3 a pound, does the demand curve shift toward demand curve $D_1$, $D_2$, or neither? Explain your answer.

## Long Response Questions

1. Explain the difference between a change in quantity demanded and a change in demand.

2. What is the difference between a movement along a demand curve and a shift in a demand curve?

## CHECKPOINT 4.2

■ **Distinguish between quantity supplied and supply and explain what determines supply.**

### Quick Review

- *Change in quantity supplied* A change in the quantity of a good that suppliers plan to sell that results from a change in the price of the good.

- *Change in supply* A change in the quantity that suppliers plan to sell when any influence on selling plans, other than the price of the good, changes. These other determinants include: prices of related goods, prices of inputs, expectations, number of sellers, productivity, technology, and the time period available for production.

### Additional Practice Problems 4.2

1. In the market for scooters, several events occur, one at a time. Explain the influence of each event on the quantity supplied of scooters and on the supply of scooters. Illustrate the effects of each event either by a movement along the supply curve or a shift in the supply curve for scooters and say which event (or events) illustrates the law of supply in action. These events are:

   a. The price of a scooter rises.

   b. The price of the steel used to make scooters rises.

   c. The number of firms making scooters decreases.

   d. New technology is developed that increases the productivity of the factories making scooters.

| Price | Quantity supplied (tons of plywood per month) | | | |
|---|---|---|---|---|
| (dollars per ton of · plywood) | Eddy | Franco | George | Helen |
| 100 | 2 | 2 | 1 | 1 |
| 75 | 2 | 1 | 1 | 1 |
| 50 | 1 | 1 | 1 | 0 |
| 25 | 0 | 0 | 1 | 0 |

■ **FIGURE 4.6**

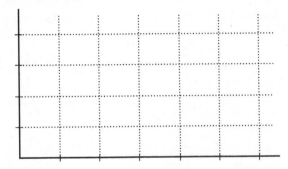

2. Each month Eddy, Franco, George, and Helen are willing and able to sell plywood as shown in the table above.

   a. Label the axes in Figure 4.6.

   b. Graph the market supply curve.

### Solutions to Additional Practice Problems 4.2

1a. This problem emphasizes the distinction between a change in the quantity supplied and a change in supply. A rise in the price of a scooter brings an increase in the quantity

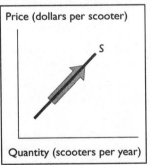

supplied of scooters, which is illustrated by a movement up along the supply curve for scooters as shown in the figure. There is no change in the supply and the supply curve does not shift. This event illustrates the law of supply in action.

1b. When the price of the steel used to make scooters rises, the cost of producing scooters rises. As a result, the supply of scooters de-creases. The supply curve

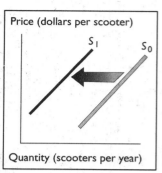

shifts leftward as illustrated in the figure by the shift from supply curve $S_0$ to supply curve $S_1$.

1c. A decrease in the number of firms producing scooters decreases the supply of scooters. The supply curve shifts leftward, as illus-trated in the figure above.

1d. New technology increases the supply of scooters. The supply curve shifts rightward, as illustrated in the figure to the right by the shift from supply curve $S_0$ to supply curve $S_1$.

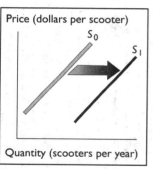

2a. The axes are labeled in Figure 4.7.

| Price (dollars per ton of plywood) | Quantity supplied (tons per month) |
|---|---|
| 100 | 6 |
| 75 | 5 |
| 50 | 3 |
| 25 | 1 |

2b. The market supply curve is derived by add-ing the quantities supplied by Eddy, Franco, George, and Helen at each price. The table above gives the resulting sum and the mar-ket supply curve is illustrated in Figure 4.7.

■ **FIGURE 4.7**

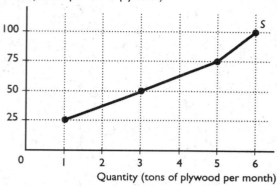

Price (dollars per ton of plywood)

Quantity (tons of plywood per month)

■ **AP Self Test 4.2**

**True or false**

1. The law of supply states that other things remaining the same, if the price of a good rises, the supply of the good increases.

2. When new technology for producing com-puters is used by manufacturers, the supply of computers increases.

3. Other things constant, if the wage rate paid to chefs rises, the supply of restaurant meals will increase.

4. If the price of coffee is expected to rise next month, the supply of coffee this month will decrease.

5. The supply of a good will increase and there will be a movement up along the supply curve of the good if the price of one of its substitutes in production falls.

**Multiple choice**

1. The quantity supplied of a good, service, or resource is ____ during a specified period and at a specified price.
   a. the amount that people are able to sell
   b. the amount that people are willing to sell
   c. the amount that people are able and will-ing to sell
   d. the amount that people are willing and able to buy
   e. the amount sold

2. One reason supply curves have an upward slope is because
   a. increased supply will require increased technology.
   b. people will pay a higher price when less is supplied.
   c. a higher price brings a greater profit, so firms want to sell more of that good.
   d. to have more of the good supplied requires more firms to open.
   e. None of the above answers is correct because supply curves have a downward slope.

3. Which of the following indicates that the law of supply applies to makers of soda?
   a. An increase in the price of a soda leads to an increase in the demand for soda.
   b. An increase in the price of a soda leads to an increase in the supply of soda.
   c. An increase in the price of a soda leads to an increase in the quantity of soda supplied.
   d. A decrease in the price of a soda leads to an increase in the quantity of soda demanded.
   e. A decrease in the price of a soda leads to an increase in the supply of soda.

4. The market supply curve is the ____ of the ____.
   a. horizontal sum; individual supply curves
   b. vertical sum; individual supply curves
   c. horizontal sum; individual supply curves minus the market demand
   d. vertical sum; individual supply curves minus the market demand
   e. vertical average; individual supply curves

5. If the costs of producing pizza increase, which will occur?
   a. The supply of pizza will decrease.
   b. The quantity of pizzas supplied will increase as sellers try to cover their costs.
   c. Pizza will cease to be produced and sold.
   d. The demand curve for pizza will shift leftward when the price of a pizza increases.
   e. The demand curve for pizza will shift rightward when the price of a pizza increases.

6. A rise in the price of a substitute in production for a good leads to
   a. an increase in the supply of that good.
   b. a decrease in the supply of that good.
   c. no change in the supply of that good.
   d. a decrease in the quantity of that good supplied.
   e. no change in either the supply or the quantity supplied of the good.

7. An increase in the productivity of producing jeans results in
   a. the quantity of jeans supplied increasing.
   b. the supply of jeans increasing.
   c. buyers demanding more jeans because they are now more efficiently produced.
   d. buyers demanding fewer jeans because their price will fall, which signals lower quality.
   e. some change but the impact on the supply of jeans is impossible to predict.

8. Suppose the price of leather used to produce shoes increases. As a result, there is ____ in the supply of shoes and the supply curve of shoes ____.
   a. an increase; shifts rightward
   b. an increase; shifts leftward
   c. a decrease; shifts rightward
   d. a decrease; shifts leftward
   e. no change; does not shift

■ **FIGURE 4.8**
Price (dollars per pizza)

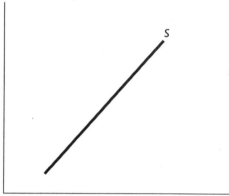

9. The shift of the supply curve of pizza illustrated in Figure 4.8 could be the result of
   a. a rise in the price of cheese used to produce pizza.
   b. a decrease in the number of firms producing pizza.
   c. an increase in the productivity of the firms producing pizza.
   d. a rise in the price of a substitute in production.
   e. a rise in the price of a pizza.

10. The shift of the supply curve of pizza illustrated in Figure 4.8 could be the result of
    a. a rise in income if pizza is a normal good.
    b. a fall in the price of soda, a consumer complement for pizza.
    c. an increase in the number of firms producing pizza.
    d. a fall in the price of a pizza.
    e. a rise in the wage paid the workers who make pizza.

**Short Response Questions**

| Price (dollars per bundle of cotton candy) | Quantity (bundles of cotton candy per month) |
|---|---|
| 1 | 4,000 |
| 2 | 8,000 |
| 3 | 10,000 |
| 4 | 12,000 |

1. The supply schedule for cotton candy is given in the table above. In Figure 4.4, you previously drew a demand curve for cotton candy. Now use the supply schedule to draw the supply curve in Figure 4.4.
   a. If the price of cotton candy is $2 a bundle, what is the quantity supplied?
   b. If the price of cotton candy is $3 a bundle, what is the quantity supplied?
   c. Does the supply curve you drew slope upward or downward?

■ **FIGURE 4.9**
Price (dollars per ton of rubber bands)

S

Quantity (tons of rubber bands per year)

2. Figure 4.9 shows a supply curve for rubber bands. Suppose the productivity of producing rubber bands increases. In Figure 4.9, illustrate the effect of this event.

3. What is the law of supply?

4. What determinant(s) of supply leads to a change in the quantity supplied?

5. What determinant(s) of supply leads to a change in supply?

## CHECKPOINT 4.3

■ **Explain how demand and supply determine the price and quantity in a market and explain the effects of changes in demand and supply.**

*Quick Review*

• *Market equilibrium* When the quantity demanded equals the quantity supplied.

• *Surplus* When the quantity demanded is less than the quantity supplied.

- *Shortage* When the quantity demanded exceeds the quantity supplied.

### Additional Practice Problems 4.3

1. Hot dogs are an inferior good and people's incomes rise. What happens to the equilibrium price and quantity of hot dogs?

2. New technology is developed for the production of hot dogs. What happens to the equilibrium price and quantity of hot dogs?

3. The price of a hot dog bun falls and, simultaneously, the number of hot dog producers increases. The effect of the fall in the price of a hot dog bun is less than the effect of the increase in the number of producers. What happens to the equilibrium price and quantity of hot dogs?

### Solutions to Additional Practice Problems 4.3

1. When income increases, the demand for an inferior good decreases and the demand curve shifts leftward. The supply does not change and the supply curve does not shift. As a result, the equilibrium price of a hot dog falls, from $3 to $1 because at a price of $3 there is a surplus of hot dogs which creates downward pressure on the price. The equilibrium quantity decreases to 20 million hot dogs.

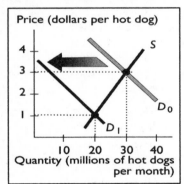

2. With new technology, the productivity of producing a good increases, so the supply of the good increases and the supply curve shifts

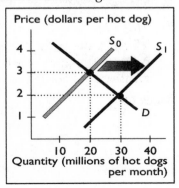

rightward. The demand does not change and so the demand curve does not shift. The equilibrium price falls, to $2 in the figure, because at the initial price there is a surplus of hot dogs. The equilibrium quantity increases, to 30 million in the figure.

3. The fall in the price of a complement, hot dog buns, increases the demand for hot dogs and the demand curve for hot dogs shifts rightward. The increase in the number of producers increases the supply of hot dogs and the supply curve shifts rightward. Because the increase in supply exceeds the increase in demand, the price of a hot dog falls, from $3 to $1 in the figure, and the quantity increases, from 10 million to 30 million in the figure.

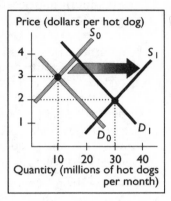

## ■ AP Self Test 4.3

### True or false

1. If the price of asparagus is below the equilibrium price, there is a shortage of asparagus and the price of asparagus will rise until the shortage disappears.

2. When the demand for skateboards decreases and the supply of skateboards remains unchanged, the quantity supplied of skateboards decreases as the price rises.

3. Automakers expect the price of an SUV to fall next year. If the demand for SUVs does not change, the equilibrium price of an SUV today will fall and the equilibrium quantity today will increase.

4. As summer comes to an end and winter sets in, the demand for and supply of hamburger buns decrease. The price of a hamburger bun definitely remains the same.

5. The number of buyers of grapefruit juice increases and at the same time severe frost decreases the supply of grapefruit juice. The price of grapefruit juice will rise.

### Multiple choice

1. The equilibrium price of a good occurs if the
   a. quantity of the good demanded equals the quantity of the good supplied.
   b. quantity of the good demanded is greater than the quantity of the good supplied.
   c. quantity of the good demanded is less than the quantity of the good supplied.
   d. demand for the good is equal to the supply of the good.
   e. price of the good seems reasonable to most buyers.

2. Which of the following is correct?
   i. A surplus puts downward pressure on the price of a good.
   ii. A shortage puts upward pressure on the price of a good
   iii. There is no surplus or shortage at equilibrium.
   a. i and ii..
   b. i and iii.
   c. ii and iii.
   d. i, ii, and iii.
   e. only iii.

3. The number of buyers of ceiling fans increases, so there is an increase in the
   a. quantity of ceiling fans demanded and a surplus of ceiling fans.
   b. demand for ceiling fans and a rise in the price of a ceiling fan.
   c. demand for ceiling fans and a surplus of ceiling fans.
   d. supply of ceiling fans and no change in the price of a ceiling fan.
   e. demand for ceiling fans and in the supply of ceiling fans.

4. Which of the following is the best explanation for why the price of gasoline increases during the summer months?
   a. Oil producers have higher costs of production in the summer.
   b. Sellers have to earn profits during the summer to cover losses in the winter.
   c. There is increased driving by families going on vacation.
   d. There is less competition among oil refineries in the summer.
   e. The number of gas stations open 24 hours a day rises in the summer months and so the price must rise to cover the higher costs.

5. Suppose that the price of lettuce used to produce tacos increases. As a result, the equilibrium price of a taco ____ and the equilibrium quantity ____.
   a. rises; increases
   b. rises; decreases
   c. falls; increases
   d. falls; decreases
   e. does not change; decreases

6. The technology associated with manufacturing computers has advanced enormously. This change has ____ the price of a computer ____ and ____ the quantity.
   a. raised; increased
   b. raised; decreased
   c. lowered; increased
   d. lowered; decreased
   e. lowered; not changed

7. Candy makers accurately anticipate the increase in demand for candy for Halloween so that the supply of candy and the demand for candy increase the same amount. As a result, the price of candy ____ and the quantity of candy ____.
   a. rises; does not change
   b. falls; increases
   c. does not change; increases
   d. does not change; does not change
   e. rises; rises

8. During 2005 the supply of petroleum decreased while at the same time the demand
for petroleum increased. If the magnitude of
the increase in demand was greater than the
magnitude of the decrease in supply, then
the equilibrium price of gasoline ____ and
the equilibrium quantity ____.
  a. increased; increased
  b. increased; decreased
  c. increased; did not change
  d. decreased; did not change
  e. did not change; increased

## Short Response Questions

1. In Checkpoint 4.1 you drew a demand curve
in Figure 4.4; in Checkpoint 4.2, you drew a
supply curve in that figure. Return to Figure
4.4 and answer the following questions.
  a. If the price of cotton candy is $1, what is
the situation in the market?
  b. If the price of cotton candy is $3, what is
the situation in the market?
  c. What is the equilibrium price and equilibrium quantity of cotton candy?

| Price (dollars per sweatshirt) | Quantity demanded (sweatshirts per season) Hockey team | Soccer team | Quantity supplied (sweatshirts per season) |
|---|---|---|---|
| 35 | 5 | 8 | 32 |
| 30 | 6 | 9 | 25 |
| 25 | 8 | 11 | 19 |
| 20 | 12 | 15 | 12 |
| 15 | 17 | 20 | 8 |

2. The table gives the demand and supply
schedules for sweatshirts. What is the market
demand schedule? At what price will the
quantity demanded be equal to the quantity
supplied? What is the equilibrium quantity?

■ **FIGURE 4.10**

Price (dollars per piece of gold jewelry)

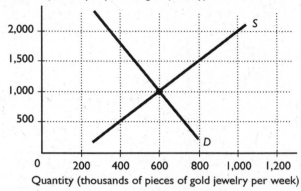

Quantity (thousands of pieces of gold jewelry per week)

3. Figure 4.10 shows the supply and demand
for gold jewelry. In the figure, show what
happens to the price and quantity if gold
jewelry is a normal good and people's incomes rise.

■ **FIGURE 4.11**

Price (dollars per piece of gold jewelry)

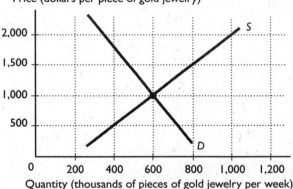

Quantity (thousands of pieces of gold jewelry per week)

4. Figure 4.11 shows the supply and demand
for gold jewelry. Suppose that consumers
think that silver jewelry is a substitute for
gold jewelry. In Figure 4.11, show what happens to the price and quantity if the price of
silver jewelry falls.

■ **FIGURE 4.12**

Price (dollars per piece of gold jewelry)

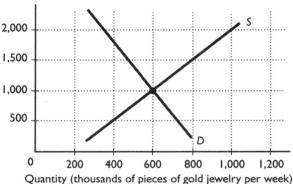

Quantity (thousands of pieces of gold jewelry per week)

5. Figure 4.12 shows the supply and demand for gold jewelry. Suppose the price of the gold that is used to produce gold jewelry rises. In the figure, show what happens to the price and quantity of gold jewelry.

■ **FIGURE 4.13**

Price (dollars per pair of blue jeans)

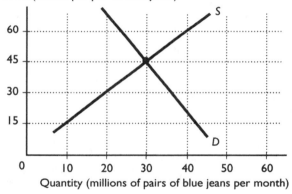

Quantity (millions of pairs of blue jeans per month)

6. Figure 4.13 shows the supply and demand for blue jeans. Suppose consumers' tastes for blue jeans has changed and fewer teens want to wear jeans. Simultaneously, blue jean manufacturers have developed a new dyeing process that allows the production to be less expensive. In the figure, show what happens to the price and quantity of blue jeans.

7. A freeze, which destroyed a good portion of the South American coffee crop in the mid-1970s, lead to an increase in the price of tea.
   a. Explain how the weather increased the price of tea.

b. Use a correctly labeled supply and demand graph of the tea market to show the effect of this weather related event. Be sure to label the price and quantity before and after the freeze.

8. People read that drinking orange juice helps prevent heart disease. What is the effect on the equilibrium price and quantity of orange juice?

9. The cost of memory chips used in computers falls. What is the effect on the equilibrium price and quantity of computers?

**Long Response Questions**

1. Consumers' incomes rise and steaks are a normal good. The supply of beef cattle has fallen recently due to a harsh winter in the western United States.
   a. Explain how these two events will impact the steak market.
   b. Use a correctly labeled graph of the steak market and show the price of a steak and the quantity of steaks after the incomes of consumers rise and the supply problem with cattle occurs:

2. Consumer information becomes available that there is a shock hazard with hair dryers. Workers who produce hair dryers have signed a wage agreement that gives them a 10 percent pay increase. The effect of the new information is greater than the effect of the wage hike.
   a. Explain how these two events will impact the market for hair dryers.
   b. Use a correctly labeled graph of the hair dryer market and show the price of a hair dryer and the quantity of hair dryers following the new consumer information and the increase in the workers' wages.

3. New cars are a normal good and people's incomes increase. Simultaneously, auto manufacturers must pay more for their workers' health insurance. What is the effect on the price and quantity of new cars?

4. These conditions in the table below are changing in the market for oranges. Taking each change separately, complete the table. Use + for increase, — for decrease or NC for no change.

| | Change in Demand | Change in Supply | Effect on Price | Effect on Quantity |
|---|---|---|---|---|
| a. The growing season in Florida is shortened by 20 days of frost | | | | |
| b. The price of tangerines (a close substitute for consumers) falls by 20 percent | | | | |
| c An announcement by the Surgeon General that oranges are a healthy source of nutrition | | | | |
| d. The wages paid to orange grove workers increases by 10 percent | | | | |
| e. Technology gains are made in harvesting equipment for oranges | | | | |
| f. Consumers anticipate an increase in the price of oranges in the near future. | | | | |
| g. The consumers' incomes fall by 10 percent and oranges are a normal good | | | | |
| h. The "Sunshine" ads promoting oranges as quick snack are paying off for sellers. | | | | |

# YOUR AP SELF TEST ANSWERS

## ■ CHECKPOINT 4.1

### True or false
1. False; page 91
2. False; page 94
3. True; page 95
4. False; page 95
5. False; page 96

### Multiple choice
1. d; page 91
2. b; page 91
3. a; page 95
4. c; page 95
5. a; page 95
6. a; page 95
7. b; page 95
8. d; page 96
9. d; page 96
10. d; page 95-96

### Short Response Questions
■ **FIGURE 4.14**

Price (dollars per bundle of cotton candy)

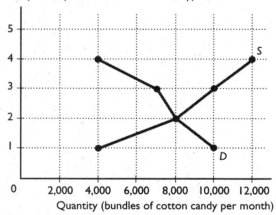

Quantity (bundles of cotton candy per month)

1. a. Figure 4.14 illustrates the demand curve, labeled *D* in the diagram. (The supply curve is from the first "Short Response Question" question in Checkpoint 4.2.)
   a. 8,000 bundles per month
   b. 7,000 bundles per month

c. The demand curve slopes downward; pages 96.

■ **FIGURE 4.15**

Price (dollars per pound of butter)

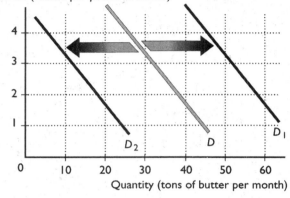

Quantity (tons of butter per month)

2. a. The demand increases and the demand curve shifts rightward, as shown in Figure 4.15 by the shift to $D_1$; page 96
   b. The demand decreases and the demand curve shifts leftward, as shown in Figure 4.15 by the shift to $D_2$; page 96
   c. The demand curve does not shift. The fall in the price of butter leads to an increase in the quantity demanded and a movement along the demand curve, not a shift of the demand curve; page 96.

### Long Response Questions
1. A change in the quantity demanded occurs when the price of the good changes. A change in demand occurs when any other determinants of demand other than the price of the good changes. So a change in prices of related goods, income, expectations, number of buyers, preferences; and consumer information change demand; page 94.
2. A movement along a demand curve reflects a change in the quantity demanded and is the result of a change in the price of the product. A shift in a demand curve reflects a change in demand and is the result of a change in any factor, other than the price, that affects demand; page 96.

# ■ CHECKPOINT 4.2

**True or false**

1. False; page 98
2. True; page 102
3. False; page 102
4. True; page 102
5. False; page 102

**Multiple choice**

1. c; page 98
2. c; page 98
3. c; page 98
4. a; page 100
5. a; page 102
6. b; page 102
7. b; page 102
8. d; page 103
9. c; page 102
10. c; page 102

**Short Response Questions**

1. The supply curve is illustrated in Figure 4.14, labeled $S$ in the diagram.
   a. 8,000 bundles per month.
   b. 10,000 bundles per month.
   c. The supply curve slopes upward; page 99.

**■ FIGURE 4.16**
Price (dollars per box of rubber bands)

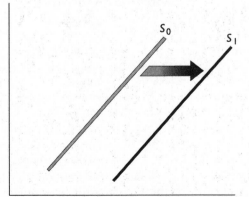

Quantity (boxes of rubber bands per year)

2. Figure 4.16 illustrates the shift; pages 102-103.

3. Other things constant, when the price of a good or service falls (rises), sellers decrease (increase) the quantity they supply. page 98.

4. The only factor that leads to a change in the quantity supplied is a change in the price of the product itself. Changes in all other determinants of supply lead to changes in the supply, *not* in the quantity supplied; page 103.

5. The factors that lead to changes in supply include changes in: prices of related goods; prices of resources and other inputs; expectations; number of sellers; productivity; new technology; and the time passing after a price change; page 103.

# ■ CHECKPOINT 4.3

**True or false**

1. True; page 106
2. False; page 107
3. True; page 108
4. False; page 110
5. True; page 110

**Multiple choice**

1. a; page 105
2. d; page 106
3. b; page 107
4. c; page 107
5. b; page 108
6. c; page 108
7. c; page 110
8. a; page 110

**Short Response Questions**

1. a. A shortage of 6,000 bundles a month; page 106.
   b. A surplus of 3,000 bundles a month; page 106.
   c. The equilibrium price is $2 a bundle of cotton candy and the equilibrium quantity is 8,000 bundles a month; page 106.

| Price (dollars per sweatshirt) | Quantity demanded (sweatshirts per season) |
|---|---|
| 35 | 13 |
| 30 | 15 |
| 25 | 19 |
| 20 | 27 |
| 15 | 37 |

2. The market demand schedule is obtained by summing the Hockey team's demand and the Soccer team's demand and is in the table above. The price that equates the quantity demanded to the quantity supplied is $25 and the equilibrium quantity is 19 sweatshirts; page 106.

■ **FIGURE 4.18**

Price (dollars per piece of gold jewelry)

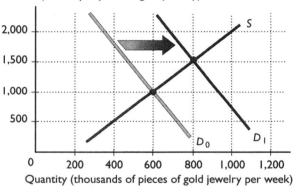

Quantity (thousands of pieces of gold jewelry per week)

3. Figure 4.18 shows the effect of the increase in income. The increase in income increases the demand for normal goods, such as gold jewelry. The demand curve shifts rightward and the supply curve does not shift. The price of gold jewelry rises, to $1,500 in the figure, and the quantity increases, to 800 pieces per week in the figure; page 107.

■ **FIGURE 4.19**

Price (dollars per piece of gold jewelry)

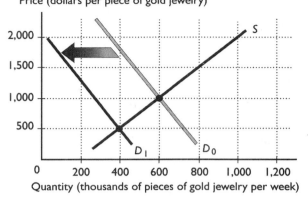

Quantity (thousands of pieces of gold jewelry per week)

4. Figure 4.19 shows the effect of the fall in price of silver jewelry. A fall in the price of a substitute decreases the demand gold jewelry. The demand curve shifts leftward and the supply curve does not shift. The price of gold jewelry falls, to $500 in the figure, and the quantity decreases, to 400 pieces per week in the figure; page 107.

■ **FIGURE 4.20**

Price (dollars per piece of gold jewelry)

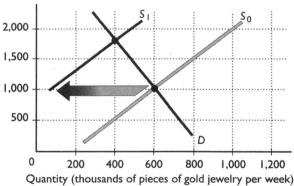

Quantity (thousands of pieces of gold jewelry per week)

5. Figure 4.20 shows the effect of the fall in the price of gold. The price of gold is a cost to the producers of gold jewelry. A rise in the cost decreases the supply of the good. The supply curve shifts leftward and the demand curve does not shift. The price of gold jewelry rises, to $1,750 in the figure, and the quantity decreases, to 400 pieces per week in the figure; page 108.

**■ FIGURE 4.21**

Price (dollars per pair of blue jeans)

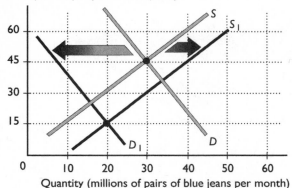

Quantity (millions of pairs of blue jeans per month)

**■ FIGURE 4.22**

Price (dollars per ton of tea)

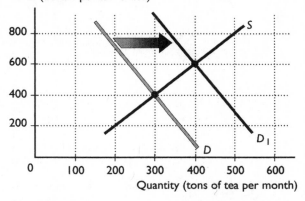

Quantity (tons of tea per month)

6. The change in tastes for wearing blue jeans decreases the demand for blue jeans and shifts the demand curve leftward. The improvement in the technology for producing blue jeans increases the supply and shifts the supply curve rightward. These changes definitely lower the price but the change in the quantity change is indeterminate because we do not know the relative magnitude of the changes in demand and supply. In Figure 4.21, the decrease in demand exceeds the increase in supply, so the equilibrium quantity decreases, but if the increase in supply exceeded the decrease in demand, the equilibrium quantity increases; page 110.

7. a. Coffee and tea are substitute goods. When the price of a substitute increases, the quantity demanded of the good under consideration decreases. Weather problems decrease the supply of coffee and thereby raise the price of coffee. Buyers switch to the substitute, tea and the demand for tea increases, shifting the demand curve for tea rightward. The price of tea rises and the quantity increases; page 107.

  b. Figure 4.22 shows the tea market. In it the demand curve shifts rightward to $D_1$. The supply curve does not shift. As a result of the increase in demand both the price and quantity sold of tea increase; page 107.

8. The increase in consumers' information increases the demand for orange juice and the demand curve shifts rightward. The price of orange juice rises and the quantity increases; page 107.

9. The fall in cost increases the supply of computers. The supply curve of computers shifts rightward. The price falls and the quantity increases; page 108.

**Long Response Questions**

1. a. When incomes rise, consumers will purchase more beef in the form of steaks. The demand for beef will increase and the demand curve shifts rightward. At the same time, the supply of beef will decrease because the harsh winter weather has made the stock of cattle be lower than normal. The supply curve shifts leftward; pages 107-108.

  b. Because both the demand and supply change and we do not know the relative sizes of the two changes, either the price or the quantity will be indeterminate. In this case, by itself the increase in demand leads to a higher price and the decrease in supply, also by itself, leads to a higher price. So the combined effect of the two will be raise the price of a steak. However, taken by itself the increase in demand leads to a higher quantity and the decrease in supply leads to a lower quantity. So the combined effect of the two changes

## ■ FIGURE 4.23
Price (dollars per pound of steak)

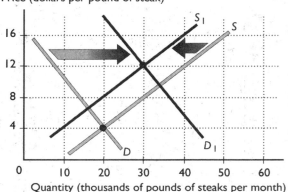

Quantity (thousands of pounds of steaks per month)

## ■ FIGURE 4.24
Price (dollars per hair dryer)

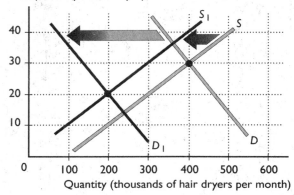

Quantity (thousands of hair dryers per month)

is indeterminate unless we know which change is larger. Figure 4.23 illustrates the case in which the change in demand exceeds the change in supply. In Figure 4.23, the demand curve shifts rightward from $D$ to $D_1$ and the supply curve shifts leftward from $S$ to $S_1$. As a result, the equilibrium price of a steak rises from $4 per pound to $12 per pound and the equilibrium quantity increases from 20,000 pounds per month to 40,000 pounds per month; page 110.

2. a. The market for hairdryers is impacted by shifts in both the demand curve and the supply curve. The additional consumer information regarding the shock hazard decreases the demand for hairdryers and the demand curve shifts leftward. The wage hike increases the cost of producing hairdryers, so the supply decreases and the supply curve shifts leftward; pages 107-108.

   b. In Figure 4.24, the demand curve shifts leftward from $D$ to $D_1$ and the supply curve shifts leftward from $S$ to $S_1$. The decreases in both demand and supply lead to a decrease in the quantity of hairdryers But the decrease in demand leads to a lower price while the decrease in supply leads to a higher price. In this case, however, we are told that the effect of the additional information exceeds the effect of the wage hike. So, as Figure 4.24 illustrates,

the quantity falls from 400,000 hair dryers per month to 200,000 hair dryers per month and the price falls from $30 per hair dryer to $20 per hair dryer; page 110.

3. The increase in income increases the demand for normal goods and shifts the demand curve for new cars rightward. The increase in health insurance premiums decreases the supply of new cars and shifts the supply curve of new cars leftward. The price of a new car definitely rises because both the change in demand and change in supply lead to a higher price. But the effect on the quantity is indeterminate: it rises if the demand effect is larger, falls if the supply effect is larger, and does not change if the two effects are the same size; page 110.

4. These answers are in the table below.

| | Change in Demand | Change in Supply | Effect on Price | Effect on Quantity |
|---|---|---|---|---|
| a. The growing season in Florida is shortened by 20 days of frost;  page 108 | NC | — | + | — |
| b. The price of tangerines (a close substitute for consumers) falls by 20 percent;  page 107 | — | NC | — | — |
| c. An announcement by the Surgeon General that oranges are a healthy source of nutrition;  page 107 | + | NC | + | + |
| d. The wages paid to orange grove workers increases by 10 percent;  page 108 | NC | — | + | — |
| e. Technology gains are made in harvesting equipment for oranges;  page 108 | NC | + | — | + |
| f. Consumers anticipate an increase in the price of oranges in the near future;  page 107 | + | NC | + | + |
| g. The incomes of consumers fall by 10 percent and oranges are a normal good;  page 107 | — | NC | — | — |
| h. The "Sunshine" ads promoting oranges as quick snack are paying off for sellers;  page 107 | + | NC | + | + |

# Elasticities of Demand and Supply

## Chapter 5

In Chapter 5 we study the price elasticity of demand, the price elasticity of supply, the cross elasticity of demand, and the income elasticity of demand.

■ **Define, explain the factors that influence, and calculate the price elasticity of demand.**

The price elasticity of demand is a measure of the extent to which the quantity demanded of a good changes when the price of the good changes and all other influences on buyers' plans remain the same. The price elasticity of demand equals the percentage change in the quantity demanded divided by the percentage change in price, with the negative sign ignored. Demand is elastic if the percentage change in the quantity demanded exceeds the percentage change in price. Demand is unit elastic if the percentage change in the quantity demanded equals the percentage change in price. Demand is inelastic if the percentage change in the quantity demanded is less than the percentage change in price. Elasticity is a *units-free* measure. Along a linear demand curve demand is unit elastic at the midpoint of the curve, demand is elastic at all points above the midpoint of the curve, and demand is inelastic at all points below the midpoint of the curve. The total revenue from the sale of a good equals the price of the good multiplied by the quantity sold. If a price change changes total revenue in the opposite direction, demand is elastic. If a price change leaves total revenue unchanged, demand is unit elastic. If a price change changes total revenue in the same direction, demand is inelastic.

■ **Define, explain the factors that influence, and calculate the price elasticity of supply.**

The price elasticity of supply is a measure of the extent to which the quantity supplied of a good changes when the price of the good changes and all other influences on sellers' plans remain the same. The two main influences on the price elasticity of supply are production possibilities and storage possibilities. If the good can be stored, supply is more elastic. The price elasticity of supply equals the percentage change in the quantity supplied divided by the percentage change in the price. If the price elasticity of supply is greater than 1, supply is elastic. If the price elasticity of supply equals 1, supply is unit elastic. If the price elasticity of supply is less than 1, supply is inelastic.

■ **Define and explain the factors that influence the cross elasticity of demand and the income elasticity of demand.**

The cross elasticity of demand is a measure of the responsiveness of the demand for a good to a change in the price of a substitute or complement, other things remaining the same. The cross elasticity of demand is positive for substitutes and negative for complements. The income elasticity of demand is a measure of the responsiveness of the demand for a good to a change in income changes, other things remaining the same. The income elasticity of demand is positive for a normal good and negative for an inferior good.

## EXPANDED CHAPTER CHECKLIST

**When you have completed this chapter, you will be able to:**

**1 Define, explain the factors that influence, and calculate the price elasticity of demand.**

- Define price elasticity of demand.
- Use the midpoint method to calculate the percentage change in price and the percentage change in the quantity demanded.
- Define elastic demand, unit elastic demand, and inelastic demand.
- Use a graph to illustrate perfectly elastic demand and perfectly inelastic demand.
- List and explain the influences on the price elasticity of demand.
- Calculate the price elasticity of demand.
- Discuss elasticity along a linear demand curve.
- Use the total revenue test to determine the price elasticity of demand.
- Discuss the relationship between farm prices and total revenue.
- Explain how we can use price elasticity of demand to design effective policies for dealing with addiction to drugs.

**2 Define, explain the factors that influence, and calculate the price elasticity of supply.**

- Define the price elasticity of supply.
- Define elastic supply, unit elastic supply, and inelastic supply.
- Use a graph to illustrate perfectly elastic supply and perfectly inelastic supply.
- List and explain the influences on the price elasticity of supply.
- Calculate the price elasticity of supply.

**3 Define and explain the factors that influence the cross elasticity of demand and the income elasticity of demand.**

- Define and calculate the cross elasticity of demand.
- Explain why the cross elasticity of demand is positive for substitutes and negative for complements.
- Define and calculate the income elasticity of demand.
- Discuss the three ranges into which the income elasticity of demand falls.

## YOUR AP TEST HINTS

### AP Topics

| Topic on your AP test | Corresponding textbook section |
|---|---|
| **Nature and function of product markets** | |
| Elasticity | Chapter 5 |
| • Price elasticity of demand | Checkpoint 5.1 |
| • Income and cross elasticity of demand | Checkpoint 5.3 |
| • Price elasticity of supply | Checkpoint 5.2 |

### AP Vocabulary

- On the AP test, the elasticity of demand is sometimes referred to as $E_P$, the elasticity of supply is $E_S$, the income elasticity of demand is $E_I$, and the cross elasticity of demand is $E_X$.

## CHECKPOINT 5.1

**■ Define, explain the factors that influence, and calculate the price elasticity of demand.**

### Quick Review

- *Price elasticity of demand* The price elasticity of demand equals the magnitude of the percentage change in the quantity demanded divided by the percentage change in the price.

- *Elastic demand* When the percentage change in the quantity demanded exceeds the percentage change in price. The elasticity of demand is greater than 1 in value.
- *Inelastic demand* When the percentage change in the quantity demanded is less than the percentage change in price. The elasticity of demand is less than 1 in value.
- *Factors affecting elasticity* The demand for a good is more elastic if a substitute is easy to find. The factors that influence the ability to find a substitute for a good are whether the good is a luxury or a necessity, how narrowly it is defined, and the amount of time available to find a substitute for it.
- *Total revenue test* If the demand for a good is elastic, a price hike lowers the total revenue spent on the good; if the demand is inelastic, a price hike raises the total revenue spent on the good; and if the demand is unit elastic, a price hike does not change the total revenue spent on the good. A price cut has the opposite effects on total revenue (for example, if the demand for a good is elastic, a price cut *raises* the total revenue spent on the good).

## Additional Practice Problems 5.1

1. For each of the following price changes, calculate the price elasticity of demand. Is the demand elastic, unit elastic, or inelastic?
   a. A 10 percent increase in price results in a 5 percent decrease in the quantity demanded.
   b. A 6 percent increase in price results in a 12 percent decrease in the quantity demanded.
   c. A 4 percent increase in price results in a 4 percent decrease in the quantity demanded.

| Price (dollars per bag of cat food) | Quantity (bags of cat food per year) | Total revenue (dollars) |
|---|---|---|
| 5 | 4 | ___ |
| 4 | 8 | ___ |
| 3 | 12 | ___ |
| 2 | 16 | ___ |
| 1 | 20 | ___ |

2. The table above gives the demand schedule for bags of cat food. A graph of this demand schedule gives a linear demand curve.
   a. Finish the table by calculating the total revenue for each row.
   b. When is the demand elastic? inelastic? unit elastic?
   c. Explain your answers to part (b).

## Solutions to Additional Practice Problems 5.1

1a. The price elasticity of demand equals the magnitude of the percentage change in the quantity demanded divided by the percentage change in the price. So the elasticity of demand equals (5 percent) ÷ (10 percent) = 0.5. Because the elasticity of demand is less than 1, demand is inelastic.

1b. The price elasticity of demand equals (12 percent) ÷ (6 percent) =2.0. Because the elasticity of demand is greater than 1, demand is elastic.

1c. The price elasticity of demand equals (4 percent) ÷ (4 percent) = 1.0. Because the elasticity of demand equals 1, demand is unit elastic.

| Price (dollars per bag of cat food) | Quantity (bags of cat food per year) | Total revenue (dollars) |
|---|---|---|
| 5 | 4 | 20 |
| 4 | 8 | 32 |
| 3 | 12 | 36 |
| 2 | 16 | 32 |
| 1 | 20 | 20 |

2a. The completed table is above. Total revenue equals the price times the quantity sold.

2b. The demand is elastic at prices greater than $3 a bag. The demand is inelastic at prices less than $3 a bag. The demand is unit elastic at a price of $3 a bag.

2c. Demand is unit elastic at the midpoint of the demand curve. When demand is unit elastic, a price change leaves total revenue unchanged. The midpoint of the curve occurs when the price is $3 a bag, so demand is unit elastic at a price of $3 a bag.

Demand is elastic at all points above the midpoint of the demand curve. So when the price is greater than $3 a bag, demand is elastic. When demand is elastic, price and total revenue change in opposite directions. For example, when the price *rises* from $4 to $5, total revenue *decreases* from $32 to $20.

Demand is inelastic at all points below the midpoint of the demand curve. So when the price is less than $3 a bag, demand is inelastic. When demand is inelastic, price and total revenue change in the same direction. For example, when the price *rises* from $1 to $2, total revenue *increases* from $20 to $32.

## ■ AP Self Test 5.1

### True or false

1. The price elasticity of demand equals the magnitude of the slope of the demand curve.

2. If the price increases by 10 percent and the quantity demanded decreases by 8 percent, the price elasticity of demand equals 1.25.

3. As the price of a good increases, if the quantity demanded of it remains the same, then demand for the good is perfectly inelastic.

4. Above the midpoint of a straight-line demand curve, demand is elastic.

5. When the price of a service increases by 5 percent and the quantity demanded decreases by 5 percent, total revenue remains unchanged.

6. If the price of tuna increases by 5 percent and the total revenue of tuna producers increases, then the demand for tuna is inelastic.

### Multiple choice

1. The price elasticity of demand is a measure of the extent to which the quantity demanded of a good changes when _____

changes and all other influences on buyers' plans remain the same.
   a. income
   b. the price of a related good
   c. the price of the good
   d. the demand alone
   e. both the demand and supply simultaneously

2. Suppose the price of a movie falls from $9 to $7. Using the midpoint method, what is the percentage change in price?
   a. 33 percent
   b. −33 percent
   c. 25 percent
   d. −25 percent
   e. −97 percent

3. Suppose the price of a tie rises from $45 to $55. Using the midpoint method, what is the percentage change in price?
   a. 10 percent
   b. −10 percent
   c. 20 percent
   d. −20 percent
   e. 100 percent

4. Demand is elastic if
   a. consumers respond strongly to changes in the product's price.
   b. a large percentage change in price brings about a small percentage change in quantity demanded.
   c. a small percentage change in price brings about a small percentage change in quantity demanded.
   d. the quantity demanded is not responsive to price changes.
   e. the demand curve is vertical.

5. If substitutes for a good are readily available, the demand for that good
   a. does not change substantially if the price rises.
   b. does not change substantially if the price falls.
   c. is inelastic.
   d. is elastic.
   e. Both answers (a) and (b) are correct.

6. During the winter of 2005–2006, the price of electric power increased enormously but the quantity demanded decreased only a little. This response indicates that the demand for electric power was
   a. inelastic.
   b. elastic.
   c. unit elastic.
   d. perfectly elastic.
   e. perfectly inelastic.

7. If the price of a product increases by 5 percent and the quantity demanded decreases by 5 percent, then the elasticity of demand is
   a. 0.
   b. 1.
   c. indeterminate.
   d. 5.
   e. 25.

8. The price of a bag of pretzels rises from $2 to $3 and the quantity demanded decreases from 100 to 60. Using the midpoint method, what is the price elasticity of demand?
   a. 1.0
   b. 1.25
   c. 40.0
   d. 20.0
   e. 0.80

9. When a firm raises the price of its product, what happens to total revenue?
   a. If demand is elastic, total revenue decreases.
   b. If demand is unit elastic, total revenue increases.
   c. If demand is inelastic, total revenue decreases.
   d. If demand is elastic, total revenue increases.
   e. If demand is unit elastic, total revenue decreases.

## Short Response Questions

### ■ FIGURE 5.1

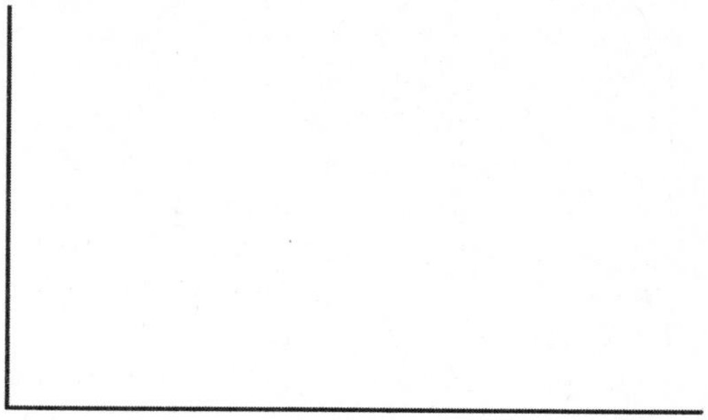

1. In Figure 5.1, label the axes and then draw a demand curve for a good that has a perfectly elastic demand.

### ■ FIGURE 5.2

2. In Figure 5.2, label the axes and then draw a demand curve for a good that has a perfectly inelastic demand.

|   | Percentage change in price | Percentage change in quantity demanded | Price elasticity of demand |
|---|---|---|---|
| A | 5 | 10 | ____ |
| B | 8 | 4 | ____ |
| C | 3 | 0 | ____ |
| D | 6 | 6 | ____ |
| E | 1 | 8 | ____ |

3. Complete the table above by calculating the price elasticity of demand.
   a. Which row has the most elastic demand?
   b. Which row has the least elastic demand?

■ **FIGURE 5.3**

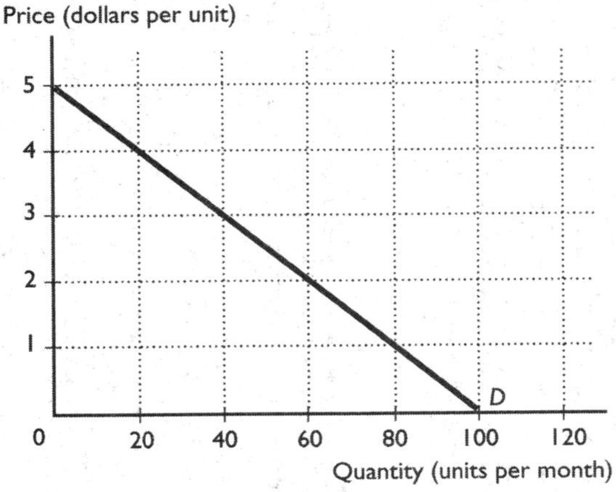

Price (dollars per unit)

4. In Figure 5.3, darken the part of the demand curve along which demand is elastic. Label the point on the demand curve at which demand is unit elastic.

5. Suppose the price elasticity of demand for oil is 0.3. If the quantity of oil decreases by 6 percent, what is the effect on the price of oil?

## Long Response Questions

1. What does it mean when the demand for a good is inelastic?

2. What is the relationship between how narrowly a good is defined and the number of substitutes it has?

3. List factors that make demand elastic.

4. What is the relationship between a rise in price, the elasticity of demand for the good, and the change in total revenue? What is the relationship between a rise in price, the elasticity of demand for the good, and your expenditure on the good?

5. Recently the publisher of a Food Network cookbook raised its price from $20 to $30 and the number of books sold per year fell from 200,000 to 100,000. What is the elasticity of demand for this cookbook? Is the demand elastic or inelastic? What happened to the total revenue from sales of this book—did it increase or decrease? Relate the change in total revenue to the price elasticity of demand.

## CHECKPOINT 5.2

■ **Define, explain the factors that influence, and calculate the price elasticity of supply.**

### Quick Review

- *Price elasticity of supply* A measure of the extent to which the quantity supplied of a good changes when the price of the good changes and all other influences on sellers' plans remain the same.

### Additional Practice Problems 5.2

1. For each of the following price changes, calculate the price elasticity of supply.
   a. A 10 percent increase in price results in a 15 percent increase in the quantity supplied.
   b. A 6 percent increase in price results in a 3 percent increase in the quantity supplied.
   c. A 7 percent increase in price results in a 7 percent increase in the quantity supplied.

2. Over one month the elasticity of supply of avocados is 0.1 and over 5 years the elasticity of supply of avocados is 2.0. If the price of avocados rises 10 percent, what is the increase in the quantity supplied in one month and in 5 years? Why is there a difference in the quantities?

### Solutions to Additional Practice Problems 5.2

1a. The elasticity of supply equals the percentage change in the quantity supplied divided by the percentage change in price, which is (15 percent) ÷ (10 percent) = 1.5.

1b. The elasticity of supply equals (3 percent) ÷ (6 percent) = 0.5.

1c. The elasticity of supply equals (7 percent) ÷ (7 percent) = 1.0.

2. The increase in the quantity supplied equals the percentage change in the price times the elasticity of supply. In one month the quantity supplied increases by (10 percent) × (0.1), which is 1 percent. In 5 years the quantity supplied increases by (10 percent ) × (2.0), which is 20 percent. The increase in the quantity supplied is much greater after 5

years because more changes can be made as more time passes. Existing avocado trees can be more carefully cultivated and additional fertilizer used. Eventually additional avocado trees can be planted, mature, and then be harvested. The supply of avocados increases as time passes, making the supply more elastic.

## ■ AP Self Test 5.2

**True or false**

1. If the percentage change in the quantity supplied is zero when the price changes, supply is perfectly elastic.

2. Goods that can be produced at a constant (or very gently rising) opportunity cost have an elastic supply.

3. The supply of apples is perfectly elastic on the day of a price change.

4. The supply of a storable good is perfectly inelastic.

5. When the price of a pizza is $20, 10 pizzas are supplied and when the price rises to $30 a pizza, 14 pizzas are supplied. Using the midpoint method, the price elasticity of supply of pizzas is 0.83.

6. If a 5 percent increase in price increases the quantity supplied by 10 percent, the elasticity of supply equals 2.0.

**Multiple choice**

1. The price elasticity of supply is a measure of the extent to which the quantity supplied of a good changes when only the
   a. cost of producing the product increases.
   b. quantity of the good demanded increases.
   c. supply increases.
   d. price of the good changes.
   e. number of firms changes.

2. When the percentage change in the quantity supplied exceeds the percentage change in price, then supply is
   a. elastic.
   b. inelastic.
   c. unit elastic.
   d. perfectly inelastic.
   e. perfectly elastic.

3. The supply of beachfront property on St. Simon's Island is
   a. elastic.
   b. unit elastic.
   c. negative.
   d. inelastic.
   e. perfectly elastic.

4. For a product with a rapidly increasing opportunity cost of producing additional units,
   a. demand is price elastic.
   b. supply is price elastic.
   c. demand is price inelastic.
   d. supply is price inelastic.
   e. the demand curve is vertical.

5. The greater the amount of time that passes after a price change, the
   a. less elastic supply becomes.
   b. more elastic supply becomes.
   c. more negative supply becomes.
   d. steeper the supply curve becomes.
   e. more vertical the supply curve becomes.

6. The price elasticity of supply equals the percentage change in the
   a. quantity demanded divided by the percentage change in the price of a substitute or complement.
   b. quantity supplied divided by the percentage change in price.
   c. quantity demanded divided by the percentage change in price.
   d. supply divided by the percentage change in the demand.
   e. quantity supplied divided by the percentage change in income.

7. If a firm supplies 200 units at a price of $50 and 100 units at a price of $40, using the

midpoint formula what is the price elasticity of supply?

a. 0.33
b. 1.00
c. 3.00
d. 5.00
e. 8.50

8. If the quantity supplied increases by 8 percent when the price rises by 2 percent, the price elasticity of supply is ____ percent.

a. 10.0
b. 6.0
c. 0.25
d. 16.0
e. 4.0

9 If the price of a good increases by 10 percent and the quantity supplied increases by 5 percent, then the elasticity of supply is

a. greater than one and supply is elastic.
b. negative and supply is inelastic.
c. less than one and supply is elastic.
d. less than one and supply is inelastic.
e. greater than one and supply is inelastic.

**Short Response Questions**

■ **FIGURE 5.4**

1. In Figure 5.4, label the axes and then draw a supply curve for a good that has a perfectly inelastic supply.

2. Suppose the elasticity of supply of wheat is 0.3 and the elasticity of supply of magazines is 1.3. If the price of wheat rises 10 percent, what is the increase in the quantity of wheat supplied? If the price of a magazine rises 10 percent, what is the increase in the quantity of magazines supplied?

| | Price (dollars) | Quantity supplied (units per week) |
|---|---|---|
| A | 5 | 10 |
| B | 15 | 30 |
| C | 25 | 50 |
| D | 35 | 90 |

3. The table above gives a supply schedule. Using the midpoint formula, calculate the price elasticity of supply between points A and B; between points B and C; and between points C and D.

| | Percentage change in price | Percentage change in quantity supplied | Price elasticity of supply |
|---|---|---|---|
| A | 6 | 8 | ____ |
| B | 8 | 4 | ____ |
| C | 4 | 8 | ____ |

4. Complete the table above by calculating the price elasticity of supply.

**Long Response Questions**

1. Describe the elasticity of supply of a good that can be stored.

2. Why does the elasticity of supply increase as time passes after a price change?

### CHECKPOINT 5.3

■ **Define and explain the factors that influence the cross elasticity of demand and the income elasticity of demand.**

*Quick Review*

- *Cross elasticity of demand* A measure of the extent to which the demand for a good changes when the price of a substitute or complement changes, other things remaining the same.

- *Income elasticity of demand* A measure of the extent to which the demand for a good changes when income changes, other things remaining the same.

## Additional Practice Problems 5.3

1. For each of the following, calculate the cross elasticity of demand. Are the goods substitutes or complements?
   a. A 10 percent increase in the price of lettuce results in a 15 percent increase in the quantity of spinach demanded.
   b. A 5 percent increase in the price of beef results in a 10 percent increase in the quantity of pork demanded.
   c. A 4 percent increase in the price of a golf club results in a 2 percent decrease in the quantity of golf balls demanded.

2. For each of the following, calculate the income elasticity of demand. Are the goods normal or inferior goods?
   a. A 3 percent increase in income results in a 1 percent increase in the quantity demanded.
   b. A 6 percent increase in income results in a 3 percent decrease in the quantity demanded.
   c. A 2 percent increase in income results in a 4 percent increase in the quantity demanded.

3. Pepsi and Coke are substitutes. Pepsi and Tropicana orange juice also are substitutes. But quite likely the two cross elasticities of demand differ in size. Which cross elasticity do you think is larger and why?

## Solutions to Additional Practice Problems 5.3

1a. The cross elasticity of demand equals the percentage change in the quantity demanded of one good divided by the percentage change in the price of the other good, which is (15 percent) ÷ (10 percent) = 1.5. The cross elasticity of supply is positive for substitute and negative for complements, so lettuce and spinach are substitutes.

1b. The cross elasticity of demand equals (10 percent) ÷ (5 percent) = 2.0. Beef and pork are substitutes.

1c. The cross elasticity of demand equals (–2 percent) ÷ (4 percent) = –0.5. Golf clubs and golf balls are complements.

2a. The income elasticity of demand equals the percentage change in the quantity demanded divided by the percentage change in income, which is (1 percent) ÷ (3 percent) = 0.33. The income elasticity is positive for a normal good and negative for an inferior good, so this good is a normal good.

2b. The income elasticity of demand equals (–3 percent) ÷ (6 percent) = –0.5. The good is an inferior good.

2c. The income elasticity of demand equals (4 percent) ÷ (2 percent) = 2.0. The good is a normal good.

3. The cross elasticity between Pepsi and Coke is likely much larger than the cross elasticity between Pepsi and Tropicana orange juice. For many people, Pepsi and Coke are close to indistinguishable. Even a slight rise in the price of a Coke will increase the quantity of Pepsi demanded significantly, so their cross elasticity is large. Pepsi and Tropicana orange juice are less close substitutes. So, although an increase in the price of Tropicana orange juice will increase the demand for Pepsi, the increase will be relatively slight and the cross elasticity will be small.

## ■ AP Self Test 5.3

### True or false

1. If the cross elasticity of demand is negative, the two goods are substitutes.

2. If the cross elasticity between hamburgers and hot dogs is positive, then hamburgers and hot dogs are substitutes.

3. An inferior good has a negative income elasticity of demand.

4. When the income elasticity of demand is positive, the good is a normal good.

5. A normal good is a good that has a positive cross elasticity of demand.

**Multiple choice**

1. The measure used to determine whether two goods are complements or substitutes is called the
   a. price elasticity of supply.
   b. cross elasticity of demand.
   c. price elasticity of demand.
   d. income elasticity.
   e. substitute elasticity of demand.

2. If beef and pork are substitutes, the cross elasticity of demand between the two goods is
   a. negative.
   b. positive.
   c. indeterminate.
   d. elastic.
   e. greater than one.

3. When the price of a pizza is $10, the quantity of soda demanded is 300 drinks. When the price of pizza is $15, the quantity of soda demanded is 100 drinks. The cross elasticity of demand equals
   a. −0.25.
   b. −0.40.
   c. −2.50.
   d. −25.00.
   e. 4.0.

4. When the price of going to a movie rises 5 percent, the quantity of DVDs demanded increases 10 percent. The cross elasticity of demand equals
   a. 10.0.
   b. 0.50.
   c. −0.50.
   d. −2.0.
   e. 2.0.

5. If two goods have a cross elasticity of demand of −2, then when the price of the one increases, the demand curve of the other good
   a. shifts rightward.
   b. shifts leftward.
   c. remains unchanged.
   d. may shift rightward, leftward, or remain unchanged.
   e. remains unchanged but the supply curve shifts leftward.

6. The income elasticity of demand is the percentage change in the ____ divided by the percentage change in ____.
   a. quantity demanded; the price of a substitute or complement
   b. quantity supplied; price
   c. quantity demanded; price
   d. quantity demanded; income
   e. quantity demanded when income changes; the quantity supplied

7. When income increases from $20,000 to $30,000 the number of home-delivered pizzas per year increases from 22 to 40. The income elasticity of demand for home-delivered pizza equals
   a. 1.45.
   b  0.69.
   c. 0.58.
   d. 0.40.
   e. 2.86.

8. When income increases by 6 percent, the demand for potatoes decreases by 2 percent. The income elasticity of demand for potatoes equals
   a. −2.00.
   b. 3.00.
   c. −3.00.
   d. 0.33.
   e. −0.33.

9. If a product is a normal good, then its income elasticity of demand is
   a. zero.
   b. positive.
   c. negative.
   d. indeterminate.
   e. greater than one.

10. The income elasticity of demand for used cars is less than zero. So, used cars are
    a. an inferior good.
    b. a normal good.
    c. an inelastic good.
    d. a perfectly inelastic good.
    e. substitute goods.

## Short Response Questions

### ■ FIGURE 5.5

Price (dollars per large screen television)

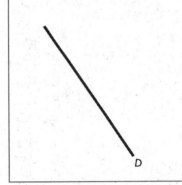

Quantity (large screen televisions per year)

1. The income elasticity of demand for large screen televisions is positive. In Figure 5.5, show the change when income increases.

| | Percentage change in price of good A | Percentage change in quantity demanded of good B | Cross elasticity of demand |
|---|---|---|---|
| A | 3 | 6 | ____ |
| B | 5 | −10 | ____ |
| C | −4 | −8 | ____ |
| D | 8 | 4 | ____ |

2. Complete the table above. Which row has substitutes and which row has complements?

| | Percentage change in income | Percentage change in quantity demanded | Income elasticity of demand |
|---|---|---|---|
| A | 5 | 10 | ____ |
| B | 5 | −10 | ____ |
| C | 5 | 2 | ____ |
| D | 6 | 6 | ____ |

3. Complete the table above. Which row indicates an inferior good and which row indicates a good that is income elastic?

## Long Response Questions

1. The income elasticity of demand for inter-city bus trips is negative. What does this fact tell you about inter-city bus trips?

## YOUR AP SELF TEST ANSWERS

### ■ CHECKPOINT 5.1

**True or false**
1. False;  page 122
2. False;  page 122
3. True;  page 120
4. True;  page 124
5. True;  page 126
6. True;  page 126

**Multiple choice**
1. c;  page 118
2. d;  page 118
3. c;  page 119
4. a;  page 120
5. d;  page 120
6. a;  page 120
7. b;  page 122
8. b;  page 122
9. a;  page 126

**Short Response Questions**
1. Figure 5.6 labels the axes and illustrates a demand curve for a good with a perfectly elastic demand; page 121.
2. Figure 5.7 labels the axes and illustrates a demand curve for a good with a perfectly inelastic demand; page 121.

### ■ FIGURE 5.6
Price (dollars)

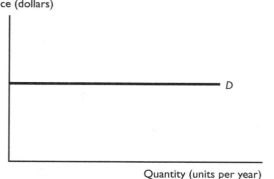

Quantity (units per year)

### ■ FIGURE 5.7
Price (dollars)

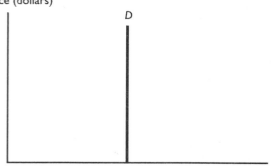

Quantity (units per year)

|   | Percentage change in price | Percentage change in quantity demanded | Price elasticity of demand |
|---|---|---|---|
| A | 5 | 10 | 2.0 |
| B | 8 | 4 | 0.5 |
| C | 3 | 0 | 0.0 |
| D | 6 | 6 | 1.0 |
| E | 1 | 8 | 8.0 |

3. The complete table is above;  page 122.
   a. The most elastic demand is in row E; page 122.
   b. The least elastic demand is in row C (the demand is perfectly inelastic); page 122.

### ■ FIGURE 5.8
Price (dollars per unit)

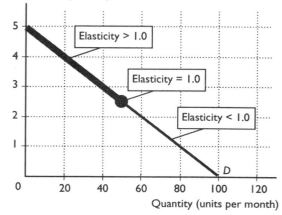

Quantity (units per month)

4. In Figure 5.8, demand is elastic along the dark portion of the demand curve. Demand is unit elastic at the midpoint of curve.

Demand is inelastic along the demand curve below the midpoint; page 124.

5. The price rises by 20 percent; page 122.

### Long Response Questions

1. Demand is inelastic if the percentage change in the quantity demanded is less than the percentage change in the price. In this case the price elasticity of demand is less than one; page 120.

2. The more narrow the definition of the good, the more substitutes exist. For example, there are more substitutes for a slice of Pizza Hut pizza than for pizza in general; page 122.

3. Demand is more elastic the more substitutes exist. Luxury goods and narrowly defined goods have more substitutes and so have more elastic demands. The more time that is available to find substitutes also increases the number of substitutes and so increases the elasticity of demand. In addition, the greater the proportion of income spent on the good, the more elastic the demand; pages 120, 122.

4. When the price of a good rises, total revenue increases if demand is inelastic, does not change if demand is unit elastic, and decreases if demand is elastic. When the price of a good rises, your expenditure on the good increases if demand is inelastic, does not change if demand is unit elastic, and decreases if demand is elastic; page 126.

5. The change in the quantity is 67 percent (100,000 change divided by 150,000 average quantity) and the change in the price is 40 percent ($10 change divided by $25 average price). So the price elasticity of demand is 1.675 (67 percent divided by 40 percent). The price elasticity of supply exceeds one, which means that the demand for the cookbooks is elastic. The buyers are very responsive to the change in price. The total revenue fell as the price increased. When the demand is elastic, a price hike decreases total revenue; pages 119-127.

### ■ CHECKPOINT 5.2

#### True or false.

1. False; page 130
2. True; page 130
3. False; page 132
4. False; page 132
5. True; page 132
6. True; page 132

#### Multiple choice

1. d; page 130
2. a; page 130
3. d; page 130
4. d; page 130
5. b; page 132
6. b; page 132
7. c; page 132
8. e; page 132
9. d; page 132

#### Short Response Questions

#### ■ FIGURE 5.9

Price (dollars)

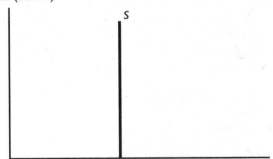

Quantity (units per year)

1. Figure 5.9 labels the axes and illustrates a supply curve for a good with a perfectly inelastic supply; page 131.

2. If the price of wheat rises 10 percent, the increase in the quantity supplied equals (10 percent) × (0.3), which is 3 percent. If the price of a magazine rises 10 percent, the increase in the quantity supplied equals (10 percent) × (1.3), which is 13 percent; pages 130 and 132.

3. The price elasticity of supply between points A and B is 1.00; between points B and C is 1.00; and between points C and D is 1.71; page 132.

| | Percentage change in price | Percentage change in quantity supplied | Price elasticity of supply |
|---|---|---|---|
| A | 6 | 8 | 1.33 |
| B | 8 | 4 | 0.50 |
| C | 4 | 8 | 2.00 |

4. The completed table is above; page 132.

## Long Response Questions

1. The elasticity of supply of a good that can be stored depends on the decision to keep the good in storage or offer it for sale. A small price change can make a big difference to this decision, so the supply of a storable good is highly elastic; page 132.

2. As time passes after a price change, it becomes easier to change production plans and supply becomes more elastic. For example, many manufactured goods have an inelastic supply if production plans have had only a short period in which to change. But after all the technologically possible ways of adjusting production have been exploited, supply is extremely elastic for most manufactured items; page 132.

## ■ CHECKPOINT 5.3

### True or false

1. False; page 135
2. True; page 135
3. True; page 136
4. True; page 136
5. False; page 136

### Multiple choice

1. b; page 135
2. b; page 135
3. c; page 135
4. e; page 135
5. b; page 136

6. d; page 136
7. a; page 136
8. e; page 136
9  b; page 136
10. a; page 136

## Short Response Questions

### ■ FIGURE 5.10

Price (dollars per large screen television)

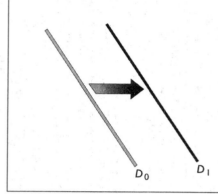

Quantity (large screen televisions per year)

1. Because the income elasticity of demand is positive, we know that large screen televisions are a normal good. In Figure 5.10 an increase in income shifts the demand curve rightward from $D_0$ to $D_1$; page 136.

| | Percentage change in price of good A | Percentage change in quantity demanded of good B | Cross elasticity of demand |
|---|---|---|---|
| A | 3 | 6 | 2.0 |
| B | 5 | −10 | −2.0 |
| C | −4 | −8 | 2.0 |
| D | 8 | 4 | 0.5 |

2. The completed table is above. The goods in row B are complements; the goods in rows A, C, and D are substitutes; page 135.

|   | Percentage change in income | Percentage change in quantity demanded | Income elasticity of demand |
|---|---|---|---|
| A | 5 | 10 | <u>2.0</u> |
| B | 5 | −10 | <u>−2.0</u> |
| C | 5 | 2 | <u>0.4</u> |
| D | 6 | 6 | <u>1.0</u> |

3. The completed table is above. The good in Row B is an inferior good. The good in row A is income elastic; page 136.

**Long Response Questions**

1. The fact that the income elasticity of demand for inter-city bus trips is negative indicates that an inter-city bus trip is an inferior good. When people's incomes increase, they take fewer inter-city bus trips and instead fly, drive, or take the train. So when people's incomes rise, the demand for inter-city bus trips decreases and the demand curve shifts leftward; page 136.

# Efficiency and Fairness of Markets

# *Chapter* 6

In Chapter 6 we study markets to determine if they are efficient. Chapter 6 also studies the main ideas about fairness and determines if competitive markets result in fair outcomes.

■ **Describe alternative methods of allocating scarce resources.**

Because resources are scarce, they must be allocated. Different ways of allocating resources include: by market price; command; majority rule; contest; first-come, first-served; sharing equally; lottery; personal characteristics; and force. In our economy, we generally rely upon the market price for allocation.

■ **Distinguish between value and price and define consumer surplus.**

Value is what buyers get and price is what buyers pay. In economics, the idea of value is called *marginal benefit*, which is the maximum price that buyers are willing to pay for another unit of the good or service. The demand curve tells us this price. A demand curve is a marginal benefit curve. Consumer surplus is the marginal benefit from a good or service minus the price paid for it, summed over the quantity consumed.

■ **Distinguish between cost and price and define producer surplus.**

Cost is what a seller must give up to produce a good and price is what a seller receives when the good is sold. The cost of producing one more unit of a good or service is its *marginal cost*. It is just worth producing one more unit of a good or service if the price for which it can be sold equals marginal cost. The supply curve tells us this price. A supply curve is a marginal cost curve. When the price exceeds marginal cost, the firm obtains a producer surplus. Producer surplus is the price of a good minus the marginal cost of producing it, summed over the quantity produced.

■ **Evaluate the efficiency of the alternative methods of allocating scarce resources.**

Markets are efficient when resources are used to produce the goods and services people value most highly. When marginal benefit equals the marginal cost, the efficient quantity is produced. The sum of consumer surplus and producer surplus is maximized at a competitive equilibrium. According to Adam Smith, each participant in a competitive market is "led by an invisible hand" to promote the efficient use of resources. Underproduction and overproduction create a deadweight loss. Government imposed price and quantity regulations, taxes and subsidies, externalities, public goods, common resources, monopoly, and high transactions costs are obstacles to efficiency.

■ **Explain the main ideas about fairness and evaluate the fairness of competitive markets and other allocation schemes.**

Two views of fairness are: it's not fair if the *result* isn't fair and it's not fair if the *rules* aren't fair. Utilitarianism is a principle that states that we should strive to achieve "the greatest happiness for the greatest number." The utilitarian idea of complete equality ignores the cost of making income transfers, which leads to the big tradeoff between efficiency and fairness. When private property and property rights are protected and exchanges are voluntary, competitive markets are fair according to the rules view of fairness.

## EXPANDED CHAPTER CHECKLIST

**When you have completed this chapter, you will be able to:**

**1 Describe alternative methods of allocating scarce resources**

- Describe and give examples of how our economy allocates resources using market price; command; majority rule; contest; first-come, first-served; sharing equally; lottery; personal characteristics; and force.

**2 Distinguish between value and price and define consumer surplus.**

- Discuss the difference between value and price.
- Explain how an economist measures marginal benefit.
- Explain why the demand curve is a marginal benefit curve.
- Define consumer surplus and illustrate it in a figure.

**3 Distinguish between cost and price and define producer surplus.**

- Discuss the difference between cost and price.
- Explain why the supply curve is a marginal cost curve.
- Define producer surplus and illustrate it in a figure.

**4 Explain the conditions in which markets are efficient and inefficient.**

- Explain why competitive markets are efficient.
- Discuss the "invisible hand."
- List the obstacles to achieving an efficient allocation of resources.
- Define and illustrate the deadweight loss.

**5 Explain the main ideas about fairness and evaluate the fairness of competitive markets and other allocation schemes.**

- Discuss the two broad views of fairness.
- Define utilitarianism and discuss the one big problem with the utilitarian idea of complete equality.
- Discuss fairness in the face of a natural disaster.

## YOUR AP TEST HINTS

### AP Topics

| Topic on your AP test | Corresponding textbook section |
|---|---|
| **Nature and function of product markets** | |
| • Consumer surplus | Checkpoint 6.2 |
| • Producer surplus | Checkpoint 6.3 |
| • Market efficiency | Checkpoint 6.4 |

### AP Vocabulary

- The AP test calls the situation in a market in which marginal benefit equals marginal cost "allocative efficiency" referring to the point that this outcome is allocating resources so that the efficient quantity is produced. Recall also that this quantity is the quantity that society most values.
- The AP test does *not* have questions dealing with market fairness, so utilitarianism is *not* part of the AP test.

## CHECKPOINT 6.1

■ **Describe alternative methods of allocating scarce resources.**

**Quick Review**

- *Allocation methods* Resources can be allocated by: using the market price; command; majority rule; a contest, first-come, first served; sharing equally; lottery; personal characteristics; and force.

**Additional Practice Problems 6.1**

1. Why is it necessary to allocate resources?

2. Suppose the price of a new BMW is $40,000. Which two kinds of people decide not to buy these BMWs? Is it true that when resources are allocated by market price, the rich always consume everything?

3. What is the command method of allocating resources?

### Solutions to Additional Practice Problems 6.1

1. Resources are scarce, so not everyone's wants can be fulfilled. As a result, some method must be used to determine whether or not resources are to be allocated to fulfilling each specific want.

2. The people who do not buy these BMWs are the people cannot afford to pay $40,000 for the new BMW and the people who can afford to pay but choose not to pay it. The fact that people can decide not to buy a particular good or service shows that the rich do not necessary consume everything; they buy and consume only the goods and services for which they choose to pay the market price .

3. The command method of allocating resources relies upon someone in authority to order how resources shall be allocated. The former Soviet Union and currently North Korea and Cuba are examples of entire economies in which command was (and is for North Korea and Cuba) the major allocation method.

### ■ AP Self Test 6.1

**True or false**
1. When market prices are used to allocate resources, only the people who are able and willing to pay get the resources.

2. A boss telling a worker what to do is an example of a command system of allocating resources.

3. In the U.S. economy, resources are never allocated according to random chance.

4. In the U.S. economy, force is used as an allocation method force only for illegal activities such as theft.

**Multiple choice**
1. Allocating resources by the order of someone in authority is a ____ allocation method.
   a. first-come, first-served
   b. market price
   c. contest
   d. majority rule
   e. command

2. Often people trying to withdraw money from their bank must wait in line, which reflects a ____ allocation method.
   a. first-come, first-served
   b. market price
   c. contest
   d. majority rule
   e. command

3. When the city of Fresno holds a referendum to determine if taxes will be raised to pay for road repairs, the city is using a ____ allocation method.
   a. majority rule
   b. market price
   c. contest
   d. personal characteristics
   e. command

4. If a person will rent an apartment only to married couples over 30 years old, that person is allocating resources using a ____ allocation method.
   a. first-come, first-served
   b. market price
   c. contest
   d. personal characteristics
   e. command

### Short Response Questions
1. Is there any method of allocating resources that eliminates the scarcity of resources?

2. Only one person can become President of Sony, yet many of Sony's top executives would like that job. What allocation method is typically used to determine who becomes President? How does this allocation method benefit Sony?

## CHECKPOINT 6.2

### ■ Distinguish between value and price and define consumer surplus.

#### Quick Review

- *Value* In economics the idea of value is called marginal benefit, which we measure as the maximum price that people are willing to pay for another unit of a good or service.
- *Consumer surplus* Consumer surplus is the marginal benefit from a good or service minus the price paid for it, summed over the quantity consumed.

#### Additional Practice Problem 6.2

1. The figure shows the demand curve for magazines and the market price of a magazine. Use the figure to answer the following questions.

Price (dollars per magazine)

Quantity (magazines per week)

a. What is the value of the 1st magazine? What is the marginal benefit of the 1st magazine? What is the consumer surplus of the 1st magazine?

b. What is the marginal benefit of the 2nd magazine? What is the consumer surplus of the 2nd magazine?

c. What is the total quantity of magazines bought and the consumer surplus?

d. If the price of a magazine rises to $10, what is the quantity bought and what is the consumer surplus?

#### Solutions to Additional Practice Problems 6.2

1a. The value of the 1st magazine equals the maximum price a consumer is willing to pay for the magazine. The figure shows that the maximum price for the 1st magazine is $15, so the value of the magazine equals $15. The marginal benefit of the magazine is equal to the maximum price the consumer will pay,

which is $15. The consumer surplus is equal to the marginal benefit of the 1st magazine ($15) minus the price of the magazine ($5) so the consumer surplus is $10.

Price (dollars per magazine)

Market price

Quantity (magazines per week)

1b. The marginal benefit of the magazine equals the maximum price a consumer will pay. The figure shows that the maximum price for the 2nd magazine is $10, so the marginal benefit of the magazine equals $5. The consumer surplus is equal to $5.

Price (dollars per magazine)

Market price

Quantity (magazines per week)

1c. The quantity bought is 3 magazines because the demand curve shows that the quantity demanded at the price of $5 is 3 magazines. The consumer surplus equals the

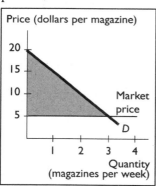

Price (dollars per magazine)

Market price

Quantity (magazines per week)

area of the darkened triangle in the figure. Calculating the area of the consumer surplus triangle, which is equal to one half the base of the triangle multiplied by the height or 1/2 × (3 − 0) × ($20 − $5), which is $22.50.

1d. If the price of a magazine rises to $10, the quantity bought is 2 magazines. The consumer surplus now equals 1/2 × (2 − 0) × ($20 − $10), which is $10.00.

# ■ AP Self Test 6.2

## True or false

1. In economics, value and price refer to the same thing.

2. The consumer surplus from one unit of a good is the marginal benefit from the good minus the price paid for it.

3. Consumer surplus always equals zero because consumers always pay for the goods and services they consume.

## Multiple choice

1. Value is
   a. the price we pay for a good.
   b. the cost of resources used to produce a good.
   c. objective so that it is determined by market forces, not preferences.
   d. the marginal benefit we get from consuming another unit of a good or service.
   e. the difference between the price paid for a good and the marginal cost of producing that unit of the good.

2. A marginal benefit curve
   a. is the same as a demand curve.
   b. is the same as a supply curve.
   c. slopes upwards.
   d. is a vertical line at the efficient quantity.
   e. is U-shaped.

3. In general, as the consumption of a good or service increases, the marginal benefit from consuming that good or service
   a. increases.
   b. decreases.
   c. stays the same.
   d. at first increases and then decreases.
   e. at first decreases and then increases.

4. The difference between the marginal benefit from a new pair of shoes and the price of the new pair of shoes is
   a. the consumer surplus from that pair of shoes.
   b. what we get.
   c. what we have to pay.
   d. the price when the marginal benefit is maximized.
   e. the consumer's expenditure on the shoes.

5. Suppose the price of a scooter is $200 and Cora Lee is willing to pay $250. Cora Lee's
   a. consumer surplus from that scooter is $200.
   b. consumer surplus from that scooter is $50.
   c. marginal benefit from that scooter is $200.
   d. consumer surplus from that scooter is $200.
   e. consumer surplus from that scooter is $250.

6. If the price of a pizza is $10 per pizza, the consumer surplus from the first pizza consumed ____ the consumer surplus from the second pizza consumed.
   a. is greater than
   b. equals
   c. is less than
   d. cannot be compared to
   e. None of the above answers is correct because more information is needed about the marginal cost of producing the pizzas to answer the question.

## Short Response Questions

1. Define consumer surplus.

| Price (dollars per MP3 player) | Quantity (millions of MP3 players per year) | Consumer surplus (dollars) |
|---|---|---|
| 500 | 4 | ____ |
| 400 | 8 | ____ |
| 300 | 12 | ____ |
| 200 | 16 | ____ |
| 100 | 20 | ____ |

2. The table above gives the demand schedule for MP3 players. Suppose the price of an MP3 player is $200.
   a. Complete the table by calculating the con-

sumer surplus. In the first row, calculate the consumer surplus for the 4 millionth MP3 player; in the second row, calculate the consumer surplus for the 8 millionth MP3 player; and so on.

b. As more MP3 players are purchased, what happens to the consumer surplus of the last unit purchased? Why?

### ■ FIGURE 6.1

Price (dollars per pair of roller blades)

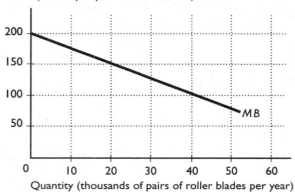

Quantity (thousands of pairs of roller blades per year)

3. Figure 6.1 shows the demand curve for roller blades.

   a. What is the marginal benefit of the 20,000th pair of roller blades?

   b. What is the marginal benefit of the 40,000th pair of roller blades?

   c. If the price of a pair of roller blades is $100, what is the consumer surplus on the 20,000th pair of roller blades?

   d. If the price of a pair of roller blades is $100, what is the consumer surplus on the 40,000th pair of roller blades?

   e. If the price of a pair of roller blades is $100, what is the quantity of roller blades purchased? What is the amount of the consumer surplus?

### ■ FIGURE 6.2

Price (dollars per bag of potato chips)

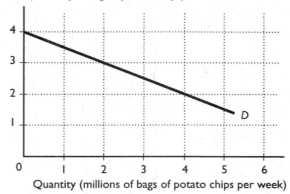

Quantity (millions of bags of potato chips per week)

4. Figure 6.2 shows the demand curve for bags of potato chips.

   a. What is the maximum price a consumer is willing to pay for the 2 millionth bag of chips?

   b. What is the marginal benefit from the 2 millionth bag of chips? What is the relationship between your answer to part (a) and your answer to this part?

   c. If the price of a bag of chips equals $2, in Figure 6.2 shade the area that equals the amount of the consumer surplus.

   d. If the price of a bag of chips equals $2, what is the amount of the consumer surplus?

## Long Response Questions

1. What is the relationship between the value of a good, the maximum price a consumer is willing to pay for the good, and the marginal benefit from the good?

2. What is the relationship between the marginal benefit of a slice of pizza, the price paid for the slice, and the consumer surplus of the slice?

## CHECKPOINT 6.3

■ **Distinguish between cost and price and define producer surplus.**

### Quick Review

- *Cost* Cost is what the seller must give up to produce a good.
- *Marginal cost* The cost of producing one additional unit of a good or service.
- *Producer surplus* The producer surplus of a good equals the price of a good minus the marginal cost of producing it.

### Additional Practice Problems 6.3

1. The figure shows the supply curve of magazines and the market price of a magazine. Use it to answer the following questions.

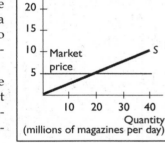

   a. What is the marginal cost of the 10 millionth magazine?
   b. What is the minimum supply price of the 10 millionth magazine?
   c. What is the producer surplus on the 10 millionth magazine?
   d. What are the quantity of magazines sold and the total producer surplus?

2. Why is the minimum price for which a seller will produce a product equal to the product's marginal cost?

### Solutions to Additional Practice Problems 6.3

1a. The marginal cost of the 10 millionth magazine is equal to the minimum supply price of the 10 millionth magazine. The supply curve, which is also the marginal cost

curve, shows this price. In the figure, the supply curve shows that the marginal cost of 10 millionth magazine is $2.50.

1b. The minimum supply price of the 10 millionth magazine equals its marginal cost, $2.50.

1c. The producer surplus on the 10 millionth magazine is equal to its market price minus its marginal cost, which is $5 − $2.50 = $2.50.

1d. At the market price of $5, 20 million magazines are sold. The producer surplus equals the area of the darkened triangle in the figure. Calculating the area of the triangle as one half the base multiplied by the height, or 1/2 × (20 million − 0) × ($5 − 0), the producer surplus equals $50 million.

2. A seller is willing to produce a good as long as the price the seller receives covers all the costs of producing the good. So the minimum price for which a seller is willing to produce a unit of the good must be the amount that just equals the cost of the producing that unit. But the cost of producing any unit of a good is its marginal cost, so the minimum supply price equals the good's marginal cost.

■ **AP Self Test 6.3**

### True or false

1. In economics, cost and price are the same thing.

2. The minimum price for which Bobby will grow another pound of rice is 20¢, so the marginal cost of an additional pound of rice is 20¢.

3. A supply curve is a marginal benefit curve.

4. Producer surplus equals the marginal benefit of a good minus the cost of producing it.

## Multiple choice

1. Cost
   a. is what the buyer pays to get the good.
   b. is always equal to the marginal benefit for every unit of a good produced.
   c. is what the seller must give up to produce the good.
   d. is greater than market price.
   e. means the same thing as price.

2. If a firm is willing to supply the 1,000th unit of a good at a price of $23 or more, we know that $23 is the
   a. highest price the seller hopes to realize for this output.
   b. minimum price the seller must receive to produce this unit.
   c. average price of all the prices the seller could charge.
   d. price that sets the marginal benefit equal to the marginal cost.
   e. only price for which the seller is willing to sell this unit of the good.

3. A supply curve shows the _____ of producing one more unit of a good or service.
   a. producer surplus
   b. consumer surplus
   c. total benefit
   d. marginal cost
   e. marginal benefit to the producer

4. Producer surplus is
   a. equal to the marginal benefit from a good minus its price.
   b. equal to the price of a good minus the marginal cost of producing it.
   c. always equal to consumer surplus.
   d. Both answers (a) and (c) are correct.
   e. Both answers (b) and (c) are correct.

5. You're willing to tutor a student for $10 an hour and the student pays you $15 an hour. Your producer surplus is
   a. $5 an hour.
   b. $10 an hour.
   c. $15 an hour.
   d. $25 an hour.
   e. more than $25 an hour.

6. In a figure that shows a supply curve and a demand curve, producer surplus is the area
   a. below the demand curve and above the market price.
   b. below the supply curve and above the market price.
   c. above the demand curve and below the market price.
   d. above the supply curve and below the market price.
   e. between the demand curve and the supply curve.

## Short Response Questions

### ■ FIGURE 6.3

Price (dollars per bag of potato chips)

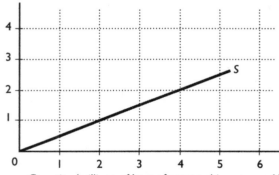

1. Figure 6.3 shows the supply curve for bags of potato chips.
   a. What is the minimum price for which a supplier is willing to produce the 2 millionth bag of chips?
   b. What is the marginal cost of the 2 millionth bag of chips? What is the relationship between your answer to part (a) and your answer to this part?
   c. If the price of a bag of chips equals $2, in Figure 6.3 shade the area that equals the amount of the producer surplus.
   d. If the price of a bag of chips equals $2, calculate the producer surplus.

## Long Response Questions

1. What is the relationship between the minimum price a supplier must receive to pro-

duce a slice of pizza and the marginal cost of the slice of pizza? What is the relationship between the marginal cost curve and the supply curve?

2. What is producer surplus? As the price of a good or service rises and the supply curve does not shift, what happens to the amount of the producer surplus?

## CHECKPOINT 6.4

■ **Explain the conditions in which markets are efficient and inefficient.**

### Quick Review

- *Efficiency of competitive equilibrium* The condition that marginal benefit equals marginal cost delivers an efficient use of resources. It allocates resources to the activities that create the greatest possible value. Marginal benefit equals marginal cost at a competitive equilibrium, so a competitive equilibrium is efficient.

- *Total surplus* The total surplus from a good or service is the sum of the consumer surplus plus the producer surplus.

- *Deadweight loss* The decrease in consumer surplus and producer surplus that results from an inefficient level of production.

### Additional Practice Problems 6.4

1. The figure shows the market for paper. Use the figure to answer the following questions.

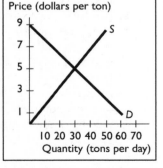

Price (dollars per ton)

10 20 30 40 50 60 70
Quantity (tons per day)

   a. What are the equilibrium price and the equilibrium quantity of paper? What is the efficient quantity of paper?

   b. In the market equilibrium, use the figure above to shade the consumer surplus and the producer surplus.

   c. What does the consumer surplus equal? What does the producer surplus equal? What does the total surplus equal?

   d. Is the market for paper efficient? Why or why not? Can the total surplus be any larger at any other level of production?

2. Who benefits from a deadweight loss?

### Solutions to Additional Practice Problems 6.4

1a. The equilibrium is shown in the figure and is where the supply and demand curves intersect. The equilibrium price is $5 a ton and the equilibrium quantity is 30 tons a day. The efficient

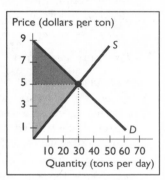

Price (dollars per ton)

10 20 30 40 50 60 70
Quantity (tons per day)

quantity is where the marginal benefit and marginal cost curves intersect. Because the demand curve is the marginal benefit curve and the supply curve is the marginal cost curve, the efficient quantity is 30 tons a day.

1b. The consumer surplus is illustrated in the figure as the area of the top, dark triangle. The producer surplus equals the area of the lower, lighter triangle.

1c. The consumer surplus equals the area of the darker triangle, or 1/2 × (30 tons) × ($4 per ton) = $60, where $4 a ton is the height of the triangle, $9 a ton − $5 a ton. The producer surplus equals the area of the lighter triangle, or 1/2 × (30 tons) × ($5 per ton) = $75, where $5 a ton is the height of the triangle, $5 a ton − $0 a ton. The total surplus equals the sum of the consumer surplus plus the producer surplus, which is $135.

1d. The efficient use of resources occurs when marginal benefit equals marginal cost. The market equilibrium is efficient because the marginal benefit of a ton of paper equals its marginal cost. The sum of the consumer surplus and producer surplus, which equals the total surplus, is at its maximum at the efficient level of production so the total surplus cannot be larger at any other amount of production.

2. No one gains from a deadweight loss. Deadweight loss is a decrease in consumer surplus and producer surplus that results from an inefficient level of production. The deadweight loss is borne by the entire society. It is not a loss for the consumers and a gain for the producer. It is a social loss.

## ■ AP Self Test 6.4

### True or false

1. When the demand curve is the marginal benefit curve and the supply curve is the marginal cost curve, the competitive equilibrium is allocatively efficient.

2. When the allocatively efficient quantity of a good is produced, the consumer surplus is always zero.

3. According to Adam Smith, the invisible hand suggests that competitive markets require government action to ensure that resources are allocated efficiently.

4. Producing less than the efficient quantity of a good results in a deadweight loss but producing more than the efficient quantity does not result in a deadweight loss.

### Multiple choice

1. When a market is efficient the
   a. sum of consumer surplus and producer surplus is maximized.
   b. deadweight gain is maximized.
   c. quantity produced is maximized.
   d. marginal benefit of the last unit produced exceeds the marginal cost by as much as possible.
   e. total benefit equals the total cost.

■ **FIGURE 6.4**

Price (dollars per computer)

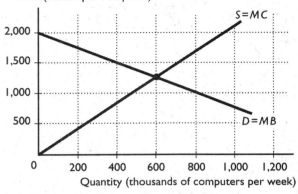

2. Figure 6.4 shows the market for computers. What is the equilibrium quantity of computers?
   a. 0 computers per week
   b. 200,000 computers per week
   c. 400,000 computers per week
   d. 600,000 computers per week
   e. more than 600,000 computers per week

3. Figure 6.4 shows the market for computers. What is the efficient quantity of computers?
   a. 0 computers per week
   b. 200,000 computers per week
   c. 400,000 computers per week
   d. 600,000 computers per week
   e. more than 600,000 computers per week

4. Which of the following occurs when a market is efficient?
   a. producers earn the highest income possible
   b. production costs equal total benefit
   c. consumer surplus equals producer surplus
   d. scarce resources are used to produce the goods and services that people value most highly
   e. every consumer has all of the good or service he or she wants.

5. The concept of "the invisible hand" suggests that markets
   a. do not produce the efficient quantity.
   b. are always fair.
   c. produce the efficient quantity.
   d. are unfair though they might be efficient.
   e. allocate resources unfairly and inefficiently.

6. When underproduction occurs,
   a. producers gain more surplus at the expense of consumers.
   b. marginal cost is greater than marginal benefit.
   c. consumer surplus increases to a harmful amount.
   d. there is a deadweight loss that is borne by the entire society.
   e. the deadweight loss harms only consumers.

7. Which of the following can result in a market producing an inefficient quantity of a good?
   i.   competition
   ii.  an external cost or an external benefit
   iii. a tax
   a. i only.
   b. ii only.
   c. iii only.
   d. ii and iii.
   e. i and iii.

## Short Response Questions

1. In Figure 6.5, what is the equilibrium quantity of automobiles? What is the efficient quantity of automobiles? Shade the consumer surplus and the producer surplus and calculate their amounts.

2. Figure 6.6 is identical to Figure 6.5.
   a. Suppose that 80,000 automobiles are produced. Shade the deadweight loss light gray and calculate its amount.
   b. Suppose that 40,000 automobiles are produced. Shade the deadweight loss dark gray and calculate its amount.

■ **FIGURE 6.5**
Price (thousands of dollars per automobile)

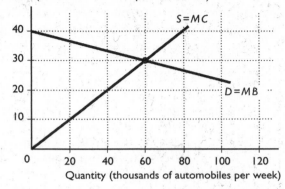

Quantity (thousands of automobiles per week)

■ **FIGURE 6.6**
Price (thousands of dollars per automobile)

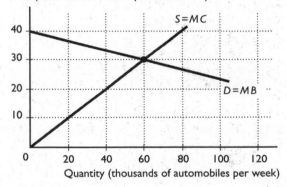

Quantity (thousands of automobiles per week)

## Long Response Questions

1. What is the relationship between a competitive market, efficiency, and the invisible hand?

2. Suppose the demand for cotton clothing increases. What effect does the increase in demand have on the equilibrium quantity and on the efficient quantity?

3. What factors might lead a market to produce an inefficient amount of a product?

## CHECKPOINT 6.5

■ **Explain the main ideas about fairness and evaluate claims that competitive markets result in unfair outcomes.**

### Quick Review

- *Utilitarianism* A principle that states that we should strive to achieve "the greatest happiness for the greatest number."
- *Big tradeoff* The big tradeoff is the tradeoff between efficiency and fairness that results when income transfers are made.

### Additional Practice Problem 6.5

1. If Bill Gates gives $1,000 to a homeless person, would the transaction be fair? If Mr. Gates is taxed $1,000 by the government and the government gives the $1,000 to the same homeless person, would the transaction be fair? Comment on your answers.

### Solution to Additional Practice Problem 6.5

1. If Mr. Gates gives $1,000 to a homeless person, the action is considered fair. The exchange is fair according to the fair rules principle because the exchange is voluntary. And the outcome is fair according to the fair results, utilitarian principle because there is more equality of income. If Mr. Gates is taxed by the government, the outcome is fair according to the fair results principle because there is more equality of income. But the transaction is not fair according to the fair rules principle because the exchange does not occur voluntarily; pages 161-163.

## ■ AP Self Test 6.5

### True or false

1. The principle that "it's not fair if the result isn't fair" might often conflict with the principle that "it's not fair if the rules aren't fair."

2. The goal of utilitarianism is to achieve the greatest happiness for the greatest number of people.

3. The big tradeoff is the tradeoff between efficiency and happiness.

### Multiple choice

1. The idea that unequal incomes is unfair generally uses the _____ principle of fairness.
   a. big tradeoff
   b. involuntary exchange
   c. voluntary exchange
   d. it's not fair if the result isn't fair
   e. it's not fair if the rules aren't fair

2. The principle that states that we should strive to achieve "the greatest happiness for the greatest number" is
   a. equity.
   b. fairness.
   c. market equilibrium.
   d. utilitarianism.
   e. the big tradeoff.

3. Which of the following is an example in which "the big tradeoff" can occur?
   a. the government redistributes income from the rich to the poor
   b. Ford increases the price of a pickup truck
   c. a basketball player signs a $5 million contract
   d. a college lowers tuition
   e. the price of personal computers falls year after year

4. The "fair-rules" view of fairness is based on
   a. income transfers from the rich to the poor.
   b. property rights and voluntary exchange.
   c. utilitarianism.
   d. the big tradeoff.
   e. allocating resources using majority rule.

### Short Response Questions

1. In the United States, richer people generally pay a larger fraction of their income as taxes than do poorer people. Is this arrangement fair? Answer from a fair-results view and from a fair-rules view.

2. Suppose that during their working lifetimes, Matt and Pat have earned identical incomes as computer programmers. The only difference between the two is that

Matt spent all of his income while Pat saved a large portion of hers. Now that they are retired, Pat's income is substantially higher than Matt's because of Pat's saving. Is it fair for Pat's income to be higher than Matt's? Answer from a fair results and from a fair rules perspective.

**Long Response Questions**

1. What is the effect of the big tradeoff in transferring income from people with high incomes to people with low incomes?

# YOUR AP SELF TEST ANSWERS

## ■ CHECKPOINT 6.1

**True or false**
1. True; page 144
2. True; page 144
3. False; page 146
4. False; page 147

**Multiple choice**
1. e; page 144
2. a; page 145
3. a; page 145
4. d; page 146

**Short Response Questions**
1. No allocation method can eliminate the scarcity of resources because people's wants will always exceed the ability of the resources to satisfy their wants; page 144.
2. Sony is using a contest allocation method. Sony benefits from this allocation scheme because all the top executives who want to be President will work extremely hard for Sony in an effort to win the contest; page 145.

## ■ CHECKPOINT 6.2

**True or false**
1. False; page 148
2. True; page 149
3. False; page 149

**Multiple choice**
1. d; page 148
2. a; page 148
3. b; page 148
4. a; page 149
5. b; page 149
6. a; page 149

**Short Response Questions**
1. Consumer surplus is the marginal benefit from a good or service minus the price paid for it, summed over the quantity consumed; page 149.

| Price (dollars per MP3 player) | Quantity (millions of MP3 players per year) | Consumer surplus (dollars) |
|---|---|---|
| 500 | 4 | 300 |
| 400 | 8 | 200 |
| 300 | 12 | 100 |
| 200 | 16 | 0 |
| 100 | 20 | 0 |

2. a. The table above contains the consumer surpluses. The consumer surplus is zero for the 20 millionth MP3 player because when the price of an MP3 player is $200, the 20 millionth MP3 player is not purchased. For the remaining quantities, the consumer surplus is the marginal benefit, which equals the maximum price consumers are willing to pay minus the price; page 149.
   b. The consumer surplus decreases as more MP3 players are purchased because the value of an additional MP3 player decreases as more are purchased; page 149.
3. a. The marginal benefit of the 20,000th pair of roller blades is the maximum price a consumer is willing to pay for that pair, which is $150; page 148.
   b. The marginal benefit of the 40,000th pair of roller blades is the maximum price a consumer is willing to pay for that pair, which is $100; page 148.
   c. The consumer surplus is the difference between the marginal benefit, $150, minus the price paid, $100, or $50; page 149.
   d. The consumer surplus is the difference between the marginal benefit, $100, minus the price paid, $100, or $0; page 149.
   e. If the price is $100, then 40,000 pairs of roller blades will be purchased. The consumer surplus equals $1/2 \times (\$200 - \$100) \times (40,000 - 0)$, or $40,000,000; page 149.
4. a. The maximum price is $3; page 148.
   b. The marginal benefit is $3. The marginal benefit is the maximum price a consumer is willing to pay for another bag of potato chips; page 148.

■ **FIGURE 6.7**

Price (dollars per bag of potato chips)

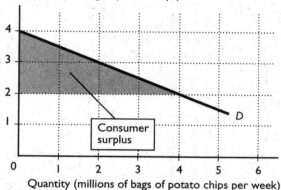

Quantity (millions of bags of potato chips per week)

c. Figure 6.7 shades the area of the consumer surplus; page 149.

d. The consumer surplus equals the area of the shaded triangle in Figure 6.7, which is $1/2 \times (\$4 - \$2) \times 4$ million = $4 million; page 149.

**Long Response Questions**

1. The value of a good is equal to the maximum price a buyer is willing to pay. The maximum price of the buyer is willing to pay also equals the marginal benefit. So the maximum price the buyer is willing to pay equals the value equals the marginal benefit; page 148.

2. The consumer surplus on a slice of pizza equals the difference between the marginal benefit of the slice minus the price paid for the slice. So the price paid for the slice plus the consumer surplus on that slice equals the consumer's marginal benefit from that slice; page 149.

■ **CHECKPOINT 6.3**

**True or false**

1. False; page 151
2. True; page 151
3. False; page 151
4. False; page 152

**Multiple choice**

1. c; page 151
2. b; page 151
3. d; page 151

4. b; page 152
5. a; page 152
6. d; page 152

**Short Response Questions**

1. a. The minimum price is $1; page 151.

   b. The marginal cost is $1. The marginal cost of the 2 millionth bag is the minimum price for which a supplier is willing to produce that bag of chips; page 151.

■ **FIGURE 6.8**

Price (dollars per bag of potato chips)

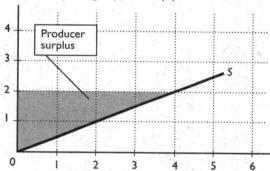

Quantity (millions of bags of potato chips per week)

c. Figure 6.8 shades the area of the producer surplus; page 152.

d. The producer surplus equals the area of the shaded triangle in Figure 6.7, so producer surplus is $1/2 \times (\$2 - \$0) \times 4$ million, which equals $4 million; page 152.

**Long Response Questions**

1. The minimum price for which a firm will produce a slice of pizza equals the marginal cost of producing that slice. It is just worth producing one more slice of pizza if the price for which it can be sold equals its marginal cost. The supply curve tells us this price. So the supply curve is the same as the marginal cost curve; page 151.

2. Producer surplus equals the price of a good or service minus the marginal cost of producing it. As the price of a good or service rises and the supply curve does not shift, the producer surplus increases; page 152.

# ■ CHECKPOINT 6.4

## True or false

1. True; page 154
2. False; page 155
3. False; page 155
4. False; page 157

## Multiple choice

1. a; page 155
2. d; page 154
3. d; page 154
4. d; page 154
5. c; page 155
6. d; page 157
7. d; page 158

## Short Response Questions

### ■ FIGURE 6.9
Price (thousands of dollars per automobile)

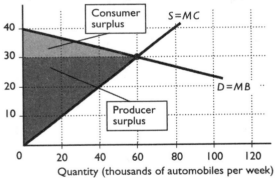

Quantity (thousands of automobiles per week)

1. In Figure 6.9 the equilibrium quantity of automobiles is 60,000 a week. The efficient quantity of automobiles is also 60,000 a week because that is the quantity at which the marginal benefit equals the marginal cost. The consumer surplus and producer surplus are the shown in the figure. The consumer surplus is the area of the light gray triangle, which is 1/2 × ($40.00 − $30.00) × (60,000) = $600,000. The producer surplus is the area of the dark gray triangle, which is 1/2 × ($30.00 − $0.00) × (60,000) = $900,000; page 154.

2. a. When 80,000 automobiles are produced, there is a deadweight loss from overproduction because for the last 20,000 auto

### ■ FIGURE 6.10
Price (thousands of dollars per automobile)

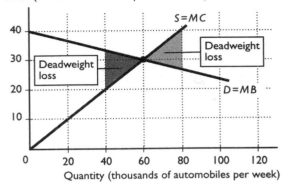

Quantity (thousands of automobiles per week)

mobiles, the marginal cost exceeds the marginal benefit. The deadweight loss is the area of the light gray triangle in Figure 6.10, which is 1/2 × ($40.00 − $26.67) × (80,000 − 60,000) = $13,300; page 157.

b. If 40,000 automobiles are produced, there again is a deadweight loss, because automobiles for which the marginal benefit exceeds the marginal cost are not produced. The amount of the deadweight loss is the area of dark gray triangle in Figure 6.10, which is 1/2 × ($33.33 − $20.00) × (60,000 − 40,000) = $13,300; page 157.

## Long Response Questions

1. Adam Smith was the first to suggest that competitive markets send resources to the uses in which they have the highest value so that competitive markets are efficient. Smith said that each participant in a competitive market is "led by an invisible hand to promote an end [the efficient use of resources] which is no part of his intention;" page 155.

2. If the demand for cotton clothing increases, the demand curve for cotton clothing shifts rightward and the equilibrium quantity increases. The demand curve is the marginal benefit curve, so when the demand curve shifts rightward, the marginal benefit curve also shifts rightward. As a result, the efficient quantity of cotton clothing increases; page 154.

3. Governments influence markets by setting price and quantity regulations as well as taxes and subsidies, all of which can create

inefficiency. Other obstacles to achieving an efficient allocation of resources are externalities, public goods, common resources, monopoly, and high transactions costs; pages 158-159.

# ■ CHECKPOINT 6.5

## True or false
1. True;  page 161
2. True;  page 162
3. False; page 162

## Multiple choice
1. b; page 161
2. d; page 162
3. a; page 162
4. b; page 163

## Short Response Questions
1. The tax arrangement is fair from a fair-results view because it leads to a greater equality of income. The tax arrangement is not fair from a fair-results view because the tax is not a voluntary exchange;  pages 161-163.
2. From a fair-results view, it is not fair for Pat's income to be substantially higher than Matt's. From a fair-rules view, it is fair because Pat and Matt had the same opportunities; pages 161-163.

## Long Response Questions
1. Income can be transferred from people with high incomes to people with low incomes only by taxing incomes, which discourages work. This tax results in the quantity of labor being less than the efficient quantity. Similarly, taxing income from capital discourages saving, which results in the quantity of capital being less than the efficient quantity. With less labor and less capital than the efficient amounts, the total amount of production is less than the efficient amount. So the greater the amount of income redistribution through income taxes, the greater is the inefficiency and the smaller is the economic pie;  page 162.

# Chapter 7

# Government Influences on Markets

In Chapter 7 we study how governments influence markets when they collect taxes. We also look at the inefficiency that is created when the government applies a rent ceiling in the housing market or a minimum wage in the labor market.

- **Explain how a price ceiling works and show how a rent ceiling creates a housing shortage, inefficiency, and unfairness.**

A price ceiling is an *upper* limit on the price at which it is legal to trade a particular good, service, or factor of production. A rent ceiling is an example of a price ceiling. A rent ceiling set above the equilibrium rent is ineffective. A housing shortage occurs when a rent ceiling is set below the equilibrium rent because the quantity of housing demanded exceeds the quantity of housing supplied. A black market is an illegal market that operates alongside a government regulated market. When a rent ceiling creates a shortage of housing, search activity, which is the time spent looking for someone with whom to do business, increases. A rent ceiling creates a deadweight loss and decreases consumer surplus and producer surplus. Rent ceilings violate the fair-rules view of fairness because they block voluntary exchange. Rent ceilings exist because of political support from current renters.

- **Explain how a price floor works and show the minimum wage creates unemployment, inefficiency, and unfairness.**

A minimum wage law is a government regulation that makes hiring labor for less than a specified wage illegal. A minimum wage law is an example of a price floor. A minimum wage set below the equilibrium wage rate is ineffective. Unemployment occurs when the minimum wage is set above the equilibrium wage rate because the quantity of labor supplied exceeds the quantity of labor demanded. A minimum wage increases job search activity and illegal hiring when some firms and workers agree to do business at an illegal wage rate below the minimum wage. The minimum wage creates a deadweight loss. The minimum wage is unfair because it delivers an unfair result and imposes unfair rules.

- **Explain how a price support in the market for agricultural produce creates a surplus, inefficiency, and unfairness.**

When governments intervene in agricultural markets, they isolate the domestic market from global competition by limiting imports. The government introduces a price floor, which in an agricultural market is called a price support. The price support leads to a surplus, so the government pays the farmers a subsidy by purchasing the surplus to keep the price at the support level. Consumers are worse off because the price rises and the quantity they purchase decreases. Consumer surplus shrinks. Farmers are better off because the price is higher and the government purchases the surplus to keep the price higher. A deadweight loss is created. Farmers in developing economies are harmed two ways: First, their exports to the domestic nation are limited and, second, the government sells the surplus it has purchased in the rest of the world, thereby lowering the price these farmers receive.

## EXPANDED CHAPTER CHECKLIST

**When you have completed this chapter, you will be able to:**

**1  Explain how a price ceiling works and show how a rent ceiling creates a housing shortage, inefficiency, and unfairness.**

- Define price ceiling and rent ceiling.
- Explain why a rent ceiling that exceeds the equilibrium price is ineffective.
- Illustrate the effects of a rent ceiling set below the equilibrium rent and discuss how a rent ceiling can lead to a black market and increased search activity.
- Illustrate the deadweight loss created by a rent ceiling.
- Discuss the fairness of rent ceilings and why we have them.

**2  Explain how a price floor works and show the minimum wage creates unemployment, inefficiency, and unfairness.**

- Define price floor and minimum wage law.
- Explain why a minimum wage below the equilibrium wage rate is ineffective.
- Illustrate the effects of a minimum wage set above the equilibrium wage rate and discuss how a minimum wage can lead to unemployment and increased job search.
- Illustrate the deadweight loss created by a minimum wage.
- Discuss the fairness of the minimum wage and why we have it.

**3  Explain how a price support in the market for agricultural produce creates a surplus, inefficiency, and unfairness.**

- Discuss how the government intervenes in agricultural markets.
- Explain why a price support leads to a surplus and tell what the government must do

with the surplus.
- Discuss the effect a price support has on consumers, producers, and society.

## YOUR AP TEST HINTS

*AP Topics*

| Topic on your AP test | Corresponding textbook section |
|---|---|
| **Nature and function of product markets** | |
| Price and quantity controls | Chapter 7 |
| • Price ceiling | Checkpoint 7.1 |
| • Price floor | Checkpoint 7.2 |
| • Price supports | Checkpoint 7.3 |

*Extra AP material*

- When a price control creates a shortage, some rationing scheme must still be used to allocate the good or service to consumers. Methods used include first-come, first served; favoritism; rationing so everyone gets some amount; and, black markets.

## CHECKPOINT 7.1

■  **Explain how a price ceiling works and show how a rent ceiling creates a housing shortage, inefficiency, and unfairness.**

*Quick Review*

- *Price ceiling* A government regulation that places an *upper* limit on the price at which a particular good, service, or factor of production may be traded.
- *Rent ceiling* A government regulation that makes it illegal to charge more than a specified rent for housing.
- *Effective rent ceiling* When a rent ceiling is set below the equilibrium rent, the quantity of housing demanded is greater than the equilibrium quantity and the quantity of housing supplied is less than the equilibrium quantity. A housing shortage occurs.

## Additional Practice Problems 7.1

1. The figure shows the rental market for apartments in Ocala, Florida.

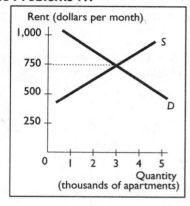

a. With no government intervention in this market, what is the rent and how many apartments are rented?

b. If the government imposes a rent ceiling of $500 a month, what is the rent and how many apartments are rented?

c. Tell why with a strictly enforced $500 rent ceiling the housing market is inefficient. What is the amount of the deadweight loss?

d. With a strictly enforced $500 rent ceiling, is there a shortage or surplus of apartments?

| Price (dollars per round of golf) | Quantity demanded | Quantity supplied |
|---|---|---|
| | (rounds per week) | |
| 50 | 2,000 | 2,800 |
| 40 | 2,300 | 2,700 |
| 30 | 2,600 | 2,600 |
| 20 | 2,900 | 2,500 |
| 10 | 3,200 | 2,400 |

2. The table above gives the supply and demand schedules for rounds of golf.

a. What is the equilibrium price and equilibrium quantity of rounds of golf?

b. Suppose the city government imposes a price ceiling of $40 a round of golf. What will be the price and quantity of rounds of golf? Is there a shortage?

c. Suppose the city government imposes a price ceiling of $20 a round of golf. What will be the price and quantity of rounds of golf? Is there a shortage?

## Solutions to Additional Practice Problems 7.1

1a. In the figure, the equilibrium rent and the equilibrium quantity are determined at the point where the demand curve and the supply curve intersect. The rent is $750 a month and 3,000 apartments are rented.

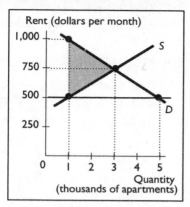

1b. To answer this practice problem remember that a rent ceiling is effective only when it is set below the equilibrium price. The rent ceiling of $500 per month is below the equilibrium rent, so it has an effect. The quantity of apartments rented decreases to 1,000 and the rent is $500.

1c. The market is inefficient because the marginal benefit of the last apartment rented, the 1,000th apartment, exceeds the marginal cost of the apartment. Because the housing market is inefficient a deadweight loss arises. In the figure the deadweight loss is shown by the gray triangle. The amount of the deadweight loss equals the area of the gray triangle. This area is 1/2 × ($1,000 − $500) × (3,000 − 1,000) = $500,000.

1d. There is a shortage of apartments. At the $500 rent ceiling, the quantity of apartments demanded is 5,000 and the quantity supplied is 1,000. So there is a shortage of 4,000 apartments.

2a. The equilibrium price is $30 a round of golf and the equilibrium quantity is 2,600 rounds a week.

2b. The price ceiling is above the equilibrium price, so the price remains at $30 a round and the quantity remains at 2,600 rounds a week. There is no shortage.

2c. The price ceiling is below the equilibrium price. The price falls to $20 a round. The quantity played equals the quantity supplied at $20, which is 2,500 rounds a week. There is a shortage of 400 rounds a week.

## ■ AP Self Test 7.1

### True or false

1. A rent ceiling always lowers the rent paid.
2. When a rent ceiling is higher than the equilibrium rent, a black market emerges.
3. The opportunity cost of a dorm room is equal to its rent plus the value of the search time spent finding the dorm room.
4. Rent ceilings are efficient because they lower the cost of housing to low-income families.
5. The total loss from a rent ceiling exceeds the deadweight loss.

### Multiple choice

1. A price ceiling is a government regulation that makes it illegal to charge a price
   a. below the equilibrium price.
   b. above the equilibrium price.
   c. for a good or service.
   d. above some specified level.
   e. that is not equal to the equilibrium price.

2. When a price ceiling is set below the equilibrium price, the quantity supplied ____ the quantity demanded and ____ exists.
   a. is less than; a surplus
   b. is less than; a shortage
   c. is greater than; a surplus
   d. is greater than; a shortage
   e. equals; an equilibrium

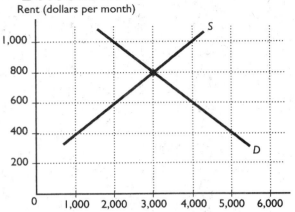

■ **FIGURE 7.1**

Rent (dollars per month)

3. Figure 7.1 shows a housing market. If the government imposes a rent ceiling of $1,000 per month, there will be a
   a. surplus of 2,000 units.
   b. shortage of 2,000 units.
   c. surplus of 4,000 units.
   d. shortage of 1,000 units.
   e. neither a shortage nor a surplus of units.

4. Figure 7.1 shows a housing market. If the government imposes a rent ceiling of $400 per month, there will be a
   a. shortage of 1,000 units.
   b. shortage of 2,000 units.
   c. shortage of 3,000 units.
   d. shortage of 4,000 units.
   e. neither a shortage nor a surplus of units.

5. Figure 7.1 shows a housing market. Of the rent ceilings listed below, the deadweight loss from a rent ceiling is largest when the rent ceiling equals ____ per month.
   a. $1,000
   b. $800
   c. $600
   d. $400
   e. More information is needed to determine which of the rent ceilings has the largest deadweight loss.

6. In a housing market with a rent ceiling set below the equilibrium rent,
   a. some people seeking an apartment to rent will not be able to find one.
   b. the total cost of renting an apartment will decrease for all those seeking housing.
   c. some landlords will not be able to find renters to fill available apartments.
   d. search will decrease because renters no longer need to search for less expensive apartments.
   e. None of the above answers are correct because to have an impact the rent ceiling must be set *above* the equilibrium rent.

7. An effective rent ceiling on housing creates a problem of allocating the available housing units because
   a. the demand for housing decreases and the demand curve shifts leftward.
   b. the supply of housing increases and the supply curve shifts rightward.
   c. a shortage of apartments occurs.
   d. a surplus of apartments occurs.
   e. it eliminates search, which is one of the major ways housing units are allocated.

8. An effective rent ceiling
   a. increases search activity.
   b. results in surpluses.
   c. creates efficiency.
   d. benefits producers.
   e. must be set below the equilibrium rent.

9. Suppose that the government imposes a price ceiling on gasoline that is below the equilibrium price. The black market for gasoline is ____ market in which the price ____ the ceiling price.
   a. a legal; exceeds
   b. an illegal; exceeds
   c. a legal; is less than
   d. an illegal; is less than
   e. an illegal; equals

10. A rent ceiling creates a deadweight loss
    a. if it is set below the equilibrium rent.
    b. if it is set equal to the equilibrium rent.
    c. if it set above the equilibrium rent.
    d. if it decreases the taxes the government collects in the housing market.
    e. never, because if it did create a dead-weight loss, the government would not impose it.

**Short Response Questions**

■ **FIGURE 7.2**
Price (dollars per purse)

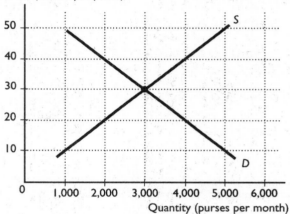

1. Figure 7.2 shows the market for purses.
   a. What is the equilibrium price and quantity of purses?
   b. Suppose the government imposes a $20 price ceiling. With the price ceiling, what is the quantity of purses demanded and the quantity of purses supplied? What is the shortage? Indicate the shortage in the figure.
   c. The price ceiling creates a deadweight loss. Show the deadweight loss in the figure.

| Price (dollars per carton) | Quantity demanded | Quantity supplied |
|---|---|---|
| | (cartons per day) | |
| 1.00 | 200 | 110 |
| 1.25 | 175 | 130 |
| 1.50 | 150 | 150 |
| 1.75 | 125 | 170 |
| 2.00 | 100 | 190 |

2. The table above gives the demand and supply schedules for milk.
   a. What is the market equilibrium in the milk market?
   b. Suppose the government imposes a price ceiling of $1.25 per carton. What is the price of a carton of milk and what quantity is purchased? Is there a shortage or surplus of milk?
   c. Suppose the government imposes a price ceiling of $1.75 per carton. What is the price of a carton of milk and what quantity is purchased? Is there a shortage or surplus of milk?

| Rent (dollars per month) | Quantity demanded | Quantity supplied |
|---|---|---|
| | (housing units per month) | |
| 900 | 200 | 350 |
| 800 | 300 | 300 |
| 700 | 400 | 250 |
| 600 | 500 | 200 |
| 500 | 600 | 150 |

3. The table above gives the demand and supply schedules for housing in a small town. In Figure 7.3, graph the demand and supply curves. Label the axes.
   a. What is the equilibrium rent and quantity of housing?
   b. Suppose the government imposes a $600 a month rent ceiling. With the rent ceiling, what is the quantity of housing demanded and the quantity of housing supplied?
   c. Does the rent ceiling result in a shortage or a surplus of housing? Indicate the shortage or surplus in Figure 7.3.

■ **FIGURE 7.3**

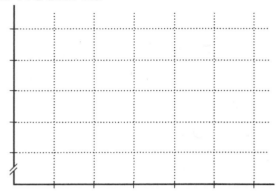

**Long Response Questions**
1. What is a price ceiling? In your answer, discuss whether an effective price ceiling is above, below, or equal to the equilibrium price, who is helped and who is harmed by a price ceiling, and the relationship between a price ceiling and a black market.
2. Are rent ceilings efficient?

## CHECKPOINT 7.2

■ **Explain how a price floor works and show the minimum wage creates unemployment, inefficiency, and unfairness.**

*Quick Review*

• *Price floor* A government regulation that places a *lower* limit on the price at which a particular good, service, or factor of production may be traded.

• *Minimum wage law* A government regulation that makes hiring labor for less than a specified wage illegal.

• *Effective minimum wage law* When the minimum wage is set above the equilibrium wage rate, the quantity of labor demanded is less than the equilibrium quantity and the quantity of labor supplied is greater than the equilibrium quantity. Unemployment occurs.

### Additional Practice Problems 7.2

1. The figure shows the market for fast food workers in Lake City Florida.

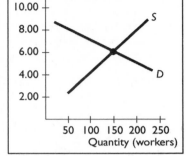

   a. What is the equilibrium wage rate of the workers and what is the equilibrium quantity of workers employed?

   b. If Lake City introduces a minimum wage for fast food workers of $8 an hour, how many fast food workers are employed?

   c. With the minimum wage, is there a surplus or a shortage of fast food workers? Indicate the amount of any shortage or surplus in the figure.

| Price (cents per pound) | Quantity demanded | Quantity supplied |
|---|---|---|
| | (tons of sugar per year) | |
| 10 | 300 | 225 |
| 15 | 275 | 275 |
| 20 | 250 | 325 |
| 25 | 225 | 375 |
| 30 | 200 | 425 |

2. The above table gives the supply and demand schedules for sugar.

   a. What is the equilibrium price and quantity of sugar?

   b. Suppose the government imposes a price floor of 25¢ a pound. What is the quantity demanded and the quantity supplied? Is there a shortage or surplus and, if so, how much?

### Solutions to Additional Practice Problems 7.2

1a. The equilibrium wage rate and the equilibrium quantity of the workers are determined where the labor demand curve and the labor supply curve intersect. The equilibrium wage rate is $6.00 an hour and the equilibrium quantity of workers is 150.

1b. In the figure, 50 fast food workers are employed. This amount equals the quantity of labor demanded when the wage rate is $8 an hour.

1c. The minimum wage creates a surplus of workers. At the $8 wage rate, 200 workers are willing to work but firms are willing to hire only 50 workers. There is a surplus of 150 workers, that is, there are 150 workers unemployed. In the figure, the length of the arrow shows the 150 unemployed workers.

2a. The equilibrium price is 15¢ a pound and the equilibrium quantity is 275 tons a year.

2b. The quantity demanded at 25¢ a pound is 225 tons and the quantity supplied is 375 tons. There is a surplus of 150 tons.

### ■ AP Self Test 7.2

**True or false**

1. Firms hire labor, so they determine how much labor to supply in a market.

2. A minimum wage is effective when it is set above the equilibrium wage rate.

3. A minimum wage law can lead to increased job search activity and illegal hiring.

4. When a minimum wage is set above the equilibrium wage rate, the employee's marginal cost of working exceeds the employer's marginal benefit from hiring labor.

5. A minimum wage is fair because low-income workers receive an increase in take-home pay.

### Multiple choice

1. A price floor
   a. is the highest price at which it is legal to trade a particular good, service, or factor of production.
   b. is the lowest price at which it is legal to trade a particular good, service, or factor of production.
   c. is an illegal price to charge.
   d. is the equilibrium price when the stock market crashes.
   e. is the lowest price for which the quantity demanded equals the quantity supplied.

2. To be effective in raising people's wages, a minimum wage must be set
   a. above the equilibrium wage rate.
   b. below the equilibrium wage rate.
   c. equal to the equilibrium wage rate.
   d. below $5.
   e. either above or below the equilibrium wage depending on whether the supply curve of labor shifts rightward or leftward in response to the minimum wage.

3. A minimum wage set above the equilibrium wage rate
   a. increases the quantity of labor supplied.
   b. decreases the quantity of labor supplied.
   c. has no effect on the quantity of labor supplied.
   d. shifts the labor supply curve rightward.
   e. shifts the labor supply curve leftward.

4. Suppose the current equilibrium wage rate for lifeguards in Houston is $7.85 an hour. A minimum wage law that creates a price floor of $8.50 an hour leads to
   a. a surplus of lifeguards in Houston.
   b. a shortage of lifeguards in Houston.
   c. no changes in the lifeguard market.
   d. a change in the quantity of lifeguards supplied but no change in the quantity of lifeguards demanded.
   e. an increase in the number of lifeguards employed.

5. An increase in the minimum wage ____ employment and ____ unemployment.
   a. increases; increases
   b. increases; decreases
   c. decreases; increases
   d. decreases; decreases
   e. does not change; increases

■ **FIGURE 7.4**

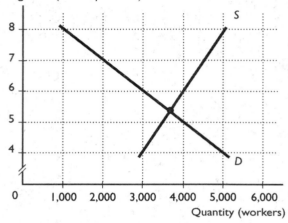

Wage rate (dollars per hour)

6. Figure 7.4 shows the market for fast food workers in San Francisco. A minimum wage of $8 per hour leads to unemployment of ____ workers.
   a. 1,000
   b. 2,000
   c. 3,000
   d. 4,000
   e. 5,000

7. In Figure 7.4, which of the following minimum wages creates the most unemployment?
   a. $4 an hour
   b. $5 an hour
   c. $6 an hour
   d. $7 an hour
   e. $8 an hour

8. If a minimum wage is introduced that is above the equilibrium wage rate,
   a. the quantity of labor demanded increases.
   b. job search activity increases.
   c. the supply of labor increases and the supply of labor curve shifts rightward.
   d. unemployment decreases because more workers accept jobs at the higher minimum wage rate.
   e. the quantity of labor supplied decreases because of the increase in unemployment.

9. The minimum wage is set above the equilibrium wage rate. Does the minimum wage create inefficiency?
   a. Yes.
   b. No.
   c. Only if the supply of labor is perfectly inelastic.
   d. Only if the supply of labor is perfectly elastic.
   e. Only if employment exceeds the efficient amount.

10. When the minimum wage is raised, the _____ union labor _____.
   a. demand for; increases
   b. demand for; decreases
   c. supply of; increases
   d. supply of; decreases
   e. demand for; does not change

### Short Response Questions

| Wage rate (dollars per hour) | Quantity demanded | Quantity supplied |
|---|---|---|
| | (workers per day) | |
| 4 | 3,500 | 2,750 |
| 5 | 3,000 | 3,000 |
| 6 | 2,500 | 3,250 |
| 7 | 2,000 | 3,500 |
| 8 | 1,500 | 3,750 |

1. The table above gives the demand and supply schedules for labor in a small town.
   a. In Figure 7.5, on the next page, label the axes. Draw the labor demand and labor supply curves. What is the equilibrium wage rate and employment.

**■ FIGURE 7.5**

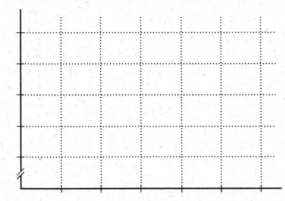

   b. Suppose the government imposes a $4 an hour minimum wage. What is the effect on the wage rate and levels of employment and unemployment?
   c. Suppose the government raises the minimum wage from $4 an hour to $7 an hour. What is the effect on the wage rate and levels of employment and unemployment? Indicate any unemployment.

**■ FIGURE 7.6**

Wage rate (dollars per hour)

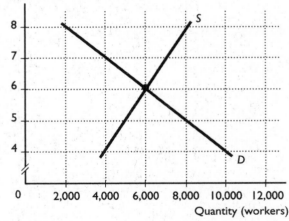

2. Figure 7.6 shows the labor demand and labor supply curves for Rochester, New York. Suppose the city is considering instituting a minimum wage. Indicate the minimum wages that lead to unemployment by dark-

ening the vertical axis for all the minimum wages that create unemployment.

### Long Response Questions

1. What is the effect of a minimum wage set below the equilibrium wage rate? Explain your answer.

2. How does a minimum wage affect the time needed to find a job?

3. Do all low-wage workers benefit from a minimum wage?

## CHECKPOINT 7.3

■ **Explain how a price support in the market for agricultural produce creates a surplus, inefficiency, and unfairness.**

### Quick Review

• *Price support* A price support is a price floor in an agricultural market maintained by a government guarantee to buy any surplus output at that price. The price support is the minimum price for which the product may be sold.

### Additional Practice Problems 7.3

1. The figure shows the market for sugar.

   a. What are the equilibrium price and quantity of sugar?

   b. Suppose the government puts in place a price support for sugar at $4 per pound. In the figure above, indicate this price support.

   c. With the price support, how much sugar is produced? How much sugar is pur-

chased by private consumers? How much is purchased by the government?

   d. With the price support, what is the subsidy received by sugar producers?

   e. Are consumers made better off or worse off with the price support?

   f. Without the price support, is the market efficient? With the price support, is the market efficient?

2. With a price support, the government pays a subsidy to farmers by buying part of the crop. Why is this purchase necessary?

### Solutions to Additional Practice Problems 7.3

1a. The equilibrium price and quantity of sugar are determined where the demand curve and the supply curve intersect. The figure shows that the equilibrium price is $2 a pound and the

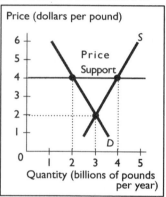

equilibrium quantity is 3 billion pounds a year.

1b. The price support is shown in the figure as the solid line at $4 per pound.

1c. With the price support, the supply curve shows that at $4 per pound, 4 billion pounds of sugar are produced. The demand curve shows that at this price consumers buy 2 billion pounds. The government buys the surplus quantity of sugar, 2 billion pounds.

1d. The government buys 2 billion pounds of sugar at $4 per pound, so the subsidy is 2 billion pounds × $4 per pound, which is $8 billion.

1e. Consumers are worse off with the price support. With the price support the price they must pay for sugar increases, from $2 per pound to $4 per pound. In response consumers decrease the quantity of sugar they consume from 3 billion pounds to 2 billion pounds.

1f. Without the price support, the market is efficient. With the price support, the market is not efficient.

2. The price support leads to a surplus of the crop. If the government did not buy the surplus, the farmers would not be able to cover their costs because there would be part of the crop left unsold.

## ■ AP Self Test 7.3

**True or false**

1. In order to have an effective price support, the government isolates the domestic market from the world market by restricting imports.

2. A price support sets the maximum price for which farmers may sell their crop.

3. In order to keep the price of a crop at supported price, the government must buy some of the crop.

4. Because they decrease production, price supports decrease producer surplus.

5. Price supports are efficient because they guarantee production of the good.

**Multiple choice**

1. Price supports are generally used in
   a. labor markets.
   b. industrial markets.
   c. housing markets.
   d. markets for services.
   e. agricultural markets.

2. A price support directly sets the
   a. amount of production.
   b. subsidy the government must receive from producers.
   c. equilibrium quantity.
   d. lowest price for which the good may be sold.
   e. highest price for which the good may be sold.

3. To have an effective price support program, the government must
   i. isolate the domestic market from the world market
   ii. pay the farmers a subsidy
   iii. introduce a price floor
   a. i only.
   b. ii only.
   c. iii only.
   d. ii and iii.
   e. i, ii, and iii.

4. To keep the price at the level set by the price support, the government must
   a. buy some of the good.
   b. sell some of the good.
   c. receive a subsidy from the producers.
   d. insure that imports are readily available.
   e. be careful to always set the price support below the equilibrium price.

## ■ FIGURE 7.7

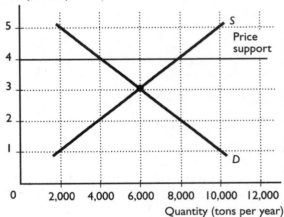

Price (dollars per ton)

5. Figure 7.7 shows a price support program in an agricultural market. The amount of the subsidy necessary to keep the price at the price support is
   a. $4.
   b. $32,000.
   c. $8,000.
   d. $16,000.
   e. $24,000.

6. With a price support program, who receives a subsidy?
   a. only consumers
   b. only producers
   c. the government
   d. importers
   e. both consumers and producers receive a subsidy

7. A price support ____ producers and ____ a deadweight loss.
   a. has no effect on; does not create
   b. benefits; creates
   c. harms; creates
   d. benefits; does not create
   e. harms; does not create

## Short Response Questions

| Price (dollars per bushel) | Quantity demanded | Quantity supplied |
|---|---|---|
| | (millions of bushels per year) | |
| 3 | 3,500 | 2,000 |
| 4 | 3,000 | 3,000 |
| 5 | 2,500 | 4,000 |
| 6 | 2,000 | 5,000 |
| 7 | 1,500 | 6,000 |

1. The table gives the demand and supply schedules for wheat.
   a. In Figure 7.8 label the axes. Draw the demand curve and supply curve and indicate the equilibrium price and quantity.

### ■ FIGURE 7.8

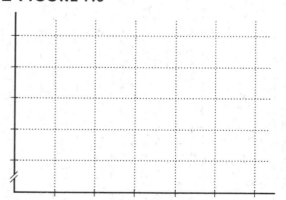

   b. Suppose the government imposes a price support of $5 per bushel. What is the ef-

fect on the price of wheat, the quantity of wheat produced and the marginal cost of a bushel of wheat? Is there a deadweight loss?
   c. With the $5 per bushel price support, how much wheat do consumers buy? What is the subsidy the government must pay to producers?

### ■ FIGURE 7.9

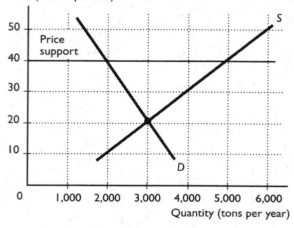

2. Figure 7.9 shows the demand and supply curves for peanuts. There is a price support of $40 per ton of peanuts.
   a. At the support price, what is the quantity of peanuts produced? What is the quantity consumers buy? How many tons of peanuts must the government buy? Indicate the amount the government must buy in Figure 7.9.
   b. How much is the subsidy paid by the government to producers?

## Long Response Questions

1. The government imposes a price floor in the agricultural market. Why must a price support be set above the equilibrium price in order to have an effect? Suppose the price support is set so that it has an effect.
   a. How is the price of the agricultural product and the quantity purchased by consumers affected?
   b. Within the domestic economy, who is ad-

versely affected by the imposition of the price support?

c. What situation is created by the price support?

d. What must the government do to keep the price equal to the price support?

2. "A price support program benefits producers and harms consumers. But there is no overall net effect on society." Comment on the above assertion. Is it correct or incorrect?

## YOUR AP SELF TEST ANSWERS

### ■ CHECKPOINT 7.1

**True or false**

1. False;  page 172
2. False;  pages 172-173
3. True;  page 174
4. False;  page 176
5. True;  page 176

**Multiple choice**

1. d;  page 172
2. b;  pages 172-173
3. e;  page 172
4. d;  page 173
5. d;  page 176
6. a;  page 173
7. c;  page 173
8. a;  page 174
9. b;  pages 173-174
10. a;  page 176

**Short Response  Questions**

### ■ FIGURE 7.10

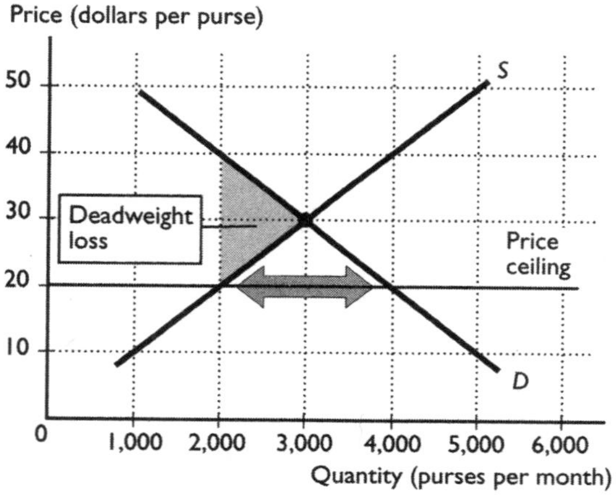

Price (dollars per purse)

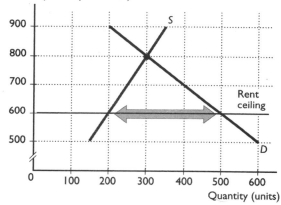

Quantity (purses per month)

1. a. The equilibrium price is $30 per purse and the equilibrium quantity is 3,000 purses.
   b. The quantity of purses demanded is 4,000, the quantity of purses supplied is 2,000, and the shortage equals 2,000 purses. In Figure 7.10, the shortage equals the length of the double-headed arrow;  page 173.

c. The deadweight loss is shown in Figure 7-10;  page 176.

2. a. The equilibrium price is $1.50 a carton and the quantity is 150 cartons a day.
   b. The price is $1.25 a carton and 130 cartons a day are purchased. There is a shortage of 45 cartons a day;  page 173.
   c. The price ceiling is above the equilibrium price, and is ineffective. The price is $1.50 a carton, 150 cartons a day are purchased, and there is neither a shortage nor a surplus;  page 172.

### ■ FIGURE 7.11

Rent (dollars per month)

3.    Figure 7.11 shows the demand curve and supply curve. The equilibrium rent is $800 a month and the quantity is 300 housing units a month.
   a. The quantity of housing demanded is 500 units a month; the quantity supplied is 200 units a month;  page 174.
   b. The shortage of 300 units a month is indicated by the arrow;  page 174.

**Long Response Questions**

1. A price ceiling is the highest price at which it is legal to trade a particular good, service, or factor of production. Price ceilings are designed to lower the price paid by consumers, so to be effective a price ceiling is set below the equilibrium price. Price ceilings help consumers who can buy at the lower price and

harm all producers and consumers who cannot buy at the lower price. An effective price ceiling leads to a shortage and, as a result, a black market often develops so that those who are willing to transact in the black market can buy more of the good or service; pages 172-177.

2. An effective rent ceiling helps renters who can find housing at the lower rent. It harms all sellers and those renters who, because of the shortage of housing, cannot find housing. The harm outweighs the benefit, so a rent ceiling creates a deadweight loss and is not efficient; page 176.

## ■ CHECKPOINT 7.2

**True or false**
 1. False; page 179
 2. True; page 180
 3. True; page 181
 4. False; page 182
 5. False; page 183

**Multiple choice**
 1. b; page 179
 2. a; page 180
 3. a; page 180
 4. a; page 180
 5. c; pages 180-181
 6. d; page 180
 7. e; pages 180-181
 8. b; page 181
 9. a; page 182
 10. a; page 183

**Short Response Questions**
 1. a. Figure 7.12 shows the demand and supply curves. The equilibrium wage rate is $5.00 an hour and the equilibrium employment is 3,000 workers a day.
   b. The $4 minimum wage is below the equilibrium wage and has no effect; page 180.
   c. The $7 minimum wage raises the wage rate to $7. Employment decreases to 2,000 workers. The number of workers looking

**■ FIGURE 7.12**

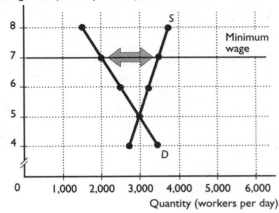

Wage rate (dollars per hour)

for work is 3,500. Unemployment equals 3,500 − 2,000, which is 1,500 people. The amount of unemployment is shown by the arrow in Figure 7.12; page 180.

**■ FIGURE 7.13**

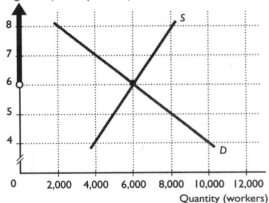

Wage rate (dollars per hour)

2. In order to have an effect in the market, the minimum wage must be set above the equilibrium wage. As Figure 7.13 shows, any minimum wage above $6 per hour creates unemployment; page 180.

**Long Response Questions**
 1. A minimum wage set below the equilibrium wage rate has no effect on the wage rate or amount of employment. A minimum wage has an effect *only* when it exceeds the equilibrium wage rate because only in this case

does it make the equilibrium wage rate illegal. If the minimum wage is set below the equilibrium wage rate, then the equilibrium wage rate remains legal and no changes occur in the market; page 180.

2. A minimum wage set above the equilibrium wage rate decreases the quantity of labor demand and increases the quantity of labor supplied, thereby creating unemployment. As a result, it increases the time spent unemployed workers spend searching for a job; page 181.

3. A minimum wage does not help all low-wage workers. In particular, it harms low-wage workers who lose their jobs or cannot find jobs because of the minimum wage; page 183.

## ■ CHECKPOINT 7.3

**True or false**
    1. True;  page 185
    2. False; page 185
    3. True;  page 186
    4. False; page 187
    5. False; page 187

**Multiple choice**
    1. e; page 185
    2. d; page 185
    3. e; page 185
    4. a; page 186
    5. d; page 186
    6. b; page 186
    7. b; page 187

**Short Response Questions**
1. a. Figure 7.14 shows the demand and supply curves. The equilibrium price is $4 a bushel and the equilibrium quantity is 3,000 million bushels a year.
   b. The $5 per bushel price support is illustrated in the figure. This price support raises the price of wheat to $5 per bushel. The quantity of wheat produced increases to 4,000 million bushels per year and the

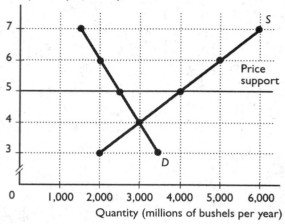

**■ FIGURE 7.14**

Price (dollars per bushel)

marginal cost of the last bushel of wheat produced increases to $5. There is a deadweight loss because the marginal cost exceeds the marginal benefit; page 186.

   c. There is a surplus of 1,500 million bushels (4,000 million bushels produced minus $2,500 million purchased by consumers) that the government must buy. The government pays a subsidy of $5 per bushel × 1,500 million bushels, which is $7.5 billion; page 186.

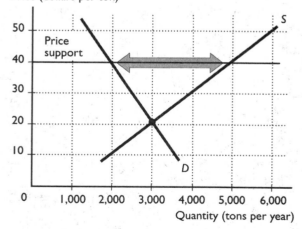

**■ FIGURE 7.15**

Price (dollars per ton)

2. a. Figure 7.15 shows that at the support price of $40 per ton, 5,000 tons are produced and consumers buy 2,000 tons. The gov-

ernment must buy the surplus, 3,000 tons. The amount the government must buy is equal to the length of the arrow in Figure 7.15; page 186.

b. To buy the surplus, the government pays a subsidy to producers of $40 per ton × 3,000 tons, which is $120,000; page 186.

## Long Response Questions

1. If a price support is set below the equilibrium price, it does not make the equilibrium price illegal and so is ineffective. If a price support is set above the equilibrium price, it makes the equilibrium price illegal and is effective; page 185.

a. The price is set above the equilibrium price, so the price of the agricultural product rises. With the rise in price, the quantity demanded by consumers decreases and so the quantity purchased by consumers decreases; page 186.

b. Consumers are adversely affected by the price support because the price of the product is raised; page 186.

c. The price support increases the quantity supplied and decreases the quantity demanded. As a result, a surplus is created; page 186.

d. In order to keep the price at the support level, the government must purchase the surplus that is produced because otherwise the surplus would push the price back to its equilibrium level; page 186.

2. The first assertion is correct: by raising the price of the product, a price support program increases producer surplus (which benefits producers) and decreases consumer surplus (which harms consumers). But the second assertion is incorrect. There is a net negative effect on society because a deadweight loss is created, which harms society. The loss to consumers exceeds the gain to producers; page 187.

# Taxes

## Chapter

# 8

In Chapter 8 we study how taxes affect markets, who pays a tax, the effect of an income tax and a Social Security tax, and review ideas about the fairness of taxes.

■ **Explain how taxes change prices and quantities, are shared by buyers and sellers, and create inefficiency.**

Taxes raise the price and decrease the quantity of the good that is taxed. Tax incidence is the division of the burden of a tax between the buyers and the sellers; generally sellers and buyers both pay part of a tax. Tax incidence between the buyers and the sellers depends on the elasticities of demand and supply and *not* upon who sends the government a check. The excess burden of a tax is the amount by which the burden of a tax exceeds the tax revenue received by the government—the deadweight loss from a tax. For a given elasticity of supply, the buyers pay a larger share of the tax the more inelastic is the demand for the good. The buyers pay the entire tax when demand is perfectly inelastic or supply is perfectly elastic. Similarly, for a given elasticity of demand, the sellers pay a larger share of the tax the more inelastic is the supply of the good. The sellers pay the entire tax when demand is perfectly elastic or supply is perfectly inelastic. Finally, the more inelastic the demand or supply, the smaller is the excess burden of the tax.

■ **Describe the effects of income taxes and social security taxes, determine who pays these taxes, and explain which taxes create the greatest inefficiency.**

The marginal tax rate is the percentage of an additional dollar that is paid in tax; the average tax rate is the percentage of income that is paid in tax. With a progressive tax, the average tax rate rises as income increases; with a proportional tax, the average tax rate is constant at all income levels; with a regressive tax, the average tax rate decreases as income increases. A tax on labor income decreases employment and creates a deadweight loss. Both the employer and the worker pay part of the tax. A tax on capital income decreases the quantity of capital and creates a deadweight loss. The supply of capital is highly elastic. If the supply of capital is perfectly elastic, firms, pay the entire tax. A tax on land or other unique resource does not decrease the quantity and creates no deadweight loss because supply is perfectly inelastic. The entire burden of the tax falls on the owner of the resource. The Social Security tax laws are written so that both workers and employers pay equal shares. But the incidence actually depends only on the elasticities of demand and supply and not on who the law says pays the tax.

■ **Review ideas about the fairness of the tax system.**

The benefits principle is the proposition that people should pay taxes equal to the benefits received from public services. This arrangement is fair because those who benefit the most pay the most. The ability-to-pay principle is the proposition that people should pay taxes according to how easily they can bear the burden. For fairness, the ability-to-pay principle compares people along vertical and horizontal dimensions. The fairness and efficiency of taxes can conflict, leading to the big tradeoff.

## EXPANDED CHAPTER CHECKLIST

When you have completed this chapter, you will be able to:

**1 Describe the effects of sales taxes and excise taxes, determine who pays these taxes, and explain why taxes create inefficiencies.**

- Define tax incidence.
- Explain how the incidence of a tax depends on the elasticities of demand and supply.
- Determine who bears the tax if demand or supply is perfectly inelastic or perfectly elastic.
- Define the excess burden of a tax and illustrate the deadweight loss from a tax.

**2 Describe the effects of income taxes and social security taxes, determine who pays these taxes, and explain which taxes create the greatest inefficiency.**

- Define taxable income, marginal tax rate, and average tax rate.
- Define progressive, regressive, and proportional taxes.
- Describe how the effect of an income tax depends upon the elasticity of supply.
- Illustrate the effects of a tax on labor income.
- Describe the difference in tax incidence when labor income, capital income, and land income are taxed. Discuss the size of the deadweight loss in each case.
- Show how a payroll tax and the income tax can deliver the same outcome.

**3 Review ideas about the fairness of the tax system.**

- Discuss the benefits principle and ability-to-pay principle of fairness of taxes.
- Describe horizontal equity and vertical equity.

## YOUR AP TEST HINTS

*AP Topics*

| Topic on your AP test | Corresponding textbook section |
|---|---|
| **Nature and function of product markets** | |
| • Tax incidence, elasticity, and deadweight loss | Checkpoint 8.1 |
| • Fairness and tax equity | Checkpoint 8.3 |

*Extra AP material*

- In a study of the U.S. tax structure, the general consensus is that the federal system of taxation is progressive, the state and local tax structures are generally regressive, making the overall United States tax system slightly progressive.
- The AP test will not ask about capital income or land income taxation. But understanding these topics will help you better grasp the effects of income and social security taxes on wage income.

## CHECKPOINT 8.1

■ **Explain how taxes change prices and quantities, are shared by buyers and sellers, and create inefficiency..**

**Quick Review**

- *Effect of a sales tax on the supply curve* A sales tax decreases the supply of the good and the supply curve shifts leftward. The vertical distance between the supply curve without the tax and the supply curve with the tax equals the amount of the tax.
- *Tax incidence and elasticities of demand and supply* For a given elasticity of supply, the more inelastic the demand, the larger the share of a tax paid by the buyer. And, for a given elasticity of demand, the more inelastic the supply, the larger the share of a tax paid by the seller.

## Additional Practice Problem 8.1

1. The figure illustrates the initial equilibrium in the markets for Coke and Pepsi. The price of a 2 liter bottle of a Coke and a Pepsi are the same, $1.50, and the quantity of each are the same, 12 million

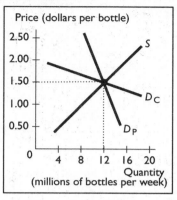

bottles a week. The supply of Coke is identical to the supply of Pepsi and both are given by supply curve S in the figure. However, as shown in the figure with the demand curve Dc for Coke and Dp for Pepsi, the demand for Coke is more elastic than the demand for Pepsi. The government now imposes a $1 per bottle sales tax on Coke and Pepsi.

   a. Does the price paid by consumers for a Coke rise by more than, less than, or the same amount as the price paid for a Pepsi?

   b. Do the consumers of Coke pay more of their tax than do consumers of Pepsi? Do the producers of Coke pay more of their tax than do the producers of Pepsi?

   c. Does the quantity of Coke decrease by more than, less than, or the same amount as the quantity of Pepsi?

   d. Does the government collect more than, less than, or the same amount of tax revenue from the tax on Coke as it does from the tax on Pepsi?

   e. Is the deadweight loss from the tax on Coke larger than, less than, or the same amount as the deadweight loss from the tax on Pepsi?

## Solution to Additional Practice Problem 8.1

1a. A tax is like an increase in the suppliers' costs, so a tax decreases the supply and shifts the supply curve leftward. The vertical distance between the supply curve with the tax and the supply curve without the tax is equal to

the amount of the tax, $1 per bottle in this problem. The figure shows this effect, with the supply curves for Coke and Pepsi both shifting to the curve labeled S+tax.

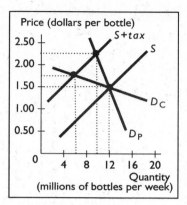

The demand for Coke is more elastic, so the price paid by consumers for a Coke rises only to $1.75, a 25¢ increase. The demand for Pepsi is less elastic, so the price paid for a Pepsi rises to $2.25, a 75¢ increase.

1b. The demand for Coke is more elastic, so consumers play less of the tax imposed on Coke. The price paid by consumers for a Coke rises 25¢, so consumers pay 25¢ of this tax and producers pay the remaining 75¢. The demand for Pepsi is more inelastic, so consumers pay more of a tax imposed on Pepsi. The price paid by consumers for a Pepsi rises 75¢, so consumers pay 75¢ of this tax and producers pay 25¢.

1c. The quantity of Coke decreases by more than the quantity of Pepsi because the demand for Coke is more elastic than the demand for Pepsi. In the figure, the equilibrium quantity of Coke decreases to 6 million bottles per week and the equilibrium quantity of Pepsi decreases only to 10 million bottles per week.

1d. The total amount of tax revenue equals the tax multiplied by the quantity sold. Because the decrease in the quantity of Coke is greater than the decrease in the quantity of Pepsi, less Coke than Pepsi is sold after the tax is imposed, and the government collects less tax revenue from the tax on Coke.

1e. Because the decrease in the quantity of Coke is greater than the decrease in the quantity of Pepsi, the deadweight loss of the tax is greater for Coke than for Pepsi.

## ■ AP Self Test 8.1

### True or false

1. When the government imposes a tax on the sale of a good, the burden of the tax falls entirely on the buyer.

2. A tax on fast-food meals does not create a deadweight loss because the elasticity of supply of fast-food meals equals 1.0.

3. For a given elasticity of supply, the more inelastic the demand for a good, the smaller the share of the tax paid by the buyer.

4. When the government taxes a good that has a perfectly elastic supply, the buyer pays the entire tax.

### Multiple choice

1. Tax incidence refers to
   a. how government taxes are spent by the government.
   b. the incidences of tax revolts by the tax payers.
   c. the amount of a tax minus its burden.
   d. the division of the burden of a tax between the buyers and the sellers.
   e. tax revenue minus excess burden.

2. Neither the supply of nor demand for a good is perfectly elastic or perfectly inelastic. So imposing a tax on the good results in a ____ in the price paid by buyers and ____ in the equilibrium quantity.
   a. rise; an increase
   b. rise; a decrease
   c. fall; an increase
   d. fall; a decrease
   e. rise; no change

3. Neither the supply of nor demand for a good is perfectly elastic or perfectly inelastic. So imposing a tax on the good results in a ____ in the price received by sellers and a ____ in the price paid by buyers.
   a. rise; rise
   b. rise; fall
   c. fall; rise
   d. fall; fall
   e. no change; rise

4. A sales tax ____ consumer surplus and ____ producer surplus.
   a. increases; increases
   b. increases; decreases
   c. decreases; increases
   d. decreases; decreases
   e. does not change; does not change

### ■ FIGURE 8.1

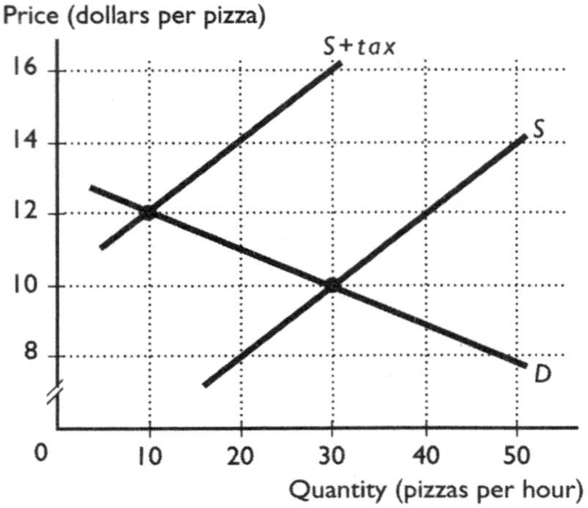

Price (dollars per pizza)

5. Figure 8.1 shows the market for delivered pizza. The government has imposed a tax of ____ per pizza.
   a. $6
   b. $8
   c. $10
   d. $12
   e. $16

6. In Figure 8.1, before the tax was imposed consumers paid ____ for a pizza and after the tax is imposed consumers pay ____ for a pizza.
   a. $10: $16
   b. $12; $16
   c. $10; $12
   d. $12; $16
   e. $10; $6

7. In Figure 8.1, consumers pay ____ of the tax and suppliers pay ____ of the tax.
   a. $6: $0
   b. $3; $3
   c. $0; $6
   d. $4; $2
   e. $2; $4

8. The deadweight loss from a tax is called the
   a. marginal benefit of the tax.
   b. marginal cost of the tax.
   c. excess burden of the tax.
   d. net gain from taxation.
   e. net loss from taxation.

9. A sales tax creates a deadweight loss because
   a. there is some paperwork opportunity cost of sellers paying the sales tax.
   b. demand and supply both decrease.
   c. less is produced and consumed.
   d. citizens value government goods less than private goods.
   e. the government spends the tax revenue it collects.

10. To determine who bears the greater share of a tax, we compare
    a. the number of buyers to the number of sellers.
    b. the elasticity of supply to the elasticity of demand.
    c. the size of the tax to the price of the good.
    d. government tax revenue to the revenue collected by the suppliers.
    e. the pre-tax quantity to the post-tax quantity.

### Short Response Question
1. Define the term "incidence of a tax."

### Long Response Questions
1. The supply curve and the demand curve for pizza slices are in Figure 8.2. The price is in dollars per slice and the quantity is thousands of pizza slices per day. Label the axes.
   a. What is the equilibrium price and quantity of pizza slices?
   b. The government imposes a sales tax of $4 a slice of pizza. In Figure 8.2, draw the new supply curve after the tax is imposed.

2. The supply curve and the demand curve for pizza slices are again shown in Figure 8.3. The price is in dollars per slice and the quantity is thousands of pizza slices per day. Once again, label the axes.

■ **FIGURE 8.2**

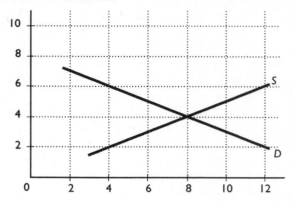

■ **FIGURE 8.3**

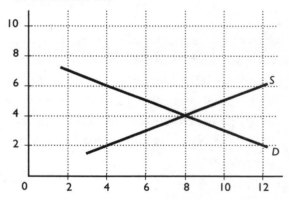

a. The government imposes a tax on buyers of $4 a slice of pizza. In Figure 8.2, draw the new demand curve after the tax is imposed.

3. In problem 1, the government imposed a tax on sellers. In problem 2 the government imposed the same tax on buyers.
   a. After the tax is imposed on sellers, what is the price paid by buyers for a slice of pizza? What is the price received by sellers for a slice of pizza? What is the incidence of the tax?
   b. After the tax is imposed on buyers, what is the price paid by buyers for a slice of pizza? What is the price received by sellers for a slice of pizza? What is the incidence of the tax?
   c. How do the prices paid and the tax inci-

dence in this question compare when the tax is imposed on sellers as opposed to on buyers? What general principle does your answer uncover?

d. In Figure 8.1, darken the area of the deadweight loss from the tax. What is the amount of the deadweight loss?

4. The government decides to tax high blood pressure medicine. The supply by drug companies is elastic; the demand by patients is inelastic. Do the drug companies bear the entire tax burden? Is there much deadweight loss from this tax?

5. What is the relationship between the deadweight loss of a tax and the excess burden of a tax? Why does a tax create a deadweight loss?

## CHECKPOINT 8.2

■ **Describe the effects of income taxes and social security taxes, determine who pays these taxes, and explain which taxes create the greatest inefficiency.**

### Quick Review

- *Progressive tax* A tax is progressive if the average tax rate increases as income increases.
- *Proportional tax* A tax is proportional if the average tax rate remains constant at all income levels.
- *Regressive tax* A tax is regressive if the average tax rate decreases as income increases.

### Additional Practice Problems 8.2

1. The supply of land is perfectly inelastic. The income from land is rent. If a tax is imposed on the income from land, who pays the tax: the demanders of land or the suppliers? Explain your answer.

2. In Hong Kong, the marginal tax rates on salaries ranges from 2 percent to 20 percent with a maximum average tax of 15 percent, which is reached on incomes of about $59,000. Compare the tax rates in Hong Kong with the U.S. federal tax rate. In which country is the personal income tax (tax on salaries) more progressive? Why?

### Solutions to Additional Practice Problems 8.2

1. Because the supply of land is perfectly inelastic, the suppliers pay all of the tax. The demanders pay none of the tax. Supply being perfectly inelastic means that suppliers have no other choice but to supply their land. Demanders determine the maximum price they are willing to pay for this quantity of land and that is the price. If a tax is imposed on land, demanders will not pay any of the tax because they are already paying the maximum price they are wiling to pay. So suppliers pay the entire tax.

2. The personal income tax in the United States is more progressive because the average tax rate increases to higher levels in the United States. Because Hong Kong's marginal tax rates are lower than U.S. marginal tax rates, Hong Kong's average tax rate remains lower than the U.S. average tax rate.

### ■ AP Self Test 8.2

#### True or false

1. When Hank earns an additional dollar, he pays 30 cents in additional tax. Hank's marginal tax rate is 30 percent.

2. If the average tax rate increases as income increases, the tax is a progressive tax.

3. Sam has $40,000 of taxable income and pays $4,000 income tax. Bert has $50,000 of taxable income and pays $4,500 income tax. Sam and Bert live in a country with a progressive income tax.

4. An income tax on labor creates a deadweight loss.

**Multiple choice**

1. The percentage of an additional dollar of income that is paid in tax is the
   a. sales tax.
   b. excise tax.
   c. marginal tax rate.
   d. personal income tax.
   e. regressive tax.

2. If the average tax rate is constant as income increases, then the tax is called
   a. regressive.
   b. progressive.
   c. proportional.
   d. an average tax.
   e. efficient.

3. If we tax labor income, the tax
   a. increases the quantity employed because the demand for labor increases.
   b. decreases the quantity employed because the supply of labor decreases.
   c. increases the quantity employed because the supply of labor increases.
   d. decreases the quantity employed because the demand for labor increases.
   e. does not change the quantity employed because people must have jobs in order to earn any income.

4. The incidence of an income tax on labor income is generally that the tax is
   a. paid only by workers.
   b. paid only by employers.
   c. shared equally between workers and employers.
   d. shared but not necessarily equally between workers and employers.
   e. funded by the deadweight loss.

5. If the supply of capital is perfectly elastic, the incidence of a tax on capital income is
   a. paid entirely by the suppliers of capital.
   b. paid entirely by firms.
   c. shared between firms and the suppliers of capital.
   d. shared but not equally between firms that demand capital and the suppliers of capital.
   e. unknown.

■ **FIGURE 8.4**

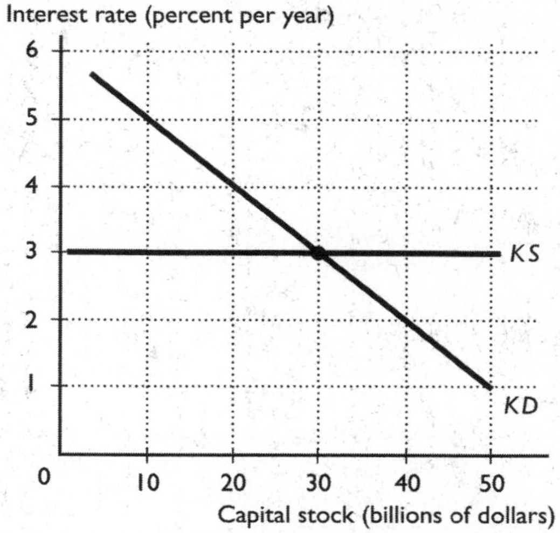

6. Figure 8.4 shows the capital market. If the government imposes a 2 percent tax on capital income, the interest rate ____.
   a. stays at 3 percent.
   b. rises to 4 percent.
   c. rises to 5 percent.
   d. falls to 2 percent.
   e. falls to 1 percent.

7. Figure 8.4 shows the capital market. If the government imposes a 2 percent tax on capital income, the equilibrium quantity of capital becomes
   a. $10 billion.
   b. $20 billion.
   c. $30 billion.
   d. $40 billion.
   e. $50 billion.

8. A tax on income from land in Montana is borne entirely by landowners because the
   a. demand for land is perfectly inelastic.
   b. supply of land is perfectly inelastic.
   c. supply of land is perfectly elastic.
   d. demand for land is perfectly elastic.
   e. deadweight loss from the tax would otherwise be infinite.

## Long Response Questions

### ■ FIGURE 8.5

Wage rate (dollars per hour)

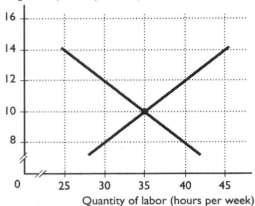

1.  Figure 8.5 shows the labor market.
    a. Label the curves. What is the equilibrium wage rate and quantity of labor?
    b. Suppose the government imposes an income tax of $4 an hour on labor income. Illustrate the effect of this tax in the figure.
    c. After the tax is imposed, what is the wage rate paid by firms and what is the amount received by households?
    d. If a deadweight loss is created, shade its area. If a deadweight loss is not created, explain why not.

### ■ FIGURE 8.6

Rent (dollars per acre per year)

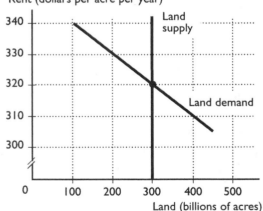

2.  Figure 8.6 shows the market for land.
    a. What is the equilibrium rent and quantity of land?

b. Suppose the government imposes a tax on land income of $10 an acre. What is the new equilibrium rent paid by renters and what is the amount of rent kept by landowners? What is the equilibrium quantity of land?
c. If a deadweight loss is created, shade its area. If a deadweight loss is not created, explain why not.

### ■ FIGURE 8.7

Wage rate (dollars per hour)

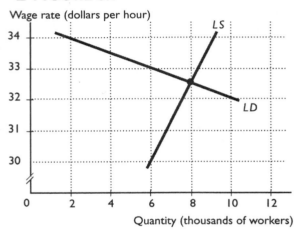

Quantity (thousands of workers)

3.  Figure 8.7 shows a labor supply curve and labor demand curve. The initial equilibrium wage rate is $32.50 an hour. The government imposes a $3 an hour Social Security tax on firms.
    a. In the figure, show the effect of this tax. What is the wage that workers receive before the tax and after the tax?
    b. Even though the Social Security tax has been imposed on the firms, how is the burden of the tax split?

| Taxable Income | Tax |
|---|---|
| $10,000 | $0 |
| 20,000 | 1,000 |
| 30,000 | 3,000 |
| 40,000 | 6,000 |
| 50,000 | 10,000 |

4.  The table above shows taxable income and the tax paid.
    a. Is the tax regressive, proportional, or pro-

gressive? Explain your answer.

b. What is the average tax rate at $40,000 of taxable income? At $50,000?

c. What is the marginal tax rate when income changes from $40,000 to $50,000 of taxable income?

5. Why is the supply of capital highly elastic? Who pays the tax on capital income if the supply of capital is perfectly elastic?

6. The government mandates that half of a Social Security tax has to be paid by the employer and the other half has to be paid by the worker. Does this law mean that the burden of the tax is shared equally by the employer and worker?

## CHECKPOINT 8.3

### ■ Review ideas about the fairness of the tax system.

**Quick Review**

- *Benefits principle* People should pay taxes equal to the benefits they receive from public services.
- *Ability-to-pay principle* People should pay taxes according to how easily they can bear the burden.

**Additional Practice Problem 8.3**

1. "The only fair taxes are user fees, such as toll roads. The gas tax is fair because the funds raised go for road maintenance. All government-provided services need to be funded through user fees. To pay for parks, we need to charge entrance fees. The cost of garbage collection must be based on how much garbage the household creates. Any tax except a user fee is unfair and must be abolished!" Comment on the fairness principle being used. Is it possible for *all* government programs to be funded through user fees?

**Solution to Additional Practice Problem 8.3**

1. The speaker is advocating the benefits principle of taxation, which is the proposition that people should pay taxes equal to the

benefits they receive from public services. Although user fees have merit, it is not possible to fund all government programs through user fees. First, for public goods such as national defense, everyone consumes the same amount. It is impossible to determine how much any particular person benefits and therefore not possible to determine the proper fee. Second, some programs are designed to redistribute income to poorer people. It would be ludicrous to tax welfare recipients an amount equal to the benefits they received, which is the case under a user-fee arrangement.

### ■ AP Self Test 8.3

**True or false**

1. The benefits principle asserts that those people who are harmed by the deadweight loss of a tax should not pay the tax.

2. If the revenue from gasoline taxes is used to pay for road repairs, the tax reflects the ability-to-pay principle.

3. The U.S. income tax, which uses progressive income taxes, can be considered fair based on the principle of vertical equity.

4. Both vertical and horizontal equity can be achieved and the marriage tax problem eliminated if married couples are taxed as two single persons.

5. The taxes with the largest deadweight loss are taxes on capital income, and the people who pay these taxes generally have the greatest ability to pay taxes.

**Multiple choice**

1. The proposition that people should pay taxes according to how easily they can bear the burden is the ____ principle
   a. regressive tax
   b. benefits
   c. ability-to-pay
   d. fairness principle.
   e. incidence of fairness principle.

2. Which of the following taxes best illustrates the benefits principle of taxation?
   a. sales tax on clothing used to fund food stamps
   b. state income tax used to fund state universities
   c. medicare tax used to fund medical care for the elderly
   d. gasoline tax used to fund road repairs
   e. federal income tax used to fund NASA spending

3. The government once imposed a luxury tax on very expensive jewelry. This tax followed the ____ principle.
   a. benefits
   b. ability-to-pay
   c. vertical equity
   d. horizontal equity
   e. fair-tax incidence

4. The proposition that taxpayers with the same ability to pay should pay the same taxes is called
   a. the benefits principle.
   b. the ability-to-pay imperative.
   c. vertical equity.
   d. horizontal equity.
   e. fair-tax incidence principle.

5. Joan's income is $60,000 and she pays $6,000 in taxes. Juan's income is $40,000 and he pays $7,000 in taxes. This situation violates
   a. the benefits principle.
   b. the big tradeoff.
   c. vertical equity.
   d. horizontal equity.
   e. the fair-tax incidence principle.

6. Vertical equity implies that
   i.  tax rates should be equal for all tax payers.
   ii. people with higher incomes should pay more in taxes.
   iii. people with higher incomes should pay a lower average tax rate.
   a. i only.
   b. ii only.
   c. iii only.
   d. i and ii.
   e. ii and iii.

7. Because the U.S. income tax is a progressive tax, taxing married couples as two single persons can violate
   a. the benefits principle.
   b. the ability-to-pay imperative.
   c. vertical equity.
   d. horizontal equity.
   e. the government's need for more revenue.

**Short Response Questions**

1. Define the benefits principle of taxation.

2. Define the ability-to-pay principle of taxation.

3. Is a tax on gasoline used to build roads an example of the benefits principle of taxation or the ability-to-pay principle of taxation? Is the federal income tax an example of the benefits principle of taxation or the ability-to-pay principle of taxation?

**Long Response Questions**

1. There are a variety of welfare programs, such as food stamps, designed to boost the income of poor families. Does it make sense to raise the tax revenue necessary to fund these programs by using the benefits principle of taxation?

2. What is the marriage tax problem? If a married couple is taxed as two single individuals, what problem is created?

# YOUR AP SELF TEST ANSWERS

## ■ CHECKPOINT 8.1

### True or false
1. False; page 194
2. False; page 196
3. False; page 197
4. True; page 198

### Multiple choice
1. d; page 194
2. b; page 195
3. c; page 195
4. d; page 196
5. a; page 195
6. c; page 195
7. e; page 195
8. c; page 196
9. c; page 196
10. b; page 197

### Short Response Question
1. Tax incidence is the division of a tax between the buyers and the sellers; page 194.

### Long Response Questions
#### ■ FIGURE 8.8

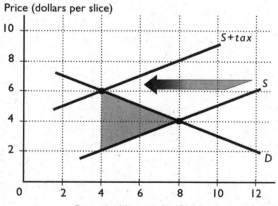

Price (dollars per slice)

Quantity (thousands of pizza slices per day)

1. The axes are labeled in Figure 8.8.
   a. The price is $4 a slice and the quantity is 8,000 slices a day; pages 195.
   b. Figure 8.8 shows the supply curve after the tax is imposed; page 195.

#### ■ FIGURE 8.9

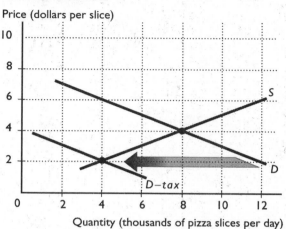

Price (dollars per slice)

Quantity (thousands of pizza slices per day)

2. The axes are labeled in Figure 8.9.
   a. Figure 8.9 shows the demand curve after the tax is imposed; page 195.
3. a. Buyers pay $6 a slice; sellers receive $2 a slice. The tax is split equally; page 195.
   b. Buyers still pay $6 a slice; sellers still receive $2 a slice. The tax is still split equally; page 195.
   c. The price paid and the tax incidence is the same in problem 1, when the tax is imposed on sellers, and in problem 2, when the tax is imposed on buyers. The general principle is that the tax incidence depends on the elasticity of demand and the elasticity of supply, not on who sends the tax to the government; pages 195, 197.
   d. The deadweight loss is the gray triangle in Figure 8.8. The amount of the deadweight loss equals 1/2 × ($6 per slice – $2 per slice) × (8,000 slices – 4,000 slices), or $8,000; page 194.
4. The burden of the tax will fall mainly upon buyers, not the drug companies, because demand is inelastic and supply is elastic. Because the demand is inelastic, the decrease in the quantity will not be large and so the deadweight loss from the tax is small; page 197.

5. The excess burden of a tax is the same as the deadweight loss. The deadweight loss arises because the tax leads to less of the good or service being produced and consumed. In particular, if the quantity before the tax was the allocatively efficient amount, then after the tax is imposed, there is underproduction and a deadweight loss; page 196.

## ■ CHECKPOINT 8.2

**True or false**
1. True; page 201
2. True; page 201
3. False; page 201
4. True; page 202

**Multiple choice**
1. c; page 201
2. c; page 201
3. b; page 202
4. d; page 202
5. b; page 203
6. c; page 203
7. a; page 203
8. b; page 205

**Long Response Questions**

### ■ FIGURE 8.10

Wage rate (dollars per hour)

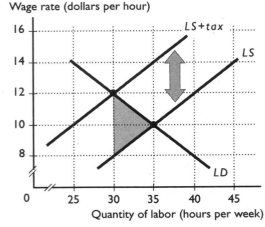

Quantity of labor (hours per week)

1. a. The curves are labeled *LD* and *LS* in Figure 8.10. The equilibrium wage rate is $10

an hour and the equilibrium quantity of labor is 35 hours a week; page 202.

b. The income tax decreases the supply of labor. The labor supply curve shifts leftward from *LS* to *LS + tax*. The vertical distance between the two supply curves, indicated by the arrow, is equal to the $4 tax; page 202.

c. Firms pay a wage rate of $12 an hour; workers receive a wage rate of $8 an hour; page 202.

d. The deadweight loss is the gray triangle in Figure 8.10; page 202.

2. a. The equilibrium rent is $320 an acre per year and the equilibrium quantity of land is 300 billion acres; page 205.

b. After the tax, renters pay $320 an acre and landowners keep $310 an acre. The equilibrium quantity of land is 300 billion acres, the same as before the tax was imposed; page 205.

c. There is no deadweight loss created because the equilibrium quantity does not change. The amount produced remains the efficient quantity; page 205.

### ■ FIGURE 8.11

Wage rate (dollars per hour)

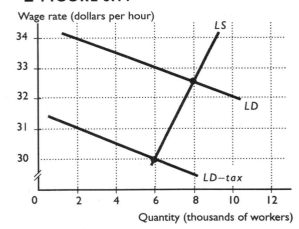

Quantity (thousands of workers)

3. a. Figure 8.11 shows the effect of the tax. Because the tax is imposed on firms, the tax decreases the demand for labor and shifts the labor demand curve leftward. The vertical distance between the initial supply curve, *LD*, and the new supply curve,

$LD + tax$, is the amount of the tax, $3 an hour. The workers received $32.50 per hour before the tax and $30.00 after the tax; page 207.

b. Even though the tax is imposed on firms, the workers pay $2.50 of the $3.00 Social Security tax and the firms pay $0.50; page 207.

4. a. This tax is a progressive tax because the average tax rate rises as income increases; page 201.

b. The average tax rate at $40,000 is equal to $6,000 ÷ $40,000, or 15 percent. The average tax rate at $50,000 is equal to $10,000 ÷ $50,000, or 20 percent; page 201.

c. The marginal tax rate between $40,000 and $50,000 of taxable income is equal to the change in taxes divided by the change in come, or ($10,000 − $6,000) ÷ ($50,000 − $40,000) which is 40 percent; page 201.

5. Because capital is internationally mobile, its supply is highly (perhaps perfectly) elastic. The demand for capital comes from firms. If the supply of capital is perfectly elastic, firms pay the entire tax on capital income. More generally, the more elastic the supply of capital, the greater the share of the tax paid by the demanders of capital, that is, by firms; page 203.

6. The burden of the Social Security tax is determined by the elasticity of supply and the elasticity of demand of labor, not by the law splitting the tax. If the demand for labor is more elastic than supply, the burden falls more on the workers and less on the employers. Conversely, if the demand for labor is less elastic than the supply of labor, the burden falls more on the employer and less on the workers. Probably the demand for labor is more elastic than the supply, so it is likely that most of the tax burden falls on workers. The government can legislate how the tax is collected, but cannot legislate the division of the tax's burden; pages 206-207.

## ■ CHECKPOINT 8.3

### True or false
1. False; page 210
2. False; page 210
3. True; page 211
4. False; pages 211-212
5. True; page 212

### Multiple choice
1. c; page 210
2. d; page 210
3. b; page 210
4. d; page 210
5. c; page 211
6. b; page 211
7. d; page 211

### Short Response Questions
1. The benefits principle of taxation is that people should pay taxes equal to the benefits they receive from public goods and services; page 210.

2. The ability-to-pay principle of taxation is that people according to how easily they can bear the tax burden; page 210.

3. The gasoline tax is an example of the benefits principle because the people who pay the tax benefit from the roads funded by the tax. The federal income tax is an example of the ability-to-pay principle because higher income people pay more taxes; page 210.

### Long Response Questions
1. If the taxes necessary to fund the various welfare programs, such as food stamps, were assessed using the benefits principle of taxation, poor families would be required to pay the tax because they are the ones who benefit from the programs. But this outcome would defeat the purpose of the programs, which are designed to increase these families' incomes. The benefits principle of taxation does not work for government programs designed to increase the incomes of the poor; page 210.

2. The marriage tax problem is that a working couple pays more taxes if they are married than if they are single. Taxing the couple as single taxpayers violates horizontal equity because then two married couples with the same total income could pay different taxes depending on how much each partner earned; pages 211-212.

# Externalities

# *Chapter* 9

## CHAPTER IN PERSPECTIVE

An externality in an unregulated market leads to inefficiency and creates a deadweight loss. Chapter 9 explains the role of the government in markets where an externality is present and how government intervention can result in an efficient level of production.

- ■ **Explain why negative externalities lead to inefficient overproduction and how property rights, pollution charges, and taxes can achieve a more efficient outcome.**

Marginal private cost is the cost of producing an additional unit of a good or service that is borne by the producer of that good or service. Marginal external cost is the cost of producing an additional unit of a good or service that falls on people other than the producer. And marginal social cost, which is the marginal cost incurred by the entire society, is the sum of marginal private cost and marginal external cost. Producers take account only of marginal private cost and overproduce when there is a marginal external cost, such as pollution. Sometimes it is possible to reduce the inefficiency arising from an externality by establishing a property right where one does not currently exist. The Coase theorem is the proposition that if property rights exist, only a small number of parties are involved, and transactions costs are low, then private transactions are efficient and the outcome is not affected by who is assigned the property right. When property rights cannot be assigned, the three main methods that governments can use to cope with externalities are emission charges (which set a price per unit of pollution that a firm must pay), marketable permits (each firm is issued permits that allow a certain amount of pollution and firms can buy and sell the permits), and taxes (the government imposes a tax equal to the marginal external cost).

- ■ **Explain why positive externalities lead to inefficient underproduction and how public provision, subsidies, vouchers, and patents can achieve a more efficient outcome.**

Marginal private benefit is the benefit from an additional unit of a good or service that the consumer of that good or service receives. Marginal external benefit is the benefit from an additional unit of a good or service that people other than the consumer of the good or service enjoy. And marginal social benefit, which is the marginal benefit enjoyed by society, is the sum of marginal private benefit and marginal external benefit. External benefits from education arise because better-educated people are better citizens, commit fewer crimes, and support social activities. External benefits from research arise because once someone has worked out a basic idea, others can copy it. When people make decisions about how much schooling to obtain, they neglect its external benefit. The result is that if education were provided only by private schools that charged full-cost tuition, we would produce too few graduates. Four devices that governments can use to overcome the inefficiency created by external benefits are public provision, private subsidies, vouchers, and patents and copyrights.

## EXPANDED CHAPTER CHECKLIST

**When you have completed this chapter, you will be able to:**

**1 Explain why negative externalities lead to inefficient overproduction and how property rights, pollution charges, and taxes can achieve a more efficient outcome.**

- Give an example of a negative externality.
- Define marginal private cost, marginal external cost, and marginal social cost.
- Draw a figure that shows the relationship between marginal private cost, marginal external cost, and marginal social cost.
- Draw a figure that shows the inefficiency with an external cost.
- Explain the Coase theorem.
- Describe how emission charges, marketable permits, and taxes can lead to efficiency in a market with an external cost.

**2 Explain why positive externalities lead to inefficient underproduction and how public provision, subsidies, vouchers, and patents can achieve a more efficient outcome.**

- Give and example of a positive externality.
- Define marginal private benefit, marginal external benefit, and marginal social benefit.
- Draw a figure that shows the relationship between marginal private benefit, marginal external benefit, and marginal social benefit.
- Draw a figure that shows the inefficiency with an external benefit.
- Describe how public provision, private subsidies, vouchers, and patents and copyrights can lead to efficiency in a market with an external benefit.

## YOUR AP TEST HINTS

*AP Topics*

| Topic on your AP test | Corresponding textbook section |
|---|---|
| **Market failure and the role of government** | |
| Externalities | Chapter 9 |
| • Positive externality | Checkpoint 9.1 |
| • Negative externality | Checkpoint 9.2 |
| • Remedies | Checkpoints 9.1, 9.2 |

*AP Vocabulary*

- On the AP test, the terms "spillover" and "externality" are interchangeable

*Extra AP material*

- In discussing a negative externality, keep in mind that that the marginal private cost is less than the marginal social cost and hence there is an over allocation of resources dedicated to the production of the good or service. Similarly, in discussing a positive externality, keep in mind that the marginal private benefit is less than the marginal social benefit and hence there is an under allocation of resources dedicated to the production of the good or service.
- Other solutions to correct a negative externality are liability rules, so that a polluter might be required to pay a fine for the pollution, and lawsuits, so that victims of an externality can go to court in an effort to end or be compensated for the externality.

## CHECKPOINT 9.1

■ **Explain why negative externalities lead to inefficient overproduction and how property rights, pollution charges, and taxes can achieve a more efficient outcome.**

**Quick Review**

- *Marginal external cost* The cost of producing an additional unit of a good or service that falls on people other than the producer.

- *Efficiency* Efficiency is achieved when the marginal social benefit equals the marginal social cost.

- *Coase theorem* If property rights exist, only a small number of parties are involved, and transactions costs are low, then private transactions are efficient and the outcome is not affected by who is assigned the property right.

## Additional Practice Problems 9.1

1. The figure illustrates the unregulated market for paper. When the factories produce paper, they also create air pollution. The cost of the pollution is $1,500 per ton. The pollution is a marginal external cost.

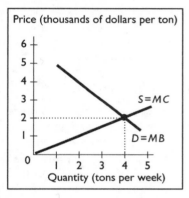

a. What is the quantity of paper produced in an unregulated market? What is the price of a ton of paper?

b. Draw the marginal social cost curve in the figure. What is the efficient quantity of paper to produce?

c. If the government imposed a tax on the firms, what must the tax equal to have the efficient quantity of paper produced? With this tax imposed, what is the equilibrium price of a ton of paper?

2. Two factories each emit 10 tons of the pollutant sulfur dioxide a week. The cost to eliminate a ton of sulfur dioxide to Factory A is $4 and the cost to Factory B is $2. The government wants to eliminate 10 tons of sulfur dioxide a week.

a. If the government requires that Firm A decrease emissions by 10 tons a week, what is the cost of eliminating the pollution?

b. If the government requires that Firm B decrease emissions by 10 tons a week, what is the cost of the eliminating the pollution?

c. If the government gives each firm 5 marketable permits, each good for 1 ton of pollution, what will occur?

## Solutions to Additional Practice Problems 9.1

1a. The equilibrium is determined by the intersection of the demand and supply curves. So the equilibrium quantity is 4 tons of paper per week and the equilibrium price is $2,000 per ton.

1b. The figure shows the marginal social cost curve, labeled MSC. At 1 ton of paper this curve lies $1,500 above the supply curve; at 2 tons of paper

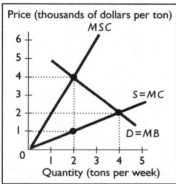

it lies $3,000 above the supply curve; and so on. The efficient quantity is where the marginal social cost equals the marginal benefit, which the figure shows is 2 tons of paper.

1c. To lead to efficiency, the tax must equal the marginal external cost. So the tax should be $1,500 per ton. At the efficient quantity of 2 tons, the tax is $3,000. With this tax, the equilibrium price is $4,000 per ton of paper.

2a. The cost for Firm A to decrease emissions is $4 a ton multiplied by 10 tons, or $40 a week.

2b. The cost for Firm B to decrease emissions is $2 a ton multiplied by 10 tons, which is $20 a week.

2c. Firm A is willing to buy permits from Firm B for any price less than $4 per permit; Firm B is willing to sell permits to Firm A for any price greater than $2 per permit. The two companies will settle on a price and Firm A will buy 5 permits from Firm B. Only Firm B will decrease its pollution and incur a cost of $20 a week.

## ■ AP Self Test 9.1

**True or false**

1. All externalities are negative.

2. Smoking on a plane creates a negative externality.

3. Marginal social cost equals marginal private cost minus marginal external cost.

4. Copper mining creates land pollution. If the copper mining industry is unregulated, then the quantity of copper mined is less than the efficient quantity.

5. The Coase theorem concludes that if property rights to a polluted river are assigned to the polluter, the quantity of pollution will increase.

6. Emission charges allow the government to set the price for a unit of pollution.

7. By issuing marketable permits, the government sets the price for each unit of pollution produced.

8. If the government imposes a pollution tax on lead mining equal to its marginal external cost, the quantity of lead mined will be the efficient quantity.

**Multiple choice**

1. Which of the following best describes an externality?
   a. something that is external to the economy
   b. a sales tax on a good in addition to the market price
   c. an effect of a transaction felt by someone other than the consumer or producer
   d. anything produced in other countries
   e. a change from what is normal

2. Pollution is an example of a ____ externality.
   a. negative production
   b. positive production
   c. negative consumption
   d. positive consumption
   e. Coasian

3. The cost of producing one more unit of a good or service that is borne by the producer of that good or service
   a. always equals the benefit the consumer derives from that good or service.
   b. equals the cost borne by people other than the producer.
   c. is the marginal private cost.
   d. is the external cost.
   e. is the marginal social cost.

4. The cost of producing an additional unit of a good or service that falls on people other than the producer is
   a. the marginal cost.
   b. represented by the demand curve.
   c. represented by the supply curve.
   d. the marginal external cost.
   e. the marginal social cost.

5. Which of the following is an example of something that creates an external cost?
   i. second-hand smoke
   ii. sulfur emitting from a smoke stack
   iii. garbage on the roadside
   a. i only.
   b. ii only.
   c. iii only.
   d. ii and iii.
   e. i, ii, and iii.

6. The marginal cost of production that is borne by the entire society is the marginal
   a. private cost.
   b. social cost.
   c. external cost.
   d. public cost.
   e. user cost.

7. If the marginal private cost of producing one kilowatt of power in California is five cents and the marginal social cost of each kilowatt is nine cents, then the marginal external cost equals ____ a kilowatt.
   a. five cents
   b. nine cents
   c. four cents
   d. zero cents
   e. fourteen cents

8. When the production of a good has a marginal external cost, which of the following will occur in an unregulated market?
   i. Overproduction relative to the allocatively efficient level will occur
   ii. The market price is less than the marginal social cost at the equilibrium quantity
   iii. A deadweight loss will occur
   a. i only.
   b. ii only.
   c. iii only.
   d. i and ii.
   e. i, ii, and iii.

■ **FIGURE 9.1**

Price (dollars per ton)

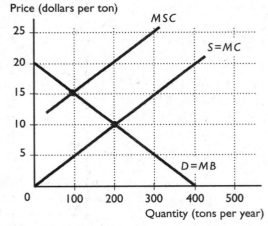

9. Figure 9.1 shows the market for a good with an external cost. The external cost equals _____ per ton.
   a. $5
   b. $10
   c. $15
   d. $20
   e. $25

10. Figure 9.1 shows the market for a good with an external cost. If the market is unregulated, the equilibrium quantity is _____ tons per year.
    a. 0
    b. 100
    c. 200
    d. 300
    e. 400

11. Figure 9.1 shows the market for a good with an external cost. The efficient quantity is _____ tons per year.
    a. 0
    b. 100
    c. 200
    d. 300
    e. 400

12. The Coase theorem is the proposition that if property rights exist and are enforced, private transactions are
    a. inefficient.
    b. efficient.
    c. inequitable.
    d. illegal.
    e. unnecessary.

13. A marketable permit
    a. allows firms to pollute all they want without any cost.
    b. allows firms to buy and sell the right to pollute at government controlled prices.
    c. eliminates pollution by setting the price of pollution permits above the marginal cost of polluting.
    d. allows firms to buy and sell the right to pollute.
    e. is the Coase solution to pollution.

14. If we compare air pollution today to air pollution in 1975, we see that
    a. pollution of all forms has increased.
    b. pollution of all forms has been substantially reduced.
    c. pollution of most types has been decreased.
    d. pollution from lead has increased.
    e. pollution of most types has not changed.

**Short Response Questions**
1. If the marginal social cost curve lies above the marginal private cost curve, is there an external cost or benefit from production of the good or service?

| Quantity (tons of pesticide per day) | Marginal private cost (dollars per ton) | Marginal external cost (dollars per ton) | Marginal social cost (dollars per ton) |
|---|---|---|---|
| 1 | 100 | ___ | 130 |
| 2 | 120 | 40 | ___ |
| 3 | ___ | 60 | 210 |
| 4 | 190 | ___ | 280 |
| 5 | 240 | 120 | ___ |

2. The table above shows the costs of producing pesticide. Complete the table.

| Quantity (megawatts per day) | Marginal private cost (dollars per megawatt) | Marginal social cost (dollars per megawatt) | Marginal benefit (dollars per megawatt) |
|---|---|---|---|
| 1 | 5 | 10 | 50 |
| 2 | 10 | 20 | 40 |
| 3 | 15 | 30 | 30 |
| 4 | 20 | 40 | 20 |

3. Generating electricity can create pollution. The table above shows the marginal private cost, marginal social cost, and marginal benefit schedules for generating electricity.

a. In Figure 9.2, label the axes and then plot the marginal private cost curve, the marginal social cost curve, and the marginal benefit curve.

■ **FIGURE 9.2**

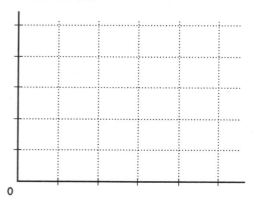

b. How much electricity will an unregulated market produce? What is the marginal external cost at this amount of production?

c. What is the efficient amount of electricity? Illustrate the deadweight loss resulting

from the market equilibrium.

d. At the allocatively efficient quantity of electricity, what is the marginal external cost?

e. If the government imposes a tax on producing electricity to produce the allocatively efficient quantity, what should be the amount of tax? How much electricity is generated and what is its price?

f. If the government sets an emission charge for the pollution created when electricity is produced, what must be the charge per megawatt to lead to the production of the allocatively efficient quantity of electricity?

**Long Response Questions**

1. Why is the allocatively efficient quantity of pollution not equal to zero?

2. According to the Coase theorem, when are private transactions efficient?

3. What is a marketable permit? What advantage do marketable permits have over the government assigning each firm a limit on how much it can pollute?

4. The production of fertilizer creates water pollution. How do emission charges and taxes result in an efficient quantity of production? What role might the court system play in this situation?

## CHECKPOINT 9.2

■ **Explain why positive externalities lead to inefficient underproduction and how public provision, subsidies, vouchers, and patents can achieve a more efficient outcome.**

**Quick Review**

• *Marginal external benefit* The benefit from an additional unit of a good or service that people other than the consumer of the good or service enjoy.

## Additional Practice Problems 9.2

1. The figure shows the marginal private benefit, marginal social benefit, and marginal cost of a college education.

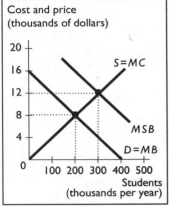

a. How much does the marginal external benefit equal?

b. If colleges are private and government has no involvement in college education, how many people will undertake a college education and what will be the tuition?

c. What is the efficient number of students?

d. If the government decides to provide public colleges, what tuition will these colleges charge to achieve the efficient number of students? What is the marginal cost of educating this many students? Why is it justified to charge a tuition that is less than the marginal cost?

2. A vaccine for chicken pox was recently developed. The company that developed the vaccine, Merck Incorporated, was required to submit a document comparing the costs and benefits of vaccinating children. The government would approve the drug only if the benefit of vaccination exceeded the cost. The producer reports that the marginal cost of a dose of vaccine is $80. The marginal benefit to the child being vaccinated is estimated to be $30 and an additional marginal benefit to the child's parents is estimated at $60.

a. How much is the marginal private benefit and the marginal external benefit?

b. Based on these data, should the government have approved the vaccine?

## Solutions to Additional Practice Problems 9.2

1a. The marginal external benefit equals the vertical distance between the marginal social benefit curve, *MSB*, and the marginal private benefit curve, *MB*. In the figure the difference is $8,000, so the marginal external benefit equals $8,000.

1b. If the government has no involvement, the equilibrium tuition and number of students is determined by the equilibrium between supply and demand. The supply curve is the marginal private cost curve, $S = MC$, and the demand curve is the marginal private benefit curve, *MB*. The figure shows that the equilibrium tuition equals $8,000 a year and the equilibrium enrollment is 200,000 students a year.

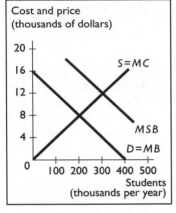

1c. The efficient number of students is 300,000 because this the quantity at which the marginal cost equals the marginal social benefit.

1d. The demand curve, which is the same as the marginal private benefit curve, shows that tuition must be $4,000 in order for 300,000 students to attend college. The marginal cost of educating 300,000 students is $12,000 students per year. It is justified to charge a tuition that is less than the marginal cost because education has external benefits so that society as well as the student benefits from the college education.

2a. The marginal private benefit is the benefit to the child being vaccinated and is $30. The marginal external benefit is the benefit to the child's parents and is $60.

2b. Based on the data that were submitted, the government should have approved the vaccine. The marginal social benefit equals the marginal private benefit to the child of $30 plus the marginal external benefit to the parent of $60, which is $90. The marginal social benefit from the vaccine is greater than the marginal cost.

## ■ AP Self Test 9.2

**True or false**

1. The marginal private benefit from a good or service must exceed the marginal external benefit.

2. The expanded job opportunities from a college degree is a marginal private benefit enjoyed by college graduates.

3. A flu vaccination has an external benefit, so the marginal private benefit curve for flu vaccinations lies above the marginal social benefit curve for flu vaccinations.

4. An unregulated market underproduces products with external benefits, such as education.

5. A public community college is an example of public provision of a good that has an external benefit.

6. To overcome the inefficiency in the market for a good with an external benefit, the government can either tax or subsidize the good.

7. Vouchers can help overcome the inefficiency created by a good with an external cost but not the inefficiency created by a good with an external benefit.

8. A patent protects intellectual property rights by giving the patent holder a monopoly.

**Multiple choice**

1. The benefit the consumer of a good or service receives is the
   a. social benefit.
   b. external benefit.
   c. private benefit.
   d. public benefit.
   e. consumption benefit.

2. An external benefit is a benefit from a good or service that someone other than the ____ receives.
   a. seller of the good or service
   b. government
   c. foreign sector
   d. consumer
   e. market maker

3. When Ronald takes another economics class, other people in society benefit. The benefit to these other people is called the marginal ____ benefit of the class.
   a. social
   b. private
   c. external
   d. opportunity
   e. extra

4. Marginal social benefit equals
   a. marginal external benefit.
   b. marginal private benefit.
   c. marginal private benefit minus marginal external benefit.
   d. marginal private benefit plus marginal external benefit
   e. marginal external benefit minus marginal private benefit.

5. If an external benefit is present, then the
   a. marginal private benefit curve lies above the marginal private cost curve.
   b. marginal social benefit curve lies above the marginal private benefit curve.
   c. marginal social cost curve lies above the marginal private benefit curve.
   d. marginal social benefit is equal to the marginal social cost.
   e. marginal social benefit curve is the same as the marginal private benefit curve.

6. In an unregulated market with an external benefit, the
   a. quantity produced is greater than the efficient quantity.
   b. price charged is too high for efficiency.
   c. quantity produced is less than the efficient quantity.
   d. producer is causing pollution but not paying for it.
   e. government might impose a tax to help move the market toward the efficient amount of production.

■ **FIGURE 9.3**

Price (hundreds of thousands of dollars per unit)

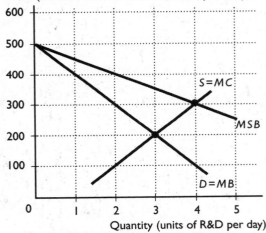

Quantity (units of R&D per day)

7. Figure 9.3 shows the market for research and development, which has ____.
   a. only external costs
   b. only external benefits
   c. both external costs and external benefits
   d. neither external costs nor external benefits
   e. might have external benefits or external costs, but more information is needed

8. Figure 9.3 shows the market for research and development. If the market is unregulated, the equilibrium quantity of R&D is ____ units per day.
   a. 0
   b. 2
   c. 3
   d. 4
   e. 5

9. Figure 9.3 shows the market for research and development. The efficient quantity of R&D is ____ units per day.
   a. 0
   b. 2
   c. 3
   d. 4
   e. 5

10. If all education in the United States were provided by private, tuition-charging schools,
    a. too much education would be consumed.
    b. too little education would be consumed.
    c. the efficient level of education would be provided.
    d. the government would provide *both* students and schools with vouchers.
    e. education would no longer have an external benefit.

11. Which of the following is a method used by government to cope with the situation in which production of a good creates an external benefit?
    a. removing property rights
    b. paying subsidies
    c. issuing marketable permits
    d. running a lottery
    e. imposing a Coasian tax

12. If tuition at a college is $30,000 and the external benefit of graduating from this college is $10,000, then
    i.   in the absence of any government intervention, the number of students graduating is less than the efficient number
    ii.  the government could increase the number of graduates by giving the college a $10,000 subsidy per student
    iii. the government could increase the number of graduates by giving the students $10,000 vouchers
    a. i only.
    b. i and ii.
    c. i and iii.
    d. ii and iii.
    e. i, ii, and iii.

13. Public universities are a service that is an example of
    a. patent protection.
    b. vouchers.
    c. private subsidies.
    d. public provision.
    e. an emission charge.

14. Which of the following is an example of a voucher?
    a. the postal service
    b. police services
    c. social security
    d. food stamps
    e. a patent on a pharmaceutical drug

15. Which government device is associated with intellectual property rights?
    a. public provision
    b. private subsidies
    c. vouchers
    d. patents and copyrights
    e. taxes

**Short Response Questions**

■ **FIGURE 9.4**

Price (dollars per pound of honey)

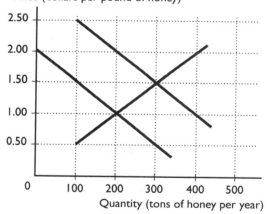

Quantity (tons of honey per year)

1. Figure 9.4 illustrates the market for honey.
    a. Label the curves in the figure.
    b. Based on Figure 9.4, does the production of honey create an external cost? An external benefit?

c. What is the efficient quantity of honey? What is the quantity that will be produced in an unregulated market?
d. Shade the area that equals the deadweight loss in an unregulated market.

| Quantity (units of R&D per day) | Marginal private cost (dollars per unit of R&D) | Marginal private benefit (dollars per unit of R&D) | Marginal social benefit (dollars per unit of R&D) |
|---|---|---|---|
| 100 | 100 | 250 | 340 |
| 200 | 120 | 200 | 290 |
| 300 | 150 | 150 | 240 |
| 400 | 190 | 100 | 190 |
| 500 | 240 | 50 | 140 |

2. The table above shows the benefits and costs of research and development, R&D.
    a. Based on the table, what is the amount of the marginal external benefit?
    b. If the market for R&D was left unregulated, what would be the competitive amount of R&D?
    c. What is the efficient amount of R&D?
    d. Would a subsidy or a tax be the proper government policy to make the market for R&D more efficient?

3. Is a private subsidy or a tax the correct government policy for a product that has an external benefit?

**Long Response Questions**

2. Is efficiency guaranteed when production is such that the marginal private benefit equals the marginal private cost? Or does efficiency require that the marginal social benefit equal the marginal social cost?

3. Most elementary schools require that children be vaccinated before allowing the child to attend school. Can this policy be justified using economic analysis?

4. What is a voucher? How do vouchers work? Why is a voucher a proper policy to deal with the inefficiency created by a good or service that has an external benefit?

**■ FIGURE 9.5**

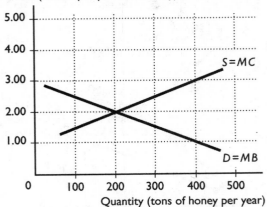

Price (dollars per pound of honey)

4. The Bee Queen Company produces a product that generates positive externalities.

   a. Define positive externality.

   b. Figure 9.5 shows the demand curve and supply curve for honey. If the marginal positive externality is $2.00 per ton, draw the marginal social benefit curve.

   c. Describe the problem that arises with a positive externality in terms of the allocation of resources. What is the equilibrium quantity of honey and the efficient quantity of honey if the marginal positive externality is $2.00 per ton?

   d. Describe the problem that arises with a positive externality in terms of marginal cost and marginal benefit.

   e. Explain how public provision, a subsidy to the sellers, and a voucher to the buyers can help eliminate the deadweight loss from a positive externality.

## YOUR AP SELF TEST ANSWERS

### ■ CHECKPOINT 9.1

**True or false**

1. False; page 218
2. True; page 219
3. False; page 220
4. False; page 222
5. False; page 224
6. True; page 225
7. False; page 225
8. True; page 226

**Multiple choice**

1. c; page 218
2. a; page 218
3. c; page 220
4. d; page 220
5. e; page 220
6. b; page 220
7. c; page 220
8. e; page 222
9. b; page 221
10. c; page 222
11. b; page 222
12. b; page 224
13. d; page 225
14. c; page 226

**Short Response Questions**

1. If the marginal social cost curve lies above the marginal private cost curve, production of the good creates an external cost; page 221.

| Quantity (tons of pesticide per day) | Marginal private cost (dollars per ton) | Marginal external cost (dollars per ton) | Marginal social cost (dollars per ton) |
|---|---|---|---|
| 1 | 100 | <u>30</u> | 130 |
| 2 | 120 | 40 | <u>160</u> |
| 3 | <u>150</u> | 60 | 210 |
| 4 | 190 | <u>90</u> | 280 |
| 5 | 240 | 120 | <u>360</u> |

2. The completed table is above; page 220.

### ■ FIGURE 9.6

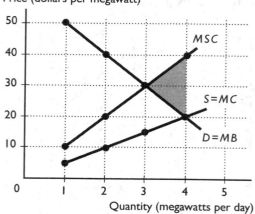

Price (dollars per megawatt)

3. a. Figure 9.6 shows the *MSC*, *MC*, and *MB* curves; page 222.

b. An unregulated market will produce 4 megawatts of electricity a day. The marginal external cost at this production is $20 per megawatt; page 222.

c. The allocatively efficient amount of electricity is 3 megawatts a day. The deadweight loss is illustrated in the figure; page 222.

d. At the efficient quantity of electricity, the marginal external cost is $15 a megawatt.

e. The tax is $15 a megawatt. With the tax, 3 megawatts of electricity are produced and the price is $30 per megawatt; page 227.

f. The emission charge is $15 per megawatt; page 225.

**Long Response Questions**

1. Pollution occurs when some goods are produced. The allocatively efficient quantity of *any* good is the quantity at which the marginal social benefit equals the marginal social cost. At this quantity, *all* the marginal costs of producing the good, including the marginal pollution cost, are equal to the marginal social benefit. Whatever is the quantity of pollution at this amount of production is the allocatively efficient quantity; page 222.

2. According to the Coase theorem, if property rights are assigned, the number of people involved is small, and transactions costs are low, then private transactions are efficient. In this situation, there are no externalities and hence no need for government intervention to remedy the situation of an external cost; page 224.

3. A marketable permit is a government-issued permit given to firms that allows the company to pollute up to the limit of the permit. Permits can be bought and sold amongst firms. The advantage marketable permits have over assigning each firm a limit for its pollution is information. In order to assign each firm a limit and achieve efficiency, the government must know each firm's marginal cost schedule. Marketable permits do not require that the government know this information; page 225.

4. Emission charges and taxes are designed to charge polluting firms the cost of their pollution. By forcing a firm to pay this cost, the firm's marginal private cost becomes equal to the marginal social cost. To use emission charges or taxes to overcome the problem of pollution, the government must know the marginal external cost at different levels of output. The nation's legal system might play a role if the victims of the spillover costs file suit to either prevent the pollution or else require that the perpetrator pay the costs imposed on the victims; page 225.

## ■ CHECKPOINT 9.2

**True or false**
1. False; page 230
2. True; page 230
3. False; page 230
4. True; page 231
5. True; page 232
6. False; page 232
7. False; page 234
8. True; page 235

**Multiple choice**
1. c; page 230
2. d; page 230
3. c; page 230
4. d; page 230
5. b; page 230
6. c; page 231
7. b; page 230
8. c; page 231
9. d; page 231
10. b; page 231
11. b; page 232
12. e; page 232
13. d; page 232
14. d; page 234
15. d; page 235

**Short Response Questions**

■ **FIGURE 9.7**
Price (dollars per pound of honey)

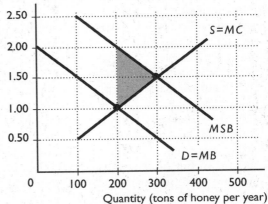

1. a. Figure 9.7 labels the curves; page 231.
   b. The production of honey has an external benefit but no external cost; page 231.
   c. The efficient quantity of honey is 300 tons, a year, at the intersection of the *MSB* curve and the *S = MC* curve. In an unregulated market, the equilibrium quantity is 200 tons a year, at the intersection of the *D = MB* curve and the *S = MC* curve; page 231.

d. Figure 9.7 shades the deadweight loss; page 231.

2. a. The marginal external benefit equals the difference between the marginal social benefit and the marginal social cost, so it is $90 per unit of R&D; page 230.

b. The competitive equilibrium is where the marginal private cost (which determines the supply) equals the marginal private benefit (which determines the demand), so the equilibrium amount of R&D is 300 units per day; page 231.

c. The efficient quantity is produced when the marginal social benefit equals the marginal cost, so the efficient amount is 400 units of R&D per day; page 231.

d. A subsidy would be a proper government policy; page 233.

3. The correct government action to deal with a good or service that has an external benefit is a private subsidy, not a tax; page 232.

**Long Response Questions**
1. Efficiency is not guaranteed when production sets the marginal private benefit equal to the marginal cost. The allocatively efficient quantity is produced when the marginal social benefit equals marginal cost. If there is an external cost, then the marginal social cost exceeds the marginal private cost and if there is an external benefit, then the marginal social benefit exceeds the marginal private benefit. In both of these cases, producing so that the marginal private benefit equals the marginal private cost leads to inefficiency and a deadweight loss; page 231.

2. Vaccination protects not only the child who is vaccinated, but also makes it less likely for classmates to catch the disease. So a vaccination has an external benefit. Although the marginal cost of a vaccination can be greater than the marginal private benefit of a vaccination, the marginal social benefit exceeds the marginal private benefit. The market might be efficient when vaccination is required; page 231.

3. A voucher is a token that the government gives to households which they can use to buy specified goods or services. Vouchers increase the demand for the product and shift the demand curve (which is the same as the marginal private benefit curve, or *MB* curve) rightward, closer to the marginal social benefit curve. Vouchers reduce the inefficiency created by a good or service with an external benefit; page 234

4. a. An external benefit occurs when the production or consumption of a good creates an external benefit. An external benefit is the benefit from an additional unit of a good or service that people other than the consumer of the good or service enjoy; pages 218, 230.

■ **FIGURE 9.8**

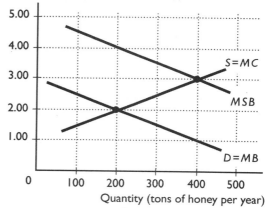

Price (dollars per pound of honey)

b. Figure 9.8 shows the marginal social benefit curve. It lies above the marginal private benefit curve (the demand curve) by the amount of the marginal positive externality, $2.00 per ton; page 231.

c. If a good has a positive externality, in an unregulated market less than the efficient quantity of the good is produced and consumed, so fewer resources than the allocatively efficient quantity are devoted to producing the good or service. In this case, the equilibrium quantity is 200 tons of honey per year and the efficient quantity is 400 tons of honey; page 231.

d. If a good has a positive externality, in an unregulated market at the equilibrium quantity the marginal social benefit of the good exceeds its marginal (social) cost; page 231

e. To eliminate the deadweight loss from the underproduction, the quantity of the good produced must be increased. Public provision, where the government produces the good, can lead to an increase in the quantity produced because the government can sell the good below cost and use tax revenue to make up the shortfall. A subsidy, which is a payment by the government to producers, increases the supply and so increases the equilibrium quantity. A voucher, which is a token the government gives to buyers that can be used to help pay for a good or service, increases the demand and so increases the equilibrium quantity; pages 232-234.

# Chapter

# Public Goods and Common Resources

# 10

Chapter 10 studies the types of goods and services provided by the government.

■ **Distinguish between public goods, private goods, and common resources.**

An excludable good, service, or resource is one for which it is possible to prevent someone from benefiting from it; a nonexcludable good, service, or resource is one for which it is impossible to prevent someone from benefiting from it. A rival good, service, or resource is one for which its consumption by one person decreases the quantity available for someone else; a nonrival good, service, or resource is one for which its consumption by one person does not decrease the quantity available to someone else. A private good is excludable and rival. A public good is a good or service that can be consumed simultaneously by everyone and from which no one can be excluded. A public good is nonexcludable and nonrival. A common resource is a resource that is nonexcludable and rival.

■ **Explain the free-rider problem and how public provision can help to overcome that problem.**

Public goods create a free-rider problem, a person who enjoys the benefits of a good or service without paying for it. The economy's marginal benefit curve of a public good is the vertical sum of the individual marginal benefit curves. The efficient quantity of a public good is the quantity where marginal benefit equals marginal cost. Because of the free-rider problem, public goods are under-provided by private firms so public provision of public goods might lead efficiency. The tendency for political parties to propose identical policies to appeal to the maximum number of voters is an example of the principle of minimum differentiation. Rational ignorance is the decision not to acquire information because the marginal cost of doing so exceeds the expected marginal benefit. Rational ignorance, combined with the bureaucratic desire to maximize budgets, can lead to inefficient overprovision of public goods.

■ **Explain the tragedy of the commons and review the possible solutions to that problem.**

Common resources suffer from the tragedy of the commons, which is the absence of incentives to prevent the overuse and depletion of a commonly owned resource. Fish are an example of a common resource. The marginal private benefit of an additional boat is that boat's catch. But the quantity of fish caught by each boat decreases as more boats fish. The marginal social benefit of an additional boat is the change in the total catch that results from that additional boat. Efficiency occurs when the marginal social benefit from a resource equals its marginal cost. But the marginal private benefit is more than the marginal social benefit, so in an unregulated market overuse of the resource occurs. The government can help bring about an efficient use of the common resource by assigning property rights to the resource, or by setting quotas on the amount of the resource that can be used, or by creating a program of individual transferable quotas (ITQ). An individual transferable quota is a production limit that the owner can transfer to someone else.

## EXPANDED CHAPTER CHECKLIST

**When you have completed this chapter, you will be able to:**

**1  Distinguish between public goods, private goods, and common resources.**

- Define nonrival and rival, and nonexcludable and excludable.
- Define public good, private good, and common resource and discuss how they differ along the two dimensions of rivalry and excludability.

**2  Explain the free-rider problem and how public provision can help to overcome that problem.**

- Explain the free-rider problem.
- Describe how the marginal benefit for a public good is calculated.
- Explain why the economy's marginal benefit curve for a public good is different from the market demand curve for a private good.
- Show on a figure the efficient quantity of a public good.
- Define the principle of minimum differentiation and explain how it applies to the proposals of political parties.
- Define rational ignorance.
- Explain why the government is large and growing.

**3  Explain the tragedy of the commons and review the possible solutions to that problem.**

- Define the tragedy of the commons.
- Discuss why the marginal private benefit of a common resource exceeds the marginal social benefit of the resource.
- Illustrate and describe why a common resource is overused.
- Discuss how property rights, quotas, and individual transferable quotas can result in the efficient use of a common resource.

## YOUR AP TEST HINTS

### AP Topics

| Topic on your AP test | Corresponding textbook section |
|---|---|
| **Market failures and the role of government** | |
| Public Goods | Chapter 10 |
| • Public versus private goods | Checkpoint 10.1 |
| • Provision of public goods | Checkpoint 10.1 |

### AP Vocabulary

- On the AP test, the term "shared consumption" is another term used for "nonrival." In both cases the terms mean that more than one person can consume the same unit of a good or service.
- On the AP test, the "exclusion principle" states that buyers who pay for a good or service can obtain them, but those who do not pay cannot obtain the good or service. This idea relates to the textbook terms of excludable and nonexcludable.
- In the four-fold classification of goods, the term "natural monopolies" might be defined as "toll goods," but the same characteristics--nonrival    and    excludable— generally apply. More specifically, a toll good is non-rival, until congestion sets in after which the good is rival, and excludable. An example is a movie theater. The theater is a toll good until it becomes so crowded that allowing another person means that someone else must be removed.
- The term "tragedy of the commons" is the same as the "problem of the commons."

## CHECKPOINT 10.1

■  **Distinguish between public goods, private goods, and common resources.**

### Quick Review

- *Public good* A public good is nonrival (or, equivalently, has shared consumption) and nonexcludable.

- *Private good* A private good is rival and excludable (or, equivalently, meets the exclusion principle).
- *Common resource* A common resource is rival and nonexcludable.

## Additional Practice Problem 10.1

1. It's a balmy, pleasant Sunday afternoon on a fall day on Long Island, where the U.S. Open Tennis Men's Singles Finals are being played. A variety of goods and services are being consumed. Classify each of the list of goods and services as rival, nonrival (or shared consumption), excludable, and nonexcludable. State if they are a public good, a private good, or a common resource.

    a. U.S. Lawn Tennis Association membership

    b. tennis lessons

    c. racquets

    d. watching the Men's Singles Championship

    e. a pleasant, sunny afternoon

    f. sunset seen over Fire Island

    g. shrimp eaten at a tailgate party

## Solution to Additional Practice Problem 10.1

1a. Membership in the U.S. Lawn Tennis Association is nonrival (and so has shared consumption) and is excludable.

1b. Tennis lessons are rival and excludable and are a private good.

1c. Racquets are rival and excludable and hence are a private good.

1d. Watching the Men's Singles Championship is excludable. Whether it is rival depends on whether the match is a sell out. If it is a sell out, then watching the championship is rival because in order for one other person to watch, someone else must be deprived of watching, and so it is a private good. In the event that it is not sold out and seats remain available, it is nonrival (and has shared consumption) because another person can watch the match. This event is therefore a toll good.

1e. The pleasant afternoon is nonrival (shared consumption) and nonexcludable and so is a public good.

1f. The sunset is nonrival (shared consumption) and nonexcludable and so is a public good.

1g. The shrimp are rival and excludable and so are a private good.

## ■ AP Self Test 10.1

### True or false

1. A good is nonexcludable if it is impossible to prevent someone from benefiting from it.

2. A private good is nonrival and nonexcludable.

3. A taco from Taco Bell is a public good.

4. A common resource is nonrival and excludable.

5. Fish in the ocean are rival and nonexcludable.

### Multiple choice

1. The fact that Heidi's enjoyment of a sunset on Saint Simon's Island does not preclude Mounette from enjoying the same sunset is an example of
   a. a good that is nonrival and has shared consumption.
   b. a good that is excludable.
   c. a private good.
   d. the rival nature of consumption.
   e. a common resource.

2. A private good is ____ and ____.
   a. rival; excludable
   b. rival; nonexcludable
   c. nonrival; excludable
   d. nonrival; nonexcludable
   e. scarce; expensive

3. If I order a pizza and invite my neighbors to eat it, the pizza is
   a. a private good.
   b. a common resource.
   c. a public good because many people ate it.
   d. either a common resource or a public good depending on whether it is overused.
   e. produced by a natural monopoly.

4. A public good is ____ and ____.
   a. rival; excludable
   b. rival; nonexcludable
   c. nonrival; excludable
   d. nonrival; nonexcludable
   e. cheap; available

5. A public good
   a. can only be consumed by one person at a time.
   b. can be consumed simultaneously by many people.
   c. is any good provided by a company owned by a member of the public.
   d. is any good provided by government.
   e. is both rival and excludable.

6. Which of the following is the best example of a public good?
   a. national defense
   b. a Ford Thunderbird
   c. a cell phone
   d. a Mountain Dew
   e. a satellite radio

7. Which of the following is the best example of a common resource?
   a. national defense
   b. a Ford Thunderbird
   c. fishing in the Yosemite river
   d. a Mountain Dew
   e. a cable television network

**Short Response Questions**

|  | Exclusive (excludable) | Not exclusive (nonexcludable) |
|---|---|---|
| **Rival** |  |  |
| **Nonrival (shared consumption)** |  |  |

1. Label each of the squares in the table above as "private goods," "public goods," "common resources," and "natural monopoly (toll goods)." For the list below, put the letter for each good in its correct square.
   a. a Pepsi

b. a fireworks display on the Fourth of July
c. fishing in the Yellowstone River
d. a non-crowded movie theater
e. a bridge crossing a creek
f. home
g. a used car
h. levees along the Mississippi to prevent floods

2. What does it mean for a good to be nonexcludable? Nonrival?

**Long Response Question**

1. Goods can be excludable or nonexcludable, rival or nonrival. Using these criteria, what is a public good, a private good, and a common resource?

### CHECKPOINT 10.2

■ **Explain the free-rider problem and how public provision can help to overcome that problem.**

**Quick Review**

- *Free rider* A free rider enjoys the benefits of a good or service without paying for the good or service.

**Additional Practice Problems 10.2**

| Quantity (square miles per day) | Abe's marginal benefit (dollars per day) | Bee's marginal benefit (dollars per day) | Kris's marginal benefit (dollars per day) |
|---|---|---|---|
| 1 | 20 | 20 | 30 |
| 2 | 35 | 35 | 50 |
| 3 | 48 | 42 | 60 |
| 4 | 60 | 45 | 65 |
| 5 | 70 | 47 | 68 |

1. A (small) city that is exactly 5 square miles in size has three people in it, Abe, Bee, and Kris. The table above gives the marginal benefit of each from a mosquito control program.
   a. Is mosquito spraying a public good or a private good? Explain your answer.
   b. Calculate the marginal social benefit for spraying 1, 2, 3, 4, and 5 square miles a day.

c. If the marginal cost of spraying was constant at $150 for a square mile, what it is the efficient number of miles that should be sprayed?

d. How many square miles would the bureau head of the city's mosquito control project lobby the city commissioners to spray?

2. How do rational ignorance and bureaucrats' goal of budget maximization combine to lead to inefficient overprovision of public goods?

**Solutions to Additional Practice Problems 10.2**

1a. Mosquito spraying is a public good because it's both nonrival—everyone can simultaneously enjoy not being bitten—and nonexcludable—even if one of the residents does not pay, the mosquitoes still do not bite that resident.

1b. The marginal social benefit is equal to the sum of the benefits of all the residents for each quantity. So the marginal social benefit for spraying 1 square mile is equal to $20 + $20 +$30 = $70. The rest of the answers in the table are calculated similarly.

| Quantity (square miles per day) | Marginal social benefit (dollars per day) |
|---|---|
| 1 | 70 |
| 2 | 120 |
| 3 | 150 |
| 4 | 170 |
| 5 | 185 |

1c. The marginal social cost equals the marginal social benefit when 3 square miles are sprayed, so 3 square miles is the efficient quantity of spraying.

1d. The head of the city's mosquito control commission wants to maximize the budget of the commission, so the head will lobby to spray 5 square miles.

2. If voters knew the marginal social benefit and marginal social cost of a public good, they could elect politicians who would deliver the efficient quantity. But voters generally are rationally ignorant about the marginal social benefit and marginal social cost of most public goods. So bureaucrats, who want to increase their budget, and special interest groups, such as the producers of a public good, lobby politi-

cians to provide more than the efficient amount of public goods. Politicians accede to the lobbying because they know that (rationally ignorant) voters will not realize that too much of the public good is provided.

## ■ AP Self Test 10.2

**True or false**

1. Beth is a free rider when she is protected by the nation's military but does not pay anything for the protection.

2. The marginal benefit curve for a public good slopes downward.

3. The efficient quantity of a public good is the quantity at which marginal benefit equals marginal cost.

4. A private firm would produce too much of a public good.

5. Rational ignorance can lead to the provision of more than the efficient amount of a public good.

**Multiple choice**

1. When someone enjoys the benefit of a good or service but does not pay for it, that person
   a. is a free range consumer.
   b. is a free rider.
   c. receives no marginal benefit from the good.
   d. must be consuming an excludable good
   e. is contributing to the tragedy of the commons.

2. The marginal benefit of a public good is the
   a. sum of the marginal benefits of all the individuals at each quantity.
   b. marginal benefit of the individual person who places the lowest value on the good, multiplied by the number of people in the economy.
   c. marginal benefit of the individual person who places the highest value on the good, multiplied by the number of people in the economy.
   d. benefit of the last person's consumption.
   e. average of the marginal benefits of all the individuals at each quantity.

3. The marginal benefit curve of a public good
   a. slopes downward.
   b. slopes upward.
   c. is vertical.
   d. is horizontal.
   e. is U-shaped.

4. Sue and Mark are the only two members of a community. Sue's marginal benefit from one lighthouse is $2,000 and Mark's marginal benefit is $1,000. If the marginal cost of one lighthouse is $2,500 and if a lighthouse is a public good, then for efficiency the lighthouse should
   a. be built but only Sue should be allowed to use it.
   b. be built but only Mark should be allowed to use it.
   c. be built and both Sue and Mark should be allowed to use it.
   d. not be built because its marginal cost exceeds Sue's marginal benefit.
   e. not be built because its marginal cost exceeds both Sue's and Mark's marginal benefit.

5. The efficient quantity of a public good is
   a. the quantity produced by private firms.
   b. the quantity at which the marginal benefit equals the marginal cost.
   c. impossible to determine because each person's marginal benefit is different.
   d. the quantity at which the marginal benefit exceeds the marginal cost by as much as possible.
   e. where the demand curve and supply curve of the good intersects.

6. The efficient quantity of a public good can't be produced by private firms because
   a. only government has the necessary resources.
   b. it is impossible to determine the efficient amount.
   c. consumers have an incentive to free ride and not pay for their share of the good.
   d. private firms aren't large enough.
   e. the price would be too high if private firms produced the goods.

7. Government bureaucracies over-provide public goods and grow larger because of their goal of ____ combined with ____ of the voters.
   a. budget maximization; rational ignorance
   b. budget minimization; irrational intelligence
   c. budget maximization; minimum differentiation
   d. budget maximization; irrational exuberance
   e. minimum differentiation; budget maximization

### Short Response Questions

| Quantity (lighthouses) | Marginal benefit, Firm A (dollars) | Marginal benefit, Firm B (dollars) | Marginal benefit, Firm C (dollars) |
| --- | --- | --- | --- |
| 1 | 50,000 | 50,000 | 50,000 |
| 2 | 45,000 | 45,000 | 45,000 |
| 3 | 40,000 | 40,000 | 40,000 |
| 4 | 35,000 | 35,000 | 35,000 |

1. Three shipping firms serve the west coast of a nation. The table has the firms' marginal benefit schedules for lighthouses. Lighthouses are a public good and the marginal cost of constructing a lighthouse is constant at $120,000.

   a. Complete the table below. Then graph the economy's marginal benefit and marginal cost curves in Figure 10.1.

| Quantity (lighthouses) | Marginal benefit, (dollars per lighthouse) |
| --- | --- |
| 1 | |
| 2 | |
| 3 | |
| 4 | |

   b. What is the efficient number of lighthouses to build?

   c. If all three firms agree to split the cost of building lighthouses equally, how much would each firm pay per lighthouse and how many lighthouses will be built?

   d. Suppose that one firm decides to free ride and not pay for the construction of any lighthouses. How much would each of the two other firms pay per lighthouse and how many lighthouses will be built?

■ **FIGURE 10.1**

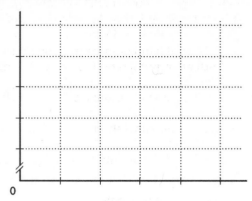

e. In the situation described in part (d), how might government action overcome the problem?

**Long Response Question**

1. A very small nation has 10 citizens. Each resident has a $10 marginal benefit from 1 unit of a private good. In addition, each has a $10 marginal benefit from 1 unit of a public good. What is one combination of marginal benefit and quantity on the economy's marginal benefit curve for the private good and what is one combination on the economy's marginal benefit curve for the public good? Explain the difference.

2. What is a free rider? Why is free riding not a problem for private goods? How does free riding affect the private provision of a public good? How does rational ignorance affect the public provision of a public good?

3. Provide two reasons to explain why street lighting is usually provided as a public good.

## CHECKPOINT 10.3

■ **Explain the tragedy of the commons and review the possible solutions to that problem.**

**Quick Review**

- *Tragedy of the commons* The absence of incentives to prevent the overuse and de-

pletion of a commonly owned resource.

- *Marginal private benefit* The benefit received by an individual from using a common resource.

- *Marginal social benefit* The benefit received by society when an individual uses a common resource.

**Additional Practice Problem 10.3**

1. Suppose Tom, Dick, and Harry are three potential fishermen. If Tom fishes by himself, the total catch is 50 fish. If Dick joins Tom fishing, the total catch is 90 fish, split evenly between the two. If Harry joins Tom and Dick fishing, the total catch is 105 fish, split evenly between the three.

   a. What is Dick's marginal private benefit from fishing? What is the marginal social benefit from Dick's fishing?

   b. What is Harry's marginal private benefit from fishing? What is the marginal social benefit from Harry's fishing?

   c. The fish that Tom, Dick, and Harry are catching are a common resource. For a common resource, why is the marginal social benefit less than the marginal private benefit?

   d. If fishing is unregulated, will the amount of fish caught equal the efficient quantity, be more than the efficient quantity, or be less that the efficient quantity?

**Solution to Additional Practice Problem 10.3**

1a. Dick's marginal private benefit is 45 fish, the quantity that he catches. The marginal social benefit of Dick's fishing is 40 fish, the difference in the total catch with Tom and Dick fishing (90 fish) versus Tom alone fishing (50 fish).

1b. Harry's marginal private benefit is 35 fish, the quantity that he catches. The marginal social benefit of Harry's fishing is 15 fish, the difference in the total catch with Tom, Dick, and Harry fishing (105 fish) versus just Tom and Dick fishing (90 fish).

1c. The marginal private benefit measures *only* the benefit going to an individual from his or her use of a common resource. But when someone uses a common resource, he or she decreases the benefit going to other users. The marginal social benefit takes account of this decrease. In the case at hand, when Dick goes fishing, while he catches 45 fish, 5 of these fish would already have been caught when Tom alone fished. So Dick's marginal social benefit is his marginal private benefit (45 fish) minus the decrease in Tom's catch (5 fish), or 40 fish. Dick adds only 40 *new* fish to the total catch. Dick's marginal social benefit from the common resource is less than his marginal private benefit.

1d. The amount of fish caught will exceed the efficient quantity because people will fish until their marginal private benefit equals the marginal cost. Since the marginal private benefit exceeds the marginal social benefit, more than the efficient quantity of fish will be caught; the fish will be subject to the tragedy of the commons.

## ■ AP Self Test 10.3

### True or false

1. The tragedy of the commons is the absence of incentives that prevent the overuse and depletion of a commonly owned resource.

2. The marginal benefit curve of a common resource slopes upward.

3. The efficient use of a common resource occurs when the marginal private benefit equals the marginal cost.

4. At the efficient level of use, the marginal private benefit of a common resource exceeds the marginal social benefit.

5. Property rights and quotas are potential solutions to the problem of the commons.

### Multiple choice

1. The tragedy of the commons is the absence of incentives to
   a. correctly measure the marginal cost.
   b. prevent under use of the common resource.
   c. prevent overuse and depletion of the common resource.
   d. discover the resource.
   e. prevent the free-rider problem.

2. For a common resource such as fish, the marginal private benefit of an additional boat is the ____ and the marginal social benefit is the ____.
   a. catch per boat; quantity of fish that one more boat catches
   b. quantity of fish that one more boat catches; change in the total catch from an additional boat
   c. change in the total catch from an additional boat; catch per boat
   d. change in the total catch from an additional boat; change in the total catch from an additional boat
   e. quantity of fish that one more boat catches; catch per boat

3. For a common resource, the equilibrium with no government intervention is such that ____ equals ____.
   a. marginal private benefit; marginal cost
   b. marginal social benefit; marginal cost
   c. marginal private benefit; marginal social benefit
   d. social benefit; cost
   e. total social benefit; total social cost

4. For a common resource, the marginal private benefit of the resource is
   a. greater than the marginal social benefit.
   b. equal to the marginal social benefit.
   c. less than the marginal social benefit.
   d. not comparable to the marginal social benefit.
   e. not defined because the resource is non-excludable.

■ **FIGURE 10.2**

Sustainable harvest per logger (tons per month)

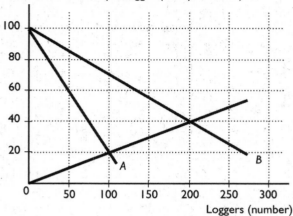

Loggers (number)

5. Figure 10.2 shows a market for logging in a tropical rainforest, which is a common resource. In the figure, curve *A* is the ____ and curve *B* is the ____.
   a. *MSB; MC*
   b. *MSB; MPB*
   c. *MPB; MSB*
   d. *MC; MSB*
   e. *MC; MPB*

6. Figure 10.2 shows a market for logging in a tropical rainforest, which is a common resource. The efficient number of loggers is ____ and if the market is unregulated, the equilibrium number of loggers is ____.
   a. 0; 100
   b. 0; 200
   c. 200; 100
   d. 100; 0
   e. 100; 200

7. For a common resource, the marginal private benefit curve ____ and the marginal social benefit curve ____.
   a. slopes upward; slopes upward
   b. slopes upward; slopes downward
   c. slopes downward; slopes upward
   d. slopes downward; slopes downward
   e. is vertical; is horizontal

8. For a common resource, efficiency requires that the ____ equals the ____.
   a. marginal private benefit; marginal cost
   b. marginal social benefit; marginal cost
   c. marginal private benefit; marginal social benefit
   d. marginal social cost; marginal cost
   e. marginal private benefit; marginal social cost

9. If the government assigns private property rights to a common resource, then the
   a. resource is under-utilized.
   b. marginal private benefit becomes equal to the marginal social benefit.
   c. government needs to set a quota to achieve efficiency.
   d. resource becomes subject to the free riding problem.
   e. resource cannot be utilized.

10. The market price of an individual transferable quota is equal to the
    a. marginal private benefit.
    b. marginal social benefit.
    c. marginal private benefit minus the marginal cost.
    d. marginal social benefit minus the marginal cost.
    e. marginal private benefit plus the marginal cost.

## Short Response Questions

■ **FIGURE 10.3**

Sustainable catch per boat (tons per month)

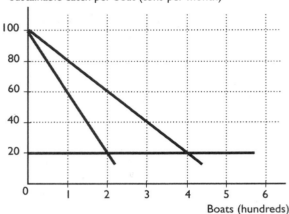

1. Figure 10.3 shows the marginal cost, marginal private benefit, and marginal social benefit curves for swordfish, a common resource. Label each curve.
   a. What is the equilibrium number of boats and sustainable catch? What is the efficient number of boats and sustainable catch?
   b. If the government sets a quota, what quota achieves the efficient outcome?
   c. If the government issues individual transferable quotas (ITQ), what is the market price of an ITQ?

## Long Response Questions

1. What is the problem of the commons and why does it occur? Give an example of how the problem of the commons affects the world's fisheries.

2. For a common resource, why does the marginal private benefit not equal the marginal social benefit? Which is smaller?

3. The table above in the right column gives the quantity of meat per year and marginal social benefit of grazing sheep on a common pasture. The marginal cost of raising a sheep is 50 pounds of meat per year.
   a. Complete the table by calculating the marginal private benefit.

| Number of sheep | Meat (pounds per year) | Marginal private benefit (pounds per year) | Marginal social benefit (pounds per year) |
|---|---|---|---|
| 0 | 0 | | |
| 10 | 2,000 | _____ | 150 |
| 20 | 3,000 | _____ | 50 |
| 30 | 3,000 | _____ | −50 |
| 40 | 2,000 | _____ | −150 |
| 50 | 0 | _____ | |

■ **FIGURE 10.4**

Meat output (pounds per year)

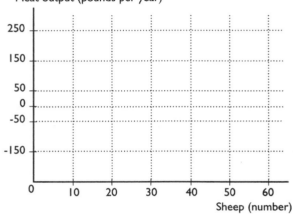

b. In Figure 10.4, plot the marginal cost curve, the marginal private benefit curve, and the marginal social cost curve.
c. What is the equilibrium number of sheep and the equilibrium quantity of meat?
d. What is the efficient number of sheep and the efficient quantity of meat?

## YOUR AP SELF TEST ANSWERS

### ■ CHECKPOINT 10.1

**True or false**
1. True; page 242
2. False; page 242
3. False; page 242
4. False; page 243
5. True; page 243

**Multiple choice**
1. a; page 242
2. a; page 242
3. a; page 242
4. d; page 243
5. b; page 243
6. a; page 243
7. c; page 243

**Short Response Questions**

|  | Exclusive (excludable) | Not exclusive (nonexcludable) |
|---|---|---|
| **Rival** | Private good<br>a<br>f<br>g | Common resource<br>c |
| **Nonrival (shared consumption)** | Natural monopoly (toll good)<br>d | Public good<br>b<br>e<br>h |

1. The table above labels each square and puts each good in its proper square; pages 242-243.
2. A public good is nonrival and nonexcludable. A private good is rival and excludable. A common resource is rival and nonexcludable; pages 242-243.

**Long Response Question**
1. A good is nonexcludable if it is impossible (or extremely costly) to prevent someone from benefiting from it. For example, the national defense provided by a fighter plane benefits everyone and so is nonexcludable. A good is nonrival if its use by one person does not decrease the quantity available for some-

one else. For example, the national defense provided by a fighter plane to you does not decrease the amount of defense it provides to your neighbor and so is nonrival; page 242.

### ■ CHECKPOINT 10.2

**True or false**
1. True; page 245
2. True; page 247
3. True; page 248
4. False; page 248
5. True; page 251

**Multiple choice**
1. b; page 245
2. a; pages 246-247
3. a; page 247
4. c; page 248
5. b; page 248
6. c; page 248
7. a; page 252

**Short Response Questions**

| Quantity (lighthouses) | Economy's marginal benefit (dollars) |
|---|---|
| 1 | 150,000 |
| 2 | 135,000 |
| 3 | 120,000 |
| 4 | 105,000 |

1. a. The complete table is above and the completed figure is Figure 10.5 (on the next page); pages 246-247.
   b. The efficient number of lighthouses to build is 3; page 248.
   c. Each firm pays $40,000 per lighthouse and three lighthouses are built; page 248.
   d. If one firm free rides, the other firms would need to pay $60,000 a lighthouse. No lighthouses would be built because $60,000 exceeds each firm's marginal benefit from any lighthouse; page 248.

■ **FIGURE 10.5**

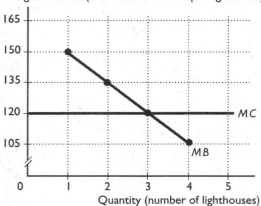

Marginal benefit (thousands of dollars per lighthouse)

e. The government could tax each firm $40,000 per lighthouse and use the tax revenue to build three lighthouses; page 249.

## Long Response Questions

1. For the private good, one combination on the economy's marginal benefit curve is: $10 marginal benefit and 10 units. For the public good, one combination is: $100 marginal benefit and 1 unit. The difference occurs because for the rival private good, all residents need their own unit of the good in order to consume it, whereas for the nonrival public good, each citizen will consume the same unit. So to obtain the economy's marginal benefit curve for a private good, we sum the quantities demanded at each price. To obtain the economy's marginal benefit curve for a public good, we sum the marginal benefits of all individuals at each quantity; pages 246-247.

2. A free rider is a person who enjoys the benefits of a good or service without paying for it. Free riding is not a problem for private goods because private goods are excludable. Because everyone can consume the same quantity of a public good and no one can be excluded from enjoying its benefits, no one has an incentive to pay for it. Everyone has an incentive to free ride. Because of the free-

rider problem, the market would provide too small a quantity of a public good.

Bureaucrats who maximize their budgets and voters who work in the industry exert a larger influence on public policy than voters who are rationally ignorant. This set of circumstances leads to overprovision; pages 245, 248, and 252.

3. Because one person's use of a street light does not diminish another person's consumption of light, street lighting is nonrival or has shared consumption. In addition, the light is nonexcludable: It is not possible to prevent one person from benefiting while others benefit based on whether one had paid or not paid for the service. As a result, the free-rider problem arises. In particular, a person can consume the service without having paid for it. To overcome the problem, street lighting is provided in the public sector through tax dollars or other mandatory fees. By eliminating the free-rider problem, the government can (potentially) move the economy toward the efficient provision of street lights; pages 248-249.

## ■ CHECKPOINT 10.3

### True or false
1. True;  page 254
2. False;  page 255
3. False;  pages 256-257
4. True;  page 257
5. True;  page 258

### Multiple choice
1. c;  page 254
2. b;  pages 255-256
3. a;  page 255
4. a;  page 256
5. b;  pages 256-257
6. e;  pages 255-257
7. d;  page 257
8. b;  pages 256-257
9. b;  page 258
10. c;  page 259

## Short Response Question

### ■ FIGURE 10.6

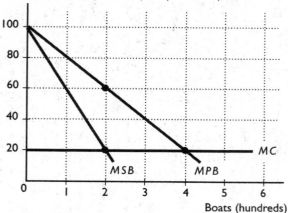

Sustainable catch per boat (tons per month)

1.   Figure 10.6 labels the curves.; page 247.

a. The equilibrium number of boats is determined by the intersection of the marginal cost curve and the marginal private benefit curve, so the equilibrium number of boats is 400 and the sustainable catch is 20 tons of swordfish a month. The efficient number of boats is determined by the intersection of the marginal cost curve and the marginal social benefit curve, so the efficient number of boats is 200 and the sustainable catch is 60 tons of swordfish a month from the marginal social benefit curve; pages 255-257.

b. If the government sets the quota at the efficient quantity, the quota for total production is set at the quantity at which marginal social benefit equals marginal cost. Here, that quantity is what 200 boats can produce; page 258.

c. The market price of an individual transferable quota (ITQ) equals the marginal private benefit minus the marginal cost at the quota level of fish. The government issues ITQs to 200 boats and so the market price of an ITQ is 60 tons a month, the marginal private benefit, minus 20 tons a month, the marginal cost, which equals a market price of 40 tons a month; page 259.

## Long Response Questions

1. The problem of the commons is that there is no incentive to prevent the overuse and depletion of a commonly used resource. As more boats fish, the quantity of fish that one boat can catch decreases. But no individual takes account of the *decrease* in the average catch because each person is concerned about what he or she catches As a result, additional boats continue to fish until their marginal private benefit equals the marginal cost of fishing. Each boat considers only its marginal private benefit. With this many boats fishing, marginal cost is greater than marginal social benefit and the fish stock is depleted; pages 254-255.

2. The marginal private benefit of using a common resource does not equal the marginal social benefit because the marginal private benefit does not take account of the effect that using the resource has on others. As a common resource is used more intensively, each additional person's use decreases *everyone else's* benefit from the resource. But the marginal private benefit ignores the decrease in other people's benefit. The marginal social benefit takes account of *both* the added benefit to the new user (the marginal private benefit) *and* the decrease in everyone else's benefit. So the marginal social benefit is less than the marginal private benefit; pages 256-257.

| Number of sheep | Meat (pounds per year) | Marginal private benefit (pounds per year) | Marginal social benefit (pounds per year) |
|---|---|---|---|
| 0 | 0 | | |
| 10 | 2,000 | 200 | 150 |
| 20 | 3,000 | 150 | 50 |
| 30 | 3,000 | 100 | −50 |
| 40 | 2,000 | 50 | −150 |
| 50 | 0 | 0 | |

3. a. The completed table is above. The marginal private benefit of a sheep is the quantity of meat per sheep. For 10 sheep the marginal private benefit is 2,000 pounds ÷ 10 sheep, which is 200 pounds; page 255.

■ **FIGURE 10.7**

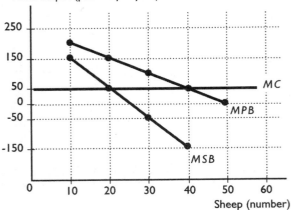

Meat output (pounds per year)

b. Figure 10.7 shows the marginal cost curve, the marginal private benefit curve, and the marginal social benefit curve; pages 255, 257.

c. The equilibrium number of sheep is determined by the intersection of the marginal private benefit curve and the marginal cost curve. The equilibrium number of sheep is 40 sheep. The equilibrium quantity of meat with 40 sheep is 2,000 pounds a year; page 255.

d The efficient number of sheep is determined by the intersection of the marginal social benefit curve and the marginal cost curve. The equilibrium number of sheep is 20 sheep. The equilibrium quantity of meat with 20 sheep is 3,000 pounds a year; page 257.

# Chapter

# Consumer Choice and Demand

# 11

Chapter 11 presents a model of consumer choice based on marginal utility and the fundamental idea that people make rational choices. We use marginal utility theory to derive a demand curve and explain the paradox of value.

■ **Calculate and graph a budget line that shows the limits to a person's consumption possibilities.**

The budget line describes the limits to a consumer's consumption possibilities. A consumer can afford any combination on the budget line and inside it, but cannot afford any combination outside the budget line. When the price of a good changes, the slope of the budget line changes. The relative price is the price of one good in terms of another good—an opportunity cost. It equals the price of one good divided by the price of another good. The slope of the budget line equals the relative price of the good plotted on the *x*-axis. An increase in the budget shifts the budget line rightward, and a decrease in the budget shifts the budget line leftward.

■ **Explain marginal utility theory and use it to derive a consumer's demand curve.**

Utility is the benefit or satisfaction a person gets from the consumption of a good or service. Total utility is the total benefit that a person gets from the consumption of a good or service; marginal utility is the change in total utility that results from a one-unit increase in the quantity of a good consumed. As the quantity of a good consumed increases, its total utility increases but its marginal utility decreases. A consumer maximizes total utility when he or she allocates his or her entire available budget and makes the marginal utility per dollar the same for all goods. The marginal utility per dollar is the increase in total utility that comes from the last dollar spent on a good. If the price of a good falls, the marginal utility per dollar for that good rises at the current consumption level and the consumer buys more of that good. So when the price of a good falls, there is an increase in the quantity demanded and a movement down along the demand curve.

■ **Use marginal utility theory to explain the paradox of value: Why water is vital but cheap while diamonds are relatively useless but expensive.**

The paradox of value is that water, which is essential to life, is cheap, while diamonds, which are relatively useless, are expensive. We solve this puzzle by distinguishing between total utility and marginal utility. The total utility from water is enormous. But we use so much water that its marginal utility is a small value. The total utility from diamonds is small. But we have few diamonds so their marginal utility is high. Diamonds have a high price and a high marginal utility while water has a low price and a low marginal utility. When the high marginal utility of diamonds is divided by the high price of a diamond, the result is a number that equals the low marginal utility of water divided by the low price of water. Water is cheap but provides a large consumer surplus, while diamonds are expensive but provide a small consumer surplus.

## EXPANDED CHAPTER CHECKLIST

**When you have completed this chapter, you will be able to:**

**1** **Calculate and graph a budget line that shows the limits to a person's consumption possibilities.**

- Define and draw a budget line.
- Discuss how the slope of the budget line changes when a price changes.
- Discus the relationship between the slope of the budget line, opportunity cost, and relative price of a good or service.
- Show the effect of an increase or decrease in the consumer's budget on the budget line.

**2** **Explain marginal utility theory and use it to derive a consumer's demand curve.**

- Define utility and total utility.
- Define and calculate marginal utility.
- Explain the principle of diminishing marginal utility.
- Use the utility-maximizing rule to choose the consumption combination that maximizes utility.
- Derive a demand curve using marginal utility theory.

**3** **Use marginal utility theory to explain the paradox of value: Why water is vital but cheap while diamonds are relatively useless but expensive.**

- Explain how marginal utility theory resolves the paradox of value.
- Discuss the difference between the price and consumer surplus of water and diamonds.

## YOUR AP TEST HINTS

*AP Topics*

| Topic on your AP test | Corresponding textbook section |
|---|---|
| **Nature and function of product markets** | |
| Theory of consumer choice | Chapter 11 |
| • Total utility and marginal utility | Checkpoint 11.2 |
| • Utility maximization: Equalizing marginal utility per dollar | Checkpoint 11.2 |

*AP Vocabulary*

- On the AP test, the utility maximizing rule (equalize marginal utility per dollar) is said to result in the "consumer equilibrium."

*Extra AP material*

- The principle of diminishing marginal utility is one explanation of the down-sloping nature of the demand curve. The AP test might also ask about two other factors: the "income effect" and the "substitution effect." The income effect is the impact of a change in the price of the product on consumers' real incomes. When the price falls, consumers' real incomes (or purchasing power) increase so that they are able to buy more than before and will buy more normal goods. The substitution effect is the impact of a change in the price of the product relative to its substitutes. If the price of a product falls, its price is now relatively lower compared to other substitute goods. Consumers respond by purchasing more of the relatively less expensive product. Both responses are reflected as movements along the demand curve.
- As total utility rises, marginal utility falls. At the peak of total utility, marginal utility is zero. As total utility declines, marginal utility is negative.
- The material on budget lines in Checkpoint 11.1 and on indifference curves in the appendix is not covered on the AP test.

# CHECKPOINT 11.1

■ **Calculate and graph a budget line that shows the limits to a person's consumption possibilities.**

## Quick Review

- *Budget line* A line that describes the limits to consumption choices and that depends on a consumer's budget and the prices of goods and services.

## Additional Practice Problems 11.1

1. Mark, a chemistry major at Cal State Hayward, dines by himself at the local Pizza Hut. He has $30 per week to spend. Pizza is $15 and a salad is $5.

   a. List the combinations of pizza and salads he can buy.

   b. Graph Mark's budget line in the figure to the right.

   c. What is the opportunity cost of a pizza?

   d. What is the relative price of a pizza?

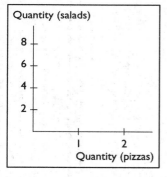

2. Sue is a student at Chabot Junior College. She has a budget of $240 that she will spend on purses and/or shoes. The price of a purse is $40 and the price of a pair of shoes is $60.

   a. Draw a graph of Sue's budget line in the figure to the right.

   b. If purses rise in price to $60, in the figure show what happens to Sue's budget line.

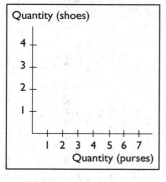

## Solutions to Additional Practice Problems 11.1

1a. The combinations of pizza and salads that Mark can afford are listed in the table. To construct this table, select the combinations of pizza and salads that spend all of Mark's $30 budget.

| Pizza | Salads |
|-------|--------|
| 0 | 6 |
| 1 | 3 |
| 2 | 0 |

1b. The figure shows Mark's budget line. The maximum number of pizzas he can buy is 2 and the maximum number of salads he can buy is 6.

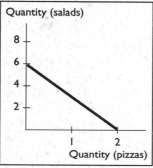

1c. The slope of the budget line is the opportunity cost of a pizza. The slope is (6 salads) ÷ (2 pizzas), which equals 3 salads per pizza. So consuming 1 pizza means Mark forgoes 3 salads.

1d. The opportunity cost of a pizza is also its relative price. The relative price of a pizza is 3 salads per pizza.

2a. The figure shows Sue's budget line as the grey line. The maximum number of purses Sue can buy is 6, where the budget line intersects the x-axis, and the maximum number of shoes Sue can buy is 4, where the budget line intersects the y-axis.

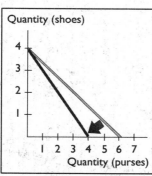

2b. When the price of a purse rises, the maximum number of purses that can be purchased decreases to 4 but the maximum number of shoes is unchanged. The budget line rotates inward as shown in the figure by the dark budget line.

■ **AP Self Test 11.1**

**True or false**

1. Dian's budget line shows the limits to what Dian can consume.

2. When Stan's budget increases, his budget line shifts outward.

3. The slope of the budget line measures the opportunity cost of one more unit of the good plotted on the $x$-axis.

**Multiple choice**

1. A budget line describes the
   a. limits to production possibilities.
   b. limits to production opportunities.
   c. the slope of the demand curve.
   d. limits to consumption possibilities.
   e. way the demand curve shifts if the consumer's budget changes.

2. Linda has $10 a month to spend on ice cream cones and chocolate bars. If the price of an ice cream cone is $2 a cone and the price of a chocolate bar is $1 a bar, which of the following is a point on Linda's budget line?
   a. 4 cones and 0 chocolate bars
   b. 1 cone and 8 chocolate bars
   c. 3 cones and 1 chocolate bar
   d. 5 cones and 10 chocolate bars
   e. 0 cones and 0 chocolate bars

3. If a consumer's budget increases, the budget line
   a. rotates outward and its slope changes.
   b. rotates inward and its slope changes.
   c. shifts outward and its slope does not change.
   d. shifts inward and its slope does not change.
   e. does not change.

4. If a budget line rotates inward and becomes steeper, then the
   a. consumer's budget decreased.
   b. consumer's budget increased.
   c. price of one of the goods decreased.
   d. price of one of the goods increased.
   e. price of both of the goods must have decreased.

■ **FIGURE 11.1**

Quantity (movies per month)

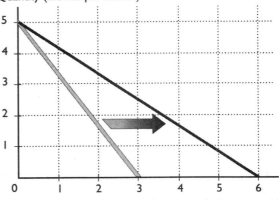

Quantity (hours playing paintball per month)

5. _____ will change Bobby's budget line as shown by the change from the gray budget line to the black budget line in Figure 11.1.
   a. An increase in Bobby's budget
   b. A decrease in Bobby's budget
   c. A fall in the price of playing paintball
   d. A rise in the price playing paintball
   e. A rise in the price of a movie

6. A relative price is the
   a. price of a substitute.
   b. price of a related good.
   c. price of one good divided by the price of another.
   d. absolute price of a good.
   e. price of one good multiplied by the price of another.

## Short Response Questions

### ■ FIGURE 11.2

Quantity (magazines per week)

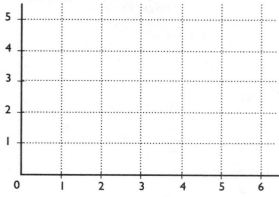

Quantity (hamburgers per week)

1. Jack buys two things: magazines, which have a price of $3 each, and hamburgers, which have a price of $4 each. Jack's income is $12.

   a. In Figure 11.2, draw Jack's budget line.

   b. What does the slope of the budget line equal? What is the interpretation of this slope?

   c. Can Jack buy 2 magazines and 1 hamburger? Can he buy 2 magazines and 3 hamburgers?

   d. Suppose the price of a hamburger falls to $2. In Figure 11.2, draw Jack's new budget line.

   e. What does the slope of the new budget line equal? How does the slope compare to your answer to part (b)?

## Long Response Questions

1. How is a budget line similar to a production possibilities frontier? How is it dissimilar?

2. What does the slope of a budget line equal?

3. What is the relationship between the relative price of a good and its opportunity cost?

## CHECKPOINT 11.2

### ■ Explain marginal utility theory and use it to derive a consumer's demand curve.

**Quick Review**

- *Marginal utility* The change in total utility that results from a one-unit increase in the quantity of a good consumed.
- *Marginal utility per dollar* The increase in total utility that comes from the last dollar spent on the good.

### Additional Practice Problems 11.2

| Orange juice | | Cookies | |
|---|---|---|---|
| Quantity per week | Total utility | Quantity per week | Total utility |
| 0 | 0 | 0 | 0 |
| 1 | 20 | 1 | 60 |
| 2 | 32 | 2 | 100 |
| 3 | 40 | 3 | 120 |
| 4 | 44 | 4 | 130 |
| 5 | 46 | 5 | 145 |

1. The table above shows Tommy's total utility from orange juice and cookies.

   a. Calculate Tommy's marginal utility schedule from orange juice and from cookies by completing the table below.

| Orange juice | | Cookies | |
|---|---|---|---|
| Quantity per week | Marginal utility | Quantity per week | Marginal utility |
| 0 | XX | 0 | XX |
| 1 | ___ | 1 | ___ |
| 2 | ___ | 2 | ___ |
| 3 | ___ | 3 | ___ |
| 4 | ___ | 4 | ___ |
| 5 | ___ | 5 | ___ |

   b. If the price of a carton of orange juice is $2, what is Tommy's marginal utility per dollar for orange juice when Tommy buys 2 cartons of orange juice a week?

   c. If the price of a box of cookies is $4, what is Tommy's marginal utility per dollar for cookies when Tommy buys 3 boxes of cookies a week?

   d. If Tommy's budget for orange juice and cookies is $10 per week and orange juice is

$2 per carton and cookies are $4 per box, what combination of orange juice and cookies will Tommy buy? Why does Tommy buy this combination? What is his total utility?

e. Tommy could afford to buy 5 cartons of orange juice a week. Why does he not buy 5 cartons?

2. If Jenny is allocating her entire available budget on movies and popcorn, explain the rule she follows to maximize her total utility.

### Solutions to Additional Practice Problems 11.2

| Orange juice | | Cookies | |
|---|---|---|---|
| Quantity per week | Marginal utility | Quantity per week | Marginal utility |
| 0 | XX | 0 | XX |
| 1 | 20 | 1 | 60 |
| 2 | 12 | 2 | 40 |
| 3 | 8 | 3 | 20 |
| 4 | 4 | 4 | 10 |
| 5 | 2 | 5 | 5 |

1a. The completed table is above. Marginal utility equals the change in total utility from a one-unit increase in the quantity of the good consumed. So the marginal utility of the second box of cookies equals 100 − 60, which is 40.

1b. The marginal utility per dollar is 12 ÷ $2 = 6.

1c. The marginal utility per dollar is 20 ÷ $4 = 5.

1d. Tommy buys 2 boxes of cookies and 1 carton of orange juice. This combination allocates his entire budget and the marginal utility per dollar for orange juice, 10, equals the marginal utility per dollar for cookies, 10. This combination gives Tommy total utility of 120.

1e. Tommy does not buy 5 cartons of orange juice because his total utility would be only 46, well less than his total utility from the utility-maximizing combination derived in the answer to part (d).

2. If the marginal utility per dollar for movies exceeds the marginal utility per dollar for popcorn, then Jenny sees more movies and buys less popcorn because this action increases her total utility; if the marginal utility per dollar for popcorn exceeds the marginal utility per dollar for movies, Jenny buys more popcorn and sees fewer movies because this action increases her total utility. More generally, if the marginal gain from an action exceeds the marginal loss, take the action. Jenny is maximizing her total utility when the marginal utility per dollar for movies equals the marginal utility per dollar for popcorn.

### ■ Self Test 11.2

**True or false**

1. As Katie consumes more sushi, her marginal utility from sushi increases.

2. Bobby maximizes his utility whenever he allocates his entire available budget.

3. Tommy is allocating his entire available budget. If Tommy's marginal utility per dollar for tacos is 8 and the marginal utility per dollar for burritos is 10, then Tommy is NOT maximizing his total utility.

4. Diminishing marginal utility theory implies that other things remaining the same, the higher the price of a good, the greater is the quantity demanded of that good.

**Multiple choice**

1. Marginal utility is the
   a. change in total utility that results from a one-unit increase in the quantity of a good consumed.
   b. total benefit from the consumption of a good or service.
   c. quantity of a good a consumer prefers.
   d. average utility per unit consumed.
   e. change in total utility that results from a one dollar change in the price of a good consumed.

2. Sushi costs $3 per piece. Cynthia's total utility after eating one piece is 30 and her total utility after eating 2 pieces is 51, so her marginal utility from the second piece is
   a. 17.
   b. 10.
   c. 51.
   d. 7.
   e. 21.

3. As Tommy drinks additional cups of tea at breakfast, Tommy's
   a. marginal utility from tea decreases.
   b. total utility from tea increases.
   c. total utility from tea decreases.
   d. Both answers (a) and (b) are correct.
   e. Both answers (b) and (c) are correct.

4. Marginal utility per dollar is calculated by ____ the price of the good.
   a. multiplying the marginal utility of a good by
   b. dividing the marginal utility of a good by
   c. multiplying the total utility of a good by
   d. dividing the total utility of a good by
   e. averaging the marginal utility of the good with

5. Sushi costs $3 per piece. Cynthia's total utility after eating one piece is 30 and her total utility after eating 2 pieces is 51, so her marginal utility per dollar from the second piece is
   a. 17.
   b. 10.
   c. 51.
   d. 7.
   e. 21.

6. When a household maximizes its total utility, then its entire available budget is allocated in such a way that the
   a. marginal utility of all goods is equal.
   b. marginal utility per dollar is equal for all goods.
   c. marginal utility is as large as possible for goods.
   d. marginal utility will start decreasing if it consumes fewer goods.
   e. quantities consumed of each good are equal.

7. Suppose that Jennifer likes pizza and hotdogs. If her marginal utility per dollar for pizza is 6 and for hotdogs is 5, Jennifer
   a. is maximizing her total utility.
   b. could increase her total utility by buying more hotdogs and less pizza.
   c. could increase her total utility by buying more pizza and fewer hotdogs.
   d. is maximizing her marginal utility.
   e. must obtain more income in order to reach her consumer equilibrium.

8. You can use marginal utility theory to find the demand curve by changing
   a. only the price of one good.
   b. only income.
   c. the utility schedule.
   d. only the prices of both goods.
   e. income and the prices of both goods.

9. Suppose that Hank consumes only Mountain Dew and pizza. If Hank's total utility from all amounts of both Mountain Dew and pizza double from what they were before, then Hank's demand for
   a. both goods must double.
   b. one of the goods must double.
   c. both goods must decrease by one-half.
   d. one of the goods must decrease by one-half.
   e. neither good changes.

**Short Response Questions**

| Quantity (bottles of Aquafina per day) | Total utility | Marginal utility |
|---|---|---|
| 0 | 0 | |
| 1 | 25 | ____ |
| 2 | 45 | ____ |
| 3 | 60 | ____ |
| 4 | 70 | ____ |
| 5 | 75 | ____ |
| 6 | 76 | ____ |

1. Carlos drinks Aquafina bottled water. The table above gives his total utility from this water. Calculate his marginal utility.

| Pizza | | | Soda | | |
|---|---|---|---|---|---|
| Quantity (slices per day) | Total utility, pizza | Marginal utility, pizza | Quantity (cans per day) | Total utility, soda | Marginal utility, soda |
| 0 | 0 | | 0 | 0 | |
| 1 | 45 | — | 1 | 25 | — |
| 2 | 85 | — | 2 | 45 | — |
| 3 | 120 | — | 3 | 60 | — |
| 4 | 150 | — | 4 | 70 | — |
| 5 | 175 | — | 5 | 75 | — |
| 6 | 195 | — | 6 | 76 | — |

2. Bertha consumes only soda and pizza. The table above gives Bertha's total utility from soda and pizza slices.

   a. Complete the marginal utility columns of the table.

   b. The price of a can of soda is $1 and the price of a slice of pizza is $2. If Bertha's budget is $6, how many cans of soda and slices of pizza will she consume?

   c. Suppose the price of a slice of pizza rises to $3, while the price of a can of soda and Bertha's budget does not change. Now how many cans of soda and slices of pizza will she consume?

   d. What are two points on Bertha's demand curve for slices of pizza? Assuming her demand curve is a straight line, in Figure 11.3 label the axes and then draw her demand curve.

■ **FIGURE 11.3**

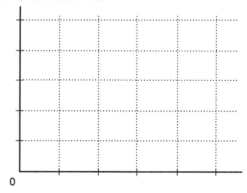

**Long Response Questions**

1. Lisa eats tacos and hamburgers. The quantities and marginal utilities from each are in the table below. Lisa's budget is $8.

   a. If the price of taco is $1 and the price of a hamburger is $2, what quantity of tacos and hamburgers will Lisa purchase?

   b. If the price of a taco rises to $2 while neither Lisa's income nor the price of a hamburger change, what quantity of tacos and hamburgers will Lisa purchase?

   c. How does Lisa respond to a change in the price of a taco?

   d. What is the slope of Lisa's demand curve and what role does diminishing marginal utility play?

| Quantity (tacos per week) | Marginal utility | Quantity (hamburgers per week) | Marginal utility |
|---|---|---|---|
| 0 | 0 | 0 | 0 |
| 1 | 50 | 1 | 80 |
| 2 | 40 | 2 | 40 |
| 3 | 30 | 3 | 20 |
| 4 | 20 | 4 | 10 |
| 5 | 10 | 5 | 5 |

2. What does it mean to "allocate the entire available budget?" How does saving fit into the picture?

3. What is marginal analysis? Why is making the marginal utility per dollar necessary for a consumer to maximize his or her utility?

4. How do the income and substitution effects of a price change lead to the negative slope of a demand curve?

## CHECKPOINT 11.3

■ **Use marginal utility theory to explain the paradox of value: Why water is vital but cheap while diamonds are relatively useless but expensive.**

**Quick Review**

• *The paradox of value* Why is water, which is essential to life, cheap, but diamonds, which are useless compared to water, expensive?

### Additional Practice Problem 11.3

1. Anthony buys 30,000 gallons of water a month. His marginal utility from a gallon of water is 100 units. The price of a gallon of water is $0.001. Anthony also buys 4 boxes of Krispy Kreme doughnuts a month. He pays $5 for a box. Anthony is maximizing his utility.

    a. What is the marginal utility from a box of Krispy Kreme doughnuts?

    b. Why does Anthony receive a lower marginal utility from his consumption of water?

### Solution to Additional Practice Problem 11.3

1a. Because Anthony is maximizing his utility, the marginal utility per dollar he spends on water equals the marginal utility per dollar he spends on doughnuts. The marginal utility per dollar for water equals 100 units ÷ $0.001 = 100,000. So the marginal utility of a box of doughnuts divided by the price of a box of doughnuts ($5) must equal 100,000. In terms of a formula, $MU ÷ 5 = 100,000$, so the marginal utility of a box of doughnuts equals $5 \times 100,000$, which is 500,000.

1b. Anthony buys 30,000 gallons of water a month and (only) 4 boxes of doughnuts a month. As the quantity of a good consumed increases, the marginal utility decreases. Because Anthony is consuming much more water than doughnuts, his total utility from water is almost surely greater than his total utility from doughnuts, but his marginal utility from water is much less than his marginal utility from doughnuts.

### ■ Self Test 11.3

**True or false**

1. Susan's demand curve for curry shows the quantity of curry she demands at each price when her total utility is maximized.

2. Marginal benefit is the maximum price a consumer is willing to pay for an extra unit of a good or service when total utility is maximized.

3. The paradox of value is solved by noting that the total utility from water is small while the marginal utility from water is large.

4. The consumer surplus from water is greater than the consumer surplus from diamonds.

**Multiple choice**

1. At all points on a demand curve, the

    i. consumer's budget has been allocated to maximize total utility.

    ii. quantity describes the quantity demanded at each price when total utility is maximized.

    iii. price represents the marginal benefit the consumer gets from an extra unit of a good.

    a. i only.

    b. ii only.

    c. i and ii.

    d. i and iii.

    e. i, ii, and iii.

2. As more of a good is consumed, the marginal utility of an additional unit \_\_\_\_, so consumers are willing to pay \_\_\_\_ for an additional unit.

    a. decreases; less

    b. increases; less

    c. decreases; more

    d. increases; more

    e. does not change; less

3. The paradox of value refers to the

    a. utility maximizing rule.

    b. fact that water is vital but cheap while diamonds are relatively useless but expensive.

    c. fact that consumers have different preferences and utility schedules.

    d. law of demand.

    e. issue of why the consumer surplus from water equals the consumer surplus from diamonds.

## Short Response Questions

**■ FIGURE 11.4**

Price (dollars per thousand gallons)

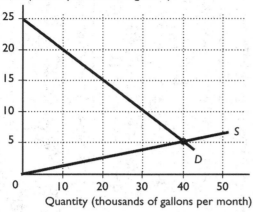

Quantity (thousands of gallons per month)

1. Figure 11.4 shows the market for water. What is the equilibrium quantity? Indicate the equilibrium price and shade in the area of the consumer surplus. What is the amount of the consumer surplus?

**■ FIGURE 11.5**

Price (thousands of dollars per carat)

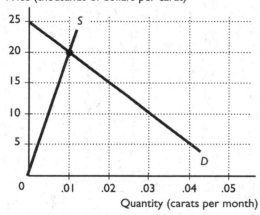

Quantity (carats per month)

2. Figure 11.5 shows the market for rubies. What is the equilibrium quantity? Indicate the equilibrium price and shade in the area of the consumer surplus. What is the amount of the consumer surplus?

3. Based on Figures 11.4 and 11.5, is there more consumer surplus for water or rubies? Which is larger: the marginal utility of a gallon of water or a carat of rubies?

## Long Response Questions

1. Bobby consumes potato chips and Gatorade and is maximizing his utility. His marginal utility from the last bag of chips he eats is 40 and his marginal utility from the last bottle of Gatorade he drinks is 60. The price of a bag of chips is $2. What must be the price of a bottle of Gatorade?

2. What is the paradox of value and what is its solution?

## YOUR AP SELF TEST ANSWERS

### ■ CHECKPOINT 11.1

**True or false**

1. True;  page 266
2. True;  page 267
3. True;  page 269

**Multiple choice**

1. d;  page 266
2. b;  page 266
3. c;  page 267
4. d;  page 269
5. c;  page 268
6. c;  page 270

**Short Response Questions**

#### ■ FIGURE 11.6

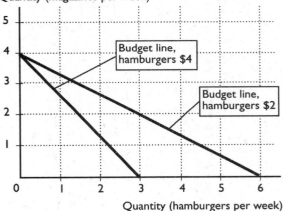

Quantity (magazines per week)

Budget line, hamburgers $4

Budget line, hamburgers $2

Quantity (hamburgers per week)

1. a. The budget line in Figure 11.6 labeled "hamburgers $4" is Jack's budget line; page 266.
   b. The slope of the budget line equals (–4 magazines/3 hamburgers), which is –1 1/3 of a magazine per hamburger. The slope is the opportunity cost of a hamburger, which is the relative price of a hamburger; page 269.
   c. Jack can buy 2 magazines and 1 hamburger. Jack cannot buy 2 magazines and 3 hamburgers because that combination is outside his budget line;  page 266.

d. The new budget line is in Figure 11.6, labeled "Hamburgers $2";  page 266.

e. The slope of the new budget line is –2/3 of a magazine per hamburger. Compared to the slope in part (b), the opportunity cost of a hamburger is lower when its price falls;  page 270.

**Long Response Questions**

1. A budget line is similar to the production possibilities frontier. Both curves show a limit to what is feasible. The *PPF* is a technological limit that does not depend on prices. But the budget line does depend on prices. Consumption possibilities change when prices or the available budget change;  page 266.

2. The slope of the budget line equals the opportunity cost and the relative price of the good measured along the *x*-axis;  page 269.

3. The relative price is the price of one good in terms of another good. The relative price is an opportunity cost. It equals the price of one good divided by the price of another good;  page 270.

### ■ CHECKPOINT 11.2

**True or false**

1. False;  page 273
2. False;  page 276
3. True;  page 277
4. False;  page 279

**Multiple choice**

1. a;  page 273
2. e;  page 273
3. d;  page 273
4. b;  page 277
5. d;  page 277
6. b;  page 277
7. c;  page 277
8. a;  page 279
9. a;  page 280

## Short Response Questions

| Quantity (bottles of Aquafina per day) | Total utility | Marginal utility |
|---|---|---|
| 0 | 0 | |
| 1 | 25 | 25 |
| 2 | 45 | 20 |
| 3 | 60 | 15 |
| 4 | 70 | 10 |
| 5 | 75 | 5 |
| 6 | 76 | 1 |

1. The completed table is above; page 273.

| | Pizza | | | Soda | |
|---|---|---|---|---|---|
| Quantity (slices per day) | Total utility, pizza | Marginal utility, pizza | Quantity (cans per day) | Total utility, soda | Marginal utility, soda |
| 0 | 0 | | 0 | 0 | |
| 1 | 45 | 45 | 1 | 25 | 25 |
| 2 | 85 | 40 | 2 | 45 | 20 |
| 3 | 120 | 35 | 3 | 60 | 15 |
| 4 | 150 | 30 | 4 | 70 | 10 |
| 5 | 175 | 25 | 5 | 75 | 5 |
| 6 | 195 | 20 | 6 | 76 | 1 |

2. a. The completed table is above; page 273.
   b. Bertha will consume 2 cans of soda and 2 slices of pizza. This combination allocates all her budget and equalizes the marginal utility per dollar for soda and pizza at 20; page 276.
   c. Bertha will now consume 3 cans of soda and 1 slice of pizza. This combination allocates all of her budget and equalizes the marginal utility per dollar for soda and pizza at 15; page 276.
   d. One point on her demand curve is $2 and 2 slices of pizza; another point is $3 and 1 slice of pizza. Figure 11.7 shows Bertha's demand curve; page 279.

## Long Response Questions

1. a. Lisa will buy 4 tacos and 2 hamburgers because this combination allocates her entire budget and sets the marginal utility per dollar of tacos equal to the marginal utility per dollar of hamburgers; page 278.
   b. Lisa will buy 2 tacos and 2 hamburgers because this combination allocates all her

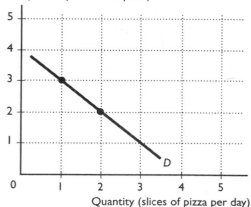

■ **FIGURE 11.7**
Price (dollars per slice of pizza)

Quantity (slices of pizza per day)

budget and equalizes the marginal utility per dollar for tacos and hamburgers at 20; page 278.
   c. When the price of a taco rises, the quantity of tacos demanded decreases; page 279.
   d. Lisa's demand curve will be downward sloping—when the price of a taco rises, the quantity of tacos demanded decreases. The principle of diminishing marginal utility plays a key role in this result. When the price of a taco rises, the marginal utility per dollar for a taco is less than that for a hamburger. In order to restore her consumer equilibrium, Lisa must increase the marginal utility per dollar for a taco. She does so by decreasing the quantity of tacos she consumes, which, according to the principle of diminishing marginal utility, increases the marginal utility of a taco and thereby increase the marginal utility per dollar for a taco; pages 273-280.

2. To "allocate the entire available budget" means that we use the entire available budget. Using the entire budget doesn't mean not saving anything. The available budget is the amount available after choosing how much to save; page 276.

3. Marginal analysis compares the marginal gain from having more of one good with the marginal loss from having less of another good. The "equalize the marginal utility per

dollar" rule is the result of marginal analysis. Suppose the marginal utility per dollar for a blouse exceeds that of a dollar for a purse. Marginal analysis indicates that the consumer can increase her total utility by spending a dollar less on purses and spending a dollar more on blouses because the gain in utility from the dollar spent on blouses exceeds the loss in utility from the dollar reduction on purses; page 280.

4. The income effect refers to the impact a price change has on consumers' real incomes, that is, on their purchasing power. If the price of a good falls, consumers are able to buy more of that good and/or more of other goods. In this case, consumers' real incomes have increased and so they wind up buying more normal goods. Hence a fall in the price of a normal good increases the quantity consumers purchase. The substitution effect refers to a change in the relative price of a good. If the price of a good falls, its relative price, that is, its price compared to the prices of other goods, falls. As a result, consumers increase their purchases of this good in place of other goods. By substituting more of the relatively cheaper good for other goods, consumers increase the quantity they purchase. Both the income and substitution effects lead to an increase in the quantity demanded of a good when its price falls, which means that the good's demand curve is downward sloping.

## ■ CHECKPOINT 11.3

**True or false**

1. True; page 282
2. True; page 282
3. False; page 282
4. True; page 282

**Multiple choice**

1. e; page 282
2. a; page 282
3. b; page 282

**Short Response Questions**

### ■ FIGURE 11.8

Price (dollars per thousand gallons)

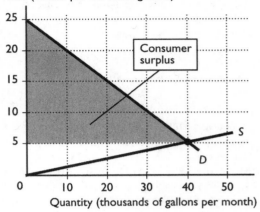

1. The equilibrium quantity is 40,000 gallons per month. The equilibrium price is $5 per thousand gallons of water. The consumer surplus is the gray triangle in Figure 11.8. The consumer surplus equals ½ × (40,000 gallons − 0 gallons) × ($25 − $5) = $400,000; page 283.

### ■ FIGURE 11.9

Price (thousands of dollars per carat)

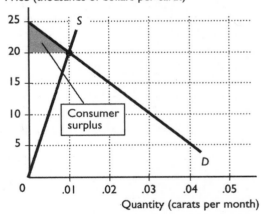

2. The equilibrium quantity is .01 carats per month. The equilibrium price is $20,000 a carat. Figure 11.9 shows the consumer surplus. The consumer surplus equals ½ × (0.01 carats − 0 carats) × ($25,000 − $20,000) = $25; page 283.

3. There is more consumer surplus for water than rubies. Because the price of a carat of rubies is much greater than the price of a gallon of water, it must be the case that the marginal utility of a carat of rubies is much greater than the marginal utility of a gallon of water; page 283.

## Long Response Questions

1. Bobby maximizes his total utility by consuming the combination of chips and Gatorade such that the marginal utility per dollar for chips equals the marginal utility per dollar for Gatorade. The marginal utility from the last bag of chips is 40 and the price of a bag of chips is $2, so the marginal utility per dollar is 40 ÷ $2 = 20. Because the marginal utility of the Gatorade is 60, the price is $3 to make the marginal utility per dollar equal to 20; page 282.

2. The paradox of value is that water, which is essential for life, is cheap while diamonds are relatively useless but expensive. The solution to the paradox is that people consume a lot of water, so the marginal utility of an additional gallon of water is very low. People consume only a few diamonds, so the marginal utility of an additional diamond is quite high. A household maximizes its total when the marginal utility per dollar is equal for all goods. So water has a low marginal utility and a low price and diamonds have a high marginal utility and a high price; page 282.

# Chapter

# Production and Cost

# 12

## CHAPTER IN PERSPECTIVE

In Chapter 12 we study how a firm's costs are determined and how these costs vary as the firm varies its output.

### ■ Explain how economists measure a firm's cost of production and profit.

The firm's goal is to maximize its profit. The highest-valued alternative forgone is the opportunity cost of a firm's production. A cost paid in money is an explicit cost. A firm incurs an implicit cost when it uses a factor of production but does not make a direct money payment for its use. The return to entrepreneurship is normal profit and is part of the firm's costs because it compensates the entrepreneur for not running another business. A firm's economic profit equals total revenue minus total cost, which is the sum of explicit costs and implicit costs and is the opportunity cost of production.

### ■ Explain the relationship between a firm's output and labor employed in the short run.

The short run is the time frame in which the quantities of some resources are fixed; the long run is the time frame in which the quantities of all resources can be varied. Marginal product is the change in total product that results from a one-unit increase in the quantity of labor employed. As firms hire labor, initially increasing marginal returns occur but eventually decreasing marginal returns set in. Average product is total product divided by the quantity of an input. When marginal product exceeds the average product, the average product curve slopes upward and average product increases as more labor is employed. And when marginal product is less than average product, the average product curve slopes downward and average product decreases as more labor is employed.

### ■ Explain the relationship between a firm's output and costs in the short run.

Total cost is the sum of total fixed cost and total variable cost. Marginal cost is the change in total cost that results from a one-unit increase in total product. Average total cost is the sum of average fixed cost and average variable cost. The U-shape of the average total cost curve arises from the influence of two opposing forces: spreading total fixed cost over a larger output and decreasing marginal returns. The marginal cost curve intersects the average variable cost and average total cost curves at their minimum points. The average cost curve and the marginal cost curve shift when technology changes or when the price of a factor of production changes.

### ■ Derive and explain a firm's long-run average cost curve.

In the long run, all costs are variable. When a firm changes its plant size, it might experience economies of scale, diseconomies of scale, or constant returns to scale. The long-run average cost curve is a curve that shows the lowest average cost at which it is possible to produce each output when the firm has had sufficient time to change both its plant size and labor employed. The long-run average cost curve slopes downward with economies of scale and upward with diseconomies of scale.

## EXPANDED CHAPTER CHECKLIST

**When you have completed this chapter, you will be able to:**

### 1 Explain how economists measure a firm's cost of production and profit.

- Explain the firm's goal.
- Compare the economic view and the accounting view of cost and profit.
- Define and give examples of explicit cost and implicit cost.
- Define normal profit and explain why it is part of a firm's opportunity costs.
- Define economic profit.

### 2 Explain the relationship between a firm's output and labor employed in the short run.

- Define the short run and the long run.
- Define total product and draw a total product curve.
- Define and calculate marginal product.
- Explain why increasing marginal returns and decreasing marginal returns occur.
- Define and calculate average product.
- Use a graph to explain the relationship between marginal product and average product.

### 3 Explain the relationship between a firm's output and costs in the short run.

- Define total cost, total fixed cost, and total variable cost, and illustrate the total cost curves.
- Define and calculate marginal cost.
- Define average total cost, average variable cost, and average fixed cost, and illustrate the average cost curves and the marginal cost curve.
- Explain why the average total cost curve is U-shaped.

### 4 Derive and explain a firm's long-run average cost curve.

- Define economies of scale, diseconomies of scale, and constant returns to scale.
- Explain how the long-run average cost curve is constructed and use it to illustrate economies and diseconomies of scale.

## YOUR AP TEST HINTS

### AP Topics

| Topic on your AP test | Corresponding textbook section |
|---|---|
| **Nature and function of product markets** | |
| Production and Costs | Chapter 12 |
| • Accounting versus economic profit | Checkpoint 12.1 |
| • Normal profit | Checkpoint 12.1 |
| • Marginal product and diminishing returns | Checkpoint 12.2 |
| • Short run costs | Checkpoint 12.3 |
| • Long run costs and economies of scale | Checkpoint 12.4 |

### AP Vocabulary

- Normal profit can be defined as a payment made to the entrepreneur to retain his or her services in the business; it is the minimum income that the entrepreneur accepts to stay in the business.
- Marginal cost rather than total cost is most often used in the graphical analysis of a firm's decisions.

### Extra AP material

- Accounting profit is the total revenue minus the explicit costs while economic profit is the total revenue minus the explicit and implicit costs (including the normal profit).

## CHECKPOINT 12.1

■ **Explain how economists measure a firm's cost of production and profit.**

### Quick Review

- *Explicit cost* A cost paid in money.
- *Implicit cost* A cost incurred by using a factor of production but for which no direct money payment is made.
- *Economic profit* Total revenue minus total opportunity cost.

### Additional Practice Problem 12.1

1. Gary manufactures toy gliders made of balsa wood. Each week, Gary pays $200 in wages, buys balsa wood for $400, pays $50 to lease saws and sanders, and pays $150 in rent for the workspace. To fund his operations, Gary withdrew his life's savings, $162,500, from his savings account at the bank, which paid interest of $250 a week. The normal profit for a glider company is $250 a week. Gary sells $1,500 worth of gliders a week.
   a. How much are the weekly explicit costs?
   b. How much are the weekly implicit costs?
   c. What does an accountant compute for the weekly (accounting) profit?
   d. What does an economist compute for the weekly economic profit?

### Solution to Additional Practice Problem 12.1

1a. The explicit costs are the wages, the balsa wood, the leased saws and sanders, and rent. The weekly explicit costs are $200 + $400 + $50 + $150, which equals $800.

1b. The implicit costs are the forgone interest and the normal profit. The weekly implicit costs are $250 + $250, which equals $500.

1c. Accountants calculate profit as total revenue minus explicit costs, which is $1,500 − $800 = $700.

1d. Economic profit is total revenue minus total cost. Total cost is the sum of explicit and implicit costs. So Gary's total cost is $800 + $500, which is $1,300. Gary's economic profit equals $1,500 − $1,300, which is $200.

## ■ AP Self Test 12.1

### True or false

1. The firm's goal is to maximize profit.
2. An accountant measures profit as total revenue minus opportunity cost.
3. All of a firm's costs must be paid in money.
4. If a firm earns an economic profit, the return to the entrepreneur exceeds normal profit.

### Multiple choice

1. The paramount goal of a firm is to
   a. maximize profit.
   b. maximize sales.
   c. maximize total revenue.
   d. minimize its costs.
   e. force its competitors into bankruptcy.

2. For a business, opportunity cost measures
   a. only the cost of labor and materials.
   b. only the implicit costs of the business.
   c. the cost of all the factors of production the firm employs.
   d. only the explicit costs the firm must pay.
   e. all of the firm's costs including its normal profit *and* its economic profit.

3. Costs paid in money to hire a resource is
   a. normal profit.
   b. an implicit cost.
   c. an explicit cost.
   d. an alternative-use cost.
   e. economic profit.

4. Which of the following is an example of an implicit cost?
   a. wages paid to employees
   b. interest paid to a bank on a building loan
   c. the cost of using capital an owner donates to the business
   d. dollars paid to a supplier for materials used in production
   e. liability insurance payments made only once a year

5. The opportunity cost of a firm using its own capital is
   a. economic depreciation.
   b. standard ownership depreciation.
   c. economic loss.
   d. normal loss.
   e. capital loss.

6. The difference between a firm's total revenue and its total cost is its ____ profit.
   a. explicit
   b. normal
   c. economic
   d. accounting
   e. excess

**Short Response Questions**

1. What is likely to happen to a firm that does not maximize profit?

2. What is an implicit cost? An explicit cost? What is a firm's economic profit?

3. Why are wages a cost to a business? Why is a normal profit a cost to a business?

**Long Response Question**

1. Bobby quits his job as a veterinarian to open a model train store. Bobby made $80,000 a year as a veterinarian. The first year his train store is open, Bobby pays a helper $26,000. He also pays $24,000 in rent, $10,000 in utilities, and buys $200,000 of model trains. Bobby had a good year because he sold all of his model trains for $300,000. The normal profit from a train store is $30,000.
   a. What would an accountant calculate as Bobby's profit?
   b. What is Bobby's total opportunity cost? What is his economic profit?

## CHECKPOINT 12.2

■ **Explain the relationship between a firm's output and labor employed in the short run.**

**Quick Review**

• *Marginal product* The change in total product that results from a one-unit increase in the quantity of labor employed.

• *Formula for the marginal product* The marginal product equals:

Change in total product ÷ change in quantity of labor

**Additional Practice Problems 12.2**

1. Bobby runs a cat grooming service. Bobby hires students to groom the cats. The table to the right shows how many cats Bobby's service can groom when Bobby changes the number of students he hires.

| Labor (students per day) | Total product (cats groomed per day) |
|---|---|
| 0 | 0 |
| 1 | 5 |
| 2 | 12 |
| 3 | 18 |
| 4 | 22 |
| 5 | 25 |

| Labor (students per day) | Average product (cats groomed per day) | Marginal product (cats groomed per day) |
|---|---|---|
| 1 | ____ | ____ |
| 2 | ____ | ____ |
| 3 | ____ | ____ |
| 4 | ____ | ____ |
| 5 | ____ | ____ |

a. Complete the table above.

b. Draw Bobby's average product curve and his marginal product curve. When does the marginal product equals the average product?

2. The first five members of the men's basketball squad are each 6 feet tall. A sixth player, whose height is 7 feet, is added. Has the average height increased or decreased with the addition of this player? A seventh player, whose height is 5 feet, is added. What happens to the team's average height? An eighth player, whose height is 6 feet, is added. What is the effect on the average height? What is the general rule about how the marginal player's height changes the average height of the team?

### Solutions to Additional Practice Problems 12.2

| Labor (students per day) | Average product (cats groomed per day) | Marginal product (cats groomed per day) |
|---|---|---|
| 1 | 5.0 | |
| | | 5.0 |
| 2 | 6.0 | |
| | | 7.0 |
| 3 | 6.0 | |
| | | 6.0 |
| 4 | 5.5 | |
| | | 4.0 |
| 5 | 5.0 | |
| | | 3.0 |

1a. The completed table is above. The average product equals: total product ÷ total labor and the marginal product equals: change in total product ÷ change in quantity of labor.

1b. The figure is to the right. The marginal product equals the average product when the average product is at its maximum. Both equal 6 cats groomed per day.

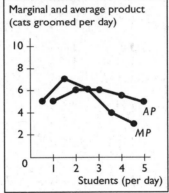

2. The 7-foot player is above the average height, so adding him to the team increases the average height. The 5-foot player is below the average height, so adding him decreases the average height. When the 6-foot player is added, the team's average height equals 6 feet, so his addition has no effect on the average height. The general rule is that when a marginal value lies above the average, the average rises. When the marginal value is below the average, the average falls. And when the marginal value equals the average, the average does not change.

### ■ AP Self Test 12.2

**True or false**

1. In the short run, the firm's fixed inputs cannot be changed.

2. Points on and below the total product curve are efficient.

3. Most production processes initially have decreasing marginal returns followed eventually by increasing marginal returns.

4. When the marginal product of labor exceeds the average product of labor, the average product curve is downward sloping.

**Multiple choice**

1. The short run is a time period during which
   a. some of the firm's resources are fixed.
   b. all of the firm's resources are fixed.
   c. all of the firm's resources are variable.
   d. the fixed cost equals zero.
   e. the firm cannot increase its output.

2. In the short run, firms can increase output by
   a. only increasing the size of their plant.
   b. only decreasing the size of their plant.
   c. only increasing the amount of labor used.
   d. only decreasing the amount of labor used.
   e. either increasing the amount of labor used or increasing the size of their plant.

3. Which of the following is correct?
   a. The short run for a firm can be longer than the long run for the same firm.
   b. The short run is the same for all firms.
   c. The long run is the time frame in which the quantities of all resources can be varied.
   d. The long run is the time frame in which all resources are fixed.
   e. The long run does not exist for some firms.

4. Marginal product equals
   a. the total product produced by a certain amount of labor.
   b. the change in total product that results from a one-unit increase in the quantity of labor employed.
   c. total product divided by the total quantity of labor.
   d. the amount of labor needed to produce an increase in production.
   e. total product minus the quantity of labor.

5. If 5 workers can wash 30 cars a day and 6 workers can wash 33 cars a day, then the marginal product of the 6th worker equals
   a. 30 cars a day.
   b. 33 cars a day.
   c. 5 cars a day.
   d. 5.5 cars a day.
   e. 3 cars a day.

6. Increasing marginal returns occur when the
   a. average product of an additional worker is less than the average product of the previous worker.
   b. marginal product of an additional worker exceeds the marginal product of the previous worker.
   c. marginal product of labor is less than the average product of labor.
   d. total output of the firm is at its maximum.
   e. total product curve is horizontal.

7. If 25 workers can pick 100 flats of strawberries an hour, then average product is
   a. 100 flats an hour.
   b. 125 flats an hour.
   c. 75 flats an hour.
   d. 4 flats an hour.
   e. More information is needed about how many flats 24 workers can pick.

**Short Response Questions**

| Quantity of labor (workers) | Total product (turkeys per day) | Average product (turkeys per worker) | Marginal product (turkeys per worker) |
|---|---|---|---|
| 0 | 0 | xx | |
| | | | 100 |
| 1 | 100 | 100 | |
| | | | ___ |
| 2 | 300 | ___ | |
| | | | ___ |
| 3 | 450 | ___ | |
| | | | 30 |
| 4 | ___ | ___ | |
| | | | ___ |
| 5 | ___ | 100 | |

1. The table gives the total product schedule at Al's Turkey Town Farm.
   a. Complete this table. (The marginal product is entered midway between rows to emphasize that it is the result of changing inputs, that is, moving from one row to the next.)

■ **FIGURE 12.1**

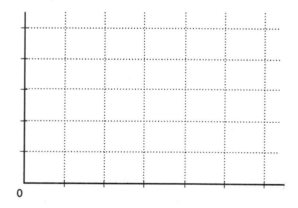

   b. In Figure 12.1 label the axes and plot the marginal product (*MP*) and average product (*AP*) curves. (Plot the *MP* curve midway between the quantities of labor.) Where do the two curves intersect?
   c. When the *MP* curve is above the *AP* curve, is the *AP* curve rising or falling? When the *MP* curve is below the *AP* curve, is the *AP* curve rising or falling?

2. If the marginal product of a new worker exceeds the average product, what happens to the average product?

**Long Response Questions**

1. What is the difference between the short run and the long run?

2. Pizza Hut opens a new store nearby. As the owner adds workers, what happens to their marginal product? Why?

3. What is the law of decreasing returns?

| Labor | Output | TC | MC | TC | MC |
|-------|--------|----|----|----|----|
| 0 | 0 | ___ | | ___ | |
| | | | ___ | | ___ |
| I | I | ___ | | ___ | |
| | | | ___ | | ___ |
| 2 | 5 | ___ | | ___ | |
| | | | ___ | | ___ |
| 3 | 9 | ___ | | ___ | |
| | | | ___ | | ___ |
| 4 | 12 | ___ | | ___ | |
| | | | ___ | | ___ |
| 5 | 14 | ___ | | ___ | |
| | | | ___ | | ___ |
| 6 | 15 | ___ | | ___ | |

## CHECKPOINT 12.3

■ **Explain the relationship between a firm's output and costs in the short run.**

*Quick Review*

- *Total cost* The cost of all the factors of production used by a firm. Total cost equals the sum of total fixed cost and total variable cost.
- *Marginal cost* The cost that arises from a one-unit increase in output.
- *Average total cost* Total variable cost per unit of output, which equals total variable cost divided by output.
- *Average total cost* Total cost per unit of output, which equals average fixed cost plus average variable cost as well as total cost divided by output.

**Additional Practice Problems 12.3**

1. Pearl owns a company that produces pools. Pearl has total fixed cost of $2,000 a month and pays each of her workers $2,500 a month. The table in the next column shows the number of pools Pearl's company can produce in a month.

   a. Complete the left side of the table.
   b. Suppose that the wage Pearl pays her workers increases to $3,000 a month. Complete the right side of the table.
   c. What was the effect of the wage hike on Pearl's marginal cost?

2. In the figure to the right is an *ATC* curve. In this figure sketch an *AVC* curve and a *MC* curve. Tell what relationships these curves must obey so that they are drawn correctly.

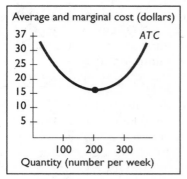

Average and marginal cost (dollars)

**Solutions to Additional Practice Problems 12.3**

| Labor | Output | TC | MC | TC | MC |
|-------|--------|--------|-------|--------|-------|
| 0 | 0 | 2,000 | | 2,000 | |
| | | | 2,500 | | 3,000 |
| I | I | 4,500 | | 5,000 | |
| | | | 625 | | 750 |
| 2 | 5 | 7,000 | | 8,000 | |
| | | | 625 | | 750 |
| 3 | 9 | 9,500 | | 11,000 | |
| | | | 833 | | 1,000 |
| 4 | 12 | 12,000 | | 14,000 | |
| | | | 1,250 | | 1,500 |
| 5 | 14 | 14,500 | | 17,000 | |
| | | | 2,500 | | 3,000 |
| 6 | 15 | 17,000 | | 20,000 | |

1a. The completed table is above. Total cost, *TC*, equals the sum of total fixed cost and total variable cost. For example, when Pearl hires 6 workers, total cost is ($2,000) + (6 × $2,500), which is $17,000. Marginal cost equals the change in the total cost divided by the change in output. For example, when output increases from 14 to 15 pools, marginal cost is ($17,000 − $14,500) ÷ (15 − 14), which is $2,500.

1b. The completed table is above.

1c. The increase in the wage rate increased Pearl's marginal cost at every level of output.

2. The completed figure is to the right. To be drawn correctly, there are three requirements: First, the *AVC* curve must reach its minimum at a lower level of output than does the *ATC* curve. Second, the vertical distance between the *ATC* and *AVC* curves must decrease as output increases. Finally the *MC* curve must go through the minimum points on both the *AVC* and *ATC* curves.

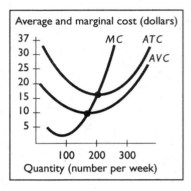

Average and marginal cost (dollars)

## ■ AP Self Test 12.3

### True or false

1. In the short run, total fixed cost does not change when the firm changes its output.

2. Marginal cost is always less than average total cost.

3. The average total cost curve is U-shaped.

4. An increase in the wage rate shifts the marginal cost curve upward.

### Multiple choice

1. Total cost is equal to the sum of
   a. total revenue and total cost.
   b. total variable cost and total product.
   c. total variable cost and total fixed cost.
   d. total fixed cost and total product.
   e. the marginal cost plus the total fixed cost plus the total variable cost.

2. Total fixed cost is the cost of
   a. labor.
   b. production.
   c. a firm's fixed factors of production.
   d. only implicit factors of production.
   e. only explicit factors of production.

3. Jay set up his hot dog stand near the business district. His total variable cost includes the
   a. annual insurance for the hot dog stand.
   b. cost of buying the hot dog stand.
   c. cost of the hot dogs and condiments.
   d. interest he pays on the funds he borrowed to pay for advertising.
   e. revenue he gets when he sells his first hot dog each day.

4. Marginal cost is equal to
   a. the total cost of a firm's production.
   b. the difference between total cost and fixed cost.
   c. a cost that is not related to the quantity produced.
   d. the change in total cost that results from a one-unit increase in output.
   e. the change in fixed cost that results from a one-unit increase in output.

5. To produce 10 shirts, the total cost is $80; to produce 11 shirts, the total cost is $99. The marginal cost of the 11th shirt is equal to
   a. $8.
   b. $9.
   c. $80.
   d. $99.
   e. $19.

6. Average total cost equals
   a. marginal cost divided by output.
   b. average fixed cost plus average variable cost.
   c. total fixed cost plus total variable cost.
   d. marginal cost plus opportunity cost.
   e. marginal cost multiplied by the quantity of output.

7. To produce 10 shirts, the total cost is $80; to produce 11 shirts, the total cost is $99. The average total cost of the 11th shirt is equal to
   a. $8.
   b. $9.
   c. $80.
   d. $99.
   e. $19.

8. One of the major reasons for the U-shaped average total cost curve is the fact that
   a. there are increasing returns from labor regardless of the number of workers employed.
   b. there eventually are decreasing returns from labor as more workers are employed.
   c. prices fall as output increases.
   d. the average fixed cost increases as more output is produced.
   e. the variable cost decreases as more output is produced.

## Short Response Questions

| Labor | Output | TC | ATC | MC |
|-------|--------|-----|-----|-----|
| 0 | 0 | ___ | xx | |
| 1 | 10 | ___ | ___ | ___ |
| 2 | 25 | ___ | ___ | ___ |
| 3 | 35 | ___ | ___ | ___ |
| 4 | 40 | ___ | ___ | ___ |
| 5 | 43 | ___ | ___ | ___ |
| 6 | 45 | ___ | ___ | ___ |

1. Sue hires workers to produce subs at Sue's Super Supper Sub Shop. Sue pays her workers $10 an hour and has fixed costs of $30 an hour. The table shows Sue's total product schedule.
   a. Complete the table.
   b. Plot Sue's *ATC* and *MC* curves in figure 12.2. (Plot the *MC*s midway between the quantities

■ **FIGURE 12.2**

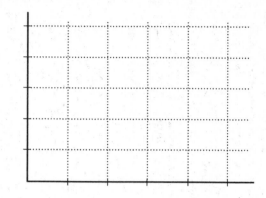

| Labor | Output | TC | ATC | MC |
|-------|--------|-----|-----|-----|
| 0 | 0 | ___ | xx | |
| 1 | 10 | ___ | ___ | ___ |
| 2 | 25 | ___ | ___ | ___ |
| 3 | 35 | ___ | ___ | ___ |
| 4 | 40 | ___ | ___ | ___ |
| 5 | 43 | ___ | ___ | ___ |
| 6 | 45 | ___ | ___ | ___ |

   c. Sue's rent increases so her fixed cost rises to $75 an hour. Complete the table above and then plot Sue's new *ATC* and *MC* curves in Figure 12.2.
   d. How does the increase in fixed cost change Sue's average total cost curve? Her marginal cost curve?

2. Discuss the statement "Average fixed cost initially decreases as output increases but then eventually increases as output increases."

3. Is marginal cost equal to the difference between the total cost and the total variable cost?

■ **FIGURE 12.3**

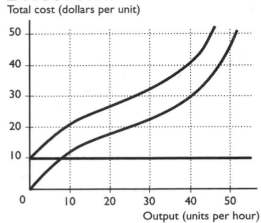

4. Label the cost curves in Figure 12.3.
5. What two factors shift the cost curves?

### Short answer and numeric questions

1. If a firm closes and produces nothing, does it still have any costs?
2. What is the difference between marginal cost and average total cost?
3. Why is the average total cost curve U-shaped?
4. Where does the marginal cost curve intersect the average variable cost and average total cost curves?

## CHECKPOINT 12.4

### ■ Derive and explain a firm's long-run average cost curve.

**Quick Review**

- *Long-run average cost curve* The long-run average cost curve shows the lowest average cost at which it is possible to produce each output when the firm has had sufficient time to adjust its labor force and its plant.

**Additional Practice Problems 12.4**

1. The figure shows three average total cost curves for A1 Sewing, a company that sells sewing machines. The company can use three different sized stores, which account for the different cost curves.

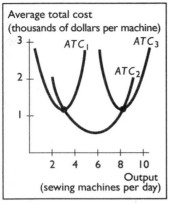

a. Which average cost curve occurs when A-1 uses the smallest store? The largest store?
b. Indicate A1's long-run average cost curve, *LRAC* in the figure.
c. If A1 plans to sell 6 sewing machines per day, what sized store will A1 use?
d. Over what range of output does A1 Sewing have economies of scale? Diseconomies of scale?

2. Describe economies of scale and diseconomies of scale along a long-run average total cost curve.

**Solutions to Additional Practice Problems 12.4**

1a. When A1 uses the smallest store, its plant size is the smallest and so its average total cost curve is *ATC*₁ in the figure. When A1 uses the largest store, its plant size is the largest and so its average total cost curve is *ATC*₃ in the figure.

1b. The long-run average cost curve is the curve that shows the lowest average total cost to produce each output. In the figure to the right, the *LRAC* curve is the darkened parts

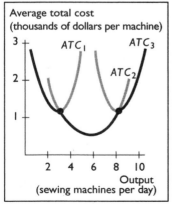

of the three average total cost curves.

1c. If A1 plans to sell 6 sewing machines, it will use the middle sized store because that is the store that gives it the lowest average total cost when selling 6 sewing machines a day.

1d. A1 has economies of scale when selling from 0 to 6 sewing machines per day. It has diseconomies of scale when it sells more than 6 sewing machines per day.

2. When economies of scale are present, the *LRAC* curve slopes downward. When the *LRAC* curve is horizontal, constant returns to scale are present. And when the *LRAC* curve slopes upward, diseconomies of scale are present.

## ■ AP Self Test 12.4

**True or false**

1. All costs are fixed in the long run.

2. When a firm increases its plant size and labor, greater specialization of capital and labor can lead to economies of scale.

3. Constant returns to scale occur when the firm increases its plant size and labor employed by the same percentage and output increases by the same percentage.

4. The long-run average cost curve is derived from the marginal cost curves for different possible plant sizes.

**Multiple choice**

1. Economies of scale occur whenever
   a. marginal cost decreases as production increases.
   b. total cost increases as production is increased by increasing all inputs by the same percentage.
   c. marginal product increases as labor increases and capital decreases.
   d. a firm increases its plant size and labor employed, and its output increases by a larger percentage.
   e. marginal product decreases as labor increases and capital increases.

2. The main source of economies of scale is
   a. better management.
   b. constant returns to plant size.
   c. specialization.
   d. long-run cost curves eventually sloping downward.
   e. increases in the labor force not matched by increases in the plant size.

3. Diseconomies of scale can occur as a result of which of the following?
   a. increasing marginal returns as the firm increases its size
   b. lower total fixed cost as the firm increases its size
   c. management difficulties as the firm increases its size
   d. greater specialization of labor and capital as the firm increases its size
   e. increases in the labor force not matched by increases in the plant

4. Constant returns to scale occur when an equal percentage increase in plant size and labor
   a. increases total cost.
   b. does not change total cost.
   c. increases average total cost.
   d. does not change average total cost.
   e. does not change production.

5. A firm's long-run average cost curve shows the ____ average cost at which it is possible to produce each output when the firm has had ____ time to change both its labor force and its plant.
   a. highest; sufficient
   b. lowest; sufficient
   c. lowest; insufficient
   d. highest insufficient
   e. average; sufficient

6. Economies of scale and diseconomies of scale explain
   a. cost behavior in the short run.
   b. profit maximization in the long run.
   c. the U-shape of the long-run cost curve.
   d. the U-shape of the short-run cost curves.
   e. the U-shape of the marginal cost curves.

■ **FIGURE 12.4**

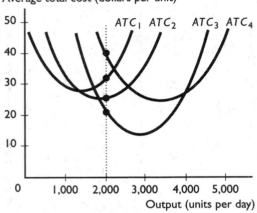

Average total cost (dollars per unit)

7. Figure 12.4 shows four of a firm's *ATC* curves. If the firms produces 2,000 units per day, it will use the plant size that corresponds to
   a. $ATC_1$.
   b. $ATC_2$.
   c. $ATC_3$.
   d. $ATC_4$.
   e. either $ATC_1$ or $ATC_4$.

**Short Response Questions**

■ **FIGURE 12.5**

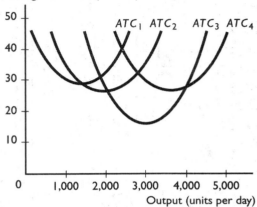

Average total cost (dollars per unit)

1. In Figure 12.5, darken the firm's long-run average total cost curve. Show over which range of output the firm has economies of scale and over which range of output the firm has diseconomies of scale.

**Long Response Questions**

1. Describe how a long-run average cost curve is constructed.

2. What are economies of scale? What leads to economies of scale?

3. What is the difference between "decreasing marginal returns" and "diseconomies of scale"

# YOUR AP SELF TEST ANSWERS

## ■ CHECKPOINT 12.1

### True or false

1. True;  page 296
2. False;  page 296
3. False;  page 297
4. True;  pages 297-298

### Multiple choice

1. a; page 296
2. c; page 296
3. c; page 297
4. c; page 297
5. a; page 297
6. c; page 297

### Short Response Questions

1. A firm that does not seek to maximize profit is either driven out of business or bought by firms that do seek that goal;  page 296.
2. An implicit cost is an opportunity cost incurred by a firm when it uses a factor of production for which it does not make a direct money payment. An explicit cost is a cost paid in money. Economic profit equals the total revenue minus *both* the explicit and the implicit costs.
3. Wages are a (explicit) cost because they are paid to hire a factor of production, labor. A normal profit is a (implicit) cost because it is paid to obtain the use of another factor of production, entrepreneurship;  page 297.

### Long Response Question

1. a. An accountant calculates profit as total revenue minus explicit costs. Bobby's explicit costs are $26,000 + $24,000 + $10,000 + $200,000, which equals $260,000. The accountant calculates profit as $300,000 − $260,000, which is $40,000;  page 296.
   b. Bobby's opportunity cost is the sum of his explicit costs and his implicit costs. Bobby's explicit costs are $260,000. His implicit costs are the sum of his income forgone as a veterinarian, $80,000, and normal profit, $30,000. So Bobby's implicit

costs are $110,000. His total opportunity cost is $260,000 + $110,000, which is $370,000. Bobby's economic profit is his total revenue minus his opportunity cost, which is $300,000 − $370,000 = −$70,000. Bobby incurs an economic loss;  pages 297-298.

## ■ CHECKPOINT 12.2

### True or false

1. True;  page 300
2. False;  page 302
3. False;  page 302
4. False;  page 304

### Multiple choice

1. a; page 300
2. c; page 300
3. c; page 300
4. b; page 302
5. e; page 302
6. b; page 302
7. d; page 304

### Short Response Questions

| Quantity of labor | Total product (turkeys per day) | Average product (turkeys per worker) | Marginal product (turkeys per worker) |
|---|---|---|---|
| 0 | 0 | xx | |
| | | | 100 |
| 1 | 100 | 100 | |
| | | | 200 |
| 2 | 300 | 150 | |
| | | | 150 |
| 3 | 450 | 150 | |
| | | | 30 |
| 4 | 480 | 120 | |
| | | | 20 |
| 5 | 500 | 100 | |

1. a. The completed table is above;  pages 301-304.
   b. Figure 12.6 (on the next page) plots the *MP* and *AP* curves. The curves intersect where the *AP* curve is at its maximum; page 304.

**■ FIGURE 12.6**

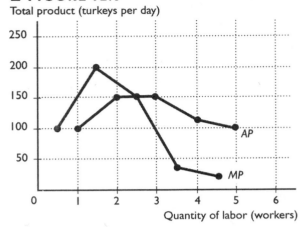

Total product (turkeys per day)

Quantity of labor (workers)

c. When the *MP* curve is above the *AP* curve, the *AP* curve is rising. When the *MP* curve is below the *AP* curve, the *AP* curve is falling; page 304.

2. If the marginal product of a worker exceeds the average product, then hiring the worker increases the average product. This result reflects the general relationship between an average value and a marginal value; page 305.

### Long Response Questions

1. The short run is the time frame in which the quantities of some resources (the plant) are fixed. The long run is the time frame in which the quantities of *all* resources can be changed. The amount of actual calendar time for the short run and long run varies among different companies. It might take Intel 6 years to be able to increase the quantities of all its resources, including building a new factory whereas it might take Taco Bell 8 months to increase the quantities of all its resources, including a new restaurant; page 300.

2. As Pizza Hut initially adds workers, the marginal product of each additional worker exceeds the marginal product of the previous worker. The marginal product increases because the workers can specialize. Some workers can make the pizzas and others can deliver them. As more workers are added, eventually the marginal product of each additional worker is less than the marginal

product of the previous worker. The marginal product decreases because more workers are using the same equipment, so there is less productive work for each new worker; page 302.

3. The law of decreasing returns states that as a firm uses more of a variable input, with a given quantity of fixed inputs, the marginal product of the variable input eventually decreases. For example, if a firm hires more and more workers to work in its (fixed) plant, eventually the marginal product of another worker is less than the marginal product of the previous worker; page 304.

### ■ CHECKPOINT 12.3

#### True or false

1. True; page 307
2. False; page 310
3. True; page 310
4. True; page 313

#### Multiple choice

1. c; page 307
2. c; page 307
3. c; page 307
4. d; page 308
5. e; page 308
6. b; page 309
7. b; page 309
8. b; page 310

#### Short Response Questions

| Labor | Output | TC | ATC | MC |
|-------|--------|-----|------|------|
| 0 | 0 | 30 | xx | |
| | | | | 1.00 |
| 1 | 10 | 40 | 4.00 | |
| | | | | 0.67 |
| 2 | 25 | 50 | 2.00 | |
| | | | | 1.00 |
| 3 | 35 | 60 | 1.71 | |
| | | | | 2.00 |
| 4 | 40 | 70 | 1.75 | |
| | | | | 3.33 |
| 5 | 43 | 80 | 1.86 | |
| | | | | 5.00 |
| 6 | 45 | 90 | 2.00 | |

1. a. The completed table is above; page 309.

■ **FIGURE 12.7**

Average and marginal cost (dollars per sub)

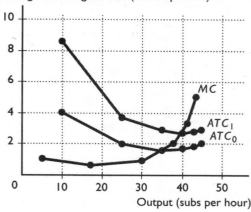

■ **FIGURE 12.8**

Total cost (dollars per unit)

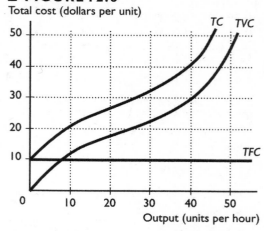

b. Figure 12.7 plots the curves as $ATC_0$ and MC.

| Labor | Output | TC | ATC | MC |
|-------|--------|-----|------|------|
| 0 | 0 | <u>75</u> | xx | |
| | | | | 1.00 |
| 1 | 10 | <u>85</u> | <u>8.50</u> | |
| | | | | 0.67 |
| 2 | 25 | <u>95</u> | <u>3.80</u> | |
| | | | | 1.00 |
| 3 | 35 | <u>105</u> | <u>3.00</u> | |
| | | | | 2.00 |
| 4 | 40 | <u>115</u> | <u>2.88</u> | |
| | | | | 3.33 |
| 5 | 43 | <u>125</u> | <u>2.91</u> | |
| | | | | 5.00 |
| 6 | 45 | <u>135</u> | <u>3.00</u> | |

c. The completed table is above. Figure 12.7 plots the new curves as $ATC_1$ and MC; page 309.

d. The average cost curve shifts upward; the marginal cost curve does not change; page 312.

2. The statement is incorrect. Average fixed cost equals total fixed cost divided by output. Because the total fixed cost does not change as the output increases, the average fixed cost *always* decreases as output increases; pages 309-310.

3. Marginal cost is not equal to the difference between the total cost and the total variable cost. Marginal cost is equal to the change in total cost brought about by a one-unit change in total output; page 308.

4. The labeled figure, Figure 12.8, is above; page 308.

5. Cost curves shift if there is a change in technology or a change in the price of a factor of production; pages 312-313.

**Long Response Questions**

1. Yes, even a closed firm might still have fixed costs. So even if zero output is produced, the firm might have (fixed) costs such as interest payments on a loan or rent on a lease that has not expired; page 307

2. Marginal cost is the change in total cost that results from a one-unit increase in output. Average total cost is total cost per unit of output, which equals average fixed cost plus average variable cost; pages 308-309.

3. When output increases, the firm spreads its total fixed cost over a larger output and its average fixed cost decreases—its average fixed cost curve slopes downward.

Decreasing marginal returns means that as output increases, ever larger amounts of labor are needed to produce an additional unit of output. So average variable cost eventually increases, and the AVC curve eventually slopes upward.

Initially as output increases, both average fixed cost and average variable cost decrease, so average total cost decreases and the ATC curve slopes downward. But as output increases further and decreasing marginal returns set in, average variable cost begins to increase. Eventually, average variable cost increases more quickly than average fixed cost decreases, so average total cost increases and the *ATC* curve slopes upward; page 311.

4. The marginal cost curve intersects the average variable cost curve and the average total cost curve at the point where they are the minimum; page 310.

## ■ CHECKPOINT 12.4

**True or false**
1. False; page 315
2. True; page 315
3. True; page 316
4. False; page 316

**Multiple choice**
1. d; page 315
2. c; page 315
3. c; page 316
4. d; page 316
5. b  page 316
6. c; page 316
7. c; page 317

**Short Response Question**
1. Figure 12.9 (above) darkens the firm's long-run average total cost curve. As indicated by the dotted line, the firm has economies of scale at all output levels less than 3,000 and has diseconomies of scale at all output levels greater than 3,000; page 317.

**Long Response Questions**
1. A long-run average cost curve is a curve that shows the lowest average total cost at which it is possible to produce each output when the firm has had sufficient time to change both its plant size and labor employed. Suppose a newspaper publisher can operate with four different plant sizes. The segment of

### ■ FIGURE 12.9

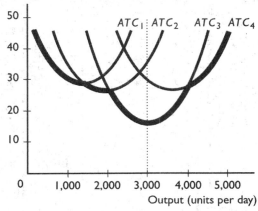

each of the four average total cost curves for which that plant has the lowest average total cost is the scallop-shaped curve that is the long-run average cost curve; page 315.

2. Economies of scale occurs when a firm increases its plant size and labor force by the same percentage, its output increases by a larger percentage and its long-run average cost decreases. The main source of economies of scale is greater specialization of both labor and capital; page 315.

3. Decreasing marginal returns occurs when the marginal product of an additional worker is less than the marginal product of the previous worker. Decreasing marginal returns is a short-run condition because *only* the quantity of labor is changed. Decreasing marginal returns occur because more and more workers must share and use the same amount of capital equipment. Diseconomies of scale occur when a firm increases the size of all its inputs—its plant and its labor—by the same percentage and its output increases by a smaller percentage. Because all inputs are changed, diseconomies of scale is a long-run condition. It occurs because as a firm gets larger, eventually controlling the firm becomes complex and so the complexity increases the average total cost; pages 302, 316.

# Perfect Competition

# Chapter 13

In Chapter 13 we study perfect competition, the market that arises when the demand for a product is large relative to the output of a single producer.

■ **Explain a perfectly competitive firm's profit-maximizing choices and derive its supply curve.**

Perfect competition exists when: many firms sell an identical product to many buyers; there are no restrictions on entry into (or exit from) the market; established firms have no advantage over new firms; and sellers and buyers are well informed about prices. A firm in perfect competition is a price taker—it cannot influence the price of its product. The market demand curve is downward sloping. A perfectly competitive firm faces a perfectly elastic demand so its demand curve is horizontal. Marginal revenue is the change in total revenue that results from a one-unit increase in the quantity sold. In perfect competition, marginal revenue equals price. A firm maximizes its profit at the output level at which total revenue exceeds total cost by the largest amount. Another way to find the profit-maximizing output is to use marginal analysis. A firm maximizes its profit at the output level at which marginal revenue equals marginal cost. The shutdown point is the output and price at which the firm just covers its total variable cost. A firm's supply curve is its marginal cost curve above minimum average variable cost.

■ **Explain how output, price, and profit are determined in the short run.**

The market supply curve in the short run shows the quantity supplied at each price by a fixed number of firms. Market demand and market supply determine the price and quantity bought and sold. Each firm takes the price as given and produces its profit-maximizing output. A perfectly competitive firm earns an economic profit when price exceeds average total cost and incurs economic loss when price is less than average total cost.

■ **Explain how output, price, and profit are determined in the long run and explain why perfect competition is efficient.**

Economic profit is an incentive for new firms to enter a market, but as they do so, the price falls and the economic profit of each existing firm decreases. Economic loss is an incentive for firms to exit a market, and as they do so the price rises and the economic loss of each remaining firm decreases. In the long run, a firm earns a normal profit and there is no entry or exit. A In a market undergoing technological change, firms that adopt the new technology make an economic profit. Firms that stick with the old technology incur economic losses. They either exit the market or switch to the new technology. Competition eliminates economic profit in the long run. Perfect competition is efficient because in a perfectly competitive market the market demand curve is the same as the marginal benefit curve and the market supply curve is the same as the entire market's marginal cost curve.

## EXPANDED CHAPTER CHECKLIST

**When you have completed this chapter, you will be able to:**

**1  Explain a perfectly competitive firm's profit-maximizing choices and derive its supply curve.**

- Describe the four market types.
- Explain why a firm in perfect competition is a price taker.
- Describe the market demand curve and a firm's demand curve in perfect competition.
- Discuss how a perfectly competitive firm determines its profit-maximizing output.
- Explain when a firm makes the decision to temporarily shut down and locate the shut-down point on a graph.
- Derive and draw a firm's short-run supply curve.

**2  Explain how output, price, and profit are determined in the short run.**

- Derive the market supply curve in the short run.
- Illustrate a perfectly competitive firm that is earning an economic profit and calculate the amount of the economic profit.
- Illustrate a perfectly competitive firm that is incurring an economic loss and calculate the amount of the economic loss.

**3  Explain how output, price, and profit are determined in the long run and explain why perfect competition is efficient.**

- Illustrate the case of a perfectly competitive firm in long-run equilibrium, when it earns only a normal profit.
- Explain how economic profit attracts entry, and discuss the effect entry has on the market supply, the price, and the existing firms' economic profit.
- Explain how economic loss creates exit, and discuss the effect exit has on the market supply, the price, and the surviving firms' economic loss.
- Define and graph the long-run market supply curve.
- Describe the forces at work in markets with technological change
- Discuss the efficiency and fairness of perfect competition.

## YOUR AP TEST HINTS

### AP Topics

| Topic on your AP test | Corresponding textbook section |
|---|---|
| **Nature and function of product markets** | |
| Perfect Competition | Chapter 13 |
| • Profit maximization | Checkpoint 13.1 |
| • Short-run supply and shutdown decision | Checkpoints 13.2, 13.3 |
| • Behavior of firms and markets in the short and long run | Checkpoints 13.2, 13.3 |

### AP Vocabulary

- On the AP test, the discussion of the slope of the short-run supply curve in is not tested on the AP exam. The test will use an upward sloping market supply curve. The market supply curve is the sum of the supply curves of each of the firms in the industry. And the firms' supply curves are the portion of the marginal cost curve that is above the average variable cost.

### Extra AP material

- Short run supply curves are derived from summing each firm's supply curve, which is the portion of the marginal cost curve above the average variable cost. The long run supply curve shows how the price and quantity supplied change in the long run. It has industry characteristics based on how the firms' costs change when the number of firms in the industry change. There are three situations: constant cost industry; increasing cost industry; and decreasing cost industry.

- A **constant cost industry** is an industry for which the entry of new firms does not change each firm's costs. This situation occurs when the industry's demand for the resources used by the firms is a small part of the overall demand, which is most likely in industries that use unspecialized resources. In this industry, in the short run an increase in demand raises the price. The higher price increases economic profit and attracts entry. In the long run, entry forces the profit back to a normal profit and the price back to equality with the *unchanged* average total cost. The long-run market supply curve is horizontal at this price and hence the long-run supply is perfectly elastic.

- An **increasing cost industry** is an industry for which the entry of new firms raises each firm's costs. This situation occurs when the industry's demand for the resources used by the firms is a large part of the overall demand, which is most likely in industries that use very specialized resources. In this case, increased output raises the demand for the resources so the price of the resources rise and hence the costs of the firms increase. In this industry, in the short run an increase in demand raises the price. The higher price increases economic profit and attracts entry. In the long run, entry forces the profit back to a normal profit and the price back to equality with the *now higher* average total cost. The long-run market supply curve is upward sloping.

- A **decreasing cost industry** is an industry for which the entry of new firms lowers each firm's costs. This situation occurs when increased output raises the demand for resources and the suppliers of resources can now afford to create more specialized and more efficient inputs for the firms to use. As a result of the increased efficiency, the costs of the firms decrease. In this industry, in the short run

an increase in demand raises the price. The higher price increases economic profit and attracts entry. In the long run, entry forces the profit back to a normal profit and the price back to equality with the *now lower* average total cost. The long-run market supply curve is downward sloping.

## CHECKPOINT 13.1

- **Explain a perfectly competitive firm's profit-maximizing choices and derive its supply curve.**

### Quick Review

- $P = MR$ The price equals the marginal revenue for a firm in perfect competition.
- $MC = MR$ Profit is maximized when production is such that marginal cost equals marginal revenue.
- *A firm's short-run supply curve* At prices less than its minimum average variable cost, the firm shuts down. At prices above the minimum average variable cost, the supply curve is the marginal cost curve.
- *Shutdown point* The output and price at which price equals the minimum average variable cost.

### Additional Practice Problem 13.1

1. Patricia is a perfectly competitive wheat farmer. Her average variable cost curve and her marginal cost are shown in the figure.
   a. If the price of a bushel of wheat is $6 per bushel, how much wheat will Patricia produce?
   b. If the price of a bushel of wheat falls to $3

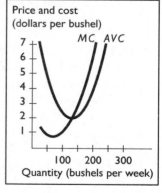

per bushel, how much wheat will Patricia produce?

c. What are two points on Patricia's supply curve?

d. What is the lowest price for which Patricia will produce wheat rather than shut down?

e. Suppose that when the price of a bushel of wheat is $6, Patricia produces a quantity of wheat such that her marginal revenue is greater than marginal cost. Explain why she is not maximizing her profit.

**Solution to Additional Practice Problem 13.1**

1a. When the price of a bushel of wheat is $6 per bushel, Patricia's marginal revenue curve is shown in the figure as $MR_1$. To maximize her profit, Patricia produces 200 bushels of wheat, the quantity at which marginal revenue equals marginal cost.

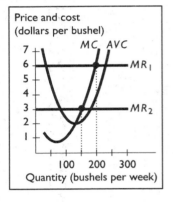

Price and cost (dollars per bushel)

1b. If the price of wheat falls to $3 per bushel, Patricia's marginal revenue curve is shown in the figure as $MR_2$. She decreases the quantity of wheat she produces to 150 bushels per week because that is the quantity at which marginal revenue equals marginal cost.

1c. One point on Patricia's supply curve is a price of $6 and 200 bushels. Another point is a price of $3 and a quantity of 150 bushels.

1d. The lowest price for which Patricia produces rather than shuts down is the price equal to her minimum average variable cost, which, as the figure shows, is equal to $2 per bushel.

1e. If marginal revenue exceeds marginal cost, then the extra revenue from selling one more bushel of wheat exceeds the extra cost incurred to produce it. So if Patricia produces one more bushel of wheat, the marginal revenue that she receives from selling that bushel is greater than the cost to produce

that bushel and this bushel increases her profit. To maximize profit, Patricia must increase her output until she reaches the point where the marginal revenue equals the marginal cost.

## ■ AP Self Test 13.1

### True or false

1. A perfectly competitive market has many firms.

2. A firm in perfect competition is a price taker.

3. When a perfectly competitive firm is maximizing its profit, the vertical difference between the firm's marginal revenue curve and its marginal cost curve is as large as possible.

4. A perfectly competitive firm's short-run supply curve is its average total cost above minimum average variable cost.

### Multiple choice

1. The four market types are
   a. perfect competition, imperfect competition, monopoly, and oligopoly.
   b. oligopoly, monopsony, monopoly, and imperfect competition.
   c. perfect competition, monopoly, monopolistic competition, and oligopoly.
   d. oligopoly, oligopolistic competition, monopoly, and perfect competition.
   e. perfect competition, imperfect competition, monopoly, and duopoly.

2. A requirement of perfect competition is that
   i. many firms sell an identical product to many buyers.
   ii. there are no restrictions on entry into (or exit from) the market, and established firms have no advantage over new firms.
   iii. buyers are well informed about prices.
   a. i only.
   b. i and ii.
   c. iii only.
   d. i and iii.
   e. i, ii, and iii.

3.  A perfectly competitive firm is a price taker because
    a. many other firms produce the same product.
    b. only one firm produces the product.
    c. many firms produce a slightly differentiated product.
    d. a few firms compete.
    e. it faces a vertical demand curve.

4.  The demand curve faced by a perfectly competitive firm is
    a. horizontal.
    b. vertical.
    c. downward sloping.
    d. upward sloping.
    e. U-shaped.

5.  For a perfectly competitive corn grower in Nebraska, the marginal revenue curve is
    a. downward sloping.
    b. the same as the demand curve.
    c. upward sloping.
    d. U-shaped.
    e. vertical at the profit maximizing quantity of production.

6.  A perfectly competitive firm maximizes its profit by producing at the point where
    a. total revenue equals total cost.
    b. marginal revenue is equal to marginal cost.
    c. total revenue is equal to marginal revenue.
    d. total cost is at its minimum.
    e. total revenue is at its maximum.

■ **FIGURE 13.1**

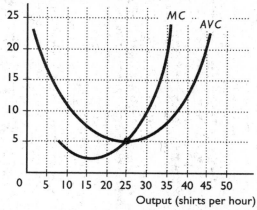

7.  Figure 13.1 shows cost curves for Wring Around the Collar, a perfectly competitive dry cleaner. If the price of dry cleaning a shirt is $20 per shirt, the firm will dry clear ____ shirts per hour.
    a. 0
    b. between 1 and 24
    c. 25
    d. 30
    e. 35

8.  In Figure 13.1, if the price of dry cleaning a shirt is $10 per shirt, the firm will dry clear ____ shirts per hour.
    a. 0
    b. between 1 and 24
    c. 25
    d. 30
    e. 35

9.  Based on Figure 13.1, the lowest price for which the company might remain open is
    a. $25 per shirt.
    b. $20 per shirt.
    c. $15 per shirt.
    d. $10 per shirt.
    e. $5 per shirt.

10. If the market price is lower than a perfectly competitive firm's average total cost, the firm will
    a. immediately shut down.
    b. continue to produce if the price exceeds the average fixed cost.
    c. continue to produce if the price exceeds the average variable cost.
    d. shut down if the price exceeds the average fixed cost.
    e. shut down if the price is less than the average fixed cost.

11. One part of a perfectly competitive trout farm's supply curve is its
    a. marginal cost curve below the shutdown point.
    b. entire marginal cost curve.
    c. marginal cost curve above the shutdown point.
    d. average variable cost curve above the shutdown point.
    e. marginal revenue curve above the demand curve.

**Short Response Questions**

1. What are the conditions that define perfect competition?

2. What is a "price taker?" Why are perfectly competitive firms price takers?

3. Willy, a perfectly competitive wheat farmer, can sell 999 bushels of wheat for $3 per bushel or 1,000 bushels for $3 per bushel. What is Willy's marginal revenue and total revenue if he sells 1,000 bushels of wheat?

4. Figure 13.2 shows a perfectly competitive firm's cost curves.
   a. Label the curves.
   b. If the market price is $40, what is the firm's equilibrium output and price?
   c. If the market price is $20, what is the firm's equilibrium output and price?
   d. What is the firm's shutdown price?
   e. Darken the firm's supply curve.

■ **FIGURE 13.2**

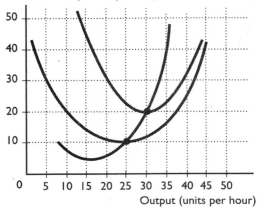

Price and cost (dollars per unit)

**Long Response Questions**

1. What is the difference between a perfectly competitive firm's demand curve and the market demand curve?

| Quantity (hogs) | Total cost (dollars) | Total revenue (dollars) | Economic profit (dollars) |
|---|---|---|---|
| 0 | 300 | ___ | ___ |
| 1 | 350 | ___ | ___ |
| 2 | 425 | ___ | ___ |
| 3 | 575 | ___ | ___ |
| 4 | 825 | ___ | ___ |
| 5 | 1,200 | ___ | ___ |

2. Peter owns Peter's Porkers, a small hog farm. The above table gives Peter's total cost schedule. Peter is in a perfectly competitive market and can sell each hog for $200.
   a. Complete the table.
   b. What is Peter's profit-maximizing number of hogs and what price will Peter set?
   c. When Peter increases his production from 2 hogs to 3 hogs, what is the marginal cost? Is the third hog profitable for Peter?
   d. When Peter increases his production from 3 hogs to 4 hogs, what is the marginal cost? Is the fourth hog profitable for Peter?
   e. What is the marginal cost of the third hog?

3. When will a firm temporarily shut down?

## CHECKPOINT 13.2

■ **Explain how output, price, and profit are determined in the short run.**

### Quick Review

- *Economic profit* If the price exceeds the average total cost ($P > ATC$), the firm earns an economic profit. If $P > ATC$, then $P \times q > ATC \times q$. Because $P \times q$ equals total revenue and $ATC \times q$ is total cost, then $P > ATC$ means that total revenue > total cost.
- *Economic loss* If the price is less than the average total cost, the firm incurs an economic loss.

### Additional Practice Problem 13.2

| Quantity (roses per week) | Average total cost | Marginal cost |
|---|---|---|
| | (dollars per rose) | |
| 100 | 2.00 | 1.50 |
| 200 | 1.50 | 1.50 |
| 300 | 1.67 | 2.50 |
| 400 | 2.00 | 5.00 |

1. Growing roses is a perfectly competitive industry. There are 100 rose growers and all have the same cost curves. The above table gives the costs of one of the growers, Rosita's Roses. The market demand schedule for roses is in the table to the right.

| Price (dollars per rose) | Quantity (roses per week) |
|---|---|
| 1.00 | 50,000 |
| 1.50 | 45,000 |
| 2.00 | 40,000 |
| 2.50 | 30,000 |
| 3.00 | 20,000 |

a. Plot the market supply curve and the market demand curve in the figure.

b. What is the equilibrium price of a rose?

c. How many roses does Rosita produce? What is her economic profit or loss?

Price and cost (dollars per rose)

Quantity (thousands of roses per week)

### Solution to Additional Practice Problem 13.2

1a. The market demand curve and market supply curve are plotted in the figure. The quantity supplied in the market at any price is the sum of the 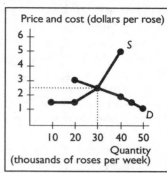 quantities supplied by each firm at that price. Because each firm is identical, the market quantity supplied is 100 times the quantity supplied by any one firm. The firm's supply curve is its marginal cost curve above the minimum average variable cost. For instance, when the price is $2.50 a rose, Rosita's marginal cost schedule shows she will supply 300 roses a week. So the quantity supplied in the market equals $100 \times (300$ roses a week), which is 30,000 roses a week.

1b. The figure shows that the equilibrium price of a rose is $2.50.

1c. In the short run, a firm can make an economic profit or incur an economic loss. A firm earns an economic profit when price exceeds average total cost and incurs an economic loss when price is less than average total cost. In the case at hand, Rosita produces 300 roses. Rosita earns an economic profit. Rosita's economic profit per rose equals the price of a rose minus the average total cost, which is $2.50 − $1.67 = $0.83. She produces 300 roses, a week so her total economic profit is (300 roses a week) × ($0.83) = $249 a week.

■ **AP Self Test 13.2**

### True or false

1. The market supply curve in the short run shows the quantity supplied at each price by a fixed number of firms.

2. Market supply in a perfectly competitive market is perfectly elastic at all prices.

3. A perfectly competitive firm earns an economic profit if price equals average total cost.

4. In a perfectly competitive industry, a firm's economic profit is equal to price minus marginal revenue multiplied by quantity.

5. A perfectly competitive firm has an economic loss if price is less than the marginal cost.

**Multiple choice**

1. If the market supply curve and market demand curve for a good intersect at 600,000 units and there are 10,000 identical firms in the market, then each firm is producing
   a. 600,000 units.
   b. 60,000,000,000 units.
   c. 60,000 units.
   d. 60 units.
   e. 10,000 units.

2. A perfectly competitive firm earns an economic profit in the short run if price is
   a. equal to marginal cost.
   b. equal to average total cost.
   c. greater than average total cost.
   d. greater than marginal cost.
   e. greater than average variable cost.

3. If a perfectly competitive firm is maximizing its profit and earning an economic profit, which of the following is correct?
   i.   price equals marginal revenue
   ii.  marginal revenue equals marginal cost
   iii. price is greater than average total cost
   a. i only.
   b. i and ii only.
   c. ii and iii only.
   d. i and iii only.
   e. i, ii, and iii.

■ **FIGURE 13.3**

Price and cost (dollars per unit)

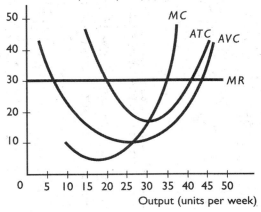

4. Figure 13.3 shows the marginal revenue and cost curves for a perfectly competitive firm. The firm
   a. is incurring an economic loss.
   b. will shut down and will incur an economic loss.
   c. will shut down and will earn zero economic profit.
   d. is earning zero economic profit.
   e. is earning an economic profit.

5. The market for watermelons in Alabama is perfectly competitive. A watermelon producer earning a normal profit could earn an economic profit if the
   a. average total cost of selling watermelons does not change.
   b. average total cost of selling watermelons increases.
   c. average total cost of selling watermelons decreases.
   d. marginal cost of selling watermelons does not change.
   e. marginal cost of selling watermelons does not change.

6. Juan's Software Service Company is in a perfectly competitive market. Juan has total fixed cost of $25,000, average variable cost for 1,000 service calls is $45, and marginal revenue is $75. Juan's makes 1,000 service calls a month. What is his economic profit?
   a. $5,000
   b. $25,000
   c. $45,000
   d. $75,000.
   e. $50,000

7. If a perfectly competitive firm finds that price is less than its *ATC*, then the firm
   a. will raise its price to increase its economic profit.
   b. will lower its price to increase its economic profit.
   c. is earning an economic profit.
   d. is incurring an economic loss.
   e. is earning zero economic profit.

8. A perfectly competitive video-rental firm in Phoenix incurs an economic loss if the average total cost of each video rental is
   a. greater than the marginal revenue of each rental.
   b. less than the marginal revenue of each rental.
   c. equal to the marginal revenue of each rental.
   d. equal to zero.
   e. less than the price of each video.

9. In the short run, a perfectly competitive firm
   a. must make an economic profit.
   b. must suffer an economic loss.
   c. must earn a normal profit.
   d. might make an economic profit, incur an economic loss, or make a normal profit.
   e. must earn an economic profit.

## Short Response Questions

### ■ FIGURE 13.4

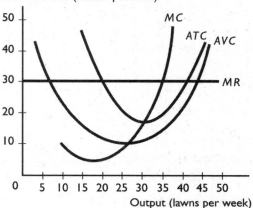
Price and cost (dollars per lawn)

1. Moe's Mowers is a perfectly competitive lawn mowing company. Moe's costs and marginal revenue are illustrated in Figure 13.4.
   a. How many lawns does Moe mow?
   b. Is Moe earning an economic profit or incurring an economic loss? Darken the area that shows the economic profit or loss. What is the amount of economic profit or loss?

### ■ FIGURE 13.5

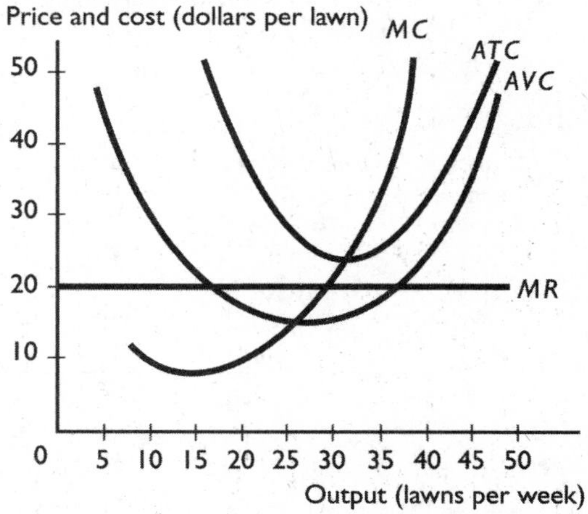

Price and cost (dollars per lawn)

2. Larry's Lawns is (another) perfectly competitive lawn mowing company in another city. Larry's costs and marginal revenue are illustrated in Figure 13.5.
   a. How many lawns does Larry mow?

b. Is Larry earning an economic profit or incurring an economic loss? Darken the area that shows the economic profit or loss. In the short run, will Larry remain open or shut down?

### Long Response Questions

1. In a perfectly competitive market, how is the market supply calculated?

2. If price is less than average total cost, is the firm earning an economic profit or incurring an economic loss?

### CHECKPOINT 13.3

■ **Explain how output, price, and profit are determined in the long run and explain why perfect competition is efficient.**

### Quick Review

- *Entry* Economic profit is an incentive for new firms to enter a market, but as they do so, the price falls and the economic profit of each existing firm decreases.
- *Exit* Economic loss is an incentive for firms to exit a market, but as they do so, the price rises and the economic loss of each remaining firm decreases.

### Additional Practice Problem 13.3

| Quantity (roses per week) | Average total cost (dollars) | Marginal cost (dollars) |
|---|---|---|
| 100 | 2.00 | 1.50 |
| 200 | 1.50 | 1.50 |
| 300 | 1.67 | 2.50 |
| 400 | 2.00 | 5.00 |

1. Growing roses is a perfectly competitive industry. Initially there are 100 rose growers and all have the same cost curves. The above table gives the costs of one of the growers, Rosita's Roses. The table to the right has the market demand schedule for roses.

| Price (dollars per rose) | Quantity (roses per week) |
|---|---|
| 1.00 | 50,000 |
| 1.50 | 45,000 |
| 2.00 | 40,000 |
| 2.50 | 30,000 |
| 3.00 | 20,000 |

The equilibrium price for a rose initially is $2.50.

a. Plot Rosita's marginal cost curve and her marginal revenue curve in the figure to the right. Is Rosita earning an economic profit or is Rosita incurring an economic loss?

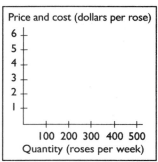

b. As time passes, what takes place in the market?

c. What will be the long-run price of a rose? What will be Rosita's profit in the long run? In the long run, how many growers will be in the market?

### Solution to Additional Practice Problem 13.3

1a. The figure shows Rosita's marginal cost curve and marginal revenue curve. The figure shows that she is producing 300 roses a week. Rosita is earning an economic profit because the price of a rose, $2.50, exceeds her average total cost of producing 300 roses, $1.67.

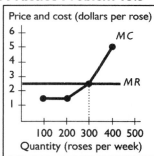

1b. A perfectly competitive firm earns a normal profit in the long run. A firm will not incur an economic loss in the long run because it will shut down. And a perfectly competitive firm cannot earn an economic profit in the long run because the presence of an economic profit attracts entry, which drives down the price and eliminates economic profit. Competitive firms cannot prevent entry into their market because there are no barriers to entry and so they cannot protect any economic profit.

In the case of the rose growers, rose growers are earning an economic profit, so more rose growers enter the market. The supply of roses increases and the market supply curve shifts rightward. The equilibrium price of a rose falls and the market equilibrium quantity increases.

1c. The long-run price of a rose will be $1.50 because that is the minimum average total cost. At that price, all rose growers, including Rosita, earn a normal profit. Indeed, the fact that they are earning only a normal profit is what removes the incentive for further firms to enter the industry. When the price of a rose is $1.50, the demand schedule shows that the quantity demanded is 45,000 roses. At a price of $1.50, each grower produces 200 roses. There will be 225 growers, each producing 200 roses.

## ■ AP Self Test 13.3

### True or false

1. When price equals average total cost, the firm earns a normal profit.

2. Entry into a perfectly competitive market lowers the price.

3. In the long run, firms respond to an economic loss by exiting a perfectly competitive market.

4. New technology shifts a firm's cost curves upward and the market supply curve leftward.

5. Perfect competition is efficient because it results in the efficient quantity being produced.

### Multiple choice

1. In the long run, new firms enter a perfectly competitive market when
   a. normal profits are greater than zero.
   b. economic profits are equal to zero.
   c. normal profits are equal to zero.
   d. economic profits are greater than zero.
   e. the existing firms are weak because they are incurring economic losses.

2. In a perfectly competitive market, if firms are earning an economic profit, the economic profit
   a. attracts entry by more firms, which lowers the price.
   b. can be earned both in the short run and the long run.
   c. is less than the normal profit.
   d. leads to a decrease in market demand.
   e. generally leads to firms exiting as they seek higher profit in other markets.

3. If firms in a perfectly competitive market are earning an economic profit, then
   a. the market is in its long-run equilibrium.
   b. new firms enter the market and the equilibrium profit of the initial firms decreases.
   c. new firms enter the market and the equilibrium profit of the initial firms increases.
   d. firms exit the market and the equilibrium profit of the remaining firms decreases.
   e. firms exit the market and the equilibrium profit of the remaining firms increases.

4. Firms exit a competitive market when they incur an economic loss. In the long run, this exit means that the economic losses of the surviving firms
   a. increase.
   b. decrease until they equal zero.
   c. decrease until economic profits are earned.
   d. do not change.
   e. might change but more information is needed about what happens to the price of the good as the firms exit.

5. If firms in a perfectly competitive market have economic losses, then as time passes firms ____ and the market ____.
   a. enter; demand curve shifts leftward
   b. enter; supply curve shifts rightward
   c. exit; demand curve shifts leftward
   d. exit; supply curve shifts rightward
   e. exit; supply curve shifts leftward

6. In the long run, a firm in a perfectly competitive market will
   a. earn zero economic profit, that is, it will earn a normal profit.
   b. earn zero normal profit but it will earn an economic profit.
   c. remove all competitors and become a monopolistically competitive firm.
   d. incur an economic normal loss but not earn a positive economic profit.
   e. remove all competitors and become a monopoly.

7. Technological change brings a ____ to firms that adopt the new technology.
   a. permanent economic profit
   b. temporary economic profit
   c. permanent economic loss
   d. temporary economic loss
   e. temporary normal profit

**Short Response Questions**

■ **FIGURE 13.6**
Price and cost (dollars per unit)

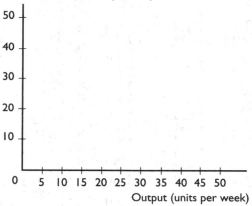

1. In Figure 13.6, suppose that the price of the good is $20. Show the long-run equilibrium for a perfectly competitive firm that produces 30 units per week.

2. Figure 13.7 shows cost curves for two firms in an industry undergoing technological change. Firm 1 uses the old technology and has an average total cost curve $ATC_1$ and marginal cost curve $MC_1$. Firm 2 uses the new technology and has an average total cost

■ **FIGURE 13.7**
Price and cost (dollars per unit)

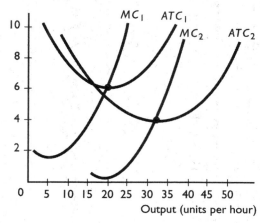

curve $ATC_2$ and marginal cost curve $MC_2$. Initially the price of the product was $6.

a. At the price of $6, do firm 1 and firm 2 earn an economic profit, normal profit, or incur economic loss?
b. As more firms adopt the new technology, what happens to market supply and price? Do firms 1 and 2 earn an economic profit, normal profit, or incur an economic loss?
c. In the long run, what will be the new price? Will firm 1 earn an economic profit, a normal profit, or incur an economic loss? Will firm 2 earn an economic profit, a normal profit, or incur an economic loss?

**Long Response Questions**
1. Why are perfectly competitive firms unable to earn an economic profit in the long run? Why won't they incur an economic loss in the long run?
2. Is perfect competition allocatively efficient?
3. What is the slope of the long-run market supply curve if the industry is an increasing cost industry?

# YOUR AP SELF TEST ANSWERS

## ■ CHECKPOINT 13.1

### True or false
1. True;  page 324
2. True;  page 325
3. False;  page 327
4. False;  pages 329-330

### Multiple choice
1. c;  page 324
2. e;  page 324
3. a;  page 325
4. a;  pages 325-326
5. b;  page 326
6. b;  page 328
7. e;  page 328
8. d;  page 328
9. e;  page 330
10. c;  page 329
11. c;  page 330

### Short Response Questions
1. Perfect competition exists when many firms sell an identical product to many buyers; there are no restrictions on entry into (or exit from) the market; established firms have no advantage over new firms; and sellers and buyers are well informed about prices;  page 324.

2. A price taker is a firm that cannot influence the price of the good or service it produces. Perfectly competitive firms are price takers because there are many competing firms selling an identical product. Any individual firm is such a small part of the market that its actions cannot affect the price;  page 325.

3. Willy's marginal revenue equals the price of a bushel of wheat, which is $3. His total revenue equals price multiplied by quantity, which is $3,000;  page 326.

4. a. Figure 13.8 labels the curves;  page 330.
   b. Output is 35 units and the price is $40; page 328.
   c. Output is 30 units and the price is $20; page 328.

### ■ FIGURE 13.8
Price and cost (dollars per unit)

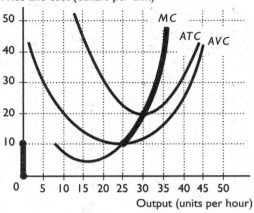

d. The shutdown price is $10;  pages 329-330.
e. The firm's supply curve is darkened in Figure 13.8;  page 330.

### Long Response Questions
1. A perfectly competitive firm's demand is perfectly elastic because all sellers produce goods that are perfect substitutes. So the firm's demand curve is horizontal. The market demand curve is downward sloping; pages 325-326.

| Quantity (hogs) | Total cost (dollars) | Total revenue (dollars) | Economic profit (dollars) |
|---|---|---|---|
| 0 | 300 | 0 | −300 |
| 1 | 350 | 200 | −150 |
| 2 | 425 | 400 | −25 |
| 3 | 575 | 600 | 25 |
| 4 | 825 | 800 | −25 |
| 5 | 1,200 | 1,000 | −200 |

2. a.  The completed table is above;  page 326.
   b. The profit-maximizing number of hogs is 3. Peter charges $200 a hog;  page 327.
   c. The marginal cost is the change in total cost that results from producing the third hog. So marginal cost is $150. This is a profitable hog because the marginal revenue from the hog exceeds its marginal cost;  page 328.

d. The marginal cost is $250. This hog is not profitable; page 328.

e. The marginal cost of the third hog is $200, which is the average of the marginal cost of increasing production from 2 to 3 hogs and of increasing production from 3 to 4 hogs. Because the marginal cost of the third hog equals the marginal revenue, 3 hogs is the profit-maximizing output; page 328.

3. If a firm shuts down, it incurs an economic loss equal to total fixed cost. If the firm produces some output, it incurs an economic loss equal to total fixed cost plus total variable cost minus total revenue. If total revenue exceeds total variable cost, the firm's economic loss is less than total fixed cost. It pays the firm to produce. But if total revenue is less than total variable cost, the firm's economic loss exceeds total fixed cost. The firm shuts down; page 329.

## ■ CHECKPOINT 13.2

**True or false**

1. True;  page 332
2. False;  page 332
3. False;  page 333
4. False;  page 333
5. False;  page 334

**Multiple choice**

1. d;  page 332
2. c;  page 333
3. e;  page 333
4. e;  page 333
5. c;  page 333
6. a;  page 333
7. d;  page 334
8. a;  page 334
9. d;  pages 333-334

**Short Response Questions**

1. a. Moe mows 35 lawns per day because that is the quantity at which marginal revenue equals marginal cost; page 333.

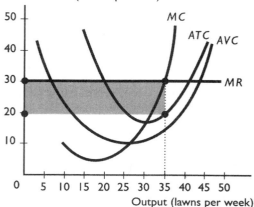

**■ FIGURE 13.9**
Price and cost (dollars per lawn)

b. Moe is earning an economic profit. Figure 13.9 illustrates the economic profit. The economic profit per lawn equals price minus average total cost, which is $30 – $20 = $10 per lawn. The quantity is 35 lawns, so the total economic profit equals ($10 per lawn) × (35 lawns), which is $350 a week; page 329.

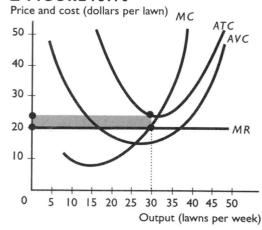

**■ FIGURE 13.10**
Price and cost (dollars per lawn)

2. a. Larry mows 30 lawns per day because that is the quantity at which marginal revenue equals marginal cost; page 333.

b. Larry has an economic loss. Figure 13.10 illustrates the economic loss as the darkened rectangle. Even though he has an economic loss, Larry remains open in the short run because the price exceeds his average variable cost; page 334.

### Long Response Questions

1. The market supply in the short run is the quantity supplied at each price by a fixed number of firms. The quantity supplied at a given price is the sum of the quantities supplied by all firms at that price. For example, if there are 100 firms in the geranium market and each produces 50 geraniums when the price is $3, then the quantity supplied in the market at $3 is 5,000 geraniums; page 332.

2. The firm is suffering an economic loss. If the price is less than average total cost, the firm is incurring an economic loss on each unit produced and has an overall economic loss; page 334.

### ■ CHECKPOINT 13.3

**True or false**

1. True; page 336
2. True; page 337
3. True; page 338
4. False; page 340
5. True; page 342

**Multiple choice**

1. d; page 337
2. a; page 337
3. b; page 337
4. b; page 338
5. e; pages 338-339
7. a; pages 337-339
8. b; page 340

**Short Response Questions**

1. Figure 13.11 shows a perfectly competitive firm in long-run equilibrium. The marginal revenue curve is horizontal at the price of $20. The firm produces 30 units because that is the quantity at which marginal revenue equals marginal cost. The firm has zero economic profit because the price, $20 per unit,

**■ FIGURE 13.11**

Price and cost (dollars per unit)

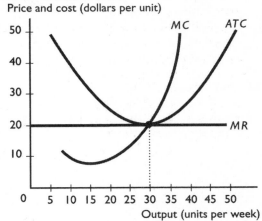

equals the average total cost, also $20 per unit; page 336.

**■ FIGURE 13.12**

Price and cost (dollars per unit)

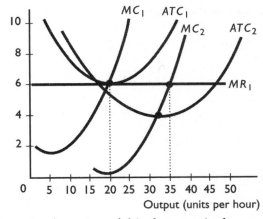

2. a. At the price of $6, the marginal revenue curve is $MR_1$ in Figure 13.12. Firm 1 produces 20 units and earns a normal profit because the $6 price equals average total cost. Firm 2 produces 35 units and earns an economic profit because the $6 price exceeds average total cost; pages 336, 340.

   b. Market supply increases and the price falls. Firm 1 now incurs an economic loss and Firm 2 earns a smaller economic profit; pages 340-341.

   c. In the long run, the new price will $4 because that is the minimum of the new average total cost. Firm 1 will either have adopted the new technology and be earning a normal profit or will have exited the industry. Firm 2 will earn a normal profit; pages 340-341.

### Long Response Questions

1. Perfectly competitive firms cannot earn an economic profit in the long run because the existence of an economic profit invites entry by new firms. As these new firms enter, the market supply increases, driving down the price and eventually eliminating the economic profit. No firm will incur an economic loss in the long run because it will close; pages 337-339.

2. Perfect competition is allocatively efficient. In a perfectly competitive market, equilibrium occurs at the intersection of the supply and demand curves. But the supply curve also is the marginal cost curve and the demand curve also is the marginal benefit curve. So the equilibrium quantity also is the quantity at which the marginal cost equals the marginal benefit, which is the efficient quantity; pages 342-343.

3. Suppose that the market starts out at equilibrium and then the demand for the good or service increases. In the short run the price rises and the firms in the market earn an economic profit. This profit attracts entry into the industry by new firms. Entry increases the supply, thereby increasing the equilibrium quantity and lowering the price. Entry continues until the price is lowered back to equality with the average total cost. At that time the firms are once again earning only a normal profit and the market is back in its long-run equilibrium. If the industry is an increasing cost industry, as more firms enter the industry, the costs of all the firms increase. In this case, entry shifts the average total cost curve upward. As a result, the price does not fall back to its initial level. Instead, the price equals the (higher) average total cost at a level that is higher than the original price. So in the long run, the equilibrium price rises and the equilibrium quantity increases. The equilibrium quantity also is the equilibrium quantity supplied (and the equilibrium quantity demanded). The long-run supply curve, shows how the price and quantity supplied change in the long run when the number of firms changes. So for an increasing cost industry, the long run supply curve is upward sloping because in the long both the (equilibrium) price and the quantity supplied increase.

# Chapter
# Monopoly | 14

In Chapter 14 we study how a monopoly chooses its price and quantity, and discuss whether a monopoly is efficient or fair.

■ **Explain how monopoly arises and distinguish between single-price monopoly and price-discriminating monopoly.**

A monopoly is a market with a single supplier of a good or service that has no close substitutes and in which natural, ownership, or legal barriers to entry prevent competition. A monopoly faces a tradeoff between price and the quantity sold. A single-price monopoly is a monopoly that must sell each unit of its output for the same price to all its customers. A price-discriminating monopoly is a monopoly that is able to sell different units of a good or service for different prices. Simpler

■ **Explain how a single-price monopoly determines its output and price.**

The demand curve for a monopoly is the downward sloping market demand curve. For a single-price monopoly, marginal revenue is less than price, so the marginal revenue curve lies below the demand curve. A monopoly maximizes profit by producing the quantity at which marginal revenue equals marginal cost and finding the highest price at which it can sell this output on the demand curve.

■ **Compare the performance of a single-price monopoly with that of perfect competition.**

Compared to perfect competition, a single-price monopoly produces a smaller output and charges a higher price. A monopoly is inefficient because it creates a deadweight loss. A monopoly redistributes consumer surplus so that the producer gains and the consumers lose. Rent seeking is the act of obtaining special treatment by the government to create an economic profit or divert consumer surplus or producer surplus away from others. Rent seeking restricts competition and can create a monopoly.

■ **Explain how price discrimination increases profit.**

To be able to price discriminate, a firm must be able to identify and separate different types of buyers and sell a product that cannot be resold. Price discrimination converts consumer surplus into economic profit so price discrimination increases the firm's profit. Perfect price discrimination charges every consumer the maximum price the consumer is willing to pay. Perfect price discrimination leaves no consumer surplus but is efficient.

■ **Explain why monopolies can sometimes achieve a better allocation of resources than competition can.**

Monopolies have two potential advantages over a competitive alternative. First, monopolies can capture economies of scale and thereby produce at lower average cost than could a larger number of smaller firms. Second, monopolies have incentives to innovate. The profits from an innovation sometimes can be protected by a patent.

## EXPANDED CHAPTER CHECKLIST

**When you have completed this chapter, you will be able to:**

**1 Explain how monopoly arises and distinguish between single-price monopoly and price-discriminating monopoly.**

- Define monopoly and state the two conditions under which monopoly arises.
- Define natural barrier and natural monopoly.
- Give examples of legal barriers that create legal monopoly.
- Describe how a price-discriminating monopoly differs from single-price monopoly.

**2 Explain how a single-price monopoly determines its output and price.**

- Calculate marginal revenue and explain why marginal revenue is less than price for a single-price monopoly.
- Explain the relationship between marginal revenue and elasticity.
- Use a total revenue curve and a total cost curve to find the profit-maximizing level of output for a single-price monopoly.
- Use a marginal revenue curve, a marginal cost curve, and a demand curve to find the profit-maximizing level of output and price for a single-price monopoly.

**3 Compare the performance of a single-price monopoly with that of perfect competition.**

- Compare the output and price of perfect competition and single-price monopoly.
- Discuss the efficiency and fairness of monopoly.
- Define rent seeking and discuss its effects.

**4 Explain how price discrimination increases profit.**

- State the two conditions necessary for price discrimination.

- Explain how a firm profits from price discrimination.
- Define perfect price discrimination and explain how a perfectly price-discriminating monopoly chooses its level of output.
- Discuss the relationship between price discrimination and efficiency.

**5 Explain why monopolies can sometimes achieve a better allocation of resources than competition can.**

- List two potential advantages of monopoly over perfect competition.

## YOUR AP TEST HINTS

*AP Topics*

| Topic on your AP test | Corresponding text-book section |
| --- | --- |
| **Nature and function of product markets** | |
| Monopoly | Chapter 14 |
| • Sources of market power | Checkpoint 14.1 |
| • Profit maximization | Checkpoints 14.2, 14.3 |
| • Inefficiency of monopoly | Checkpoint 14.3 |
| • Price discrimination | Checkpoint 14.4 |

*AP Vocabulary*

- On the AP test, three factors are deemed necessary to price discriminate. The first factor is "ability to segment the market," which means the ability to identify and separate different types of buyers. The second condition is "no resale of the good or service." The "no resale" condition is sometimes called "no arbitrage." And the third condition is that there must be some market power, that is, the firm must be able to set the price it charges. This last requirement means that firms in perfect competition cannot price discriminate because they are price takers and have no influence over the price they charge. In addition, discriminating among groups of buyers is related to the elasticity of the buyers: Buyers with an inelastic demand pay a higher price than buyers with an elastic demand.

### Extra AP material

- In a graph with the demand curve and the marginal revenue curve, eventually the marginal revenue crosses the horizontal axis. Extending a vertical line upward to the demand curve from this crossing point locates the point on the demand curve where demand is unit elastic. Above this point is the portion of the demand curve where demand is elastic and below this point is the portion of the demand curve where demand is inelastic.
- A single-price monopoly is neither allocative efficient nor productive efficient since the price is greater than both the marginal cost and the minimum average cost.

## CHECKPOINT 14.1

- **Explain how monopoly arises and distinguish between single-price monopoly and price-discriminating monopoly.**
  - *Barrier to entry* A natural, ownership, or legal constraint that protects a firm from competitors.

### Additional Practice Problem 14.1

1. What is the source of the monopoly for each of the following situations? What sort of barrier to entry protects these producers?
   a. The U.S. Postal Service has a monopoly on first class mail delivery.
   b. DeBeer's, while not truly a monopoly, nonetheless controls about 80 percent of the world's diamond sales.
   c. Tampa Electric is the only electric utility company supplying power to Tampa, Florida.

### Solution to Additional Practice Problem 14.1

1a. The U.S. Postal Service derives its monopoly status by a government franchise to deliver first class mail. So the U.S. Postal Service is

protected by a legal barrier to entry. Though it retains its franchise on first class mail delivery, it faces competition from the overnight services provided by FedEx, United Parcel Service, and others.

1b. DeBeers gained its monopoly power in diamond sales by buying up supplies of diamonds from sources throughout the world. So DeBeers is protected by an ownership barrier to entry.

1c. Tampa Electric has been granted a public franchise to be the only distributor of electricity in Tampa. Although Tampa Electric might be a natural monopoly, the public franchise, a legal barrier to entry, is perhaps the most immediate source of monopoly.

## ■ AP Self Test 14.1

### True or false

1. A legal barrier creates a natural monopoly.
2. A firm experiences economies of scale along a downward-sloping long-run average total cost curve.
3. A monopoly always charges all customers the same price.

### Multiple choice

1. A monopoly market has
   a. a few firms.
   b. a single firm.
   c. two dominating firms in the market.
   d. only two firms in it.
   e. some unspecified number of firms in it.

2. Two of the three types of barriers to entry that can protect a firm from competition are
   a. legal and illegal.
   b. natural and legal.
   c. natural and illegal.
   d. natural and rent seeking.
   e. ownership and rent seeking.

3. A natural monopoly is one that arises from
   a. patent law.
   b. copyright law.
   c. a firm buying up all of a natural resource.
   d. economies of scale.
   e. ownership of a natural resource.

4. A legal barrier is created when a firm
   a. has economies of scale, which allow it to produce at a lower cost than two or more firms.
   b. is granted a public franchise, government license, patent, or copyright.
   c. produces a unique product or service.
   d. produces a standardized product or service.
   e. has an ownership barrier to entry.

5. Pizza producers charge one price for a single pizza and almost give away a second one. This is an example of
   a. monopoly.
   b. a barrier to entry.
   c. behavior that is not profit-maximizing.
   d. price discrimination.
   e. rent seeking.

### Short Response Questions
1. What conditions define monopoly?
2. What are the two types of barriers to entry?

### Long Response Questions
1. What are the two pricing strategies a monopoly can use? Why don't perfectly competitive firms have these same strategies?

---

## CHECKPOINT 14.2

■ **Explain how a single-price monopoly determines its output and price.**

### Quick Review
- *Marginal revenue* The change in total revenue resulting from a one-unit increase in the quantity sold.
- *Maximize profit* A single-price monopoly maximizes its profit by producing where $MR = MC$ and then using the demand curve to determine the price for this quantity of output.

---

**Additional Practice Problems 14.2**

| Quantity (pizzas per hour) | Total cost (dollars per pizza) | Average total cost (dollars per pizza) | Marginal cost (dollars per pizza) |
|---|---|---|---|
| 0 | 1.00 | | |
| 1 | 6.00 | ____ | ____ |
| 2 | 13.00 | ____ | ____ |
| 3 | 22.00 | ____ | ____ |
| 4 | 33.00 | ____ | ____ |

1. In a small town, Leonardo's Pizza is the sole restaurant. The table above gives Leonardo's total cost schedule. Complete the table.

| Quantity demanded (pizzas per hour) | Price (dollars per pizza) | Marginal revenue (dollars per pizza) |
|---|---|---|
| 0 | 16.00 | |
| 1 | 14.00 | ____ |
| 2 | 12.00 | ____ |
| 3 | 10.00 | ____ |
| 4 | 8.00 | ____ |

2. The table above gives the demand schedule for Leonardo's pizzas. Complete the table.

3. In a figure, plot Leonardo's demand curve, average total cost curve, marginal cost curve, and marginal revenue curve.
   a. What is Leonardo's equilibrium quantity and price?
   b. What is Leonardo's economic profit or loss? In the figure show the economic profit or loss.

## Solutions to Additional Practice Problems 14.2

| Quantity (pizzas per hour) | Total cost (dollars per pizza) | Average total cost (dollars per pizza) | Marginal cost (dollars per pizza) |
|---|---|---|---|
| 0 | 1.00 | | |
| | | | 5.00 |
| 1 | 6.00 | 6.00 | |
| | | | 7.00 |
| 2 | 13.00 | 6.50 | |
| | | | 9.00 |
| 3 | 22.00 | 7.33 | |
| | | | 11.00 |
| 4 | 33.00 | 8.25 | |

1.   The completed table is above.

| Quantity demanded (pizzas per hour) | Price (dollars per pizza) | Marginal revenue (dollars per pizza) |
|---|---|---|
| 0 | 16.00 | |
| | | 14.00 |
| 1 | 14.00 | |
| | | 10.00 |
| 2 | 12.00 | |
| | | 6.00 |
| 3 | 10.00 | |
| | | 2.00 |
| 4 | 8.00 | |

2.   The completed table is above.

3.   The figure shows Leonardo's demand curve, average total cost curve, marginal cost curve, and marginal revenue curve.

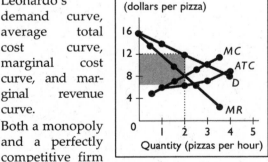

3a.   Both a monopoly and a perfectly competitive firm maximize their profit by producing the quantity at which marginal revenue equals marginal cost. So Leonardo's maximizes its profit by producing 2 pizzas per hour. The price, from the demand curve, is $12 per pizza.

3b.   Leonardo's sells each pizza for $12.00. The average total cost for 2 pizzas is $6.50. So for each pizza Leonardo's earns an economic profit of $5.50 for a total economic profit of $5.50 per pizza × 2 pizzas, or $11.00. This economic profit is equal to the area of the darkened rectangle in the figure.

## ■ AP Self Test 14.2

### True or false

1.   For a single-price monopoly, marginal revenue exceeds price.

2.   Marginal revenue is always positive for a monopoly.

3.   A single-price monopoly maximizes profit by producing the quantity at which marginal revenue equals marginal cost.

### Multiple choice

1.   For a single-price monopoly, price is
   a. greater than marginal revenue.
   b. one half of marginal revenue
   c. equal to marginal revenue.
   d. unrelated to marginal revenue.
   e. always less than average total cost when the firm maximizes its profit.

2.   A single-price monopoly can sell 1 unit for $9.00. To sell 2 units, the price must be $8.50 per unit. The marginal revenue from selling the second unit is
   a. $17.50.
   b. $17.00.
   c. $8.50.
   d. $8.00.
   e. $9.00.

3.   When demand is elastic, marginal revenue is
   a. positive.
   b. negative.
   c. zero.
   d. increasing as output increases.
   e. undefined.

4. To maximize profit, a single-price monopoly produces the quantity at which
   a. the difference between marginal revenue and marginal cost is as large as possible.
   b. marginal revenue is equal to marginal cost.
   c. average total cost is at its minimum.
   d. the marginal cost curve intersects the demand curve.
   e. the marginal revenue curve intersects the horizontal axis.

5. Once a monopoly has determined how much it produces, it will charge a price that
   a. is determined by the intersection of the marginal revenue and marginal cost curves.
   b. minimizes marginal cost.
   c. is determined by its demand curve.
   d. is independent of the amount produced.
   e. is equal to its average total cost.

### Short Response Questions

1. What is the relationship between the elasticity of demand and marginal revenue?

| Quantity (hamburgers per hour) | Price (dollars) | Marginal revenue (dollars) |
|---|---|---|
| 1 | 8.00 | |
| | | ___ |
| 2 | 7.00 | |
| | | ___ |
| 3 | 6.00 | |
| | | ___ |
| 4 | 5.00 | |
| | | ___ |
| 5 | 4.00 | |

2. The table above gives the demand schedule for Bud's Burgers, a monopoly seller of hamburgers in a small town. Complete the table by calculating the marginal revenue.
   a. In Figure 14.1 draw the demand curve and marginal revenue curve.
   b. Suppose the marginal cost is $3 no matter how many hamburgers Bud's produces. Draw the marginal cost curve in the figure. To maximize his profit, how many burgers will Bud grill in an hour and what will be their price?

■ **FIGURE 14.1**
Price and marginal revenue (dollars per hamburger)

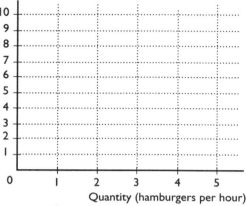

Quantity (hamburgers per hour)

■ **FIGURE 14.2**
Price and cost (dollars per unit)

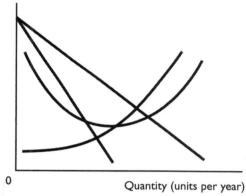

Quantity (units per year)

3. Figure 14.2 shows a monopoly. Label the curves. Identify the quantity produced by labeling it $Q$ and the price charged by labeling it $P$. Is the monopoly earning an economic profit or incurring an economic loss? Darken the area that shows the economic profit or economic loss.

### Long Response Questions

1. Both perfectly competitive and monopoly firms maximize their profit by producing where $MR = MC$. Why do both use the same rule?

2. Why can a monopoly earn an economic profit in the long run but a perfectly competitive firm cannot?

## CHECKPOINT 14.3

■ **Compare the performance of a single-price monopoly with that of perfect competition.**

### Quick Review

• *Monopoly and competition compared* Compared to perfect competition, a single-price monopoly produces a smaller output and charges a higher price.

### Additional Practice Problems 14.3

1. In River Bend, Mississippi, suppose that the owners of the Acme cab company have convinced the city government to grant it a public franchise so it is the only cab company in town. Prior to this, the cab market in River Bend was perfectly competitive. The figure shows the demand and marginal revenue curves for cab rides as well as the marginal cost curve.

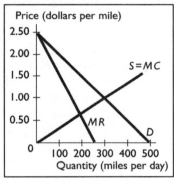

a. Before the government granted Acme its monopoly, how many miles of taxi rides were driven and what was the price?

b. As a monopoly, how many miles of taxi rides will Acme drive? What is the price Acme sets?

c. What is the efficient number of miles?

d. On the graph, show the deadweight loss that results from Acme's monopoly.

2. Suppose that Acme is put up for sale. Looking at the entire future, say Acme's total economic profit is $2 million. If the bidding for Acme is a competitive process, what do you expect will be the price for which the company is sold? What result are you illustrating?

### Solutions to Additional Practice Problems 14.3

1a. Before the monopoly was granted, the equilibrium number of miles and price were determined by the demand and supply curves. As the figure shows, the

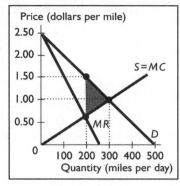

equilibrium number of miles was 300 miles per day and the price was $1.00 per mile.

1b. To maximize its profit, the figure shows that Acme drives 200 miles per day because that is the quantity at which marginal revenue equals marginal cost. The price is set from the demand curve and is $1.50 per mile.

1c. The efficient quantity is the quantity at which marginal benefit equals marginal cost. The demand curve is the marginal benefit curve, so the figure shows that the efficient quantity is 300 miles a day.

1d. Single-price monopolies create a deadweight loss because a monopoly produces where $MR = MC$ but efficiency requires production where $MB = MC$. The figure illustrates the deadweight loss as the darkened triangle.

2. Bidders are willing to pay up to $2 million for Acme because if they can buy it for any price less than $2 million, they receive an economic profit. Because the bidding is competitive, the price of Acme will be bid up to $2 million, so that the winning bidder earns a normal profit. This result demonstrates rent-seeking equilibrium in which the rent-seeking costs exhaust the economic profit.

■ **AP Self Test 14.3**

### True or false

1. A monopoly charges a higher price than a perfectly competitive industry would charge.

2. A monopoly redistributes consumer surplus so that the consumers gain and the producer loses.

3. The buyer of a monopoly always makes an economic profit.

**Multiple choice**

1. If a perfectly competitive industry is taken over by a single firm that operates as a single-price monopoly, the price will ____ and the quantity will ____.
   a. fall; decrease
   b. fall; increase
   c. rise; decrease
   d. rise; increase
   e. not change; decrease

■ **FIGURE 14.3**
Price and costs (dollars per gallon)

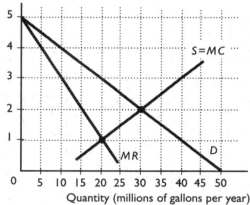

2. Figure 14.3 shows the market for gasoline in a town. If the market is perfectly competitive, the price is ____ per gallon and if the market is taken over by a firm that operates as a single-price monopoly, the price is ____.
   a. $1; $2
   b. $1; $3
   c. $1; $1
   d. $2; $1
   e. $2; $3

3. Figure 14.3 shows the market for gasoline in a town. If the market is perfectly competitive, the market quantity is ____ million gallons a year and if the market is taken over by a firm that operates as a single-price monopoly, the quantity is ____ million gallons a year.
   a. 50; 20
   b. 50; 30
   c. 30; 20
   d. 50; 10
   e. 20; 30

4. Comparing single-price monopoly to perfect competition, monopoly
   a. increases the amount of consumer surplus.
   b. has the same amount of consumer surplus.
   c. has no consumer surplus.
   d. decreases the amount of consumer surplus.
   e. decreases the amount of economic profit.

5. Is a single-price monopoly efficient?
   a. Yes, because it creates a deadweight loss.
   b. No, because it creates a deadweight loss.
   c. Yes, because consumers gain and producers lose some of their surpluses.
   d. Yes, because consumers lose and producers gain some of their surpluses.
   e. Yes, because it produces the quantity at which $MR=MC$.

6. Monopolies
   a. are always fair but are not efficient.
   b. might or might not be fair and are always efficient.
   c. might or might not be fair and are generally inefficient.
   d. are always fair and are always efficient.
   e. are never fair and are always efficient.

7. In equilibrium, rent seeking eliminates the
   a. deadweight loss.
   b. economic profit.
   c. consumer surplus.
   d. demand for the product.
   e. opportunity to price discriminate.

## Short Response Questions

■ **FIGURE 14.4**

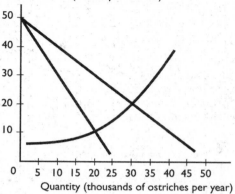

Price and costs (dollars per ostrich)

Quantity (thousands of ostriches per year)

1. Figure 14.4 shows the market for ostrich farming, an industry that is initially perfectly competitive. Then one farmer buys all the other farms and operates as a single-price monopoly. In the figure, label the curves. What was the competitive price and quantity? What is the monopoly price and quantity? Darken the deadweight loss area.

2. What happens to consumer surplus with a single-price monopoly?

### Long Response Questions

1. How does the quantity produced and the price set by a single-price monopoly compare to set in a perfectly competitive market? Does a monopoly produce the allocatively efficient quantity of output?

2. What is rent seeking? How does rent seeking affect society and what is a rent-seeking equilibrium?

## CHECKPOINT 14.4

■ **Explain how price discrimination increases profit.**

### Quick Review

- *Price discrimination* Price discrimination is selling a good at a number of different prices.
- *Consumer surplus* The consumer surplus

of a good is its marginal benefit, which is the maximum price the consumer is willing to pay, minus the price paid for it.

### Additional Practice Problems 14.4

1. Frequently the price of the first scoop of ice cream in a cone is less than the price of the second scoop. Why is this the case?

2. Why is the price to attend a movie less on a weekday afternoon than on a weekend evening?

3. How does price discrimination affect the amount of consumer surplus? The amount of the firm's economic profit?

### Solutions to Additional Practice Problems 14.4

1. The ice cream store is price discriminating among units of the good by charging different prices for different scoops of ice cream. The store knows that consumers' marginal benefits from ice cream decrease, so that the consumer is willing to pay less for the second scoop than for the first scoop. By charging less for the second scoop, the store will sell more scoops and increase its profit.

2. If the price to attend a movie is less on a weekday afternoon than on a weekend evening, the movie theater is practicing price discrimination among two groups of buyers. Each group has a different average willingness to pay to see a movie. By having two different prices, the movie theater maximizes profit by converting consumer surplus into economic profit.

3. Price discrimination decreases consumer surplus because it allows the business to set a price that is closer to the maximum the consumer is willing to pay. Price discrimination increases the firm's profit, which is why firms price discriminate.

### ■ Self Test 14.4

#### True or false

1. Price discrimination lowers a firm's profit.

2. Price discrimination converts producer surplus into consumer surplus.

3. With perfect price discrimination, the demand curve becomes the marginal revenue curve.

## Multiple choice

1. Which of the following must a firm be able to do to successfully price discriminate?
   i. divide buyers into different groups according to their willingness to pay
   ii. prevent resale of the good or service
   iii. identify into which group (high willingness to pay or low willingness to pay) a buyer falls
   a. ii only.
   b. i and ii.
   c. i and iii.
   d. iii only.
   e. i, ii, and iii.

2. Which of the following is (are) price discrimination?
   i. charging different prices based on differences in production cost
   ii. charging business flyers a higher airfare than tourists
   iii. charging more for the first pizza than the second
   a. i only.
   b. ii only.
   c. ii and iii.
   d. i and iii.
   e. i, ii, and iii.

3. When a monopoly price discriminates, it
   a. increases the amount of consumer surplus.
   b. decreases its economic profit.
   c. converts consumer surplus into economic profit.
   d. converts economic profit into consumer surplus.
   e. has no effect on the deadweight loss.

4. If a monopoly is able to perfectly price discriminate, then consumer surplus is
   a. equal to zero.
   b. maximized.
   c. unchanged from what it is with a single-price monopoly.
   d. unchanged from what it is in a perfectly competitive industry.
   e. not zero but is less than with a single-price monopoly.

5. With perfect price discrimination, the quantity of output produced by the monopoly is _____ the quantity produced by a perfectly competitive industry.
   a. greater than but not equal to
   b. less than
   c. equal to but not greater than
   d. not comparable to
   e. either greater than or equal to

## Short Response Question

### ■ FIGURE 14.5

Price and cost (dollars per article of clothing)

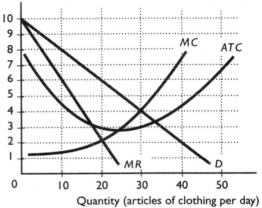

Quantity (articles of clothing per day)

1. Figure 14.5 shows the cost and demand curves for a dry-cleaner that has a monopoly in a small town.
   a. In the figure, lightly darken the area of the economic profit for a single-price monopoly. What is the amount of economic profit this firm earns?
   b. Suppose the firm can price discriminate and set one price for the first 10 articles of clothing and another price for the second 10 articles of clothing. What prices would it set? Darken the additional economic profit the firm earns. What is the amount of the firms economic profit now?
   c. Suppose the firm is able to perfectly price discriminate. More heavily darken the additional economic profit the firm now earns. What is the amount of the firm's economic profit now?

## Long Response Questions

1. Explain the effect of price discrimination on consumer surplus and economic profit.

2. When does a price discriminating monopoly produce the efficient quantity of output?

## CHECKPOINT 14.5

■ **Explain why monopoly can sometimes achieve a better allocation of resources than competition can.**

### Quick Review

- *Economies of scale* Economies of scale occur when a firm increases its plant size and labor force by the same percentage, its output increases by a larger percentage so that its average total costs decrease.

- *Patents* A legal right given the developer of a new product or process that allows the developer to have a monopoly on producing or using the product or process.

### Additional Practice Problem 14.5

1. Pharmaceutical drug companies are granted patents on the drugs they develop. It is currently estimated that it costs about $800 million to develop and test a new drug.

   a. How does the patent affect the pharmaceutical companies' incentives to develop new drugs?

   b. Some less developed nations have threatened to "break" the patents held by companies that produce drugs which fight AIDs. If these countries break the patents by allowing other firms to produce the drugs, what happens to the incentive to develop new AIDs drugs?

   c. When a drug patent expires, other generic drug companies are allowed to produce identical copies of the drug. After the patent expires, what happens to the price of the drug and the profits of the pharma-

ceutical company that initially developed the drug?

### Solution to Additional Practice Problem 14.5

1a. The patent gives the pharmaceutical drug company the incentive to develop new drugs. The company knows that if it succeeds, it will be granted a monopoly on the drug for some period of time and thereby can recoup the funds it spent developing the drug.

1b. If the countries break the patents, the profit from these AIDs drugs will be much less. Pharmaceutical companies will realize that if they develop new AIDs drugs, the odds of them making a profit are smaller, so the incentive to develop new AIDs drugs is significantly weakened.

1c. After the patent expires, the price plunges as new competitors enter the market. The profit of the company that developed the drug also plummets.

## ■ Self Test 14.5

### True or false

1. Compared to competitive markets, monopolies have no potential benefits.

2. Economies of scale can lead to natural monopolies.

3. A monopoly market is likely to lead to more innovations than a competitive market.

4. Patents strengthen the incentive to innovate.

### Multiple choice

1. What are the potential advantages for the economy of monopoly over competition?
   a. Monopolies can take advantage of the nation's patent laws.
   b. Monopolies earn more profit.
   c. Monopolies have a higher rate of productivity growth.
   d. Economies of scale and incentives to innovate are potential advantages.
   e. Monopolies set lower prices.

2. If a single firm can meet the entire market demand at a lower average total cost than could a larger number of smaller firms, then the industry is
   a. a perfectly price discriminating monopoly.
   b. perfectly competitive.
   c. a legal monopoly.
   d. a single-price monopoly.
   e. a natural monopoly.

3. Most societies ____ natural monopolies.
   a. break up firms that are
   b. regulate
   c. outlaw price discrimination by
   d. refuse to grant patents to
   e. give incentives to firms to become

4. Patents
   a. are granted only to competitive firms and not monopolies.
   b. require that monopolies increase the amount they produce.
   c. increase the incentive to capture economies of scale.
   d. increase the incentive to innovate.
   e. grant the holder a monopoly that lasts forever.

5. Patents
   a. are a legal barrier to entry.
   b. remove legal barriers to entry.
   c. create economies of scale.
   d. decrease the incentive to innovate.
   e. are prohibited in the United States.

**Short Response Questions**
1. How might a monopoly provide society with more benefits than would a competitive market?

**Long Response Questions**
1. What incentives do firms need to innovate? How do patents affect these incentives? For society, what are the advantages and disadvantages of patents?

## YOUR AP SELF TEST ANSWERS

### ■ CHECKPOINT 14.1

**True or false**
1. False; page 350
2. True; page 351
3. False; page 352

**Multiple choice**
1. b; page 350
2. b; page 350
3. d; page 350
4. b; page 351
5. d; page 352

**Short Response Question**
1. Monopoly occurs when there is a market with a single firm selling a good or service that has no close substitutes and in which the firm is protected by either a natural, ownership, or a legal barrier to entry; page 350.
2. Barriers to entry are anything that protects a firm from the entry of new competitors. Barriers to entry are either natural barriers, ownership barriers, or legal barriers; page 350.

**Long Response Question**
1. A monopoly can sell each unit of its output for the same price to all its customers or it can price discriminate by selling different units of its good or service at different prices. A perfectly competitive firm cannot affect the price so it must charge a single price determined by market demand and market supply; page 352.

### ■ CHECKPOINT 14.2

**True or false**
1. False; page 354
2. False; page 355
3. True; page 356

**Multiple choice**
1. a; page 354
2. d; page 354

3. a; page 355
4. b; page 356
5. c; page 356

**Short Response Questions**
1. If demand is elastic, marginal revenue is positive; if demand is unit elastic, marginal revenue is zero; and if demand is inelastic, marginal revenue is negative; page 354.

| Quantity (hamburgers per hour) | Price (dollars) | Marginal revenue (dollars) |
|---|---|---|
| 1 | 8.00 | |
| | | 6.00 |
| 2 | 7.00 | |
| | | 4.00 |
| 3 | 6.00 | |
| | | 2.00 |
| 4 | 5.00 | |
| | | 0.00 |
| 5 | 4.00 | |

2. The completed table is above
   a. Figure 14.6 plots the demand and marginal revenue curves; page 357.
   b. Figure 14.6 shows the marginal cost curve. To maximize his profit, Bud produces the quantity at which marginal revenue equals marginal cost. So Bud prepares 3 hamburgers per hour. From the demand curve, the price of a hamburger is $6; pages 363-357.

### ■ FIGURE 14.6

Price and marginal revenue (dollars per hamburger)

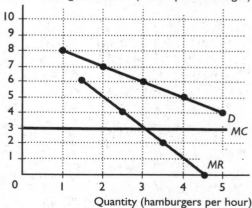

Quantity (hamburgers per hour)

■ **FIGURE 14.7**

Price and cost (dollars per unit)

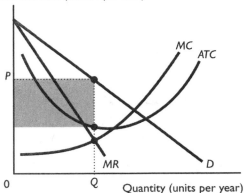

3. The curves, quantity, price, and economic profit are labeled and illustrated in Figure 14.7; page 357.

## Long Response Questions

1. Both perfectly competitive and monopoly firms maximize profit by producing where $MR = MC$. They use the same rule because for *any* firm, a unit of output is produced if $MR > MC$ because producing that unit adds to the firm's profit. And a unit of output is not produced if $MR < MC$ because producing that unit would lower the firm's profit. As long as $MR > MC$, *any* firm increases its total profit by continuing to produce additional output until the firm reaches the point at which $MR = MC$. If the firm continued to produce additional units, it would produce units for which $MR < MC$ and hence decrease its profit. So *any* firm will produce until it reaches the point where $MR = MC$ because at this point the firm has maximized its profit; page 356.

2. A monopoly can earn an economic profit in the long run because it is protected by a barrier to entry. Other firms want to enter the market in order also to earn some economic profit, but they cannot do so. A firm in perfect competition is not protected by barriers to entry, so if it is earning an economic profit, other firms will enter the market and compete away the economic profit; page 357.

## ■ CHECKPOINT 14.3

### True or false

1. True;  page 359
2. False;  page 360
3. False;  page 362

### Multiple choice

1. c;  page 359
2. e;  page 359
3. c;  page 359
4. d;  page 360
5. b;  page 360
6. c;  page 361
7. b;  page 362

### Short Response Questions

■ **FIGURE 14.8**

Price and cost (dollars per ostrich)

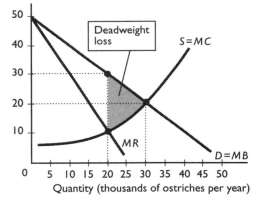

1. Figure 14.8 shows that the perfectly competitive price is $20 an ostrich and the quantity is 30,000 ostriches. The monopoly price is $30 an ostrich and the quantity is 20,000 ostriches a year. The deadweight loss is the dark triangular area;  page 360.

2. Consumer surplus decreases with a single-price monopoly. Consumer surplus decreases because the monopoly produces less output and charges a higher price;  page 360.

### Long Response Questions

1. The price set by a monopoly exceeds the price in a competitive market and the quantity produced by a monopoly is less than the quantity produced in a competitive market.

The quantity produced in a perfectly competitive market is the allocatively efficient amount. Because a monopoly produces less output, a monopoly produces less than the allocatively efficient amount. So a monopoly results in a deadweight loss; page 359.

2. Rent seeking is the act of obtaining special treatment by the government to create economic profit or to divert consumer surplus or producer surplus away from others. Rent seeking harms society because in a competitive rent-seeking equilibrium, the amount of the deadweight loss increases. In a rent seeking equilibrium, the amount of resources devoted to acquiring the monopoly equals the (potential) economic profit. These resources used in rent seeking add to the deadweight loss. So in a rent seeking equilibrium, the total deadweight loss of the monopoly is equal to the sum of the "conventional" deadweight loss triangle which occurs because the firm produces less than the allocatively efficient quantity plus the amount of the economic profit; page 362.

## ■ CHECKPOINT 14.4

**True or false**

1. False; page 364
2. False; page 364
3. True; page 367

**Multiple choice**

1. e; page 364
2. c; page 364
3. c; page 364
4. a; pages 367
5. c; page 368

**Short Response Question**

1. a. The economic profit is the light gray rectangle in Figure 14.9. The economic profit equals the area of the rectangle, which is $60 a day; page 365.
   b. The firm will set a price of $8 for each of the first 10 articles and $6 for each of the second 10 articles. The added profit is the

■ **FIGURE 14.9**

Price and cost (dollars per article of clothing)

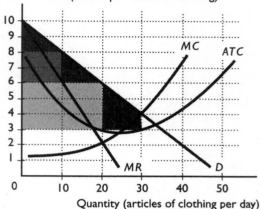

darker gray rectangle for the first 10 articles. The total economic profit the firm now earns is $80 a day; page 366.
   c. The economic profit is increased by the addition of the three very dark gray areas. The economic profit is now $120 a day; page 367.

**Long Response Questions**

1. Price discrimination decreases consumer surplus and increases economic profit. Price discrimination allows the firm to charge a price closer to the maximum the consumer is willing to pay, which is the marginal benefit of the good. Because the price is higher, the monopoly collects more revenue from the consumer, thereby converting consumer surplus into economic profit; page 364.

2. With perfect price discrimination, the charges every consumer the maximum price he or she is willing to pay. In this case, the monopoly increases output to the point at which price equals marginal cost. This output is identical to that of perfect competition and so is allocatively efficient. Deadweight loss with perfect price discrimination is zero because perfect price discrimination produces the efficient quantity; page 368.

## ■ CHECKPOINT 14.5

### True or false

1. False; page 370
2. True; page 370
3. True; page 371
4. True; page 372

### Multiple choice

1. d; page 370
2. e; page 370
3. b; page 370
4. d; page 372
5. a; page 372

### Short Response Questions

1. A monopoly might be able to capture economies of scale, so that it can produce at lower average total cost than could competitive firms. A monopoly also has a greater incentive to innovate because a monopoly can earn enough profit to cover the cost of innovation; pages 370-371.

### Long Response Questions

1. Innovation is costly, so firms need the incentive that they will likely be able to earn enough profit to repay the costs of innovation. The advantage of patents is that they increase firms' incentives to innovate by developing new products and new processes. They do so by granting the innovator a temporary monopoly over the patented product or process and thereby the opportunity to earn a temporary economic profit. Thus patents benefit society by making more innovations available. However, a firm granted a patent has a legal monopoly. A monopoly sets a higher price and produces less than the allocatively efficient quantity thereby creating a deadweight loss. Giving firms a monopoly and resulting deadweight loss is a drawback to society of patents; pages 370-372.

# Monopolistic Competition

# *Chapter* 15

In Chapter 15 we study a market structure that lies between the extremes of perfect competition and monopoly: monopolistic competition.

## ■ Describe and identify monopolistic competition.

Monopolistic competition is a market structure in which a large number of firms compete; each firm produces a differentiated product; firms compete on product quality, price, and marketing; and firms are free to enter and exit. Product differentiation is making a product that is slightly different from the products of competing firms. Product differentiation allows the firm to compete on product quality, price, and marketing. There are no barriers to entry in monopolistic competition. The four-firm concentration ratio and the Herfindahl-Hirschman Index (HHI) measure the extent to which a market is dominated by a small number of firms. The four-firm concentration ratio is the percentage of the value of the sales accounted for by the four largest firms in the industry. The Herfindahl-Hirschman Index is the square of the percentage market share of each firm summed over the 50 largest firms in the market.

## ■ Explain how a firm in monopolistic competition determines its output and price in the short run and the long run.

A firm in monopolistic competition has a downward-sloping demand curve. A firm in monopolistic competition makes its output and price decisions just like a monopoly firm does. It maximizes profit by producing the output at which marginal revenue equals marginal cost. The price is determined from the demand curve and is the highest price for which the firm can sell the quantity it produces. In the short run, the firm might have an economic profit or an economic loss. Entry and exit result in zero economic profit in the long run. In the long run a firm in monopolistic competition has excess capacity because it produces less than the efficient scale. In monopolistic competition price exceeds marginal cost—which indicates inefficiency—but the inefficiency arises from product variety—a gain for consumers.

## ■ Explain why advertising costs are high and why firms use brand names in monopolistic competition.

To maintain economic profit, firms in monopolistic competition innovate and develop new products, and incur huge costs to ensure that buyers appreciate the differences between their own products and those of their competitors. Selling costs, such as advertising, increase a firm's *total* cost, but they might lower *average* total cost if they increase the quantity sold by a large enough amount. Firms advertise to send a signal to the consumer that the product is high quality. Brand names also send a signal to the consumer about the product's quality. They also give the firm the incentive to maintain the expected level of product quality. Advertising and brand names provide consumers with information, but the opportunity cost of the additional information must be weighed against the gain to the consumer. So the efficiency of monopolistic competition is ambiguous.

## EXPANDED CHAPTER CHECKLIST

When you have completed this chapter, you will be able to:

**1 Describe and identify monopolistic competition.**

- Describe the market structure of monopolistic competition.
- Define product differentiation and discuss how it leads to competition on quality, price, and marketing.
- Calculate the four-firm concentration ratio and the Herfindahl-Hirschman Index.

**2 Explain how a firm in monopolistic competition determines its output and price in the short run and the long run.**

- Illustrate the firm's profit-maximizing decisions in monopolistic competition in the short run and long run.
- Explain why firms in monopolistic competition earn zero economic profit in the long run.
- Illustrate the excess capacity of firms in monopolistic competition.
- Discuss efficiency of monopolistic competition.

**3 Explain why advertising costs are high and why firms use brand names in monopolistic competition.**

- Explain why firms in monopolistic competition are continuously developing new products.
- Discuss the efficiency of product innovation.
- Illustrate how an increase in sales brought about by advertising can lower average total cost.
- Explain how advertising and brand names send a signal to the consumer.
- Discuss the efficiency of advertising and brand names.

## YOUR AP TEST HINTS

### AP Topics

| Topic on your AP test | Corresponding textbook section |
|---|---|
| **Nature and function of product markets** | |
| Monopolistic Competition | Chapter 15 |
| • Product differentiation and role of advertising | Checkpoint 15.1 |
| • Profit maximization | Checkpoint 15.2 |
| • Short-run and long-run equilibrium | Checkpoint 15.2 |
| • Excess capacity and inefficiency | Checkpoint 15.2 |

### Extra AP material

- The demand curve for a monopolistically competitive firm is more elastic than the demand curve for a monopoly because there are more close substitutes for the product produced by a monopolistically competitive firm.
- In the long run, a monopolistically competitive firm is not allocatively efficient because price is greater than marginal cost because the marginal benefit of a unit of the good to the consumer, which equals the price, exceeds the marginal cost of producing the unit. In the long run, a monopolistically competitive firm also is not production efficient because price exceeds the minimum average total cost.
- The material that is in Checkpoint 15.3 about advertising costs, brand names, and innovation is not on the AP test..

## CHECKPOINT 15.1

■ **Describe and identify monopolistic competition.**

### Quick Review

- *Four-firm concentration ratio* The four-firm concentration ratio is the percentage of the value of sales accounted for by the four largest firms in an industry.

- *Herfindahl-Hirschman Index (HHI)* The HHI is the square of the percentage market share of each firm summed over the largest 50 firms (or summed over all the firms if there are fewer than 50) in a market.

### Additional Practice Problem 15.1

| Firm | Total revenue (millions of dollars) | Percent of total revenue (percent) |
|---|---|---|
| McDonald's | 1,200 | ____ |
| Burger King | 600 | ____ |
| Wendy's | 600 | ____ |
| Hardee's | 300 | ____ |
| Checker's | 180 | ____ |
| Other 20 smaller firms | 720 | ____ |

1. The table gives some hypothetical data on sales in the fast-food hamburger market. Suppose that the total revenue of each of the 20 smallest firms is the same and each has total revenue of $36 million.
   a. Complete the table.
   b. Calculate the four-firm concentration ratio.
   c. Calculate the Herfindahl-Hirschman Index.
   d. Based on the hypothetical concentration ratios, in what market structure would you classify the fast-food hamburger market?

### Solution to Additional Practice Problem 15.1

| Firm | Total revenue (millions of dollars) | Percent of total revenue (percent) |
|---|---|---|
| McDonald's | 1,200 | 33.3 |
| Burger King | 600 | 16.7 |
| Wendy's | 600 | 16.7 |
| Hardee's | 300 | 8.3 |
| Checker's | 180 | 5.0 |
| Other 20 smaller firms | 720 | 20.0 |

1a. The total revenue shares are in the table above. To calculate the total revenue shares, first determine the total revenue within the market, which is $3,600 million. A firm's total revenue equals its total revenue divided by $3,600 million and then multiplied by 100.

1b. The four-firm concentration ratio is the percentage of the total revenue accounted for by the four largest firms in the industry, which is 33.3 percent + 16.7 percent + 16.7 percent + 8.3 percent = 75.0 percent.

1c. To calculate the Herfindahl-Hirschman Index (HHI), square and then sum the market shares of the firms. The market shares are equal to each firm's percentage of total revenue. Each of the 20 smaller firms has total revenue of $36 million, so each has a 1 percentage point market share. So the HHI = $(33.3)^2 + (16.7)^2 + (16.7)^2 + (8.3)^2 + (5.0)^2 + (1.0)^2 \times 20$ = 1,108.89 + 278.89 + 278.89 + 68.89 + 25.00 + 20.00, which is 1,780.56.

1d. Based on concentration ratios, the fast-food hamburger market is just on the borderline between monopolistic competition and oligopoly.

### ■ AP Self Test 15.1

**True or false**
1. Firms in monopolistic competition are free to enter or exit the market.
2. Each firm in monopolistic competition constantly tries to collude with its competitors.
3. The goods and services produced by firms in monopolistic competition all have virtually the same, if not identical, quality.
4. The larger the four-firm concentration ratio, the more competitive the industry.

**Multiple choice**
1. In monopolistic competition there
   a. are a large number of firms.
   b. are several large firms.
   c. is one large firm.
   d. might be many, several, or one firm.
   e. are many firms but only a few buyers.

2. A firm in monopolistic competition has a ____ market share and ____ influence the price of its good or service.
   a. large; can
   b. large; cannot
   c. small; can
   d. small; cannot
   e. large; might be able to

3. Product differentiation means
   a. making a product that has perfect substitutes.
   b. making a product that is entirely unique.
   c. the inability to set your own price.
   d. making a product that is slightly different from products of competing firms.
   e. making your demand curve horizontal.

4. A firm in monopolistic competition has ____ demand curve.
   a. a downward-sloping
   b. an upward-sloping
   c. a vertical
   d. a horizontal
   e. a U-shaped

5. Firms in monopolistic competition compete on
   i. quality.
   ii. price.
   iii. marketing.
   a. i and ii.
   b. ii only.
   c. ii and iii.
   d. i and iii.
   e. i, ii, and iii.

6. The absence of barriers to entry in monopolistic competition means that in the long run firms
   a. earn an economic profit.
   b. earn zero economic profit.
   c. incur an economic loss.
   d. earn either an economic profit or a normal profit.
   e. earn either a normal profit or suffer an economic loss.

7. Each of the ten firms in an industry has 10 percent of the industry's total revenue. The four-firm concentration ratio is
   a. 80.
   b. 100.
   c. 1,000
   d. 40.
   e. 10.

8. Each of the four firms in an industry has a market share of 25 percent. The Herfindahl-Hirschman Index equals
   a. 3,600.
   b. 100.
   c. 625.
   d. 25.
   e. 2,500.

9. If the four-firm concentration ratio for the market for pizza is 28 percent, then this industry is best characterized as
   a. a monopoly.
   b. monopolistic competition.
   c. an oligopoly.
   d. perfect competition.
   e. oligoplistic competition.

10. The larger the four-firm concentration, the ____ competition within an industry; the larger the Herfindahl-Hirschman Index, the ____ competition within an industry.
    a. more; more
    b. more; less
    c. less; more
    d. less; less
    e. The premise of the question is wrong because the four-firm concentration ratio applies only to markets with four firms in it and these markets are, by definition, not competitive.

**Short Response Questions**

| Firm | Total revenue (millions of dollars) | Percent of total revenue (percent) |
| --- | --- | --- |
| Dell | 1,000 | _____ |
| HP | 800 | _____ |
| IBM | 500 | _____ |
| Toshiba | 400 | _____ |
| Other 46 smaller firms | 2,300 | _____ |

1. The table gives some hypothetical data on sales in the desktop computer market. Suppose that the total revenue of each of the 46 smallest firms is the same and each has total revenue of $50 million.
   a. Complete the table.
   b. Calculate the four-firm concentration ratio.
   c. Calculate the Herfindahl-Hirschman Index.

2. Industry A has 1 firm with a market share of 57 percent and 43 other firms, each with a market share of 1 percent. Industry B has 4 firms, each with a market share of 15 percent, and 40 other firms, each with a market share of 1 percent.
   a. Calculate the four-firm concentration ratio for the two industries.
   b. Calculate the Herfindahl-Hirschman Index for the two industries.

## Long Response Question

1. What conditions define monopolistic competition?

## CHECKPOINT 15.2

■ **Explain how a firm in monopolistic competition determines its output and price in the short run and the long run.**

### Quick Review

- *Profit maximization* A firm in monopolistic competition produces where marginal revenue equals marginal cost. The price is determined from the demand curve.

### Additional Practice Problems 15.2

1. The figure shows the demand and costs for Bernie's Burger barn, a firm in monopolistic competition.

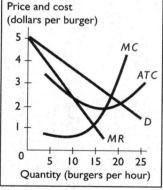

   a. To maximize its profit, how many burgers does Bernie produce in an hour? What is the price of a hamburger?
   b. Is the firm earning an economic profit or loss and, if so, how much?
   c. Does this figure show the firm in the short run or the long run? Explain your answer.

2. The Piece A' Pie company is a pizza restaurant in competition with many other pizza restaurants. Piece A' Pie produces 50 pizzas an hour.
   a. If Piece A' Pie's average total cost is $10 a pizza and its price is $12 a pizza, what is its economic profit?
   b. If Piece A' Pie's average total cost is $12 a pizza and its price is $12 a pizza, what is its economic profit?
   c. If Piece A' Pie's average total cost is $15 a pizza and its price is $12 a pizza, what is its economic profit?
   d. Which of the three situations outlined in parts (a), (b), and (c) can represent a short-run equilibrium? A long-run equilibrium? Why?

### Solutions to Additional Practice Problems 15.2

1a. To maximize its profit, Bernie's will produce where $MR = MC$. So Bernie's produces 15 burgers per hour. Bernie's demand curve shows that Bernie will set a price of $3 for a burger.

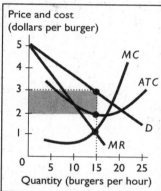

1b. Bernie's is earning an economic profit, because its price is greater than its average total cost. Its economic profit equals the area of the darkened rectangle in the figure. Bernie's earns an economic profit of $1 (its price, $3, minus its average total cost, $2) on each burger and so its total economic profit is $1 × 15 = $15.

1c. Bernie's is in its short-run equilibrium. It is not in its long-run equilibrium because the firm is earning an economic profit. Firms in monopolistic competition cannot earn an economic profit in the long run; they can earn an economic profit only in the short run.

2a. Piece A' Pie's economic profit on a pizza is equal to price minus average total cost. So Piece A' Pie earns an economic profit of $12 a pizza minus $10 a pizza, which is $2 a pizza. Piece A' Pie produces 50 pizzas an hour, so its total economic profit is $2 a pizza × 50 pizzas an hour, which is $100 an hour.

2b. Piece A' Pie's economic profit on a pizza is equal to price minus average total cost. So Piece A' Pie earns an economic profit of $12 a pizza minus $12 a pizza, which is zero dollars a pizza. Piece A' Pie earns zero economic profit so it earns a normal profit.

2c. Piece A' Pie's economic profit on a pizza is equal to price minus average total cost. So Piece A' Pie earns an economic profit of $12 a pizza minus $15 a pizza, which is −$3 a pizza. Piece A' Pie produces 50 pizzas an hour, so its total economic profit is −$3 a pizza × 50 pizzas an hour, which is −$150 an hour. So Piece A' Pie incurs an economic loss of $150 an hour.

2d. In the short run, depending on market conditions, a firm in monopolistic competition can earn an economic profit, can earn zero economic profit, or can incur an economic loss. Only the situation in part (b) can represent a long-run equilibrium. In the long run, the absence of barriers to entry means that firms in monopolistic competition earn zero economic profit.

## ■ AP Self Test 15.2

### True or false

1. A firm in monopolistic competition makes its output decision just like a monopoly and produces the quantity where marginal revenue equals marginal cost.

2. A firm in monopolistic competition can earn an economic profit in the short run.

3. A firm in monopolistic competition can never incur an economic loss.

4. A firm in monopolistic competition has a positive markup.

5. In a broader view of efficiency, monopolistic competition brings gains for consumers.

### Multiple choice

1. A firm in monopolistic competition maximizes profit by equating
   a. price and marginal revenue.
   b. price and marginal cost.
   c. demand and marginal cost.
   d. marginal revenue and marginal cost.
   e. price and average total cost.

2. Once a firm in monopolistic competition has determined how much to produce, the firm determines its price by referring to its
   a. demand curve.
   b. marginal cost curve.
   c. marginal revenue curve.
   d. average total cost curve.
   e. average variable cost curve.

### ■ FIGURE 15.1

Price and cost (dollars per lunch)

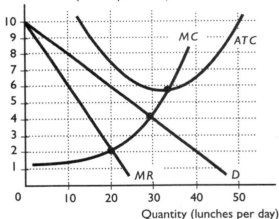

3. Figure 15.1 shows Louie's Lunches, a lunch counter in competition with many other restaurants. To maximize its profit, Louie's produces ____ lunches per day.
   a. 10
   b. 20
   c. 30
   d. between 31 and 40
   e. more than 40

4. Figure 15.1 shows demand and cost curves for Louie's Lunches. To maximize its profit, Louie's sets a price of ____ per lunch.
   a. $2
   b. $4
   c. between $5.00 and $5.99
   d. $6
   e. more than $6.01

5. Figure 15.1 shows demand and cost curves for Louie's Lunches. Louie's is in the ____ and is ____.
   a. short run; earning an economic profit
   b. short run; earning a normal profit
   c. short run; incurring an economic loss
   d. long run; earning an economic profit
   e. long run; earning a normal profit

6. A firm in monopolistic competition definitely incurs an economic loss if
   a. price equals marginal revenue.
   b. price is less than average total cost.
   c. marginal revenue equals marginal cost.
   d. marginal revenue is less than average total cost.
   e. price is greater than marginal cost.

7. In the long run, a firm in monopolistic competition
   a. earns zero economic profit.
   b. produces at a minimum average total cost.
   c. has deficient capacity.
   d. can earn either a normal profit or an economic profit.
   e. produces a quantity where its demand curve is upward sloping.

8. In the long run, a firm in monopolistic competition ____ excess capacity and a firm in perfect competition ____ excess capacity.
   a. has; has
   b. has; does not have
   c. does not have; has
   d. does not have; does not have
   e. might have; might have

9. In the long run, a firm in monopolistic competition ____ a markup of price over marginal cost and a firm in perfect competition ____ a markup of price over marginal cost.
   a. has; has
   b. has; does not have
   c. does not have; has
   d. does not have; does not have
   e. might have; might have

## Short Response Questions

1. What rule do firms in monopolistic competition follow to determine their profit-maximizing quantity of output? How does this rule compare to the rule followed by a monopoly?

### ■ FIGURE 15.2

Price and cost (dollars per pizza)

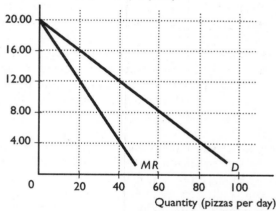

2. Figure 15.2 shows the demand curve and marginal revenues curve for Seaside Pizza, a firm in monopolistic competition. Draw the average total cost curve and marginal cost curve so that Seaside's output is 40 pizzas a day and its economic profit is $160. Is this a short-run or long-run equilibrium?

■ **FIGURE 15.3**

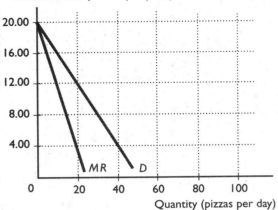

3. Figure 15.3 shows the demand curve and the marginal revenues curves for Surf Pizza, a firm in monopolistic competition. Draw the average total cost curve and marginal cost curve so that Surf's output is 20 pizzas a day and Surf's earns zero economic profit. Is this a short-run or long-run equilibrium?

4. What is a firm's markup?

**Long Response Questions**

1. What is the difference between the demand curve faced by a firm in perfect competition versus the demand curve faced by a firm in monopolistic competition?

2. Why do firms in monopolistic competition earn zero economic profit in the long run?

3. Is monopolistic competition allocatively efficient?

**CHECKPOINT 15.3**

■ **Explain why advertising costs are high and why firms use brand names in monopolistic competition.**

**Quick Review**

• *Selling costs* Selling costs such as advertising expenditures might lower average total cost if they increase the quantity sold by a large enough amount.

**Additional Practice Problem 15.3**

1. The figure to the right shows a firm in monopolistic competition.

   a. What quantity does the firm produce and what is the price?

   b. How much is the firm's markup?

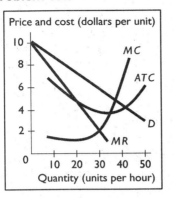

**Solution to Additional Practice Problem 15.3**

1a. As the figure shows, the firm produces 30 units and sets price of $6 per unit.

1b. The markup equals the difference between the price and the marginal cost. The price is $6 and the marginal cost is $2, so the markup is $4.

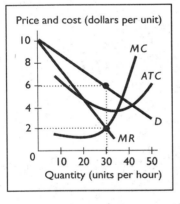

■ **AP Self Test 15.3**

**True or false**

1. Firms in monopolistic competition innovate without regard to cost.

2. Because advertising increases the demand for a firm's product, increasing the amount of advertising shifts the firm's cost curves downward.

3. Brand names give the firm an incentive to achieve a high and consistent standard of quality.

4. Whether monopolistic competition is efficient depends on the value people place on product variety.

## Multiple choice

1. Because economic profits are eliminated in the long run in monopolistic competition, to earn an economic profit firms continuously
   a. shut down.
   b. exit the industry.
   c. innovate and develop new products.
   d. declare bankruptcy.
   e. decrease their costs by decreasing their selling costs.

2. A firm in monopolistic competition that introduces a new and differentiated product will temporarily have a ____ demand for its product and is able to charge ____.
   a. less elastic, a lower price than before
   b. less elastic, a higher price than before
   c. more elastic, a lower price than before
   d. more elastic, a higher price than before
   e. less elastic, the same price as before

3. The decision to innovate
   a. depends on the marketing department's needs.
   b. depends on whether the firm wants to benefit its customers.
   c. is based on the marginal cost and the marginal revenue of innovation.
   d. is unnecessary in a monopolistically competitive market.
   e. None of the above answers is correct.

4. Advertising costs and other selling costs are
   a. efficient.
   b. fixed costs.
   c. variable costs.
   d. marginal costs.
   e. considered as part of demand because they affect the demand for the good.

5. For a firm in monopolistic competition, selling costs
   a. increase costs and reduce profits.
   b. always increase demand.
   c. can change the quantity produced and lower the average total cost.
   d. can lower total cost.
   e. has no effect on the quantity sold.

6. If advertising increases the number of firms in an industry, each firm's demand
   a. increases.
   b. does not change.
   c. decreases.
   d. might increase or decrease depending on whether the new firms produce exactly the same product or a product that is slightly differentiated.
   e. None of the above answers is correct.

7. One reason a company advertises is to
   a. signal consumers that its product is high quality.
   b. lower its total cost.
   c. produce more efficiently.
   d. lower its variable costs.
   e. lower its fixed costs.

## Short Response Question

1. Why do firms in monopolistic competition engage in innovation and product development?

## Long Response Question

1. How does advertising act as a signal?

## YOUR AP SELF TEST ANSWERS

### ■ CHECKPOINT 15.1

**True or false**
1. True; page 378
2. False; page 378
3. False; page 379
4. False; page 380

**Multiple choice**
1. a; page 378
2. c; page 378
3. d; page 378
4. a; page 379
5. e; page 379
6. b; page 379
7. d; page 380
8. e; page 381
9. b; page 381
10. d; pages 380-381

**Short Response Questions**

| Firm | Total revenue (millions of dollars) | Percent of total revenue (percent) |
|---|---|---|
| Dell | 1,000 | 20 |
| HP | 800 | 16 |
| IBM | 500 | 10 |
| Toshiba | 400 | 8 |
| Other 46 smaller firms | 2,300 | 46 |

1  a. The total revenue shares are in the table above. The total revenue within the market is $5,000 million. A firm's total revenue share equals its total revenue divided by $5,000 million and then multiplied by 100.

b. The four-firm concentration ratio is the percentage of the total revenue accounted for by the four largest firms in the industry, which is 20 percent + 16 percent + 10 percent + 8 percent = 54 percent; page 380.

c. To calculate the Herfindahl-Hirschman Index (HHI), square and then sum the market shares of the firms. The market shares are equal to each firm's percentage of total revenue. Each of the 20 smaller firms has total revenue of $50 million, so

each has a 1 percentage point market share. So the HHI = $(20)^2 + (16)^2 + (10)^2 + (8)^2 + (1.0)^2 \times 46 = 400 + 256 + 100 + 64 + 46$, which is 866; page 381.

2. a. The four-firm concentration ratios are the same for both industries, 60 percent; page 380.

b. The Herfindahl-Hirschman Index is 3,292 for Industry A and 940 for Industry B; page 381.

**Long Response Question**
1. Monopolistic competition occurs when a large number of firms compete; each firm produces a differentiated product, the firms compete on product quality; price, and marketing; and firms are free to enter and exit. The key difference between monopolistic competition and perfect competition is the presence of differentiated products in monopolistic competition. Because each firm produces a slightly different version of a product compared to its competitors, each monopolistically competitive firm faces a downward sloping demand curve; page 378.

### ■ CHECKPOINT 15.2

**True or false**
1. True; page 384
2. True; page 384
3. False; page 385
4. True; page 387
5. True; page 388

**Multiple choice**
1. d; page 384
2. a; page 384
3. b; page 384
4. d; page 384
5. c; page 385
6. b; page 385
7. a; page 386
8. b; page 387
9. b; page 387

## Short Response Questions

1. Firms in monopolistic competition produce the quantity at which marginal revenue equals marginal cost. This rule is the same rule that a monopoly follows; page 384.

**■ FIGURE15.4**

Price and cost (dollars per pizza)

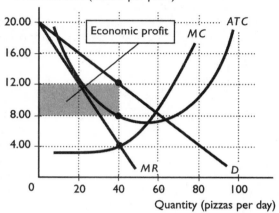

2. Figure 15.4 shows the average total cost curve and marginal cost curve so that Seaside Pizza's output is 40 pizzas a day and economic profit is $160. The figure shows a short-run equilibrium because Seaside is earning an economic profit; page 384.

**■ FIGURE15.5**

Price and cost (dollars per pizza)

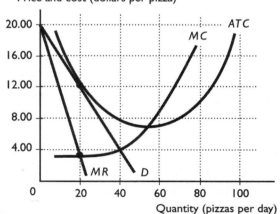

3. Figure 15.5 shows the average total cost curve and marginal cost curve so that Surf Pizza's output is 20 pizzas a day and it earns zero economic profit. The figure shows a long-run equilibrium because Surf is earning zero economic profit; page 386.

4. The markup is the amount by which the price exceeds the marginal cost; page 387.

## Long Response Questions

1. A perfectly competitive firm produces a product that is identical to that produced by its competitors. As a result of the fact that there are many perfect substitutes, the demand faced by a for firm in perfect competition is perfectly elastic so that its demand curve is horizontal. A monopolistically competitive firm produces a product that is differentiated from those produced by its competitors. Because these products are not perfect substitutes, the demand faced by a firm in monopolistic competition not perfectly elastic, so its demand curve is downward sloping; page 384.

2. There is no restriction on entry in monopolistic competition, so if firms in an industry are making an economic profit, other firms have an incentive to enter the industry. The entry of new firms decreases the demand for each firm's product. The demand curve and marginal revenue curve for the existing firms shift leftward, which lowers the firm's price and economic profit. When all firms in the industry are earning zero economic profit, there is no new incentive for new firms to enter and the industry is in long-run equilibrium. Similarly, if firms in an industry are incurring an economic loss, firms have an incentive to exit the industry. Exit raises the price and thus reduces the economic loss of the surviving firms. In the long run the remaining firms make zero economic profit; page 386.

3. In monopolistic competition, price exceeds marginal revenue and marginal revenue equals marginal cost, so price exceeds marginal cost—a sign of allocative inefficiency. But this inefficiency arises from product differentiation that consumers value and for which they are willing to pay. So the loss

that arises because marginal benefit exceeds marginal cost must be weighed against the gain that arises from greater product variety; page 388.

## ■ CHECKPOINT 15.3

### True or false
1. False; page 390
2. False; page 392
3. True; page 395
4. True; page 395

### Multiple choice
1. c; page 390
2. b; page 390
3. c; page 390
4. b; page 392
5. c; page 392
6. c; page 393
7. a; page 394

### Short Response Question
1. Firms innovate and develop new products to increase the demand for their product and earn an economic profit; page 390.

### Long Response Question
1. Advertising sends a signal to the consumer that the product being advertised is high quality. Producers are willing to pay for expensive advertising only if they know that their product is of high enough quality that the consumer will buy it repeatedly; pages 394-395.

# Oligopoly

# Chapter 16

In Chapter 16 we study the last market structure, oligopoly. Oligopoly is characterized by having a small number of firms competing. It lies between the extremes of perfect competition and monopoly.

## ■ Describe and identify oligopoly and explain how it arises.

An oligopoly is a market structure in which a small number of firms compete and natural or legal barriers prevent the entry of new firms. Because there are a small number of firms in the market, the firms are interdependent because each firm's actions affect the other firms. So firms in oligopoly have a temptation to form a cartel and collude to limit output, raise price, and increase economic profit. A duopoly is a market with only two firms. The key feature to identifying an oligopoly is uncovering whether the firms are so few that they recognize the interdependence among them. The Herfindahl-Hirschman Index is larger for oligopoly than for monopolistic competition; if the HHI exceeds 1,800, the industry is usually oligopoly.

## ■ Explore the range of alternative price and quantity outcomes and describe the dilemma faced by firms in oligopoly.

A cartel is a group of firms acting together to limit output, raise price, and thereby increase economic profit. Firms in oligopoly make zero economic profit if they act as perfectly competitive firms. They make the same economic profit as a monopoly if they act together in a cartel to restrict output to the monopoly level. In the cartel, each firm can make a bigger economic profit by increasing production, but this action decreases the economic profit of the other firms. The dilemma faced by a firm in an oligopoly cartel is that if each firm in the cartel increases output to maximize profit, then each firm ends up making a smaller economic profit.

## ■ Use game theory to explain how price and quantity are determined in oligopoly.

Game theory is the tool economists use to analyze strategic behavior. Games have rules, strategies, and payoffs. The prisoners' dilemma is a game between two prisoners that shows why it is hard to cooperate, even when it would be beneficial to both players to do so. The equilibrium of a game occurs when each player takes the best possible action given the action of the other player. This equilibrium concept is called Nash equilibrium. The equilibrium of the prisoners' dilemma game (each confesses) is not the best outcome for the prisoners. The duopolist's dilemma is like the prisoners' dilemma. Collusion is difficult to attain, and so the firms reach a Nash equilibrium in which they produce more and have lower profit than if they restricted production to the joint profit-maximizing quantity. In a repeated game, a punishment strategy can produce a monopoly output, a monopoly price, and an economic profit. If the firms can successfully collude, they produce an inefficient quantity. Firms in oligopoly also might operate at a higher average total cost than firms in perfect competition or a monopoly because their advertising and research budgets are higher than the efficient amounts.

## EXPANDED CHAPTER CHECKLIST

**When you have completed this chapter, you will be able to:**

### 1 Describe and identify oligopoly and explain how it arises.

- Define oligopoly and explain how one firm's actions can decrease the profits of the other firms.
- Define cartel.
- Explain why barriers to entry can create oligopoly.

### 2 Explore the range of possible price and quantity outcomes and describe the dilemma faced by firms in oligopoly.

- Discuss why the outcomes in an oligopoly range from the competitive outcome to the monopoly outcome.
- Explain why collusion usually breaks down.

### 3 Use game theory to explain how price and quantity are determined in oligopoly.

- Define game theory and discuss the three features of games. Describe the prisoner's dilemma.
- Define Nash equilibrium and recognize the Nash equilibrium in a payoff matrix.

## YOUR AP TEST HINTS

*AP Topics*

| Topic on your AP test | Corresponding textbook section |
|---|---|
| **Nature and function of product markets** | |
| Oligopoly | Chapter 16 |
| • Interdependence, collusion, and cartels | Checkpoint 16.1, 16.2 |
| • Game theory and strategic behavior | Checkpoint 16.3 |

*Extra AP material*

- The AP test will require that students know these game theory concepts:
  - A dominant strategy is a strategy that always yields the highest payoff regardless of what choice the other player makes.
  - A Nash equilibrium is the equilibrium in which each player takes the best possible action given the action of the other player.
  - The payoff matrix for a duopoly.
- The Concentration Ratio and the Herfindahl-Hirschman Index, which were discussed in Chapter 15.1, are relevant to identifying oligopoly.

## CHECKPOINT 16.1

### ■ Describe and identify oligopoly and explain how it arises.

**Quick Review**

- *Oligopoly* An oligopoly is characterized by having a small number of firms competing with natural or legal barriers preventing the entry of new firms.

**Additional Practice Problems 16.1**

1. What is the key difference between oligopoly and monopolistic competition?

2. What does it mean for firms to be interdependent? Why are firms in oligopoly interdependent?

**Solutions to Additional Practice Problems 16.1**

1. The key difference between oligopoly and monopolistic competition is that oligopoly is characterized by having only a small number of interdependent firms. Monopolistic competition has a large number of competing firms. Because there are only a few firms in oligopoly and because they are interdependent, the firms in oligopoly face the temptation to collude, which is an incentive missing from monopolistic competition.

2. Firms are interdependent when one firm's actions have an impact on another firm's profit. Firms in oligopoly are interdependent because there are only a few firms. In this case, one firm's actions have a major effect on the profits of its few competitors.

## ■ AP Self Test 16.1

**True or false**

1. Oligopoly is a market in which a small number of firms compete.

2. The aim of a cartel is to lower price, increase output, and increase economic profit.

3. Only legal barriers to entry can create oligopoly.

4. Economies of scale can limit the number of firms that are in a market.

5. A market in which the HHI exceeds 1,800 is usually an oligopoly.

**Multiple choice**

1. Oligopoly is a market structure in which
   a. many firms each produce a slightly differentiated product.
   b. one firm produces a unique product.
   c. a small number of firms compete.
   d. many firms produce an identical product.
   e. the number of firms is so small that they do not compete with each other.

2. The fact that firms in oligopoly are interdependent means that
   a. there are barriers to entry.
   b. one firm's profits are affected by other firms' actions.
   c. they can produce either identical or differentiated goods.
   d. there are too many firms for any one firm to influence price.
   e. they definitely compete with each other so that the price is driven down to the monopoly level.

3. Collusion results when a group of firms
   i. act separately to limit output, lower price, and decrease economic profit.
   ii. act together to limit output, raise price, and increase economic profit.
   iii. in the United States legally fix prices.
   a. i only.
   b. ii only.
   c. iii only.
   d. i and iii.
   e. ii and iii.

4. A cartel is a group of firms
   a. acting separately to limit output, lower price, and decrease economic profit.
   b. acting together to limit output, raise price, and increase economic profit.
   c. legally fixing prices.
   d. acting together to erect barriers to entry.
   e. that compete primarily with each other rather than the other firms in the market.

5. A market with only two firms is called a
   a. duopoly.
   b. two-firm monopolistic competition.
   c. two-firm monopoly.
   d. cartel.
   e. two-firm quasi-monopoly.

6. The efficient scale of one firm is 20 units and the average total cost at the efficient scale is $30. The quantity demanded in the market as a whole at $30 is 40 units. This market is
   a. a natural duopoly.
   b. a legal duopoly.
   c. a natural monopoly.
   d. a legal monopoly.
   e. monopolistically competitive.

7. Even though four firms can profitably sell hotdogs downtown, the government licenses only two firms. This market is a
   a. natural duopoly.
   b. legal duopoly.
   c. natural monopoly.
   d. legal monopoly.
   e. market-limited oligopoly.

### Short Response Questions

1. What conditions define oligopoly?
2. What is a cartel?
3. How does the HHI for monopolistic competition compare to the HHI for oligopoly?

### Long Response Question

1. Firms in oligopoly are interdependent. Firms in monopolistic competition are not. What accounts for the difference? Why is the difference important?

## CHECKPOINT 16.2

■ **Explore the range of alternative price and quantity outcomes and describe the dilemma faced by firms in oligopoly.**

### Quick Review

- *Duopoly* A market with only two firms.
- *Range of outcomes* The price and quantity in a duopoly can range from the competitive outcome to the monopoly outcome.

### Practice Problem 16.2

1. Just as in the textbook, Isolated Island has two natural gas wells, one owned by Tom and the other owned by Jerry. Each well has a valve that controls the rate of flow of gas, and the marginal cost of producing gas is zero. The table gives the demand schedule for gas on this island. Suppose Tom and Jerry agree to operate as a monopoly. A monopoly produces 6 units and charges $6 a unit. Tom and Jerry

| Price (dollars per unit) | Quantity demanded (units per day) |
|---|---|
| 12 | 0 |
| 11 | 1 |
| 10 | 2 |
| 9 | 3 |
| 8 | 4 |
| 7 | 5 |
| 6 | 6 |
| 5 | 7 |
| 4 | 8 |
| 3 | 9 |
| 2 | 10 |
| 1 | 11 |
| 0 | 12 |

agree that each will produce 3 units and charge $6. There are no fixed costs

a. If neither Tom nor Jerry cheat on the agreement what is Tom's profit? Jerry's profit? The combined profit?
b. Suppose Tom decides to cheat on the agreement by producing 4 units. Jerry sticks to the agreement. If 7 units are produced, what is the price? What is Tom's profit? Jerry's profit? The combined profit?
c. Why would Tom ever consider cheating on the agreement he made with Jerry?

### Solution to Additional Practice Problem 16.2

1a. Profit is equal to total revenue because total cost is zero. Tom's profit is $18, Jerry's profit is $18, and the combined profit is $36.

1b. If 7 units are produced, the price is $5 a unit. Tom's profit on his 4 units is $20 and Jerry's profit on his 3 units is $15. Combined profit is $35.

1c. Tom considers cheating because cheating increases his profit. Tom realizes that if he alone cheats, his profit will be more, $20 versus $18. Jerry's profit falls more than Tom's rises but Tom is concerned only about his own profit.

■ **AP Self Test 16.2**

### True or false

1. In a duopoly, the highest price that the firms might set is the perfectly competitive price.
2. The only possible outcome for a duopoly is the monopoly outcome.
3. Once a duopoly has achieved the monopoly outcome, neither firm can increase its total profit.
4. A duopoly is currently making, in total, the same economic profit as a monopoly. If one firm increases its output, the economic profit of the other firm increases.
5. A duopoly's total profit is the largest when it produces more than the monopoly level of output.

**Multiple choice**

■ **FIGURE 16.1**

Price and cost (dollars per bottle of shampoo)

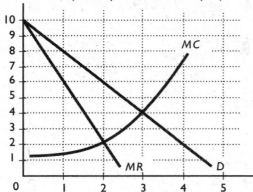

Quantity (millions of bottles of shampoo per day)

1. Suppose only two companies make shampoo. Figure 16.1 shows the market demand curve and associated marginal revenue curve. It also shows the combined marginal cost curve of the two companies. If these companies formed a cartel that operated as a monopoly, production would be ____ million bottles of shampoo and the price would be ____ per bottle of shampoo.
   a. 5; $4
   b. 2; $6
   c. 3; $6
   d. 2; $2
   e. 3; $4

2. Suppose the two companies that make shampoo illustrated in Figure 16.1 operate as perfect competitors. In this case, production would be ____ million bottles of shampoo and the price would be ____ per bottle of shampoo.
   a. 5; $4
   b. 2; $6
   c. 3; $6
   d. 2; $2
   e. 3; $4

3. For a duopoly, the highest price is charged when the duopoly achieves
   a. the competitive outcome.
   b. the monopoly outcome.
   c. an outcome between the competitive outcome and the monopoly outcome.
   d. its noncooperative equilibrium.
   e. Both answers (a) and (d) are correct because both refer to the same price.

4. For a duopoly, the smallest quantity is produced when the duopoly achieves
   a. the competitive outcome.
   b. the monopoly outcome.
   c. an outcome between the competitive outcome and the monopoly outcome.
   d. its noncooperative equilibrium.
   e. Both answers (a) and (d) are correct because both refer to the same quantity.

5. For a duopoly, the maximum total profit is reached when the duopoly produces
   a. the same amount of output as the competitive outcome.
   b. the same amount of output as the monopoly outcome.
   c. an amount of output that lies between the competitive outcome and the monopoly outcome.
   d. more output than the competitive outcome.
   e. less output than the monopoly outcome.

6. If a duopoly has reached the monopoly outcome, a firm can increase its profit if it and it alone ____ its price and ____ its production.
   a. raises; increases
   b. raises; decreases
   c. lowers; increases
   d. lowers; decreases
   e. raises; does not change

7. If a duopoly has reached the monopoly outcome and only one firm increases its production, that firm's profit _____ and the other firm's profit _____.
   a. increases; increases
   b. increases; decreases
   c. decreases; increases
   d. decreases; decreases
   e. increases; does not change

8. Suppose a duopoly had reached the monopoly outcome and then the first firm increased its production. If the second firm next increases its production, the second firm's profit _____ and the first firm's profit _____.
   a. increases; increases
   b. increases; decreases
   c. decreases; increases
   d. decreases; decreases
   e. increases; does not change

9. If both firms in a duopoly increase their production by one unit beyond the monopoly output, each firm's profit _____ and the *total* profit of the duopoly _____.
   a. increases; increases
   b. does not change; does not change
   c. decreases; decreases
   d. does not change; increases
   e. decreases; does not change

10. The very best outcome possible for the firms in a duopoly is to produce the
   a. monopoly level of output.
   b. perfectly competitive level of output.
   c. output level that maximizes total revenue.
   d. output level that minimizes total cost.
   e. Nash equilibrium level of output if the game is not repeated.

## Short Response Questions

| Quantity (thousands of newspapers per day) | Price (cents) | Marginal revenue (cents) |
|---|---|---|
| 0 | 60 | 60 |
| 2 | 50 | 40 |
| 4 | 40 | 20 |
| 6 | 30 | 0 |
| 8 | 20 | −20 |

1. Anytown, USA has two newspapers that have a duopoly in the local market. The table contains information on the market demand and marginal revenue for newspapers. The marginal cost of a newspaper is 20 cents.

   a. Graph the demand curve, marginal revenue curve, and marginal cost curve in Figure 16.2.

**■ FIGURE 16.2**

Price and marginal revenue (cents per newspaper)

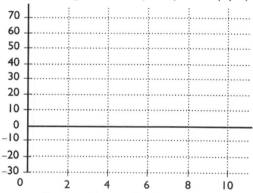

Quantity (thousands of newspapers per day)

   b. What price and quantity represent the competitive outcome?
   c. What price and quantity represent the monopoly outcome?
   d. What range of price and quantity represent the potential duopoly outcomes?

## Long Response Questions

1. In oligopoly, one firm's profit-maximizing actions might decrease its competitors' profits. Why is this fact a problem for firms in oligopoly?

2. Why do firms in an oligopoly have an incentive to form a collusive cartel that boosts the price and decreases the output? Why does each firm have the incentive to cheat on the cartel agreement to limit production and raise the price?

## CHECKPOINT 16.3

■ **Use game theory to explain how price and quantity are determined in oligopoly.**

### Quick Review

- *Game theory* The tool that economists use to analyze strategic behavior—behavior that recognizes mutual interdependence and takes account of the expected behavior of others.
- *Payoff matrix* A table (or matrix) showing each participant's payoffs and how they depend on the strategies adopted by the players.
- *Nash equilibrium* An equilibrium in which each player takes the best possible action given the action of the other player.

### Additional Practice Problem 16.3

1. Coke and Pepsi are engaged in an advertising game. They each know that if they both limit their advertising, they will make the maximum attainable joint economic profit of $400 million, divided so that each has an economic profit of $200 million. They also know that if either of them advertises while the other does not, the one advertising makes an economic profit of $300 million and the one that does not advertise incurs an economic loss of $100 million dollars. And they also know that if they both advertise, they both earn zero economic profit.

   a. Construct a payoff matrix for the game that Coke and Pepsi must play.
   b. Find the Nash equilibrium. How is this game similar to the prisoners' dilemma?
   c. What is the equilibrium if this game is played repeatedly?

d. Suppose that Coke and Pepsi are both playing a tit-for-tat strategy and that last time both did not advertise. Today, however, Coke really needs some extra income. So Coke advertises. What takes place today and in the future?

### Solution to Additional Practice Problem 16.3

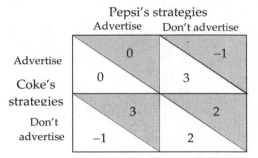

Pepsi's strategies

1a. A payoff matrix is a table that shows payoffs for every possible action by each player, Coke and Pepsi, given every possible action by the other player. The payoff matrix is above. The number in each square is the economic profit in millions of dollars.

1b. To find the Nash equilibrium of a game, place yourself in the position of the first player. Ask yourself "what if" your opponent takes one action: What will you do? Then ask "what if" the opponent takes the other action: now what will you do? This analysis allows you to determine the first player's action. Then place yourself in the position of the second player and repeat the "what if" analysis to determine the second player's action. So, to find Coke's strategy, ask what Coke will do for each of Pepsi's choices. If Pepsi advertises (the first column of the payoff matrix), Coke advertises because that gives Coke a larger profit ($0 versus a loss of $1 million). If Pepsi does not advertise (the second column of the payoff matrix), Coke advertises gallons because that gives Coke a larger profit ($3 million versus $2 million). Regardless of Pepsi's action, Coke advertises. Similar reasoning shows that Pepsi also advertises. So the Nash equilibrium is for each to advertise and earn zero economic profit. The game is similar to a prisoners' dilemma game because there is a conflict between each player's incentives to do what is best for the player versus what is best for both of them taken together. In the prisoners' dilemma game, both prisoners confess, leading to the worst joint outcome. In this game, both players advertise, again leading to the worst joint outcome.

1c. In a repeated game, Coke and Pepsi both do not advertise and earn the maximum joint economic profit. This outcome occurs if they use a tit-for-tat strategy.

1d. Today, Coke earns an economic profit of $3 million and Pepsi incurs an economic loss of $1 million. But in the second year, Pepsi will advertise. Coke might go back to not advertising to induce Pepsi to not advertise in the third year. So in the second year, Pepsi earns an economic profit of $3 million and Coke incurs an economic loss of $1 million. Over the two years, Coke earns a total economic profit of $2 million (and Pepsi also earns a total economic profit of $2 million.) But if Coke had not "cheated" on the agreement and advertised in the first year, then over the two years Coke's total economic profit would have been $4 million, not just $2 million. So, by cheating on the agreement Coke earns more profit immediately but over the longer haul earns less profit.

## ■ Self Test 16.3

### True or false

1. Game theory is used to analyze strategic behavior.

2. A prisoners' dilemma has no equilibrium.

3. A Nash equilibrium is the best outcome for all players in a prisoners' dilemma game.

4. The monopoly outcome is more likely in a repeated game than in a one-play game.

5. If firms in oligopoly play a repeated game and end up restricting their output, then oligopoly is efficient.

### Multiple choice

1. One of the main tools economists use to analyze strategic behavior is
   a. the Herfindahl-Hirschman Index.
   b. game theory.
   c. cartel theory.
   d. the collusion index.
   e. dual theory, which is used to study duopolies.

2. A Nash equilibrium occurs
   a. when each player acts without considering the actions of the other player.
   b. when each player takes the best possible action given the action of the other player.
   c. only when players use the tit-for-tat strategy.
   d. only if the game is played in Nashville, TN.
   e. when each player takes the action that makes the combined payoff for all players as large as possible.

3. Game theory reveals that
   a. the equilibrium might not be the best solution for the parties involved.
   b. firms in oligopoly are not interdependent.
   c. each player looks after what is best for the industry.
   d. if all firms in an oligopoly take the action that maximizes their profit, then the equilibrium will have the largest possible combined profit of all the firms.
   e. firms in an oligopoly choose their actions without regard for what the other firms might do.

4. The prisoners' dilemma game
   a. shows that prisoners are better off if they cooperate.
   b. shows it is easy to cooperate.
   c. has an equilibrium in which both prisoners are made as well off as possible.
   d. would have the same outcome even if the prisoners can communicate and cooperate.
   e. has an equilibrium in which one prisoner is made as well off as possible and the other prisoner is made as worse off as possible.

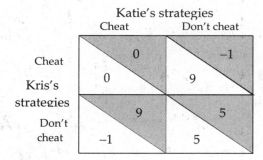

**Katie's strategies**

| | Cheat | Don't cheat |
|---|---|---|
| Cheat | 0 / 0 | −1 / 9 |
| Don't cheat | 9 / −1 | 5 / 5 |

5. Katie and Kris are duopolists who formed a collusive agreement to boost prices and decrease production. Their payoff matrix is above and the entries are millions of dollars of economic profit. They now have the choice of cheating on the agreement or not cheating. If Kris cheats, then
   a. Kris definitely earns an economic profit of $9 million.
   b. Kris definitely earns $0.
   c. Kris definitely incurs an economic loss of $1 million.
   d. Kris definitely earns an economic profit of $5 million.
   e. Kris might earn an economic profit of $9 million or might earn $0 depending on what Katie does.

6. Based on the payoff matrix above, the Nash equilibrium is for
   a. Kris to cheat and Katie to cheat.
   b. Kris to not cheat and Katie to not cheat.
   c. Kris to cheat and Katie to not cheat.
   d. Kris to not cheat and Katie to cheat.
   e. Kris and Katie to invite a third person to determine what each of them should do.

7. Based on the payoff matrix above, in the Nash equilibrium the total profit that Katie and Kris earn together is ____ million.
   a. $8
   b. $9
   c. $10
   d. $0
   e. −$1

8. A collusive agreement to form a cartel is difficult to maintain because
   a. each firm can increase its own profits by cutting its price and selling more.
   b. forming a cartel is legal but frowned upon throughout the world.
   c. supply will decrease because of the high cartel price.
   d. demanders will rebel once they realize a cartel has been formed.
   e. each firm can increase its profit if it decreases its production even more than the decrease set by the cartel.

9. Firms in oligopoly can achieve an economic profit
   a. always in the long run.
   b. if they cooperate.
   c. only if the demand for their products is inelastic.
   d. only if the demand for their products is elastic.
   e. if they reach the non-cooperative equilibrium.

10. When duopoly games are repeated and a "tit-for-tat" strategy is used,
   a. the competitive outcome is more likely to be reached than when the game is played once.
   b. the monopoly outcome is more likely to be reached than when the game is played once.
   c. both firms begin to incur economic losses.
   d. one firm goes out of business.
   e. because the game is repeated it is impossible to predict whether the competitive or the monopoly outcome is more likely.

11. Oligopoly is
   a. always efficient.
   b. efficient only if the firms cooperate.
   c. efficient only if they play non-repeated games.
   d. generally not efficient.
   e. efficient only if the firms innovate.

## Short Response Questions

Cameron's strategies

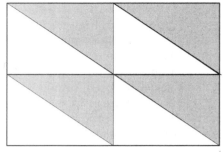

Art's strategies

1. Art and Cameron own the only two movie theaters in a small, isolated town. They have recently agreed to an illegal cartel agreement in which they will boost their ticket prices. If they both comply with the agreement, both will make $1 million of economic profit. If one cheats by lowering his price, the cheater will make $1.5 million of economic profit and the other will suffer an economic loss if $0.5 million. If they both cheat by lowering their prices, each makes zero economic profit.

   a. Complete the payoff matrix above.
   b. What is the Nash equilibrium of this game?

Intel's strategies

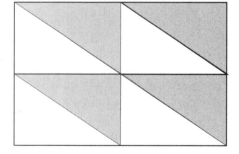

AMD's strategies

2. Intel and AMD are involved in a game to determine the amount they will spend on research and development. If they each spend $2 billion, their economic profit is zero. If they each spend $1 billion, their economic profit is $500 million. And if one spends $2 billion and the other spends $1 billion, the one spending $2 billion has an economic profit of $1,500 million and the other has an economic loss of $100 million.

   a. Complete the payoff matrix above.
   b. What is the Nash equilibrium of this game?

## Long Response Questions

1. What are "strategies" in game theory?
2. In game theory, what does the term "dominant strategy" mean?
3. In a prisoners' dilemma, why don't the players cooperate?
4. In the duopolists' dilemma, why don't the players cooperate?
5. How does the number of players in a game affect its outcome?

# YOUR AP SELF TEST ANSWERS

## ■ CHECKPOINT 16.1

**True or false**

   1. True;  page 402

   2. False;  page 402

   3. False;  page 402

   4. True;  page 403

   5. True;  page 404

**Multiple choice**

   1.  c;  page 402

   2.  b;  page 402

   3.  b;  page 402

   4.  b;  page 402

   5.  a;  page 402

   6.  a;  page 403

   7.  b;  page 404

**Short Response Questions**

   1. Oligopoly occurs when a small number of firms compete and natural or legal barriers prevent the entry of new firms; page 402.

   2. A cartel is a group of firms acting together to limit output and raise price in order to increase their economic profit;  page 402.

   3. The HHI for monopolistic competition is less than that for oligopoly. For monopolistic competition, the HHI usually lies between 1,000 and 1,800. For oligopoly, the HHI usually lies above 1,800; page 404.

**Long Response Question**

   1. The difference is because there are only a small number of firms in oligopoly. Because there are only a small number of firms, one firm's actions affect the profits of all its (few) competitors. This result reflects the fact that the firms are interdependent, which is the difference between oligopoly and monopolistic competition. Because of the interdependency, we cannot study each firm in isolation; we must take account of interaction between the firms' behaviors;  page 402.

## ■ CHECKPOINT 16.2

**True or false**

   1. False;  page 407

   2. False;  page 407

   3. False;  page 407

   4. False;  page 407

   5. False;  page 407

**Multiple choice**

   1. b;  page 406

   2. e;  page 406

   3. b;  page 407

   4. b;  page 407

   5. b;  page 407

   6. c;  page 407

   7. b;  page 407

   8. b;  page 408

   9. c;  page 408

  10. a;  page 408

**Short Response Questions**

### ■ FIGURE 16.3

Price and marginal revenue (cents per newspaper)

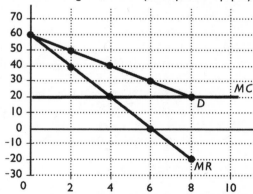

Quantity (thousands of newspapers per day)

   1. a. The curves are graphed in Figure 16.3.

      b. The competitive equilibrium is 8,000 newspapers a day and a price of 20¢ a newspaper; page 406.

c. The monopoly equilibrium is 4,000 newspapers a day and a price of 40¢ a newspaper; pages 406-407.

d. The exact price and quantity can't be predicted, but it will be somewhere between the competitive and monopoly outcomes. The price will be between 40¢ and 20¢ a newspaper and the output will be between 4,000 and 8,000 newspapers a day; pages 406-408.

### Long Response Questions

1. The point that one firm's actions can decrease another firm's profits is what makes competition difficult in an oligopoly. The firms would be better off cooperating by raising their prices and restricting their outputs. In this case, each firm's profit increases. But, each firm, trying to increase its profit still more, has the incentive to boost its output from the restricted amount and cut its price from the higher level. If that firm and that firm alone boosts its output and cuts its price, its profit increases, though the profits of its competitors decrease. Because each firm faces the same incentives, each firm takes actions that lead the profits of its competitors to decrease, so that *all* the firms wind up worse off; pages 406-408.

2. If the firms can form and maintain a cartel that boosts the price and decreases the output, all the firms' profits can increase. But then every firm has the incentive to cheat on an output-limiting agreement because if it and it alone cheats by boosting its output and cutting its price, its economic profit will increase still more; page 407.

### ■ CHECKPOINT 16.3

### True or false

1. True; page 411
2. False; pages 412, 413
3. False; page 413
4. True; page 416
5. False; page 416

### Multiple choice

1. b; page 411
2. b; page 412
3. a; page 413
4. a; page 413
5. e; page 412
6. a; page 414
7. d; page 414
8. a; page 414
9. b; page 414
10. b; page 416
11. d; page 416

### Short Response Questions

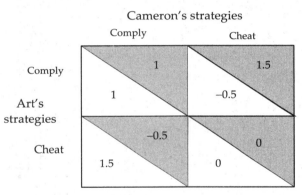

Cameron's strategies

Comply    Cheat

Art's strategies — Comply | 1 / 1 | 1.5 / −0.5

Art's strategies — Cheat | −0.5 / 1.5 | 0 / 0

1. a. The completed payoff matrix is above. The payoffs are in millions of dollars; page 412.

   b. The Nash equilibrium is for both Cameron and Art to cheat on the collusive agreement and each earn zero economic profit; pages 414.

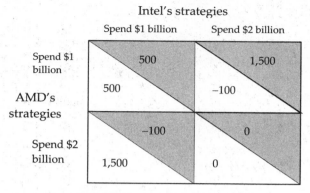

Intel's strategies

1. a. The completed payoff matrix is above. The payoffs are in millions of dollars; page 412.

   b. The Nash equilibrium is for both Intel and AMD to spend $2 billion on research and development and each earn zero economic profit; page 415.

## Long Response Questions

1. Strategies are all the possible actions of each player. In the prisoners' dilemma game, strategies are "to confess" or "to deny;" in the Airbus/Boeing duopoly game, strategies are "to produce 4 airplanes a week" or "to produce 3 airplanes a week;" in an advertising game, the strategies are "advertise" or "do not advertise;" and so on. The player must select which strategy to use, which might depend upon what strategy the other player selects; page 412.

2. A dominant strategy is a strategy that always yields the highest payoff regardless of what choice the other player makes. For instance, in the prisoners' dilemma game, the strategy "confess" is always better than the strategy "deny" regardless of whether the other player confesses or denies. As a result, the strategy "confess" is the dominant strategy. If a game has two players and each has a dominant strategy, then the Nash equilibrium has each player using his or her dominant strategy.

3. In the prisoners' dilemma game, the players do not cooperate because they do not see cooperation as being in their best interest. Regardless of what the second player does, the first player is better off confessing. Regardless of what the first player does, the second player is better off confessing. Because it is in each player's separate best interest to confess rather than cooperate by denying, both players confess even though the outcome with both players confessing is the worst possible outcome for the two players taken together; pages 408-413.

4. In the duopolists' dilemma game, the players do not cooperate for precisely the same reason they do not cooperate in the prisoners' dilemma game: The players do not see cooperation as being in their best interest. For each player, the strategy of cheating on a collusive agreement to boost price and restrict output increases the firm's profit. As a result, because each player's profit-maximizing actions harm the other player, the equilibrium can be the worst outcome for both; page 414.

5. Firms in oligopolistic industries are mutually interdependent and must consider the actions of their rival when making decisions. Collusion is likely among firms to fix price and production. Collusion can help to charge higher price and hence earn higher profits. Indeed, if the firms can collude so as to achieve the monopoly outcome and Collusion, however, provides the incentive to cheat on these agreements because greed tempts firms to play games to gain more. The more players in a game, that is, the more firms involved in the collusive agreement, the harder it is to maintain the agreement. So the more players in a game, the less likely is the monopoly outcome; page 414.

# Regulation and Antitrust Law

## Chapter 17

## CHAPTER IN PERSPECTIVE

Competitive markets produce the efficient quantity and do not need government intervention. Monopoly and oligopoly markets produce less than the efficient quantity and so face regulation and antitrust laws. Studying the regulation of monopolies and U.S. antitrust law applies your knowledge of how markets work. The chapter discusses two explanations of governmental regulation of business: public interest theory and capture theory. The first leads to efficient resource use while the second favors producers over consumers.

### ■ Explain the effects of regulation of natural monopoly and oligopoly.

Regulation is rules administered by a government agency that determine prices, product standards and types, and the conditions under which new firms may enter an industry. In the United States since the mid-1970s, there has been deregulation of many industries. Regulation generally sets the prices a regulated firm can charge. The public interest theory of regulation is that regulation seeks an efficient use of resources. The capture theory of regulation is that regulation helps producers maximize economic profit. Natural monopolies, industries in which one firm can supply the market at a lower average total cost than can two or more firms, are almost always regulated. A marginal cost pricing rule sets price equal to marginal cost. A marginal cost pricing rule achieves an efficient level of output but the regulated firm incurs an economic loss. An average cost pricing rule sets price equal to average total cost. An average cost pricing rule enables the firm to earn a normal profit but it creates a deadweight loss. Average cost pricing is typically achieved using rate of return regulation, in which the regulators set the price at a level that enables the firm to cover all of its costs and earn a target percent return on its capital. Price cap regulation and earnings sharing regulation try to increase the firm's incentive to cut its costs and operate efficiently. Oligopolies are occasionally regulated. Often regulation designed to increase quality control in an oligopoly or a competitive industry winds up increasing the monopoly profit of the regulated producers.

### ■ Describe U.S. antitrust law and explain three antitrust policy debates.

Antitrust law regulates and prohibits certain kinds of market behavior, such as monopoly and monopolistic practices. The Sherman Act of 1890 was the first federal antitrust law in the United States. Section 1 outlaws "every contract, combination in the form of a trust or otherwise, or conspiracy in restraint of trade." Section 2 declares that "every person who shall monopolize, or attempt to monopolize, ... shall be deemed guilty of a felony." The Clayton, Robinson-Patman, and Celler-Kefauver Acts prohibit practices if they "substantially lessen competition or create monopoly." Price fixing is *always* illegal. But resale price maintenance and tying arrangements are more controversial because they might lead to efficiency or inefficiency. Economists think predatory pricing is unlikely to occur. The Department of Justice uses guidelines based on the Herfindahl-Hirschman Index (HHI) to determine which mergers it will challenge. The higher the HHI, the more likely the merger will be challenged.

## EXPANDED CHAPTER CHECKLIST

When you have completed this chapter, you will be able to:

### 1 Explain the effects of regulation of natural monopoly and oligopoly.

- Define regulation and deregulation.
- Discuss the two economic theories of regulation.
- Define natural monopoly and illustrate it in a figure.
- Explain the marginal cost pricing rule and show that it achieves an efficient output in a regulated industry.
- Explain the average cost pricing rule and show the deadweight loss created by it as the result of restricting output and raising price.
- Describe how rate of return regulation can lead to the producer exaggerating its costs.
- Define incentive regulation.
- Discuss regulation of oligopolies, and describe how the public interest theory and the capture theory would treat a cartel.

### 2 Describe U.S. antitrust law and explain three antitrust policy debates.

- Discuss the Sherman Act and explain the activities prohibited by Sections 1 and 2.
- Discuss the Clayton Act and its amendments and describe the practices they prohibit.
- Define "resale price maintenance," "tying arrangement," and "predatory pricing," and explain why they are controversial among antitrust economists.
- Describe the United States versus Microsoft antitrust case.
- Explain how the Department of Justice uses the Herfindahl-Hirschman Index in deciding whether to challenge a merger.

## YOUR AP TEST HINTS

### AP Topics

| Topic on your AP test | Corresponding textbook section |
| --- | --- |
| Market failure and the role of government | |
| Public policy to promote competition | Chapter 17 |
| • Antitrust policy | Checkpoint 17.1 |
| • Regulation | Checkpoint 17.2 |

### AP Vocabulary

- On the AP test, a marginal cost pricing rule can be termed as setting the "social optimum price". An average cost pricing can be called the "fair return price."

### Extra AP material

- The history of regulation and the regulatory process as discussed in 17.1 is not addressed nor tested on the AP exam.
- The public interest theory and capture theory are not included on the AP test.
- Recent anti-trust court cases, as discussed in Checkpoint 17.2, are not addressed nor tested on the AP exam.

## CHECKPOINT 17.1

### ■ Explain the effects of regulation of natural monopoly and oligopoly.

#### Quick Review

- *Marginal cost pricing rule* A price rule for a natural monopoly that sets price equal to marginal cost. On the AP test, this rule can be referred to as setting the "social optimum price."
- *Average cost pricing rule* A price rule for a natural monopoly that sets price equal to average cost. On the AP test, this rule can be referred to as setting the "fair return price."

## Additional Practice Problem 17.1

1. The figure shows the demand and cost curves for the local water distributing company. The company is a natural monopoly.

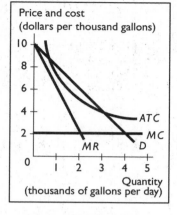

Price and cost
(dollars per thousand gallons)

Quantity
(thousands of gallons per day)

a. If the company is unregulated, what price does it charge for water and how much is distributed? Does the firm earn an economic profit, a normal profit, or an economic loss?

b. If the company is regulated using an average cost pricing rule or fair return price, what price does it charge for water and how much is distributed? Does the firm earn an economic profit, a normal profit, or an economic loss?

c. If the company is regulated using a marginal cost pricing rule or social optimum price, what price does it charge for water and how much is distributed? Does the firm earn an economic profit, a normal profit, or an economic loss?

## Solution to Additional Practice Problem 17.1

1a. An unregulated monopoly produces the quantity where marginal revenue equals marginal cost and the price is determined by the demand curve. In the figure, marginal revenue equals marginal cost when 2 thousand gallons of water per day

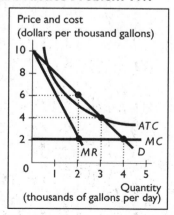

Price and cost
(dollars per thousand gallons)

Quantity
(thousands of gallons per day)

are distributed. The price is $6 per thousand gallons. The firm earns an economic profit.

1b. If an average cost pricing rule is used, price and quantity are determined by where the average total cost curve intersects the demand curve. From the figure, the price is $4 per thousand gallons and the quantity is 3 thousand gallons per day. The firm earns a normal profit.

1c. If a marginal cost pricing rule is used, price and quantity are determined by where the marginal cost curve intersects the demand curve. From the figure, the price is $2 per thousand gallons and the quantity is 4 thousand gallons per day. The firm incurs an economic loss.

## ■ AP Self Test 17.1

### True or false

1. Regulatory rules are administered by the regulated company.

2. In a regulated industry, firms are free to determine the price they charge but the regulating agency determines the production technology they must use.

3. Public interest theory assumes that the political process introduces regulation that eliminates deadweight loss.

4. The capture theory predicts that regulations benefit large interest groups.

5. A regulated natural monopoly produces the efficient quantity of output when it is regulated to use a marginal cost pricing rule.

6. Rate of return regulation sets the price at a level that allows the regulated firm to earn a specified target percent return on its capital.

7. Price cap regulation is designed to give firms the incentive to raise the price of their output, provided competition in the market increases.

8. Regulation with the purpose of quality control can achieve a monopoly price for the regulated producers.

**Multiple choice**

1. Regulation
   a. consists of rules administered by a government agency.
   b. is a theory that resources are used efficiently.
   c. consists of rules administered by private industry to avoid government interference.
   d. is a theory that firms maximize profits if government agencies assist.
   e. is illegal in the United States.

2. Deregulation is the process of ____ restrictions on prices, product standards and types, and entry conditions.
   a. increasing
   b. not changing
   c. evaluating
   d. decreasing
   e. fine-tuning

3. The first national regulatory agency to be set up in the United States was the
   a. Atomic Energy Commission.
   b. Securities and Exchange Commission.
   c. Interstate Commerce Commission.
   d. Food and Drug Administration.
   e. Federal Energy Regulatory Commission.

4. The theory that regulation seeks an efficient use of resources is the
   a. public interest theory.
   b. producer surplus theory.
   c. consumer surplus theory.
   d. capture theory.
   e. deadweight loss theory.

5. Which of the following best describes the capture theory of regulation?
   i. Regulation seeks an efficient use of resources
   ii. Regulation is aimed at keeping prices as low as possible
   iii. Regulation helps firms maximize economic profit
   a. i only.
   b. ii only.
   c. iii only.
   d. i and ii.
   e. i, ii, and iii.

6. At a level of output when regulators require a natural monopoly to set a price that is equal to marginal cost, the firm
   a. earns a normal profit.
   b. earns an economic profit.
   c. incurs an economic loss.
   d. earns a normal-economic profit.
   e. earns either a normal profit or an economic profit, depending on whether the firm's average total cost equals or is less than the marginal cost.

7. If a natural monopoly is told to set price equal to average cost, then the firm
   a. is not able to set marginal revenue equal to marginal cost.
   b. automatically also sets price equal to marginal cost.
   c. will earn a substantial economic profit.
   d. will incur an economic loss
   e. sets a price that is lower than its marginal cost.

## ■ FIGURE 17.1

Price and cost (dollars per month)

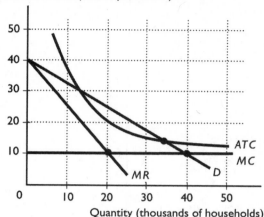

Quantity (thousands of households)

8. If the natural monopoly illustrated in Figure 17.1 was regulated using a marginal cost pricing rule and thereby setting the social optimum price, the price would be ____.
   a. $10
   b. between $10.01 and $20.00
   c. between $20.01 and $30.00
   d. between $30.01 and $40.00
   e. more than $40.01

9. If the natural monopoly illustrated in Figure 17.1 was regulated using an average total cost pricing rule and thereby setting a fair return price, the price would be ____.
   a. $10
   b. between $10.01 and $20.00
   c. between $20.01 and $30.00
   d. between $30.01 and $40.00
   e. more than $40.01

10. If the natural monopoly illustrated in Figure 17.1 was unregulated, the price would be ____.
   a. $10
   b. between $10.01 and $20.00
   c. between $20.01 and $30.00
   d. between $30.01 and $40.00
   e. more than $40.01

11. Rate of return regulation is designed to allow a natural monopoly to
   a. earn an economic profit.
   b. set its price equal to its average total cost.
   c. underestimate its average cost.
   d. compete with any firm entering the market.
   e. earn zero normal profit.

12. When a regulatory agency uses rate of return regulation, the
   a. agency is able to eliminate the deadweight loss.
   b. regulated firm has no incentive to cut costs.
   c. regulated firm's profit must be maximized for the market to be efficient.
   d. the regulated firm must receive a government subsidy.
   e. the agency is using a form of marginal cost pricing and setting the social optimum price.

13. A regulation that motivates the firm to operate efficiently and keep its costs under control is called
   a. an output regulation.
   b. a subsidy.
   c. price cap regulation.
   d. deregulation.
   e. a price-capture theory regulation.

14. Under price-cap regulation, the regulators set the ____ price that can be charged and hold that cap for several years.
   a. minimum
   b. maximum
   c. average fixed cost
   d. average variable cost
   e. marginal

15. Why would members of a cartel be in favor of regulation by a government agency?
    a. Regulation follows the public interest theory.
    b. Industry output can be controlled at the monopoly level, and the regulation means that members cannot cheat.
    c. Costs are reduced.
    d. Regulation can increase the demand for the product.
    e. Cartel members are never in favor of regulation.

## Short Response Questions

### ■ FIGURE 17.2
Price and cost (dollars per month)

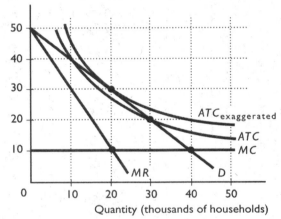

1. Figure 17.2 shows both the actual and exaggerated average total cost curves of a cable TV company that is a regulated monopoly. Also given are the demand curve and marginal revenue curve. Answer questions (a) through (c) based on the assumption that regulators know the true costs of production.
    a. What price would the regulator set using the marginal cost pricing rule, that is, setting the social optimum price?
    b. What price would the regulator set using the average cost pricing rule, that is, setting the fair return price?
    c. What price would the firm set if it was unregulated?

d. Now assume that the monopoly successfully exaggerates its cost of production. What price would the regulator set using the average cost pricing rule?

### ■ FIGURE 17.3
Price and cost (dollars per meal)

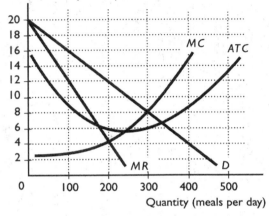

Quantity (meals per day)

2. A small town has only five restaurants. Figure 17.3 shows the demand curve, marginal revenue curve, and marginal cost curve for the restaurant market in this town.
    a. What are the competitive price and quantity?
    b. What price and quantity would result if the firms colluded and acted like a monopoly?
    c. Suppose the restaurants are regulated. What price and quantity would prevail under the public interest theory of regulation?
    d. If the restaurants are regulated, what price and quantity would prevail under the capture theory?

3. What is the goal of price cap regulation?

## Long Response Questions

1. Why doesn't the government regulate all industries?

2. What is the advantage of using a marginal cost pricing rule to regulate a natural monopoly? The disadvantage? Why does this rule lead to the "social optimum" price?

3. What is rate of return regulation? Does it attempt to set the regulated firm's price equal to its marginal cost or its average total cost? If a firm regulated using rate of return regulation exaggerates its costs, what occurs?

## CHECKPOINT 17.2

### Describe U.S. antitrust law and explain three antitrust policy debates.

#### Quick Review

- *Sherman Act* The first antitrust law, Section 1 of the Sherman Act prohibits conspiring with others to restrict competition and Section 2 outlaws attempts to monopolize.

- *Clayton Act* The second antitrust law, the Clayton Act prohibits certain business practices if they substantially lessen competition or create monopoly.

#### Additional Practice Problem 17.2

1. Cooperative agreements among firms such as the New York Yankees and the Chicago White Sox that limit the number of games played and that restrict the number of teams for which an athlete can play show cartel-like behavior. Except for professional sports teams, cartels are generally illegal in the United States. Microsoft and Hewlett Packard do not draft college graduates and so they cannot agree that a particular college graduate will work for Microsoft and not Hewlett Packard. Why do you think the Supreme Court made a decision in the case of professional sporting teams to permit cartel-like behavior?

#### Solution to Additional Practice Problem 17.2

1. Under competitive conditions, rich teams such as the New York Yankees, with plenty of fans and lucrative media contracts, would be able to purchase all the best players. Putting all the best players on a single team would prevent another team from winning. The teams unable to win would be unable to entice fans to their stadiums. The entire sports industry would die

if only one team were profitable and dominant. This situation is unlike the case with Microsoft and Hewlett Packard because if one of these firms becomes dominant, its absolute dominance would not spell the end of the industry. The sports leagues, in an exception to general American policy, are allowed to limit output, that is, the number of games. They also are allowed to have league rules that seek through drafts to apportion talent equally to preserve the competitive nature of the sport.

### ■ AP Self Test 17.2

#### True or false

1. The first antitrust law in the United States was the Grant Act, passed in 1890.

2. The Sherman Act outlaws contracts and conspiracies in restraint of trade.

3. The Clayton Act outlaws all price discrimination.

4. Price fixing is *always* illegal.

5. Resale price maintenance always leads to efficiency.

6. Tying arrangements always lead to inefficiency.

7. The Department of Justice's suit against Microsoft claims that Microsoft has violated the Clayton Act's prohibition of acquiring a competitor's assets.

8. The Department of Justice uses the four-firm concentration ratio as the guideline to determine which mergers it will examine and possibly block.

#### Multiple choice

1. The first antitrust act was____ passed in ____.
   a. the Clayton Act; 1890
   b. the Sherman Act; 1890
   c. the Clinton Act; 1999
   d. the Rockefeller Act; 1890
   e. the Clayton Act; 1914

2. Which antitrust law has two main provisions, one against conspiring with others to restrict competition and the other making it

a felony to monopolize or attempt to monopolize?
a. Sherman Act
b. Clayton Act
c. Robinson-Patman Act
d. Celter-Kefauver Act
e. Bade-Parkin Act

3. The Clayton Act
a. replaced the Sherman Act.
b. along with its amendments, outlawed several business practices if they substantially lessened competition or created monopoly.
c. along with its amendments, prohibited all business practices that substantially lessen competition or create monopoly.
d. was the first anti-trust law in the United States.
e. was repealed in 1985.

4. Which of the following is (are) prohibited if it substantially lessens competition or creates a monopoly?
i.  price discrimination
ii.  tying arrangements
iii.  exclusive dealing
a. i only.
b. ii only.
c. ii and iii.
d. iii only.
e. i, ii, and iii.

5. If Polka Cola prevents all its retail outlets from selling any other competing soft drink, it is engaged in
a. a tying arrangement.
b. a requirement contract.
c. an exclusive deal.
d. territorial confinement.
e. resale price maintenance.

6. If Polka Cola agrees to sell its cola to a retailer only if the retailer also buys a lemon-lime drink, Polka Up, then Polka Cola is engaged in
a. a tying arrangement.
b. a requirement contract.
c. an exclusive deal.
d. territorial confinement.
e. price discrimination.

7. Which of the following is *always* illegal?
a. possessing a very large market share
b. selling at a price below other producers because of efficiency
c. price fixing
d. attempting to merge with a competitor
e. price discrimination

8. Resale price maintenance
a. can lead to efficiency by preventing low-price shops from being free riders.
b. can lead to inefficiency by preventing low-price shops from being free riders.
c. is always legal.
d. is a clear example of predatory pricing.
e. is an example of a tying arrangement.

9. Predatory pricing occurs when a firm sets a _____ price to drive competitors out of business with the intention of then setting a _____ price.
a. monopoly; high
b. monopoly; low
c. low; monopoly
d. low; low
e. high; monopoly

10. Department of Justice guidelines state that it will examine mergers in markets for which the Herfindahl-Hirschman Index is
a. a positive number.
b. below 1,000 points.
c. between 1,000 and 1,800 and the merger would reduce the index by 100 points.
d. between 1,000 and 1,800, and the merger would increase the index by 100 points.
e. more than 1,800.

11. In a concentrated industry with a Herfindahl-Hirschman Index that exceeds 1,800,

the Department of Justice will challenge any merger that increases the Herfindahl-Hirschman index by a minimum of

a. 50 points.
b. 100 points.
c. 1,000 points.
d. 1,800 points.
e. 10,000 points.

## Short Response Questions

1. What is the law about price fixing?

| Company | Market share (percent) |
|---|---|
| Acme | 27 |
| ABC | 18 |
| Banks | 10 |
| Cooper | 8 |
| 37 individual firms | 1 each |

2. The table above has a list of companies that make up the market for steel, along with each companies' share of the market.

a. What is the Herfindahl-Hirschman Index for this market? How would you describe the competitiveness of this market?

b. If Acme acquires Banks, what is the new Herfindahl-Hirschman Index? Would the Department of Justice challenge this acquisition? Why or why not? How would you describe the competitiveness of this market if the merger occurs?

## Long Response Questions

1. General Motors is a huge company, with total revenue exceeding $190 billion a year in 2004. Why doesn't the government challenge General Motors and take it to court for antitrust violations?

2. Airlines routinely price discriminate, charging pleasure travelers a significantly lower price than business travelers. The Clayton Act, however, mentioned price discrimination as one of the business practices it covers and prohibits. Why can airlines routinely price discriminate?

# YOUR AP SELF TEST ANSWERS

## ■ CHECKPOINT 17.1

### True or false

1. False; page 424
2. False; page 425
3. True; page 425
4. False; page 425
5. True; pages 427
6. True; page 428
7. False; page 430
8. True; page 432

### Multiple choice

1. a; page 424
2. d; page 424
3. c; page 424
4. a; page 425
5. c; page 425
6. c; pages 426-427
7. a; page 427
8. a; pages 426-427
9. b; pages 427-428
10. c; page 430
11. b; pages 424-429
12. b; page 429
13. c; page 430
14. b; page 430
15. b; page 431

### Short Response Questions

1. a. Using marginal cost pricing, the regulator sets a price of $10 a month; pages 426-427.
   b. Using average cost pricing, the regulator sets a price of $20 a month; pages 427-428.
   c. The firm serves 20,000 household, where marginal revenue equals marginal cost, and sets the price at $30 a month.
   d. If the firm successfully exaggerates its costs, the regulator sets a price of $30 a month; pages 427-428.
2. a. The competitive price is $8 a meal and the competitive quantity is 300 meals a day; page 431.
   b. The monopoly price is $12 a meal and the quantity is 200 meals a day; page 431.
   c. The price is $8 a meal and the quantity is 300 meals a day, the same as the competitive outcome; page 431.
   d. The price is $12 a meal and the quantity is 200 meals a day, the same as the monopoly outcome; page 432.
3. Price cap regulation gives regulated firms the incentive to cut their costs and produce efficiently, without exaggerating their costs or wasting resources; page 430.

### Long Response Questions

1. The government does not regulate all industries because not all industries need to be regulated. Competitive industries do not need regulation because competition produces an efficient outcome. But a natural monopoly is not a competitive industry and so government regulation might help move the monopoly toward producing the allocatively efficient amount of output; pages 424-427.

2. The advantage of using a marginal cost pricing rule is that the firm produces the allocatively efficient quantity of output. The disadvantage is that the firm incurs an economic loss. The reason this rule sets the "social optimum" price is because the firm produces the allocatively efficient quantity of output. As a result, there is no deadweight loss in the production of this good or service and so society is as well off as possible; pages 426-427.

3. Rate of return regulation is a regulation that sets the price at a level that enables the regulated firm to earn a specified target percent return on its capital. The target rate of return is determined with reference to what is normal in competitive industries. This rate of return is part of the opportunity cost of the natural monopoly and is included in the firm's average total cost. Rate of return regulation sets the price equal to average to-

tal cost. If the firm inflates its costs, the regulators might allow the firm to increase the price it charges so that it can cover all of its now higher costs; pages 428-429.

# ■ CHECKPOINT 17.2

## True or false

1. False; page 434
2. True; page 434
3. False; page 435
4. True; page 435
5. False; page 436
6. False; page 436
7. False; page 437
8. False; page 438

## Multiple choice

1. b; page 434
2. a; page 434
3. b; page 435
4. e; page 435
5. c; page 435
6. a; page 435
7. c; page 435
8. a; page 436
9. c; page 437
10. d; page 438
11. a; page 438

## Short Response Questions

1. The law about price fixing is clear: It is *always* illegal. If price fixing can be proven, the firms are automatically guilty because there can be no acceptable excuse; page 435.

2. a. HHI = $27^2 + 18^2 + 10^2 + 8^2 + 37 = 1,254$. Because this falls between 1,000 and 1,800, the market is moderately concentrated; page 438.

   b. HHI = $37^2 + 18^2 + 8^2 + 37 = 1,794$. The Department of Justice would challenge this acquisition because it increases the index by more than 100 points. After this merger, the market remains moderately concentrated; page 438.

## Long Response Questions

1. General Motors is, indeed, a huge company. But it competes with other huge companies in a gigantic market, the new car market. Ford had total revenue over $170 billion in 2004; Toyota's total revenue also was over $170 billion in 2004. There are other extremely large competitors in the automobile market. Antitrust laws deal with markets where there is little competition, not with markets where the many competitors are large. So there is no need for antitrust action against General Motors; page 434.

2. The Clayton Act prohibited several businesses practices *only if* they "substantially lessen competition or create monopoly." If the acts do not "substantially lessen competition or create monopoly," they are legal. Price discrimination by the airlines does not substantially lessen competition or create a monopoly. As a result, price discrimination by the airlines is legal; page 435.

# Demand and Supply in Factor Markets

# Chapter 18

**CHAPTER IN PERSPECTIVE**

In this we chapter study demand, supply, and equilibrium in factor markets.

■ **Describe the anatomy of the markets for labor, capital, and land.**

The four factors of production are labor, capital, land, and entrepreneurship. The wage rate is the price of labor, the interest rate is the price of capital, and rent is the price of land. A labor market is a collection of people and firms who are trading labor services. A financial market is a collection of people and firms who are lending and borrowing to finance the purchase of physical capital. A commodity market is a market in which raw materials are traded. Factor markets with many buyers and sellers are competitive markets.

■ **Explain how the value of marginal product determines the demand for a factor of production.**

The demand for a factor of production is derived from the demand for the goods and services it is used to produce. The value of the marginal product is the value to a firm of hiring one more unit of a factor of production. The value of the marginal product equals the price of a unit of output multiplied by the factor's marginal product. To maximize profit, a firm hires labor up to the point at which the value of the marginal product equals the wage rate. A firm's demand for labor curve is also its value of the marginal product curve. The demand for labor changes and the demand for labor curve shifts when the price of the firm's output, the prices of other factors of production, or technology change.

■ **Explain how wage rates and employment are determined.**

An individual's labor supply curve can be backward bending at higher wage rates so that an increase in the wage rate decreases the quantity of labor supplied. The key factors that change the supply of labor are the adult population, preferences, and time spent in school and training. The labor market equilibrium determines the wage rate and employment.

■ **Explain how interest rates, borrowing, and lending are determined.**

Other things remaining the same, the higher the interest rate, the smaller is the quantity of capital demanded. The quantity of financial capital supplied results from people's saving decisions. Other things remaining the same, the higher the interest rate, the greater is the quantity of saving supplied. Financial market equilibrium occurs at the interest rate where the quantity of capital demanded equals the quantity of capital supplied.

■ **Explain how rents and natural resource prices are determined.**

Natural resources are either renewable or nonrenewable. The quantity of land is fixed, so the supply of each particular block of land is perfectly inelastic. Economic rent is the income received by *any* factor of production over and above the amount required to induce a given quantity of the factor to be supplied. The known quantity of a nonrenewable resource increases over time because advances in technology enable ever less accessible sources to be discovered.

## EXPANDED CHAPTER CHECKLIST

**When you have completed this chapter, you will be able to:**

**1 Describe the anatomy of the markets for labor, capital, and land.**

- Identify the four factors of production.
- Describe the labor markets, financial markets, and land markets.

**2 Explain how the value of marginal product determines the demand for a factor of production.**

- Explain why the demand for a factor of production is a derived demand.
- Calculate the value of marginal product.
- Explain how a firm decides the number of workers to hire.
- Explain the relationship between the value of marginal product curve and the demand for labor curve.
- State the factors that change the demand for labor.

**3 Explain how wage rates and employment are determined.**

- Describe an individual's labor supply curve.
- List the key factors that change the supply of labor.
- Illustrate labor market equilibrium.

**4 Explain how interest rates, borrowing, and lending are determined.**

- Explain the relationship between the interest rate and the quantity of capital demanded.
- Discuss the two main factors that change the demand for capital.
- Explain the relationship between the interest rate and quantity of saving supplied.
- Discuss the main influences on the supply of saving.
- Use a graph to determine the equilibrium interest rate and quantity of capital.

**5 Explain how rents and natural resource prices are determined.**

- Describe the two categories of natural resources and provide examples of each.
- Illustrate the market for land.
- Define economic rent and illustrate the components of a factor's income.

## YOUR AP TEST HINTS

*AP Topics*

| Topic on your AP test | Corresponding textbook section |
|---|---|
| **Factor markets** | |
| • Derived demand | Checkpoint 18.1 |
| • Marginal revenue product | Checkpoint 18.2 |
| • Labor market | Checkpoint 18.3 |

*AP Vocabulary*

- The AP test uses the term "Marginal Revenue Product ($MRP$)" rather than "Value of the Marginal Product." The value of the marginal product equals $P \times MP$ and the marginal revenue product equals $MR \times MP$. For a firm in perfect competition, $P = MR$ and the two concepts are the same.
- On the AP test, the wage rate can be referred to as the "marginal resource cost." The point is that the wage rate is the *cost* to the firm of hiring one more (a *marginal*) worker (which is a labor *resource*).
- With the two vocabulary definitions above, the profit-maximizing quantity of a resource to hire is the amount that sets the marginal revenue product ($MRP$) equals to the marginal resource cost ($MRC$).
- The AP test refers to three factors that change the demand for a resource as: changes in the demand for the product being produced (which change the price of the product); changes in productivity (which can be the result of changes in technology, changes in the quantities of other resources, or changes in the quality of other resources); and changes in the prices of other resources.

## Extra AP material

- The elasticity of demand for a resource measures the sensitivity of producers to a change in the resource's price. Factors that influence the elasticity are the rate of decline of the marginal product (the more the marginal product decreases when use of the resource increases, the larger the elasticity of demand for the resource); the ease of resource substitutability (the more easily resources can be substituted for each other, the larger the elasticity of demand for the resource); the elasticity of demand for the product produced using the resource (the larger the elasticity of demand for the product, the greater the increase in the quantity produced when the supply increases as a result of a fall in wages); and the proportion of the total cost taken up by the resource (the larger the proportion, the larger the elasticity of demand for the resource).

- A competitive labor market has a large number of firms demanding labor. Each firm is a "wage taker;" that is, a single firm cannot affect the equilibrium wage rate. A monopsony labor market has only a single firm demanding labor. This firm is a "wage maker" because it can determine what wage rate it will pay. The firm pays the lowest wage rate possible in order to employ any given quantity of labor. If it wants to increase the quantity employed, the firm must boost its wage rate. This makes the supply curve of labor upward sloping. Because the form pays all its workers the same wage rate, the marginal resource cost (*MRC*) of hiring an additional worker exceeds the wage rate (since *all* workers will get a wage increase if another worker is hired) so the *MRC* curve lies above the labor supply curve. A monopsonist maximizes its profit by equating *MRC* to *MRP*, and then uses the labor supply curve to determine the lowest wage rate necessary to hire that number of workers. The wage rate is lower and the quantity of workers hired

is fewer by a monopsony than by a perfectly competitive firm.

- Firms can use different combinations of resources to produce goods and services. The issue of the optimum combination of resources deals the question: What is the least costly combination of resources? The Least Cost rule states that the cost of any output is minimized when the marginal product per dollar cost of each resource is the same. For instance, if the marginal product of labor is 20 units per hour and the wage rate is $10 per hour, then the marginal product per dollar is 20 units per hour ÷ $10 per hour, or $2 per unit.

## CHECKPOINT 18.1

■ **Describe the anatomy of the markets for labor, capital, and land.**

### Quick Review

- *Factors of production* The four factors of production are labor, capital, land, and entrepreneurship.

### Additional Practice Problems 18.1

1. Tell whether each of the following are land, labor, capital, or entrepreneurship.
    a. oil
    b. an oil worker
    c. an oil platform in the Gulf of Mexico
    d. the Chief Executive Officer of Exxon
    e. a professor
    f. a beach in Florida

2. What is the difference between a stock and a bond?

### Solutions to Additional Practice Problems 18.1

1a. Oil is a gift of nature and so it is part of land.

1b. An oil well worker is part of labor.

1c. The oil platform is part of capita.

1d. The Chief Executive Officer is in charge of running Exxon and so is part of entrepreneurship.

1e. The professor is part of labor.

1f. The beach is a gift of nature and so is part of land.

2. A share of the stock of a company is an entitlement to a share in the profits of the company. A bond is a promise to pay specified amounts of money on specified dates.

■ **AP Self Test 18.1**

**True or false**
1. The amount that an entrepreneur is paid is determined in a factor market.
2. Stocks and bonds are traded in a stock market.
3. As a factor of production, coal is considered to be land.

**Multiple choice**
1. The wage rate paid to labor is
   a. a factor output.
   b. a factor price.
   c. a factor input.
   d. an input of the workforce.
   e. part of the firm's normal profit.

2. ____ capital consists of the funds that firms use to buy and operate capital.
   a. Human
   b. Physical
   c. Financial
   d. Logistical
   e. Actual

3. Which of the following would be traded in the commodity market?
   a. 1,200 shares of Coca-Cola stock
   b. bonds issued by Cisco
   c. interest-bearing securities of the federal government
   d. petroleum
   e. labor

**Short Response Questions**
1. For what are factors of production used?
2. Petroleum is categorized as what type of factor of production?
3. What is the difference between capital and financial capital?

## CHECKPOINT 18.2

■ **Explain how the value of marginal product determines the demand for a factor of production.**

**Quick Review**
- *Value of marginal product* The value to a firm of hiring one more unit of a factor of production, which equals the price of a unit of output multiplied by the marginal product of the factor of production.

**Additional Practice Problem 18.2**
Casey's lawn service, The Other Side of the Fence, hires workers to mow lawns. The market for lawn mowing is perfectly competitive, and the price of mowing a lawn is $20.00. The labor market is competitive, and the wage rate is $40 a day. The table shows the workers' total product, *TP*:

| Workers | Lawns per day |
|---------|---------------|
| 1 | 3 |
| 2 | 7 |
| 3 | 14 |
| 4 | 18 |
| 5 | 20 |
| 6 | 21 |

a. Calculate the marginal product of hiring the third worker.
b. Calculate the marginal revenue product of the third worker.
c. Complete the table to the right showing the marginal revenue product.

| Workers | MRP |
|---------|-----|
| 1 | ____ |
| 2 | ____ |
| 3 | ____ |
| 4 | ____ |
| 5 | ____ |
| 6 | ____ |

d. How many workers will Casey hire to maximize his profit?
e. How many lawns a day will Casey mow to maximize its profit?
f. What is Casey's total revenue if he hires 4 workers? What is Casey's total revenue if he hires 5 workers? What is the change in total revenue if Casey hires 5 workers?

**Solution to Additional Practice Problem 18.2**
1a. The marginal product of hiring the third worker equals the total product of hiring

three workers, which is 14 lawns, minus the total product of hiring two workers, which is 7 lawns. So the marginal product of hiring the third worker is 7 lawns.

1b. To calculate the marginal revenue product, multiply the marginal product of the third worker by the marginal revenue of mowing a lawn. Because the firm is perfectly competitive, the marginal revenue equals the price. So the marginal revenue product of the third worker is 7 lawns a day × $20.00, which is $140 a day.

1c. The completed table is to the right.

| Workers | MRP |
|---------|------|
| 1 | $60 |
| 2 | $80 |
| 3 | $140 |
| 4 | $80 |
| 5 | $40 |
| 6 | $20 |

1d. To answer this practice problem, recall that to maximize profit, a firm hires labor up to the point at which the marginal revenue product equals the marginal resource cost, which, for workers, is the wage rate. So, to maximize his profit, Casey hires up to the point at which the marginal revenue product equals the wage rate. The wage rate is $40 a day and the answer to part (c) shows that the marginal revenue product of the fifth worker is also $40 a day. Casey hires 5 workers.

1e. To maximize his profit, Casey hires 5 workers and the 5 workers mow 20 lawns.

1f. When Casey hires 4 workers, Casey's company mows 18 lawns. Total revenue is 18 lawns a day × $20, which is $360 a day. When Casey hires 5 workers, Casey's company mows 20 lawns a day. Total revenue is 20 lawns a day × $20, which is $400 a day. Casey's total revenue increases by $40 when Casey hires the fifth worker.

## ■ AP Self Test 18.2

### True or false

1. The demand for labor is derived from the demand for the goods and services that the labor is hired to produce.

2. A firm's demand for labor curve is also its value of marginal product curve.

3. A rise in the wage rate decreases the quantity of labor demanded.

### Multiple choice

1. The demand for labor is derived from the
   a. supply of labor.
   b. wage rate.
   c. supply of the good the labor is used to produce.
   d. demand for the goods and services the labor helps produce.
   e. supply of all the other factors of production that can be substituted for labor.

2. Which of the following is true?
   a. The increase in revenue to a firm of hiring another worker is the worker's marginal revenue product.
   b. A firm will hire more workers if the wage rate is greater than the marginal revenue product.
   c. The marginal revenue product is the cost of hiring a worker.
   d. The marginal revenue product increases as more workers are hired.
   e. The marginal revenue product equals the marginal revenue of the good produced divided by the marginal product.

3. The value of the marginal product of labor is equal to the marginal product of labor ____ the price of a unit of output.
   a. divided by
   b. multiplied by
   c. minus
   d. plus
   e. squared and then multiplied by

4. The rule for maximizing profit is to hire labor up to the point at which the value of the marginal product
   a. equals the wage rate.
   b. is greater than the wage rate.
   c. is less than the wage rate.
   d. is a mirror image of the wage rate.
   e. equals the price of the product produced.

5. An increase in the price of a firm's output leads to a
   a. movement up along the demand for labor curve.
   b. movement down along the demand for labor curve.
   c. rightward shift of the demand for labor curve.
   d. leftward shift of the demand for labor curve
   e. rightward shift of the supply of labor curve.

6. The demand for labor is more elastic
   a. if the marginal product of labor does not change much as employment changes.
   b. no other input can take the place of labor.
   c. wages account for a large proportion of the total cost.
   d. Both answers A and B are correct.
   e. Both answers .A and C are correct.

### Short Response Questions

| Quantity of labor (workers) | Marginal product (lawns per week) | Value of marginal product 1 (dollars) | Value of marginal product 2 (dollars) |
|---|---|---|---|
| 1 | 13 | ___ | ___ |
| 2 | 12 | ___ | ___ |
| 3 | 11 | ___ | ___ |
| 4 | 10 | ___ | ___ |
| 5 | 9 | ___ | ___ |

1. Gene's Lawn Service hires workers to mow lawns. The market for lawns is perfectly competitive and Gene charges $25 a lawn. The table above shows the workers' marginal product schedule.
   a. Calculate the value of the marginal product for each quantity of workers and record your answers in the "Value of the marginal product 1" column. In Figure 18.1, plot Gene's demand for labor curve. Label it *LD1*.
   b. If the wage rate is $300 per week, how many workers will Gene hire? If it is $250 per week, how many workers will Gene hire?
   c. Suppose the price of mowing a lawn rises to $30 per lawn. Calculate the new value of the marginal products and record them in the "Value of the marginal product 2"

■ **FIGURE 18.1**

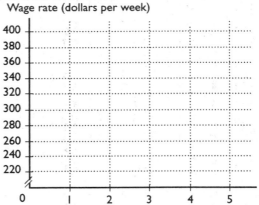

Wage rate (dollars per week)

column. In Figure 18.1, plot Gene's new demand for labor curve and label it *LD2*. How did the increase in the price of mowing a lawn change Gene's demand for labor curve?

2. What is the relationship between the demand for labor curve and the value of the marginal product curve?

### Long Response Questions

1. Why do the value of the marginal product and the marginal revenue product decrease as more workers are employed?

2. What factors change the demand for labor and shift the demand for labor curve?

3. Suppose that Wings Over Buffalo is a company making buffalo wings in Buffalo New York. It produces its wings using only labor and capital. A worker is paid a wage rate of $10 per hour and a unit of capital costs $4 per hour. The marginal product of labor is 100 wings per hour and the marginal product of capital is 10 wings per hour.
   a. What is the marginal product per dollar for a worker? For a unit of capital?
   b. Is Wings Over Buffalo using the least cost combination of labor and capital? Explain your answer. If it is not, how should the company change the combination of labor and capital?

# CHECKPOINT 18.3

■ **Explain how wage rates and employment are determined.**

### Quick Review

* *Changes in the demand for labor* The demand for labor depends on the price of the firm's output, the prices of other factors of production, and technology.

* *Changes in the supply of labor* The key factors that change the supply of labor are the adult population, preferences, and time spent in school and training.

### Additional Practice Problems 18.3

1. Why does an individual labor supply curve bend backward?

2. Tell how each of the events given below affects the labor market. Draw a labor supply and labor demand diagram to determine the effect on the equilibrium wage rate and employment.

   a. More workers reach retirement age and retire.

   b. New technology increases workers' productivity.

   c. Suppose that the price of clothing falls. What is the impact of this change in the labor market for textile workers.

### Solutions to Additional Practice Problems 18.3

1. To see how the wage rate influences the quantity of labor supplied, think about Emma's labor supply decision. Emma enjoys leisure time but, if her boss offers her $20 an hour, Emma chooses to work 30 hours a week. This wage rate is high enough to make Emma regard working as the best available use of her time. If Emma were offered a higher wage rate, she would want to work even longer hours, but only up to a point. If Emma is offered $50 an hour, she would be willing to work a 45-hour week. But if the wage rate is increased above $50 an hour, Emma might cut back on her work hours and take more leisure. For wages greater than $50 per hour, Emma believes that she is earning enough income even when she works less than 45 hours per week. At these wage rates, Emma would prefer more hours not working to more income. So her labor supply curve bends backward at a wage rate of $50 per hour.

2a. When more workers reach retirement age and then retire, the supply of labor decreases. The labor supply curve shifts leftward, as shown in the figure by the shift from $LS_0$ to $LS_1$. As a result, the equilibrium wage rate rises and the equilibrium quantity of employment decreases.

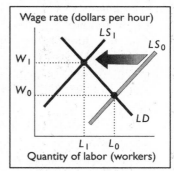

2b. By making workers more productive, the new technology, increases the demand for labor. The labor demand curve shifts rightward, in the figure from $LD_0$ to $LD_1$. The equilibrium wage rate rises and the equilibrium amount of employment increases.

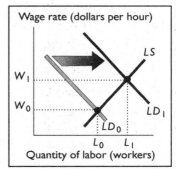

2c. A fall in the price of clothing decreases the value of marginal product of textile workers. As a result, the demand for labor decreases and the labor demand curve shifts leftward, from $LD_0$ to $LD_1$ in the figure. The equilibrium wage rate

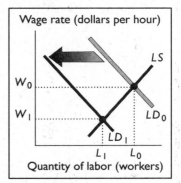

falls and the equilibrium amount of employment decreases.

# ■ AP Self Test 18.3

## True or false

1. An individual's supply of labor curve shows that the quantity of labor supplied always increases when the wage rate rises.

2. An increase in college enrollment decreases the supply of low-skilled labor.

3. If the wage rate is less than the equilibrium wage rate, the wage rate will rise to eliminate the surplus of labor.

## Multiple choice

1. An individual's labor supply curve eventually bends backward because at a high enough wage rate,
   a. people are willing to work more hours.
   b. employers are willing to hire more workers.
   c. people desire more leisure time.
   d. very few workers are hired.
   e. more people enter the labor market to search for jobs.

2. The supply of labor curve shifts leftward if
   a. the population increases.
   b. the demand for labor curve shifts leftward.
   c. the supply of labor increases.
   d. the wage rate falls.
   e. the supply of labor decreases.

3. If the wage rate is above the equilibrium wage rate, the quantity of labor demanded is _____ the quantity of labor supplied.
   a. greater than
   b. less than
   c. equal to
   d. the negative of
   e. not comparable to

4. The more people who remain in school for full-time education and training, the _____ is the _____ low-skilled labor.
   a. smaller; demand for
   b. smaller; supply of
   c. larger; supply of
   d. larger; demand for
   e. less elastic; demand for

5. If the supply of labor decreases, then the equilibrium wage rate _____ and equilibrium employment _____.
   a. does not change; decreases
   b. rises; increases
   c. rises; decreases
   d. falls; increases
   e. falls; decreases

## Short Response Questions

1. How does an increase in the adult population change the supply of labor?

### ■ FIGURE 18.2

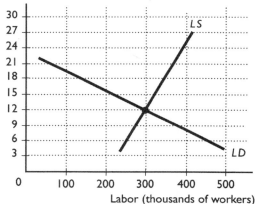

Wage rate (dollars per hour)

2. Figure 18.2 shows the labor market for sales associates. If JCPenney wishes to hire a sales associate, what wage rate must JCPenney pay? In Figure 18.3 (on the next page) draw the labor supply curve faced by JCPenney.

■ **FIGURE 18.3**

Wage rate (dollars per hour)

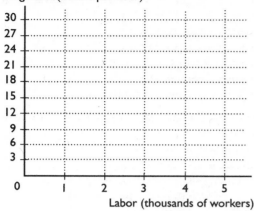

Labor (thousands of workers)

■ **FIGURE 18.4**

Wage rate (dollars per hour)

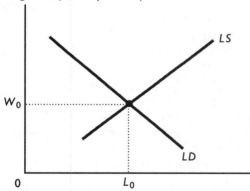

Quantity of labor (number of workers)

3. Figure 18.4 shows the labor market for Internet security programmers. Suppose that more companies start conducting more of their business on the Internet and so need more Internet security. In Figure 18.4, illustrate the effect in the market for these programmers. What happens to the equilibrium wage rate and number of programmers?

**Long Response Questions**

1. What are the similarities between a firm that has a monopoly selling its product and a firm that has a monopsony in hiring labor?

2. If more people decide to obtain an advanced education, after they graduate what is the effect on the supply of high-skilled labor? What is the effect on the equilibrium wage rate for high-skilled workers? Use a labor market diagram to illustrate your answer.

## CHECKPOINT 18.4

■ **Explain how interest rates, borrowing, and lending are determined.**

### Quick Review

• *Factors that change the demand for capital* Two main factors that change the demand for capital are population growth and technological change.

• *Factors that change the supply of savings* The main influences on the supply of saving are population, current income, and expected future income.

### Additional Practice Problems 18.4

1. Tell how each of the events given below affects the financial capital market. Draw a financial capital supply and financial capital demand diagram to determine the effect on the equilibrium interest rate and quantity of financial capital.

　a. More households come to expect higher incomes in the future.

　b. New technology increases the demand for physical capital.

2. Describe the financial market equilibrium over time.

### Solutions to Additional Practice Problems 18.4

1a. When more households expect higher incomes in the future, households save less and the supply of financial capital decreases. The supply curve of financial capital

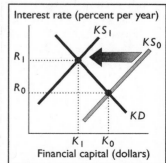

shifts leftward, as shown in the figure by the shift from $KS_0$ to $KS_1$. The equilibrium interest rate rises and the equilibrium quantity of financial capital decreases.

1a. New technology that increases the demand for physical capital also increases the demand for financial capital to fund the purchases of the physical capital. So the financial capital demand curve shifts rightward, as shown in the figure. The equilibrium interest rate rises and the equilibrium quantity of financial capital increases.

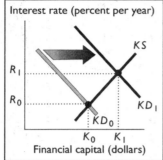

2. Over time, the demand for capital and the supply of capital increase. Population growth increases the demand for capital. And as the increased population earns a larger income, the supply of capital increases. Technological advances increase the demand for capital and bring higher incomes, which in turn increase the supply of capital. The quantity of capital increases because both the demand for capital and supply of capital increase over time, but the interest rate does not persistently increase or decrease.

## ■ AP Self Test 18.4

### True or false

1. A rise in the interest rate decreases the quantity of capital supplied.

2. If a household's current income is low and its expected future income is high, the household will have a low level of saving.

### Multiple choice

1. The demand for financial capital stems from a firm's
   a. need to pay for benefits.
   b. requirement to pay for union wages.
   c. demand for physical capital.
   d. demand for labor.
   e. supply of physical capital.

2. When the interest rate falls, the ____ financial capital ____.
   a. demand for; increases
   b. demand for; decreases
   c. quantity demanded of; increases
   d. quantity demanded of; decreases
   e. supply of; increases

3. The quantity of financial capital supplied results from people's ____ decisions.
   a. saving
   b. spending
   c. investing
   d. employment
   e. labor supply

4. The higher the interest rate, the
   a. more incentive people have to consume.
   b. less incentive people have to save.
   c. higher the opportunity cost of current consumption.
   d. lower the opportunity cost of current consumption.
   e. larger the demand for investment.

5. If a household's current income is ____ and its expected future income is low, it will have ____.
   a. zero; a high level of saving
   b. high; a negative level of saving
   c. high; no saving
   d. high; a high level of saving
   e. low, but not zero; a high level of saving

### Short Response Questions

1. What is the source of the supply of financial capital?

2. If people expect an increase in future income, what is the effect on the interest rate?

| Interest rate (percent) | Demand for financial capital (billions of dollars) | Supply of financial capital (billions of dollars) |
|---|---|---|
| 4 | 150 | 90 |
| 5 | 130 | 100 |
| 6 | 110 | 110 |
| 7 | 90 | 120 |
| 8 | 70 | 130 |

3. The table above gives the demand and supply schedules for financial capital.
   a. What is the equilibrium interest rate and quantity of financial capital?
   b. Suppose that population growth increases the quantity of financial capital demanded by $20 billion at each interest rate and also increases the quantity of financial capital supplied by $20 billion at each interest rate. Now what is the equilibrium interest rate and quantity of financial capital?

### Long Response Questions
1. How does technological change affect the demand for capital?
2. How does an increase in population affect the equilibrium interest rate and amount of financial capital?

## CHECKPOINT 18.5

### ■ Explain how rents and natural resource prices are determined.

### Quick Review
- *Renewable natural resources* Natural resources that can be used repeatedly.
- *Nonrenewable natural resources* Natural resources that can be used only once and that cannot be replaced once they have been used.

### Additional Practice Problem 18.5
1. Petroleum is a nonrenewable natural resource and is constantly being used. Simultaneously there are new technologies being developed that allow petroleum to be discovered in new locations and also new technologies being developed that make more efficient use of petroleum. What effects do these changes have on the supply of petroleum, the demand for petroleum, and the price of petroleum?

### Solution to Additional Practice Problem 18.5
1. Using a natural resource such as petroleum decreases its supply, which, by itself, raises the price. But new technologies that lead to the discovery of previously unknown reserves increase the supply, which, by itself, lowers the price. And the new technologies that enable a more efficient use of a nonrenewable natural resource decrease the demand for the resource, which, by itself, lowers the price. So whether the supply increases or decreases and whether the price rises or falls depends on which effect is larger.

### ■ AP Self Test 18.5
**True or false**
1. Forestland is a renewable natural resource.
2. The demand for land is perfectly elastic, and the supply of land is perfectly inelastic.
3. The price of a natural resource can only rise over time.

**Multiple choice**
1. A natural resource is renewable if it
   a. never has to rest.
   b. can be used repeatedly.
   c. cannot be replaced once it has been used.
   d. is available at a price of zero.
   e. has a perfectly elastic supply.

2. Oil is an example of
   a. a nonrenewable natural resource.
   b. a renewable natural resource.
   c. physical capital.
   d. a resource for which the true value of the resource cannot be measured.
   e. a resource with a perfectly inelastic demand.

3. The supply of each particular block of land is
   a. perfectly elastic.
   b. unit elastic.
   c. elastic.
   d. perfectly inelastic.
   e. inelastic but not perfectly inelastic.

4. Economic rent is the income over and above
   a. opportunity cost.
   b. average cost.
   c. factor income.
   d. marginal cost.
   e. variable cost.

### Short Response Questions

1. There are billions of barrels of petroleum still in the ground. Why, then, is petroleum considered a nonrenewable natural resource?

### Long Response Questions

1. The table above shows the demand for land. The supply of land is fixed at 20,000 square acres.
   a. In Figure 18.5, label the axes and graph the demand curve and the supply curve of land.
   b. What is the equilibrium rent and quantity?
   c. Lightly darken the area that represents economic rent. More heavily darken the area that represents the opportunity cost.

| Rent (dollars per acre per month) | Land (thousands of acres) |
| --- | --- |
| 400 | 10 |
| 350 | 20 |
| 300 | 30 |
| 250 | 40 |
| 200 | 50 |

■ **FIGURE 18.5**

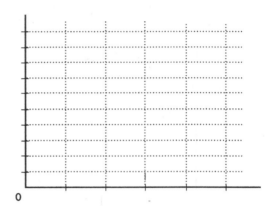

2. John Travolta is reported to receive approximately $18 million to star in a movie. Suppose Mr. Travolta would act in a movie as long as he received $100,000 which is what he would earn in his next best occupation as, say, a motivational speaker. What is his opportunity cost and what is his economic rent? If Mr. Travolta would act in a movie for $100,000, why is he paid $18 million?

# YOUR AP SELF TEST ANSWERS

## ■ CHECKPOINT 18.1

**True or false**

1. False; page 446
2. False; page 447
3. True; page 448

**Multiple choice**

1. b; page 446
2. c; page 447
3. d; page 448

**Short Response Questions**

1. Factors of production are used to produce goods and services; page 446.

2. Petroleum is one of the gifts of nature, so it is part of land; page 448.

3. Capital consists of the tools, instruments, machines, buildings, and other items that have been produced in the past and businesses now use to produce goods and services. Financial capital is the funds businesses use to purchase and operate capital; page 447.

## ■ CHECKPOINT 18.2

**True or false**

1. True; page 449
2. True; page 451
3. True; pages 451-452

**Multiple choice**

1. d; page 449
2. a; page 449
3. b; page 449
4. a; page 450
5. c; page 452
6. c; page 452

**Short Response Questions**

1. a. The completed table is above and Figure 18.6 plots the demand for labor curve $LD_1$; pages 449-451.

   b. If the wage rate is $300 per week, Gene hires 2 workers; if it is $250 per week, Gene hires 4 workers; pages 449-452.

| Quantity of labor (workers) | Marginal product (lawns per week) | Value of marginal product 1 (dollars) | Value of marginal product 2 (dollars) |
|---|---|---|---|
| 1 | 13 | 325 | 390 |
| 2 | 12 | 300 | 360 |
| 3 | 11 | 275 | 330 |
| 4 | 10 | 250 | 300 |
| 5 | 9 | 225 | 270 |

### ■ FIGURE 18.6

Wage rate (dollars per week)

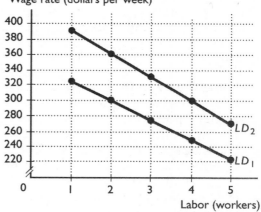

c. The completed table is above and Figure 18.6 plots the demand for labor curve $LD_2$. The increase in the price of mowing a lawn increases Gene's demand for labor and his demand for labor curve shifts rightward; page 452.

2. The demand for labor curve and the value of the marginal product curve are the same; page 451.

**Long Response Questions**

1. The value of the marginal product equals the price of a unit of the output multiplied by the marginal product of labor. The marginal revenue product equals the marginal revenue multiplied by the marginal product of labor. As more labor is employed, its marginal product decreases, and as a result, the value of the marginal product and the marginal revenue product decrease. In addition,

as the firm hires more workers, the firm produces more output. Unless the firm is a perfect competitor, its marginal revenue decreases as the quantity increases, which is another reason the marginal revenue product decreases when employment increases; page 449.

2. Three factors change the demand for labor and shift the demand for labor curve. The first is changes in the price of the firm's output, which can occur when the demand for the product being produced changes. An increase in demand raise the price and increases the demand for labor. The second factor is changes in the prices of other resources. For instance, an increase in the price of capital will (eventually) increase the demand for labor as firms substitute labor for capital. Finally, the third factor is changes in the productivity of labor. Often this change occurs as a result of an advance in technology. An increase in productivity of labor increases the demand for labor; page 452.

3. a. The marginal product per dollar for labor equals 100 wings per hour ÷ $10 per hour, which is 10 wings per dollar. The marginal product per dollar for capital equals 10 wings per hour ÷ $4 per hour, which is 2.5 wings per dollar.

   b. Wings Over Buffalo is not using the least cost combination of labor and capital because the marginal product per dollar for labor does not equal that of capital. The company should hire more labor and less capital. For instance, if the company decreased its capital by 10 units, it would save $40 per hour and lose 100 wings. If the company then hired 1 worker, it would increase its costs by $10 and gain 100 wings. So if the company cut its capital by 10 units and hired one worker, the company would produce the same number of wings at a lower total cost. *Anytime the marginal product per dollar of its inputs are not equal, the company can decrease its costs by using more of the input with the larger marginal product per dollar and less of the input with the lower marginal product per dollar.

## ■ CHECKPOINT 18.3

### True or false

1. False; page 454
2. True; page 456
3. False; page 456

### Multiple choice

1. c; page 454
2. e; page 456
3. b; page 456
4. b; page 456
5. c; page 457

### Short Response Questions

1. An increase in the adult population increases the supply of labor; page 456.

### ■ FIGURE 18.7

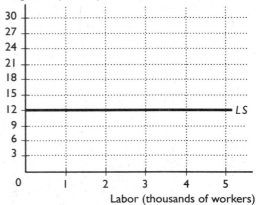

Wage rate (dollars per hour)

2. The equilibrium wage rate is $12 per hour, so JCPenney can hire as many workers as it wants for $12 an hour. JCPenney faces a labor supply that is perfectly elastic at the equilibrium wage rate, so as Figure 18.7 shows, JCPenney faces a labor supply curve that is horizontal at $12 an hour.

## ■ FIGURE 18.8

Wage rate (dollars per hour)

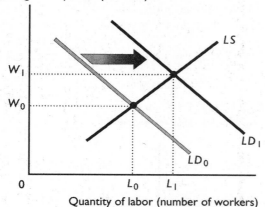

Quantity of labor (number of workers)

3. In Figure 18.8 the demand for Internet security programmers increases. The demand for labor curve shifts rightward from $LD_0$ to $LD_1$. The equilibrium wage rate rises and the quantity of these programmers employed increases; page 457.

### Long Response Questions

1. A monopoly exploits its market power by setting a higher price and thereby selling less than an otherwise identical competitive firm. Similarly a monopsony exploits its market power by setting a paying a lower wage rate and thereby hiring fewer workers than an otherwise identical competitive firm. When selling any given quantity, a monopoly sets the highest price possible. If the firm wants to increase the quantity it sells, the firm must lower its price so that all consumers pay a lower price. As a result, $MR$ is less than $P$ and the $MR$ curve lies below the demand curve. A monopoly produces where $MR = MC$ and then uses the demand curve to set the highest price that enables it to sell the quantity it produces. A monopsony behaves analogously. When hiring any given quantity of labor, a monopsony sets the lowest wage rate possible. If the firm wants to increase the quantity of workers it hires, the firm must raise its wage rate so that all workers receive a higher wage. As a result, $MRC$ is greater than $W$ and the $MRC$ curve lies above the la-

bor supply curve. A monopsony hires where $MRC = W$ and then uses the labor supply curve to set the lowest wage rate that enables it to hire the quantity of labor it employs.

## ■ FIGURE 18.9

Wage rate (dollars per hour)

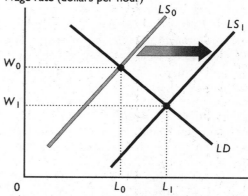

Quantity of labor (number of workers)

2. As more people obtain advanced degrees the supply of high-skilled labor increases. The labor supply curve of high-skilled labor shifts rightward as illustrated in Figure 18.9. As a result, the equilibrium wage rate for high-skilled labor falls, from $W_0$ to $W_1$ in the figure; page 456.

## ■ CHECKPOINT 18.4

### True or false

1. False; page 459
2. True; page 460

### Multiple choice

1. c; page 459
2. c; page 459
3. a; page 459
4. c; page 459
5. d; page 461

### Short Response Questions

1. The supply of financial capital results from people's saving; page 459.

2. If people expect an increase in future income, they save less now and the supply of capital decreases. The equilibrium interest rate rises; page 460.

3. a. The equilibrium interest rate is 6 percent because this is the interest rate at which the quantity of financial capital demanded equals the quantity of financial capital supplied. The equilibrium quantity of financial capital is $110 billion; page 461.

   b. In this question, both the demand and supply of financial have increased by the same amount. So the equilibrium interest rate remains the same, 6 percent, and the equilibrium quantity of financial capital increases to $130 billion; page 461.

### Long Response Questions

1. Advances in technology increase the demand for some types of capital and decrease the demand for other types. For example, the development of desktop computers increased the demand for office computing equipment, decreased the demand for electric typewriters, and increased the overall demand for capital in the office. So the demand for financial capital increased; page 459.

2. An increase in population increases both the demand for financial capital and the supply of financial capital. As a result, both the demand curve and supply curve shift rightward. The equilibrium quantity of financial capital increases. But the effect on the interest rate is indeterminate. If the demand increases by more than the supply, the interest rate rises; if the supply increases by more than the demand, the interest rate falls; and if the supply increases by the same amount as the demand, the interest rate does not change; pages 459-461.

### ■ CHECKPOINT 18.5

**True or false**
1. True; page 463
2. False; page 463
3. False; page 465

**Multiple choice**
1. b; page 463
2. a; page 463
3. d; page 463

4. a; page 464

### Short Response Questions
1. Petroleum is a nonrenewable natural resource because once any particular barrel is used, that barrel cannot be used again; page 463.

### Long Response Questions
■ **FIGURE 18.10**

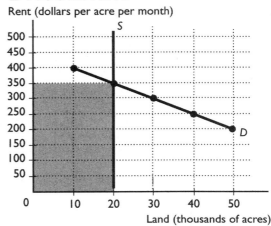

Rent (dollars per acre per month)

1. a. Figure 18.10 shows the completed figure; page 463.

   b. The equilibrium rent is $350 an acre per month and the equilibrium quantity is 20,000 acres; page 463.

   c. The gray area in Figure 18.10 is the economic rent. The opportunity cost is zero because all the income is economic rent. Whenever the supply of a resource is perfectly inelastic, all the income is economic rent; page 464.

2. Mr. Travolta's opportunity cost is $100,000 because this is the amount he forgoes by acting. His economic rent is the difference between his equilibrium salary, which is $18 million, and his opportunity cost, so his economic rent is $17.9 million. Mr. Travolta is willing to act in a movie for $100,000 but demand among producers for his acting services increases his equilibrium salary to $18 million a picture. It is the demand that sets the price for a good or service that has a perfectly inelastic supply; page 464.

# Inequality and Poverty

# Chapter 19

## CHAPTER IN PERSPECTIVE

In chapter 19 we conclude our study of income determination by looking at the extent and sources of economic inequality and examining how taxes and government programs redistribute income.

■ **Describe the economic inequality and poverty in the United States.**

Income and wealth are distributed unequally. The extent of inequality is measured using a Lorenz curve. A Lorenz curve graphs the cumulative percentage of income (or wealth) against the cumulative percentage of households. The farther the Lorenz curve is from the 45° line of equality, the more unequally income (or wealth) is distributed. In the United States, inequality has increased over the past few decades and economic mobility, moving up or down 1 quintile in the distribution of income, has decreased. Education, household size, martial status, and age of householder are important factors affecting a household's income. Poverty is a state in which a household's income is too low to buy the quantities of food, shelter, and clothing that are deemed necessary. Poverty rates for blacks and Hispanics fell during the 1990s but still exceed those for white households. The longer poverty lasts, the larger the problem for the household. For 30 percent of poor households poverty lasts for more than 9 months.

■ **Explain how economic inequality and poverty arise.**

Human capital is people's accumulated skill and knowledge. Differences in skills lead to large differences in earnings. High-skilled labor has a greater value of marginal product of skill than low-skilled labor, so at a given wage rate, the quantity of high-skilled labor demanded exceeds that of low-skilled labor. Skills are costly to acquire, so at a given wage rate, the quantity of high-skilled labor supplied is less than that of low-skilled labor. The equilibrium wage rate of high-skilled labor is higher than that of low-skilled labor. Discrimination according to race and/or sex is another possible source of inequality. High income people typically own large amounts of physical and financial capital. Some have great entrepreneurial ability. Personal and family characteristics also affect an individual's income.

■ **Explain why governments redistribute income and describe the effects of redistribution on economic inequality and poverty.**

The government redistributes income using income taxes, income maintenance programs, and subsidized services. Income maintenance programs include Social Security, unemployment compensation, and welfare programs. Market income is a household's income earned from the markets for factors of production and with no government redistribution. The distribution of income after taxes and benefits is more equal than the market distribution. Utilitarianism suggest that more equality is fairer. But government redistribution weakens work incentives both for the recipient and the wage earner and creates the big tradeoff between equity and efficiency. A major challenge is to insure that welfare programs do not weaken the incentive to acquire human capital; the current approach attempts to avoid weakening these incentives. The negative income tax is a redistribution scheme that provides every household with a guaranteed minimum annual income and taxes all earned income above the minimum at a fixed rate.

## EXPANDED CHAPTER CHECKLIST

**When you have completed this chapter, you will be able to:**

**1 Describe the economic inequality and poverty in the United States.**

- Describe the distribution of income and wealth, and explain how they have changed over time.
- Define, construct, and interpret a Lorenz curve.
- Define poverty and discuss its extent in the United States.

**2 Explain how economic inequality arises.**

- Discuss the demand for and the supply of high-skilled labor and low-skilled labor.
- Illustrate the market for high-skilled labor and the market for low-skilled labor.
- Analyze the effect of discrimination in the labor market.

**3 Explain the effects of taxes, social security, and welfare programs on economic inequality.**

- Describe how income taxes, income maintenance programs, and subsidized services redistribute income.
- Define market income.
- Define the big tradeoff and give two reasons why redistribution shrinks the size of the economic pie.

## YOUR AP TEST HINTS

### AP Topics

| Topic on your AP test | Corresponding textbook section |
|---|---|
| **Market failure and the role of government** | |
| Income Distribution | Chapter 19 |
| • Equity | Checkpoint 19.1 |
| • Sources of income inequality | Checkpoint 19.2 |
| • Market distribution of income | Checkpoint 19.3 |

### Extra AP material

- The different approaches to fairness of taxation, the benefit approach and the ability to pay approach, can be related to the fairness of redistributing income more equally.

## CHECKPOINT 19.1

■ **Describe the economic inequality and poverty in the United States.**

### Quick Review

- *Lorenz curve* A curve that graphs the cumulative percentage of income (or wealth) against the cumulative percentage of households. The farther the Lorenz curve is from the line of equality, the greater is the inequality.

### Additional Practice Problems 19.1

| 1978 | |
|---|---|
| **Households** | **Income (percentage)** |
| Lowest 20 percent | 4.3 |
| Second 20 percent | 10.3 |
| Third 20 percent | 16.9 |
| Fourth 20 percent | 24.7 |
| Highest 20 percent | 43.8 |

1. The table above shows the distribution of income in the United States in 1978:
   a. Draw the Lorenz curve for the United States in 1978.
   b. Was the distribution of income in the United States more or less equal than in recent years?

2. The figure shows Lorenz curves for three nations, *A*, *B*, and *C*. In which nation is income distributed most unequally? Most equally? In which nation is average income the highest?

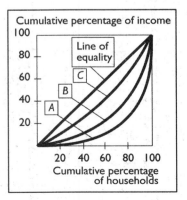

## Solutions to Additional Practice Problems 19.1

| 1978 | |
| --- | --- |
| Households (cumulative percent) | Income (cumulative percent) |
| 20 percent of households | 4.3 |
| 40 percent of households | 14.6 |
| 60 percent of households | 31.5 |
| 80 percent of households | 56.2 |
| 100 percent of households | 100.0 |

1a.  When drawing a Lorenz curve, the key is that it plots the *cumulative* percentage of income against the *cumulative* percentage of households. To create a Lorenz curve calculate cumulative percentages, which is done by adding the income owned by *all* the people who fall in the income group in and below the percentage being calculated. So, to draw the Lorenz curve, we first need to calculate the cumulative percentage of households and the cumulative percentage of income.      The table      above has these per- centages.    The Lorenz    curve in   the   figure plots   the   cu- mulative     per- centage        of income    and cumulative percentage of households from the table.

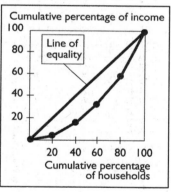

1b. The distribution of income in the United States in recent years is less equal that what it was in 1978.

2.  Income is distributed the most unequally in nation *A* because its Lorenz curve is farthest from the line of equality. Income is distributed the most equally in nation *C* because its Lorenz curve is the closest to the line of equality. Based on the Lorenz curves it is impossible to determine in which nation average income is the highest. Lorenz curves give information about the distribution of income, *not* about its amount.

## ■  AP Self Test 19.1

### True or false

1.  The Lorenz curve always lies above the line of equality.

2.  Since 1967, the percentage of the total income received by the richest 20 percent of households decreased.

3.  In the United States, poverty is distributed equally across the races, with approximately 15 percent of households of each race living in poverty.

### Multiple choice

1.  Which of the following is correct about the United States?
    a.  Income is equally distributed.
    b.  Wealth is equally distributed.
    c.  Income is equally distributed but wealth is unequally distributed because of inheritances.
    d.  Both wealth and income are unequally distributed.
    e.  Both wealth and income are equally distributed.

2.  If the income distribution is more unequal than the wealth distribution, then the
    a.  Lorenz curve for income will be farther away from the line of equality than the Lorenz curve for wealth.
    b.  government has imposed a higher tax rate on income.
    c.  Lorenz curve for wealth will be farther away from the line of equality than the Lorenz curve for income.
    d.  Lorenz curve for wealth will lie above the Lorenz curve for income.
    e.  It is not possible to draw the Lorenz curve for wealth on the same figure with the Lorenz curve for income.

■ **FIGURE 19.1**

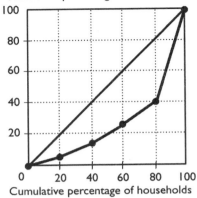

Cumulative percentage of income

Cumulative percentage of households

3. In Figure 19.1, the richest 20 percent of households receive ____ percent of total income.
   a. 20
   b. 100
   c. 80
   d. 40
   e. 60

4. In the United States in 1998, the wealthiest 1 percent of households held approximately ____ percent of all wealth.
   a. 1
   b. 13
   c. 27
   d. 38
   e. 88

5. Of all the characteristics that lead to income inequality, the factor with the largest impact is
   a. race.
   b. sex.
   c. age.
   d. education.
   e. location.

6. Which of the following statements about poverty is (are) correct?
   i. Blacks and Hispanics have higher poverty rates than whites.
   ii. Over the last 40 years, poverty rates for all groups have generally increased.
   iii. Most household spells of poverty last well beyond 9 months.
   a. i only.
   b. ii only.
   c. iii only.
   d. ii and iii.
   e. i, ii, and iii.

**Short Response Questions**

1. What does the distance between a Lorenz curve for income and the line of equality tell about the distribution of income?

2. Is the distribution of annual or lifetime income more equal? Why?

**Long Response Questions**

1. Can a Lorenz curve ever lie above the line of equality? Why or why not?

| Household percentage | Percentage of income | Cumulative percentage of income |
|---|---|---|
| Lowest 20 percent | 5.0 | ____ |
| Second 20 percent | 9.0 | ____ |
| Third 20 percent | 20.0 | ____ |
| Fourth 20 percent | 26.0 | ____ |
| Highest 20 percent | 40.0 | ____ |

■ **FIGURE 19.2**

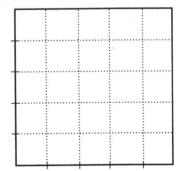

2. The table above has data for the nation of Beta. Complete the table by calculating the

cumulative percentages for the last column. In Figure 19.2, plot the Lorenz curve for Beta.

3. How has the distribution of income and the amount of economic mobility changed in the United States over the past few decades?

4. What is poverty? How many Americans live in poverty? How have poverty rates changed over the last few decades?

## CHECKPOINT 19.2

■ **Explain how economic inequality and poverty arise.**

### Quick Review

- *Demand for high-skilled labor and low-skilled labor* The vertical distance between the demand curve for low-skilled labor and the demand curve for high-skilled labor is equal to the value of marginal product of skill.

- *Supply of high-skilled labor and low-skilled labor* The vertical distance between the supply curve of low-skilled labor and the supply curve of high-skilled labor is equal to the compensation that high-skilled workers require for the cost of acquiring the skill.

### Additional Practice Problem 19.2

1. The figure shows the demand and supply curves for high-skilled and low-skilled labor at the beginning of the 1990s. ("H" indicates "high-skilled and "L" indicates "low-skilled.") Since then, new technology has increased the value of the marginal product of skill. In the figure, show the effect of this change. Is the income difference between high-skilled labor and low-skilled labor greater now or in 1990?

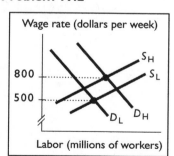

### Solution to Additional Practice Problem 19.2

1. This practice problem studies the relationship between skill differentials and the wage rate. Remember that high-skilled labor has a higher value of marginal product than low-skilled labor and the technology changes increased the value of the marginal product even more. As a result, the demand for high-skilled labor increased and the demand curve shifted rightward. As the figure shows, the wage rate paid to high skilled-workers increased. So the difference in income between high-skilled labor and low-skilled labor is greater now than in 1990.

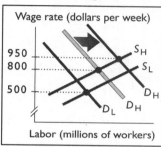

## ■ AP Self Test 19.2

### True or false

1. At a given wage rate, the quantity of high-skilled labor demanded exceeds the quantity of low-skilled labor demanded.

2. The horizontal distance between the demand curve for high-skilled labor and the demand curve for low-skilled labor measures the value of marginal product of skill.

3. The greater the cost of acquiring a skill, the greater is the vertical distance between the supply curve of high-skilled labor and the supply curve of low-skilled labor.

4. The equilibrium wage rate paid high-skilled workers exceeds that paid low-skilled workers.

5. Discriminating against some group of workers has no cost to a prejudiced employer.

**Multiple choice**

1. Differences in skills
   i. can arise partly from differences in education and/or partly from differences in on-the-job training.
   ii. can lead to large differences in earnings.
   iii. result in different demand curves for high-skilled and low-skilled labor.
      a. i only.
      b. ii only.
      c. ii and iii.
      d. i and iii.
      e. i, ii, and iii.

2. Other things being equal, the demand curve for low-skilled workers ____ the demand curve for high-skilled workers.
   a. lies below
   b. lies above
   c. is the same as
   d. is not comparable to
   e. at high wages lies below and at low wages lies above

3. The cost of acquiring a skill accounts for why the
   a. demand for high-skilled workers is different than the demand for low-skilled workers.
   b. supply of high-skilled workers is different than the supply of low-skilled workers.
   c. demand for high-skilled workers is different from the supply of high-skilled workers.
   d. demand for high-skilled workers is different from the supply of low-skilled workers.
   e. supply curves of high-skilled and low-skilled workers cross.

4. The vertical distance between the supply curves for neurosurgeons and for fast-food servers
   a. represents the difference in the demand for these two occupations.
   b. is the compensation that neurosurgeons require for the cost of acquiring this skill.
   c. is the difference in the value of the marginal product of the two professions.
   d. is the difference in on-the-job training.
   e. equals the difference in the equilibrium wages paid these two professions..

5. The wage rate that high-skilled workers receive is ____ the wage rate that low-skilled workers receive.
   a. greater than or equal to
   b. equal to
   c. less than or equal to
   d. greater than
   e. less than

6. If discrimination against women decreases their value of marginal product, then you would expect women to have ____ wage rate than men and there will be ____ high-paying jobs for women.
   a. a lower; more
   b. a higher; fewer
   c. a lower; fewer
   d. a higher; more
   e. the same; fewer

## ■ FIGURE 19.3

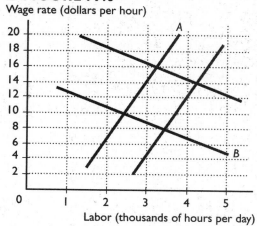

Wage rate (dollars per hour)

7. Figure 19.3 shows supply and demand curves for high-skilled and low-skilled labor. The curve labeled *A* is the supply curve for ____ workers and the curve labeled *B* is the demand curve for ____ workers.
   a. both high-skilled and low-skilled; both high-skilled and low-skilled
   b. high-skilled; high-skilled
   c. high-skilled; low-skilled
   d. low-skilled; high-skilled
   e. low-skilled; low-skilled

8. Figure 19.3 shows supply and demand curves for high-skilled and low-skilled labor. The wage rate paid to high-skilled workers is ____ per hour and the wage rate paid to low-skilled workers is ____ per hour.
   a. $14; $10
   b. $16; $14
   c. $14; $10
   d. $16; 10
   e. $16; $8

9. Inequality in the distribution of income and wealth is increased by
   a. the fact that, on the average, rich people marry rich partners.
   b. saving to redistribute an uneven income over the life cycle.
   c. marrying outside one's own socioeconomic class.
   d. donating money to charities.
   e. the U.S. income tax.

## Short Response Questions

### ■ FIGURE 19.4

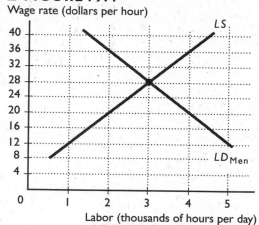

Wage rate (dollars per hour)

1. Suppose the supply of labor for men and women is identical and Figure 19.4 shows this supply curve, labeled *LS*. It also shows the demand curve for men, labeled *LD*Men.
   a. Suppose men and women have equal values of marginal products but employers are prejudiced against women. As a result, at any wage rate employers demand 2,000 fewer hours of female labor. Draw the demand curve for women in Figure 19.4.
   b. What is the wage rate paid men? Women?
   c. Do these wage rates make it costly for employers to discriminate against women?

### ■ FIGURE 19.5

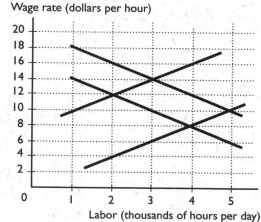

Wage rate (dollars per hour)

2. Figure 19.5 shows demand and supply curves

for high-skilled and low-skilled workers.

a. Label the demand curve for the high-skilled workers $D_H$ and the demand curve for low-skilled workers $D_L$. Label the supply curves similarly, using $S_H$ and $S_L$.

b. What is the value of marginal product of skill?

c. What is the compensation required for the cost of acquiring the skill?

d. What is the equilibrium wage rate for high-skilled workers and low-skilled workers?

### Long Response Questions

1. What is the opportunity cost of acquiring a skill?

2. a. How does the demand for high-skilled workers compare to the demand for low-skilled workers? How does the supply of high-skilled workers compare to the supply of low-skilled workers?

   b. How does the wage rate of high-skilled workers compare to the wage rate of low-skilled workers?

   c. How does the quantity of high-skilled workers employed compare to the quantity of low-skilled workers employed?

3. Why is discrimination costly for a prejudiced employer?

### CHECKPOINT 19.3

■ **Explain why governments redistribute income and describe the effects of redistribution on economic inequality and poverty.**

### Quick Review

- *Market income* Market income equals income earned from factors of production with no government redistribution.

- *Money income* Money income equals market income plus money benefits paid by the government.

### Additional Practice Problem 19.3

| Households | Income (millions of dollars per year) | Income (percentage of total income) |
|---|---|---|
| Lowest 20 percent | 5 | 2.5 |
| Second 20 percent | 15 | 7.5 |
| Third 20 percent | 35 | 17.5 |
| Fourth 20 percent | 55 | 27.5 |
| Highest 20 percent | 90 | 45.0 |

1. The table above shows the distribution of market income in an economy.

   a. Suppose the government imposes a proportional income tax of 10 percent upon everyone. It then distributes the funds it collects by paying benefits to the bottom two percentile income groups. The lowest 20 percent group receives one half of the funds collected and the second lowest receives the other half. Calculate the income shares of each 20 percent of households after tax and redistribution

   b. Draw the Lorenz curves for this economy before and after taxes and benefits. Have the government's taxes and benefits made the distribution more or less equal?

### Solution to Additional Practice Problem 19.3

| Household percentage | Tax paid (millions of dollars) | Income after tax and benefits (millions of dollars) | Income (percentage of total income) |
|---|---|---|---|
| Lowest 20 percent | 0.5 | 14.5 | 7.25 |
| Second 20 percent | 1.5 | 23.5 | 11.75 |
| Third 20 percent | 3.5 | 31.5 | 15.75 |
| Fourth 20 percent | 5.5 | 49.5 | 24.75 |
| Highest 20 percent | 9.0 | 81.0 | 40.50 |

1a. To solve this practice problem, subtract the amount paid as income tax and add the income received as benefits to obtain the new amount of income of each group. Then construct the Lorenz curve for the new income shares. In the above table, the second column shows the tax paid by each group. Total taxes collected are $20 million. The lowest and second lowest 20 percentile groups each receive half of this amount, so each receives $10 million in benefits. The third column adds benefits to the market income and subtracts the tax. The last column has the income shares. To find a group's income share divide income after tax and benefits by total income, which is $200 million, and multiply by 100.

| Household percentage | Cumulative percentage (before) | Cumulative percentage (after) |
|---|---|---|
| Lowest 20 percent | 2.50 | 7.25 |
| Second 20 percent | 10.00 | 19.00 |
| Third 20 percent | 27.50 | 34.75 |
| Fourth 20 percent | 55.00 | 59.50 |
| Highest 20 percent | 100.00 | 100.00 |

1b. The above table has the cumulative percentage of income before tax and benefits and after tax and benefits. These cumulative percentages are plotted in the

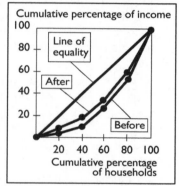

Lorenz curve in the figure. The Lorenz curve after the taxes and benefits is closer to the line of equality so the government's taxes and benefits have made the distribution of income more equal.

## ■ AP Self Test 19.3

### True or false
1. In general, U.S. federal and state taxes are progressive.
2. Subsidized services from the government go to only households with below-average incomes.
3. The distribution of income after taxes and benefits is more equal than the market distribution of income.
4. The redistribution of income creates the big tradeoff between earning an income and losing welfare benefits.

5. Under a negative income tax, some households would receive more money from the government than they would pay in taxes.

### Multiple choice
1. Which of the following is a way income is redistributed in the United States?
   i. subsidizing services
   ii. income taxes
   iii. income maintenance programs
   a. i only.
   b. ii only.
   c. ii and iii.
   d. ii and iii.
   e. i, ii, and iii.

2. A ____ tax is one that taxes income at an average rate that increases with the level of income.
   a. regressive
   b. progressive
   c. flat
   d. consumption
   e. proportional

3. Richer families pay a smaller fraction of their income in sales tax than do poorer families. The sales tax is definitely ____ tax.
   a. a regressive
   b. a progressive
   c. a flat
   d. an unfair
   e. a proportional

4. In a small island nation, families with an income of $10,000 pay $2,000 in income taxes and families with an income of $100,000 pay $20,000 in income taxes. This income tax is a ____ tax.
   a. regressive
   b. progressive
   c. kinked
   d. constant-amount
   e. proportional

5. Of the following types of income tax systems, the one that provides the greatest amount of redistribution from the rich to the poor is a
   a. progressive income tax.
   b. proportional income tax.
   c. regressive income tax.
   d. flat-rate income tax.
   e. money-income tax.

6. A household's income earned from the markets for factors of production and with no government redistribution is
   a. money income.
   b. welfare.
   c. market income.
   d. exploitative income.
   e. factored income.

7. Which of the following measures shows the most equality?
   a. money income
   b. market income
   c. income after taxes and before benefits
   d. wealth
   e. money wealth

8. When government redistributes income, one dollar collected from a rich person translates into ____ received by a poor person.
   a. one dollar
   b. less than one dollar
   c. more than one dollar
   d. zero dollars
   e. either exactly one dollar or, with some programs, more than one dollar

**Short Response Questions**

1. Define a "progressive" tax and a "regressive" tax.
2. Define market income and money income.
3. What are the nation's three main types of income maintenance programs?

**Long Response Questions**

1. Would progressive or regressive income taxes redistribute more money from the rich to the poor? Why?
2. Currently the government more heavily taxes high-income households and transfers money to low-income households. What are the likely reactions of the recipients of the money? Of the taxpayers? How do these reactions reflect the big tradeoff?
3. Suppose a negative income tax plan is passed so that a household is guaranteed an income of $20,000 and market income is taxed at a rate of 25 percent.
   a. What is the total income of a household that has a market income of $20,000?
   b. What is the total income of a household that has a market income of $60,000?

## YOUR AP SELF TEST ANSWERS

### ■ CHECKPOINT 19.1

**True or false**
1. False; page 473
2. False; page 474
3. False; page 477

**Multiple choice**
1. d; page 472
2. a; page 473
3. e; page 473
4. d; page 474
5. d; page 475
6. a; page 477

**Short Response Questions**
1. The farther the Lorenz curve is from the line of equality, the less equal is the distribution of income; page 473.
2. The distribution of lifetime income is more equal than the distribution of annual income because in any given year, different households are at different stages in their life cycle; page 476.

**Long Response Questions**
1. A Lorenz curve can never lie above the line of equality. The Lorenz curve plots the cumulative percentage of income against the cumulative percentage of households. Because the households are arranged by order of income, the cumulative percentage of income must always be less (except at 0 percent and 100 percent) than the cumulative percentage of households; page 472.
2. The table and Lorenz curve (in Figure 19.6) are in the next column. The cumulative percentage of income for an income group equals its percentage of income plus the percentages of income of all groups lower than it. The Lorenz curve plots these cumulative percentages of income against the cumulative percentage of households; page 472.

| Household percentage | Percentage of income | Cumulative percentage of income |
|---|---|---|
| Lowest 20 percent | 5.0 | 5.0 |
| Second 20 percent | 9.0 | 14.0 |
| Third 20 percent | 20.0 | 34.0 |
| Fourth 20 percent | 26.0 | 60.0 |
| Highest 20 percent | 40.0 | 100.0 |

**■ FIGURE 19.6**

Cumulative percentage of income

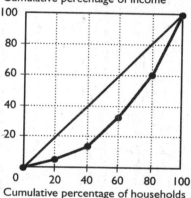

Cumulative percentage of households

3. The distribution of income has become less equal in the United States over the last few decades. The distribution of income changed because higher income groups have gained more income than the lower income groups. Economic mobility has decreased over the same years. Fewer families are now moving up or down 1 or more quintile in the distribution of income and more families are remaining in the same quintile; pages 474-476.

4. Poverty is a state in which a household's income is too low to buy the quantities of food, shelter, and clothing that are deemed necessary. Approximately 37 million Americans lived in poverty in 2004. Over the last several decades, poverty rates for whites and blacks have generally decreased, while poverty rates for Hispanics at first rose and then decreased, strikingly, during the 1990s; page 477.

## ■ CHECKPOINT 19.2

**True or false**

1. True;  pages 480-481
2. False;  page 481
3. True;  pages 480-481
4. True;  pages 481-482
5. False;  page 483

**Multiple choice**

1. e;  pages 480-482
2. a;  page 481
3. b;  pages 480-481
4. b;  page 481
5. d;  pages 481-482
6. c;  page 483
7. c;-page 481
8. e;  page 481
9. a;  page 484

**Short Response Questions**

### ■ FIGURE 19.7

Wage rate (dollars per hour)

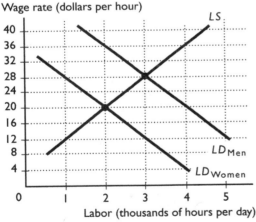

Labor (thousands of hours per day)

1. a. Figure 19.7 shows the demand curve for women. It lies to the left of the demand curve by men by 2,000 hours of labor at every wage rate;  page 483.

   b. Men are paid a wage of $28 an hour and women are paid a wage of $20 an hour;  page 483.

   c. If a firm discriminates against women, it costs the firm $28 an hour to hire a man when it could get the same output if it

hired a woman for $20. A discriminating firm's costs are higher as a result of its discrimination;  page 483.

### ■ FIGURE 19.8

Wage rate (dollars per hour)

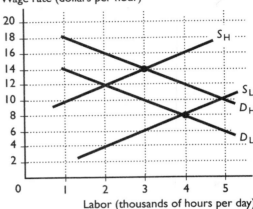

Labor (thousands of hours per day)

2. a. Figure 19.8 labels the curves.

   b. The value of marginal product of skill is $4 an hour because that is the vertical distance between the demand curve for high-skilled workers and the demand curve for low-skilled workers;  page 481.

   c. The compensation required for the cost of acquiring the skill is $8 an hour because that is the vertical distance between the supply curve for high-skilled workers and the supply curve for low-skilled workers;  page 481.

   d. The equilibrium wage rate for high-skilled workers is $14 an hour and the equilibrium wage rate for low-skilled workers is $8 an hour;  page 481.

**Long Response Questions**

1. The opportunity cost of acquiring a skill includes actual expenditures on tuition and books, as well as costs in the form of lost or reduced earnings while the skill is being acquired. When a person goes to school full time, that cost is the total earnings forgone. When a person receives on-the-job training, he or she is paid a lower wage than one who is doing a comparable job but not undergoing training. In this case, the cost of acquiring the skill is equal to the wage paid to a person

not being trained minus the wage paid to a person being trained; page 480.

2. a. Because the value of the marginal product of high-skilled workers exceeds that of low-skilled workers, the demand for high-skilled workers exceeds the demand for low-skilled workers. Because skills are costly to attain, the supply of high-skilled workers is less than the supply of low-skilled workers; pages 480-481.

   b. The demand for high-skilled workers exceeds the demand for low-skilled workers and the supply of high-skilled workers is less than the supply of low-skilled workers. So the wage rate received by high-skilled workers exceeds the wage rate received by low-skilled workers; page 482.

   c. The quantity of high-skilled workers employed compared to the quantity of low-skilled workers employed depends on the positions of the demand and supply curves of both types of labor. The demand curve for high-skilled labor lies to the right of the demand curve for low-skilled labor. The supply curve of high-skilled labor lies to the left of the supply curve of low-skilled labor. Because the positions of these curves determine the quantity of labor employed, we cannot say with certainty how the quantity of high-skilled workers employed compares that the quantity of low-skilled workers employed; page 481.

3. Discrimination is costly for employers because it means that they hire the higher-priced favored group of workers rather than the lower-priced unfavored group of workers. As a result, the firm's costs are higher than necessary and so its profit is less than it could. The shortfall in the profit is the opportunity cost a prejudiced employer must pay; page 483.

## ■ CHECKPOINT 19.3

### True or false
1. True; page 486
2. False; page 487
3. True; page 488
4. False; page 489
5. True; page 491

### Multiple choice
1. e; page 486
2. b; page 486
3. a; page 486
4. e; page 486
5. a; page 486
6. c; page 488
7. a; page 488
8. b; page 489

### Short Response Questions
1. A progressive tax is a tax for which the average tax rate rises with income. A regressive tax is a tax for which the average tax rate falls with income; page 486.

2. Market income is household income earned from the markets for factors of production with *no* government redistribution effort. Money income is market income plus money benefits paid the government. These money benefits are often called transfer payments; pages 487-488.

3. The three types of income maintenance programs are Social Security programs, unemployment compensation, and welfare programs; page 486.

### Long Response Questions
1. A progressive income tax will redistribute more income away from the rich to the poor. A progressive income tax has a higher average tax rate as income rises. As a result, the rich pay a greater amount of taxes than do the poor because the rich have more income and because the average tax rate on that income is higher; page 486.

2. The recipients of the money payments likely will work less. If they were to work more, they might earn enough to move into a higher tax bracket and lose the money the government is giving to them. The taxpayers also will tend to work less. On both counts, people work less and so the nation's total income decreases. These effects illustrate the force of the big tradeoff: By making incomes more equal, the government program has blunted people's incentives to work, lessened economic efficiency, and decreased the overall size of the nation's income; page 489.

3. a. The household receives its $20,000 guaranteed income. Then, on its market income of $20,000, it pays ($20,000) × (25 percent) = $5,000 in taxes, leaving $15,000 in income after taxes. Its total income is $20,000 + $15,000 = $35,000. This household receives a "negative income tax" payment of $15,000; page 491.

b. The household receives its $20,000 guaranteed income. Then, on its market income of $60,000, it pays ($60,000) × (25 percent) = $15,000 in taxes, leaving $45,000 in income after taxes. Its total income is $20,000 + $45,000 = $65,000. This household receives a "negative income tax" payment of $5,000; page 491.

# GDP and the Standard of Living

# Chapter 20

■ **Define GDP and explain why the value of production, income, and expenditure are the same for an economy.**

The standard of living is the level of the consumption of the goods and services that people enjoy, on the average. It is measured by the average income per person. Gross Domestic Product, GDP, is the market value of all the final goods and services produced within a country in a given time period. Only final goods and services are included in GDP; intermediate goods and services are not included. Expenditures are consumption expenditure (C), investment (I), government expenditures on goods and services (G), and net exports (NX). Total expenditure equals $C + I + G + NX$. Firms pay out everything they receive as incomes to the factors of production. We call total income Y. The circular flow shows that total expenditure equals total income so that $Y = C + I + G + NX$.

■ **Describe how economic statisticians measure GDP in the United States.**

GDP is measured using the expenditure approach and the income approach. The expenditure approach adds the four sources of expenditure: consumption expenditure, investment, government expenditures on goods and services, and net exports. Expenditures on used goods and financial assets are not in GDP. The income approach adds two categories of income (wages plus interest, rent, and profit). This sum is net domestic product at factor cost. To get to GDP from this, subsidies are subtracted, and indirect taxes and depreciation are added. A statistical discrepancy is added or subtracted so that GDP using the income approach equals GDP using the expenditure approach. Disposable person income is the income received by households minus the personal income taxes paid.

■ **Distinguish between nominal GDP and real GDP and define the GDP deflator.**

Real GDP is the value of final goods and services produced in a given year expressed in the prices of a base year; nominal GDP is the value of final goods and services produced in a given year using prices of that year. The chained-dollar method of calculating real GDP links the prices used to compute real GDP to the base year by calculating and then averaging annual growth rates of real GDP using current year prices and past year prices. The GDP deflator is an average of current prices expressed as a percentage of base-year prices. It equals (nominal GDP ÷ real GDP) × 100.

■ **Describe and explain the limitations of real GDP as a measure of the standard of living.**

Real GDP per person can be used to compare the standard of living over time or across nations. Real GDP fluctuates in a business cycle, going from an expansion to a peak to a recession to a trough. GDP is not a perfect measure of the standard of living because it does not measure household production, underground production, the value of leisure time, the environmental quality, health and life expectancy, or political freedom and justice.

## EXPANDED CHAPTER CHECKLIST

**When you have completed this chapter, you will be able to:**

**1 Define GDP and explain why the value of production, income, and expenditure are the same for an economy.**

- Define GDP.
- Explain the difference between a final good or service and an intermediate good or service, and tell why only final goods and services are included in GDP.
- Discuss the four types of expenditure.
- State why the value of production equals income, which equals expenditure.

**2 Describe how economic statisticians measure GDP in the United States.**

- Explain the expenditure approach to measuring GDP.
- Discuss why used goods and financial assets are not included in GDP.
- Explain the income approach to measuring GDP and discuss each of the components.
- State what adjustments must be made to net domestic product at factor cost to convert it to GDP.

**3 Distinguish between nominal GDP and real GDP and define the GDP deflator.**

- Define nominal GDP and real GDP, and explain the difference between them.
- Calculate real GDP.
- Define the GDP deflator and calculate it.

**4 Describe and explain the limitations of real GDP as a measure of the standard of living.**

- List the goods and services omitted from GDP and explain why each of these goods and services are not measured in GDP.
- Discuss how these omitted factors affect the standard of living.

## YOUR AP TEST HINTS

*AP Topics*

| Topic on your AP test | Corresponding textbook section |
|---|---|
| **Measurement of economic performance** | |
| GDP | Chapter 20 |
| • Measuring GDP | Checkpoint 20.1 |
| • Components of GDP | Checkpoints 20.2, 20.3 |
| • Nominal versus real GDP | Checkpoint 20.3 |
| • GDP deflator | Checkpoint 20.3 |
| • GDP and the standard of living | Checkpoint 20.4 |

*AP Vocabulary*

- On the AP test, "depreciation" can also be called "consumption of fixed capital."
- On the AP test, the "underground economy" can also be known as the "black market."

*Extra AP material*

- Net investment equals investment minus depreciation. When net investment is growing, generally GDP is expanding and the economy is either in an expansion or pulling out of a recession. However, when net investment is falling, generally the economy is struggling with GDP possibly decreasing or growing slowly and the economy either in or close to a recession.

## CHECKPOINT 20.1

**■ Define GDP and explain why the value of production, income, and expenditure are the same for an economy.**

*Quick Review*

- *Total expenditure* Total expenditure is the

total amount received by producers of final goods and services and equals $C + I + G + NX$.

- *Total income* Total income is the income paid to all factors of production and equals total expenditure.

## Additional Practice Problems 20.1

1. Last year consumption expenditure was $70 billion, investment was $16 billion, government purchases of goods and services were $12 billion, exports were $4 billion, and imports were $3 billion.
   a. What did GDP last year equal?
   b. This year imports increased to $5 billion. If all the other types of expenditure stay the same, what does GDP this year equal?

2. Suppose that GDP equals $12 trillion, consumption expenditure equals $7 trillion, investment equals $3.5 trillion, and government expenditure on goods and services equals $2.5 trillion. What does net exports equal?

3. One of the four expenditure categories is net exports. How can net exports be negative?

## Solutions to Additional Practice Problems 20.1

1a. To solve this problem use the equality between GDP and expenditure, GDP = $C + I + G + NX$. Last year's GDP = $70 billion + $16 billion + $12 billion + ($4 billion − $3 billion) = $99 billion.

1b. This year, imports increased from $3 billion to $5 billion, so replace the $3 billion in the calculation with $5 billion and GDP for this year is $97 billion. The $2 billion increase in imports results in a $2 billion decrease in GDP.

2. GDP = $C + I + G + NX$. So $NX$ = GDP − $C$ − $I$ − $G$. In this case, $NX$ = $12 trillion − $7 trillion − $3.5 trillion − $2.5 trillion, which equals −$1 trillion.

3. Net exports equals the value of exports of goods and services minus the value of imports of goods and services. If, as is the case in the United States, the value of imports exceeds the value of exports, net exports will be negative.

## ■ AP Self Test 20.1

### True or false

1. The computer chip that Dell Corp. buys from Intel Corp. is a final good.
2. Expenditure on a bulldozer is consumption expenditure.
3. The value of net exports of goods and services can be negative.
4. The value of production equals income, which equals expenditure.

### Multiple choice

1. The abbreviation "GDP" stands for
   a. Gross Domestic Product.
   b. Gross Domestic Prices.
   c. General Domestic Prices.
   d. Great Domestic Prices.
   e. Government's Domestic Politics.

2. GDP is equal to the ____ value of all the final goods and services produced within a country in a given period of time.
   a. production
   b. market
   c. wholesale
   d. retail
   e. typical

3. The following are all *final* goods except
   a. flour used by the baker to make cup cakes.
   b. bread eaten by a family for lunch.
   c. pencils used by a 6th grader in class.
   d. Nike shoes used by a basketball player.
   e. a computer used by Intel to design new computer chips.

4. Investment is defined as
   a. the purchase of a stock or bond.
   b. financial capital.
   c. what consumers do with their savings.
   d. the purchase of new capital goods by firms.
   e. spending on capital goods by governments.

5. In one year, a firm increases its production by $9 million and increases sales by $8 mil-

lion. All other things in the economy remaining the same, which of the following is true?

  a. GDP increases by $8 million and inventory investment decreases by $1 million.

  b. GDP increases by $9 million and inventory investment increases by $1 million.

  c. Inventory investment decreases by $1 million.

  d. GDP increases by $8 million and investment increases by $1 million.

  e. GDP increases by $17 million.

6. Total expenditure equals

  a. $C + I + G + NX$.

  b. $C + I + G - NX$.

  c. $C + I - G + NX$.

  d. $C - I + G + NX$.

  e. $C - I - G - NX$.

### Short Response Questions

1. Classify each of the following into the components of U.S. GDP: consumption expenditure, investment, government purchases of goods and services, exports, or imports.

  a. The purchase of a Sony DVD player made in Japan.

  b. A family's purchase of a birthday cake at the local Safeway grocery store.

  c. Microsoft's purchase of 1,000 Dell computers.

  d. The purchase of a new pizza oven by Pizza Hut.

  e. The government's purchase of 15 stealth fighters.

2. Additions to inventories are counted in what component of GDP? Can the inventory addition ever be negative?

### Long Response Questions

1. Why aren't intermediate goods or services counted in GDP?

2. Why does total expenditure equal total income?

---

## CHECKPOINT 20.2

■ **Describe how economic statisticians measure GDP in the United States.**

### Quick Review

- *Expenditure approach* GDP equals the sum of consumption expenditure, investment, government purchases, and net exports.

- *Income approach* GDP equals the sum of wages plus interest, rent, and profit minus subsidies plus indirect taxes and depreciation plus or minus any statistical discrepancy. The sum of the first two income categories is net domestic product at factor.

### Additional Practice Problem 20.2

| Item | Amount (billions of dollars) |
|---|---|
| **Wages** | 5,875 |
| **Consumption expenditure** | 6,987 |
| **Indirect taxes less subsidies** | 630 |
| **Interest, rent, and profit** | 2,248 |
| **Depreciation** | 1,329 |
| **Investment** | 1,586 |
| **Statistical discrepancy** | 0 |
| **Net exports** | −349 |

1. The table above gives some of the items in the U.S. National Income and Product Accounts in 2001.

  a. Calculate U.S. GDP in 2001.

  b. Did you use the expenditure approach or the income approach to make this calculation?

  c. What was the government's expenditure on goods and services in 2001?

### Solution to Additional Practice Problem 20.2

1a. This question focuses on calculating GDP. To solve problems such as this, you need to know how to use the expenditure approach and the income approach. The expenditure approach adds four categories of expenditure while the income approach adds the two income categories and then makes a few additional adjustments.

To calculate GDP using the expenditure approach the four categories of expenditure you need to know are: consumption, investment, government expenditure, and net exports. The table does not give the value of government expenditures on goods and services, so you cannot find GDP using the expenditure approach.

To calculate GDP using the income approach you need to know the values of wages and of interest, rent, and profit. Adding these two together yields net domestic income at factor cost. To adjust to GDP, you need also indirect taxes less subsidies, depreciation, and any statistical discrepancy. All these items are listed in the table, so GDP can be calculated using the income approach. In this case, GDP = $5,875 billion + $2,248 + $630 billion + $1,329 billion + $0, which is $10,082 billion.

1b  The only way GDP can be calculated in part (a) is by the income approach, which is the approach used.

1c. GDP was calculated in part (a) using the income approach. The expenditure approach notes that GDP = $C + I + G + NX$. Subtract $C$, $I$, and $NX$ from both sides of the equation to show that $G = GDP - C - I - NX$. Using the values of GDP, $C$, $I$, and $NX$ yields $G$ = $10,082 billion − $6,987 billion − $1,586 billion + $349 billion = $1,858 billion. (The net exports were negative, so −(−$349 billion) equals + $349 billion).

## ■ AP Self Test 20.2

### True or false

1. The expenditure approach measures GDP by using data on consumption expenditure, investment, government expenditures on goods and services, and net exports of goods and services.

2. In the United States, expenditure on used goods is becoming an increasingly large fraction of GDP.

3. The income approach uses data on consumption expenditure, investment, government purchases of goods and services, and net exports of goods and services to calculate GDP.

4. Personal disposable income is usually larger than GDP.

### Multiple choice

1. In calculating GDP, economists
   a. measure total expenditure as the only true measure.
   b. can measure either total expenditure or total income.
   c. measure total income as the only true measure.
   d. measure total income minus total expenditure.
   e. measure total income plus total expenditure.

2. The expenditure approach to measuring GDP is based on summing
   a. wages, interest, rent, and profit.
   b. each industry's production.
   c. the total values of final goods, intermediate goods, used goods, and financial assets.
   d. consumption expenditure, investment, government expenditures on goods and services, and net exports of goods and services.
   e. consumption expenditure, investment, government expenditures on goods and services, and net exports of goods and services minus wages, interest, rent, and profit.

3. Suppose GDP is $10 billion, consumption expenditure is $7 billion, investment is $2 billion, and government expenditures on goods and services is $2 billion. Net exports of goods and services must be
   a. $1 billion.
   b. −$1 billion.
   c. $2 billion.
   d. −$2 billion.
   e. $10 billion.

4. According to the expenditure approach to measuring GDP, in the United States the largest component of GDP is
   a. consumption expenditure.
   b. investment.
   c. government expenditures on goods and services.
   d. net exports of goods and services.
   e. wages.

5. Which of the following is <u>NOT</u> one of the income categories used in the income approach to measuring GDP?
   a. wages
   b. rent
   c. interest
   d. taxes paid by persons
   e. profit

6. If the statistical discrepancy equals zero, then once income is totaled across the income categories, to calculate GDP we must
   a. add the amount of income saved and spent.
   b. add indirect taxes and depreciation and subtract subsidies.
   c. subtract indirect taxes and subsidies and then add depreciation.
   d. do nothing because the income sum equals GDP.
   e. add subsidies and then subtract depreciation and indirect taxes.

### Short Response Question

| Item | Amount (dollars) |
|---|---|
| **Wages** | 3,900 |
| **Consumption expenditure** | 4,000 |
| **Indirect taxes minus subsidies** | 400 |
| **Interest, rent, and profit** | 1,400 |
| **Government expenditures** | 1,000 |
| **Investment** | 1,100 |
| **Net exports** | 300 |
| **Statistical discrepancy** | 300 |
| **Depreciation** | 700 |

1. The table above gives data for a small nation:
   a. What is the nation's GDP? Did you use the expenditure or income approach to calculate GDP?

b. What does net investment equal?
c. What is the net domestic product at factor cost?

### Long Response Question

1. What adjustments must be made to net domestic product at factor cost to convert it to GDP? Why must these adjustments be made?

2. What adjustments must be made to GDP to calculate GNP? To calculate disposable personal income?

### CHECKPOINT 20.3

### ■ Distinguish between nominal GDP and real GDP and define the GDP deflator.

#### Quick Review

- *Real GDP* The value of the final goods and services produced in a given year valued at the prices of a base year.
- *Nominal GDP* The value of the final goods and services produced in a given year valued at the prices that prevailed in that year.

#### Additional Practice Problems 20.3

1. In a small, lush tropical nation suppose real GDP in 2004 was $5 billion and nominal GDP in 2004 was $10 billion. In 2005, nominal GDP was $12 billion. If GDP in 2005, measured using 2004 prices was $11.5 billion and GDP in 2004, measured using 2005 prices was $11 billion, what does real GDP in 2005 equal?

2. Nominal GDP = $10 trillion, real GDP = $9 trillion. What is the GDP deflator?

3. Real GDP = $8 trillion, GDP deflator = 120. What is nominal GDP?

4. Nominal GDP = $12 trillion, GDP deflator = 120. What is real GDP?

#### Solution to Practice Problem 20.3

1. This question gives you practice in how real GDP is calculated. To determine the answers,

take each part step-by-step:

First we need the growth rate of GDP from 2004 to 2005 measured using 2004 prices. Nominal GDP in 2004 (which is GDP in 2004 measured using 2004 prices) was $10 billion and GDP in 2005 measured using 2004 prices was $11.5 billion. So the growth in GDP using 2004 prices was [($11.5 billion – $10.0 billion) ÷ $10 billion] × 100, or 11.5 percent.

Next we need the growth rate of GDP from 2004 to 2005 measured using 2005 prices. GDP in 2004 measured with 2005 prices was $11 billion and nominal GDP in 2005 (which is GDP in 2005 measured using 2005 prices) was $12 billion. So the growth in GDP using 2005 prices was [($12 billion – $11 billion) ÷ $11 billion] × 100, which is 9.1 percent.

Finally, we average the two growth rates to give a growth rate of 10.3 percent between 2004 and 2005. This percentage change is applied to real GDP in 2004, $5 billion, to give real GDP in 2005, so that real GDP in 2005 equals ($5 billion) × (1.103) or $5.52 billion.

2.  GDP deflator = (Nominal GDP ÷ Real GDP) × 100 = ($10 trillion ÷ $9 trillion) × 100 = 111.1.

3.  Rearranging the formula used in problem 2 gives (GDP deflator × Real GDP) ÷ 100 = Nominal GDP, so (120 × $8 trillion) ÷ 100 = $9.6 trillion.

4.  Once again rearranging the formula used in problem 2 gives (Nominal GDP ÷ GDP deflator) × 100 = Real GDP, so ($12 trillion ÷ 120) × 100 = $10 trillion.

## ■ AP Self Test 20.3

### True or false

1.  Nominal GDP increases only if the production of final goods and services increases.

2.  Real GDP is just a more precise name for GDP.

3.  Real GDP equals nominal GDP in the base year.

4.  If real GDP is $600 billion and nominal GDP is $750 billion, then the GDP deflator is 125.

### Multiple choice

1.  Nominal GDP can change
    a. only if prices change.
    b. only if the quantities of goods and services change.
    c. only if prices increase.
    d. if either prices or the quantities of goods and services change.
    e. only if prices *and* the quantities of the goods and services change.

2.  The difference between nominal GDP and real GDP is
    a. the indirect taxes used in their calculations.
    b. the prices used in their calculations.
    c. that nominal GDP includes the depreciation of capital and real GDP does not.
    d. that nominal GDP includes net exports of goods and services and real GDP includes net imports.
    e. that real GDP includes the depreciation of capital and nominal GDP does not.

3.  Real GDP measures the value of goods and services produced in a given year valued using
    a. base year prices.
    b. prices of that same year.
    c. no prices.
    d. future prices.
    e. government approved prices.

4.  If nominal GDP increases, then real GDP
    a. must decrease.
    b. must increase.
    c. must not change.
    d. could increase, decrease, or not change.
    e. could either increase or not change but cannot decrease.

5.  The GDP deflator is a measure of
    a. taxes and subsidies.
    b. changes in quantities.
    c. prices.
    d. depreciation.
    e. changes in nominal GDP.

6. The GDP deflator is calculated as
   a. (nominal GDP ÷ real GDP) × 100.
   b. (real GDP ÷ nominal GDP) × 100.
   c. (nominal GDP + real GDP) ÷ 100.
   d. (nominal GDP − real GDP) ÷ 100.
   e. (real GDP − nominal GDP) ÷ 100.

7. Nominal GDP is $12.1 trillion and real GDP is $11.0 trillion. The GDP deflator is
   a. 90.1.
   b. 121.
   c. 1.10.
   d. 91.0.
   e. 110.

**Short Response Questions**

| Item | Data for 2005 | | Data for 2006 | |
|------|---------------|-------|---------------|-------|
|      | Quantity | Price | Quantity | Price |
| Pizza | 100 | $10.00 | 150 | $20.00 |
| Soda  | 50  | $2.00  | 75  | $4.00  |

1. An economy produces only pizza and soda. The table above gives the quantities produced and prices in 2005 and 2006. The base year is 2005.
   a. What is nominal GDP in 2005?
   b. What is real GDP in 2005?
   c. What is nominal GDP in 2006?
   d. What is real GDP in 2006?

2. Calculate the price level for each of the following combinations of nominal GDP and real GDP.
   a. Nominal GDP = $12 trillion, real GDP = $10 trillion.
   b. Nominal GDP = $12 trillion, real GDP $16 trillion.
   c. Nominal GDP = $8 trillion, real GDP = $4 trillion.

**Short Response Questions**

1. If you want to measure the change in production, is it better to use nominal GDP or real GDP? Why?

2. How does the chained-dollar method of calculating real GDP link the current year's real GDP to the base year's real GDP?

## CHECKPOINT 20.4

■ **Describe and explain the limitations of real GDP as a measure of the standard of living.**

### Quick Review

- *Standard of living* The standard of living among different nations or over a period of time can be compared using real GDP per person.
- *Goods and services omitted from GDP* Household production, underground production, leisure time, and environmental quality are omitted from GDP.

### Additional Practice Problems 20.4

1. How has real GDP per person changed in the United States since 1964?

2. How do you think the standard of living in the United States today compares with the standard of living 150 years ago?

### Solutions to Additional Practice Problems 20.4

1. Real GDP per person has increased substantially since 1964. In fact, real GDP per person has more than doubled since 1964. Historically, in the United States for the past 100 years real GDP per person has doubled about every 30 years.

2. The standard of living now is dramatically higher than it was 150 years ago. First, even though no totally accurate data on real GDP per person is available from 150 years ago, it is certain that real GDP per person is much higher today even after taking account of the fact that household production was more common 150 years ago. The underground economy is larger today, which boosts today's standard of living, and people today enjoy significantly more leisure time, which also boosts today's standard of living. Perhaps the edge on environment quality goes to the past. Considering health and life expectancy, and political freedom and social justice, people today are much better off than people 150 years ago. It is likely true that no

country in history has ever enjoyed a standard of living as high as that in the United States today.

## ■ AP Self Test 20.4

### True or false

1. As currently measured, real GDP does not include the value of home production.

2. Production in the underground economy is part of the "investment" component of GDP.

3. The production of anti-pollution devices installed by electric utilities is not counted in GDP because the devices are designed only to eliminate pollution.

4. The measure of a country's real GDP does not take into account the extent of political freedom in the country.

### Multiple choice

1. Which of the following is <u>NOT</u> part of the business cycle?
   a. recession
   b. peak
   c. inflation
   d. trough
   e. expansion

2. In the business cycle, what immediately precedes the time when real GDP is falling?
   a. recession
   b. peak
   c. depression
   d. trough
   e. expansion

3. The measurement of GDP handles household production by
   a. estimating a dollar value of the goods purchased to do housework.
   b. estimating a dollar value of the services provided.
   c. ignoring it.
   d. including it in exactly the same way that all other production is included.
   e. including it in real GDP but not in nominal GDP because there are no prices paid for the work.

4. You hire some of your friends to help you move to a new house and pay them a total of $200 and buy them dinner at Pizza Hut. Which of the following is true?
   a. The $200 should be counted as part of GDP but not the dinner at Pizza Hut.
   b. If your friends do not report the $200 on their tax forms, it becomes part of the underground economy.
   c. The dinner at Pizza Hut should be counted as part of GDP but not the $200.
   d. Hiring your friends is an illegal activity and should not be counted in GDP.
   e. Neither the $200 nor the dinner should be counted in GDP because both are household production.

5. The value of leisure time is
   a. directly included in GDP and, in recent years, has become an increasing large part of GDP.
   b. excluded from GDP.
   c. zero.
   d. directly included in GDP but, in recent years, has become a decreasing large part of GDP.
   e. directly included in GDP and, in recent years, has not changed much as a fraction of GDP.

6. A new technology is discovered that results in all new cars producing 50 percent less pollution. The technology costs nothing to produce and cars do not change in price. As a result of the technology, there is a reduction in the number of visits people make to the doctor to complain of breathing difficulties. Which of the following is true?
   a. real GDP decreases as a result of fewer doctor services being provided.
   b. real GDP is not affected.
   c. nominal GDP increases to reflect the improvement in the health of the population.
   d. real GDP will decrease to reflect the decrease in pollution.
   e. nominal GDP does not change and real GDP increases because people's health increases.

7. The calculation of GDP using the income approach <u>EXCLUDES</u>
   a. rent.
   b. interest.
   c. environmental quality.
   d. wages.
   e. profit.

8. Good health and life expectancy are
   a. included in GDP but not in our standard of living.
   b. included in both GDP and in our standard of living.
   c. included in our standard of living but not in GDP.
   d. not included in either our standard of living or in GDP.
   e. sometimes included in GDP if they are large enough changes but are never included in our standard of living.

## Short Response Questions

1. What are the parts of a business cycle? What is their order?

2. If you cook a hamburger at home, what happens to GDP? If you go to Burger King and purchase a hamburger, what happens to GDP?

## Long Response Question

1. What general categories of goods and services are omitted from GDP? Why is each omitted? What is the effect of these omissions on use of GDP as a measure of the standard of living?

## ■ YOUR AP SELF TEST ANSWERS

### ■ CHECKPOINT 20.1

**True or false**

1. False; page 498
2. False; page 499
3. True; page 500
4. True; page 501

**Multiple choice**

1. a; page 498
2. b; page 498
3. a; page 498
4. d; page 499
5. b; page 499
6. a; page 500

**Short Response Questions**

2. a. Import; page 500.
   b. Consumption expenditure; page 499.
   c. Investment; page 499.
   d. Investment; page 499.
   e. Government expenditure on goods and services; 500.

2. Additions to inventory are included as part of investment. "Additions" to inventory can be negative when the amount of goods and services sold exceeds the amount produced; page 499.

**Long Response Questions**

1. Intermediate goods or services are not counted in GDP because if they were, they would be double counted. A computer produced by Dell Corp. is included in GDP. But if the Intel chip that is part of the computer is also included in GDP, then the Intel chip is counted twice: once when it is produced by Intel, and again when it is included in the computer produced by Dell; page 498.

2. Total expenditure is the amount received by producers of final goods and services from the sales of these goods and services Because firms pay out everything they receive as incomes to the factors of produc-

tion, total expenditure equals total income. From the viewpoint of firms, the value of production is the cost of production, and the cost of production is equal to income. From the viewpoint of consumers of goods and services, the value of production is the cost of buying the production, which equals expenditure; page 501.

### ■ CHECKPOINT 20.2

**True or false**

1. True; page 503
2. False; page 504
3. False; page 505
4. False; page 507

**Multiple choice**

1. b; page 503
2. d; page 503
3. b; page 503
4. a; page 503
5. d; page 505
6. b; page 506

**Short Response Question**

1. a. GDP = $6,400, which is the sum of consumption expenditure, investment, government expenditures on goods and services, and net exports. The expenditure approach was used; page 503.
   b. Net investment equals (total or gross) investment minus depreciation, so net investment equals $1,100 − $700, which is $400.
   c. Net domestic product at factor cost equals $5,300, the sum of wages plus interest, rent, and profit; page 505.

**Long Response Questions**

1. To change net domestic product at factor cost to GDP, three sets of adjustments must be made. First, net domestic product at factor cost is measured at firms' costs; to convert costs to equal the market prices paid, taxes must be added and subsidies subtracted.

Second, net domestic product does not include depreciation but GDP does. So, depreciation must be added. Finally, any statistical discrepancy must be added or subtracted; page 506.

2. To calculate GNP, net factor income from abroad must be added (or subtracted, if it is negative) from GDP. Then, to calculate disposable personal income, from GNP depreciation and retained profits must be subtracted, transfer payments must be added, and then any statistical discrepancy must be either added or subtracted; page 507.

## ■ CHECKPOINT 20.3

**True or false**

1. False; page 509
2. False; page 509
3. True; page 509
4. True; page 511

**Multiple choice**

1. d; page 509
2. b; page 509
3. a; page 509
4. d; page 509
5. c; page 511
6. a; page 511
7. e; page 511

**Short Response Questions**

1. a. Nominal GDP = (100 × $10) + (50 × $2) = $1,100, the sum of expenditure on pizza and expenditure on soda; page 509.

   b. Because 2005 is the base year, real GDP = nominal GDP, so real GDP = $1,100; page 509.

   c. Nominal GDP = (150 × $20) + (75 × $4) = $3,300, the sum of expenditure on pizza and expenditure on soda; page 509.

   d. Using 2005 prices, GDP in 2006 is (150 × $10) + (75 × $2) = $1,650. So GDP grew from $1,100 in 2005 to $1,650 in 2006, a percentage increase of 50 percent. Using

2006 prices, GDP grew 50 percent between 2005 and 2006. The average growth is 50 percent, so real GDP in 2006 is 50 percent higher than in 2005, so that real GDP in 2006 is $1,650; page 510.

2. a. GDP deflator = ($12 trillion ÷ $10 trillion) × 100 = 120; page 511.

   b. GDP deflator = ($12 trillion ÷ $16 trillion) × 100 = 75; page 511.

   c. GDP deflator = ($8 trillion ÷ $4 trillion) × 100 = 200; page 511.

**Long Response Questions**

1. To measure the change in production, it is necessary to use real GDP. Nominal GDP changes whenever production *or* prices change. Real GDP uses constant prices and changes only when production changes. The actual production is usually more important than nominal GDP because the quantity of production is related to the standard of living, employment, and other important economic factors; page 509.

2. From one year to the next, real GDP is scaled by the percentage change from the first year to the next. For instance, real GDP in 2005 is linked to real GDP in 2004 by the percentage change from 2004, and real GDP in 2006 in turn is linked to real GDP in 2005 by the percentage change from 2005, and so on. These links are like the links in a chain. They link real GDP in the current year back to the base year and the base year prices; page 510.

## ■ CHECKPOINT 20.4

**True or false**

1. True; page 515
2. False; page 515
3. False; page 516
4. True; page 517

**Multiple choice**

1. c; page 513
2. b; page 514
3. c; page 515

4. b; page 515

5. b; page 515

6. a; page 516

7. c; page 516

8. c; page 517

## Short Response Questions

1. The business cycle has four parts: the expansion phase, when real GDP is growing; the peak, when real GDP reaches its highest level; the recession phase, when real GDP is falling for at least 6 months; and the trough, when real GDP is at its lowest level. The order of the business cycle is from expansion to peak to recession to trough, and then back to expansion; pages 513-514.

2. If you cook a hamburger at home, the meat you purchased is included in GDP but the production of the hamburger is not included in GDP because it is household production. If you buy a hamburger at Burger King, the production of the hamburger is included in GDP; page 515.

## Long Response Questions

1. Goods and services omitted from GDP are household production, underground or black market production, leisure time, and environmental quality. GDP measures the value of goods and services that are bought in markets. Because household production, leisure time, and environmental quality are not purchased in markets, they are excluded from GDP. Even though underground production or black market production frequently is bought in markets, the activity is unreported and is not included in GDP. These omissions all limit GDP's use as a measure of the standard of living. For instance, household production and underground production both produce goods and services that affect people's standard of living. Leisure time also is an important contributor to people's standard of living. And degradation of the environment lowers the standard of living whereas improving the environment raises the standard of living; pages 515-516.

# Jobs and Unemployment

## Chapter 21

Chapter 21 explores one of the economy's important markets, the labor market, by defining indicators of its performance and explaining how these indicators have changed over time. Chapter 21 also discusses unemployment and its relationship to real GDP.

■ **Define the unemployment rate and other labor market indicators.**

The Current Population Survey is a monthly survey of 60,000 households across the country that is the basis for the nation's labor market statistics. The working-age population is non-institutionalized people aged 16 and over who are not in the U.S. Armed Forces. The labor force is the sum of the employed and unemployed. To be unemployed, a person must have no employment, be available for work, and either have made an effort to find a job during the previous four weeks or be waiting to be recalled to a job from which he or she was laid off. The unemployment rate is the percentage of people in the labor force who are unemployed. The labor force participation rate is the percentage of the working-age population who are members of the labor force. A discouraged worker is a person who is available and willing to work but has not made specific efforts to find a job within the previous four weeks. Full-time workers are those who usually work 35 hours or more a week. Part-time workers are those who usually work less than 35 hours per week. Involuntary part-time workers and part-time workers who are looking for full-time work. Aggregate hours are the total number of hours worked by all the people employed.

■ **Describe the trends and fluctuations in the indicators of labor market performance in the United States.**

From 1965 to 2005, the average unemployment rate was 5.9 percent. The lowest unemployment rates were achieved in the late 1960s and in the late 1990s. In the Great Depression of the 1930s, the U.S. unemployment rate reached 25 percent. From 1965 to 2005, the labor force participation rate had generally an upward trend and is a bit less than 67 percent. The labor force participation rate for men decreased and for women increased. About 17 percent of workers have part-time jobs. The involuntary part-time rate rises during recessions and falls during expansions. Aggregate hours have an upward trend. The average workweek has fallen from 38.5 hours in 1965 to just below 34 hours in 2005.

■ **Describe the sources and types of unemployment, define full employment, and explain the link between unemployment and real GDP.**

People who become unemployed are job losers, job leavers, entrants, or reentrants. People who leave unemployment are hires, recalls, or withdrawals. Unemployment is either frictional (normal labor turnover), structural (changes in necessary job skills or job locations), seasonal (changes in the seasons), or cyclical (changes in the business cycle). The duration of unemployment increases in recessions. Full employment occurs when there is no cyclical unemployment. At full employment, the unemployment rate is the natural unemployment rate. The unemployment rate rises in recessions.

## EXPANDED CHAPTER CHECKLIST

**When you have completed this chapter, you will be able to:**

**1  Define the unemployment rate and other labor market indicators.**

- Define working-age population and labor force.
- Tell the criteria the Current Population Survey uses to classify a person as employed or unemployed.
- Define and calculate the unemployment rate.
- Define and calculate the labor force participation rate.
- Define discouraged workers.
- Tell the criteria used to classify a worker as full time or part time.
- Define involuntary part-time workers.
- Define and calculate aggregate hours.

**2  Describe the trends and fluctuations in the indicators of labor market performance in the United States.**

- Describe how the unemployment rate changed since 1965.
- Tell what happens to the unemployment rate in recessions and in expansions.
- Describe how the labor force participation rate changed since 1965.

**3  Describe the sources and types of unemployment, define full employment, and explain the link between unemployment and real GDP.**

- List the sources of unemployment.
- Describe how unemployment ends.
- List and explain four types of unemployment.
- Discuss the uneven demographic impacts of unemployment.

- Identify the relationships between full employment, the natural unemployment rate, and potential GDP.

## YOUR AP TEST HINTS

### AP Topics

| Topic on your AP test | Corresponding textbook section |
|---|---|
| **Measurement of economic performance** | |
| Unemployment | Chapter 21 |
| • Define and measure | Checkpoint 21.1 |
| • Types | Checkpoint 21.3 |
| • Natural rate of unemployment | Checkpoint 21.3 |
| • Relationship between potential GDP and natural rate of unemployment | Checkpoint 21.3 |

### AP Vocabulary

- On the AP test, the working age population might be called the "civilian noninstitutional population, aged 16 years and over."

### Extra AP material

- The AP test will not ask how the unemployment rate, labor force participation rate, or aggregate hours have changed over time.

## CHECKPOINT 21.1

■ **Define the unemployment rate and other labor market indicators.**

### Quick Review

- *Unemployment rate* The unemployment rate is the percentage of the people in the labor force who are unemployed. That is,

$$\text{Unemployment rate} = \frac{(\text{Unemployed people})}{(\text{Labor force})} \times 100$$

- *Labor force participation rate* The labor force participation rate is the percentage of the working-age population who are members of the labor force. It equals

$$\text{Participation rate} = \frac{(\text{Labor force})}{(\text{Working - age people})} \times 100$$

- *Aggregate hours* The aggregate hours are the total number of hours worked by all the people employed, both full time and part time, during a year.

## Additional Practice Problems 21.1

1. Determine the labor market status of each of the following people:
   a. Don is 21 and a full-time college student.
   b. Shirley works for 20 hours a week as an administrative assistant and is looking for a full-time job.
   c. Clarence was laid off from his job selling keyboards to computer manufacturers and is actively seeking a new job.
   d. Pat quit her job as an account executive 6 months ago but, unable to find a new position, has stopped actively searching.

2. The Bureau of Labor Statistics reported that in June 2005, the labor force was 149.1 million, employment was 141.6 million, and the working-age population was 225.9 million. Average weekly hours for that month were 33.7. Calculate for that month the:
   a. Unemployment rate.
   b. Labor force participation rate.
   c. Aggregate hours worked in a week.

## Solutions to Additional Practice Problems 21.1

1a. Don is neither working nor looking for work, so he is not in the labor force.

1b. Shirley is working for pay for more than 1 hour a week, so she is employed and part of the labor force. She is working less than 35 hours a week, so she is a part-time worker. Because she is looking for a full-time job, Shirley is an involuntary part-time worker.

1c. Clarence is actively seeking a new job, so he is unemployed. Clarence is part of the labor force.

1d. Pat is neither working nor actively looking for work, so she is not in the labor force. Pat is a discouraged worker.

2a. The labor force equals the sum of the number of people employed and the number of people unemployed. Subtracting the number employed from the labor force gives the number of unemployed. The labor force is 149.1 million and the number of employed is 141.6 million, so the number unemployed is 149.1 million − 141.6 million, which is 7.5 million. To calculate the unemployment rate, divide the number of unemployed by the labor force and multiply by 100. The unemployment rate equals (7.5 million ÷ 149.1 million) × 100, which is 5.0 percent.

2b. The labor force participation rate is the percentage of the working-age population who are members of the labor force. The labor force participation rate equals the labor force divided by the working-age population all multiplied by 100, which is (149.1 million ÷ 225.9 million) × 100 = 66.0 percent.

2c. In June, 2005, 141.6 million people worked an average of 33.7 hours a week, so the aggregate hours worked in a week is 141.6 million × 33.7 hours, which is 4,771.9 million hours.

## ■ AP Self Test 21.1

### True or false

1. When contacted by the Bureau of Labor Statistics, Bob states that he has been laid off by Ford Motor Corporation, but expects to be recalled within the next three weeks. Bob is considered part of the labor force.

2. People are counted as unemployed as long as they are working less than 40 hours per week.

3. The unemployment rate decreases when unemployed workers find jobs.

4. The labor force participation rate measures the percentage of the labor force that is employed.

5. If the number of discouraged workers increases, the unemployment rate will increase.

**Multiple choice**

1. Assume the U.S. population is 300 million. If the working age population is 240 million, 150 million are employed, and 6 million are unemployed, what is the size of the labor force?
   a. 300 million
   b. 240 million
   c. 156 million
   d. 150 million
   e. 144 million

2. To be counted as employed by the BLS, you must have worked for pay _____ in the week before the survey.
   a. at least 1 hour
   b. at least 5 hours
   c. more than 20 hours
   d. 40 hours
   e. None of the above are right because the BLS counts anyone who works volunteer hours at a non-profit institution or school as employed.

3. Which of the following statements about the United States is (are) correct?
   i. The size of the labor force is greater than the number of employed people.
   ii. The size of the labor force is greater than the number of unemployed people.
   iii. The number of unemployed people is greater than the number of employed people.
   a. ii only.
   b. iii only.
   c. ii and iii.
   d. i and ii.
   e. i, ii, and iii.

4. If you are available and willing to work but have not actively looked for work in the past month then you are _____ of the labor force and are _____.
   a. part; counted as unemployed
   b. part; not counted as unemployed
   c. not part; not counted as unemployed
   d. not part; counted as unemployed only if you have had a job within the last 12 months
   e. not part; counted as unemployed regardless of whether or not you have held a job within the last 12 months

5. The unemployment rate equals
   a. (number of people without a job) ÷ (population) × 100.
   b. (number of people unemployed) ÷ (labor force) × 100.
   c. (number of people without a job) ÷ (working-age population) × 100.
   d. (number of people unemployed) ÷ (population) × 100.
   e. (working-age population − number of people employed) ÷ (labor force) × 100.

6. If the working age population is 200 million, 150 million are employed, and 6 million are unemployed, the unemployment rate is _____.
   a. 3.0 percent
   b. 25.0 percent
   c. 4.0 percent
   d. 12.0 percent
   e. 3.8 percent

7. A discouraged worker is
   a. counted as employed by the BLS but is not part of the labor force.
   b. counted as employed by the BLS and is part of the labor force.
   c. counted as unemployed by the BLS and is part of the labor force.
   d. not part of the labor force.
   e. counted as unemployed by the BLS but is not part of the labor force.

8. While in school, Kiki spends 20 hours a week as a computer programmer for Microsoft and studies 30 hours a week.
   a. Kiki is classified as a full-time worker, working 50 hours a week.
   b. Kiki is classified as a part-time worker, working 30 hours a week.
   c. Kiki is classified as a part-time worker, working 20 hours a week.
   d. Because Kiki is a student, she is not classified as working.
   e. Because Kiki is a student, she is classified as a full-time worker, working 20 hours a week at a paid job.

9. Part-time workers for noneconomic reasons are people who
   a. work less than 35 hours a week but would like to work more than 35 hours a week.
   b. work more than 35 hours a week but would like to work less than 35 hours a week.
   c. have lost their jobs within the last four weeks and are seeking another job.
   d. do not want to work full time.
   e. are discouraged workers.

## Short Response Questions

| Category | Number of people |
|---|---|
| Total population | 2,600 |
| Working-age population | 2,000 |
| Not in the labor force | 500 |
| Employed | 1,300 |

1. The table above gives the status of the population of a (small!) nation.
   a. What is the size of the labor force?
   b. What is the number of unemployed workers?
   c. What is the unemployment rate?
   d. What is the labor force participation rate?

| Category | Number of people |
|---|---|
| Working-age population | 3,000 |
| Unemployed | 100 |
| Employed | 1,900 |

2. The table above gives the status of the population of another (small!) nation.
   a. What is the size of the labor force?

b. What is the unemployment rate?
c. What is the labor force participation rate?

| Year | Working age population | Employed | Unemployed |
|---|---|---|---|
| 2002 | 175 | 150 | 25 |
| 2003 | 200 | 180 | 15 |
| 2004 | 250 | 230 | 10 |
| 2005 | 300 | 265 | 25 |

3. The table above gives the status of the population of yet another (small!) nation.
   a. What is the size of the labor force in each year?
   b. What is the unemployment rate for each year?
4. Are involuntarily part-time workers counted as employed or unemployed?

## Long Response Questions
1. What criteria must a person meet to be counted as unemployed?
2. What is a discouraged worker? Explain why a discouraged worker is not counted as part of the labor force.

## CHECKPOINT 21.2

■ **Describe the trends and fluctuations in the indicators of labor market performance in the United States.**

### Quick Review
- *Labor force participation rate* The percentage of the working-age population who are members of the labor force.
- *Aggregate hours* The total number of hours worked by all the people employed, both full time and part time, during a year.

### Additional Practice Problem 21.2
1. How does the unemployment rate change in a recession? Since 1965, when was the unemployment rate the highest and what did it equal?

2. How do aggregate hours change in a recession?

**Solutions to Additional Practice Problems 21.2**

1. The unemployment rate rises during recessions. Since 1965, the unemployment rate reached its peak of almost 10 percent during the 1982 recession.

2. Aggregate hours fall during a recession.

### ■ AP Self Test 21.2

**True or false**

1. The average unemployment rate in the United States during the 1970s and 1980s was above the average unemployment rate during the 1960s and 1990s.

2. Although the female labor force participation rate increased over the last 40 years, it is still less than the male labor force participation rate.

3. The percentage of involuntary part-time workers rises during a recession.

**Multiple choice**

1. From 1965 to 2005, the average unemployment rate in the United States was approximately
   a. 3 percent.
   b. 6 percent.
   c. 12 percent.
   d. 24 percent.
   d. 9 percent.

2. From 1990 to 2005, the unemployment rate in the United States
   a. was always lower than the unemployment rate in Japan.
   b. almost always equaled the unemployment rate in Canada.
   c. generally rose while the unemployment rate in France, Germany, and Italy fell.
   d. was lower than the unemployment rate in France, Germany, and Italy.
   e. was usually higher than the unemployment rate in Canada.

3. The total U.S. labor force participation rate increased since 1965 because
   a. the female labor force participation rate increased.
   b. more men are retiring early.
   c. fewer women are attending college.
   d. many blue-collar jobs with rigid work hours have been created in the last decade.
   e. the male labor force participation rate increased.

4. In the United States since 1965, aggregate hours have ____ and average weekly hours per worker have ____.
   a. risen; risen
   b. risen; fallen
   c. fallen; risen
   d. fallen; fallen
   e. risen; not changed

**Short Response Question**

1. During a recession, what happens to:
   a. the unemployment rate?
   b. aggregate hours?
   c. average weekly hours?

**Long Response Question**

1. How does the unemployment rate during the Great Depression compare with more recent unemployment rates?

### CHECKPOINT 21.3

### ■ Describe the sources and types of unemployment, define full employment, and explain the link between unemployment and real GDP.

*Quick Review*

- *Frictional unemployment* Unemployment that arises from normal labor market turnover.
- *Structural unemployment* Unemployment that arises when changes in technology or international competition change the

skills needed to perform jobs or change the location of jobs.

- *Seasonal unemployment* Unemployment that arises because of seasonal weather patterns.
- *Cyclical unemployment* Unemployment that fluctuates over the business cycle, rising during a recession and falling during an expansion.

### Additional Practice Problem 21.3

1. Each of the following people is actively seeking work. Classify each as either frictionally, structurally, seasonally, or cyclically unemployed:

   a. Perry lost his job because his company went bankrupt when faced with increased foreign competition.

   b. Sam did not like his boss and so he quit his job.

   c. Sherry just graduated from college.

   d. Hanna lost her job selling cotton candy on the boardwalk when winter arrived and the tourists left.

   e. Jose was fired when his company downsized in response to a recession.

   f. Pat was laid off from her job at the Gap because customers decided they liked the fashions at JCPenney better.

### Solution to Additional Practice Problem 21.3

1a. Perry is structurally unemployed.
1b. Sam is frictionally unemployed.
1c. Sherry is frictionally unemployed.
1d. Hanna is seasonally unemployed.
1e. Jose is cyclically unemployed.
1f. Pat is frictionally unemployed.

### ■ AP Self Test 21.3

**True or false**

1. If Amazon.Com Inc. must lay off 20 percent of its workers, the laid-off workers would be considered job leavers.

2. The only way to end a spell of unemployment is by finding a job.

3. The unemployment that arises when technology changes is termed technological unemployment.

4. When the U.S. economy is at full employment, the unemployment rate is zero.

5. Potential GDP is the level of real GDP produced when the economy is at full employment.

**Multiple choice**

1. Generally, most unemployed workers are ____; the fewest number of unemployed workers are ____.
   a. job losers; job leavers
   b. job leavers; reentrants and entrants
   c. job losers; reentrants and entrants
   d. reentrants and entrants; job leavers
   e. job leavers; job losers

2. Reentrants are people who
   a. are laid off.
   b. leave the labor force voluntarily.
   c. recently left school.
   d. have returned to the labor force.
   e. voluntarily leave their job.

3. Tommy graduates from college and starts to look for a job. Tommy is
   a. frictionally unemployed.
   b. structurally unemployed.
   c. cyclically unemployed.
   d. seasonally unemployed.
   e. not unemployed because he is looking for work.

4. If an entire industry relocates to a foreign country, the relocation leads to a higher rate of ____ unemployment.
   a. frictional
   b. structural
   c. seasonal
   d. cyclical
   e. structural and cyclical

5. Of the following, who is cyclically unemployed?
   a. Casey, who lost his job because the technology changed so that he was no longer needed.
   b. Katrina, an assistant manager who quit her job to search for a better job closer to home.
   c. Kathy, a steelworker who was laid off but has stopped looking for a new job because she can't find a new job.
   d. David, a new car salesman who lost his job because the economy went into a recession.
   e. Samantha, who worked part-time in JCPenney to help with the Christmas rush but was laid off in January.

6. In the United States, the highest unemployment rates occur among
   a. white female teenagers.
   b. black male teenagers.
   c. white females aged 20 and over.
   d. black males aged 20 and over.
   e. white males aged 20 and over.

7. When the economy is at full employment,
   a. the natural unemployment rate equals zero.
   b. the amount of cyclical unemployment equals zero.
   c. the amount of structural unemployment equals zero.
   d. there is no unemployment.
   e. the amount of frictional unemployment equals zero.

8. When the unemployment rate is less than the natural unemployment rate, real GDP is ____ potential GDP.
   a. greater than
   b. less than
   c. unrelated to
   d. equal to
   e. not comparable to

**Short Response Questions**
1. What are sources of unemployment? How does unemployment end?
2. What are the four types of unemployment?
3. How does the average duration of unemployment change during a recession?

**Long Response Questions**
1. What is the relationship between full employment, the natural unemployment rate, and potential GDP?
2. If the unemployment rate exceeds the natural unemployment rate, what is the relationship between real GDP and potential GDP? If the unemployment rate is less than the natural unemployment rate, what is the relationship between real GDP and potential GDP?

## YOUR AP SELF TEST ANSWERS

### ■ CHECKPOINT 21.1

**True or false**
1. True; page 524
2. False; page 524
3. True; page 525
4. False; page 526
5. False; page 526

**Multiple choice**
1. c; page 524
2. a; page 524
3. d; page 524
4. c; page 524
5. b; page 525
6. e; page 525
7. d; page 526
8. c; page 526
9. d; page 526

**Short Response Questions**
1. a. 1,500; page 524.
   b. 200; page 524.
   c. 13.3 percent; page 525.
   d. 75.0 percent; page 526.
2. a. 2,000; page 524.
   b. 5.0 percent; page 525.
   c. 66.7 percent; page 526.
3. a. The labor force is the sum of employed plus unemployed people. In 2002 the labor force is 175; in 2003 the labor force is 195; in 2004 the labor force is 240; and in 2005 the labor force is 290; page 524.
   b. The unemployment rate is the number of unemployed workers divided by the labor force and then multiplied by 100. In 2002 the unemployment rate is 14.3 percent; in 2003 the unemployment rate is 7.7 percent; for 2004 the unemployment rate is 4.2 percent; and in 2005 the unemployment rate is 8.6 percent; page 525.
4. Involuntary part-time workers are counted as employed; page 526.

**Long Response Questions**
1. People of working age can be either employed, unemployed, or not in the labor force. To be counted as unemployed, the person must be without employment, available for work, and actively searching or waiting to be recalled to a job from which he or she was laid off; page 524.
2. A discouraged worker is an unemployed worker who is not actively looking for a job. To be counted as part of the labor force, a person must be either employed or unemployed. A discouraged worker is not employed. And a discouraged worker is not unemployed because the worker is not actively seeking a job. So a discourage worker is not in the labor force; page 526.

### ■ CHECKPOINT 21.2

**True or false**
1. True; page 529
2. True; pages 530-531
3. True; page 532

**Multiple choice**
1. b; page 529
2. d; page 531
3. a; pages 530-531
4. b; pages 532-533

**Short Response Question**
1. a. The unemployment rate rises; page 529.
   b. Aggregate hours fall; page 533.
   c. Average weekly hours falls; page 533.

**Long Response Question**
1. The unemployment rate during the Great Depression was *much* higher, reaching near 25 percent, than the recent unemployment rate, which reached its peak of approximately 10 percent in 1982; pages 523-530.

## ■ CHECKPOINT 21.3

### True or false

1. False; page 535
2. False; page 536
3. False; page 537
4. False; page 539
5. True; pages 540-541

### Multiple choice

1. a; pages 535-536
2. d; page 535
3. a; page 537
4. b; page 537
5. d; page 538
6. b; page 539
7. b; page 539
8. a; page 541

### Short Response Questions

1. Sources of unemployment are job losers, job leavers, entrants, and reentrants. People who end a period of unemployment rate are hires, recalls, or withdrawals; pages 535-536.

2. Unemployment is either frictional, structural, seasonal, or cyclical; pages 537-538.

3. The average duration of unemployment (the length of time a person is unemployed) rises in a recession; page 538.

### Long Response Questions

1. When the economy is at full employment, the unemployment rate is the natural unemployment rate. When the economy is at full employment, the amount of GDP produced is potential GDP; pages 539-541.

2. If the unemployment rate exceeds the natural unemployment rate, real GDP is less than potential GDP. The relationship between the unemployment rate and potential GDP is symmetric because if the unemployment rate is less than the natural unemployment rate, real GDP is less than potential GDP; page 541.

# The CPI and the Cost of Living

# Chapter 22

Chapter 22 explores how the cost of living is measured. It discusses the Consumer Price Index, CPI, explains how it is constructed, and examines its biases. Chapter 22 demonstrates how to adjust money values for changes in the price level. In addition, Chapter 22 discusses the real wage rate and the real interest rate, and also shows how both are calculated.

■ **Explain what the Consumer Price Index (CPI) is and how it is calculated.**

The Consumer Price Index (CPI) measures the average of the prices paid by urban consumers for a fixed market basket of consumer goods and services. The CPI compares the cost of the fixed market basket of goods and services at one time with the cost of the fixed market basket in the reference base period, currently 1982–1984. The CPI in the base period is 100. If the CPI is now 150, it costs 50 percent more to buy the same goods and services than it cost in the base period. To construct the CPI market basket, households are surveyed on what they buy. Then, each month the Bureau of Labor Statistics checks the prices of the 80,000 goods and services in the basket. To calculate the CPI, the cost of the market basket using current prices is divided by the cost of the basket using base period prices and the result is multiplied by 100. The inflation rate is the percentage change in the price level from one year to the next and is equal to [(CPI in current year − CPI in previous year) ÷ (CPI in previous year)] × 100.

■ **Explain the limitations of the CPI as a measure of the cost of living.**

The CPI has four sources of bias that lead to an inaccurate measure of the cost of living. These biases are the new goods bias (new goods replace old goods), the quality change bias (goods and services increase in quality), the commodity substitution bias (changes in relative prices lead consumers to change the items they buy), and the outlet substitution bias (consumers switch to shopping more often in discount stores). The overall CPI bias has been estimated to overstate inflation by 1.1 percentage points per year. The CPI bias distorts private contracts and increases government outlays. The GDP deflator is constructed using, in part, the CPI, and so the GDP deflator inherits the same biases as the CPI. The GDP deflator is not a good measure of the cost of living because it includes prices of goods and services households never buy.

■ **Adjust money values for inflation and calculate real wage rates and real interest rates.**

Comparing values measured in dollars in different years is misleading if the value of money changes. To make the comparison, the nominal values must be converted to real values. The real wage rate measures the quantity of goods and services that an hour's work can buy and equals the nominal wage rate divided by the CPI and multiplied by 100. The real interest rate equals the nominal interest rate minus the inflation rate.

## EXPANDED CHAPTER CHECKLIST

**When you have completed this chapter, you will be able to:**

### 1 Explain what the Consumer Price Index (CPI) is and how it is calculated.

- Define the CPI and discuss the meaning of the CPI numbers.
- Explain the construction of the CPI, including the role played by the fixed CPI basket and the reference base period.
- Discuss how the cost of the CPI basket is calculated and show how the CPI is calculated.
- Define and calculate the inflation rate.

### 2 Explain the limitations of the CPI as a measure of the cost of living.

- Explain the new goods bias.
- Explain the quality change bias.
- Explain the commodity substitution bias.
- Explain the outlet substitution bias.
- State the estimated size of the CPI bias.
- Explain the consequences of the CPI bias for private contracts and government outlays.
- Compare the GDP deflator and the CPI as measures of the cost of living.

### 3 Adjust money values for inflation and calculate real wage rates and real interest rates.

- Explain how changes in the price level can be used when comparing the price of a good at different dates.
- Discuss the difference between the nominal wage rate and the real wage rate.
- Explain how the real wage rate is calculated.
- Define nominal interest rate and real interest rate.
- Explain the relationship between the nominal interest rate, the real interest rate, and the inflation rate.

- Explain how the real interest rate is calculated.

## YOUR AP TEST HINTS

*AP Topics*

| Topic on your AP test | Corresponding textbook section |
|---|---|
| **Measurement of economic performance** | |
| Inflation Measurement and Adjustment | Chapter 22 |
| • Price indexes | Checkpoint 22.1, 22.2, 22.3 |
| • Nominal versus real values | Checkpoint 22.3 |

*Extra AP material*

- The CPI and the GDP deflator are the two most common price indices. On the AP test, you might see reference to another price index: The PPI or Producer Price Index. This price index measures the average prices paid by producers (firms) for the raw material or semi-finished goods and services they buy to produce their output.

## CHECKPOINT 22.1

### ■ Explain what the Consumer Price Index (CPI) is and how it is calculated.

*Quick Review*

- *CPI market basket* The goods and services in the CPI and the relative importance attached to each of them.
- *CPI formula* The CPI equals:

$$\frac{\text{Cost of CPI basket at current period prices}}{\text{Cost of CPI basket at base period prices}} \times 100.$$

- *Inflation rate* The inflation rate equals:

$$\frac{(\text{CPI in current year} - \text{CPI in previous year})}{\text{CPI in previous year}} \times 100.$$

### Additional Practice Problem 22.1

| Item | Quantity (2005) | Price (2005) | Quantity (2006) | Price (2006) |
|---|---|---|---|---|
| Limes | 20 | $1.00 | 15 | $1.00 |
| Biscuits | 30 | $1.00 | 45 | $0.75 |
| Rum | 10 | $10.00 | 8 | $11.00 |

1. A Consumer Expenditure Survey in Scurvy shows that people consume only limes, biscuits, and rum. The Consumer Expenditure Survey for both 2005 and 2006 are in the table above. The reference base year is 2005.
   a. What and how much is in the CPI market basket?
   b. What did the CPI market basket cost in 2005? What was the CPI in 2005?
   c. What did the CPI market basket cost in 2006? What was the CPI in 2006?
   d. What was the inflation rate between 2005 and 2006?

### Solution to Additional Practice Problem 22.1

1a. The market basket is 20 limes, 30 biscuits, and 10 rums, the quantities consumed in the base year of 2005.

1b. In 2005 the market basket cost 20 × $1.00 + 30 × $1.00 + 10 × $10.00 = $150. Because this is the reference base year, the CPI = 100.0.

1c. In 2006 the market basket cost 20 × $1.00 + 30 × $0.75 + 10 × $11.00 = $152.50. The CPI in 2006 is equal to ($152.50) ÷ ($150.00) × 100, which is 101.7.

1d. The inflation rate equals [(101.7 − 100.0) ÷ 100] × 100 = 1.7 percent.

### ■ AP Self Test 22.1

**True or false**

1. In the reference base period, the CPI equals 1.0.

2. The CPI market basket is changed from one month to the next.

3. If the cost of the CPI basket at current period prices equals $320, then the CPI equals 320.

4. If the cost of the CPI basket at current period prices exceeds the cost of the CPI basket at base period prices, the inflation rate between these two periods is positive.

5. If the CPI increases from 110 to 121, the inflation rate is 11 percent.

**Multiple choice**

1. The CPI is reported once every
   a. year.
   b. quarter.
   c. month.
   d. week.
   e. other year.

2. The Consumer Price Index (CPI) measures
   a. the prices of a few consumer goods and services.
   b. the prices of those consumer goods and services that increased in price.
   c. the average of the prices paid by urban consumers for a fixed market basket of goods and services.
   d. consumer confidence in the economy.
   e. the average of the costs paid by businesses to produce a fixed market basket of consumer goods and services.

3. If a country has a CPI of 105.0 last year and a CPI of 102.0 this year, then
   a. the average prices of goods and services increased between last year and this year.
   b. the average prices of goods and services decreased between last year and this year.
   c. the average quality of goods and services decreased between last year and this year.
   d. there was an error when calculating the CPI this year.
   e. the quantity of consumer goods and services produced decreased between last year and this year.

4. The good or service given the most weight in the CPI basket when calculating the CPI is
   a. food and beverages.
   b. taxes.
   c. housing.
   d. medical care.
   e. recreation.

5. Suppose a basket of consumer goods and services costs $180 using the base period prices, and the same basket of goods and services costs $300 using the current period prices. The CPI for the current year period equals
   a. 166.7.
   b. 66.7.
   c. 160.0.
   d. 60.0.
   e. 300.0.

6. Suppose the CPI for 1980 was 82.3 and for 1981 was 90.9. Based on this information, we can calculate that the inflation rate in 1981 was
   a. 10.4 percent.
   b. 8.6 percent.
   c. 90.9 percent.
   d. 82.3 percent.
   e. 9.09 percent.

7. In the United States since 1975, on average the inflation rate in the last ten years was
   a. higher than between 1975 to 1980.
   b. higher than in the 1980s.
   c. lower than between 1975 to 1980.
   d. much higher than between 1985 to 1995.
   e. negative.

### Short Response Questions

| Item | Quantity (2005) | Price (2005) | Quantity (2006) | Price (2006) |
|------|------|------|------|------|
| Pizza | 10 | $10.00 | 15 | $10.00 |
| Burritos | 20 | $1.00 | 25 | $0.75 |
| Rice | 30 | $0.50 | 20 | $1.00 |

1. The table above gives the expenditures of households in the small nation of Studenvia. In Studenvia, 2005 is the reference base period.
   a. What is the cost of the CPI basket in 2005?
   b. What is the cost of the CPI basket in 2006?
   c. What is the CPI in 2005?
   d. What is the CPI in 2006?
   e. What is the inflation rate in 2006?

2. Suppose the CPI was 100.0 in 2002, 110.0 in 2003, 121.0 in 2004, and 133.1 in 2005. What is the inflation rate in 2003, 2004, and 2005?

3. When is the inflation rate larger: when the price level rises from 105 to 115 or when the price rises from 180 to 195?

### Long Response Questions

1. If the price level rises slowly, is the inflation rate positive or negative? Why?

## CHECKPOINT 22.2

■ **Explain the limitations of the CPI as a measure of the cost of living.**

### Quick Review

- *Commodity substitution bias* People cut back on their purchases of items that become relatively more costly and increase their consumption of items that become relatively less costly.

### Additional Practice Problem 22.2

1. Nowadays when households buy broccoli, they discard some of it because it is bruised. Suppose 20 percent is discarded. Now new, genetically engineered broccoli is developed that does not bruise so that all the broccoli that is purchased can be used. People prefer the new broccoli, so they switch to buying the new broccoli. If the price of the new broccoli is 10 percent higher than the old, what actually happens to the CPI and what should happen to the CPI?

2. When the price of textbook is $95 a book, Anthony buys his books at the bookstore closest to him. When textbooks rise in price to $125 a book at that store, Anthony drives several miles away to a store where the books are sold for only $110. How does Anthony's decision affect the CPI?

### Solution to Additional Practice Problem 22.2

1. With the introduction of the new broccoli, the CPI will rise because the new broccoli's price is higher (10 percent) than the old broccoli. But, the CPI should actually decrease because people pay only 10 percent more for 20 percent more (useable) broccoli. This problem illus-

trates how the quality change bias can bias the CPI upwards.

2. Anthony's decision reflects outlet substitution. When the price of a good rises, consumers, such as Anthony, switch the stores from which they buy goods and services to less expensive outlets. But the CPI, as constructed, does not take into account this point. The CPI will record that the price of textbooks rose by $30, from $95 to $125. For Anthony, however, the true increase in the cost was only $15, from $95 to $110 a book, plus the cost of his time and gasoline to get to the new store. The outlet substitution bias means that the CPI overstates the true rise in the cost of living.

## ■ AP Self Test 22.2

**True or false**

1. The CPI is a biased measure of the cost of living.

2. Commodity substitution bias refers to the ongoing replacement of old goods by new goods.

3. The bias in the CPI is estimated to overstate inflation by approximately 1.1 percentage points a year.

4. Inflation measured using the GDP deflator is generally lower than inflation measured using the CPI.

**Multiple choice**

1. All of the following create bias in the CPI EXCEPT the
   a. new goods bias.
   b. outlet substitution bias.
   c. commodity substitution bias.
   d. GDP deflator bias.
   e. quality change bias.

2. An example of the new goods bias in the calculation of the CPI is a price increase in
   a. butter relative to margarine.
   b. an MP3 player relative to a Walkman.
   c. a 2006 Honda Civic LX relative to a 2001 Honda Civic LX.
   d. textbooks bought through the campus bookstore relative to textbooks bought through Amazon.com.
   e. a Caribbean cruise for a couple who has never been on a cruise before.

3. Over the last decade, the price of a dishwasher has remained relatively constant while the quality of dishwashers has improved. The CPI
   a. is adjusted monthly to reflect the improvement in quality.
   b. is increased monthly to reflect the increased quality of dishwashers.
   c. has an upward bias if it is not adjusted to take account of the higher quality.
   d. has an upward bias because it does not reflect the increased production of dishwashers.
   e. should not take account of any quality changes because it is a price index not a quality index.

4. Joe buys chicken and beef. If the price of beef rises and the price of chicken does not change, Joe will
   a. buy more beef and help create a new goods bias for the CPI.
   b. buy more chicken and help create a commodity substitution bias for the CPI.
   c. buy the same quantity of beef and chicken and help create a commodity substitution bias for the CPI.
   d. buy less chicken and beef and thus help create a quality change bias for the CPI.
   e. buy more chicken and help eliminate the commodity substitution bias for the CPI.

5. The CPI bias was estimated by the Congressional Advisory Commission on the Consumer Price Index as
   a. understating the actual inflation rate by about 5 percentage points a year.
   b. understating the actual inflation rate by more than 5 percentage points a year.
   c. overstating the actual inflation rate by about 1 percentage point a year.
   d. overstating the actual inflation rate by more than 5 percentage points a year.
   e. understating the actual inflation rate by about 1 percentage point a year.

6. A consequence of the CPI bias is that it
   a. decreases government outlays.
   b. increases international trade.
   c. reduces outlet substitution bias.
   d. distorts private contracts.
   e. means that it is impossible to measure the inflation rate.

### Long Response Questions

1. What are the sources of bias in the CPI? Briefly explain each.

2. Once you graduate, you move to a new town and sign a long-term lease on a townhouse. You agree to pay $1,000 a month rent and to change the monthly rent annually by the percentage change in the CPI. For the next 4 years, the CPI increases 5 percent each year. What will you pay in monthly rent for the second, third, and fourth years of your lease? Suppose the CPI overstates the inflation rate by 1 percentage point a year. If the CPI bias was eliminated, what would you pay in rent for the second, third, and fourth years?

## CHECKPOINT 22.3

■ **Adjust money values for inflation and calculate real wage rates and real interest rates.**

### Quick Review

- *Real wage rate* The real wage rate equals the nominal wage rate divided by the CPI and multiplied by 100.

- *Real interest rate* The real interest rate equals the nominal interest rate minus the inflation rate.

### Additional Practice Problems 22.3

| Year | Minimum wage (dollars per hour) | CPI |
|------|--------------------------------|-----|
| 1955 | 0.75 | 26.7 |
| 1965 | 1.25 | 31.6 |
| 1975 | 2.10 | 56.7 |
| 1985 | 3.35 | 107.5 |
| 1995 | 4.25 | 152.4 |
| 2005 | 5.15 | 194.1 |

1. The table above shows the minimum wage and the CPI for six different years. The reference base period is 1982–1984.
   a. Calculate the real minimum wage in each year in 1982–1984 dollars.
   b. In which year was the minimum wage the highest in real terms?
   c. In which year was the minimum wage the lowest in real terms?

2. Suppose Sally has saved $1,000 dollars. Sally wants a 3 percent real interest rate on her savings. What nominal interest rate would she need to receive if the inflation rate is 7 percent?

## Solutions to Additional Practice Problems 22.3

| Year | Real minimum wage (1982-1984 dollars per hour) |
|------|------------------------------------------------|
| 1955 | 2.81 |
| 1965 | 3.96 |
| 1975 | 3.70 |
| 1985 | 3.12 |
| 1995 | 2.79 |
| 2005 | 2.65 |

1a. Using the CPI to adjust nominal values to real values is a key use of the CPI. Keep in mind that to convert a nominal price (such as the nominal wage rate) into a real price (such as the real wage rate), you divide by the CPI and multiply by 100, but to convert the nominal interest rate into the real interest rate, you subtract the inflation rate.

To convert the nominal minimum wages in the table to real prices, divide the price by the CPI in that year and then multiply by 100. In 1955, the nominal minimum wage gas was $0.75 an hour and the CPI was 26.7, so the real minimum wage is ($0.75 ÷ 26.7) × 100 = $2.81. The rest of the real minimum wages in the table above are calculated similarly.

1b. In real terms, the minimum wage was highest in 1965 when it equaled $3.96.

1c. In real terms, the minimum wage was the lowest in 2005 when it equaled $2.65.

2. The real interest rate equals the nominal interest rate minus the inflation rate. Rearranging this formula shows that the nominal interest rate equals the real interest rate plus the inflation rate. To get a 3 percent real interest rate with a 7 percent inflation rate, Sally needs the nominal interest rate to be equal to 3 percent plus 7 percent, or 10 percent.

## ■ AP Self Test 22.3

### True or false

1. The CPI was 171 in 2000 and 24.4 in 1950, so the price level in 2000 was 7 times higher than what it was in 1950.

2. A change in the real wage rate measures the change in the goods and services that an hour's work can buy.

3. The nominal interest rate is the percentage return on a loan expressed in dollars; the real interest rate is the percentage return on a loan expressed in purchasing power.

4. If the nominal interest rate is 8 percent a year and the inflation rate is 4 percent a year, then the real interest rate is 4 percent a year.

### Multiple choice

1. In 2005, in New York, apples cost $1.49 a pound. Suppose the CPI was 120 in 2005 and 140 in 2006. If there is no change in the real value of an apple in the year 2006, how much would a pound of apples sell for in 2006?
   a. $2.74
   b. $1.69
   c. $1.66
   d. $1.74
   e. $1.28

2. In 1970, the CPI was 39 and in 2000 it was 172. A local phone call cost $0.10 in 1970. What is the price of this phone call in 2000 dollars?
   a. $1.42
   b. $0.39
   c. $1.72
   d. $0.44
   e. $0.23

3. The nominal wage rate is the
   a. minimum hourly wage that a company can legally pay a worker.
   b. average hourly wage rate measured in the dollars of a given reference base year.
   c. minimum hourly wage rate measured in the dollars of a given reference base year.
   d. average hourly wage rate measured in current dollars.
   e. wage rate after inflation has been adjusted out of it.

4. In 2001, the average starting salary for an economics major was $29,500. If the CPI was 147.5, the real salary was
   a. $200.00 an hour.
   b. $20,000.
   c. $35,000.
   d. $43,513.
   e. $14,750.

5. If we compare the nominal wage versus the real wage in the United States since 1975, we see that the
   a. real wage rate increased steadily.
   b. nominal wage rate increased and the real wage rate did not change by very much.
   c. real wage rate increased more than the nominal wage rate.
   d. nominal wage rate increased at an uneven pace whereas the increase in the real wage rate was steady and constant.
   e. nominal wage rate and real wage rate both decreased.

6. The real interest rate is equal to the
   a. nominal interest rate plus the inflation rate.
   b. nominal interest rate minus the inflation rate.
   c. nominal interest rate times the inflation rate.
   d. nominal interest rate divided by the inflation rate.
   e. inflation rate minus the nominal interest rate.

7. You borrow at a nominal interest rate of 10 percent. If the inflation rate is 4 percent, then the real interest rate is
   a. the $10 in interest you have to pay.
   b. 16 percent.
   c. 2.5 percent.
   d. 6 percent.
   e. 14 percent.

8. In the United States between 1965 and 2005, the
   a. nominal and real interest rates both decreased in almost every year.
   b. nominal and real interest rates were both constant in almost every year.
   c. real interest rate was constant in most years and the nominal interest rate fluctuated.
   d. nominal interest rate was greater than the real interest rate in all years.
   e. nominal interest rate was greater than the real interest rate in about one half of the years and the real interest rate was greater than the nominal interest rate in the other half of the years.

**Short Response Questions**

| Job | Salary (dollars per year) | CPI |
|-----|-----|-----|
| Job A | 20,000 | 105 |
| Job B | 25,000 | 120 |
| Job C | 34,000 | 170 |

1. Often the cost of living varies from state to state or from large city to small city. After you graduate, suppose you have job offers in 3 locales. The nominal salary and the CPI for each job is given in the table above.
   a. Which job offers the highest real salary?
   b. Which job offers the lowest real salary?
   c. In determining which job to accept, what is more important: the real salary or the nominal salary? Why?

| Year | Real interest rate (percent per year) | Nominal interest rate (percent per year) | Inflation rate (percent per year) |
|------|------|------|------|
| 1999 | ____ | 10 | 5 |
| 2000 | ____ | 6 | 1 |
| 2001 | 4 | 6 | ____ |
| 2002 | 5 | ____ | 3 |

2. The table above gives the real interest rate, nominal interest rate, and inflation rate for various years in a foreign country. Complete the table.

**Long Response Question**

1. In 1980, the nominal interest rate was 12 percent. In 2005, the nominal interest rate was 7 percent. From this information, can you determine if you would rather have saved $1,000 in 1980 or 2005? Explain your answer.

## YOUR AP SELF TEST ANSWERS

### ■ CHECKPOINT 22.1

**True or false**

1. False; page 548
2. False; page 548
3. False; page 551
4. True; page 551
5. False; page 551

**Multiple choice**

1. c; page 548
2. c; page 548
3. b; page 548
4. c; page 549
5. a; page 551
6. a; page 551
7. c; pages 552

**Short Response Questions**

1. a. The cost is $135; page 550.
   b. The cost is $145. The quantities used to calculate this cost are the base period, 2005, quantities; page 550.
   c. The CPI is 100; page 551.
   d. The CPI is 107.4; page 551.
   e. The inflation rate is 7.4 percent; page 551.

2. The inflation rate for each year is 10 percent; page 551.

3. The inflation rate is larger when the price level rises from 105 to 115 because the inflation rate equals $\dfrac{(115-105)}{105} \times 100$ which is 9.5 percent. When the price level rises from 180 to 195, the inflation rate is equal to $\dfrac{(195-180)}{180} \times 100$ which is 8.3 percent; page 551.

**Long Response Question**

1. *Whenever* the price level rises, the inflation rate is positive. The inflation rate is the growth rate of the price level. So if the price level rises slowly, the inflation rate is small; if the price level rises rapidly, the inflation rate is large; page 551.

### ■ CHECKPOINT 22.2

**True or false**

1. True; page 554
2. False; page 555
3. True; page 555
4. True; pages 557

**Multiple choice**

1. d; page 554
2. b; page 554
3. c; pages 554-555
4. b; page 555
5. c; page 555
6. d; pages 555-556

**Long Response Questions**

1. There are four sources of bias in the CPI: the new goods bias, the quality change bias, the commodity substitution bias, and the outlet substitution bias. The new goods bias refers to the fact that new goods replace old goods. The quality change bias occurs because at times price increases in existing goods are the result of increased quality. The commodity substitution bias occurs because consumers buy fewer goods and services when their prices rise compared to other, comparable products. The fixed market basket approach taken in the CPI's calculation cannot take account of this method by which households offset higher prices. Finally, the outlet substitution bias refers to the fact that when prices rise, people shop more frequently at discount stores to take advantage of the lower prices in these stores; pages 554-555.

2. The monthly rent increases by 5 percent each year. For the second year the monthly rent equals $1,000 × 1.05, which is $1,050. For the third year the monthly

rent equals $1,050 × 1.05, which is $1,102.50. And for the fourth year the monthly rent equals $1,102.50 × 1.05, which is $1,157.63. If the CPI bias was eliminated, the monthly rent would increase by 4 percent each year. The monthly rent would be $1,040 for the second year, $1,081.60 for the third year, and $1,124.86 for the third year; page 556.

# ■ CHECKPOINT 22.3

**True or false**
1. True;  page 559
2. True;  page 561
3. True;  page 562
4. True;  page 562

**Multiple choice**
1. d; page 559
2. d; page 559
3. d; page 560
4. b; page 560
5. b; page 561
6. b; page 562
7. d; page 562
8. d; page 563

**Short Response Questions**
1. a. The real salary equals (nominal salary ÷ CPI) times 100. The real salary is $19,048 for Job A, $20,833 for Job B, and $20,000

for Job C. The real salary is highest for Job B; page 560.
   b. The real salary is lowest for Job A;  page 560.
   c. The real salary is more important than the nominal salary because the real salary measures the quantity of goods and services you will be able to buy;  pages 560-561.

| Year | Real interest rate (percent per year) | Nominal interest rate (percent per year) | Inflation rate (percent per year) |
| --- | --- | --- | --- |
| 1999 | 5 | 10 | 5 |
| 2000 | 5 | 6 | 1 |
| 2001 | 4 | 6 | 2 |
| 2002 | 5 | 8 | 3 |

2. The completed table is above;  page 562.

**Long Response Question**
1. You cannot determine when you would rather have been a saver. Savers are interested in the real interest rate because the real interest rate is the percentage return expressed in purchasing power. Thus the real interest rate gives the increase in the goods and services that a saver can purchase. Without knowing the inflation rate, there is not enough data given to compute the real interest rate and so not enough data to know when it was a better time to be a saver; page 562.

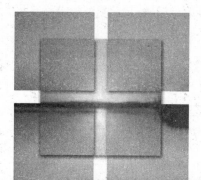

# Potential GDP and the Natural Unemployment Rate

# Chapter 23

## CHAPTER IN PERSPECTIVE

Chapter 23 studies the forces that determine potential GDP and the influences on the natural unemployment rate. It begins by introducing different macroeconomic schools of thought. The two main schools of thought are classical macroeconomics and Keynesian macroeconomics. Classical macroeconomics asserts that markets work well and, while the economy will fluctuate, no government intervention is needed. But classical macroeconomics couldn't explain why the Great Depression lasted so long. Keynesian economics was borne during the Great Depression and asserted that depressions were the result of too little spending. Keynesian economics called for government intervention to assist the economy. But it focused exclusively on the short run. The new macroeconomics developed in the 1970s. This theory focuses on how macroeconomic outcomes are the result of microeconomic choices. Most economists now believe that maintaining economic growth is more important than eliminating business cycle fluctuations because the Lucas wedge (the cost of slower economic growth) is much larger than Okun gaps (the cost of business cycle recessions).

■ **Explain the forces that determine potential GDP and the real wage rate and employment at full employment.**

Potential GDP is the amount of GDP that would be produced if the economy were at full employment. The production function shows the maximum quantity of real GDP that can be produced as the quantity of labor employed changes and all other influences on production remain the same. Its shape reflects diminishing returns, so that each additional hour of labor employed produces a successively smaller addition of real GDP. The quantity of labor employed is determined in the labor market. The quantity of labor demanded increases (decreases) as the real wage rate falls (rises). The quantity of labor supplied increases (decreases) as the real wage rate rises (falls). Labor market equilibrium occurs at the intersection of the labor supply curve and the labor demand curve. When the labor market is in equilibrium, the economy is at full employment and real GDP, determined using the production function, equals potential GDP.

■ **Explain the forces that determine the natural unemployment rate.**

The natural unemployment rate is the unemployment rate at full employment and consists of frictional and structural unemployment. Two fundamental causes of unemployment are job search, which is the activity of looking for a job, and job rationing, which occurs when the real wage rate exceeds the equilibrium wage rate creating a surplus of labor. The amount of job search depends on demographic change, unemployment benefits, and structural change. Job rationing occurs when there is an efficiency wage, a minimum wage, or a union wage because all of these factors force the real wage above the equilibrium real wage.

## EXPANDED CHAPTER CHECKLIST

**When you have completed this chapter, you will be able to:**

**1** **Explain the forces that determine potential GDP and the real wage rate and employment at full employment.**

- Distinguish between classical macroeconomics and Keynesian macroeconomics, and explain the views of each.
- Discuss how the new macroeconomics differs from classical macroeconomics and Keynesian macroeconomics.
- Discuss the Okun gap and Lucas Wedge.
- Define potential GDP.
- Describe the production function and explain how it displays diminishing returns.
- Discuss the relationship between the real wage rate and the quantity of labor demanded.
- Discuss the relationship between the real wage rate and the quantity of labor supplied.
- Discuss how equilibrium in the labor market is achieved and the relationship between the labor market equilibrium and potential GDP.

**2** **Explain the forces that determine the natural unemployment rate.**

- Define the natural unemployment rate.
- Define job search and describe the factors that influence it.
- Define job rationing and explain why it occurs.
- Explain how job rationing affects the natural unemployment rate.

## YOUR AP TEST HINTS

### AP Topics

| Topic on your AP test | Corresponding textbook section |
|---|---|
| **National Income and Price Determination** | |
| Unemployment | Chapter 23 |
| • Full employment output | Checkpoint 23.1 |
| • Natural unemployment rate | Checkpoint 23.2 |

### AP Vocabulary

- On the AP test, the "GDP gap" equals the difference between potential GDP (full employment GDP) and the GDP that is actually produced. In a recession, the GDP gap is positive.
- On the AP test, the natural unemployment rate is the same as the natural rate of unemployment.

## CHECKPOINT 23.1

- **Explain the forces that determine potential GDP and the real wage rate and employment at full employment.**

### Quick Review

- *Production function* The production function shows the relationship between the maximum quantity of real GDP that can be produced as the quantity of labor employed changes when all other influences on production remain constant.
- *Equilibrium in a market* The equilibrium in a market occurs at the intersection of the demand and supply curves.

## Additional Practice Problem 23.1

| Quantity of labor demanded (billions of hours per year) | Real GDP (hundreds of billions of 2001 dollars) | Real wage rate (2001 dollars per hour) |
|---|---|---|
| 0 | 0 | 50 |
| 10 | 5 | 40 |
| 20 | 9 | 30 |
| 30 | 12 | 20 |
| 40 | 14 | 10 |

1. The table above describes an economy's production function and its demand for labor. The table below describes the supply of labor in this economy.

| Quantity of labor supplied (billions of hours per year) | Real wage rate (2001 dollars per hour) |
|---|---|
| 0 | 10 |
| 10 | 20 |
| 20 | 30 |
| 30 | 40 |
| 40 | 50 |

   a. Make graphs of the production function and the labor market.

   b. Does the production function show diminishing returns?

   c. What is the equilibrium employment, real wage rate, and potential GDP?

   d. Suppose that the population grows so that the quantity of labor supplied increases by 20 billion hours at every real wage rate. What is the effect on the real wage rate and on potential GDP?

## Solution to Additional Practice Problem 23.2

1a. The production function is a graph of the first two columns of the first table. The figure to the right shows the relationship between labor and real GDP.

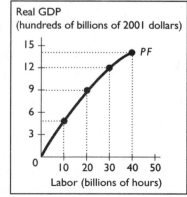

The next figure to the right shows the labor market. The labor demand curve is the first and third columns in the first table. It shows the relationship between the real wage rate and the quantity of labor demanded. The labor supply curve is from the second table and shows the relationship between the real wage rate and the quantity of labor supplied.

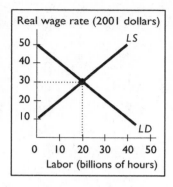

1b. The production function shows diminishing returns because every additional 10 billion hours of labor employed increases real GDP by less.

1c. Find the equilibrium in the labor market. Then use the production function to determine how much GDP this full-employment quantity of labor produces, which is the potential GDP. Equilibrium employment is where the labor demand curve and the labor supply curve intersect. The second figure in part (a) shows that the equilibrium real wage rate is $30 an hour and the equilibrium employment is 20 billion hours per year. The production function, in the first figure in part (a), shows that when 20 billion hours of labor are employed, GDP is $900 billion, so potential GDP equals $900 billion.

| Quantity of labor supplied (billions of hours per year) | Real wage rate (2001 dollars per hour) |
|---|---|
| 20 | 10 |
| 30 | 20 |
| 40 | 30 |
| 50 | 40 |
| 60 | 50 |

1d. The new labor supply schedule is given in the table above and shown in the figure on the next page. In the figure, the labor supply curve shifts rightward from $LS_1$ to $LS_2$. The equilibrium quantity of labor increases to 30 billion hours and the equilibrium real wage rate falls to $20. The production function in the first table in the practice problem shows that when

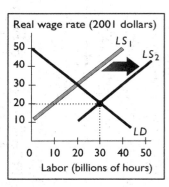

Real wage rate (2001 dollars)

Labor (billions of hours)

employment is 30 billion hours, real GDP is $1,200 billion. So, the increase in the population increases potential GDP to $1,200 billion.

## ■ AP Self Test 23.1

### True or false

1. Classical macroeconomics says that markets work well and government intervention cannot improve on the performance of markets.

2. New macroeconomists agree that the problem of business cycle fluctuations is much more important than the problem of sustaining economic growth.

3. Real GDP can exceed potential GDP permanently.

4. The production function shows how the quantity of labor hired depends on the real wage rate.

5. The nominal wage rate influences the quantity of labor demanded because what matters to firms is the number of dollars they pay for an hour of labor.

6. At the labor market equilibrium the real wage rate is such that the quantity of labor demanded equals the quantity of labor supplied.

7. When the labor market is in equilibrium, the economy is at full employment and real GDP equals potential GDP.

### Multiple choice

1. ____ adopts the view that how the economy works depends on the micro choices people make.
   a. Classical macroeconomics
   b. Keynesian economics
   c. The new macroeconomics
   d. The Lucas wedge
   e. The Okun gap

2. Potential GDP
   a. is the quantity of GDP produced when the economy is at full employment.
   b. can never be exceeded.
   c. can never be attained.
   d. is another name for real GDP.
   e. is another name for nominal GDP.

3. With fixed quantities of capital, land, and entrepreneurship and fixed technology, the amount of real GDP produced increases when ____ increases.
   i. the quantity of labor employed
   ii. the inflation rate
   iii. the price level
      a. i only.
      b. ii only.
      c. iii only.
      d. ii and iii.
      e. i, ii, and iii.

4. The production function graphs the relationship between
   a. nominal GDP and real GDP.
   b. real GDP and the quantity of labor employed.
   c. real GDP and capital.
   d. nominal GDP and the quantity of labor employed.
   e. real GDP and the supply of labor.

5. The quantity of labor demanded definitely increases if the
   a. real wage rate rises.
   b. real wage rate falls.
   c. nominal wage rate rises.
   d. nominal wage rate falls.
   e. supply of labor decreases.

6. The supply of labor curve has a ____ slope because as the real wage rate rises, ____.
   a. negative; firms hire fewer workers
   b. positive; the opportunity cost of leisure rises
   c. positive; the opportunity cost of leisure falls
   d. negative; households work more hours
   e. positive; firms offer more jobs

7. The real wage rate is $35 an hour. At this wage rate there are 100 billion labor hours supplied and 200 billion labor hours demanded. There is a
   a. shortage of 300 billion hours of labor.
   b. shortage of 100 billion hours of labor.
   c. surplus of 100 billion hours of labor.
   d. surplus of 300 billion hours of labor.
   e. shortage of 200 billion hours of labor.

■ **FIGURE 23.1**

Real wage rate (2000 dollars per hour)

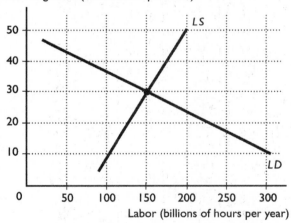

Labor (billions of hours per year)

8. In Figure 23.1, the equilibrium real wage rate is ____ and equilibrium employment is ____ billions of hours per year.
   a. $50; 200
   b. $10; 100
   c. $30; more than 300
   d. $20; 125
   e. $30; 150

9. In Figure 23.1, full employment is reached when employment is ____ billions of hours a year.
   a. 150
   b. 200
   c. 250
   d. more than 300
   e. More information is needed about the nation's production function to answer the question.

10. When the labor market is in equilibrium, real GDP ____ potential GDP.
    a. is greater than
    b. is equal to
    c. is less than
    d. might be greater than, less than, or equal to
    e. is not comparable to

11. Compared to the U.S. production function, the European production function is
    a. higher.
    b. lower.
    c. the same.
    d. lower than the U.S. production function at low levels of employment and higher than the U.S. production function at high levels of employment.
    e. higher than the U.S. production function at low levels of employment and lower than the U.S. production function at high levels of employment.

**Short Response Questions**

1. What is the relationship between equilibrium in the labor market and potential GDP? Be sure to explain the role played by the production function.

2. Suppose a nation's production function shifts upward. If the equilibrium quantity of labor does not change, what is the effect on the nation's potential GDP?

3. Suppose a nation's production function shifts upward and the equilibrium quantity of labor increases. What is the effect on the nation's potential GDP?

## Long Response Questions

| Quantity of labor (billions of hours per year) | Real GDP (billions of 2000 dollars) |
|---|---|
| 0 | 0 |
| 10 | 400 |
| 20 | 725 |
| 30 | 900 |
| 40 | 960 |
| 50 | 1,000 |

■ **FIGURE 23.2**

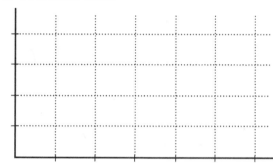

1. The above table gives data for a nation's production function. In Figure 23.2, draw the production function. Label the axes. How are diminishing returns reflected?

■ **FIGURE 23.3**

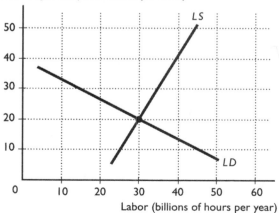

2. Figure 23.3 illustrates the labor market for the nation with the production function given in the previous problem. In the figure, identify the equilibrium real wage rate and employment. Using the production function in Figure 23.2, what is the nation's potential GDP?

3. Using the production function in Figure 23.2 and the labor market in Figure 23.3, suppose that both the labor supply and labor demand curves shift rightward by 10 billion labor hours. The production function does not change. What is the nation's potential GDP?

4. What are the differences between classical macroeconomics and Keynesian macroeconomics?

**CHECKPOINT 23.2**

■ **Explain the forces that determine the natural unemployment rate.**

### Quick Review

- *Job search* Job search is the activity of looking for an acceptable vacant job. Job search is influenced by demographic changes, unemployment benefits, and structural change.
- *Job rationing* Job rationing is a situation that arises when the real wage rate is above the full-employment equilibrium level. An efficiency wage, a minimum wage, or a union wage can lead to job rationing.

### Additional Practice Problems 23.2

1. Why do demographic changes affect the amount of job search?
2. What factors can keep the real wage rate above the full-employment level? How do these factors affect the amount of employment?
3. Since 1965, how has the real minimum wage generally changed in the United States? What effect would this trend have on the natural unemployment rate?

### Solutions to Additional Practice Problems 23.2

1. Demographic changes affect the amount of job search because younger workers conduct more job search than do older workers. In particular, older workers generally have already settled into a career, whereas younger

workers are often entering the labor market for the first time. As new entrants, younger workers must search for a job. In addition, younger workers often switch between jobs before settling upon their career and while they are switching, they are searching for a new job.

2. Job rationing, when the real wage rate is above the full-employment equilibrium level, is the result of efficiency wages, the minimum wage, and union wages. An efficiency wage is a real wage that a firm sets above the full-employment equilibrium level in order to motivate its workers to work harder. A minimum wage is a government regulation that sets the lowest wage legal to pay. A union wage is a wage rate negotiated between a labor union and a firm. Because these wage rates are above the full-employment level, the quantity of labor employed is less than it otherwise would be.

3. Since 1965 there has been a general downward trend in the real minimum wage. The drop was most pronounced between 1967 and 1988, after which the real minimum wage has generally hovered near $5 an hour. The general downward trend in the real minimum wage reduces the amount of job rationing, thereby decreasing the natural unemployment rate.

## ■ AP Self Test 23.2

**True or false**

1. The amount of job search depends on a number of factors including demographic change.
2. An increase in unemployment benefits, other things remaining the same, will increase the amount of time spent on job search.
3. Job rationing has no effect on the natural unemployment rate.
4. Job rationing results in a shortage of labor.
5. Teenage labor is not affected by the minimum wage.

**Multiple choice**

1. In the United States since 1950, the average unemployment rate was highest during the decade of the
   a. 1950s.
   b. 1960s.
   c. 1970s.
   d. 1980s.
   e. 1990s.

2. The two fundamental causes of unemployment at full employment are
   a. seasonal jobs and technological change.
   b. foreign competition and financial bankruptcies.
   c. job search and job rationing.
   d. decreases in labor productivity and retirement benefits.
   e. demographic change and decreases in the demand for labor.

3. Job search is defined as
   a. the activity of looking for an acceptable, vacant job.
   b. saying you are looking when you are actually not looking.
   c. attending school to increase your employability.
   d. equivalent to job rationing.
   e. being paid an efficiency wage.

4. The higher unemployment benefits are, the
   a. higher the opportunity cost of job search.
   b. lower the opportunity cost of job search.
   c. shorter the time spent searching and accepting a suitable job.
   d. shorter the time spent searching for a suitable job and the higher the opportunity cost of being unemployed.
   e. lower the natural unemployment rate.

5. Job rationing occurs if
   a. the minimum wage is set below the equilibrium wage rate.
   b. an efficiency wage is set below the equilibrium wage rate.
   c. a union wage is set below the equilibrium wage rate.
   d. the real wage rate is pushed above the equilibrium wage rate.
   e. the Lucas wedge is positive.

6. The existence of union wages, efficiency wages, and the minimum wage
   a. raises the real wage rate above the equilibrium wage and creates a shortage of labor.
   b. lowers the real wage rate below the equilibrium wage and creates a shortage of labor.
   c. raises the real wage rate above the equilibrium wage and raises the natural unemployment rate.
   d. does not have an impact on the equilibrium wage rate or on the amount of unemployment.
   e. raises the real wage rate above the equilibrium wage and lowers the natural unemployment rate.

7. Intel wants to attract the most productive and knowledgeable workers. To achieve this goal it could pay ____ wage.
   a. an efficiency
   b. a minimum
   c. a nominal
   d. an equilibrium
   e. a Lucas wedge

8. Collective bargaining by unions can result in a union wage rate that is ____ the equilibrium real wage rate and creates a ____ of labor.
   a. above; surplus
   b. above; shortage
   c. below; surplus
   d. below; shortage
   e. equal to; surplus

■ **FIGURE 23.4**

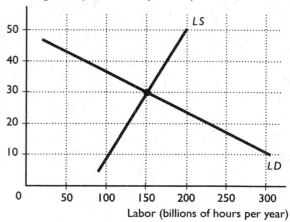

9. In Figure 23.4, of the wages listed below, there is the most job rationing and unemployment if the real wage rate equals
   a. $10 per hour.
   b. $20 per hour.
   c. $30 per hour.
   d. $40 per hour.
   e. None of the above is correct because at any real wage rate there is never any job rationing.

10. In Figure 23.4, if there is any job rationing, the real wage rate must be ____ per hour and employment is ____ billion hours.
    a. less than $30; more than 150
    b. equal to $30; equal to 150
    c. less than $30; less than 150
    d. more than $30; less than 150
    e. less than $20; less than 150

**Short Response Questions**

1. What types of unemployment are included in the natural unemployment rate? What types are not included?

2. The demographics of the United States are such that there will be an increase of young people entering the labor force between 2004 and 2012. What do you predict will be the effect on the U.S. unemployment rate?

3. Why do unemployment benefits affect the natural unemployment rate?

4. An efficiency wage is a wage that exceeds the equilibrium wage rate. Why would a firm pay an efficiency wage?

## Long Response Questions

### ■ FIGURE 23.5

Real wage rate (2000 dollars per hour)

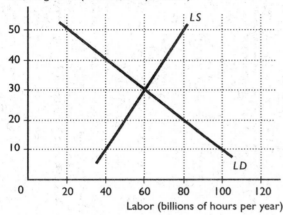

Labor (billions of hours per year)

1. Figure 23.5 illustrates the labor market.
   a. What is the equilibrium wage rate? Equilibrium employment?
   b. What must a firm do to set an efficiency wage?
   c. Suppose the government imposes a minimum wage that creates a surplus of 60 billion hours of labor a year. What is the minimum wage?

d. If a union negotiates on behalf of its members, what can you say about the range of wage rates the union will try to obtain?

e. In your answers to (b), (c), and (d), is there any unemployment? Compare your answers to parts (b), (c), and (d). How does the employment that results in these situations compare with that in part (a)?

| Real wage rate (2001 dollars per hour) | Quantity of labor demanded (billions of hours per year) | Quantity of labor supplied (billions of hours per year) |
|---|---|---|
| 10 | 180 | 150 |
| 20 | 160 | 160 |
| 30 | 140 | 170 |
| 40 | 120 | 180 |

2. The above table gives the labor demand and labor supply schedules for a nation.
   a. What is the equilibrium wage rate?
   b. Suppose firms set an efficiency wage of $30 an hour. What is the effect of this wage rate?
   c. Suppose the government sets a minimum wage of $30 an hour. What is the effect of the minimum wage?
   d. Suppose unions negotiate a wage of $30 an hour. What is the effect of the union wage?
   e. How do your answers to parts (b), (c), and (d) compare?

# YOUR AP SELF TEST ANSWERS

## ■ CHECKPOINT 23.1

**True or false**

1. True;  page 570
2. False;  page 571
3. False;  page 573
4. False;  page 574
5. False;  page 575
6. True;  page 578
7. True;  page 579

**Multiple choice**

1. c;  page 571
2. a;  page 573
3. a;  page 573
4. b;  page 574
5. b;  page 576
6. b;  pages 577-578
7. b;  pages 578-579
8. e;  page 578
9. a;  page 579
10. b;  page 579
11. b;  page 580

**Short Response Questions**

1. The equilibrium quantity of labor is the amount of full employment. The production function shows how much GDP this full-employment quantity of labor produces and this quantity of GDP is potential GDP;  page 579.
2. If the production function shifts upward, the amount of real GDP produced by every quantity of labor increases. The nation's potential GDP increases;  pages 574, 579.
3. On both counts, the upward shift of the production function and the increase in employment, potential GDP increases;  pages 574, 579.

**Long Response Questions**

1. Figure 23.6 illustrates the production function. In the table, diminishing returns are demonstrated by the fact that each additional 10 billion hours of labor increases real GDP

## ■ FIGURE 23.6

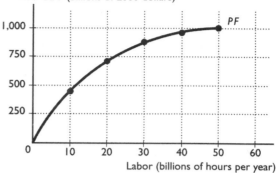

Real GDP (billions of 2000 dollars)

by a smaller amount. In the figure, diminishing returns are illustrated by the slope of the production function, which becomes less steep as the quantity of labor increases;  pages 574-575.

2. The equilibrium real wage rate is $20 an hour and the equilibrium employment is 30 billion hours. Potential GDP is $900 billion;  page 579.

3. If both the labor demand and labor supply curves shift rightward by 10 billion labor hours, then equilibrium employment increases by 10 billion hours to 40 billion hours. Potential GDP increases to $960 billion;  page 579.

4. Classical macroeconomics believes that markets work well and government intervention cannot improve the economy. Keynesian economics believes that a market economy is unstable and needs government intervention to help it reach full employment and sustained economic growth;  page 570.

## ■ CHECKPOINT 23.2

**True or false**

1. True;  page 583
2. True;  page 583
3. False;  page 584
4. False;  pages 584-586
5. False;  page 585

## Multiple choice

1. d; page 582
2. c; page 583
3. a; page 583
4. b; page 583
5. d; pages 584-585
6. c; page 585
7. a; page 585
8. a; page 585
9. d; page 586
10. d; pages 587-586

## Short Response Questions

1. The natural unemployment rate includes frictional, structural, and seasonal unemployment. It does *not* include cyclical unemployment; page 582.

2. The natural unemployment rate increases as more young people enter the labor force and search for jobs. The natural unemployment rate in the United States likely will increase between 2004 and 2012; page 583.

3. If unemployment benefits increase, the opportunity cost of job search decreases. Workers spend more time unemployed, searching for jobs and so the natural unemployment rate increases; page 583.

4. A firm pays an efficiency wage rate to motivate its employees to work hard. The employees will work hard to avoid being let go because they know that if they have to take another job, they are likely to be paid the lower equilibrium wage; page 585.

## Long Response Questions

1. a. The equilibrium wage rate is $30 and employment is 60 billion hours; page 579.

   b. An efficiency wage is set higher than the equilibrium wage rate, so the firm must set the wage rate above $30; page 585.

   c. A minimum wage of $50 an hour creates a labor surplus of 60 billion hours a year; pages 585-586.

   d. The union will strive to set a wage rate that is higher than the competitive wage, so the union will try to set a wage that is higher than $30; page 585.

   e. In each of the answers to parts (a), (b), and (c), unemployment occurs. And in each of the answers, employment is less than 60 billion hours; page 586.

2. a. The equilibrium wage rate is $20 an hour because that is the wage rate at which the quantity of labor demanded equals the quantity supplied. Employment is 160 billion hours; page 579.

   b. If firms set an efficiency wage of $30 an hour, there is a labor surplus of 30 billion hours a year (170 billion hours supplied minus 140 billion hours demanded); pages 585-586.

   c. If the government sets a minimum wage of $30 an hour, there is a labor surplus of 30 billion hour a year; pages 585-586.

   d. If unions negotiate a wage of $30 an hour, there is a labor surplus of 30 billion hours a year; pages 585-586.

   e. In each of the answers to parts (b), (c), and (d) there is a labor surplus of 30 billion hours a year. All three of the events raise the wage rate above its equilibrium and create unemployment. All three of the events lower employment; page 586.

# Investment and Saving

## Chapter 24

Chapter 24 shows how the nation's capital is replaced and increased through investment. Saving is the amount of income that is not paid in taxes or spent on consumption goods and services. At the financial market equilibrium, the quantity of saving supplied equals the quantity of investment demanded.

■ **Define and explain the relationships among capital, investment, wealth, and saving.**

Physical capital, also called capital, is the tools, machines, buildings, and other constructions that have been produced in the past and are used to produce additional goods and services. Financial capital is the funds firms use to buy and operate physical capital. Gross investment is the total amount spent on new capital goods. Net investment equals gross investment minus depreciation. Net investment is the change in the quantity of capital. Wealth is the value of all the things a person owns. Saving is the amount of income that is not paid in taxes or spent on consumption goods or services. Saving adds to wealth. Financial markets are the collection of households, firms, governments, banks, and other financial markets that lend and borrow. Financial markets determine the price of financial capital, which is expressed as an interest rate.

■ **Explain how investment and saving decisions are made and how these decisions interact in financial markets to determine the real interest rate and the amount of investment and saving.**

Firms demand investment goods. Other things remaining the same, the higher the real interest rate, the smaller is the quantity of investment demanded, and the lower the real interest rate, the larger is the quantity of investment demanded. Investment demand is the relationship between the quantity of investment demanded and the real interest rate, other things remaining the same. Investment demand changes when the expected rate of profit changes. Households supply savings. Other things remaining the same, the higher the real interest rate, the greater is the quantity of saving supplied, and the lower the real interest rate, the smaller is the quantity of saving supplied. Saving supply is the relationship between saving and the real interest rate, other things remaining the same. The three main factors that influence saving supply are disposable income, the buying power of net assets, and expected future disposable income. The financial market equilibrium occurs at the real interest rate where the quantity of investment demanded equals the quantity of saving supplied.

■ **Explain how government influences the real interest rate, investment, and saving.**

In the global economy, $I = S + (NT - G)$ where $I$ is investment, $S$ is private saving, and $NT - G$ is government saving, net taxes minus government expenditure. A government budget surplus adds to private saving, lowering the real interest rate and increasing investment. A government budget deficit decreases saving, raising the real interest rate and decreasing (crowding out) investment.

## EXPANDED CHAPTER CHECKLIST

**When you have completed this chapter, you will be able to:**

### 1 Define and explain the relationships among capital, investment, wealth, and saving.

- Define physical capital and financial capital, and state how the two are related.
- Define gross investment and net investment and explain the relationship between net investment and capital.
- Define wealth and saving and explain how the two are related.
- Describe financial markets, including stock markets, bond markets, short-term securities markets, and loan markets.

### 2 Explain how investment and saving decisions are made and how these decisions interact in financial markets to determine the real interest rate.

- Discuss the relationship between the quantity of investment demanded and the real interest rate.
- Discuss the relationship between the quantity of saving supplied and the real interest rate.

### 3 Explain how government influences the real interest rate, investment, and saving.

- Explain the formula $I = S + (NT - G)$.
- Describe and illustrate the effect a government budget surplus has on the real interest rate and quantity of investment.
- Describe and illustrate the effect a government budget deficit has on the real interest rate and quantity of investment.
- Define crowding out and describe why it occurs.

## YOUR AP TEST HINTS

### AP Topics

| Topic on your AP test | Corresponding textbook section |
|---|---|
| **National income and price determination** | |
| Aggregate Demand | Chapter 24 |
| • Determinants of aggregate demand | Checkpoint 24.2 |
| • Crowding out | Checkpoint 24.3 |
| Time Value of Money | Checkpoint 24.2 |
| Investment in Human and Physical Capital | Checkpoint 24.1 |

### AP Vocabulary

- On the AP test, private saving is also called "loanable funds." The loanable funds market is all of the financial markets taken together. It is from this market that firms finance their purchases of physical capital and governments finance any budget deficits. Hence an increase in the demand for capital or an increase in the government budget deficit increases the demand for loanable funds and raises the interest rate.

### Extra AP material

- The AP test will not ask about the Ricardo-Barro effect. The AP test also will not require that you draw a savings supply curve.

## CHECKPOINT 24.1

### ■ Define and explain the relationships among capital, investment, wealth, and saving.

#### Quick Review

- *Net investment* Net investment is the change in the quantity of capital and equals gross investment minus depreciation.
- *Wealth* Wealth is the value of all things that a person owns. Wealth at the end of the year equals wealth at the beginning of the year plus saving over the year.

### Additional Practice Problems 24.1

1. On December 31, 2004 CSX railroad had capital of $19.5 billion dollars. During 2005 CSX made investments of $1.0 billion and had $0.4 billion of capital depreciate.
   a. What was CSX's gross investment?
   b. What was CSX's net investment?
   c. What was the amount of CSX's capital stock on December 31, 2005? By how much did the capital stock change? How does this answer compare to the answer to part (b)?

2. In 2003, the 3-D graphics accelerator company Nvidia wanted to raise $200 million to build a new headquarters building and buy other physical capital. What methods could Nvidia have used to obtain the funds to purchase the capital it needed?

3. On December 31, 2004, Tommy's wealth was $25,000 he had in a savings account. During 2005, Tommy earned $125,000 as a manager of his company's server farm and he received $1,000 in interest from his saving. Tommy paid taxes of $35,000 and had consumption spending of $80,000.
   a. What was Tommy's saving during 2005?
   b. What was Tommy's wealth on December 31, 2005?

### Solutions to Additional Practice Problems 24.1

1a. CSX's gross investment is equal to their total investment, $1.0 billion.

1b. CSX's net investment is equal to its gross investment minus its depreciation, or $1.0 billion minus $0.4 billion, which is $0.6 billion.

1c. CSX's capital stock on December 31, 2005 equals its capital stock on December 31, 2004 plus its (gross) investment minus its depreciation, or $19.5 billion + $1.0 billion − $0.4 billion, which is $20.1 billion. CSX's capital increased by $0.6 billion, which is the same as CSX's net investment. It is the case that the change in the capital stock equals net investment.

2. Nvidia had a number of choices. It could have sold new shares of stock, so the current stockholders would share future profits with new stockholders. Nvidia could have sold bonds, which means it would be borrowing the funds from the buyers of the bonds. The company could have sold short-term securities. Nvida could have arranged a bank loan. If Nvidia sold bonds, short-term securities, or borrowed from a bank, Nvidia would have increased its debt and would be required at some time to repay whoever loaned it the funds. As it happens, Nvidia actually financed its new capital by selling bonds.

3a. Tommy's total income was $126,000. From this he paid $35,000 in taxes and spent $80,000 on consumption, leaving $11,000 as his savings.

3b. Tommy's wealth on December 31, 2005 equals his wealth on December 31, 2004 plus his savings in 2005. So his wealth at the end of 2005 was $25,000 + $11,000, or $36,000.

### ■ AP Self Test 24.1

#### True or false

1. Financial capital and physical capital are two different names for the same thing.
2. Net investment equals gross investment minus depreciation.
3. The nation's capital stock at the end of 2006 equals the capital stock at the beginning of 2006 plus gross investment during 2006.
4. Wealth and income are the same thing.
5. A bond issued by a firm is a certificate of ownership and claim to the profits that the firm makes.

#### Multiple choice

1. Which of the following is **NOT** an example of physical capital?
   a. a building
   b. a bond
   c. a dump truck
   d. a lawn mower
   e. a computer

2. The decrease in the value of capital that results from its use and obsolescence is
   a. appreciation.
   b. deconstruction.
   c. depreciation.
   d. gross investment.
   e. net investment.

3. Which of the following formulas is correct?
   a. Net investment = gross investment + depreciation
   b. Net investment = gross investment + capital
   c. Net investment = gross investment − depreciation
   d Net investment = gross investment − saving
   e. Net investment = gross investment − wealth

4. Intel's capital at the end of the year equals Intel's capital at the beginning of the year
   a. minus its stock dividends.
   b. plus net investment.
   c. minus depreciation.
   d. plus gross investment.
   e. plus depreciation.

5. U.S. capital at the end of 2006 equals U.S. capital at the beginning of 2006 plus
   a. nothing, because capital can't change in just one year.
   b. gross investment during 2006.
   c. gross investment during 2006 minus net investment in 2006.
   d. net investment during 2006.
   e. depreciation during 2006 minus gross investment during 2006.

| Year | Gross investment (trillions of 2000 dollars) | Depreciation (trillions of 2000 dollars) |
|---|---|---|
| 2006 | 1.9 | 0.8 |
| 2007 | 2.0 | 0.9 |

6. The table above gives a nation's investment and depreciation. If the capital stock equaled $25.0 trillion at the end of 2005, at the end of 2006 the capital stock equaled
   a. $25.0 trillion.
   b. $25.8 trillion.
   c. $24.2 trillion.
   d. $26.9 trillion.
   e. $26.1 trillion.

7. The table above gives a nation's investment and depreciation. If the capital stock equaled $23.0 trillion at the end of 2006, net investment in 2007 equaled
   a. $25.9 trillion.
   b. $25.0 trillion.
   c. $0.9 trillion.
   d. $2.0 trillion.
   e. $1.1 trillion.

8. The Ng's family's wealth at the end of the year equals their wealth at the beginning of the year
   a. minus personal income taxes.
   b. plus saving.
   c. minus consumption.
   d. plus income.
   e. plus consumption minus income.

9. Economists use the term "financial markets" or "loanable funds market" to mean the markets in which
   a. firms purchase their physical capital.
   b. firms supply their goods and services.
   c. households supply their labor services.
   d. firms get the funds that they use to buy physical capital.
   e. the government borrows to fund any budget surplus.

## Short Response Questions

1. In 2003, Regis Hair Salon purchased 10 hair dryers for $3,300 each. During the year, depreciation was $13,000. What was Regis' gross investment and net investment?

| Year | Gross investment (trillions of 2000 dollars) | Depreciation (trillions of 2000 dollars) | Net investment (trillions of 2000 dollars) |
|------|------|------|------|
| 2005 | 2.3 | 0.2 | ____ |
| 2006 | 2.5 | 0.3 | ____ |
| 2007 | 2.8 | 0.4 | ____ |

2. The table above gives gross investment and depreciation for three years.
   a. Complete the net investment column.
   b. If the capital was $22.3 trillion at the beginning of 2005, what was it at the beginning of 2006? 2007? 2008?

3. The Bouton family earns an income of $80,000 a year after taxes by directing local television shows. Their consumption expenditures during the year are $75,000.
   a. What is the amount of their saving over the year?
   b. If their wealth at the beginning of the year was $100,000, how much is their wealth at the end of the year?

## Long Response Questions

1. What is the relationship between physical capital and financial capital?

2. What is the difference between gross investment and capital?

## CHECKPOINT 24.2

■ **Explain how investment and saving decisions are made and how these decisions interact in financial markets to determine the real interest rate and the amount of investment and saving.**

### Quick Review

- *Investment demand* The relationship between the quantity of investment demanded and the real interest rate, other things remaining the same.

## Additional Practice Problems 24.2

1. Suppose you buy a lottery ticket and the top prize is $10 million. Your current income is $30,000 a year and you save $1,500 a year. Glory be, you win the lottery and your income this year is $10,030,000! Do you think you will save more or less than $1,500 this year? In your answer, focus on the amount of your income this year and what you expect it to be in the future.

2. New Cell is a biotech company that is exploring ways to rejuvenate older cells so as to restore the cell's youth. New Cell's investment demand curve is shown in the figure. Suppose that New Cell makes a breakthrough in its technology that increases the expected rate of profit from investment. In the figure, show the effect of this change on New Cell's investment demand curve.

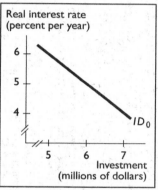

## Solutions to Additional Practice Problems 24.2

1. You will save more than $1,500 this year. First, your disposable income is much higher this year, and saving increases when disposable income increases. Second, your expected future income is much lower than your income this year because you cannot expect to win the lottery two years running! When expected future income is lower, saving increases. For both reasons you will save a *lot* more than $1,500.

2. An increase in the expected rate of profit increases investment demand and shifts the investment demand curve rightward. In the figure, First Call's investment demand curve shifts rightward from $ID_0$ to $ID_1$.

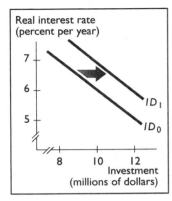

### ■ AP Self Test 24.2

**True or false**

1. Other things remaining the same, the higher the real interest rate, the smaller the quantity of investment demanded.

2. When the expected rate of profit changes, there is a movement along the investment demand curve.

3. The real interest rate is the opportunity cost of consumption expenditure.

4. An increase in the buying power of net assets leads to a decrease in saving.

5. If the real interest rate is greater than the equilibrium real interest rate, there is a shortage of saving in the loanable funds market.

**Multiple choice**

1. If the real interest rate falls, other things being the same, the quantity of investment demanded ____ and the quantity of saving supplied ____.
   a. increases; decreases
   b. increases; increases
   c. decreases; does not change
   d. does not change; decreases
   e. decreases; decreases

2. Investment demand
   a. increases in a recession.
   b. decreases in an expansion.
   c. increases when firms are optimistic about their future prospects.
   d. increases when the buying power of net assets increases.
   e. decreases when the buying power of net assets increases.

### ■ FIGURE 24.1

Real interest rate (percent per year)

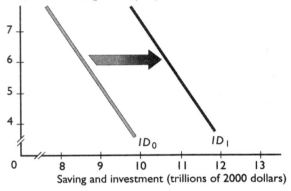

Saving and investment (trillions of 2000 dollars)

3. The shift of the investment demand curve in Figure 24.1 illustrates ____ in investment demand and could be the result of ____.
   a. an increase; a rise in the buying power of net assets
   b. an increase; a fall in the buying power of net assets
   c. a decrease; businesses being less optimistic about the future
   d. a decrease; a rise in the expected rate of profit
   e. an increase; a rise in the expected rate of profit

4. Other things remaining the same, a ____ in the real interest rate ____ the quantity of saving supplied and ____ the quantity of financial capital supplied.
   a. fall; increases; increases
   b. rise; increases; increases
   c. fall; increases; decreases
   d. fall; decreases; increases
   e. rise; increases; decreases

5. An increase in the buying power of a household's net assets leads to
   a. an increase in savings.
   b. an increase in investment.
   c. a decrease in savings.
   d. a decrease in investment.
   e. no change in either saving or investment.

6. In the financial market, the real interest rate changes until
   a. saving supply is greater than investment demand.
   b. saving supply is smaller than investment demand.
   c. saving supply and investment demand are equal.
   d. the quantity of saving supplied equals the quantity of investment demanded.
   e. the investment demand curve and the saving supply curve have shifted so that they are in equilibrium.

**Short Response Questions**

■ **FIGURE 24.2**
Real interest rate (percent per year)

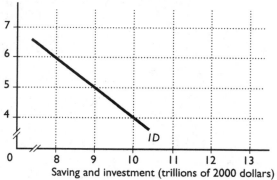

1. Figure 24.2 shows an investment demand curve. Because the economy enters an expansion, the expected rate of profit increases. Show the effect of this change on investment.

2. The table in the next column above gives a saving supply schedule and an investment demand schedule.
   a. Label the axes and then draw the saving supply curve and investment demand curve in Figure 24.3.

| Real interest rate (percent per year) | Investment (trillions of 2000 dollars) | Saving (trillions of 2000 dollars) |
|---|---|---|
| 4 | 12 | 10 |
| 5 | 11 | 11 |
| 6 | 10 | 12 |
| 7 | 9 | 13 |

■ **FIGURE 24.3**

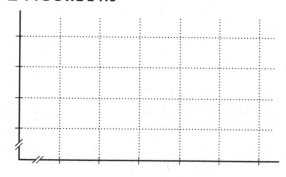

   b. What is the equilibrium real interest rate? What is the equilibrium quantity of investment and saving?
   c. Suppose that firms become more optimistic about the expected rate of profit. In Figure 24.3, show this change. What is the effect on the real interest rate and quantity of investment and saving?

**Long Response Questions**

1. Why does an increase in the real interest rate decrease the quantity of investment demanded?

2. What factors shift the investment demand curve?

3. Suppose the real interest rate is less than its equilibrium value. What forces drive the real interest rate to its equilibrium?

## CHECKPOINT 24.3

■ **Explain how government influences the real interest rate, investment, and saving.**

### Quick Review

- *Government saving* Government saving equals net taxes minus government purchases, or $NT - G$.
- *Crowding-out effect* The tendency for a government budget deficit to decrease investment.

### Additional Practice Problem 24.3

1. The table shows the investment demand schedule and the supply schedule of private saving.

| Real interest rate (percent per year) | Investment | Private saving |
|---|---|---|
| | (trillions of 2000 dollars per year) | |
| 4 | 2.7 | 2.1 |
| 5 | 2.6 | 2.2 |
| 6 | 2.5 | 2.3 |
| 7 | 2.4 | 2.4 |
| 8 | 2.3 | 2.5 |
| 9 | 2.2 | 2.6 |
| 10 | 2.1 | 2.7 |

a. If the government's budget is balanced, what is the equilibrium real interest rate, the equilibrium the quantity of private saving and the equilibrium quantity of investment?

b. If the government budget surplus is $200 billion (and there is no Ricardo-Barro effect) what is the equilibrium real interest rate and the quantity of investment?

c. If the government budget deficit is $200 billion (and there is no Ricardo-Barro effect) what is the equilibrium real interest rate, the quantity of private saving, and the quantity of investment? Is there any crowding out?

### Solution to Additional Practice Problem 24.3

1a. With no budget deficit or surplus, private saving is total saving, which means the that private saving is the total of loanable funds. The equilibrium real interest rate is 7 percent a year. The equilibrium quantity of private saving is $2.4 trillion and the equilibrium quantity of investment is $2.4 trillion.

1b. When the government has a $200 billion budget surplus, it is adding that amount to private saving so the quantity of loanable funds at every interest rate increases. At an interest rate of 7 percent, there is a surplus of saving, that is, a surplus of loanable funds. The real interest rate falls. When the real interest rate falls to 6 percent, the quantity of private saving is $2.3 trillion and the total quantity of saving, which is the total quantity of loanable funds, is $2.5 trillion. The quantity of investment demand is also $2.5 trillion. The total quantity of loanable funds equals the quantity of investment demanded. So the equilibrium real interest rate is 6 percent, the equilibrium quantity of private saving is $2.3 trillion, and the equilibrium quantity of investment is $2.5 trillion.

1c. If the government runs a $200 billion deficit, *total* saving at every real interest rate is $200 billion less than the private saving shown in the table. So the total quantity of loanable funds is decreases by $200 billion at every interest rate. When the real interest rate is 8 percent, the quantity of total loanable funds is $2.3 trillion (the $2.5 trillion private saving "plus" the negative $200 billion government saving). The quantity of investment demanded is $2.3 trillion, so the real interest rate of 8 percent is the equilibrium rate. Private saving is $2.5 trillion and investment is $2.3 trillion. In comparison to the situation with no government deficit, $100 billion of investment has been crowded out.

## ■ AP Self Test 24.3

### True or false

1. Investment, $I$, is financed by private saving, $S$, and government saving, $G - NT$.

2. With no Barro-Ricardo effect, an increase in government saving leads to a fall in the real interest rate.

3. With no Barro-Ricardo effect an increase in government saving leads to an increase in the quantity of investment.

4. The crowding-out effect is the tendency of a government budget surplus to crowd out private saving.

## Multiple choice

1. With no Ricardo-Barro effect, a government budget surplus
   a. increases total saving supply.
   b. increases investment demand.
   c. decreases total saving supply.
   d. decreases investment demand.
   e. has no effect on either saving supply or investment demand.

2. Suppose net taxes are greater than government purchases. Then
   a. private saving is equal to investment.
   b. private saving is greater than investment and government saving is positive.
   c. private saving is less than investment and government saving is positive.
   d. there is a budget deficit.
   e. private saving is greater than investment and government saving is negative.

3. $(NT - G)$ is
   a. always positive.
   b. always negative.
   c. positive if the government runs a budget surplus.
   d. negative if the government runs a budget surplus.
   e. equal to $(S - I)$.

4. The "crowding-out effect" refers to how a government budget deficit
   a. shifts only the saving supply curve leftward.
   b. shifts only the investment demand curve leftward.
   c. shifts both the investment demand curve and saving supply curve leftward.
   d. decreases the equilibrium quantity of investment.
   e. increases the equilibrium quantity of investment.

5. If there is no Ricardo-Barro effect, a government budget deficit will ____ the equilibrium real interest rate and ____ the equilibrium quantity of investment.
   a. raise; increase
   b. raise; decrease
   c. lower; increase
   d. lower; decrease
   e. not change; not change

## Short Response Questions

| Row | Net taxes | Government expenditure |
|-----|-----------|------------------------|
|     | (trillions of 2000 dollars) | |
| A   | 5         | 6                      |
| B   | 5         | 4                      |
| C   | 6         | 4                      |
| D   | 7         | 6                      |

1. The above table gives data for net taxes and government expenditure.
   a. What was government saving in Row A? Row B? Row C? Row D?
   b. In which rows did the government have a budget deficit? A budget surplus?
   c. What is the relationship between your answers to parts (a) and (b)?

2. What is the crowding-out effect?

## YOUR AP SELF TEST ANSWERS

### ■ CHECKPOINT 24.1

**True or false**

1. False; page 594
2. True; page 594
3. False; page 594
4. False; page 596
5. False; page 597

**Multiple choice**

1. b; page 594
2. c; page 594
3. c; page 594
4. b; page 594
5. d; page 595
6. e; page 595
7. e; page 595
8. b; page 596
9. d; page 596

**Short Response Questions**

1. Regis' gross investment was $33,000, and net investment, which equals gross investment minus depreciation, was $20,000; page 594.

| Year | Gross investment (trillions of 2000 dollars) | Depreciation (trillions of 2000 dollars) | Net investment (trillions of 2000 dollars) |
|------|------|------|------|
| 2005 | 2.3 | 0.2 | 2.1 |
| 2006 | 2.5 | 0.3 | 2.2 |
| 2007 | 2.8 | 0.4 | 2.4 |

2. a. Net investment is gross investment minus depreciation. The answers are in the table above; page 594.
   b. The capital changes by the amount of net investment. The capital stock at the beginning of 2006 is $24.4 trillion, at the beginning of 2007 is $26.6 trillion, and at the beginning of 2008 is $29.0 trillion; page 595.

3. a. Saving is the amount of income not paid as taxes or spent on consumption goods. So the Bouton family's saving during the year equals $80,000 − $75,000, which is $5,000; page 596.
   b. Saving adds to wealth, so the Bouton family's wealth increases by $5,000 to $105,000; page 596.

**Long Response Questions**

1. Physical capital is the tools, machines, buildings, and other constructions that have been produced in the past and are used to produce additional goods and services. Financial capital is the funds firms use to buy and operate physical capital. Hence a firm needs financial capital in order to buy a piece of physical capital; page 594.

2. Capital is the tools, machines, buildings, and other constructions that have been produced in the past and are used to produce additional goods and services. Investment is the purchase of new capital, so investment adds to the total amount of the nation's capital. Gross investment is the total amount of investment spent on new capital goods; page 594.

### ■ CHECKPOINT 24.2

**True or false**

1. True; page 599
2. False; pages 600-601
3. True; page 602
4. True; page 603
5. False; page 605

**Multiple choice**

1. a; pages 599, 602
2. c; page 601
3. e; pages 600-601
4. b; pages 599, 602
5. c; page 603
6. d; page 605

**Short Response Questions**

1. The decrease in the expected rate of profit decreases investment demand and the investment demand curve shifts leftward, from $ID_0$ to $ID_1$ in Figure 24.4 (illustrated on the next page); pages 600-601.

### ■ FIGURE 24.4

Real interest rate (percent per year)

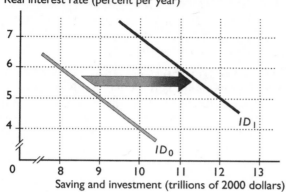

Saving and investment (trillions of 2000 dollars)

### ■ FIGURE 24.5

Real interest rate (percent per year)

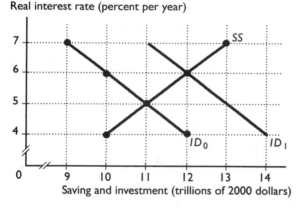

Saving and investment (trillions of 2000 dollars)

3. a. The axes are labeled and the curves are drawn in Figure 24.5. The saving supply curve is *SS* and the investment demand curve is *ID*₀; page 605.

   b. The equilibrium real interest rate is 5 percent a year. The equilibrium quantity of investment and saving is $11 trillion; page 605.

   c. The increase in optimism increases investment demand and shifts the investment demand curve rightward from *ID*₀ to *ID*₁. The real interest rate rises and the quantity of investment and saving increases; page 606.

### Long Response Questions

1. The real interest rate is the opportunity cost of the funds used to finance the purchase of capital. The funds used to finance investment might be borrowed, or they might be the financial resources of the firm's owners. The opportunity cost of both sources of funds is the real interest rate. In the case of borrowed funds, the real interest rate is the opportunity cost because it is what is really paid to the lender. In the case of the owners' funds, the real interest rate is the opportunity cost because the funds could be loaned and earn the real interest rate. An increase in the real interest rate increases the opportunity cost of financing investment and so the quantity of investment demanded decreases; page 599.

2. The investment demand curve shifts when the expected rate of profit changes. Technological change, changes in the phase of the business cycle, population growth, subjective influences, and contagion effects all change the expected rate of profit and shift the investment demand curve; pages 600-601.

3. If the real interest rate is less than the equilibrium real interest rate, the quantity of investment demanded exceeds the quantity of saving supplied. Borrowers can't find all the loans they want, but lenders are able to lend all the funds they have available. So the real interest rate rises and the quantity of investment demanded decreases, while the quantity of saving supplied increases. The equilibrium occurs when the interest rate is such that quantity of investment demanded equals the quantity of saving supplied; page 605.

## ■ CHECKPOINT 24.3

### True or false

1. False; page 608
2. True; pages 608-609
3. True; page 609
4. False; pages 609-610

### Multiple choice

1. a; page 608
2. c; page 608

3. c; page 608

4. d; pages 609-610

5. b; page 609

## Short Response Questions

1. a. Government saving is –$1 trillion in Row A; $1 trillion in Row B; $2 trillion in Row C; and $1 trillion in Row D; page 608.

   b. The government has a budget deficit in Row A and budget surpluses in Rows B, C, and D; page 608.

   c. When government saving is negative, as in Row A, the government has a budget deficit. When government saving is positive, as in Rows B, C, and D, the government has a budget surplus; page 608.

2. The crowding-out effect is the tendency for a government budget deficit to decrease private investment; pages 609-610.

# Economic Growth

## CHAPTER IN PERSPECTIVE

Chapter 25 discusses the factors that determine economic growth, studies different theories that explain economic growth, and examines possible government polices to speed economic growth.

■ **Define and calculate the economic growth rate, and explain the implications of sustained growth.**

Economic growth is a sustained expansion of production possibilities measured as the increase in real GDP over a given time period. The economic growth rate is the annual percentage change of real GDP. The standard of living depends on real GDP per person, which equals real GDP divided by the population. The Rule of 70 is that the number of years it takes a variable to double approximately equals 70 divided by the annual growth rate of the variable.

■ **Identify the main sources of economic growth.**

Real GDP grows when the quantities of the factors of production grow or when technology advances. Labor productivity is the quantity of real GDP produced by one hour of labor. When labor productivity grows, real GDP per person grows. Growth of labor productivity depends on saving and investment in more physical capital, acquisition of more human capital, and discovery of better technologies.

■ **Review the theories of economic growth that explain why growth rates vary over time and across countries.**

The classical theory predicts that labor productivity growth is temporary. If real GDP rises above the subsistence level, a population explosion occurs so that labor productivity falls and real GDP per person returns to the subsistence level. The neoclassical theory asserts that real GDP per person will increase as long as technology keeps advancing. But technological change is assumed to be random. The new growth theory emphasizes that human capital growth and technological change is the result of choices. It also says that technological discoveries bring profit and competition destroys profit, thereby creating the incentive for more technological discoveries. When labor productivity increases because of technological change or an increase in capital, the production function shifts upward. The demand for labor increases so employment increases. The increase in employment and the shift of the production function both increase real GDP. The new growth theory predicts that our unlimited wants will lead us to ever greater productivity and perpetual economic growth.

■ **Describe policies that might speed economic growth.**

The preconditions for economic growth are economic freedom, property rights, and markets. Economic freedom occurs when people are able to make personal choices, their private property is protected, and they are free to buy and sell in markets. Governments can increase economic growth by creating incentives to save, invest, and innovate; by encouraging saving; by encouraging research and development; by encouraging international trade; and by improving the quality of education.

## 1 Define and calculate the economic growth rate, and explain the implications of sustained growth.

- Define the economic growth rate.
- Calculate the growth rate of real GDP.
- Explain the relationship between the standard of living and real GDP per person.
- Calculate the growth rate of real GDP per person.
- Explain and be able to use the Rule of 70.

## 2 Identify the main sources of economic growth.

- Explain why growth in real GDP can be divided into growth in aggregate hours and growth in labor productivity.
- Tell how labor productivity is calculated, and discuss the importance of growth in labor productivity.
- List and explain the three sources of growth in labor productivity.
- Explain the law of diminishing returns.

## 3 Review the theories of economic growth that explain why growth rates vary over time and across countries.

- Describe the classical growth theory and explain why it predicts a return to the subsistence level.
- Describe the neoclassical growth theory and explain why it predicts that the national level of real GDP per person and national growth rates will converge.
- Describe the new growth theory and explain why it predicts national growth rates will not necessarily converge.
- Compare the predictions of each growth theory with the facts in the global economy.

## 4 Describe policies that might speed economic growth.

- List and explain the preconditions for economic growth.

- Describe five government policies that can achieve faster economic growth.
- Discuss the extent to which government policy can affect economic growth.

## YOUR AP TEST HINTS

### AP Topics

| Topic on your AP test | Corresponding textbook section |
|---|---|
| **Inflation, Unemployment, and Stabilization Policy** | |
| Economic Growth and Productivity | Chapter 25 |
| • R&D and technological progress | Checkpoints 25.2, 25.3, 25.4 |
| • Economic growth policy | Checkpoints 25.2, 25.4 |

### Extra AP material

- When illustrating economic growth, the AP test uses the production possibilities frontier (also called on the AP test the production possibilities curve) rather than a production function. Economic growth results in the production possibilities curve shifting outward. More rapid growth means more rapid outward shifts.

## CHECKPOINT 25.1

### ■ Define and calculate the economic growth rate, and explain the implications of sustained growth.

**Quick Review**

- *Growth rate* The growth rate of real GDP equals

$$\frac{\left(\begin{array}{c}\text{Real GDP in}\\\text{current year}\end{array}\right) - \left(\begin{array}{c}\text{Real GDP in}\\\text{previous year}\end{array}\right)}{\left(\text{Real GDP in previous year}\right)} \times 100$$

- *Growth rate of real GDP per person* The growth rate of real GDP per person equals (growth rate of real GDP)–(growth rate of population).

- *Rule of 70* The number of years it takes for the level of any variable to double is approximately 70 divided by the annual percentage growth rate of the variable.

## Additional Practice Problem 25.1

1. In the nation of Transylvania in 2007, real GDP was $3.0 million and the population was 1,000. In 2008, real GDP was $3.3 million and the population was 1,050.
    - a. What is Transylvania's economic growth in 2008?
    - b. What is the population growth rate?
    - c. What is Transylvania's growth rate of real GDP per person?
    - d. Did Transylvania's standard of living rise?
    - e. Approximately how long will it take for real GDP per person to double?

## Solution to Additional Practice Problem 25.1

1. This question uses three growth rate formulas. The first is the formula that calculates the economic growth rate; the second is the formula that calculates the growth rate of real GDP per person; the third is the Rule of 70.

1a. The economic growth rate is the growth rate of real GDP. Transylvania's economic growth rate equals [($3.3 million − $3.0 million) ÷ $3.0 million] × 100 = 10 percent.

1b. Transylvania's population growth rate equals [(1,050 − 1,000) ÷ 1,000] × 100 = 5 percent.

1c. Transylvania's real GDP per person growth rate equals the growth rate of real GDP minus the growth rate of the population, or 10 percent − 5 percent = 5 percent.

1d. Transylvania's real GDP per person rose, so Transylvania's standard of living increased.

1e. The number of years it takes for real GDP per person to double is given by the Rule of 70. Transylvania's real GDP per person is growing at 5 percent per year, so it will take approximately 70 ÷ 5 or 14 years for Transylvania's real GDP per person to double.

## ■ AP Self Test 25.1

### True or false

1. If real GDP last year was $1.00 trillion and real GDP this year is $1.05 trillion, the growth rate of real GDP this year is 5 percent.

2. Real GDP per person equals real GDP divided by the population.

3. If a nation's population grows at 2 percent and its real GDP grows at 4 percent, then the growth rate of real GDP per person is 2 percent.

4. If real GDP is growing at 2 percent a year, it will take 70 years for real GDP to double.

### Multiple choice

1. The economic growth rate is measured as the
    - a. annual percentage change of real GDP.
    - b. annual percentage change of employment.
    - c. level of real GDP.
    - d. annual percentage change of the population.
    - e. amount of population.

2. Real GDP is $9 trillion in the current year and $8.6 trillion in the previous year. The economic growth rate between these years has been
    - a. 10.31 percent.
    - b. 4.65 percent.
    - c. 5.67 percent.
    - d. 7.67 percent.
    - e. $0.4 trillion.

3. If the growth rate of population is greater than a nation's growth rate of real GDP, then its real GDP per person
    - a. falls.
    - b. rises.
    - c. does not change.
    - d. might rise or fall.
    - e. cannot be measured.

4. If real GDP increases by 6 percent and at the same time the population increases by 2 percent, then real GDP per person grows by
   a. 6 percent.
   b. 4 percent.
   c. 2 percent.
   d. 8 percent.
   e. 3 percent.

5. If a country experiences a real GDP growth rate of 4 percent a year, real GDP will double in
   a. 14 years.
   b. 17.5 years.
   c. 23.3 years.
   d. 35 years.
   e. 25 years.

### Short Response Questions

| Year | Real GDP (billions of 2000 dollars) |
|------|-------------------------------------|
| 2005 | 100.0 |
| 2006 | 110.0 |
| 2007 | 121.0 |
| 2008 | 133.1 |

1. The above table gives a nation's real GDP. What is the growth rate of real GDP in 2006? In 2007? In 2008?

| Country | Real GDP 2007 | Real GDP 2008 | Growth rate |
|---------|---------------|---------------|-------------|
| A | $248 million | $257 million | _____ |
| B | $175 million | $188 million | _____ |
| C | $453 million | $467 million | _____ |
| D | $129 million | $141 million | _____ |
| E | $373 million | $396 million | _____ |

2. The above table gives real GDPs for several different nations in two different years. Complete the table by computing the growth rate of GDP between 2007 and 2008.

| Year | Real GDP growth rate (percent) | Population growth rate (percent) |
|------|-------------------------------|----------------------------------|
| 2005 | 3 | 2 |
| 2006 | 4 | 2 |
| 2007 | 1 | 2 |
| 2008 | 4 | 4 |

3. The table above gives the growth rate of real GDP and the growth rate of population for a nation.
   a. What is the growth rate of real GDP per person for each year?
   b. In what years did the standard of living improve?

4. If a nation's real GDP grows at 3 percent a year, how long does it take for real GDP to double? If the growth rate is 4 percent, how long does it take for real GDP to double? If the growth rate is 5 percent, how long does it take real GDP to double?

### CHECKPOINT 25.2

■ **Identify the main sources of economic growth.**

**Quick Review**
- *Labor productivity* Labor productivity equals real GDP divided by aggregate hours. When labor productivity grows, real GDP per person grows.

### Additional Practice Problem 25.2

| Item | 2003 | 2004 |
|------|------|------|
| Aggregate hours (billions) | 232.2 | 234.5 |
| Real GDP (trillions of 2000 dollars) | 10.32 | 10.76 |

1. The table above provides some data on the U.S. economy in 2003 and 2004.
   a. Calculate the growth rate of real GDP in 2004.
   b. Calculate labor productivity in 2003 and 2004.
   c. Calculate the growth rate of labor productivity in 2004.
   d. How does the growth rate of labor productivity you calculated compare with the typical growth in the United States since 1960?

**Solution to Additional Practice Problem 25.2**

1a. The growth rate of real GDP in 2004 is [($10.76 trillion − $10.32 trillion) ÷ $10.32 trillion] × 100, which is 4.3 percent.

1b. Labor productivity is real GDP divided by aggregate hours. So labor productivity in 2003 is $10.32 trillion ÷ 232.2 billion hours, which is $44.44 per hour of labor. In 2004 labor productivity is $10.76 trillion ÷ 234.5 billion hours, which is $45.88 per hour of labor.

1c. The growth rate of labor productivity is labor productivity in 2004 minus the labor productivity in 2003, divided by labor productivity in 2003, all multiplied by 100. The growth rate of labor productivity equals [($45.88 per hour − $44.44 per hour) ÷ $44.44 per hour] × 100, which is 3.24 percent.

1d. The increase in labor productivity in 2004 was slower than in the early 1960s but was larger than has been the average since then.

## ■ AP Self Test 25.2

### True or false

1. Real GDP increases if aggregate hours increase or labor productivity increases.

2. If labor productivity increases and aggregate hours do not change, then real GDP per person increases.

3. Higher wages are a source of growth in labor productivity.

4. The discovery and applications of new technology has increased labor productivity.

### Multiple choice

1. If real GDP is $1,200 billion, the population is 60 million, and aggregate hours are 80 billion, labor productivity is
   a. $5.00 an hour.
   b. $6.67 an hour.
   c. $15.00 an hour.
   d. $20,000.
   e. $150 an hour.

2. If aggregate hours are 100 billion hours and labor productivity is $40 an hour, than real GDP equals
   a. $100 billion.
   b. $40 billion.
   c. $100 trillion.
   d. $2.5 trillion.
   e. $4 trillion.

3. Which of the following lists gives factors that increase labor productivity?
   a. saving and investment in physical capital, and wage increases
   b. expansion of human capital, labor force increases, and discovery of new technologies
   c. expansion of human capital, population growth, and discovery of new technologies
   d. saving and investment in physical capital, expansion of human capital, and discovery of new technologies
   e. labor force increases and wage increases

4. Growth in physical capital depends most directly upon the amount of
   a. saving and investment.
   b. years the firm has been in existence.
   c. population growth.
   d. government expenditures.
   e. human capital.

5. Human capital is
   a. the same as labor productivity.
   b. a measure of the number of labor hours available.
   c. the accumulated skills and knowledge of workers.
   d. the average number of years of schooling of the labor force.
   e. is what people are born with and cannot be changed.

## Short Response Questions

| Year | Real GDP (trillion of 2000 dollars) | Aggregate hours (billions) |
|------|-------------------------------------|----------------------------|
| 1964 | 3.00  | 133.6 |
| 1974 | 4.32  | 158.7 |
| 1984 | 5.81  | 185.3 |
| 1994 | 7.84  | 211.5 |
| 2004 | 10.76 | 234.5 |

1. The table above has data from the United States. For each year, calculate labor productivity.

2. Aggregate hours are 200 billion and labor productivity is $45 an hour. What is real GDP?

## Long Response Question

1. What three factors increase labor productivity?

## CHECKPOINT 25.3

■ **Review the theories of economic growth that explain why growth rates vary over time and across countries.**

### Quick Review

- *Classical growth theory* The clash between an exploding population and limited resources will eventually bring economic growth to an end. Income is driven to the subsistence level.

- *Neoclassical growth theory* Real GDP per person will increase as long as technology keeps advancing. No explanation is given for technological growth.

- *New growth theory* Unlimited wants will lead us to ever greater productivity and perpetual economic growth.

### Additional Practice Problem 25.3

1. How do each of the growth theories reflect the period during which they were developed?

2. Some advisors urge less developed nations to restrict their birth rate. These advisors claim that a high birth rate impoverishes a nation.

a. What growth theory are these advisors following?

b. What would a new growth theory proponent say about this recommendation?

### Solutions to Additional Practice Problems 25.3

1. The classical growth theory was developed during the industrial revolution. Observers such as Thomas Malthus, saw some technological advances and rapid population growth. They combined these two observations into the classical growth theory, which predicts a return to a subsistence level of real GDP per person.

   The neoclassical growth theory was developed in the 1950s, when rapid population growth was no longer a worry and when technological growth and the capital per hour of labor were starting to grow more rapidly. The neoclassical growth theory assigned a key role to these latter two factors and concluded that growth would persist as long as technology advanced.

   The new growth theory was developed in the 1980s, when technological growth exploded. The new growth theory assigns importance to technological growth. Based on the observation that technological growth has persisted during the past 200 years, the new growth theory concludes that technology, and so real GDP, will grow forever.

2a. These advisors are following the classical theory of economic growth. They believe that if real GDP per person rises in these nations, then the birth rate will increase and drive real GDP per person back to the subsistence level. They identify the low real GDP per person in these nations with a high birth rate and the resulting high population growth rate.

2b. A new growth theory proponent likely would disagree with the suggestion to limit the birth rate. According to this theory, the pace at which new discoveries are made and at which technology advances depends on how many people are looking for a new technology and how intensively they are looking. In this case, limiting the population leads to a reduction in the discovery of new technologies and a decrease in the growth rate of real GDP per person.

## ■ AP Self Test 25.3

### True or false

1. The classical theory of growth concludes that eventually real GDP per person returns to the subsistence level.

2. According to the neoclassical theory, the rate of technological change does not influence the rate of economic growth.

3. The new growth theory predicts that economic growth can persist indefinitely.

### Multiple choice

1. Classical growth theory predicts that increases in
   a. real GDP per person are permanent and sustainable.
   b. real GDP per person are temporary and not sustainable.
   c. resources permanently increase labor productivity.
   d. resources permanently increase real GDP per person.
   e. competition increase economic growth.

2. If real income is above the subsistence level then, according to classical growth theory,
   a. the population will increase.
   b. the population will decrease.
   c. the standard of living will continue to improve.
   d. labor productivity will increase.
   e. more technological advances occur.

3. Neoclassical growth theory predicts that economic growth is
   a. only temporary due to overpopulation.
   b. the result of technological advances.
   c. impossible due to extremes in weather.
   d. caused by women entering the work force.
   e. increased by decreasing labor productivity.

4. The new growth theory states that
   a. technological advances are the result of random chance.
   b. technological advances result from choices.
   c. technological advances are the responsibility of the government.
   d. the subsistence income level leads to technological advances.
   e. it is impossible to replicate production activities.

### Short Response Question

1. What role does population growth play in each of the three growth theories?

### Long Response Questions

1. What role do technological advances play in each of the three growth theories?

2. Which growth theory is most pessimistic about the prospects for persistent economic growth? Which is most optimistic?

## CHECKPOINT 25.4

## ■ Describe policies that might speed economic growth.

### Quick Review

- *Preconditions for economic growth* The three preconditions are economic freedom, property rights, and markets.

- *Policies to achieve growth* Five policies are to create incentive mechanisms, encourage saving, encourage research and development, encourage international trade, and improve the quality of education.

### Additional Practice Problem 25.4

1. In 1949 East and West Germany had about the same real GDP per person. By 1989 West Germany had a real GDP per person more than twice the level of East Germany's. Why did East Germany grow so much more slowly than West Germany over those 40 years?

### Solution to Additional Practice Problem 25.4

1. In 1949, East Germany was formed with state ownership of capital and land, and virtually no economic freedom. West Germany was formed with private ownership of most capital and land, and significant economic freedom.

West Germany had the preconditions for economic growth; East Germany did not. When East Germany collapsed in 1989, West Germany had more human capital, more capital per hour of labor, and better technology. The different incentives had given West German workers the incentive to acquire human capital, West German investors the incentive to acquire physical capital, and West German entrepreneurs the incentive to innovate new and better technology.

## ■ AP Self Test 25.4

### True or false

1. To achieve economic growth, economic freedom must be coupled with a democratic political system.

2. Markets slow specialization and hence slow economic growth.

3. Encouraging saving can increase the growth of capital and stimulate economic growth.

4. Limiting international trade will increase economic growth.

### Multiple choice

1. Economic freedom means that
   a. firms are regulated by the government.
   b. some goods and services are free.
   c. people are able to make personal choices and their property is protected.
   d. the rule of law does not apply.
   e. the nation's government is a democracy.

2. Property rights protect
   a. only the rights to physical property.
   b. only the rights to financial property.
   c. all rights except rights to intellectual property.
   d. rights to physical property, financial property, and intellectual property.
   e. the government's right to impose taxes.

3. Which of the following statements is FALSE?
   a. Saving helps create economic growth.
   b. Improvements in the quality of education are important for economic growth.
   c. Free international trade helps create economic growth.
   d. Faster population growth is the key to growth in real GDP per person.
   e. Economic freedom requires property rights.

4. Saving
   a. slows growth because it decreases consumption.
   b. finances investment which brings capital accumulation.
   c. has no impact on economic growth.
   d. is very low in most East Asian nations.
   e. is important for a country to gain the benefits of international trade.

5. Economic growth is enhanced by
   a. free international trade.
   b. limiting international trade so that the domestic economy can prosper.
   c. discouraging saving, because increased saving means less spending.
   d. ignoring incentive systems.
   e. increasing welfare payments to the poor so they can afford to buy goods.

### Long Response Questions

1. Does persistent economic growth necessarily occur when a nation meets all the preconditions for growth?

2. What role do specialization and trade play in determining economic growth?

## YOUIR AP SELF TEST ANSWERS

### ■ CHECKPOINT 25.1

**True or false**

1. True; page 620
2. True; page 620
3. True; page 621
4. False; page 621

**Multiple choice**

1. a; page 620
2. b; page 620
3. a; page 621
4. b; page 621
5. b; page 621

**Short Response Questions**

1. 10 percent; 10 percent; 10 percent; page 620.

| Country | Real GDP 2007 | Real GDP 2008 | Growth rate |
|---------|---------------|---------------|-------------|
| A | $248 million | $257 million | 3.6 percent |
| B | $175 million | $188 million | 7.4 percent |
| C | $453 million | $467 million | 3.1 percent |
| D | $129 million | $141 million | 9.3 percent |
| E | $373 million | $396 million | 6.2 percent |

2. The completed table is above; page 620.
3. a. 1 percent; 2 percent; –1 percent; 0 percent; page 621.
   b. 2005 and 2006; page 620.
4. Use the Rule of 70. So, 70 ÷ 3 = 23.3 years; 70 ÷ 4 = 17.5 years; 70 ÷ 5 = 14 years; page 621.

### ■ CHECKPOINT 25.2

**True or false**

1. True; page 624
2. True; page 625
3. False; page 625
4. True; page 626

**Multiple choice**

1. c; page 624
2. e; page 624
3. d; page 625
4. a; page 625
5. c; page 625

**Short Response Questions**

1. Labor productivity equals real GDP ÷ aggregate hours. So labor productivity in 1964 was $22.45 an hour; in 1974 was $27.22 an hour; in 1984 was $31.35 an hour; in 1994 was $37.07 an hour; and in 2004 was $45.88 an hour; page 624.
2. Real GDP is $9 trillion; page 624.

**Long Response Question**

1. Labor productivity is increased by three factors. First, increasing saving and investment in physical capital gives workers more capital with which to work. Second, increasing the amount of human capital makes workers more productive and increases labor productivity. Finally, discovering new technologies makes workers more productive and increases labor productivity. All of these are important for an economy because it is increases in labor productivity that leads to increases in the standard of living; pages 625-626.

### ■ CHECKPOINT 25.3

**True or false**

1. True; pages 630-631
2. False; page 632
3. False; page 635

**Multiple choice**

1. b; pages 630-631
2. a; page 630
3. b; page 632
4. b; pages 633-634

**Short Response Question**

1. Population growth plays a crucial role only in the classical growth theory. In that theory population growth leads the econ-

omy back to a subsistence real income; pages 630-631.

**Long Response Questions**

1. In the classical growth theory, advances in technology start a temporary period of economic growth but as time passes and the population grows, economic growth slows and the economy returns to a subsistence level of income. In the neoclassical growth theory, economic growth continues as long as technology advances but technological growth is assumed to be the result of random chance. In the new growth theory, technology grows indefinitely and, as a result, economic growth continues indefinitely; pages 630, 632, 633-635.

2. The most optimistic theory is the new growth theory, which concludes that economic growth can continue forever. The most pessimistic theory is the classical theory, which concludes that the economy will return to a subsistence level of real income; pages 630-631, 634-635.

## ■ CHECKPOINT 25.4

**True or false**

1. False; page 639
2. False; pages 639-640

3. True; page 640
4. False; page 641

**Multiple choice**

1. c; page 639
2. d; page 639
3. d; page 639-640
4. b; page 640
5. a; page 641

**Long Response Questions**

1. No. The preconditions for growth are necessary for growth to occur. But for growth to be persistent, people must face incentives that encourage saving and investment, expansion of human capital, and the discovery and application of new technologies; pages 639-640.

2. Growth begins when people can specialize in the activities in which they have a comparative advantage and trade with each other. As an economy reaps the benefits from specialization and trade, production and consumption grow, real GDP per person increases, and the standard of living rises; page 640.

# Money and the Monetary System

## Chapter 26

Chapter 26 defines money, describes the U.S. monetary system, and describes the functions of the Federal Reserve System.

### ■ Define money and describe its functions.

Money is any commodity or token that is generally accepted as a means of payment. Money serves three functions. It is a medium of exchange (an object that is generally accepted in return for goods and services), a unit of account (an agreed-upon measure for stating the prices of goods and services), and a store of value (any commodity or token that can be held and exchanged later for goods and services). Money consists of currency (dollar bills and coins) and deposits at banks and other financial institutions. Currency in a bank is not money. Deposits are money but checks are not money. Credit cards, debit cards, and electronic checks are not money. M1 and M2 are two official measures of money. M1 is currency held by individuals and businesses and traveler's checks plus checkable deposits owned by individuals and businesses. M2 is M1 plus savings and time deposits, and money market funds and other deposits. Some items in M2 are not technically money because they are not a means of payment.

### ■ Describe the monetary system and explain the functions of banks and other monetary institutions.

The monetary system consists of the Federal Reserve and the banks and other institutions that accept deposits and provide the services that enable people and businesses to make and receive payments. Three types of financial institutions are commercial banks, thrift institutions, and money market funds. Banks make loans at a higher interest rate than the interest rate paid on deposits. A bank has four types of assets: cash assets, interbank loans, securities, and loans. A bank's cash assets consist of its reserves and funds that are due from other banks as payments for checks that are being cleared. Monetary institutions create liquidity, lower the costs of lending and borrowing, pool risks, and make payments.

### ■ Describe the functions of the Federal Reserve System.

The Federal Reserve System is the central bank of the United States. The Fed conducts the nation's monetary policy. The Board of Governors has seven members. There are 12 regional Federal Reserve banks. The Federal Open Market Committee is the Fed's main policy-making committee and consists of the Board of Governors, the president of the Federal Reserve Bank of New York, and four presidents of other regional Federal Reserve banks. The Fed uses three tools to control the quantity of money: required reserve ratios (the minimum percentage of deposits banks must hold as reserves), discount rate (the interest rate at which the Fed stands ready to lend reserves to commercial banks), and open market operations (purchase or sale of government securities by the Fed in the open market). The monetary base is the sum of coins, Federal Reserve notes, and banks' reserves held at the Fed. To decrease the quantity of money, the Fed can increase the required reserve ratio, raise the discount rate, or sell securities in the open market.

## EXPANDED CHAPTER CHECKLIST

**When you have completed this chapter, you will be able to:**

### 1 Define money and describe its functions.

- Define money and discuss how money serves as a medium of exchange, unit of account, and store of value.
- Categorize currency in a bank, checks, credit cards, debit cards, e-checks, and e-cash as money or not money.
- Define M1 and M2.

### 2 Describe the monetary system and explain the functions of banks and other monetary institutions.

- Describe the different types of financial institutions.
- Explain how a commercial bank achieves its goal of maximizing its stockholders' long-term wealth.
- Explain the four economic functions of monetary institutions.

### 3 Describe the functions of the Federal Reserve System.

- Describe the organizational structure of the Fed and the functions of each part of the structure.
- Describe the Fed's policy tools and briefly summarize how each works.
- Define monetary base.

## YOUR AP TEST HINTS

### AP Topics

| Topic on your AP test | Corresponding textbook section |
|---|---|
| **Financial sector** | |
| Money and Banking | Chapter 26 |
| • Definition of financial assets | Checkpoint 26.1 |
| • Measures of money | Checkpoint 26.1 |
| • Loanable funds market | Checkpoint 26.2 |
| • Tools of monetary policy | Checkpoint 26.3 |

### AP Vocabulary

- On the AP test, the financial markets all taken together can be called the "loanable funds market."

## CHECKPOINT 26.1

### ■ Define money and describe its functions.

**Quick Review**

- *M1* M1 consists of currency held by individuals and businesses, and traveler's checks plus checkable deposits owned by individuals and businesses. Currency inside banks is not counted.
- *M2* M2 consists of M1 plus savings deposits and small time deposits, money market funds, and other deposits.

**Additional Practice Problems 26.1**

1. You go to the bank and withdraw $200 from your checking account. You keep $100 in cash and deposit the other $100 in your savings account. What is the change in M1? What is the change in M2?

2. Janice goes to her bank's website and transfers $300 from her checking account to her savings account. What is the change in M1? What is the change in M2

3. In January 2001, currency held by individuals and businesses was $534.9 billion; traveler's checks were $8.1 billion; checkable deposits owned by individuals and businesses were $559.3 billion; savings deposits were $1,889.7 billion; small time deposits were $1,052.6 billion; and money market funds and other deposits were $952 billion.
   a. What was M1 in January 2001?
   b. What was M2 in January 2001?

**Solutions to Additional Practice Problems 26.1**

1. Your checking account decreased by $200, your currency increased by $100, and your savings account increased by $100. M1, which includes your currency and your checkable deposit, is

changed by the decrease in the checking account and the increase in currency. The net effect on M1 is –$200 + $100 = –$100, that is, M1 decreases by $100. M2, which includes your currency, your checkable deposits, and your savings account, does not change. The change in your checkable deposits, –$200, is balanced by the change in your currency, +$100, and the change in your savings account, +100. There was no change in M2.

2. M1 decreases by $300. While the funds were in Janice's checking account, they were part of M1. But once they are transferred to her savings account, they are no longer part of M1. M2 does not change. The $300 was part of M2 when it was in Janice's checking account because funds in checking accounts are part of M1 and all of M1 is in M2. And, funds in savings accounts are also part of M2. So switching funds from a checking account to a savings account does not change M2.

3a. M1 is the sum of currency, traveler's checks, and checkable deposits owned by individuals and businesses. So, M1 equals $534.9 billion + $8.1 billion + $559.3 billion, which is $1,102.3 billion.

3b. M2 equals M1 plus savings deposits, small time deposits, and money market funds and other deposits. So M2 equals $1,102.3 billion + $1,889.7 billion + $1,052.6 billion + $952 billion, which is $4,996.6 billion.

## ■ AP Self Test 26.1

### True or false

1. Using money as a medium of exchange is called barter.

2. Prices in terms of money reflect money's role as a unit of account.

3. Currency is money but checkable deposits at banks are not money.

4. A debit card is not money.

5. M1 and M2 are official measures of money.

### Multiple choice

1. Which of the following best defines what money is now and what it has been in the past?
   a. currency
   b. currency plus checking deposits
   c. currency plus credit cards
   d. anything accepted as a means of payment
   d. anything used as a store of value

2. For something to be a "means of payment" means that the asset
   a. is valuable and backed by gold.
   b. is valuable and backed by the government.
   c. can be used to settle a debt.
   d. requires a double coincidence of wants.
   e. must be used when bartering.

3. Which of the following is not a function of money?
   i. unit of account
   ii. store of value
   iii. unit of debt
   a. i only.
   b. ii only.
   c. iii only.
   d. Both ii and iii.
   e. Both i and ii.

4. Barter is
   a. the exchange of goods and services for money.
   b. the pricing of goods and services with one agreed upon standard.
   c. the exchange of goods and services directly for other goods and services.
   d. a generally accepted means of payment.
   e. storing money for use at a later date.

5. If someone buries money in a tin can beneath a tree, the money is functioning as a
   a. medium of exchange.
   b. unit of account.
   c. means of payment.
   d. store of value.
   e. bartering tool.

6. Credit cards, debit cards, and e-checks are
   a. always counted as money.
   b. not money.
   c. sometimes counted as money, depending on how they are used.
   d. sometimes counted as money, depending on what is purchased.
   e. sometimes counted as money, depending on what measure of money is being used.

7. Which of the following counts as part of M1?
   a. $5,000 worth of gold
   b. $5,000 worth of government bonds
   c. $5,000 in a checking account
   d. $5,000 credit line on a credit card
   e. $5,000 of real estate

8. M2 equals
   a. M1 and is just another name for currency outside of banks.
   b. M1 plus savings deposits, small time deposits, and money market fund deposits.
   c. M1 minus traveler's checks because they are not really money.
   d. currency plus savings deposits, all time deposits, and money market funds and other deposits.
   e. M1 plus savings deposits and small time deposits minus money market fund deposits.

9. If currency held by individuals and businesses is $800 billion; traveler's checks are $10 billion; checkable deposits owned by individuals and businesses are $700 billion; savings deposits are $4,000 billion; small time deposits are $1,000 billion; and money market funds and other deposits are $800 billion, then M1 equals ____ billion.
   a. $7,310
   b. $5,800
   c. $2,510
   d. $1,510
   e. $710

10. If currency held by individuals and businesses is $800 billion; traveler's checks are $10 billion; checkable deposits owned by individuals and businesses are $700 billion; savings deposits are $4,000 billion; small time deposits are $1,000 billion; and money market funds and other deposits are $800 billion, then M2 equals ____ billion.
   a. $7,310
   b. $5,800
   c. $2,510
   d. $1,510
   e. $710

## Short Response Questions

1. Why was it possible at one time to use whale's teeth as money?
2. Why is currency money?
3. Why are e-checks not money?

## Long Response Questions

1. What are the functions of money?
2. In January 2005, currency held by individuals and businesses was $699.6 billion; traveler's checks were $7.5 billion; checkable deposits owned by individuals and businesses were $649.2 billion; savings deposits were $3,544.7 billion; small time deposits were $824.5 billion; and money market funds and other deposits were $711.4 billion.
   a. What was M1 in January 2005?
   b. What was M2 in January 2005?
3. Some parts of M2 are not money. Why are these parts included in M2?
4. How does the withdrawal of $50 in currency from a checking account affect the amount of M1? M2?

## CHECKPOINT 26.2

■ **Describe the monetary system and explain the functions of banks and other monetary institutions.**

### Quick Review

- *Reserves* A bank's reserves consist of the currency in its vault plus the balance on its reserve account at a Federal Reserve Bank.

### Additional Practice Problems 26.2

1. The Acme Bank just sold $100 in securities in exchange for a $100 bill. It made a $50 loan, and the borrower left with the cash. It also accepted a $60 cash deposit.
    a. How have the bank's reserves changed as a result of all these actions?
    b. How have its deposits changed?

2. A bank has the following deposits and assets: $300 in checkable deposits, $800 in savings deposits, $900 in small time deposits, $1,000 in loans to businesses, $950 in government securities, $20 in currency, and $30 in its reserve account at the Fed. Calculate the bank's:
    a. Total deposits
    b. Deposits that are part of M1
    c. Deposits that are part of M2
    d. Reserves
    e. What is the ratio of the bank's reserves to its deposits?

### Solutions to Additional Practice Problems 26.2

1a. The $100 sale of securities adds $100 to reserves. The $50 loan which the borrower then withdrew as cash removes $50 from the bank and out of its reserves, and the $60 deposit adds to reserves. The net result is +$100 − $50 + $60, which is +$110. Acme has $110 more in reserves.

1b. The $60 deposit is the only transaction that affects its deposits, so deposits rise by $60.

2a. Total deposits are the sum of checkable deposits, $300, savings deposits, $800, and small time deposits, $900, which equals a total of $2,000.

2b. The only deposits that are part of M1 are checkable deposits, $300.

2c. All of the bank's deposits are part of M2, so deposits that are part of M2 are $2,000.

2d. Reserves are the currency in the bank's vault plus the balance on its reserve account at a Federal Reserve Bank. Reserves are $20 + $30, which equals $50.

2e. The ratio of reserves to deposits is $50 ÷ $2,000, which equals 2.5 percent.

### ■ AP Self Test 26.2

#### True or false

1. A commercial bank accepts checkable deposits, savings deposits, and time deposits.

2. A commercial bank maximizes its stockholders' long-term wealth by refusing to make any risky loans.

3. When a credit union has excess reserves, it makes loans to its members at an interest rate called the federal funds rate.

4. Thrift institutions provide most of the nation's bank deposits.

5. By lending to a large number of businesses and individuals, a bank lowers the average risk it faces.

#### Multiple choice

1. A commercial bank's main goal is to
    a. provide loans to its customers.
    b. maximize the long-term wealth of its stockholders.
    c. help the government when it needs money.
    d. lend money to the Federal Reserve banks.
    e. open checking accounts.

2. A bank divides its assets into four parts:
    a. cash assets, interbank loans, securities, and loans.
    b. reserves, securities, bonds, and loans.
    c. reserves, bonds, cash securities, and interbank loans.
    d. securities, reserves, debts, and interbank cash.
    e. reserves, checkable deposits, securities, and loans.

3. A commercial bank's reserves are
    a. bonds issued by the U.S. government that are very safe.
    b. the provision of funds to businesses and individuals.
    c. currency in its vault plus the balance on its reserve account at a Federal Reserve Bank.
    d. savings and time deposits.
    e. its loans.

4. A bank has $400 in checking deposits, $800 in savings deposits, $700 in time deposits, $900 in loans to businesses, $300 in outstanding credit card balances, $500 in government securities, $10 in currency in its vault, and $20 in deposits at the Fed. The bank's deposits that are part of M1 equal
   a. $1,900.
   b. $400.
   c. $1,210.
   d. $530.
   e. $410.

5. Which of the following accepts deposits from or sell shares to the general public?
   i. money market funds.
   ii. thrift institutions.
   iii. commercial banks.
   a. i only.
   b. ii only.
   c. iii only.
   d. ii and iii.
   e. i, ii, and iii.

6. Which of the following is a thrift institution?
   a. a savings and loan association
   b. a money market fund
   c. a commercial bank
   d. a loan institution
   e. the Federal Reserve

7. Banks and other monetary institutions perform which of the following functions?
   i. create liquidity
   ii. pool the risks of lending
   iii. make loans to the Federal Reserve
   a. i only.
   b. ii only.
   c. iii only.
   d. i and ii.
   e. i, ii, and iii.

8. A liquid asset is
   a. any deposit held at a commercial bank.
   b. bank loans made to low-risk borrowers.
   c. any asset than can be converted into money easily and with certainty.
   d. any deposit held with the Federal Reserve.
   e. any liability of a commercial bank.

**Short Response Questions**

1. What are a bank's reserves? How does a bank use its account at the Federal Reserve Bank?

2. Which is a larger percentage of M1: commercial bank deposits or thrift institution deposits?

3. What economic functions are performed by the nation's monetary institutions?

**Long Response Question**

1. What does it mean for banks to "pool risk"?

## CHECKPOINT 26.3

■ **Describe the functions of the Federal Reserve System.**

*Quick Review*
- *Federal Reserve System* The Federal Reserve System is the central bank of the United States. It conducts the nation's monetary policy.

**Additional Practice Problems 26.3**
1. What are required reserve ratios?
2. What is the discount rate?
3. In August, 2005 Federal Reserve notes and coins were $785 billion, and banks' reserves at the Fed are $9 billion, the gold stock was $11 billion, and the Fed owned $742 billion of government securities. What did the monetary base equal?

**Solutions to Additional Practice Problems 26.3**
1. Banks are required by law to hold a certain fraction of their deposits as reserves. The Federal Reserve determines what fraction banks must hold as reserves. These fractions are called the banks' required reserve ratios.

2. Banks can borrow reserves from the Federal Reserve. The interest rate they pay on these loans is the discount rate.

3. The monetary base is the sum of the coins and Federal Reserve notes plus banks' reserves at the Fed. In this case the monetary base equals $785 billion + $9 billion, which is $794 billion.

## ■ AP Self Test 26.3

**True or false**

1. The Federal Reserve System is the central bank of the United States.

2. In practice, the power in the Fed resides with the Board of Governors.

3. An open market operation is the purchase or sale of government securities by the Federal Reserve from the U.S. government.

4. If banks use $1 million of reserves to buy $1 million worth of newly printed bank notes from the Fed, the monetary base does not change.

5. Federal Reserve notes are an asset of the Fed.

**Multiple choice**

1. Regulating the amount of money in the United States is one of the most important responsibilities of the
   a. State Department.
   b. state governments.
   c. Treasury Department.
   d. Federal Reserve.
   e. U.S. Mint.

2. The Board of Governors of the Federal Reserve System has
   a. 12 members appointed by the president of the United States.
   b. 12 members elected by the public.
   c. seven members appointed by the president of the United States.
   d. seven members elected by the public.
   e. seven members appointed to life terms.

3. The Fed's monetary policy is determined by the
   a. Federal Open Market Committee.
   b. Executive Council to the Governor.
   c. Regional Federal Reserve Banks.
   d. Board of Governors.
   e. Federal Monetary Policy Committee.

4. The most influential position in the Federal Reserve System is the
   a. president of the Federal Reserve Bank of New York.
   b. chairman of the Board of Governors.
   c. chairman of the Federal Reserve Bank presidents.
   d. president of the Federal Reserve Bank of Chicago.
   e. most senior member of the Board of Governors.

5. The Fed's policy tools include
   a. required reserve ratios, the discount rate, and open market operations.
   b. holding deposits for the U.S. government, reserve requirements, and the discount rate.
   c. setting regulations for lending standards and approving or rejecting loans banks make to large corporations.
   d. supervision of the banking system and buying and selling commercial banks.
   e. required reserve ratios, income tax rates, and open market operations.

6. The minimum percent of deposits that banks must hold and cannot loan is determined by the
   a. interest rate.
   b. discount rate.
   c. required reserve ratio.
   d. federal funds rate.
   e. ratio of M2 to M1.

7. The discount rate is the interest rate that
   a. commercial banks charge their customers.
   b. commercial banks charge each other for the loan of reserves.
   c. the Fed charges the government.
   d. the Fed charges commercial banks for the loan of reserves.
   e. the Fed pays commercial banks on their reserves held at the Fed.

8. The monetary base is the
   a. minimum reserves banks must hold to cover any losses from unpaid loans.
   b. sum of coins, Federal Reserve notes, and banks' reserves at the Fed.
   c. sum of gold and foreign exchange held by the Fed.
   d. sum of government securities and loans to banks held by the Fed.
   e. sum of coins, required reserves, and bank loans.

9. If Federal Reserve notes and coins are $765 billion, and banks' reserves at the Fed are $8 billion, the gold stock is $11 billion, and the Fed owns $725 billion of government securities, what does the monetary base equal?
   a. $765 billion.
   b. $773 billion.
   c. $776 billion.
   d. $744 billion.
   e. $1,509 billion.

10. If the Federal Reserve _____ the required reserve ratio, the quantity of money _____.
    a. lowers; increases
    b. lowers; decreases
    c. raises; does not change
    d. raises; increases
    e. Not enough information is given because the effect depends also on the size of the monetary base.

**Short Response Questions**

1. How many people are on the Board of Governors of the Federal Reserve System? How are they selected?

2. What is the monetary base?

3. Are U.S. government securities an asset or a liability of the Federal Reserve? Are Federal Reserve notes an asset or a liability of the Federal Reserve?

**Long Response Questions**

1. What is the FOMC and who are its members?

2. Suppose that banks' deposits are $600 billion and that the required reserve ratio is 10 percent.
   a. What is the minimum amount of reserves banks must hold?
   b. Suppose the Federal Reserve lowers the required reserve ratio to 8 percent. Now what is the minimum amount of reserves banks must hold?
   c. Suppose the Federal Reserve raises the required reserve ratio to 12 percent. Now what is the minimum amount of reserves banks must hold?

# YOUR AP SELF TEST ANSWERS

## ■ CHECKPOINT 26.1

### True or false

1. False;  page 649
2. True;  page 649
3. False;  page 650
4. True;  page 652
5. True;  page 653

### Multiple choice

1. d;  page 648
2. c;  page 648
3. c;  pages 648-649
4. c;  page 649
5. d;  page 649
6. b;  pages 651-652
7. c;  page 653
8. b;  page 653
9. d;  page 653
10. a;  page 653

### Short Response Questions

1. It was possible to use whale's teeth as money because whale's teeth were generally accepted as a means of payment. At one time, most people were willing to trade goods and services in exchange for whale's teeth;  page 648.

2. Currency is money because it is generally accepted as a means of payment. It is generally accepted because the government has declared that currency is money, so that currency is fiat money;  page 650.

3. E-checks are not money because they are instructions to transfer money from one person's deposit account to another person's deposit account;  page 652.

### Long Response Questions

1. Money has three functions. It is a medium of exchange, an object that is generally accepted in return for goods and services. It is a unit of account, an agreed-upon measure for stating the prices of goods and services. And it is a store of value, a commodity or token that can be held and exchanged at a later date for goods and services;  pages 647-648.

2. a. M1 is the sum of currency, traveler's checks, and checkable deposits owned by individuals and businesses. So, M1 equals $699.6 billion + $7.5 billion + $649.2 billion, which is $1,356.3 billion;  page 643.

   b. M2 equals M1 plus savings deposits, small time deposits, and money market funds and other deposits. So M2 equals $1,356.3 billion + $3,544.7 billion + $824.5 billion + $711.4 billion, which is $6,436.9 billion;  page 653.

3. Time deposits, money market funds, and some of the savings deposits included in M2 are not money. They are not money because they are not a means of payment. They are included in M2 because they are very easily converted into money;  page 653.

4. Withdrawing $50 in currency from a checking account has no effect on the overall size of M1 because it converts $50 of checkable deposits into $50 of currency. Similarly there is no effect on the overall size of M2.

## ■ CHECKPOINT 26.2

### True or false

1. True;  page 656
2. False;  page 657
3. False;  pages 657-658
4. False;  page 658
5. True;  page 660

### Multiple choice

1. b;  page 657
2. a;  page 657
3. c;  page 657
4. b;  page 657
5. e;  page 657
6. a;  page 658
7. d;  page 660
8. c;  page 660

**Short Response Questions**

1. A bank's reserves are the currency in its vault plus the balance on its reserve account at a Federal Reserve bank. A bank uses its account at the Fed to receive and make payments to other banks and to obtain currency; page 657.

2. Commercial bank deposits are a larger percentage of M1 than thrift institution deposits. Commercial bank deposits are about 38 percent of M1, while thrift institution deposits are about 10 percent; page 659.

3. The nation's monetary institutions perform four economic functions: They create liquidity, they lower the cost of lending and borrowing, they pool risks, and they make payments; pages 660-661.

**Long Response Question**

1. "Pooling risk" refers to the point that making loans is risky because the borrower might not repay the loan. If a lender has loaned to only one borrower who does not repay the loan, the lender suffers a large loss. Banks make loans to many different borrowers and "pool" (or gather together) the risk of the loans. Although some loans will not be repaid, the majority will be repaid and so the average risk from failure to be repaid is lower; page 660.

## ■ CHECKPOINT 26.3

**True or false**

1. True;  page 663
2. False;  page 665
3. False;  page 666
4. True;  page 666
5. False;  page 666

**Multiple choice**

1. d;  page 663
2. c;  page 664
3. a;  page 664
4. b;  page 664
5. a;  pages 665-666
6. c;  page 665
7. d;  page 665
8. b;  page 666
9. b;  page 666
10. a;  page 667

**Short Response Questions**

1. There are seven members on the Board of Governors of the Federal Reserve System. They are appointed by the president of the United States and confirmed by the U.S. Senate;  page 664.

2. The monetary base is the sum of coins, Federal Reserve notes, and banks' reserves at the Federal Reserve;  page 666.

3. U.S. government securities are the Federal Reserve's largest asset. Federal Reserve notes (currency) are the largest liability of the Fed; page 666.

**Long Response Questions**

1. The FOMC is the Federal Open Market Committee and it is the main policy-making committee of the Federal Reserve. The FOMC is the group that decides upon the nation's monetary policy. The members are the seven members of the Board of Governors, the president of the Federal Reserve Bank of New York, and, on an annual rotating basis, four presidents of the other regional Federal Reserve banks;  page 664.

2. a. If the required reserve ratio is 10 percent, banks must keep ($600 billion) × (0.10) = $60 billion as reserves;  page 665.

   b. If the required reserve ratio is lowered to 8 percent, banks must keep ($600 billion) × (0.08) = $48 billion as reserves. A decrease in the required reserve ratio decreases the total amount of reserves banks must keep. Banks will then loan the excess reserves they now possess;  page 665.

   c. If the required reserve ratio is raised to 12 percent, banks must keep ($600 billion) × (0.12) = $72 billion as reserves. An increase in the required reserve ratio increases the total amount of reserves banks must keep. Banks will now call in and reduce their outstanding loans;  page 665.

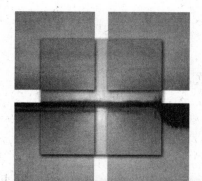

# Money Creation and Control

## Chapter 27

Chapter 27 explains how banks create money and how the money supply is controlled by the Fed.

■ **Explain how banks create money by making loans.**

Banks accept deposits. They hold some deposits as reserves and use the rest to buy government securities and make loans. Deposits are a liability of the bank; reserves, government securities, and loans are assets of the bank. When a check is written, the recipient deposits it in another bank. Deposits and reserves in the first bank decrease and in the second bank increase. The total amount of deposits, however, does not change. The required reserve ratio is the ratio of reserves to deposits that banks are required by regulation to hold. Excess reserves are actual reserves minus required reserves. Banks use excess reserves to buy government securities or make loans. When a bank makes a loan, it deposits the amount loaned in the checkable deposit of the borrower. The bank has now created money. To spend the loan, the borrower writes a check. The bank loses deposits and reserves when the check clears. The bank in which the check is deposited gains the reserves and deposits. This bank now has excess reserves, which it lends. When this loan is spent, a third bank gains reserves and deposits. The process is limited and eventually concludes because at each round the change in excess reserves shrinks. An initial increase in a bank's excess reserves leads to a larger increase in deposits because the initial increase is spread throughout different banks as the funds are repeatedly loaned and deposited throughout the banking system. The amount of the increase depends on the required reserve ratio; the larger the required reserve ratio, the smaller the increase.

■ **Explain how the Fed controls the quantity of money.**

Open market operations are the major policy tool the Fed uses to change the quantity of money. If the Fed buys government securities, banks' reserves increase and excess reserves increase. Banks lend the excess reserves, new deposits are created, and the quantity of money increases. If the Fed sells government securities, banks' reserves decrease and excess reserves decrease. Banks decrease their lending, deposits are destroyed, and the quantity of money decreases. Whether the Fed transacts with banks or the nonbank public does not change the effect of an open market operation. The monetary base changes by the amount of the open market purchase or sale but the quantity of money changes by more than the amount of the open market purchase or sale. The money multiplier is the number by which a change in the monetary base is multiplied to find the resulting change in the quantity of money. The money multiplier equals $(1 + C) \div (R + C)$ where $C$, the currency drain, is the ratio of currency to deposits and $R$ is the required reserve ratio. A currency drain is currency held outside of the banks. The larger the currency drain and the larger the required reserve ratio, the smaller is the money multiplier because banks receive fewer deposits in each round of the multiplier lending and depositing process.

## EXPANDED CHAPTER CHECKLIST

**When you have completed this chapter, you will be able to:**

**1 Explain how banks create money by making loans.**

- Define the balance sheet and describe the assets and liabilities that appear on a bank's balance sheet.
- Calculate the amount of reserves a bank must hold.
- Calculate a bank's excess reserves.
- Explain how loans made by the banking system create money and explain why the amount of loans made exceeds the initial change in reserves.

**2 Explain how the Fed controls the quantity of money.**

- Describe an open market operation and trace the impact of an open market operation on the quantity of money.
- Explain why there is a multiplier effect from an open market operation and discuss the factors that affect the size of the effect.
- Calculate the money multiplier and use it to determine the effect a change in the monetary base has on the quantity of money.

## YOUR AP TEST HINTS

*AP Topics*

| Topic on your AP test | Corresponding textbook section |
|---|---|
| **Financial sector** | |
| Banks and Money Creation | Chapter 27 |
| • Banks and money creation | Checkpoints 27.1, 27.2 |

*Extra AP material*

- Be sure to understand how the Fed's policy tools work. An open market purchase of government securities by the Fed increases banks' excess reserves. Similarly, a decrease in the required reserve ratio increases banks' excess reserves and a decrease in the discount rate increases banks' willingness to borrow reserves, which leads to an increase in excessive reserves. In *all* these cases, the increase in excess reserves starts the multiple creation of bank deposits illustrated in Figure 27.3, so in *all* these cases the quantity of money increases.

- The impact of a currency drain on the money creation process needs to be thoroughly understood. A currency drain decreases the fraction of a bank's loan that is deposited back into the banking system. The larger the currency drain, the smaller are banks' excess reserves (and hence its loans) in each round in the multiple creation of bank deposits process. As a result, the smaller is the ultimate increase in the quantity of money from an initial increase in reserves.

- Leakages in the money creation process include the currency drain and banks' willingness to hold, rather than loan, excessive reserves. In both cases, banks loan less at each round in the multiple creation of bank deposits process so that the ultimate increase in the quantity of money from an initial increase in reserves is smaller and the money multiplier is smaller.

## CHECKPOINT 27.1

- **Explain how banks create money by making loans.**

*Quick Review*

- *Excess reserves* Excess reserves equal actual reserves minus required reserves.

**Additional Practice Problem 27.1**

1. The required reserve ratio is 0.05 and banks have no excess reserves. Katie deposits $500 in currency in her bank. Calculate:
   a. The change in the bank's reserves as soon as Katie makes the deposit.

b. The bank's excess reserves as soon as Katie makes the deposit.

c. The maximum amount that Katie's bank can loan.

d. The maximum amount of new money that the banking system can create.

e. The maximum amount of loans that the banking system can make.

**Solution to Additional Practice Problem 27.1**

1a. The new deposit of $500 increases the bank's actual reserves by $500.

1b. The bank is required to keep 5 percent of deposits as reserves. So required reserves increase by 5 percent of the deposit, or ($500) × (0.05), which is $25. As a result, excess reserves, which are actual reserves minus required reserves, increase by $500 − $25, which is $475.

1c. The crucial point to keep in mind is that banks can loan their excess reserves in order to boost their revenue and profit. So Katie's bank can loan a maximum of $475.

1d. The banking system creates money by creating deposits. When a bank in the banking system makes a loan, it does so by creating a deposit. Katie's bank loans 0.95 of the initial deposit. When that $475 loan is deposited in another bank that bank will have $475 × 0.95, or $451.25 in excess reserves that it will loan. At each round in the process, the new loan and deposit is 0.95 of the previous loan and deposit. The ultimate increase in deposits equals $(1 \div [1 − L]) \times$ the initial increase in reserves, or $(1 \div [1 − 0.95]) \times \$500 = \$10,000$.

1e. As a result of the banking system, there are $10,000 of new deposits created. Of this $10,000, the initial $500 is the result of Katie's deposit in her bank. The remaining deposits are created by the banking systems' loans, which, when spent, are deposited into a bank. So the maximum amount of loans the banking system can create equals the total increase in deposits minus the initial deposit, which is $10,000 − $500 = $9,500.

## ■ AP Self Test 27.1

**True or false**

1. The first step in creating a bank is to accept deposits.

2. Checkable deposits are an asset on the bank's balance sheet.

3. A commercial bank's cash and its reserves at a Federal Reserve bank are assets on its balance sheet.

4. Excess reserves increase when the required reserve ratio increases, all other things remaining the same.

5. When banks clear checks, they create money.

6. When a bank increases its loans, it creates money.

7. The required reserve ratio has no effect on the amount of money banks can create.

8. An immigrant enters the United States and deposits $190,000 into a bank. The required reserve ratio is 5 percent. When the entire sequence of loans and deposits is completed, deposits increase by a maximum of $3.8 million.

**Multiple choice**

1. Which of the following actions is NOT carried out by a bank?
   a. buy government securities
   b. clear checks
   c. make loans
   d. print money
   e. accept deposits

2. A bank's balance sheet is a statement that summarizes
   a. only the bank's loans.
   b. only the bank's reserves.
   c. the bank's assets and liabilities.
   d. the number of banks in a community.
   e. the bank's profit and loss.

3. Cash in a bank is part of the bank's
   a. owners' equity.
   b. liabilities.
   c. assets.
   d. government securities.
   e. deposits.

4. Which of the following is a bank liability?
   a. checkable deposits
   b. government securities
   c. equipment
   d. loans
   e. reserves

5. If the required reserve ratio is 20 percent, then for every dollar that is deposited in the bank, the bank must
   a. keep 20 cents as reserves.
   b. keep 80 cents as reserves.
   c. loan 80 cents.
   d. loan 20 cents.
   e. keep 20 cents as reserves and loan 20 cents.

6. A bank has checkable deposits of $500,000, loans of $300,000, and government securities of $200,000. If the required reserve ratio is 10 percent, the amount of required reserves is
   a. $20,000.
   b. $30,000.
   c. $50,000.
   d. $500,000.
   e. $80,000.

7. Excess reserves are the
   a. same as the required reserves.
   b. amount of reserves the Fed requires banks to hold.
   c. amount of reserves held above what is required.
   d. amount of reserves a bank holds at the Fed.
   e. amount of reserves banks keep in their vaults..

8. Keisha writes a $500 check to Larry drawn on Community Bank. Larry deposits the $500 check in his checking account at Neighbors Bank. When the check clears both banks, ____ by $500.
   a. Community Bank's assets decrease
   b. Community Bank's assets increase
   c. Community Bank's liabilities increase
   d. Neighbors Bank's assets decrease
   e. Neighbors Bank's liabilities decrease

9. Banks can make loans up to an amount equal to their
   a. total deposits.
   b. total reserves.
   c. required reserves.
   d. excess reserves.
   e. total government securities.

10. The banking system can create more money than an initial increase in excess reserves
    a. because banks are sneaky.
    b. because the Fed lends it money.
    c. because excess reserves are loaned and then wind up as deposits in another bank.
    d. because banks charge more interest than they pay out.
    e. because banks' total reserves increase when their excess reserves increase.

11. The ____ the required reserve ratio, the ____ the ____ in deposits from an initial new deposit of $100,000 in currency.
    a. larger; larger; decrease
    b. larger; larger; increase
    c. larger; smaller; decrease
    d. smaller; larger; decrease
    e. smaller; larger; increase

12. If the required reserve ratio is 15 percent and banks loan all of their excess reserves, a new deposit of $20,000 leads to a total increase in deposits of
    a. $3,000.
    b. $20,000.
    c. $133,333.
    d. $200,000.
    e. $300,000.

**Short Response Questions**

| Assets | Liabilities |
| --- | --- |
| | |
| | |
| | |

1. The Bank of Townsville has reserves at the Fed of $100, owner's equity of $200, loans of $800, checkable deposits of $1,000, cash of $200, and government securities of $100. Arrange these entries in the balance sheet above.

| Round | Increase in deposits (dollars) | Increase in reserves (dollars) | Increase in excess reserves (dollars) | Loan (dollars) |
|-------|-------------------------------|-------------------------------|--------------------------------------|----------------|
| A | —— | —— | —— | —— |
| B | —— | —— | —— | —— |
| C | —— | —— | —— | —— |
| D | —— | —— | —— | —— |

2. Meg tutors 10 students during finals week and is paid $500 in cash. She deposits the $500 in her bank. The required reserve ratio is 10 percent and banks always loan the maximum possible.
   a. Starting with Meg's $500 deposit, complete the above table.
   b. After the first four rounds, what is the total increase in deposits?
   c. What will be the total increase in deposits?

**Long Response Questions**

1. The Bank of Utah has deposits of $500 million and reserves of $60 million. If the required reserve ratio is 10 percent, calculate the bank's excess reserves. How much can the bank loan? If the required reserve ratio is changed to 8 percent, calculate the bank's excess reserves. How much can the bank loan?

2. How does making a loan create a deposit?

3. Shaniq deposits $100 in cash in her checking account.
   a. If the required reserve ratio is 10 percent, what will be the total increase in deposits created by the banking system?
   b. If the required reserve ratio is 5 percent, percent, what will be the total increase in deposits created by the banking system?
   c. What is the relationship between the required reserve ratio and the total increase in deposits creates by the banking system?

## CHECKPOINT 27.2

■ **Explain how the Fed controls the quantity of money.**

*Quick Review*
- *Open market operation* The purchase or sale of government securities by the Fed in the open market.
- *Currency drain* Currency held by the public outside of banks; the currency drain equals the ratio of currency to deposits.
- *Money multiplier* The number by which a change in the monetary base is multiplied to find the resulting change in the quantity of money.

**Additional Practice Problems 27.2**

1. If the Fed makes an open market sale of $1 million of government securities to Bank of America, what initial changes occur on the Fed's balance sheet and on Bank of America's balance sheet? Be sure to tell if each change affects an asset or a liability.

2. If the required reserve ratio is 10 percent and the currency drain is 30 percent, what is the size of the money multiplier? By how much will a $10 billion increase in the monetary base change the quantity of money?

3. If the required reserve ratio is 20 percent and the currency drain is 30 percent, what is the size of the money multiplier? By how much will a $10 billion increase in the monetary base change the quantity of money?

4. Using problems 2 and 3, what is the effect of a rise in the required reserve ratio on the increase in the quantity of money?

**Solutions to Additional Practice Problems 27.2**

1. When the Fed sells $1 million of government securities, the Fed's holding of government securities decreases by $1 million. The Fed decreases Bank of America's reserves at the Fed by $1 million. One of the Fed's assets, government securities, and one of its liabilities, reserve deposits, decrease by $1 million. For Bank of America, its holdings of government securities increase by $1 million and its reserves at the Fed decrease by $1 million. For Bank of America, one of its assets, government securities, increases by $1 million, and another of its assets, reserves at the Fed, decrease by $1 million.

2. The money multiplier equals $(1 + C) \div (R + C)$ where $C$ is the currency drain and $R$ is the required reserve ratio, both expressed as decimals. So the money multiplier equals $(1 + 0.3) \div (0.1 + 0.3)$, which is 3.25. So a $10 billion increase in the monetary base increases the quantity of money by 3.25 × $10 billion, or $32.5 billion.

3. The money multiplier equals $(1 + C) \div (R + C)$ where $C$ is the currency drain and $R$ is the required reserve ratio, both expressed as decimals. So the money multiplier equals $(1 + 0.3) \div (0.2 + 0.3)$, which is 2.6. So a $10 billion increase in the monetary base increases the quantity of money by 2.6 × $10 billion, or $26 billion.

4. An increase in the required reserve ratio shrinks the amount by which the quantity of money increases.

## ■ AP Self Test 27.2

**True or false**

1. When the Fed buys securities in an open market operation, it pays for them with newly created bank reserves and money.

2. The Fed buys securities only from commercial banks.

3. When the Fed buys securities from a commercial bank, the banks' reserves and deposits at the Fed both increase.

4. When the Fed sells government securities, it decreases the quantity of banks' reserves.

5. When the Fed buys government securities, the effect on the money supply depends on whether the Fed buys the securities from a bank or the general public.

6. If the Fed increases the monetary base by $1 billion, the ultimate increase in the quantity of money will be less than $1 billion.

7. The larger the currency drain, the larger the money multiplier.

8. If the currency drain is 0.2 and the required reserve ratio is 0.1, the money multiplier is 1.675.

**Multiple choice**

1. When the Fed buys or sells securities, it is conducting ____ operation.
   a. a closed door
   b. an open market
   c. a multiplier
   d. a deposit
   e. a currency

2. When the Fed sells securities in an open market operation
   a. the monetary base increases and the money supply increases.
   b. the monetary base does not change.
   c. only commercial banks can be buyers.
   d. the federal funds rate does not change.
   e. buyers pay for the securities with money and bank reserves.

3. If the Fed buys securities from a commercial bank, the effect on the quantity of money
   a. is larger than when the Fed buys securities from the non-bank public.
   b. is less than when the Fed buys securities from the non-bank public.
   c. is the same as when the Fed buys securities from the non-bank public.
   d. depends on whether the bank was borrowing reserves from another bank.
   e. depends if the monetary base changes.

4. If the Fed buys government securities, then
   a. the quantity of money is not changed, just its composition.
   b. new bank reserves are created.
   c. the quantity of money decreases.
   d. bank reserves are destroyed.
   e. banks' excess reserves decrease.

5. The Citizens First Bank sells $100,000 of government securities to the Fed. This sale immediately
   a. decreases the quantity of money.
   b. decreases the bank's checkable deposits.
   c. increases the bank's reserves.
   d. decreases the bank's assets.
   e. increases the bank's required reserves..

6. The Fed buys $100 million U.S. government securities from Bank of America. Bank of America's balance sheet shows this transaction as ____ in total assets and ____ in reserves.
   a. no change; a $100 million decrease
   b. no change; a $100 million increase
   c. a $100 million increase; no change
   d. a $100 million increase; a $100 million increase
   e. a $100 million decrease; a $100 million decrease

7. When the Fed conducts an open market purchase, the first round changes in the money multiplier process are that excess reserves ____, bank deposits ____, and the quantity of money ____.
   a. decrease; decrease; decreases
   b. increase; do not change; increases
   c. decrease; increase; does not change
   d. do not change; increase; increases
   e. increase; increase; increases

8. A currency drain is cash
   a. lost in the drain.
   b. draining into the banks.
   c. held outside the banks.
   d. held at the Fed.
   e. held as reserves.

9. If the currency drain increases,
   a. the monetary base increases.
   b. banks' reserves decrease.
   c. the quantity of money increases.
   d. banks' reserves increase.
   e. the money multiplier increases.

10. The money multiplier is used to determine how much the
    a. monetary base increases when the Fed purchases government securities.
    b. quantity of money increases when the monetary base increases.
    c. monetary base increases when the quantity of money increases.
    d. quantity of money increases when the required reserve ratio increases.
    e. monetary base increases when the Fed sells government securities.

11. If the monetary base does not change and Fed increases the required reserve ratio, the money multiplier ____ and the quantity of money ____.
    a. increases; increases
    b. increases; decreases
    c. decreases; increases
    d. decreases; decreases
    e. decreases; does not change

12. The Fed makes an open market operation purchase of $200,000. The currency drain is 0.33 and the required reserve ratio is 0.10. By how much does the quantity of money increase?
    a. $800,000
    b. $333,333
    c. $2,000,000
    d. $618,604
    e. $465,116

### Short Response Questions

1. Increases in what factors decrease the size of the money multiplier?

| Round | Increase in deposits (dollars) | Increase in currency (dollars) | Increase in reserves (dollars) | Increase in excess reserves (dollars) |
|---|---|---|---|---|
| A |  |  | 1,000 | 1,000 |
| B | ___ | ___ | ___ | ___ |
| C | ___ | ___ | ___ | ___ |
| D | ___ | ___ | ___ | ___ |

2. Suppose the Fed buys $1,000 of government securities from Hayward National Bank. The required reserve ratio is 0.10 and the currency drain is 0.25. Suppose that all banks loan all of their excess reserves. Complete the above table. Calculate the total increase in deposits and currency following the first four rounds of the multiplier process.

| Round | Increase in deposits (dollars) | Increase in currency (dollars) | Increase in reserves (dollars) | Increase in excess reserves (dollars) |
|-------|-------------|-------------|-------------|-------------|
| A |  |  | 1,000 | 1,000 |
| B | ____ | ____ | ____ | ____ |
| C | ____ | ____ | ____ | ____ |
| D | ____ | ____ | ____ | ____ |

3. Suppose the Fed buys $1,000 of government securities from Fremont National Bank. The required reserve ratio is 0.10 and the currency drain is 1.00. Suppose that all banks loan all of their excess reserves. Complete the above table. Calculate the total increase in deposits and currency following the first four rounds of the multiplier process.

4. In which question, 1 or 2, was the increase in the quantity of money largest after four rounds?

5. Calculate the money multiplier when the required reserve ratio is 0.10 and the currency drain is 0.20. Calculate the money multiplier when the required reserve ratio is 0.10 and the currency drain is 0.60. As the currency drain increases, what happens to the magnitude of the money multiplier?

6. Calculate the money multiplier when the required reserve ratio is 0.10 and the currency drain is 0.20. Calculate the money multiplier when the required reserve ratio is 0.20 and the currency drain is 0.20. As the required reserve ratio increases, what happens to the magnitude of the money multiplier?

## Long Response Questions

1. Describe the process by which a fractional reserve banking system creates money after an open market purchases of U.S. government securities. If there is no currency drain and banks keep no excess reserves, what is the money multiplier?

2. Why does an increase in the required reserve ratio or in the currency drain decrease the magnitude of the money multiplier?

## YOUR AP SELF TEST ANSWERS

### ■ CHECKPOINT 27.1

**True or false**

1. False; page 674
2. False; page 676
3. True; page 676
4. False; page 677
5. False; pages 677-678
6. True; pages 679-680
7. False; pages 680-682
8. True; page 682

**Multiple choice**

1. d; page 674
2. c; page 674
3. c; page 674
4. a; page 676
5. a; page 676
6. c; page 676
7. c; page 677
8. a; pages 677-678
9. d; page 679
10. c; pages 680-682
11. b; page 682
12. c; page 682

**Short Response Questions**

| Assets | | Liabilities | |
|---|---|---|---|
| Cash | 200 | Deposits | 1,000 |
| Reserves at the Fed | 100 | | |
| Loans | 800 | | |
| Government securities | 100 | Owner's equity | 200 |

1. The completed balance sheet is above;  page 679.

| Round | Increase in deposits (dollars) | Increase in reserves (dollars) | Increase in excess reserves (dollars) | Loan (dollars) |
|---|---|---|---|---|
| A | 500.00 | 500.00 | 450.00 | 450.00 |
| B | 450.00 | 450.00 | 405.00 | 405.00 |
| C | 405.00 | 405.00 | 364.50 | 364.50 |
| D | 364.50 | 364.50 | 328.05 | 328.05 |

2. a. The completed table is above;  page 681.

b. The total increase in deposits after the first four rounds is $1,719.50.

c. The total increase in deposits is $(1 \div [1 - L])$ × the increase in reserves. $L$ is the proportion of a round of loans and deposits to the previous round of loans and deposits. In this case, $L$ is 0.90, so the total increase in deposits is $(1 \div [1 - 0.90])$ × $500, or 10.0 × $500.00, which equals $5,000; page 682.

**Long Response Questions**

1. The Bank of Utah's required reserves are $(0.10) \times (\$500 \text{ million}) = \$50$ million, so it has excess reserves of $10 million. It can loan the amount of its excess reserves, $10 million. If the required reserve ratio is 8 percent, the bank's required reserves are $40 million and so the bank has $20 million of excess reserves. When the required reserve ratio decreases, the amount the bank can loan increases; pages 676-677.

2. When a bank makes a loan, the bank deposits the loan in the borrower's checkable deposit. For instance, when Emma borrows $30,000 to buy machines for her business, the bank places the $30,000 in Emma's checkable deposit. As a result, when a loan is made, an equal sized deposit is created;  page 679.

3. a. The total increase in deposits is $(1 \div [1 - L])$ × the increase in reserves. $L$ is the proportion of a round of loans and deposits to the previous round of loans and deposits. In this case, $L$ is 0.90, so the total increase in deposits is $(1 \div [1 - 0.90])$ × $100, or 10.0 × $100.00, which equals $1,000; page 682.

b. When the required reserve ratio is 5 percent, $L$ is 0.95. So the total increase in deposits is $(1 \div [1 - 0.95])$ × $100, or 20.0 × $100.00, which equals $2,000; page 682.

c. When the required reserve ratio is smaller, the total increase in deposits is larger; page 682.

# ■ CHECKPOINT 27.2

## True or false

1. True;  page 684
2. False;  page 684
3. True;  page 685
4. True;  page 687
5. False;  pages 684-687
6. False;  pages 687-688
7. False;  page 689
8. False;  page 690

## Multiple choice

1. b;  page 684
2. e;  page 684
3. c;  pages 684-687
4. b;  page 685
5. c;  page 685
6. b;  page 685
7. e;  page 687
8. c;  page 687
9. b;  page 687
10. b;  page 689
11. d;  page 690
12. d;  page 690

## Short Response Questions

1. An increase in the currency drain, in the amount of excess reserves banks keep and do not loan, or in the required reserve ratio decrease the magnitude of the money multiplier; pages 689-690.

| Round | Increase in deposits (dollars) | Increase in currency (dollars) | Increase in reserves (dollars) | Increase in excess reserves (dollars) |
|---|---|---|---|---|
| A | | | 1,000.00 | 1,000.00 |
| B | 800.00 | 200.00 | 800.00 | 720.00 |
| C | 576.00 | 144.00 | 576.00 | 518.40 |
| D | 414.72 | 103.68 | 414.72 | 373.25 |

2. The completed table is above. After four rounds, currency increases by $447.68, deposits increase by $1,790.72, and the quantity of money increases by the sum of the increase in currency and the increase in deposits, which is $2,238.40;  page 689.

| Round | Increase in deposits (dollars) | Increase in currency (dollars) | Increase in reserves (dollars) | Increase in excess reserves (dollars) |
|---|---|---|---|---|
| A | | | 1,000 | 1,000 |
| B | 500.00 | 500.00 | 500.00 | 450.00 |
| C | 225.00 | 225.00 | 225.00 | 202.50 |
| D | 101.25 | 101.25 | 101.25 | 91.13 |

3. The completed table is above. After four rounds, currency increases by $826.25, deposits increase by $826.25, and the quantity of money increases by the sum of the increase in currency and the increase in deposits, which is $1,652.50;  page 689.

4. The increase in the quantity of money is greater when the currency drain is smaller, in question 1;  page 689.

5. The money multiplier equals $(1 + C) \div (C + R)$ where $C$ is the currency drain and $R$ is the required reserve ratio. The money multiplier for the first part of the question equals $(1 + 0.20) \div (0.20 + 0.10)$, or $(1.20) \div (0.30)$ which is 4.00. The money multiplier for the second part of the question is $(1 + 0.60) \div (0.60 + 0.10)$, or $(1.60) \div (0.70)$, which is 2.29. As the currency drain increases, the magnitude of the money multiplier decreases; pages 689-690.

6. The money multiplier equals $(1 + C) \div (C + R)$ where $C$ is the currency drain and $R$ is the required reserve ratio. The money multiplier for the first part of the question equals $(1 + 0.20) \div (0.20 + 0.10)$, or $(1.20) \div (0.30)$ which is 4.00. The money multiplier for the second part of the question is $(1 + 0.20) \div (0.20 + 0.20)$, or $(1.20) \div (0.40)$, which is 3.00. As the required reserve ratio increases, the magnitude of the money multiplier decreases; pages 689-690.

## Long Response Questions

1. An open market purchase of U.S. government securities increases the monetary base and increases banks' excess reserves. Banks loan the excess reserves. The recipients of the

loans spend them and the proceeds are then deposited in other banks. With fractional reserves, that is, with a required reserve less than one, banks are required to keep only a fraction of new deposits as reserves and can loan the remainder. So when the other banks' receive their new deposits, they increase their loans, which are then spent and deposited in yet other banks. These new banks, in turn, increase their loans, which are spent and then deposited in additional banks. This process continues. At each round, the increase in deposits increases the quantity of money, so the ultimate increase in the quantity of money exceeds the initial increase in the monetary base. The money multiplier is the amount by which the monetary base is multiplied to determine the final increase in the quantity of money. If banks keep no excess reserves and there is no currency drain, the money multiplier equals $1/R$ where $R$ is the required reserve ratio; pages 687-690.

2. The money multiplier exists because of the repeating process of loaning, depositing the proceeds in another bank, and then making another loan. The more each bank loans, the greater the final increase in the quantity of money and the larger the money multiplier. If the required reserve ratio increases in size, banks will be able to loan less of any additional deposit they receive. And if the currency drain increases, less is deposited in a bank and the bank will be able to loan less. Because an increase in the required reserve ratio and an increase in the currency drain decrease the amount that can be loaned, both decrease the size of the money multiplier; pages 689-690.

# Money, Interest, and Inflation

## Chapter 28

## CHAPTER IN PERSPECTIVE

Chapter 28 discusses how the quantity of money determines the nominal interest rate and studies the relationship between money and the price level. It starts by pointing out that real factors, independent of the price level, determine potential GDP and other real variables. The effects of money on the economy differ in the short run and the long run. This chapter looks at the short run and long run but not at how the long run is reached—examining these ripple effects is the task of the next two chapters.

■ **Explain what determines the demand for money and how the demand for money and the supply of money determine the _nominal_ interest rate.**

The inventory of money that households and firms choose to hold is the quantity of money demanded. The nominal interest rate is the opportunity cost of holding money. The demand for money curve shows the quantity of money demanded at each nominal interest rate. An increase in the price level or real GDP increases the demand for money and the demand for money curve shifts rightward. The supply of money is a fixed quantity. Equilibrium in the money market determines the nominal interest rate. In the short run, when the Fed increases the quantity of money, the nominal interest rate falls

■ **Explain how in the long run, the quantity of money determines the price level and money growth brings inflation.**

A one-time increase in the quantity of money lowers the nominal interest rate in the short run. In the long run, a one-time increase in the quantity of money brings an equal percentage increase in the price level and the nominal interest rate returns to its initial value. The quantity theory of money is the proposition when real GDP equals potential GDP, an increase in the quantity of money brings an equal percentage increase in the price level. The equation of exchange states that the quantity of money multiplied by the velocity of circulation equals nominal GDP. An increase in the quantity of money, with no change in potential GDP or velocity, leads to the same percentage increase in the price level. In rates of change, money growth plus velocity growth equals inflation plus real GDP growth. An increase in the growth of the quantity of money, with no change in the growth of velocity or real GDP, leads to an equal increase in the inflation rate. A hyperinflation is inflation at a rate that exceeds 50 percent a month.

■ **Identify the costs of inflation and the benefits of a stable value of money.**

The four costs of inflation are tax costs, shoe-leather costs, confusion costs, and uncertainty costs. Inflation is a tax. With inflation, households and business lose purchasing power, which is the tax on holding money. Inflation interacts with the income tax to lower saving and investment. Shoe-leather costs are costs that arise from an increase in the amount of running around that people do to try to avoid losses from the falling value of money. Confusion costs are costs of making errors because of rapidly changing prices. Uncertainty costs arise because long-term planning is difficult, so people have a shorter-term focus. Investment falls and the growth rate slows.

## EXPANDED CHAPTER CHECKLIST

**When you have completed this chapter, you will be able to:**

**1** **Explain what determines the demand for money and how the demand for money and the supply of money determine the *nominal* interest rate.**

- Discuss the factors that influence the demand for money.
- Explain the relationship between the nominal interest rate, the real interest rate, and the inflation rate.
- Draw a figure to illustrate the money market and indicate the money market equilibrium.
- Explain how the nominal interest rate changes when the Fed changes the quantity of money.

**2** **Explain how in the long run, the quantity of money determines the price level and money growth brings inflation.**

- Explain the relationship between a change in the quantity of money and the money market in the long run
- Use the quantity theory of money and the equation of exchange to describe the relationship between a change in the quantity of money and the price level.
- Explain the relationship between a change in the growth rate of the quantity of money and the inflation rate.

**3** **Identify the costs of inflation and the benefits of a stable value of money.**

- Explain why inflation is a tax.
- List and discuss the four costs of inflation.
- Explain why high inflation as well as unpredictable inflation impose costs on society.

## YOUR AP TEST HINTS

*AP Topics*

| Topic on your AP test | Corresponding text-book section |
|---|---|
| **Financial sector** | |
| Money, Banking, and Financial Markets | Chapter 28 |
| • Money demand | Checkpoint 28.1 |
| • Money market | Checkpoint 28.2 |
| • Quantity theory | Checkpoint 28.2 |
| • Real versus nominal interest rate | Checkpoint 28.1 |
| • Cost of inflation | Checkpoint 28.3 |

*AP Vocabulary*

- The AP test often uses "$Q$" instead of "$Y$" for real GDP in the equation of exchange. Hence the equation of exchange is written on the AP test as $M \times V = P \times Q$ rather than $M \times V = P \times Y$.

*Extra AP material*

- On the AP test, the demand for money can be divided into two parts: the "transactions demand" and the "asset demand." The transaction demand results from use of money as a medium of exchange and is influenced by real GDP. An increase in real GDP means more transactions take place, which increases the demand for money. The asset demand for money results from using money as a store of value and is influenced by the (nominal) interest rate. An increase in the interest rate raises the opportunity cost of holding money rather than an interest-bearing asset, which decreases the quantity of money demanded. In a diagram with the interest rate on the vertical axis, the total demand for money curve is constructed by adding the vertical transactions demand for money curve (vertical because the transactions demand does not depend on the interest rate) to the downward sloping asset demand for money curve. Add these two curves horizontally so that at any interest rate, the total quantity of money demanded equals the sum of the quantity of transaction demand money plus the quantity of asset demand money. The resulting total demand for money curve will be downward sloping.

- The AP test might ask how the cost of anticipated inflation can be less than the cost of unanticipated inflation. The AP test also frequently focuses on the difference between anticipated inflation and unanticipated inflation. Some groups are harmed (or helped) by unanticipated inflation but not by anticipated inflation. For instance, if there is unanticipated inflation, lenders are harmed (because the real interest rate they actually receive is less than what they expected to receive) and borrowers are helped because the real interest rate they actually pay is less than what they expected to pay). But if the inflation is anticipated, the nominal interest rate rises so that lenders are not harmed and borrowers are not helped. Frequently this difference is quite important on the AP test.

- For the AP test, be sure to practice how changes in the demand for money shift the demand for money curve and change the interest rate. In addition, be sure to know how the change in the interest rate affects the quantity of investment.

- The AP test might ask how changes in the price level and real GDP that result from a change in the quantity of money feed back to affect the money market. In particular, in the short run an increase in the quantity of money lowers the (nominal and real) interest rate and increases real GDP and the price level. In turn, the increase in real GDP and the price increase the demand for money, which raises the interest rate and offsets some of the initial fall. In the long run, real GDP returns to its starting value. But the price level rises. The rise in the price increases the demand for money sufficiently so that the interest rate returns to its starting value.

## CHECKPOINT 28.1

■ **Explain what determines the demand for money and how the demand for money and the supply of money determine the *nominal* interest rate.**

### Quick Review

- *Shifts in the demand for money curve* When real GDP, the price level, or financial technology change, the demand for money curve shifts.
- *Equilibrium nominal interest rate* The equilibrium nominal interest rate occurs where the demand for money curve intersects the supply curve because at this interest rate the quantity of money demanded equals the quantity supplied.

### Additional Practice Problems 28.1

1. The figure shows the money market.
   a. What is the equilibrium nominal interest rate and quantity of money?
   b. Use the figure to show what happens to the interest rate if the Fed increases the quantity of money from $4.0 trillion to $4.1 trillion.

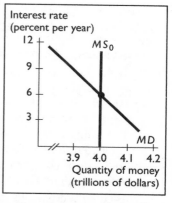

2. The table above has schedules for the transaction demand for money and asset demand for

| Interest rate (percent) | Transactions demand | Asset demand | Total demand |
|---|---|---|---|
| | (trillions of dollars) | | |
| 4 | 1.0 | 2.0 | ___ |
| 5 | 1.0 | 1.5 | ___ |
| 6 | 1.0 | 1.0 | ___ |
| 7 | 1.0 | 0.5 | ___ |

money. Complete the table by determining the total demand for money schedule.

a. In the figure to the right, draw the transactions demand, the asset demand, and the total demand curves for money.

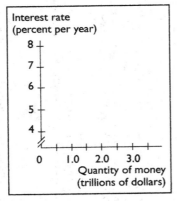

### Solutions to Additional Practice Problems 28.1

1a. This problem shows how the nominal interest rate is determined in the money market. You are using the supply and demand model introduced in Chapter 4. As the figure illustrates, the equilibrium interest rate is 6 percent because this is the interest rate at which the quantity of money demanded equals the quantity of money supplied. The equilibrium quantity of money is $4.0 trillion.

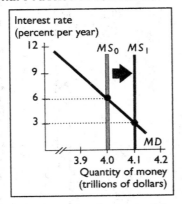

1b. The Fed's increase in the quantity of money shifts the supply of money curve rightward, from $MS_0$ to $MS_1$. As a result, the equilibrium nominal interest rate falls from 6 percent to 3 percent.

| Interest rate (percent) | Transactions demand | Asset demand | Total demand |
|---|---|---|---|
| | (trillions of dollars) | | |
| 4 | 1.0 | 2.0 | 3.0 |
| 5 | 1.0 | 1.5 | 2.5 |
| 6 | 1.0 | 1.0 | 2.0 |
| 7 | 1.0 | 0.5 | 1.5 |

2. The completed table above is above. At each

interest rate, the total demand for money equals the sum of the transaction demand plus the asset demand.

2a. The transaction demand curve for money is labeled *TD*, the asset demand curve for money is labeled *AD*, and the "total" demand curve for money is labeled *MD* in the figure to the right. The demand curve for money is equal to the horizontal sum of the transactions demand curve and the asset demand curve.

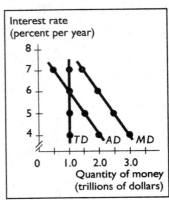

### ■ AP Self Test 28.1

**True or false**

1. The real interest rate is the opportunity cost of holding money.

2. An increase in real GDP shifts the demand for money curve leftward.

3. If the price of a government bond rises, the interest rate on the bond rises.

4. When the interest rate is above its equilibrium level, people buy bonds and the interest rate falls.

5. An increase in the quantity of money lowers the interest rate.

**Multiple choice**

1. The quantity of money demanded
   a. is infinite.
   b. has no opportunity cost.
   c. is the quantity that balances the benefit of holding an additional dollar of money against the opportunity cost of doing so.
   d. is directly controlled by the Fed.
   e. changes very infrequently.

2. Which of the following statements is correct?
   a. Nominal interest rate = Real interest rate – Inflation rate
   b. Nominal interest rate = Real interest rate + Inflation rate
   c. Nominal interest rate = Inflation rate – Real interest rate
   d. Nominal interest rate = Inflation rate + Price index
   e. Nominal interest rate = Inflation rate ÷ Real interest rate

3. The opportunity cost of holding money is the
   a. real interest rate.
   b. nominal interest rate.
   c. inflation rate.
   d. time it takes to go to the ATM or bank.
   e. growth rate of real GDP.

4. The demand for money curve shows the relationship between the quantity of money demanded and
   a. the nominal interest rate.
   b. the real interest rate.
   c. the inflation rate.
   d. real GDP.
   e. nominal GDP.

5. The demand for money ____ when the ____.
   a. increases; price level increases
   b. decreases; price level increases
   c. remains constant; price level increases
   d. increases; interest rate increases
   e. increases; supply of money decreases

6. Every day ____ adjusts to make the quantity of money demanded equal the quantity of money supplied.
   a. the inflation rate
   b. the nominal interest rate
   c. the quantity of money
   d. potential GDP
   e. real GDP

7. If the nominal interest rate is above its equilibrium level, then
   a. people sell financial assets and the interest rate falls.
   b. people buy financial assets and the interest rate falls.
   c. the demand for money curve shifts rightward and the interest rate rises.
   d. the supply of money curve shifts leftward and the interest rate rises.
   e. the demand curve for money shifts leftward and the interest rate falls.

8. When the Fed increases the quantity of money, the
   a. equilibrium interest rate falls.
   b. equilibrium interest rate rises.
   c. demand for money curve shifts rightward.
   d. supply of money curve shifts leftward.
   e. demand for money curve shifts leftward.

| Nominal interest rate (percent per year) | Quantity of money, (trillions dollars) |
|---|---|
| 5 | 3.1 |
| 6 | 3.0 |
| 7 | 2.9 |
| 8 | 2.8 |
| 9 | 2.7 |
| 10 | 2.6 |

9. The table above gives the demand for money schedule. When the Fed decreases the quantity of money from $2.9 trillion to $2.7 trillion, the interest rate ____ from ____.
   a. rises; 5 percent to 10 percent
   b. falls; 9 percent to 7 percent
   c. rises; 5 percent to 8 percent
   d. rises; 6 percent to 8 percent
   e. rises; 7 percent to 9 percent

■ **FIGURE 28.1**

Nominal interest rate (percent per year)

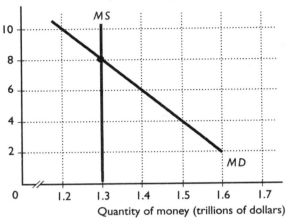

■ **FIGURE 28.2**

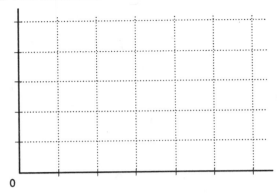

10. The figure above shows the money market. If the Fed increases the quantity of money from $1.3 trillion to $1.4 trillion, the interest rate ____ from ____.
  a. falls; 9 percent to 7 percent
  b. falls; 8 percent to 6 percent
  c. rises; 5 percent to 8 percent
  d. rises; 6 percent to 8 percent
  e. falls; 12 percent to 7 percent

### Short Response Questions

1. What are the benefits from holding money?

| Nominal interest rate (percent per year) | Quantity of money, (trillions dollars) |
|---|---|
| 5 | 1.2 |
| 6 | 1.0 |
| 7 | 0.8 |
| 8 | 0.6 |
| 9 | 0.4 |
| 10 | 0.2 |

2. The table above has the nominal interest rate and the quantity of money demanded.
  a. Using the data, label the axes and plot the demand for money curve in Figure 28.2.
  b. Suppose the Fed sets the quantity of money at $0.6 trillion. Plot this quantity in Figure 28.2. What is the equilibrium nominal interest rate?
  c. If the Fed wants to change the nominal interest rate so that it equals 6 percent a year, what action must the Fed take?

■ **FIGURE 28.3**

Nominal interest rate (percent per year)

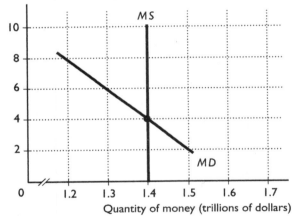

Quantity of money (trillions of dollars)

3. Figure 28.3 shows a demand for money curve and a supply of money curve.
  a. What is the equilibrium interest rate?
  b. The price level rises so that the demand for money changes by $0.2 trillion at every interest rate. Which direction does the demand for money curve shift? Draw the new demand for money curve in the figure. What is the equilibrium interest rate?
  c. From the initial situation in Figure 28.3, suppose real GDP increases so that the demand for money changes by $0.2 trillion at every interest rate. Which direction does the demand for money curve shift? Draw the new demand for money curve in the figure. What is the equilibrium interest rate?

## Long Response Questions

1. What is the opportunity cost of holding money and why is this the opportunity cost?

2. What effect will an increase in real GDP have on the demand for money curve? What effect will an increase in the price level have? What is the effect of these changes on the nominal interest rate?

3. Suppose a government bond pays $100 in interest each year. If you buy the bond for $1,000, what is the interest rate? If you buy the bond for $2,000 dollars, what is the interest rate? As the price of the bond increases, what happens to the interest rate?

4. How can the Fed lower the nominal interest rate?

## CHECKPOINT 28.2

■ **Explain how in the long run, the quantity of money determines the price level and money growth brings inflation.**

### Quick Review

- *Inflation rate in the long run* In the long run and other things remaining the same, a given percentage change in the quantity of money brings an equal percentage change in the price level.

- *Quantity theory of money* The proposition that when real GDP equals potential GDP, an increase in the quantity of money brings an equal percentage increase in the price level.

- *Equation of exchange* An equation that states that the quantity of money multiplied by the velocity of circulation equals the price level multiplied by real GDP, that is $M \times V = P \times Q$. ($Q$ and $Y$ both stand for real GDP.)

### Additional Practice Problems 28.2

1. In the short run, how does an increase in the quantity of money affect the price level? The nominal interest rate?

2. In the long run, how does an increase in the quantity of money affect the price level? The nominal interest rate?

3. In the long run, according to the quantity theory of money, how does an increase in the growth rate of the quantity of money affect the inflation rate? The nominal interest rate?

4. The quantity of money is $90 billion, real GDP is $900 billion, and the price level is 110. What is the velocity of circulation?

### Solutions to Additional Practice Problems 28.2

1. In the *immediate* short run, the price level does not change but then, as time passes, it starts to rise. In the short run, an increase in the quantity of money lowers the nominal interest rate.

2. In the long run, the price level rises. In the long run, the nominal interest rate does not change.

3. In the long run, an increase in the growth rate of the quantity of money raises the inflation rate by the same percentage. For instance, if the growth rate of the quantity of money increases by 3 percentage points, in the long run the inflation rate increases by 3 percentage points. In the long run, the nominal interest rate rises.

4. The velocity of circulation is the number of times in a year that the average dollar of money gets used to buy final goods and services. The velocity of circulation is calculated using the formula $V = (P \times Q) \div M$. Nominal GDP, which equals $P \times Q$, is $990 billion. So velocity equals ($990 billion) $\div$ $90 billion = 11.

## ■ AP Self Test 28.2

### True or false

1. If the inflation rate is 2 percent a year and the real interest rate is 4 percent a year, the nominal interest rate is 6 percent a year.

2. In the long run, an increase in the quantity of money raises the price level and leaves the nominal interest rate unchanged.

3. $M \times P = V \times Q$ is the equation of exchange.

4. According to the quantity theory of money, in the long run with other things remaining the same, a 5 percent increase in the quantity

of money brings a 5 percent increase in the price level.

5. According to the quantity theory of money, if the quantity of money grows 2 percent a year faster, the inflation rate falls by 2 percent a year.

## Multiple choice

1. In the long run, the price level adjusts
   a. so that the real interest rate equals the nominal interest rate.
   b. so that the inflation rate equals zero.
   c. to achieve money market equilibrium at the long-run equilibrium interest rate.
   d. so that the inflation rate equals the growth rate of real GDP.
   e. so that the inflation rate is moderate.

2. If the equilibrium real interest rate is 4 percent a year and the inflation rate is 4 percent a year, then the nominal interest rate is ____ percent a year.
   a. 4
   b. 8
   c. 0
   d. 6
   e. 2

3. Other things remaining the same, if the quantity of money increases by a given percentage, then in the long run the ____ by the same percentage.
   a. price level rises
   b. price level falls
   c. real interest rate rises
   d. real interest rate falls
   e. nominal interest rate falls

4. In the long run, an increase in the quantity of money ____ the price level and ____ the nominal interest rate.
   a. raises; raises
   b. raises; does not change
   c. raises; lowers
   d. does not change; raises
   e. does not change; does not change

5. Suppose that $P \times Q$ is $5,000 million a year and the quantity of money is $500 million. Then the velocity of circulation is
   a. 50.
   b. 500.
   c. 10.
   d. 20.
   e. 2,500,000.

6. The quantity theory of money is a proposition about the
   a. Fed's methods it uses to change the quantity of money.
   b. relationship between nominal and real interest rate.
   c. relationship between a change in the quantity of money and the price level.
   d. relationship between financial assets and currency demanded.
   e. relationship between the nominal interest rate and the quantity of money demanded.

7. If the quantity of money grows at 3 percent a year, velocity does not grow, and real GDP grows at 2 percent a year, then the inflation rate equals
   a. 6 percent.
   b. 5 percent.
   c. 1 percent.
   d. –1 percent.
   e. 12 percent.

8. If the quantity of money grows at 4 percent a year, velocity grows at 2 percent, and real GDP grows at 2 percent a year, then the inflation rate equals
   a. 6 percent.
   b. 2 percent.
   c. 0 percent.
   d. 8 percent.
   e. 4 percent.

9. Hyperinflation is
   a. inflation caused by negative growth in the quantity of money.
   b. inflation at a rate that exceeds 50 percent a month.
   c. inflation caused by excessive growth in the demand for money.
   d. inflation at a rate that exceeds 5 percent a month.
   e. only theoretical and has never occurred in the real world.

### Short Response Questions

1. In the long run, what is the effect of a 5 percent increase in the quantity of money, other things remaining the same?

| Year | Quantity of money (billions of dollars) | Velocity of circulation | Price level (2000 = 100) | Real GDP (billions of 2000 dollars) |
|------|------|------|------|------|
| 2005 | 100 | 11 | ____ | 1,000 |
| 2006 | 110 | 11 | ____ | 1,000 |
| 2007 | 121 | 11 | ____ | 1,000 |

2. The table above gives data for the nation of Quantoland, a small nation to the south. In 2005, 2006, and 2007, real GDP equals potential GDP.
   a. Complete the table.
   b. Calculate the percentage change in the quantity of money in 2006 and 2007. Then calculate the percentage change in the price level in 2006 and 2007.
   c. What key proposition is illustrated in your answer to part (b)?

| Year | Growth in quantity of money (percent) | Growth in velocity of circulation (percent) | Inflation rate (percent) | Growth in Real GDP (percent) |
|------|------|------|------|------|
| 2005 | 4 | 2 | ____ | 3 |
| 2006 | 7 | 2 | ____ | 3 |
| 2007 | ____ | 1 | 4 | 3 |

3. The table above gives data for the nation of Velocoland, a small nation to the north. In 2005, 2006, and 2007, real GDP equals potential GDP.
   a. Complete the table.

b. Between 2005 and 2006, by how much does the growth rate of the quantity of money change? By how much does the inflation rate change?

### Long Response Questions

1. To what factor does the quantity theory attribute increases in the inflation rate?

2. In the long run, if real GDP grows at 3 percent a year, velocity does not change, and the quantity of money grows at 5 percent a year, what is the inflation rate?

3. What is a hyperinflation? What leads to hyperinflation?

## CHECKPOINT 28.3

■ **Identify the costs of inflation and the benefits of a stable value of money.**

### Quick Review

- *The inflation rate and income tax* Inflation increases the nominal interest rate, and because income taxes are paid on nominal interest income, the true income tax rate rises with inflation.

### Additional Practice Problem 28.3

1. In the island of Atlantis where you live, the inflation rate has been varying between 3 percent a year and 10 percent a year in recent years. You are willing to lend money if you are guaranteed a real interest rate of at least 2 percent a year. There are potential borrowers, but they will borrow only if they are guaranteed a real interest rate of not more than 5 percent a year.
   a. Can you successfully make a loan if everyone can accurately predict the inflation rate?
   b. Can you successfully make a loan if neither you nor the borrowers can accurately predict the inflation rate?
   c. What bearing does your answer to part b have on the cost of inflation?

**Solution to Additional Practice Problem 28.3**

1a. If you and the potential borrowers can accurately predict the inflation rate, it is possible to make a loan. If everyone knows the inflation rate is 10 percent a year, you are willing to lend as long as you receive a nominal interest rate of at least 12 percent a year. Borrowers are willing to pay a real interest rate of no more than 5 percent a year, so borrowers are willing to agree to a loan as long as the nominal rate is no more than 15 percent a year. Because they are willing to pay up to 15 percent a year and you are willing to take as little as 12 percent a year, you can make a loan and charge a nominal interest rate between 12 percent a year and 15 percent a year. Similarly, if everyone knows the inflation rate is 3 percent a year, a loan can be made with a nominal interest rate between 5 percent a year and 8 percent a year.

1b. To receive a real interest rate of at least 2 percent a year you must receive a nominal interest rate of at least 12 percent a year in case inflation is 10 percent a year. If borrowers pay a nominal interest rate of 12 percent a year and inflation is 3 percent a year, they are paying a real interest rate of 9 percent a year, well above their maximum real interest rate of 5 percent a year. Because of the uncertainty about the inflation rate, you don't make the loan.

1c. The fact that inflation is uncertain means that the loan did not get made. Presumably the loan would benefit both the lender and the borrower. The fact that it cannot be made means that both are worse off, which reflects the uncertainty cost of inflation.

## ■ Self Test 28.3

**True or false**

1. Inflation is a tax.

2. One of the benefits of inflation is that it makes the value of money change, which benefits both borrowers and lenders.

3. When there is a high inflation rate, the growth rate slows.

4. No country in the world has experienced hyperinflation since the end of the 1950s.

**Multiple choice**

1. All of the following are costs of inflation EXCEPT
   a. tax costs.
   b. confusion costs.
   c. uncertainty costs.
   d. government spending costs.
   e. shoe-leather costs.

2. Shoe-leather costs arise from inflation because the velocity of circulation of money ____ as the inflation rate ____.
   a. increases; falls
   b. decreases; rises
   c. increases; rises
   d. does not change; rises
   e. does not change; falls

3. A consequence of hyperinflation is that people
   a. who make fixed-payment loans to others receive higher payments as inflation increases.
   b. spend time trying to keep their money holdings near zero.
   c. receive higher nominal wage hikes, which increases their purchasing power for goods and services.
   d. want to lend funds because interest rates are so high.
   e. increase the quantity of money demanded.

4. The uncertainty costs of inflation cause people to
   a. increase long-run investment.
   b. increase investment causing growth to decrease.
   c. focus on the short run, which decreases investment and slows growth.
   d. focus on the long run, which increases investment and speeds growth.
   e. incur more shoe leather costs.

5. The costs of inflation ____ when inflation is more rapid and ____ when inflation is more unpredictable.
   a. increase; increase
   b. increase; decrease
   c. decrease; increase
   d. increase; do not change
   e. do not change; increase

**Short Response Question**

1. Jose holds $600 of money. If the inflation rate is 5 percent a year, what is Joe's inflation tax?

**Long Response Questions**

1. Why does the velocity of circulation increase in a hyperinflation?

2. On what factors does the cost of inflation depend?

# YOUR AP SELF TEST ANSWERS

## ■ CHECKPOINT 28.1

### True or false
1. False; page 700
2. False; page 701
3. False; page 704
4. True; page 703
5. True; pages 704-706

### Multiple choice
1. c; page 699
2. b; page 700
3. b; page 700
4. a; pages 700-701
5. a; page 700
6. b; page 702
7. b; page 703
8. a; pages 704-705
9. e; pages 704-705
10. b; pages 704-705

### Short Response Questions
1. The sources of benefit from holding money are that you can make payments and do transactions; page 699.
2. a. Figure 28.4 plots the demand for money curve; page 700.
   b. Figure 28.4 shows the supply of money curve when the Fed sets the quantity of money at $0.6 trillion. The equilibrium nominal interest rate is 8 percent a year at the intersection of the $MD$ and $MS$ curves; page 703.
   c. If the Fed wants to lower the interest rate to 6 percent a year, it increases the quantity of money to $1.0 trillion; page 705.
3. a. The equilibrium interest rate is 4 percent; page 703.
   b. The demand for money increases and the demand for money curve shifts rightward. Figure 28.5 shows the change as the shift in the demand for money curve from $MD_0$ to $MD_1$. The new equilibrium interest rate is 8 percent; pages 701, 704-705.

## ■ FIGURE 28.4

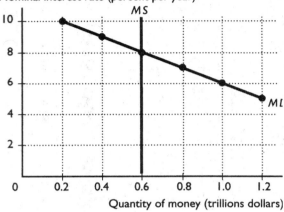

Nominal interest rate (percent per year)

## ■ FIGURE 28.5

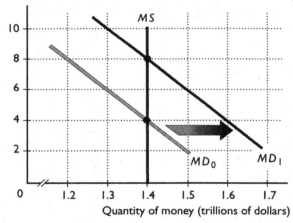

Nominal interest rate (percent per year)

   c. The demand for money increases and the demand for money curve shifts rightward. In Figure 28.5, because the demand for money increases by the same amount as in part (b), the demand for money curve shifts once again from $MD_0$ to $MD_1$. The new equilibrium interest rate is 8 percent; pages 701, 704-705.

### Long Response Questions
1. The opportunity cost of holding money is the nominal interest rate. By holding money rather than a financial asset, the nominal in-

terest rate is forgone. For instance, if Seemi can earn 5 percent a year on a bond, then holding $1,000 in money costs her $50 a year; page 700.

2. An increase in real GDP increases the demand for money and shifts the demand for money curve rightward. Similarly, an increase in the price level increases the demand for money and shifts the demand for money curve rightward. Both changes raise the equilibrium interest rate; pages 701, 704-705.

3. When the price of the bond is $1,000, the interest rate equals ($100 ÷ $1,000) × 100, which is 10 percent. When the price of the bond is $2,000, the interest rate equals ($100 ÷ $2,000) × 100, which is 5 percent. When the price of the bond increases, the interest rate falls; page 703.

4. If the Fed wants to lower the interest rate, it increases the quantity of money. As a result, the supply of money line shifts rightward and the equilibrium nominal interest rate falls; pages 704-705.

## ■ CHECKPOINT 28.2

**True or false**
1. True;  page 708
2. True;  page 710
3. False;  page 711
4. True;  page 712
5. False;  page 713

**Multiple choice**
1. c;  page 708
2. b;  page 708
3. a;  pages 710, 712
4. b;  page 710
5. c;  page 711
6. c;  page 711
7. c;  page 713
8. e;  page 713
9. b;  page 715

**Short Response Questions**

1. Other things remaining the same, in the long run a 5 percent increase in the quantity of money leads to a 5 percent increase in the price level; pages 710, 712.

| Year | Quantity of money (billions of dollars) | Velocity of circulation | Price level (2000 = 100) | Real GDP (billions of 2000 dollars) |
|------|------|------|------|------|
| 2005 | 100 | 11 | 110.0 | 1,000 |
| 2006 | 110 | 11 | 121.0 | 1,000 |
| 2007 | 121 | 11 | 133.1 | 1,000 |

2. a. The completed table is above. Use the equation of exchange to solve for the price level; pages 712.

b. In 2006, the percentage change in the quantity of money is [($110 billion − $100 billion) ÷ $100 billion] × 100, which is 10 percent.

In 2007, the percentage change in the quantity of money is [($121 billion − $110 billion) ÷ $110 billion] × 100, which also is 10 percent.

In 2006, the percentage change in the price level is [(121.0 − 110.0) ÷ 110.0] × 100, which is 10 percent.

In 2007, the percentage change in the price level is [(133.1 − 121.0) ÷ 121.0] × 100, which also is 10 percent.

c. The answer to part (b) illustrates the quantity theory of money, the proposition that, when real GDP equals potential GDP, an increase in the quantity of money brings an equal percentage increase in the price level; page 712.

| Year | Growth in quantity of money (percent) | Growth in velocity of circulation (percent) | Inflation rate (percent) | Growth in Real GDP (percent) |
|------|------|------|------|------|
| 2005 | 4 | 2 | 3 | 3 |
| 2006 | 7 | 2 | 6 | 3 |
| 2007 | 6 | 1 | 4 | 3 |

3. a. The completed table is above. Use the equation of exchange in growth rates to solve for the unknowns; page 713.

b. Between 2005 and 2006, the growth rate of the quantity of money increased by 3 percentage points. Between these two years the inflation rate also increased by 3 percentage points; page 713.

**Long Response Questions**

1. The quantity theory attributes higher inflation to more rapid growth in the quantity of money. In the long run, the inflation rate equals the money growth rate plus the velocity growth rate minus the real GDP growth rate. In the long run, changes in the growth rate of velocity and real GDP are independent of changes in the money growth rate. So an increase in the money growth leads to an increase in the inflation rate; page 713.

2. The inflation rate equals the money growth rate plus the velocity growth rate minus the real GDP growth rate. Velocity does not grow, so the inflation rate equals 5 percent a year minus 3 percent a year, which is 2 percent a year; page 713.

3. A hyperinflation is inflation at a rate that exceeds 50 percent a month. A hyperinflation is the result of extraordinarily rapid growth in the quantity of money; page 715.

## ■ CHECKPOINT 28.3

**True or false**

1. True; page 717
2. False; pages 718-719
3. True; page 720
4. False; page 720

**Multiple choice**

1. d; page 717
2. c; page 718
3. b; page 718
4. c; page 719
5. a; page 719

**Short Response Question**

1. With an inflation of 5 percent a year, Jose losses ($600 × 0.05) = $30 in purchasing power. His money will buy only $570 worth of goods and services. Jose is paying an inflation tax of $30; page 717.

**Long Response Questions**

1. The velocity of circulation increases because people try to spend their money as rapidly as possible to avoid incurring losses from the falling value of money. When people spend their money more rapidly, the velocity of circulation increases, thereby creating more shoe-leather costs; page 718.

2. The costs of an inflation depend on its rate and its predictability. The higher the inflation rate, the greater is the cost. In addition, the more unpredictable the inflation rate, the greater is the cost. These results are symmetric: The lower the inflation rate and the more predictable the inflation rate, the lower its cost; page 719.

# AS-AD and the Business Cycle

# *Chapter* **29**

■ **Provide a technical definition of recession and describe the history of the U.S. business cycle and the global business cycle.**

A business cycle has two phases, expansion and recession, and two turning points, a peak and a trough. A standard definition of recession is a decrease in real GDP that lasts for at least two quarters. The United States has experienced 33 complete business cycles since 1854. The average length of an expansion is 35 months and the average length of a recession is 18 months. Since World War II, the average recession has been 11 months and the average expansion has been 59 months.

■ **Explain the influences on aggregate supply.**

Aggregate supply is the output from all firms. Other things remaining the same, a rise in the price level increases the quantity of real GDP supplied. Moving along the aggregate supply curve, the only influence on production plans that changes is the price level. All other influences on production plans, such as the money wage rate and the money price of other resources, remain constant. Along the potential GDP line, when the price level changes, the money wage rate and the money prices of other resources change by the same percentage as the change in the price level. Aggregate supply changes when potential GDP changes, the money wage rate changes, or the money prices of other resources change.

■ **Explain the influences on aggregate demand.**

The quantity of real GDP demanded is the total amount of final goods and services produced in the United States that people, businesses, governments, and foreigners plan to buy. A change in the price level brings changes in the buying power of money, the real interest rate, and the real prices of exports and imports, which influence the quantity of real GDP demanded. An increase in the price level decreases the quantity of real GDP demanded and brings a movement along the aggregate demand curve. Factors that change aggregate demand are expectations about the future, fiscal policy and monetary policy, and the state of the world economy. The aggregate demand multiplier is an effect that magnifies changes in expenditure plans and brings potentially large fluctuations in aggregate demand.

■ **Explain how fluctuations in aggregate demand and aggregate supply create the business cycle.**

Macroeconomic equilibrium occurs at the intersection of the aggregate supply and aggregate demand curves. The macroeconomic equilibrium can be a full-employment equilibrium, real GDP equals potential GDP, an above full-employment equilibrium, or a below full-employment equilibrium. Fluctuations in aggregate demand and aggregate supply lead to changes in real GDP and the price level. If real GDP exceeds potential GDP, an inflationary gap exists, which is eliminated by a decrease in aggregate supply and a rise in the price level. If real GDP is less than potential GDP, a recessionary gap exists, which is eliminated by an increase in aggregate supply and a fall in the price level.

## EXPANDED CHAPTER CHECKLIST

**When you have completed this chapter, you will be able to:**

### 1 Provide a technical definition of recession and describe the history of the U.S. business cycle.

- State the standard definition of recession.
- Describe a business cycle.
- Discuss the history of the U.S. business cycle, including the average length of an expansion and recession, and how the length has changed since World War II.

### 2 Explain the influences on aggregate supply.

- Describe the relationship between potential GDP and the quantity of real GDP supplied over the business cycle.
- List the influence on production plans that changes the quantity of real GDP supplied and leads to a movement along the *AS* curve.
- Explain why an increase in the price level increases the quantity of real GDP supplied.
- Discuss the factors that change aggregate supply and shift the *AS* curve.

### 3 Explain the influences on aggregate demand.

- Discuss the influence of the price level for expenditure plans.
- Draw an *AD* curve and discuss the factors that change aggregate demand and shift the *AD* curve.
- Discuss the *AD* multiplier.

### 4 Explain how fluctuations in aggregate demand and aggregate supply create the business cycle.

- Describe and illustrate how fluctuations in aggregate demand change real GDP and the price level.

- Describe and illustrate how fluctuations in aggregate supply change real GDP and the price level.
- Define an inflationary gap and explain how real GDP returns to potential GDP.
- Define a recessionary gap and explain how real GDP returns to potential GDP.

## YOUR AP TEST HINTS

### AP Topics

| Topic on your AP test | Corresponding textbook section |
|---|---|
| **National income and price determination** | |
| Aggregate Supply and Aggregate Demand | Chapter 29 |
| • Long run versus short run aggregate supply | Checkpoint 29.2 |
| • Determinants of aggregate demand | Checkpoint 29.3 |
| • Real output and price level | Checkpoint 29.4 |
| • Economic fluctuations | Checkpoint 29.4 |

### AP Vocabulary

- On the AP test, the vertical line showing potential GDP is also called the "long-run aggregate supply" or *LRAS* curve. Changes in potential GDP are reflected by shifts in the production possibilities frontier (also called the production possibilities curve). When potential GDP increases (so that long-run aggregate supply increases) the production possibilities curve shifts outward.

### Extra AP material

- The aggregate demand/aggregate supply model is the main macroeconomic model of the economy. It is featured heavily in the AP test, so be certain you understand it.
- Government regulation can affect aggregate supply. If government regulation increases so that firms can produce less output, then potential GDP decreases and the *AS* curve shifts leftward.

# CHECKPOINT 29.1

■ **Provide a technical definition of recession and describe the history of the U.S. business cycle and the global business cycle.**

### Quick Review

- *Business cycle* The business cycle is the fluctuation in economic activity from an expansion to a peak to a recession to a trough and then to another expansion.
- *Recession* The conventional definition of a recession is a decrease in real GDP that lasts for at least six months.

### Additional Practice Problems 29.1

| Billions of 2000 dollars | | | | |
|---|---|---|---|---|
| | **Quarter** | | | |
| **Year** | **1** | **2** | **3** | **4** |
| 1973 | 4305 | 4355 | 4332 | 4373 |
| 1974 | 4335 | 4348 | 4306 | 4289 |
| 1975 | 4238 | 4269 | 4341 | 4398 |
| 1976 | 4497 | 4530 | 4552 | 4584 |
| 1977 | 4640 | 4731 | 4816 | 4817 |

1 The table shows real GDP in the Untied States from the first quarter of 1973 to the fourth quarter of 1977.

   a. Did the United States experience a recession during these years? If so, during which quarters?

   b. In which quarter was the United States at a business-cycle peak?

   c. In which quarter was the United States at a business-cycle trough?

   d. In what periods did the United States experience an expansion?

2. A country's real GDP grows at 5 percent a year for three quarters, slows to 0.5 percent a year for three quarters, and then increases back to 5 percent. Has the country experienced a recession?

### Solutions to Additional Practice Problems 29.1

1a. Although GDP fell in the 3rd quarter of 1973 and the first quarter of 1974, it rebounded in each of the following quarters, so these do not qualify as recessions. The United States first experienced a recession from the 3rd quarter of 1974 until the 1st quarter of 1975, when real GDP decreased for three consecutive quarters.

1b. The United States was at a business cycle peak in the 2nd quarter of 1974. In the following quarters, real GDP decreased as the economy went into a recession.

1c. The United States was at a business cycle trough in the first quarter of 1975. In the quarters prior to this quarter, real GDP was decreasing. In the quarters following it, real GDP increased.

1d. The United States experienced an expansion from the 1st quarter of 1973 to the 2nd quarter of 1974 and then from the 2nd quarter of 1975 to the fourth quarter of 1977.

2. The standard definition of a recession is a decrease in real GDP that lasts for at least two quarters. The country has not experienced a decrease in real GDP so by the standard definition, a recession has not occurred.

■ **AP Self Test 29.1**

### True or false

1. A recession begins at a trough and ends at a peak.

2. An expansion is a period during which real GDP decreases.

3. In the United States since 1854, there have been ten complete business cycles.

4. Potential GDP is not always equal to real GDP.

### Multiple choice

1. The business cycle is

   a. a regular up and down movement in production and jobs.

   b. an irregular up and down movement in production and jobs.

   c. a regular movement in price changes.

   d. an irregular movement in price changes.

   e. an irregular up and down movement in the interest rate.

2. The turning point that reflects the end of an expansion is a
   a. peak.
   b. recession.
   c. trough.
   d. trend.
   e. stoppage.

3. A standard definition of recession is a decrease in real GDP that lasts for at least two
   a. years.
   b. quarters.
   c. months.
   d. weeks.
   e. reference periods.

4. Which organization or agency identifies and dates business-cycle phases and turning points in the United States?
   a. Bureau of Economic Analysis
   b. Department of Commerce
   c. National Bureau of Economic Research
   d. Federal Reserve System
   e. Bureau of the Treasury

5. Since 1854, the NBER has identified
   a. 82 complete business cycles.
   b. 33 expansions and 25 recessions.
   c. 33 complete business cycles.
   d. 25 expansions and 33 recessions.
   e. 17 complete business cycles.

6. During the twentieth century, recessions
   a. have shortened and expansions have lengthened.
   b. were as long as expansions.
   c. have lengthened and expansions have shortened.
   d. and expansions have shortened.
   e. and expansions have not changed in length.

### Short Response Questions
1. What is a standard definition of a recession?

2. Figure 29.1 shows how GDP changes over time. In it, identify the different parts of the business cycle.

3. Identify when the economy in Figure 29.2 is experiencing recession.

■ **FIGURE 29.1**
Real GDP (trillions of 2000 dollars)

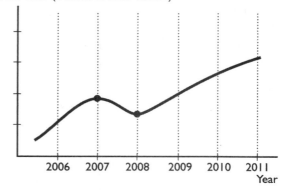

■ **FIGURE 29.2**
Real GDP (trillions of 2000 dollars)

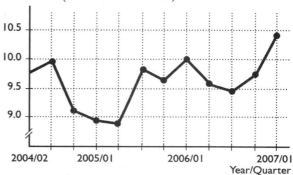

### CHECKPOINT 29.2

■ **Explain the influences on aggregate supply.**

#### Quick Review

- *Aggregate supply* The relationship between the quantity of real GDP supplied and the price level when all other influences on production plans remain the same.

- *Factors that change aggregate supply* Aggregate supply decreases and the aggregate supply curve shifts leftward when potential GDP decreases, when the money wage rate rises, or when the money price of other resources rises.

## Additional Practice Problem 29.2

1. The table shows the aggregate supply schedule for the United Kingdom.

| Price level (GDP deflator) | Real GDP supplied (billions of 1995 pounds) |
|---|---|
| 90 | 650 |
| 100 | 700 |
| 110 | 750 |
| 120 | 800 |
| 130 | 850 |

a. Plot the aggregate supply curve in the figure.

b. If the money wage rate in the United Kingdom increases, show the effect on the aggregate supply curve. Is there a movement along the aggregate supply curve or a shift of the aggregate supply curve?

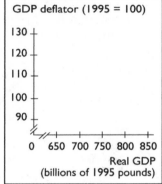

## Solution to Additional Practice Problem 29.2

1a. The aggregate supply curve is plotted in the figure as $AS_0$. The aggregate supply curve has a positive slope, so as the price level rises, the quantity of real GDP supplied increases.

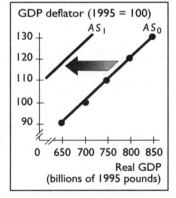

1b. To answer this Practice Problem remember that changes in the price level lead to changes in the aggregate quantity supplied and movements along the aggregate supply curve. Aggregate supply changes when any influence on production plans other than the price level changes. An increase in the money wage rate decreases aggregate supply and shifts the aggregate supply curve leftward, as illustrated by the shift to $AS_1$. A change in the money wage rate shifts the aggregate supply curve.

## ■ AP Self Test 29.2

### True or false

1. Along the aggregate supply curve, a rise in the price level decreases the quantity of real GDP supplied.

2. A rise in the price level decreases potential GDP.

3. Anything that changes potential GDP shifts the aggregate supply curve.

4. An increase in potential GDP shifts the aggregate supply curve rightward.

### Multiple choice

1. Moving along the potential GDP line, the money wage rate changes by the same percentage as the change in the price level so that the real wage rate
   a. increases.
   b. decreases.
   c. stays at the full-employment equilibrium level.
   d. might either increase or decrease.
   e. stays the same, though not necessarily at the full-employment equilibrium level.

2. As the price level rises relative to costs and the real wage rate falls, profits ____ and the number of firms in business ____.
   a. increase; increases
   b. increase; decreases
   c. decrease; increases
   d. decrease; decreases
   e. do not change; do not change

■ **FIGURE 29.3**

Price level (GDP deflator, 2000 = 100)

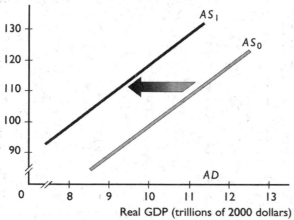

3. In Figure 29.3, which of the following might be the reason for a shift of the aggregate supply curve from $AS_0$ to $AS_1$?
   a. a fall in the money wage rate
   b. an increase in potential GDP
   c. an increase in investment
   d. a fall in the price of oil
   e. a rise in the money wage rate

4. When potential GDP increases,
   a. the $AS$ curve shifts rightward.
   b. there is a movement up along the $AS$ curve.
   c. the $AS$ curve shifts leftward.
   d. there is a movement down along the $AS$ curve.
   e. there is neither a movement along or a shift in the $AS$ curve.

5. If the money wage rate rises,
   a. the $AS$ curve shifts rightward.
   b. there is a movement up along the $AS$ curve.
   c. the $AS$ curve shifts leftward.
   d. there is a movement down along the $AS$ curve.
   e. there is neither a movement along nor a shift in the $AS$ curve.

**Short Response Questions**
1. Which of the following increase aggregate supply and shift the $AS$ rightward? Which of the following decrease aggregate supply and shift the $AS$ curve leftward? Which of the following do not shift the $AS$ curve?
   a. A fall in the money wage rate.
   b. An increase in government expenditure.
   c. An increase in quantity of money.
   d. A rise in the price of oil.
   e. An increase in productivity.
   f. An increase in taxes.
   g. The U.S. exchange rate rises.
   h. Government regulations severely restrict the amount of pollution firms can emit so firms must decrease their production.

| Price level (GDP deflator 2000 = 100) | Quantity of real GDP supplied (trillions of 2000 dollars) | Potential GDP (trillions of 2000 dollars) |
|---|---|---|
| 140 | 17 | 13 |
| 130 | 15 | 13 |
| 120 | 13 | 13 |
| 110 | 11 | 13 |
| 100 | 9 | 13 |

■ **FIGURE 29.4**

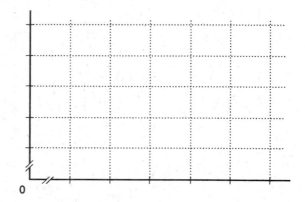

2. The table above gives the aggregate supply schedule and potential GDP schedule for a nation.
   a. Label the axes and then plot the $AS$ curve and potential GDP line in Figure 29.4.
   b. Suppose the money wage rate falls. Show the effect of this change on aggregate supply and potential GDP in Figure 29.4.

■ **FIGURE 29.5**

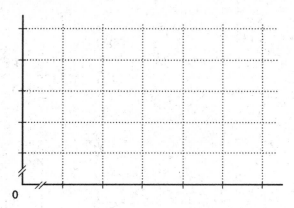

c. Use the data in the table to again plot the AS curve and potential GDP line in Figure 29.5. Be sure to label the axes.

d. Potential GDP increases by $2 trillion. Show the effect of this change on aggregate supply and potential GDP in Figure 29.5.

**Short answer and numeric questions**

1. Why does the AS curve slope upward?

2. Why does the aggregate supply curve shift when the money wage rate rises? Why doesn't the potential GDP line also shift?

3. What is the effect on aggregate supply if the money price of oil rises?

## CHECKPOINT 29.3

■ **Explain the influences on aggregate demand.**

*Quick Review*

- *Aggregate demand* The relationship between the quantity of real GDP demanded and the price level when all other influences on expenditure plans remain the same.

- *Factors that change aggregate demand* Aggregate demand changes and the aggregate demand curve shifts if expected future income, inflation, or profit change; if the government or the Federal Reserve

take steps that change expenditure plans, such as changes in taxes or in the quantity of money; or the state of the world economy changes.

**Practice Problem 29.3**

1. Draw aggregate demand curves and illustrate the effects of each event listed below either by a movement along the aggregate demand curve or a shift in the aggregate demand curve. These events are:

    a. The price level falls.

    b. Firms increase their investment because the expected future rate of profit increases.

    c. The government cuts its taxes.

**Solution to Practice Problem 29.3**

1a. To answer this Practice Problem, remember that a change in any determinant of expenditure plans other than the price level brings a change in aggregate demand and a shift in the AD 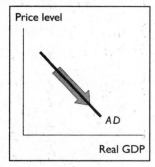 curve. In this part, it *is* the price level that changes, so there is a change in the quantity of real GDP demanded and a movement along the aggregate demand curve. Because the price level falls, there is a downward movement along the aggregate demand curve, as illustrated.

1b. An increase in firms' investment increases aggregate demand. The aggregate demand curve shifts rightward, as shown in the figure by the shift from $AD_0$ to $AD_1$.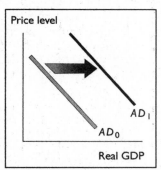

1c. When the government cuts its taxes, house-holds' incomes rise and so they increase their consumption expenditure. Aggregate demand increases and the aggregate demand curve shifts rightward, as illustrated in the previous answer.

## ■ AP Self Test 29.3

### True or false

1. As the price level falls, other things remaining the same, the quantity of real GDP demanded increases.
2. An increase in expected future income will not increase aggregate demand until the income actually increases.
3. A decrease in government purchases shifts the aggregate demand curve rightward.
4. An increase in income in Mexico decreases aggregate demand in the United States because Mexicans will buy more Mexican-produced goods.

### Multiple choice

1. When the price level rises there is a ____ the aggregate demand curve.
   a. rightward shift of
   b. movement down along
   c. leftward shift of
   d. movement up along
   e. rotation of

2. A rise in the price level
   a. raises the buying power of money.
   b. decreases the prices of exports.
   c. lowers the buying power of money.
   d. increases aggregate demand.
   e. makes the aggregate demand curve steeper.

■ **FIGURE 29.6**

Price level (GDP deflator, 2000 = 100)

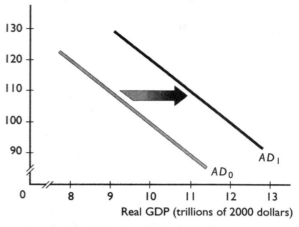

3. In Figure 29.6, the shift in the aggregate demand curve could be the result of
   a. an increase in the quantity of money.
   b. a decrease in foreign incomes.
   c. a tax hike.
   d. a fall in the price level.
   e. a decrease in the expected future rate of profit.

4. A change in which of the following factors does <u>NOT</u> shift the aggregate demand curve?
   a. expectations about the future
   b. the money wage rate
   c. monetary and fiscal policy
   d. foreign income
   e. the foreign exchange rate

5. Which of the following shifts the aggregate demand curve leftward?
   a. a decrease in government expenditures on goods and services
   b. an increase in the price level
   c. a tax cut
   d. an increase in foreign income
   e. a decrease in the price level

6. When investment increases, the ____ in aggregate demand is ____ the change in investment.
   a. increase; greater than
   b. increase; smaller than
   c. increase; the same as
   d. decrease; the same as
   e. decrease; greater than

**Short Response Questions**

1. Which of the following increase aggregate demand and shift the *AD* rightward? Which decrease aggregate demand and shift the *AD* curve leftward? Which do not shift the *AD* curve?
   a. A fall in the money wage rate.
   b. An increase in government expenditure.
   c. An increase in quantity of money.
   d. A rise in the price of oil.
   e. An increase in productivity.
   f. An increase in taxes.
   g. The U.S. exchange rate rises.
   h. Government regulations severely restrict the amount of pollution firms can emit so firms must decrease their production.

■ **FIGURE 29.7**

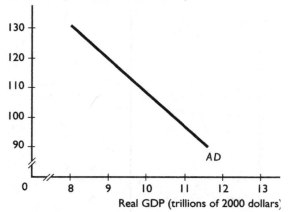

2. Figure 29.7 shows an aggregate demand curve.
   a. Suppose that government expenditures on goods and services increase. In Figure 29.7, illustrate the effect of this fiscal policy.

   b. Suppose the Federal Reserve decreases the quantity of money. In Figure 29.7, illustrate the effect of this monetary policy.

**Long Response Questions**

1. Why does an increase in the price level decrease the quantity of real GDP demanded?

2. Expected future profit increases. Explain the effect on aggregate demand.

3. The government increases its taxes. What is the effect on aggregate demand?

4. What is the aggregate demand multiplier?

## CHECKPOINT 29.4

■ **Explain how fluctuations in aggregate demand and aggregate supply create the business cycle.**

*Quick Review*

- *Effect of decrease in aggregate demand* A decrease in aggregate demand, everything else remaining the same, lowers the price level and decreases real GDP.

- *Effect of decrease in aggregate supply* A decrease in aggregate supply, everything else remaining the same, raises the price level and decreases real GDP.

**Additional Practice Problems 29.4**

1. The table shows aggregate demand and aggregate supply schedules for the United Kingdom.

   a. Plot the aggregate demand curve.

   b. Plot the aggregate supply curve.

   c. What is the macroeconomic equilibrium?

   d. If potential GDP in the United Kingdom is £800 billion, what is the type of macroeconomic equilibrium?

| Price level (GDP deflator) | Real GDP demanded | Real GDP supplied |
|---|---|---|
| | (billions of 1995 pounds) | |
| 90 | 800 | 650 |
| 100 | 775 | 700 |
| 110 | 750 | 750 |
| 120 | 725 | 800 |
| 130 | 700 | 850 |

e. If the government increases its expenditures on goods and services, what is the effect on the British economy?

## Solution to Practice Problems 29.4

1a. The aggregate demand curve is plotted in the figure to the right. The aggregate demand curve has a negative slope, so as the price level falls, the quantity of real GDP demanded increases.

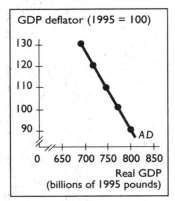

1b. The aggregate supply curve is plotted in the figure. The aggregate supply curve has a positive slope, so as the price level rises, the quantity of real GDP supplied increases.

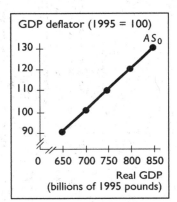

1c. The macroeconomic equilibrium is at a price level of 110 and real GDP of £750 billion. The macroeconomic equilibrium is at the intersection of the aggregate supply curve and the aggregate demand curve.

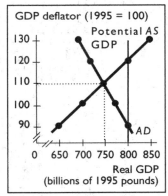

1d. Because potential GDP is £800 billion and the macroeconomic equilibrium is £750 billion, the economy is in a below full-employment equilibrium. Real GDP is less than potential GDP.

1e. If the government increases its expenditures on goods and services, the aggregate demand curve shifts rightward. As a result, the price level rises and real GDP increases, moving the nation closer to a full-employment equilibrium.

## ■ AP Self Test 29.4

### True or false

1. Starting from full employment, an increase in aggregate demand increases real GDP above potential GDP.

2. Starting from full employment, a decrease in aggregate demand shifts the aggregate demand curve leftward and creates an inflationary gap.

3. Starting from full employment, an increase in aggregate demand shifts the aggregate demand curve rightward and creates an inflationary gap.

4. A recessionary gap brings a rising price level to eliminate the gap.

### Multiple choice

1. If the quantity of real GDP supplied equals the quantity of real GDP demanded, then
   a. nominal GDP must equal real GDP.
   b. real GDP must equal potential GDP.
   c. real GDP must be greater than potential GDP.
   d. real GDP might be greater than, equal to, or less than potential GDP.
   e. real GDP must be less than potential GDP.

2. An increase in investment ____ aggregate demand, the aggregate demand curve shifts ____ and the economy is in the ____ phase of the business cycle.
   a. decreases; rightward; expansion
   b. increases; rightward; expansion
   c. decreases; leftward; recession
   d. increases; rightward; recession
   e. increases; leftward; recession

■ **FIGURE 29.8**

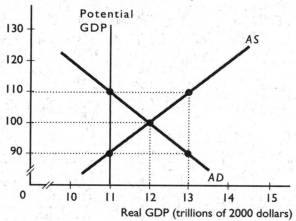

3. In Figure 29.8, the equilibrium price level is ____ and the equilibrium real GDP is ____ trillion.
   a. 110; $11
   b. 110; $13
   c. 100; $12
   d. 90; $11
   e. 90; $13

4. Figure 29.8 shows
   a. a full-employment equilibrium.
   b. an above full-employment equilibrium with an inflationary gap.
   c. an above full-employment equilibrium with a recessionary gap.
   d. a below full-employment equilibrium with an inflationary gap.
   e. a below full-employment equilibrium with a recessionary gap.

5. If government expenditure increases, real GDP ____ and the price level ____.
   a. increases; falls
   b. decreases; does not change
   c. decreases; rises
   d. does not change; does not change
   e. increases; rises

6. If the price of oil rises, the
   a. AD curve shifts rightward, real GDP increases, and the price level rises.
   b. AS curve shifts leftward, the price level rises, and real GDP decreases.
   c. AD curve and the AS curve shift leftward, real GDP decreases, and the price level rises.
   d. AD curve and the AS curve shift rightward, the price level rises, and real GDP decreases.
   e. AS curve shifts leftward, the price level rises, and real GDP increases.

7. Stagflation is a combination of ____ real GDP and a ____ price level.
   a. increasing; rising
   b. increasing; falling
   c. decreasing; rising
   d. decreasing; falling
   e. no change in; rising

8. An inflationary gap is created when
   a. real GDP is greater than potential GDP.
   b. real GDP equal to potential GDP.
   c. the inflation rate is less than potential inflation.
   d. the price level exceeds the equilibrium price level.
   e. potential GDP is greater than real GDP.

9. An economy is at full employment. If aggregate demand increases,
   a. an inflationary gap is created and the AS curve shifts leftward as the money wage rate rises.
   b. an inflationary gap is created and the AD curve shifts leftward.
   c. an inflationary gap is created and potential GDP increases to close the gap.
   d. a recessionary gap is created and the AS curve shifts leftward as the money wage rate falls.
   e. a recessionary gap is created and the AS curve shifts leftward as the money wage rate rises.

**Short Response Questions**

1. What is stagflation? What can create stagflation?

2. What is the effect on aggregate demand, aggregate supply, the price level and real GDP if the government decreases its taxes?

3. What is the effect on aggregate demand, aggregate supply, the price level and real GDP if the government decreases its expenditure?

4. What is the effect on aggregate demand, aggregate supply, the price level and real GDP if the money wage rate falls?

**Long Response Questions**

■ **FIGURE 29.9**

Price level (GDP deflator, 2000 = 100)

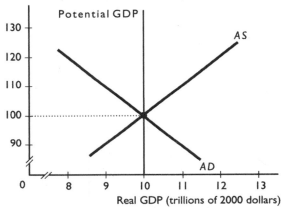

1. Figure 29.9 shows the economy. Suppose people expect an increase in the future expected rate of profit.

   a. In Figure 29.9, show the effect of the change in expectations on the price level and real GDP.

   b. In Figure 29.9, show how the economy returns to potential GDP.

■ **FIGURE 29.10**

Price level (GDP deflator, 2000 = 100)

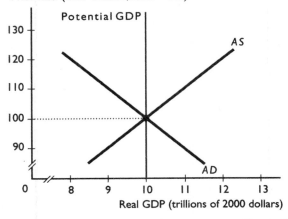

2. Figure 29.10 shows the economy. Show the effect a rise in the price of oil has on the price level and real GDP.

3. What is an inflationary gap and how is it eliminated?

## YOUR AP SELF TEST ANSWERS

### ■ CHECKPOINT 29.1

**True or false**

1. False; page 726
2. False; page 726
3. False; page 726
4. True; pages 728-729

**Multiple choice**

1. b; page 726
2. a; page 726
3. b; page 726
4. c; page 726
5. c; page 726
6. a; page 727

**Short Response Questions**

1. The standard definition of a recession is a decrease in real GDP that lasts for at least two quarters (six months); page 726.

### ■ FIGURE 29.11

Real GDP (trillions of 2000 dollars)

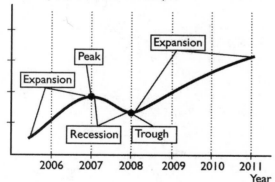

2. Figure 29.11 divides the data into the two phases and the two turning points of the business cycle; page 726.

3. A recession runs from the third quarter of 2004 to the second quarter of 2005 and from the first quarter of 2006 to the third quarter of 2006; page 726.

### ■ CHECKPOINT 29.2

**True or false**

1. False; page 732
2. False; page 732
3. True; page 735
4. True; page 735

**Multiple choice**

1. c; page 732
2. a; page 734
3. e; page 736
4. a; page 735
5. c; page 736

**Short Response Questions**

1. Parts (a) and (e) increase aggregate supply and shift the *AS* curve rightward. Parts (d) and (h) decrease aggregate supply and shift the *AS* curve leftward. Parts (b), (c), (f), and (g) do not shift the *AS* curve; pages 735-736.

### ■ FIGURE 29.12

Price level (GDP deflator, 2000 = 100)

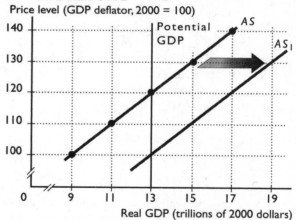

2. a. Figure 29.12 labels the axes. The aggregate supply curve is labeled *AS*; page 733.

   b. The fall in the money wage rate has no effect on potential GDP, so the potential GDP line does not change. Aggregate supply, however, increases so the *AS* curve shifts rightward, to an *AS* curve such as *AS₁*; page 736.

■ **FIGURE 29.13**

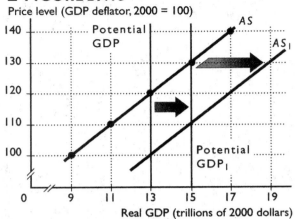

Price level (GDP deflator, 2000 = 100)

c. Figure 29.13 labels the axes. The aggregate supply curve is labeled *AS*; page 733.

d. The potential GDP line shifts rightward by $2 trillion, as indicated by the shift to Potential GDP1. The aggregate supply curve also shifts rightward by $2 trillion, as shown by the shift to *AS*1; page 736.

**Long Response Questions**

1. The movement along the *AS* curve brings a change in the real wage rate (and changes in the real cost of other resources whose money prices are fixed). If the price level rises, the real wage rate falls.

   A fall in the real wage rate boosts a firm's profit. The number of firms in business increases.

   If the price level rises relative to costs, fewer firms will want to shut down, so more firms operate.

   If the price level rises and the money wage rate does not change, an extra hour of labor that was previously unprofitable becomes profitable. So, the quantity of labor demanded increases and production increases.

   For the economy as a whole, as the price level rises, the quantity of real GDP supplied increases; pages 733-735.

2. An increase in the money wage rate increases firms' costs. The higher are firms' costs, the smaller is the quantity that firms are willing to supply at each price level. Aggregate sup-

ply decreases and the *AS* curve shifts leftward. A change in the money wage rate does not change potential GDP. Potential GDP depends only on the economy's real ability to produce and on the full-employment quantity of labor, which occurs at the equilibrium real wage rate. The equilibrium real wage rate can occur at any money wage rate; page 736.

3. If the money price of oil rises, firm's costs increase. The higher are firms' costs, the smaller is the quantity that firms are willing to supply at each price level. Aggregate supply decreases and the aggregate supply curve shifts leftward; page 736.

■ **CHECKPOINT 29.3**

**True or false**

1. True; page 738
2. False; page 740
3. False; page 741
4. False; page 742

**Multiple choice**

1. d; page 739
2. c; pages 738-739
3. a; page 741
4. b; paged 740-742
5. a; pages 740-742
6. a; page 742

**Short Response Questions**

1. Parts (b) and (c) increase aggregate demand and shift the *AD* curve rightward. Parts (f) and (g) decrease aggregate demand and shift the *AD* curve leftward. Parts (a), (d), (e), and (h) do not shift the *AD* curve; pages 740-742.

■ **FIGURE 29.14**

Price level (GDP deflator, 2000 = 100)

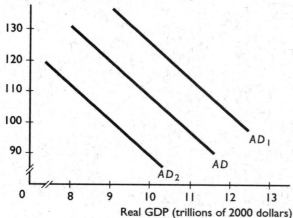

2. a. In Figure 29.14, an increase in government purchases increases aggregate demand and shifts the *AD* curve rightward, from *AD* to *AD*₁; page 741.
   b. In Figure 29.14, a decrease in the quantity of money decreases aggregate demand and shifts the *AD* curve leftward, from *AD* to *AD*₂; page 741.

**Long Response Questions**

1. An increase in the price level decreases the quantity of real GDP demanded for several reasons. First an increase in the price level lowers the buying power of money, which decreases consumption expenditure. Second it raises the demand for money which raises the equilibrium real interest rate so that investment decreases. Finally it raises the real prices of exports, and lowers the real price of imports so that net exports decrease; pages 738-740.

2. Firms are in business to earn a profit. An increase in expected future profit increases the investment that firms plan to undertake and increases aggregate demand; page 740.

3. The government can influence aggregate demand by changing taxes. When the government increases taxes, consumers disposable income falls. As a result, consumption expenditure decreases so that aggregate demand decreases; page 741.

4. The aggregate demand multiplier is an effect that magnifies changes in expenditure and increases fluctuations in aggregate demand. For example, an increase in investment increases aggregate demand and increases income. The increase in income induces an increase in consumption expenditure so aggregate demand increases by more than the initial increase in investment; page 742.

■ **CHECKPOINT 29.4**

**True or false**
   1. True; pages 744-745
   2. False; pages 744-745, 748
   3. True; pages 744-745, 748
   4. False; page 748

**Multiple choice**
   1. d; page 744
   2. b; pages 744-745
   3. c; page 744
   4. b; pages 744-745, 748
   5. e; pages 741, 745
   6. b; page 746-747
   7. c; page 746
   8. a; page 748
   9. a; page 748

**Short Response Questions**

1. Stagflation is a combination of recession (falling real GDP) and inflation (rising price level). Stagflation can be created by a decrease in aggregate supply; page 746.

2. A tax cut increases consumption expenditure, thereby increasing aggregate demand and shifting the *AD* curve rightward. The price level rises and real GDP increases; page 745.

3. A decrease in government expenditures decreases aggregate demand and shifts the *AD* curve leftward. The price level falls and real GDP decreases; page 745.

4. A fall in the money wage rate increases aggregate supply and shifts the *AS* curve

rightward. The price level falls and real GDP increases; page 746.

## Long Response Questions

### ■ FIGURE 29.15

Price level (GDP deflator, 2000 = 100)

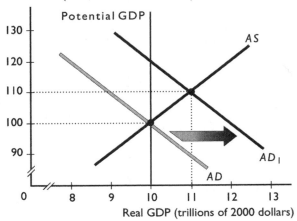

1. a. An increase in expected rate of profit increases firms' investment which increases aggregate demand. The aggregate demand curve shifts rightward from *AD* to *AD*1 in Figure 29.15. The equilibrium price level rises to 110 and equilibrium real GDP increases to $11 trillion; pages 744-746.

   b. An inflationary gap now exists. The money wage rate rises and aggregate supply decreases. In Figure 29.16 the *AS* curve shifts leftward. Eventually the *AS* curve moves to *AS*1. Real GDP returns to potential GDP, $10 trillion, and the price level rises to 120; page 748.

2. Figure 29.17 shows the effect of a rise in the price of oil. Aggregate supply decreases and the *AS* curve shifts leftward from *AS* to *AS*1. Real GDP decreases to $9 trillion and the price level rises to 110; page 746.

3. An inflationary gap is a gap that exists when real GDP exceeds potential GDP. An inflationary gap brings a rising price level. Workers have experienced a fall in the buying power of their wages, and firms' profits have

### ■ FIGURE 29.16

Price level (GDP deflator, 2000 = 100)

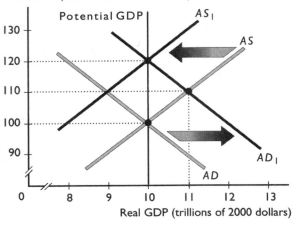

### ■ FIGURE 29.17

Price level (GDP deflator, 2000 = 100)

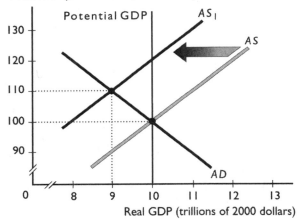

increased. Employment exceeds full employment. Workers demand higher wages. As the money wage rate rises, aggregate supply decreases and the aggregate supply curve shifts leftward. Eventually, real GDP will return to potential GDP and the inflationary gap is eliminated; page 748.

# Aggregate Expenditure

## Chapter 30

■ **Distinguish between autonomous expenditure and induced expenditure and explain how real GDP influences expenditure plans.**

Aggregate *planned* expenditure is planned consumption expenditure plus planned investment plus planned government expenditures plus planned net exports. Aggregate *planned* expenditure does not always equal real GDP. Induced expenditure are the components of aggregate expenditure that change when real GDP changes; autonomous expenditure are the components of aggregate expenditure that do not change when real GDP changes. The consumption function is the relationship between consumption expenditure and disposable income. The marginal propensity to consume, *MPC*, is the fraction of a change in disposable income that is spent on consumption. When real GDP increases, imports increase. The marginal propensity to import is the fraction of an increase in real GDP spent on imports.

■ **Explain how real GDP adjusts to achieve equilibrium expenditure.**

Equilibrium expenditure occurs when aggregate *planned* expenditure equals real GDP. It occurs at the point where the *AE* curve intersects the 45° line. If aggregate planned expenditure is less than real GDP, an unplanned increase in inventories occurs. Firms decrease production and real GDP decreases until real GDP equals aggregate planned expenditure and the economy is at equilibrium expenditure. If aggregate planned expenditure exceeds real GDP, an unplanned decrease in inventories occurs. Firms increase production and real GDP increases. The economy moves to its equilibrium expenditure.

■ **Describe and explain the expenditure multiplier.**

The expenditure multiplier is the amount by which a change in any component of autonomous expenditure is multiplied to determine the change that it creates in equilibrium expenditure and real GDP. The multiplier is greater than 1 because an increase in autonomous expenditure induces further changes in aggregate expenditure. If we ignore income taxes and imports, the multiplier equals $1 \div (1 - MPC)$. The multiplier is larger if the *MPC* is larger. Imports and income taxes reduce the size of the multiplier. In general, the multiplier equals $1 \div (1 - \text{slope of } AE \text{ curve})$. An expansion is triggered by an increase in autonomous expenditure that increases aggregate planned expenditure and real GDP.

■ **Derive the *AD* curve from equilibrium expenditure.**

The *AE* curve is the relationship between aggregate planned expenditure and real GDP, when all other influences on expenditure plans remain the same. The *AD* curve is the relationship between the quantity of real GDP demanded and the price level. When the price level rises, aggregate planned expenditure decreases, the *AE* curve shifts downward, and equilibrium expenditure decreases. When the price level rises, aggregate planned expenditure increases, the *AE* curve shifts upward, and equilibrium expenditure increases. Each point of equilibrium expenditure corresponds to a point on the *AD* curve.

## EXPANDED CHAPTER CHECKLIST

**When you have completed this chapter, you will be able to:**

**1** **Distinguish between autonomous expenditure and induced expenditure and explain how real GDP influences expenditure plans.**

- Compare autonomous expenditure and induced expenditure.
- Describe the consumption function and define the marginal propensity to consume, *MPC*.
- List the influences on consumption and describe their effect on the consumption function.

**2** **Explain how real GDP adjusts to achieve equilibrium expenditure.**

- Describe the relationship between aggregate planned expenditure and real GDP and illustrate aggregate expenditure with an *AE* curve.
- Discuss how equilibrium expenditure is determined and illustrate equilibrium expenditure using the *AE* curve and a 45° line.

**3** **Describe and explain the expenditure multiplier.**

- Define the multiplier.
- Explain the relationship between the *MPC* and the multiplier.
- Discuss why income taxes and imports reduce the size of the multiplier and state the general formula for the multiplier, $1 \div (1 - \text{slope of } AE \text{ curve})$.
- Describe what initiates a business cycle expansion or recession and discuss the impact of the multiplier in creating expansions and recessions.

**4** **Derive the *AD* curve from equilibrium expenditure.**

- Discuss the differences between the *AE* curve and the *AD* curve.

## YOUR AP TEST HINTS

### AP Topics

| Topic on your AP test | Corresponding textbook section |
|---|---|
| National income and price determination | |
| Aggregate Demand | Chapter 30 |
| • Determinants of aggregate demand | Checkpoint 30.4 |
| • Multiplier | Checkpoint 30.2 |

### Extra AP material

- On the AP test, the marginal propensity to save (*MPS*) is sometimes used. The marginal propensity to save is related to the marginal propensity to consume (*MPC*). The marginal propensity to consume is the additional consumption expenditure that results from an additional dollar of disposable income. The marginal propensity to save is the additional saving that results from an additional dollar of disposable income. Because an additional dollar of disposable income must be either spent or saved, it is the case that $MPC + MPS = 1$. This result can be rearranged to show that $MPS = 1 - MPC$. As a result, the formula for the expenditure multiplier, $1/(1 - MPC)$, can be rewritten as $1/(MPS)$.
- The aggregate expenditure model is not a major topic on the AP test.

## CHECKPOINT 30.1

■ **Distinguish between autonomous expenditure and induced expenditure and explain how real GDP influences expenditure plans.**

### Quick Review

- *Autonomous expenditure* The components of aggregate expenditure that do not change when real GDP changes.
- *Consumption function* The relationship between consumption expenditure and

disposable income, other things remaining the same.

- *Marginal propensity to consume, MPC* The fraction of a change in disposable income that is spent on consumption, which equals the change in consumption expenditure divided by the change in disposable income that brought it about.

### Additional Practice Problems 30.1

1. Suppose disposable income increases by $1.5 trillion.

   a. If the marginal propensity to consume (*MPC*) is 0.8, what is the change in consumption expenditure?

   b. If the *MPC* equals 0.6, what is the change in consumption expenditure?

   c. What is the relationship between the *MPC* and the change in consumption expenditure for a given change in disposable income?

2. The figure shows the consumption function for a small nation. Calculate the marginal propensity to consume and autonomous consumption in the nation.

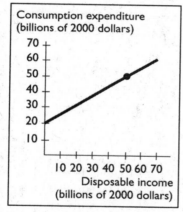

Consumption expenditure (billions of 2000 dollars)

Disposable income (billions of 2000 dollars)

### Solutions to Additional Practice Problems 30.1

1a. The change in consumption expenditure equals the *MPC* multiplied by the change in disposable income. When the *MPC* is 0.8, the change in consumption expenditure equals ($1.5 trillion) × (0.8), which is $1.2 trillion.

1b. When the *MPC* is 0.6, the change in consumption expenditure is ($1.5 trillion) × (0.6), which is $0.9 trillion.

1c. The larger the *MPC*, the greater the change in consumption expenditure for a given change in disposable income.

2. The *MPC* is the slope of the consumption function and equals the change in consumption expenditure divided by the change in disposable income that brought it about. The figure shows

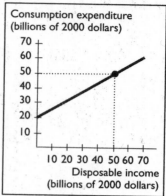

Consumption expenditure (billions of 2000 dollars)

Disposable income (billions of 2000 dollars)

that when disposable income increases from $0 to $50 billion, consumption expenditure increases from $20 billion to $50 billion. The *MPC* equals ($30 billion) ÷ ($50 billion), which is 0.60. Autonomous consumption is the amount of consumption when income equals zero and equals the *y*-axis intercept, $20 billion.

### ■ AP Self Test 30.1

**True or false**

1. Induced expenditure increases as real GDP increases.

2. The slope of the consumption function is less than the slope of the 45° line.

3. The marginal propensity to consume equals consumption expenditure divided by disposable income.

4. The consumption function shifts when the buying power of net assets changes.

**Multiple choice**

1. When disposable income increases from $9 trillion to $10 trillion, consumption expenditure increases from $6 trillion to $6.8 trillion. The *MPC* is
   a. 1.00.
   b. 0.80.
   c. 0.60.
   d. 0.68.
   e. $6.8 trillion.

■ **FIGURE 30.1**

Consumption expenditure (billions of 2000 dollars)

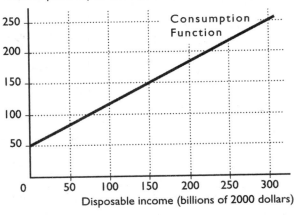

**Short Response Question**

| Disposable income (trillions of 2000 dollars) | Consumption expenditure, (trillions of 2000 dollars) |
|---|---|
| 0.0 | 0.4 |
| 1.0 | 1.2 |
| 2.0 | 2.0 |
| 3.0 | 2.8 |
| 4.0 | 3.6 |
| 5.0 | 4.4 |

■ **FIGURE 30.2**

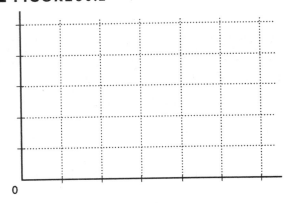

2. Figure 30.1 shows a consumption function. What is the amount of autonomous consumption?
   a. $0
   b. $50 billion
   c. $100 billion
   d. $150 billion
   e. $200 billion

3. Figure 30.1 shows a consumption function. What is the amount of induced consumption when disposable income equals $150 billion?
   a. $0
   b. $50 billion
   c. $100 billion
   d. $150 billion
   e. $200 billion

4. Figure 30.1 shows a consumption function. What does the *MPC* equal?
   a. 1.00
   b. 0.80
   c. 0.67
   d. 0.60
   e. 0.50

1. The table above has data on consumption expenditure and disposable income.
   a. Using the data, label the axes and plot the consumption function in Figure 30.2.
   b. Indicate the amount of autonomous consumption expenditure in Figure 30.2.
   c. What is the amount of saving if disposable income equals $1.0 trillion? $4.0 trillion?
   d. Calculate the marginal propensity to consume.
   e. Suppose the real interest rate falls and consumers increase their consumption by $0.6 trillion at every level of disposable income. Draw the new consumption function in Figure 30.2. What is the amount of autonomous consumption now?

2. In a graph with a consumption function, what does the *MPC* equal? What does autonomous consumption equal?

| Change in disposable income (trillions of 2000 dollars) | Change in consumption expenditure (trillions of 2000 dollars) | Marginal propensity to consume, MPC |
|---|---|---|
| 2 | 1.8 | ____ |
| 1 | 0.9 | ____ |
| 4 | 3.0 | ____ |

3. The table above shows the change in consumption expenditure when a change in disposable income occurs. Complete the table by calculating the marginal propensities to consume.

## CHECKPOINT 30.2

### ■ Explain how real GDP adjusts to achieve equilibrium expenditure.

**Quick Review**

- *Equilibrium expenditure* The level of aggregate expenditure that occurs when aggregate planned expenditure equals real GDP.

**Additional Practice Problem 30.2**

| GDP | C | I | G | X | M |
|---|---|---|---|---|---|
| 50 | 50 | 20 | 25 | 25 | 10 |
| 100 | 85 | 20 | 25 | 25 | 15 |
| 150 | 120 | 20 | 25 | 25 | 20 |
| 200 | 155 | 20 | 25 | 25 | 25 |
| 250 | 190 | 20 | 25 | 25 | 30 |
| 300 | 225 | 20 | 25 | 25 | 35 |

1. The table gives the components of real GDP in billions of dollars.
   a. Draw the aggregate expenditure curve.
   b. What is equilibrium expenditure?
   c. At what levels of GDP does aggregate planned expenditure exceed real GDP? At what levels does real GDP exceed aggregate planned expenditure?
   d. At what levels of GDP is unplanned inventory change negative? At what levels is unplanned inventory change positive?
   e. What is the relationship between your answers to parts (c) and (d)?

**Solution to Additional Practice Problem 30.2**

1a. Aggregate planned expenditure equals $C + I + G + X - M$. To construct the $AE$ curve add the components of aggregate planned expenditure together for each level of real GDP. The $AE$ curve is illustrated in the figure, along with a 45° line.

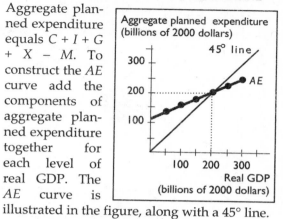

1b. Equilibrium expenditure occurs at the level of real GDP where the $AE$ curve intersects the 45° line. The equilibrium expenditure is $200 billion.

1c. For all GDP less than $200 billion, aggregate planned expenditure exceeds real GDP. For all GDP greater than $200 billion, aggregate planned expenditure exceeds real GDP.

1d. For all GDP less than $200 billion, unplanned inventory change is negative. For all GDP greater than $200 billion, unplanned inventory change is positive.

1e. For all levels of GDP for which aggregate planned expenditure exceeds real GDP, unplanned inventory change is negative. And for all levels of GDP for which real GDP exceeds aggregate planned expenditure, unplanned inventory change is positive.

### ■ AP Self Test 30.2

**True or false**

1. Equilibrium expenditure occurs at the intersection of the aggregate expenditure curve and the 45º line.

2. If planned expenditure is less than real GDP, unplanned inventories increase.

3. If aggregate planned expenditure exceeds real GDP, inventories decrease and firms decrease production.

## Multiple choice

### ■ FIGURE 30.3

Aggregate planned expenditure (trillions of 2000 dollars)

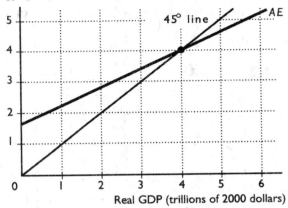

1. In Figure 30.3, equilibrium expenditure equals ____ trillion.
   a. $1
   b. $2
   c. $3
   d. $4
   e. $5

2. In Figure 30.3, if real GDP is $5 trillion, then
   a. the economy is at its equilibrium.
   b. inventories are above their target.
   c. inventories are below their target
   d. the price level will rise to restore equilibrium.
   e. the price level will fall to restore equilibrium.

3. When aggregate planned expenditure exceeds real GDP, there is
   a. a planned decrease in inventories.
   b. a planned increase in inventories.
   c. an unplanned decrease in inventories.
   d. an unplanned increase in inventory.
   e. an unplanned decrease in the price level.

4. Equilibrium expenditure is the level of expenditure at which
   a. firms' inventories are zero.
   b. firms' inventories are at the desired level.
   c. firms produce more output than they sell.
   d. aggregate planned expenditure minus planned changes in inventories equals real GDP.
   e. aggregate planned expenditure plus planned changes in inventories equals real GDP.

## Short Response Questions

| GDP | C | I | G | X | M | AE |
|-----|-----|-----|-----|-----|-----|-----|
| 0.0 | 0.6 | 0.4 | 0.2 | 0.2 | 0.2 | __ |
| 1.0 | 1.2 | 0.4 | 0.2 | 0.2 | 0.4 | __ |
| 2.0 | 1.8 | 0.4 | 0.2 | 0.2 | 0.6 | __ |
| 3.0 | 2.4 | 0.4 | 0.2 | 0.2 | 0.8 | __ |
| 4.0 | 3.0 | 0.4 | 0.2 | 0.2 | 1.0 | __ |
| 5.0 | 3.6 | 0.4 | 0.2 | 0.2 | 1.2 | __ |

### ■ FIGURE 30.4

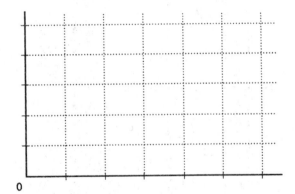

1. The table above gives the components of aggregate planned expenditure in trillions of 2000 dollars.
   a. Complete the table.
   b. Label the axes in Figure 30.4 and then plot the *AE* curve.
   c. In Figure 30.4, show the equilibrium expenditure.

2. If aggregate planned expenditure is less than real GDP, what forces drive the economy to equilibrium expenditure?

## CHECKPOINT 30.3

■ **Describe and explain the expenditure multiplier.**

### Quick Review

- *Multiplier* The expenditure multiplier is the amount by which a change in any component of autonomous expenditure is magnified or multiplied to determine the change that it generates in equilibrium expenditure and real GDP.
- *Basic multiplier formula* The defining multiplier formula is:

$$\text{Multiplier} = \frac{\text{Change in equilibrium expenditure}}{\text{Change in autonomous expenditure}}.$$

- *Multiplier and the MPC* With no imports or income taxes, the multiplier is:

$$\text{Multiplier} = \frac{1}{(1 - MPC)}.$$

- *Multiplier, imports and income taxes* With imports and income taxes, the multiplier is:

$$\text{Multiplier} = \frac{1}{(1 - \text{slope of the } AE \text{ curve})}.$$

### Additional Practice Problems 30.3

1. An economy has no imports or taxes, the *MPC* is 0.90, and real GDP is $12 trillion. If businesses increase investment by $0.1 trillion:
   a. Calculate the multiplier.
   b. Calculate the change in real GDP.
   c. Calculate the new level of real GDP.

2. An increase in autonomous expenditure of $2 trillion increases equilibrium expenditure by $4 trillion:
   a. Calculate the multiplier.
   b. Calculate the slope of the *AE* curve.

3. Suppose there are no income taxes or imports. How would the following events affect equilibrium expenditure and real GDP?
   a. Investment increases by $40 billion and the *MPC* equals 0.6.
   b. The president and Congress agree to increase military spending by $100 billion and the *MPC* is 0.8.

### Solutions to Additional Practice Problems 30.3

1a. With no taxes or imports, the multiplier equals 1 ÷ (1 − *MPC*). The *MPC* is 0.9, so the multiplier equals 1 ÷ (1 - 0.9), which equals 10.0.

1b. The change in real GDP is equal to the multiplier times the change in investment, which is 10 × $0.1 trillion = $1 trillion.

1c. Real GDP increases by $1 trillion from $12 trillion to $13 trillion.

2a. The multiplier equals the change in equilibrium expenditure divided by the change in autonomous expenditure. The multiplier equals $4 trillion ÷ $2 trillion, which is 2.

2b. The expenditure multiplier equals 1/(1 − slope of the *AE* curve). The multiplier is 2, so 2 = 1/(1 − slope of the *AE* curve). Multiply both sides by (1 − slope of the *AE* curve) to get 2 × (1 − slope of the *AE* curve) = 1. Solve for the slope of the *AE* curve, which is that the slope of the *AE* curve is 0.50.

3a. The increase in investment is an increase in autonomous expenditure. The change in equilibrium expenditure and real GDP equals the multiplier times the change in autonomous expenditure. The multiplier equals 1 ÷ (1 − *MPC*) = 1 ÷ (1 − 0.6) = 2.5. The change in equilibrium expenditure and real GDP equals (2.5) × ($40 billion), which is $100 billion. Equilibrium expenditure and real GDP increase by $100 billion.

3b. The increase in military spending is an increase in government purchases and is an increase in autonomous expenditure. The change in equilibrium expenditure and real GDP equals the multiplier times the change in autonomous expenditure. The multiplier equals 1 ÷ (1 − *MPC*). Because the *MPC* equals 0.8, the multiplier is 5.0. The change in equilibrium expenditure and real GDP equals (5.0) × ($100 billion), which is $500 billion.

## ■ AP Self Test 30.3

**True or false**

1. The multiplier is greater than 1.

2. If the multiplier equals 4, then a $0.25 trillion increase in investment increases real GDP by $1.0 trillion.

3. The smaller the marginal propensity to consume, the larger is the multiplier.

4. A country that has a high marginal tax rate has a larger multiplier than a country with a low marginal tax rate, other things being the same.

**Multiple choice**

1. The multiplier is equal to the change in ____ divided by the change in ____.
   a. autonomous expenditure; equilibrium expenditure
   b. dependent expenditure; autonomous expenditure
   c. real GDP; equilibrium expenditure
   d. equilibrium expenditure; autonomous expenditure
   e. the price level; real GDP

2. The multiplier is larger than one because
   a. an increase in autonomous expenditure induces further increases in aggregate expenditure.
   b. additional expenditure induces lower incomes.
   c. an increase in autonomous expenditure brings about a reduction in the real interest rate.
   d. an increase in autonomous expenditure induces further decreases in aggregate expenditure.
   e. the price level rises, thereby reinforcing the initial effect.

3. The multiplier equals 5 and there is a $3 million increase in investment. Equilibrium expenditure
   a. decreases by $15 million.
   b. increases by $3 million.
   c. increases by $5 million.
   d. increases by $15 million.
   e. increases by $0.60 million.

4. In an economy with no income taxes or imports, the marginal propensity to consume is 0.80. The multiplier is
   a. 0.20.
   b. 0.80.
   c. 1.25.
   d. 5.00.
   e. 10.00.

5. An increase in the marginal tax rate
   a. increases the multiplier.
   b. decreases the multiplier but cannot make it negative.
   c. has no effect on the multiplier.
   d. can either increase or decrease the multiplier.
   e. decreases the multiplier and can make it negative.

6. Which of the following increases the magnitude of the expenditure multiplier?
   a. a decrease in the marginal propensity to consume
   b. an increase in autonomous spending
   c. an increase in the marginal income tax rate
   d. a decrease in the marginal propensity to import
   e. an increase in investment

**■ FIGURE 30.5**

Aggregate planned expenditure (trillions of 2000 dollars)

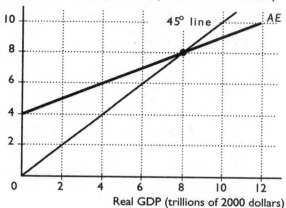

Real GDP (trillions of 2000 dollars)

**■ FIGURE 30.6**

Aggregate planned expenditure (trillions of 2000 dollars)

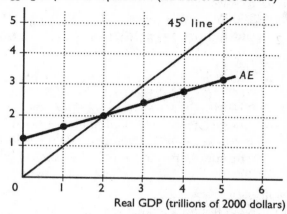

Real GDP (trillions of 2000 dollars)

7. In Figure 30.5, the slope of the $AE$ curve is ____ and the multiplier equals ____.
   a. 0.8; 5.0
   b. 0.4; 2.5
   c. 0.90; 10.0
   d. 0.50; 0.5
   e. 0.50; 2.0

8. If the slope of the $AE$ curve is 0.5, then the expenditure multiplier equals
   a. 5.
   b. 4.
   c. 3.
   d. 2.
   e. 0.5.

9. At the beginning of a recession, the multiplier
   a. offsets the initial cut in autonomous expenditure and slows the recession.
   b. reinforces the initial cut in autonomous expenditure and adds force to the recession.
   c. offsets the initial cut in autonomous expenditure and reverses the recession.
   d. reinforces the initial cut in autonomous expenditure and reverses the recession.
   e. has no effect on the recession.

**Short Response Questions**

1. Figure 30.6 shows the aggregate planned expenditure curve for a nation. Suppose that

that government purchases increase by $1.2 trillion at every level of real GDP.
   a. In Figure 30.6 plot the new aggregate expenditure curve.
   b. What is the new equilibrium expenditure? By how much did equilibrium expenditure change?
   c. What is the slope of the new (and old) $AE$ curve?
   d. What is the multiplier? Use the multiplier to find the change in equilibrium expenditure.

| Marginal propensity to consume, MPC | Multiplier |
|---|---|
| 0.9 | ____ |
| 0.8 | ____ |
| 0.7 | ____ |
| 0.6 | ____ |
| 0.5 | ____ |
| 0.4 | ____ |

2. The table gives various values for the marginal propensity to consume. Suppose there are no income taxes or imports. Complete the table by calculating the values of the multiplier. What is the relationship between the $MPC$ and the multiplier?

**Long Response Question**

1. Why is the multiplier greater than 1?

# CHECKPOINT 30.4

## ■ Derive the *AD* curve from equilibrium expenditure.

### Quick Review

- *Equilibrium expenditure* The level of aggregate expenditure that occurs when aggregate planned expenditure equals real GDP.
- *Aggregate demand* The real GDP at equilibrium expenditure and the associated price level are the aggregate demand schedule.

### Additional Practice Problem 30.4

■ **FIGURE 30.7**

Aggregate planned expenditure (trillions of 2000 dollars)

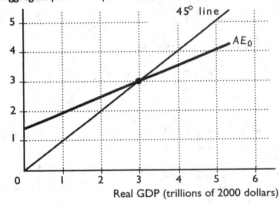

Real GDP (trillions of 2000 dollars)

1. Figure 30.7 shows the *AE* curve, *AE*₀, when the price level is 100.

   a. In the figure, show what occurs when the price level rises to 110 and aggregate planned expenditure decreases by $1 trillion at every level of real GDP. What is the new equilibrium expenditure?

   b. In the figure, show what occurs when the price level falls to 90 and aggregate planned expenditure increases by $1 trillion at every level of real GDP. What is the new equilibrium expenditure?

   c. Use the results from parts (a) and (b) to draw an aggregate demand curve in Figure 30.8.

■ **FIGURE 30.8**

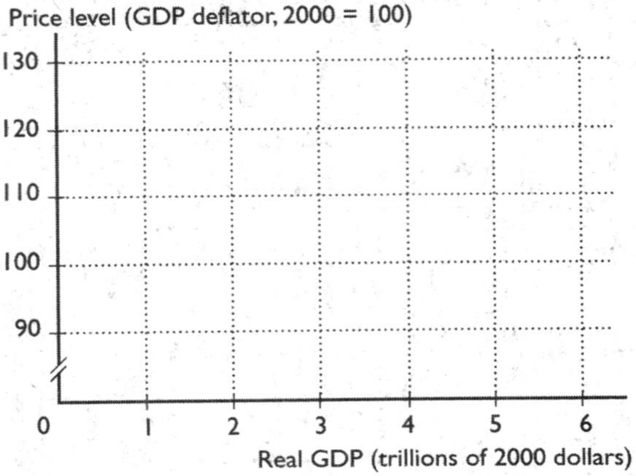

Price level (GDP deflator, 2000 = 100)

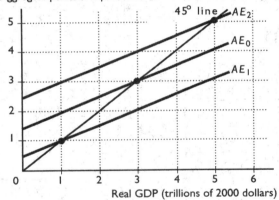

Real GDP (trillions of 2000 dollars)

### Solution to Additional Practice Problem 30.4

■ **FIGURE 30.9**

Aggregate planned expenditure (trillions of 2000 dollars)

Real GDP (trillions of 2000 dollars)

1a. Figure 30.9 shows the new aggregate expenditure curve, labeled *AE*₁. The new equilibrium expenditure is $1 trillion, where the *AE*₁ curve intersects the 45° line.

1b. Figure 30.9 shows the new aggregate expenditure curve, labeled *AE*₂. The new equilibrium expenditure is $5 trillion.

1c. Points on the aggregate demand schedule are the points of equilibrium expenditure. So each point of equilibrium expenditure corresponds to a point on the *AD* curve. When the price level is 110, real GDP is $1 trillion. When the price level is 100, real GDP is $3 trillion. And when the price level is 90, real GDP is $5 trillion. These points and the ag-

■ **FIGURE 30.10**

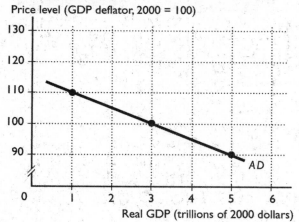

gregate demand curve are shown Figure 30.10. The aggregate demand curve has been derived from the equilibrium expenditure model.

■ **AP Self Test 30.4**

**True or false**

1. There is no relationship between equilibrium expenditure and the *AD* curve.

2. Each point of equilibrium expenditure on the *AE* curve corresponds to a point on the *AD* curve.

**Multiple choice**

1. A movement along the *AE* curve arises from a change in ____ and a movement along the *AD* curve arises from a change in ____.
   a. real GDP; the price level
   b. real GDP; investment
   c. the price level; the price level
   d. the price level; investment
   e. investment; the price level

2. The level of equilibrium expenditure at each price level determines
   a. the points on the *AD* curve.
   b. aggregate planned production.
   c. the price level.
   d. full employment.
   e. the points on the *AE* curve.

3. A change in the price level
   a. shifts the *AE* curve and creates a movement along the *AD* curve.
   b. creates a movement along the *AE* curve and shifts the *AD* curve.
   c. shifts the *AE* curve and the *AD* curve in the same direction.
   d. shifts the *AE* curve and the *AD* curve in opposite directions.
   e. creates a movement along both the *AE* curve and the *AD* curve.

4. The *AD* curve is the relationship between
   a. aggregate planned expenditure and the price level.
   b. aggregate planned expenditure and the quantity of real GDP demanded.
   c. the quantity of real GDP demanded and the price level.
   d. the quantity of real GDP demanded and the unemployment rate.
   e. aggregate planned expenditure and real GDP when the price level is fixed.

**Short Response Question**

1. What is the relationship between the *AE* curve and the *AD* curve?

## YOUR AP SELF TEST ANSWERS

### ■ CHECKPOINT 30.1

**True or false**
1. True;  page 758
2. True;  page 759
3. False;  page 760
4. True;  page 761

**Multiple choice**
1. b; page 760
2. b; page 758
3. c; page 758
4. c; page 760

**Short Response Questions**

■ **FIGURE 30.11**

Consumption expenditure (trillions of 2000 dollars)

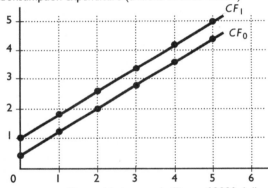

Disposable income (trillions of 2000 dollars)

1. a. Figure 30.11 plots the consumption function, labeled $CF_0$; page 759.
   b. Autonomous consumption is $0.4 trillion, the $y$-intercept of curve $CF_0$ in Figure 30.11; page 758.
   c. If disposable income is $1.0 trillion, consumption expenditure is $1.2 trillion, so saving is −$0.2 trillion. If disposable income is $4.0 trillion consumption expenditure is $3.6 trillion, so saving is $0.4 trillion; page 759.
   d. The marginal propensity to consume is 0.80; page 760.

e. The new consumption function is labeled $CF_1$ in Figure 30.11. Autonomous consumption is $1 trillion; page 758.

2. The $MPC$ equals the slope of the consumption function. Autonomous consumption equals the $y$-axis intercept; pages 758, 760.

| Change in disposable income (trillions of 2000 dollars) | Change in consumption expenditure (trillions of 2000 dollars) | Marginal propensity to consume, MPC |
|---|---|---|
| 2 | 1.8 | 0.90 |
| 1 | 0.9 | 0.90 |
| 4 | 3.0 | 0.75 |

3. The completed table is above. The marginal propensity to consume is the change in consumption expenditure divided by the change in disposable income that brought it about; page 760.

### ■ CHECKPOINT 30.2

**True or false**
1. True;  page 766
2. True;  page 767
3. False;  page 767

**Multiple choice**
1. d; page 766
2. b; page 767
3. c; page 767
4. b; page 767

**Short Response Questions**

| GDP | C | I | G | X | M | AE |
|---|---|---|---|---|---|---|
| 0.0 | 0.6 | 0.4 | 0.2 | 0.2 | 0.2 | 1.2 |
| 1.0 | 1.2 | 0.4 | 0.2 | 0.2 | 0.4 | 1.6 |
| 2.0 | 1.8 | 0.4 | 0.2 | 0.2 | 0.6 | 2.0 |
| 3.0 | 2.4 | 0.4 | 0.2 | 0.2 | 0.8 | 2.4 |
| 4.0 | 3.0 | 0.4 | 0.2 | 0.2 | 1.0 | 2.8 |
| 5.0 | 3.6 | 0.4 | 0.2 | 0.2 | 1.2 | 3.2 |

1. a. Aggregate planned expenditure equals $C + I + G + X − M$. The completed table is above; page 765.

■ **FIGURE 30.12**

Aggregate planned expenditure (trillions of 2000 dollars)

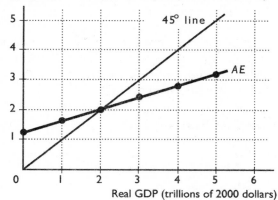

b. Figure 30.12 shows the aggregate planned expenditure curve; page 765.

c. A 45° line has been added to Figure 30.12. Equilibrium expenditure is where the 45° line intersects the aggregate expenditure curve, so equilibrium expenditure is $2 trillion; page 766.

2. If aggregate planned expenditure is less than real GDP, people are spending less than firms are producing. There is an unplanned increase in inventories. Firms decrease production, and real GDP decreases. Firms continue to decrease production until the unplanned inventory change is zero. When this occurs, real GDP and aggregate expenditure are in equilibrium; page 767.

■ **CHECKPOINT 30.3**

**True or false**

1. True; pages 770-771
2. True; page 771
3. False; page 772
4. False; page 773

**Multiple choice**

1. d; page 771
2. a; pages 771-772
3. d; page 770
4. d; page 772
5. b; page 773

6. d; pages 772-773
7. e; page 773
8. d; page 773
9. b; page 774

**Short Response Questions**

■ **FIGURE 30.13**

Aggregate planned expenditure (trillions of 2000 dollars)

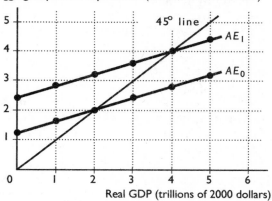

1. a. Figure 30.13 has the new $AE$ curve, labeled $AE_1$ and the initial curve labeled $AE_0$; page 771.

b. Equilibrium expenditure increases by $2 trillion to $4 trillion; page 771.

c. The slope of the $AE$ curve equals ($0.4 trillion) ÷ ($1.0 trillion), which is 0.40; page 771.

d. The formula for the multiplier is equal to $\dfrac{1}{(1 - \text{slope of the } AE \text{ curve})}$. Thus the multiplier is $\dfrac{1}{(1 - 0.4)} = 1.67$. The change is equal to the multiplier multiplied by the change in autonomous expenditure, which is (1.67) × ($1.2 trillion). The change in equilibrium expenditure is $2.0 trillion; pages 770, 773.

| Marginal propensity to consume, MPC | Multiplier |
|---|---|
| 0.9 | 10.0 |
| 0.8 | 5.0 |
| 0.7 | 3.3 |
| 0.6 | 2.5 |
| 0.5 | 2.0 |
| 0.4 | 1.7 |

2. The multiplier equals $1 \div (1 - MPC)$. The completed table is above. As the *MPC* increases in size, the multiplier increases in size; pages 772.

**Long Response Question**

1. The multiplier exceeds 1 because an initial change in autonomous expenditure leads to additional changes in induced expenditure. For instance, an initial increase in government expenditure to repair bridges destroyed by a hurricane increases the employment and income of bridge repair workers. As a result, these workers increase their consumption expenditure, which in turn increases the income of the workers who make the consumption goods that are purchased. In turn, these workers increase their consumption expenditure and the cycle continues. As a result, the final change in aggregate expenditure, which includes the government's expenditure and the (induced) consumption expenditure, exceeds the initial change in autonomous expenditure. This result creates the multiplier, the conclusion that the change in aggregate expenditure and GDP exceeds the initial change in autonomous expenditure; pages 771-772.

## ■ CHECKPOINT 30.4

**True or false**

1. False; pages 776-777
2. True; pages 776-777

**Multiple choice**

1. a; page 776
2. a; pages 776-777
3. a; pages 776-777
4. c; page 776

**Short Response Question**

1. The *AE* curve is used to derive the *AD* curve. Each point of equilibrium expenditure on the *AE* curve corresponds to a point on the *AD* curve; page 776.

# Fiscal and Monetary Policy Effects

## *Chapter* 31

Chapter 31 provides a description of both fiscal and monetary processes and policies. On the fiscal side, first the federal budget process is outlined. Then fiscal policies are identified and illustrated using the *AD-AS* model. On the monetary side, the basics of how monetary policy affects the economy are discussed, and then the *AD-AS* model is used to illustrate monetary policy. The limits to both fiscal and monetary policy are examined.

■ **Describe the federal budget process and explain the effects of fiscal policy.**

The federal budget is an annual statement of the expenditures, tax receipts, and surplus or deficit of the United States. If tax receipts exceed expenditures, the government has a budget surplus and if expenditures exceed tax receipts, the government has a budget deficit. Fiscal policy can be discretionary, which is policy initiated by an act of Congress, or automatic, which is policy that is triggered by the state of the economy. The government expenditure multiplier and the tax multiplier show that aggregate demand changes by more than an initiating change in government expenditures or taxes. If real GDP is less than potential GDP, expansionary fiscal policy, which is an increase in government expenditures or a tax cut, can move the economy to potential GDP. If real GDP is greater than potential GDP, contractionary fiscal policy, which is a decrease in government expenditures or a tax hike, can move the economy to potential GDP. A cut in taxes or an increase in government expenditures on productive services also have supply-side effects that increase potential GDP and aggregate supply. The use of discretionary fiscal policy is hampered by law-making time lags, by estimating potential GDP, and by economic forecasting. Automatic stabilizers are features of fiscal policy, such as induced taxes and needs-tested spending, that stabilize real GDP without explicit action by the government.

■ **Describe the Federal Reserve's monetary policy process and explain the effects of monetary policy.**

Monetary policy is determined by the Federal Open Market Committee (FOMC). The Fed's purchase or sale of government securities affects the nominal interest rate and, in the short run, also the real interest rate. Changes in the interest rate impact decisions regarding investment, consumption, and net exports. When the Fed increases (decreases) the quantity of money, the interest rate falls (rises) and aggregate demand increases (decreases). To fight inflation, the Fed conducts an open market sale. The interest rate rises and expenditure decreases. The multiplier decreases aggregate demand. The *AD* curve shifts leftward and real GDP and the price level both decrease. If the Fed is worried about recession, it conducts an open market purchase, which lowers the interest rate. Aggregate demand increases so that real GDP and the price level increase. Monetary policy has no law-making lag, but estimating potential GDP is hard and economic forecasting is error prone. Monetary policy also has the drawback that it depends on how private decision makers respond to a change in the interest rate.

## EXPANDED CHAPTER CHECKLIST

**When you have completed this chapter, you will be able to:**

**1 Describe the federal budget process and explain the effects of fiscal policy.**

- Define budget surplus, balanced budget, and budget deficit.
- Describe the federal budget time line.
- Define discretionary fiscal policy and automatic fiscal policy.
- Describe the government expenditures multiplier and the tax multiplier, and explain why both exist.
- Define the balanced budget multiplier.
- Explain and illustrate how fiscal policy can eliminate a recessionary gap and an inflationary gap.
- State why fiscal policy has supply-side effects.
- Discuss the limitations to discretionary fiscal policy.
- Explain the operation of the automatic stabilizers and define induced taxes and needs-tested spending.

**2 Describe the Federal Reserve's monetary policy process and explain the effects of monetary policy.**

- Describe the Fed's monetary policy process.
- Explain how the Fed influences the interest rate in the short run and long run.
- Illustrate the effects when the Fed raises and when it lowers the interest rate.
- Discuss the ripple effect of the Fed's actions and explain the role played by the multiplier.
- Explain and illustrate in an *AD-AS* figure how the Fed fights inflation and recession.
- Describe the limitations to monetary policy.

## YOUR AP TEST HINTS

*AP Topics*

| Topic on your AP test | Corresponding textbook section |
| --- | --- |
| **Inflation, unemployment, and stabilization policies** | |
| Monetary and Fiscal Policies | Chapter 31 |
| • Demand-side effects | Checkpoints 31.1, 31.2 |
| • Supply-side effects | Checkpoint 31.1 |
| • Policy mix | Checkpoint 31.1 |
| • Government deficit and debt | Checkpoint 31.1 |

*Extra AP material*

- The impact of fiscal policy on the exchange rate and net exports is important. An expansionary fiscal policy (an increase in government expenditures and/or a tax cut) increases real GDP and real income, which, in turn, increase the demand for money. In turn, the increase in demand for money raises the interest rate. The rise in the interest rate increases foreigners' demand for U.S. dollars in order buy U.S. assets with the now higher interest rate. The increase in demand for dollars by foreigners raises the U.S. exchange rate. The rise in the exchange rate makes foreign imports into the United States less expensive, which increases U.S. imports. In addition, the higher U.S. income resulting from the fiscal policy increases U.S. residents' purchases of imports. Both effects increase U.S. imports and thereby decrease U.S. net exports.

- Be certain that you can illustrate the effects of fiscal and monetary policy in aggregate demand/aggregate supply diagrams.

- It also is important for the AP test to bear in mind that fiscal policy and monetary policy are independent of each other. Fiscal policy is under the control of the federal government and monetary policy is the Federal Reserve's responsibility.

# CHECKPOINT 31.1

■ **Describe the federal budget process and explain the effects of fiscal policy.**

*Quick Review*

- *Discretionary fiscal policy* Fiscal policy action that is initiated by an act of Congress.

- *Automatic fiscal policy* Fiscal policy that is triggered by the state of the economy.

- *Government expenditure multiplier* The magnification effect of a change in government expenditures on aggregate demand.

- *Tax multiplier* The magnification effect of a change in taxes on aggregate demand.

## Additional Practice Problems 31.1

1. The figure shows the U.S. economy in 2009.

    a. What is the equilibrium price level and real GDP?

    b. Is there an inflationary gap or a recessionary gap?

    c. Should the government use an expansionary or contractionary fiscal policy to move the economy to potential GDP? What sorts of fiscal policies might be used?

    d. In the figure, show the effect of these policies after real GDP equals potential GDP. What is the new equilibrium price level and real GDP? (Ignore any supply-side effects from the policy.)

2. What is the balanced budget multiplier and why is it greater than zero?

## Solutions to Additional Practice Problems 31.1

1a. The equilibrium price level and real GDP are determined by the intersection of the aggregate demand, *AD*, curve and the aggregate supply, *AS*, curve. The figure shows that the equilibrium price is 110 and the equilibrium quantity of real GDP is $11 trillion.

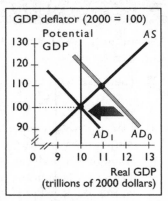

1b. Real GDP of $11 trillion exceeds potential GDP of $10 trillion, so there is an inflationary gap.

1c. In order to close the inflationary gap, the government must use contractionary fiscal policy. A contractionary fiscal policy will "contract" real GDP so that it equals potential GDP (which is also called the "long-run aggregate supply"). Contractionary fiscal policy includes an increase in taxes and/or a decrease in government expenditures.

1d. The figure shows the effect of the contractionary fiscal policy. Both an increase in taxes or a decrease in government expenditure decrease aggregate demand. The aggregate demand curve shifts leftward, from $AD_0$ to $AD_1$ in the figure. As a result, the price level falls from 110 to 100 and real GDP decreases from $11 trillion back to potential GDP of $10 trillion. The inflationary gap is eliminated.

2. The balanced budget multiplier is the magnification effect on aggregate demand of *simultaneous* changes in government expenditures and taxes that leave the budget balance unchanged. The balanced budget multiplier is not zero—it is positive—because the size of the government expenditure multiplier is larger than the size of the tax multiplier. That is, a $1 increase in government expenditures increases aggregate demand by more than a $1 increase in taxes decreases aggregate demand. So when both government expenditures and taxes increase by $1, aggregate demand still increases.

## ■ AP Self Test 31.1

### True or false

1. Other things the same, a tax cut decreases the national debt.

2. The 2002 Bush tax cut package approved by Congress in 2002 is an example of discretionary fiscal policy.

3. The government expenditure multiplier is the magnification effect that a change in aggregate demand has on government expenditures on goods and services.

4. The magnitude of the tax multiplier is smaller than the government expenditure multiplier.

5. If government expenditures and taxes increase by the same amount, aggregate demand does not change.

6. To eliminate an inflationary gap, the government could decrease its expenditures on goods and services.

7. A tax cut increases aggregate supply but does not increase aggregate demand, so it increases real GDP and lowers the price level.

8. Automatic stabilizers are features of fiscal policy that work to stabilize real GDP without explicit action by the government.

### Multiple choice

1. The annual statement of the expenditures, tax receipts, and surplus or deficit of the government of the United States is the federal
   a. surplus record.
   b. deficit record.
   c. budget.
   d. spending.
   e. debt to the public.

2. When government expenditures are less than tax receipts, the government has
   a. a budget with a positive balance.
   b. a budget deficit.
   c. a budget surplus.
   d. a budget with a negative debt.
   e. an illegal budget because expenditures must exceed tax receipts.

3. National debt decreases in a given year when a country has
   a. a budget deficit.
   b. a balanced budget.
   c. a budget supplement.
   d. a budget surplus.
   e. no discretionary fiscal policy.

4. Discretionary fiscal policy is a fiscal policy action, such as
   a. an interest rate cut, initiated by an act of Congress.
   b. an increase in payments to the unemployed, initiated by the state of the economy.
   c. a tax cut, initiated by an act of Congress.
   d. a decrease in tax receipts, initiated by the state of the economy.
   e. an increase in the quantity of money.

5. An example of automatic fiscal policy is
   a. an interest rate cut, initiated by an act of Congress.
   b. an increase in the quantity of money.
   c. a tax cut, initiated by an act of Congress.
   d. a decrease in tax receipts, triggered by the state of the economy.
   e. any change in the interest rate, regardless of its cause.

6. The government expenditure multiplier is the magnification effect of a change in government expenditures on
   a. aggregate demand.
   b. the budget deficit.
   c. tax receipts.
   d. aggregate supply.
   e. potential GDP.

7. The magnitude of the tax multiplier is ____ the magnitude of the government expenditure multiplier.
   a. equal to
   b. greater than
   c. smaller than
   d. the inverse of
   e. exactly one half

8.  If a change in the tax laws leads to a $100 billion decrease in tax receipts, then aggregate demand
    a. increases by $100 billion.
    b. increases by less than $100 billion.
    c. increases by more than $100 billion.
    d. decreases by $100 billion.
    e. decreases by more than $100 billion.

9.  An example of expansionary fiscal policy is
    a. increasing the quantity of money.
    b. lowering the interest rate.
    c. decreasing government expenditure.
    d. decreasing needs-tested spending.
    e. cutting taxes.

10. Discretionary fiscal policy works to close a recessionary gap by shifting the
    a. *AD* curve leftward.
    b. *AS* curve leftward.
    c. *AD* curve leftward and the *AS* curve leftward.
    d. *AD* curve rightward.
    e. potential GDP line leftward.

11. If the economy is at an above full-employment equilibrium, ____ gap exists and discretionary fiscal policy that ____ will return real GDP to potential GDP.
    a. an inflationary; increases aggregate demand
    b. an inflationary; decreases aggregate demand
    c. a recessionary; increases aggregate supply
    d. a recessionary; decreases aggregate supply
    e. a recessionary; decreases aggregate demand

12. Ignoring any supply-side effects, to close a recessionary gap of $100 billion with a government expenditures multiplier of 5, the government could
    a. increase government expenditures by $100 billion
    b. increase government expenditures by $20 billion.
    c. raise taxes by $100 billion.
    d. raise taxes by more than $20 billion.
    e. decrease government expenditures by $20 billion.

■ **FIGURE 31.1**

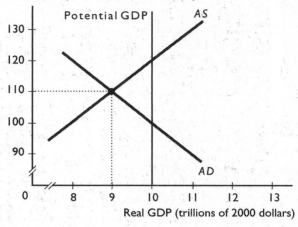

13. The figure above shows an economy with ____ gap and a fiscal policy that can eliminate this gap is ____.
    a. an inflationary; an increase in government expenditures
    b. an inflationary; a tax hike
    c. a recessionary; an increase in the quantity of money
    d. a recessionary; a tax hike
    e. a recessionary; an increase in government expenditures

14. The supply-side effects of a tax cut ____ potential GDP and ____ aggregate supply.
    a. increase; increase
    b. increase; decrease
    c. decrease; increase
    d. decrease; decrease
    e. increases; does not change

15. If a tax cut increases aggregate demand more than aggregate supply, real GDP ____ and the price level ____.
    a. increases; rises
    b. increases; falls
    c. decreases; rises
    d. decreases; falls
    e. increases; does not change

16. Discretionary fiscal policy is handicapped by
    a. law-making time lags, induced taxes, and automatic stabilizers.
    b. law-making time lags, estimation of potential GDP, and economic forecasting.
    c. economic forecasting, law-making time lags, and induced taxes.
    d. automatic stabilizers, law-making time lags, and potential GDP estimation.
    e. automatic stabilizers, the multipliers, and potential GDP estimation.

## Short Response Questions

1. What happens to the national debt if the government has a $100 billion budget deficit?

2. Give examples of a contractionary fiscal policy. An expansionary fiscal policy.

3. What is the government expenditure multiplier? Why does it exist?

4. It is not easy to determine potential GDP. Why does this fact hamper the use of discretionary fiscal policy?

## Long Response Questions

■ **FIGURE 31.2**

Price level (GDP deflator, 2000 = 100)

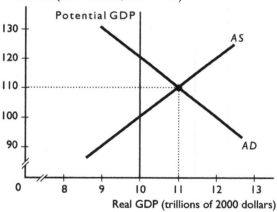

1. Figure 31.2 illustrates the economy.
   a. Is there an inflationary gap or a recessionary gap present?
   b. What type of fiscal policy might be used to restore the economy to full employment?

c. Ignoring any supply-side effects, in Figure 31.2, illustrate the effect of the policy you suggested in your answer to part (b).

■ **FIGURE 31.3**

Price level (GDP deflator, 2000 = 100)

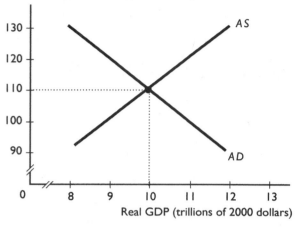

2. In Figure 31.3, illustrate the effect of an increase in government expenditure which changes aggregate demand by $2 trillion.

■ **FIGURE 31.4**

Price level (GDP deflator, 2000 = 100)

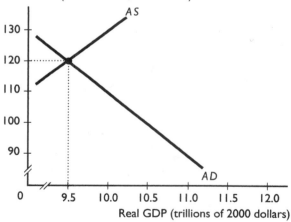

3. Figure 31.4 illustrates the economy. Potential GDP is $11 trillion. Suppose that the government cuts its taxes and that the supply-side effects are larger than the demand-side effects. If the economy moves back to potential GDP, in Figure 31.4, illustrate the effect of this government policy.

4. How can the government use fiscal policy to eliminate a recessionary gap?

5. What are the demand-side effects of a tax cut? What are the supply-side effects? Why does a tax cut have supply-side effects?

6. What are automatic stabilizers? Can they eliminate a recession?

## CHECKPOINT 31.2

■ **Describe the Federal Reserve's monetary policy process and explain the effects of monetary policy.**

### Quick Review

• *Ripple effects from monetary policy* When the Fed increases the interest rate, three events follow: investment and consumption expenditure decrease; the price of the dollar rises on the foreign exchange market and net exports decrease; a multiplier effect induces a further decrease in consumption expenditure and aggregate demand.

### Additional Practice Problems 31.2

1. If the Fed increases the quantity of money, explain how each of the following items changes:

    a. Businesses' investment

    b. The price of the dollar on foreign exchange markets

2. The figure shows the U.S. economy in 2009.

    a. Will the Fed fear inflation or recession?

    b. What policy should the Fed undertake to avoid what it fears?

    c. In the figure, illustrate the effect of the Fed's policy.

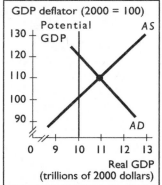

d. How does this set of answers compare to the answers of Additional Practice Problem 1 in Checkpoint 31.1?

3. What is an advantage that monetary policy has over fiscal policy?

### Solutions to Additional Practice Problems 31.2

1a. An increase in the quantity of money lowers the interest rate. The interest rate is the opportunity cost of the funds used to finance investment. When the opportunity cost of investment decreases, businesses increase their purchases of new capital equipment or, in other words, investment increases.

1b. When the interest rate in the United States falls relative to the interest rate in other countries, people sell dollars and buy other currencies. With fewer dollars demanded and more dollars supplied, the price of the dollar falls on the foreign exchange market.

2a. There is an inflationary gap in the figure and so the Fed fears inflation.

2b. In order to eliminate the potential for inflation, the Fed should decrease the quantity of money. Decreasing the quantity of money decreases aggregate demand and thereby lowers the price level and decreases real GDP, which eliminates the possibility of inflation.

2c. The figure shows the effect of the monetary policy. A decrease in the quantity of money raises the interest rate, which, in turn, decreases consumption expenditure, investment, and net exports. Aggregate demand decreases

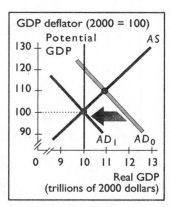

and the aggregate demand curve shifts leftward, from $AD_0$ to $AD_1$ in the figure. As a result, the price level falls from 110 to 100 and real GDP decreases from \$11 trillion back to potential GDP of \$10 trillion.

2d. The answers are very similar insofar as in both instances the correct policy was a contractionary policy. Both the contractionary fiscal policy in the earlier Practice Problem and the similarly contractionary monetary policy in this Practice Problem decrease aggregate demand and shift the *AD* cure leftward.

3. Monetary policy has an advantage over fiscal policy because it cuts out the law-making time lags. The FOMC meets eight times a year and can conduct telephone meetings between its scheduled meetings. And the actual actions that change the quantity of money are daily actions taken by the New York Fed operating under the guidelines decided by the FOMC. So monetary policy is a continuous policy process and is not subject to a long decision lag.

## ■ AP Self Test 31.2

**True or false**

1. The FOMC meets once a year in January to determine the nation's monetary policy.

2. In the short run, when the Fed changes the nominal interest rate, the real interest rate also changes.

3. If the Fed fears a recession, it lowers the interest rate.

4. A change in the interest rate changes net exports.

5. The Fed's monetary policy works by changing aggregate supply.

6. If the Fed's monetary policy raises the interest rate, aggregate demand decreases.

7. To combat a recession, the Fed lowers taxes, which increases aggregate demand and shifts the aggregate demand curve rightward.

8. Monetary policy is a perfect stabilization tool because it does not have law-making time lags.

**Multiple choice**

1. The FOMC is the
   a. report the Fed gives to Congress twice a year.
   b. group within the Fed that makes the monetary policy decisions.
   c. report that summarizes the economy across Fed districts.
   d. name of the meeting the Fed has with Congress twice a year.
   e. interest rate the Fed most directly influences.

2. The Fed affects aggregate demand through monetary policy by changing
   a. the quantity of money and influencing the interest rate.
   b. tax rates and influencing disposable income.
   c. the quantity of money and determining government expenditure.
   d. government expenditures and so influencing the budget balance.
   e. tax rates on only interest income and so influencing disposable income.

3. If the Fed sells government securities, in the short run the nominal interest rate _____ and the real interest rate _____.
   a. rises; rises
   b. does not change; rises
   c. falls; falls
   d. rises; does not change
   e. rises; falls

4. When the Fed increases the nominal interest rate, the real interest rate
   a. temporarily rises.
   b. permanently rises.
   c. temporarily falls.
   d. permanently falls.
   e. does not change.

5. In the long run, the Fed's policies can influence
   a. the real interest rate.
   b. the inflation rate.
   c. induced taxes.
   d. income taxes.
   e. the size of the tax multiplier.

6. If the Fed decreases the interest rate, which of the following occurs?
   a. Investment increases.
   b. Consumption expenditure decreases.
   c. The price of the dollar on the foreign exchange market increases.
   d. Net exports decreases.
   e. Government expenditures on goods and services increases.

7. If the Fed increases the interest rate, which of the following occur?
   a. The price of the dollar on the foreign exchange market increases.
   b. Investment increases.
   c. Aggregate demand increases.
   d. Net exports increases.
   e. Consumption expenditure increases.

8. The Fed increases the interest rate when it
   a. fears recession.
   b. wants to increase the quantity of money.
   c. fears inflation.
   d. wants to encourage bank lending.
   e. cannot change the quantity of money.

9. Decreasing the quantity of money shifts the aggregate demand curve ____, so that real GDP ____ and the price level ____.
   a. rightward; increases; rises
   b. leftward; decreases; rises
   c. rightward; increases; falls
   d. leftward; decreases; falls
   e. leftward; increases; rises

10. To fight a recession, the Fed can
    a. lower the interest rate by buying securities.
    b. lower the interest rate by selling securities.
    c. raise the interest rate by buying securities.
    d. raise the interest rate by selling securities.
    e. lower income taxes on interest income.

11. When the economy is in a recession, the Fed can ____ the interest rate, which ____ aggregate demand and ____ real GDP.
    a. lower; increases; decreases
    b. raise; decreases; increases
    c. lower; increases; increases
    d. raise; increases; decreases
    e. lower; decreases; decreases

12. An advantage monetary policy has over fiscal policy is that monetary policy
    a. can be quickly changed and implemented.
    b. is coordinated with fiscal policy.
    c. is approved by the president of the United States.
    d. affects consumption expenditure and investment without impacting international trade.
    e. has no multiplier effects.

13. Which of the following is correct?
    i. Monetary policy is subject to long law-making time lags.
    ii. Monetary policy does not require a good estimate of potential GDP.
    iii. Monetary policy can be enacted more quickly than fiscal policy.
    a. i only.
    b. ii only.
    c. iii only.
    d. both i and iii.
    e. both ii and iii.

## Short Response Questions

1. Suppose the Fed increases the quantity of money. In the short run, what is the effect on the interest rate? On investment? On aggregate demand?

2. How does monetary policy affect the price of the dollar on the foreign exchange market? In your answer, explain the case in which the Fed raises the interest rate.

## Long Response Questions

■ **FIGURE 31.5**

Price level (GDP deflator, 2000 = 100)

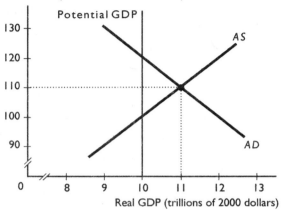

Real GDP (trillions of 2000 dollars)

1. Figure 31.5 illustrates the economy.
   a. What type of monetary policy is used to restore the economy to full employment?
   b. In Figure 31.5, illustrate the effect of the policy you suggested in your answer to part (a).

c. In question 1 from the Long Response Question section in Checkpoint 31.1, you answered a similar question about fiscal policy. Compared to using fiscal policy, what is an advantage of using monetary policy to restore the economy to potential GDP? Compared to monetary policy, what is an advantage of using fiscal policy?

2. How does the Fed keep the public informed about the state of the economy and its monetary policy decisions?

3. In the short run, how does the Fed affect the real interest rate? In the long run, how does the Fed affect the real interest rate?

4. Suppose the Fed is concerned that the economy is entering a recession. What policy can the Fed pursue and what is the effect of the policy on real GDP and the price level?

# YOUR AP SELF TEST ANSWERS

## ■ CHECKPOINT 31.1

### True or false
1. False; page 784
2. True; page 787
3. False; page 787
4. True; page 787
5. False; page 787
6. True; page 789
7. False; pages 790-792
8. True; page 794

### Multiple choice
1. c; page 784
2. c; page 784
3. d; page 784
4. c; page 784
5. d; page 784
6. a; page 787
7. c; page 787
8. c; page 787
9. e; page 788
10. d; page 788
11. b; page 789
12. b; pages 787-788
13. e; page 788
14. a; page 791
15. a; page 792
16. b; page 793

### Short Response Questions
1. If the government has a $100 billion budget deficit, the national debt increases by $100 billion; page 784.

2. A contractionary fiscal policy is a decrease in government expenditures, an increase in taxes, or a combination of the two. An expansionary fiscal policy is an increase in government expenditures, a cut in taxes, or a combination of the two; pages 788-789.

3. The government expenditure multiplier is the magnification effect of a change in government expenditure on aggregate demand. For instance, a $10 billion increase in gov-

ernment expenditure on goods and services will lead to a larger than $10 billion increase in aggregate demand. The multiplier exists because an increase in government expenditure rises real GDP and real income, which, in turn, create additional increases in consumption expenditure. The increase in consumption expenditure then serves to further increase aggregate demand; page 787.

4. It is not easy to tell whether real GDP is below, above, or at potential GDP. So a discretionary fiscal action can move real GDP *away* from potential GDP instead of toward it; page 794.

### Long Response Questions

■ **FIGURE 31.6**

Price level (GDP deflator, 2000 = 100)

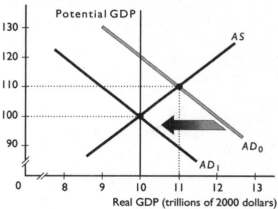

1. a. There is an inflationary gap because real GDP exceeds potential GDP; page 789.

   b. The economy will return to full employment with a tax hike or a decrease in government expenditures; page 789.

   c. Figure 31.6 shows the results of the suggested policy. Aggregate demand decreases and the *AD* curve shifts leftward from $AD_0$ to $AD_1$. Real GDP decreases from $11 trillion to $10 trillion and the price level falls from 110 to 100; page 789.

■ **FIGURE 31.7**

Price level (GDP deflator, 2000 = 100)

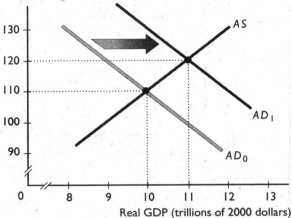

Real GDP (trillions of 2000 dollars)

2. The increase in government expenditure increases aggregate demand so that the aggregate demand curve shifts rightward by $2 trillion, as illustrated in Figure 31.7. As a result, the price level rises to 120 and real GDP increases to $11 trillion; page 788.

■ **FIGURE 31.8**

Price level (GDP deflator, 2000 = 100)

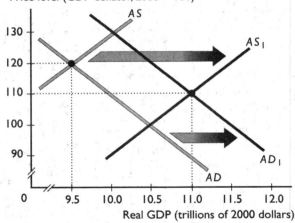

Real GDP (trillions of 2000 dollars)

3. The tax cut increases both aggregate demand and aggregate supply, so in Figure 31.8, the aggregate demand curve shifts rightward from $AD$ to $AD_1$ and the aggregate supply curve shifts rightward from $AS$ to $AS_1$. Because the effect on aggregate supply exceeds the effect on aggregate demand, the shift of the $AS$ curve is larger than the shift of the $AD$

curve. As a result, real GDP increases and the price level falls. The exact fall of the price level depends on the precise sizes of the shifts but in the figure it falls to 100; page 792.

4. A recessionary gap exists when real GDP is less than potential GDP. The government can eliminate the recessionary gap by using expansionary fiscal policy to increase aggregate demand. The government can increase aggregate demand by increasing its expenditures on goods and services or by cutting taxes; page 788.

5. A tax cut increases disposable income, which increases consumption expenditure and aggregate demand. A tax cut creates an incentive to work and save. So a tax cut increases the supply of labor and the supply of saving. An increase in the supply of labor increases the equilibrium quantity of labor employed. An increase in the supply of saving increases the equilibrium quantity of investment and capital. With larger quantities of labor and capital, potential GDP increases and so does aggregate supply. So a decrease in taxes increases aggregate supply; pages 790-791.

6. Automatic stabilizers are features of fiscal policy that stabilize real GDP without explicit action by the government. Automatic stabilizers include induced taxes and needs-tested spending. Induced taxes and needs-tested spending decrease the multiplier effect of a change in autonomous expenditure. So they moderate both expansions and recessions and make real GDP more stable. But they cannot eliminate a recession; page 794.

■ **CHECKPOINT 31.2**

**True or false**

1. False; page 796
2. True; page 797
3. True; page 798
4. True; page 799
5. False; pages 800-801

6. True; page 801
7. False; page 802
8. False; page 803

**Multiple choice**

1. b; page 796
2. a; page 797
3. a; page 797
4. a; page 797
5. b; page 797
6. a; page 799
7. a; page 799
8. c; page 801
9. d; page 801
10. a; page 802
11. c; page 802
12. a; page 803
13. c; page 803

**Short Response Questions**

1. If the Fed increases the quantity of money, the interest rate falls and investment increases. Aggregate demand increases because investment increases and because consumption expenditure and net exports also increase; page 794.

2. If the U.S. interest rate rises relative to the interest rate in other countries, some people will want to move funds into the United States from other countries to take advantage of the higher interest rate they can now earn on U.S. bank deposits and bonds. To move money into the United States, people must buy dollars and sell other currencies. With more dollars demanded, the price of the dollar rises on the foreign exchange market; page 790.

**Long Response Questions**

1. a. The economy will return to full employment with a decrease in the quantity of money; page 801.
   b. Figure 31.9 shows the results of the decrease in the quantity of money. Aggregate demand decreases and the *AD* curve shifts leftward from $AD_0$ to $AD_1$. Real

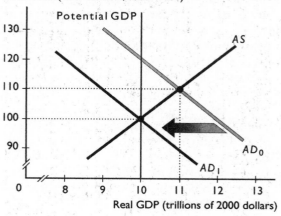

■ **FIGURE 31.9**

Price level (GDP deflator, 2000 = 100)

GDP decreases from $11 trillion to potential GDP of $10 trillion and the price level falls from 110 to 100; page 801.

   c. The advantage of using monetary policy is that there is no law-making lag. The actions that change the quantity of money are taken each day. The advantage of using fiscal policy is that the impact on aggregate demand is direct. The effects of monetary policy are indirect and depend on how private decisions respond to a change in the interest rate. These responses are hard to forecast and vary from one situation to another in unpredictable ways; page 803.

2. To keep the public informed about the state of the economy, the Fed makes available the Beige Book, which is a report that summarizes the current economic conditions in each Federal Reserve district and each sector of the economy. After each FOMC meeting the FOMC announces its decisions and describes its view of the likelihood that its goals of price stability and sustainable economic growth will be achieved. The minutes of the FOMC meeting are released only after the next meeting. The Fed is required to report twice a year to the House of Representatives Committee on Financial Services, at which time the Fed chairman testifies before the committee; page 796.

3. In the short run, the Fed can determine the nominal interest rate by changing the quantity of money in circulation. In the short run, the expected inflation rate is determined by recent monetary policy and inflation experience. So when the Fed changes the nominal interest rate, the real interest rate also changes, temporarily.

In the long run, saving supply and investment demand determine the real interest rate in global financial markets. So in the long run, the Fed influences the nominal interest rate by the effects of its policies on the inflation rate. But it does not directly control the nominal interest rate, and it has no control over the real interest rate; page 797.

4. When the Fed is concerned that the economy is entering a recession, it makes an open market purchase of government securities. Banks' reserves increase and the quantity of money increases. The interest rate falls. As a result, the quantity of investment and other interest-sensitive expenditure increases. Net exports also increases. With the increase in aggregate expenditure, the multiplier effect increases aggregate demand by even more. With the increase in aggregate demand, real GDP increases and the price level rises; page 798.

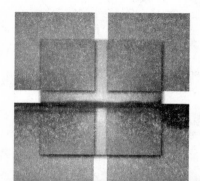

# The Short-Run Policy Tradeoff

# Chapter 32

Chapter 32 discusses the relationship between inflation and unemployment in the short run and the relationship between the long-run Phillips curve and the short-run Phillips curve. It also discusses how the Fed can influence the expected inflation rate.

## ▪ Describe the short-run tradeoff between inflation and unemployment.

The short-run Phillips curve shows the relationship between the inflation rate and the unemployment rate when the natural unemployment rate and expected inflation rate remain constant. The downward-sloping short-run Phillips curve indicates a tradeoff between inflation and unemployment: lower unemployment can be attained but at the cost of higher inflation. The short-run Phillips curve is another way of looking at the upward-sloping aggregate supply curve, because a change in real GDP also changes the unemployment rate and a change in the price level also changes the inflation rate. So moving up the aggregate supply curve, the higher price level corresponds to higher inflation and the larger real GDP corresponds to lower unemployment. The relationship between output and unemployment is called Okun's Law. Okun's Law states that for each percentage point that the unemployment rate is above the natural unemployment rate, there is a 2 percent gap between real GDP and potential GDP.

## ▪ Distinguish between the short-run and the long-run Phillips curves and describe the shifting tradeoff between inflation and unemployment.

The long-run Phillips curve is a vertical line that shows the relationship between inflation and unemployment when the economy is at full employment. At full employment, the unemployment rate is the natural unemployment rate, but the inflation rate can take on any value. So along the long-run Phillips curve, there is no long-run tradeoff between inflation and unemployment. The short-run Phillips curve intersects the long-run Phillips at the expected inflation rate. If the expected inflation rate changes, the short-run Phillips curve shifts upward or downward to intersect the long-run Phillips curve at the new expected inflation rate. The natural rate hypothesis is the proposition that when the money growth rate changes, the unemployment rate changes temporarily and eventually returns to the natural unemployment rate. If the natural unemployment rate changes, both the long-run Phillips curve and the short-run Phillips curve shift rightward (if it increases) or leftward (if it decreases).

## ▪ Explain how the Fed can influence the expected inflation rate and how expected inflation influences the short-run tradeoff.

The expected inflation rate helps set the money wage rate and other money prices. To forecast inflation, people use data about past inflation and other relevant variables, as well as economic science. If the Fed pursues a surprise inflation reduction, inflation slows but at the cost of recession. If the Fed pursues a credible announced inflation reduction, the expected inflation rate falls along with the inflation rate and there is no accompanying loss of output or increase in unemployment.

## EXPANDED CHAPTER CHECKLIST

**When you have completed this chapter, you will be able to:**

### 1 Describe the short-run tradeoff between inflation and unemployment.

- Define, describe, and illustrate the short-run Phillips curve.
- Explain why the short-run Phillips curve is another way of looking at the upward sloping aggregate supply curve.
- Explain and use Okun's Law.
- Explain why aggregate demand fluctuations that bring movements along the aggregate supply curve also bring movements along the short-run Phillips curve.

### 2 Distinguish between the short-run and the long-run Phillips curves and describe the shifting tradeoff between inflation and unemployment.

- Describe and illustrate the long-run Phillips curve and explain how it differs from the short-run Phillips curve.
- Illustrate the effect of a change in the expected inflation rate on the long-run Phillips curve and the short-run Phillips curve.
- Explain the natural rate hypothesis.
- Illustrate the effect of a change in the natural unemployment rate on the long-run Phillips curve and the short-run Phillips curve.

### 3 Explain how the Fed can influence the expected inflation rate and how expected inflation influences the short-run tradeoff.

- Define rational expectation.
- Describe the economy following a surprise inflation reduction by the Fed.
- Describe the economy following a credible announced inflation reduction by the Fed.

## YOUR AP TEST HINTS

*AP Topics*

| Topic on your AP test | Corresponding textbook section |
|---|---|
| **National income and price determination** | |
| Aggregate Supply | Chapter 32 |
| • Short run versus long run | Checkpoints 32.1, 32.2 |
| • Sticky versus flexible wages | Checkpoints 32.1, 32.2 |
| Monetary and fiscal policies | Chapter 32 |
| • Phillips curve | Checkpoint 32.1 |
| • Role of expectations | Checkpoint 32.3 |

## CHECKPOINT 32.1

■ **Describe the short-run tradeoff between inflation and unemployment.**

*Quick Review*

- *Short-run Phillips curve* A curve that shows the relationship between the inflation rate and the unemployment rate when the natural unemployment rate and the expected inflation rate remain constant.
- *Okun's Law* For each percentage point that the unemployment rate is above the natural unemployment rate, there is a 2 percent gap between real GDP and potential GDP.

**Additional Practice Problems 32.1**

1. The table describes five possible situations that might arise in 2007, depending on the level of aggregate demand in that year. Potential GDP is $7 trillion, and the natural unemployment rate is 5 percent.

| | Price level (2006 = 100) | Unemployment rate (percentage) |
|---|---|---|
| A | 101.5 | 9 |
| B | 104.0 | 6 |
| C | 105.0 | 5 |
| D | 106.5 | 4 |
| E | 109.0 | 3 |

   a. Calculate the inflation rate for each possible outcome.

b. Use Okun's Law to find the real GDP associated with each unemployment rate in the table.

c. Plot the short-run Phillips curve for 2007.

d. Plot the aggregate supply curve for 2007.

e. Mark the points *A, B, C, D,* and *E* on each curve that correspond to the data provided in the table and the data that you have calculated.

2. In the Practice Problem, what is the role played the aggregate demand curve? In the figure you have drawn with the aggregate supply curve, show an aggregate demand curve that would create an inflation rate of 5 percent. To what point on the Phillips curve does this aggregate demand/aggregate supply equilibrium correspond?

## Solutions to Additional Practice Problems 32.1

1a. The inflation rate equals the change in the price level divided by the initial price level, all multiplied by 100. So, for row *A*, the inflation rate equals

$$\frac{101.5 - 100.0}{100.0} \times 100, \text{ or } 1.5$$

| | Inflation rate (percent per year) |
|---|---|
| A | 1.5 |
| B | 4.0 |
| C | 5.0 |
| D | 6.5 |
| E | 9.0 |

percent. The rest of the inflation rates are calculated similarly.

1b. Okun's Law states that for each percentage point that the unemployment rate is above the natural unemployment rate, there is a 2 percent gap between real GDP and potential GDP. In row *A* the unemployment rate is 9 percent. The natural unemployment rate is 5 percent, so the unemployment rate is 4 percentage points above the natural unemployment rate. So real GDP is (2) × (4 percent) = 8 percent below potential GDP. Potential GDP is $7 trillion, so real GDP is (8 percent) × ($7 tril-

| | Real GDP (trillions of 2006 dollars) |
|---|---|
| A | 6.44 |
| B | 6.86 |
| C | 7.00 |
| D | 7.14 |
| E | 7.28 |

lion) = $0.56 trillion dollars below potential GDP. Real GDP equals $7 trillion minus $0.56 trillion, which is $6.44 trillion, as shown in the table in this answer. The rest of the real GDP calculations are similar.

1c. The short-run Phillips curve for 2007 shows the relationship between the inflation rate and the unemployment rate. The unemployment rates are given in the table in

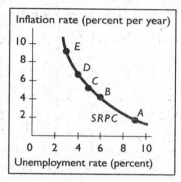

the problem and the associated inflation rates are given in the answer to part (a). The figure plots the resulting Phillips curve.

1d. The aggregate supply curve for 2007 is plotted in the figure. The price levels are given in the problem and the corresponding real GDPs are calculated from Okun's Law in part (b).

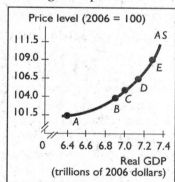

1e. The figures in part (e) and part (f) have the points labeled.

2. When aggregate demand increases, everything else remaining the same, there is a movement up along the aggregate supply curve. Real GDP increases and the price level rises. At the same time, the unemployment rate decreases and the inflation rate rises. There is a movement up along the short-run Phillips curve.

When aggregate demand decreases, everything else remaining the same, there is a movement down along the aggregate supply curve. Real GDP decreases and the price level falls. At the same time, the unemployment rate increases and the inflation rate falls. There is a movement down along the short-run Phillips curve.

Because the current price level is 100, to create an inflation rate of 5 percent, the aggregate demand curve must intersect the aggregate supply at a price level of 105. The figure shows this aggregate demand curve. This price level corresponds to point C and so this aggregate demand/aggregate supply equilibrium corresponds to point C on the short-run Phillips curve.

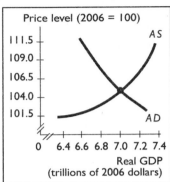

Price level (2006 = 100)

## ■ AP Self Test 32.1

**True or false**

1. The short-run Phillips curve shows the tradeoff between the natural unemployment rate and the expected inflation rate.

2. Moving along a short-run Phillips curve, the price of a lower unemployment rate is a higher inflation rate.

3. Okun's Law states that for each percentage point that real GDP is less than potential GDP, there is a 2 percent gap between the unemployment rate and the natural unemployment rate.

4. Points on the short-run Phillips curve correspond to points on the aggregate supply curve.

5. Aggregate demand fluctuations bring movements along the aggregate supply curve and along the short-run Phillips curve.

**Multiple choice**

1. The short-run Phillips curve shows the relationship between
   a. the inflation rate and the interest rate.
   b. real GDP and the inflation rate.
   c. the unemployment rate and the interest rate.
   d. the inflation rate and the unemployment rate.
   e. real GDP and the price level.

2. The short-run Phillips curve is
   a. vertical at the natural unemployment rate.
   b. upward sloping.
   c. downward sloping.
   d. horizontal at the expected inflation rate.
   e. U-shaped.

3. Moving along the short-run Phillips curve, as the unemployment rate increases the inflation rate
   a. decreases.
   b. increases.
   c. remains unchanged.
   d. initially decreases and then increases.
   e. initially increases and then decreases.

4. If real GDP exceeds potential GDP, then employment is ____ full employment and the unemployment rate is ____ the natural unemployment rate.
   a. below; above
   b. equal to; below
   c. above; below
   d. above; above
   e. equal to; equal to

5. Okun's Law states that for every percentage point that the unemployment rate is above the natural unemployment rate, there is a ____ percent gap between real GDP and potential GDP.
   a. 1
   b. 1.5
   c. 2
   d. 2.5
   e. 5

6. According to Okun's Law, if the natural unemployment rate is 5 percent, the actual unemployment rate is 4 percent, and potential GDP is $10 trillion, then actual real GDP is
   a. $12 trillion.
   b. $11 trillion.
   c. $9.6 trillion.
   d. $10.4 trillion.
   e. $10.2 trillion.

7. When a movement up along the aggregate supply curve occurs, there is also
   a. a movement down along the short-run Phillips curve.
   b. a movement up along the short-run Phillips curve.
   c. a rightward shift of the short-run Phillips curve.
   d. a leftward shift of the short-run Phillips curve.
   e. no movement along and no shift in the short-run Phillips curve.

8. When aggregate demand increases, there is a movement ____ along the *AS* curve and ____
   a. up; a movement up along the short-run Phillips curve.
   b. up; a movement down along the short-run Phillips curve.
   c. up; an upward shift of the short-run Phillips curve.
   d. down; a downward shift of the short-run Phillips curve.
   e. down; a movement down along the short-run Phillips curve.

## Short Response Questions

| Inflation rate (percent per year) | Unemployment rate (percentage) |
|---|---|
| 2 | 12 |
| 3 | 8 |
| 4 | 5 |
| 5 | 3 |
| 6 | 2 |

1. The table above has data on the inflation rate and the unemployment rate.
   a. Using the data, label the axes and plot the short-run Phillips curve in Figure 32.1.

■ **FIGURE 32.1**

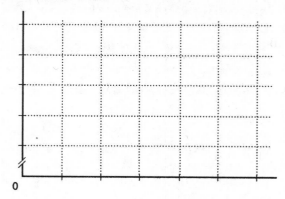

   Label the curve *SRPC*.
   b. What is the effect of a decrease in the unemployment rate from 8 percent to 5 percent? Show the effect in Figure 32.1.
   c. How does your answer to question (b) indicate the presence of a tradeoff?

## Long Response Questions

1. What does the slope of the short-run Phillips curve indicate about the tradeoff between inflation and unemployment?

| Unemployment rate (percentage) | Real GDP (trillions of 2000 dollars) |
|---|---|
| 4 | ____ |
| 5 | ____ |
| 6 | ____ |
| 7 | ____ |

2. The table above gives data for an economy. Suppose that for this economy the natural unemployment rate is 5 percent and potential GDP is $8 trillion.
   a. What is Okun's Law?
   b. Using Okun's Law, complete the table by calculating real GDP for each unemployment rate.

3. What is the effect on the aggregate supply curve and on the short-run Phillips curve of an increase in aggregate demand?

## CHECKPOINT 32.2

■ **Distinguish between the short-run and the long-run Phillips curves and describe the shifting tradeoff between inflation and unemployment.**

### Quick Review

• *Long-run Phillips curve* The long-run Phillips curve is the vertical line that shows the relationship between inflation and unemployment when the economy is at full employment.

• *Factor that shifts the long-run Phillips curve* An increase (decrease) in the natural unemployment rate shifts the long-run (and short-run) Phillips curve rightward (leftward).

### Additional Practice Problems 32.2

1. The figure shows a short-run Phillips curve and a long-run Phillips curve.

   a. What is the expected inflation rate?

   b. What is the natural unemployment rate?

   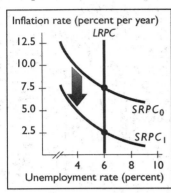

   c. If the expected inflation rate falls to 2.5 percent a year, show the new short-run and long-run Phillips curves.

   d. If the natural unemployment rate decreases to 4 percent but the expected inflation rate does not change from what it is in the figure above, show the new short-run and long-run Phillips curves.

2. Explain how the inflation rate and unemployment rate might simultaneously increase.

### Solutions to Additional Practice Problems 32.2

1a. The expected inflation rate is the inflation rate where the short-run Phillips curve and the long-run Phillips curve intersect. The expected inflation rate is 7.5 percent a year.

1b. The long-run Phillips curve is vertical at the natural unemployment rate. The natural unemployment rate is 6 percent.

1c. When the expected inflation rate decreases to 2.5 percent a year, the short-run Phillips curve shifts downward but the long-run Phillips curve does not shift. The new short-run Phillips curve intersects the long-run Phillips curve at the new expected inflation rate. The figure shows that the short-run Phillips curve shifts downward from $SRPC_0$ to $SRPC_1$.

1d. A decrease in the natural unemployment rate shifts *both* the short-run Phillips curve and the long-run Phillips curve leftward. In the figure the long-run Phillips curve shifts leftward from $LRPC_0$ to $LRPC_1$ and the short-run Phillips curve shifts leftward from $SRPC_0$ to $SRPC_1$. The new short-run Phillips curve intersects the new long-run Phillips curve at the expected inflation rate.

2. If the natural unemployment rate increases, the short-run Phillips curves shifts rightward. If, simultaneously, the inflation rate rises, it is possible to move from a point on its old short-run Phillips curve to a point on the new short-run Phillips curve such that both the inflation rate and the unemployment rate increase. For

instance, in the figure the short-run Phillips curve shifts and the inflation rate rises from 5.0 percent to 7.5 percent. The movement from point *A* on the initial short-run Phillips curve

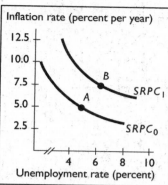

Inflation rate (percent per year)

*SRPC0* to point *B* on the new short-run Phillips curve *SRPC1* shows how both the unemployment rate and inflation rate can simultaneously increase.

### ■ AP Self Test 32.2

**True or false**

1. The long-run Phillips curve is horizontal because it shows that at the expected inflation rate, any unemployment rate might occur.

2. An increase in the expected inflation rate shifts the long-run Phillips curve.

3. An increase in the expected inflation rate shifts the short-run Phillips curve.

4. The natural rate hypothesis states that an increase in the growth rate of the quantity of money temporarily decreases the unemployment rate.

5. A change in the natural unemployment rate shifts both the short-run and long-run Phillips curves.

**Multiple choice**

1. The long-run Phillips curve is the relationship between
   a. unemployment and the price level at full employment.
   b. unemployment and the rate of inflation at the expected price level.
   c. inflation and real GDP at full employment.
   d. inflation and unemployment when the economy is at full employment.
   e. inflation and the expected inflation rate.

2. The long-run Phillips curve is
   a. upward sloping.
   b. downward sloping.
   c. horizontal.
   d. vertical.
   e. upside-down U-shaped.

3. The inflation rate that is used to set the money wage rate and other money prices is the
   a. natural inflation rate.
   b. actual inflation rate.
   c. expected inflation rate.
   d. cost of living inflation rate.
   e. wage inflation rate.

4. Burger King is paying $8 an hour to its servers. If the expected inflation rate is 10 percent a year, then to keep the real wage rate constant in a year the money wage rate must
   a. rise to $8.80 an hour.
   b. fall to $7.20 an hour.
   c. stay at $8.00 an hour.
   d. rise to $8.10 an hour.
   e. rise to $8.40 an hour.

### ■ FIGURE 32.2

Inflation rate (percent per year)

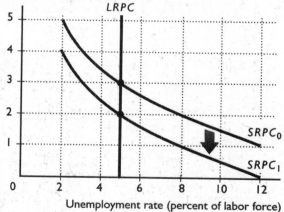

Unemployment rate (percent of labor force)

5. The shift in Figure 32.2 is the result of
   a. an increase in the expected inflation rate.
   b. a decrease in the expected inflation rate.
   c. an increase in the natural unemployment rate.
   d. a decrease in the natural unemployment rate.
   e. an increase in the inflation rate.

6. When the expected inflation rate ____, the short-run Phillips curve shifts ____.
   a. falls; upward
   b. rises; upward
   c. rises; downward
   d. None of the above because a change in the expected inflation rate leads to a movement along the short-run Phillips curve but does not shift the short-run Phillips curve.
   e. None of the above because a change in the expected inflation rate only shifts the long-run Phillips curve and has no effect on the short-run Phillips curve.

7. The natural rate hypothesis states that
   a. only natural economic policies can bring a permanent reduction in the unemployment rate.
   b. changes in the growth rate of the quantity of money temporarily change the unemployment rate.
   c. it is natural for the unemployment rate to exceed the inflation rate.
   d. it is natural for the unemployment rate to be less than the natural unemployment rate.
   e. changes in the growth rate of the quantity of money temporarily change the natural unemployment rate.

8. If the natural unemployment rate decreases, then the short-run Phillips curve ____ and the long-run Phillips curve ____.
   a. does not shift; shifts leftward
   b. shifts leftward; shifts leftward
   c. shifts rightward; shifts leftward
   d. shifts rightward; shifts rightward
   e. shifts leftward; does not shift

9. The natural unemployment rate
   a. changes because of changes in frictional and structural unemployment.
   b. never changes.
   c. always increases.
   d. decreases when the inflation rate rises.
   e. increases when the expected inflation rate rises.

**Short Response Questions**

| Inflation rate (percent per year) | Unemployment rate (percentage) |
|:---:|:---:|
| 2 | 12 |
| 3 | 8 |
| 4 | 5 |
| 5 | 3 |
| 6 | 2 |

■ **FIGURE 32.3**

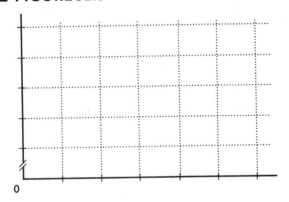

1. The table above has data on a nation's short-run Phillips curve. In this nation, the natural unemployment rate equals 5 percent.
   a. Label the axes and then draw both the short-run Phillips curve and long-run Phillips curve in Figure 32.3.
   b. What is the expected inflation rate?
   c. Suppose the expected inflation rate falls by 1 percentage point. Show the effect of this change on the short-run Phillips curve and long-run Phillips curve in Figure 32.3.

2. How does an increase in the expected inflation rate change the short-run and long-run Phillips curves?

3. How does an increase in the natural unemployment rate change the short-run and long-run Phillips curves?

**Long Response Questions**

■ **FIGURE 32.4**

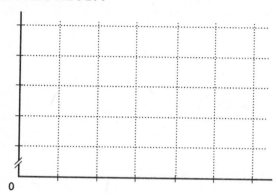

1. In Figure 32.4, redraw your initial short-run and long-run Phillips curves from Figure 32.3. Suppose that the natural unemployment rate falls to 3 percent and the expected inflation rate does not change. In Figure 32.4, show the effect of this change.

2. In the *AS-AD* model, does the aggregate demand curve, the aggregate supply curve, or the potential GDP line best correspond to the long-run Phillips curve?

3. What are the key points about the long-run Phillips curve and the relationship between the long-run Phillips curve and the short-run Phillips curve?

4. What is the natural rate hypothesis?

## CHECKPOINT 32.3

■ **Explain how the Fed can influence the expected inflation rate and how expected inflation influences the short-run tradeoff.**

### Quick Review

- *Surprise inflation reduction* A surprise inflation reduction slows inflation but at the cost of recession.
- *Credible announced inflation reduction* A credible announced inflation reduction lowers the inflation rate but with no ac-

companying loss of output or increase in unemployment.

**Additional Practice Problem 32.3**

1. The figure shows the short-run and long-run Phillips curves. The current inflation rate is 7.5 percent a year and the current unemployment rate is the natural unemployment rate, 5 percent.

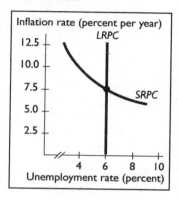

a. Suppose that the Fed announces that it will slow the money growth rate such that inflation will fall to 5 percent a year and everyone believes the Fed. Explain the effect of the Fed's action on inflation and unemployment next year.

b. Suppose that the Fed announces that it will slow the money growth rate such that inflation will fall to 5 percent a year and no one believes the Fed. The Fed actually carries out its policy. Explain the effect of the Fed's action on inflation and unemployment next year.

c. Based on your answers to this question, should the Fed be concerned about its credibility?

**Solution to Additional Practice Problem 32.3**

1a. If the Fed's announcement is credible, the expected inflation rate falls. The short-run Phillips curve shifts downward as illustrated in the figure. The economy moves from point *A* to point *B*. The inflation rate

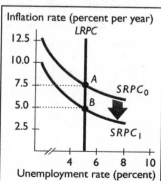

falls to 5 percent a year and the unemployment rate remains at 5 percent. In this case the reduction in the inflation rate had no effect on the unemployment rate.

1b. Because no one expected the Fed's action, the expected inflation rate does not change and the short-run Phillips curve does not shift. The economy moves along its short-run Phil-

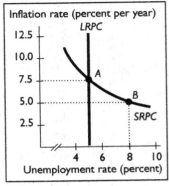

lips curve from point *A* to point *B*. As the inflation rate falls to 5 percent, the unemployment rate rises to 8 percent.

1c. The Fed should be concerned about its credibility. *Only* if the Fed has credibility can it make an announcement about reducing inflation that reduces the inflation rate without an increase in the unemployment rate.

## ■ AP Self Test 32.3

**True or false**

1. The expected inflation rate never changes.

2. One factor that can be used to predict inflation are data on past inflation and money growth.

3. A surprise inflation reduction does not increase the unemployment rate.

4. A credible announced inflation reduction leads to a large increase in the unemployment rate.

5. When the Fed slowed inflation in 1981, the consequence was recession.

**Multiple choice**

1. A rational expectation of the inflation rate is
   a. a forecast based on the forecasted actions of the Fed and other relevant determinant factors.
   b. an expected inflation rate between 1 percent and 5 percent.
   c. a forecast based only on the historical evolution of inflation over the last 100 years.
   d. an expected inflation rate between 5 percent and 10 percent.
   e. always correct.

2. Because money supply growth is a major component determining the inflation rate, in order to forecast inflation we should forecast actions by the
   a. Office of the Treasury.
   b. president.
   c. Congress.
   d. Fed.
   e. U.S. Mint.

3. If the economy begins at its natural unemployment rate and the Fed provides a surprise slowing of the inflation rate more than expected, there is a
   a. rightward shift of the long-run Phillips curve.
   b. movement upward along the short-run Phillips curve.
   c. leftward shift of the long-run Phillips curve.
   d. movement downward along the short-run Phillips curve.
   e. movement downward along the long-run Phillips curve.

4. A surprise reduction of inflation will come at the expense of
   a. a higher expected inflation rate.
   b. an increase in real GDP.
   c. recession.
   d. a decrease in the natural unemployment rate.
   e. a downward shift in the short-run Phillips curve.

5. A "credible announced" inflation reduction policy is one that
   a. has monetary policy slowly increasing the money supply.
   b. the public is told about *after* the policy change has occurred.
   c. the public is told about before policy changes have occurred and that is believed by the public.
   d. depends only on fiscal policy changes that have been publicly debated and implemented.
   e. the public is never told about.

6. If the Fed makes a credible announcement that its policy aims to reduce inflation, the
   a. long-run Phillips curve shifts downward.
   b. short-run Phillips curve shifts downward.
   c. long-run Phillips curve shifts upward.
   d. short-run Phillips curve shifts upward.
   e. long-run Phillips curve shifts rightward.

7. A credible announced inflation reduction results in _____ natural unemployment rate and _____ shift in the short-run Phillips curve.
   a. a higher; an upward
   b. a lower; an upward
   c. no change in the; an upward
   d. no change in the; a downward
   e. no change in the; no

8. In 1981, the Fed
   a. created a surprise inflation reduction policy and created an expansion.
   b. created a surprise inflation reduction policy and created a recession.
   c. credibly announced an inflation reduction policy and created a recession.
   d. credibly announced an inflation reduction policy and created an expansion.
   e. took no action so that the inflation rate skyrocketed.

## Short Response Questions
1. Must inflation reduction always result in higher unemployment?
2. In the long run, what is the effect of reducing the inflation rate?

## Long Response Questions
■ **FIGURE 32.5**

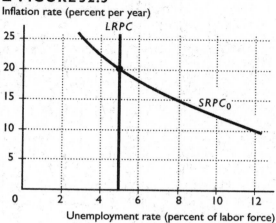

1. Figure 32.5 shows a nation's short-run and long-run Phillips curves. In this nation, the natural unemployment rate equals 5 percent and the actual and expected inflation rate is 20 percent. The nation's government decides to take actions to lower the inflation rate to 10 percent.
   a. Suppose the government announces that the inflation rate will be lowered to 10 percent but no one believes this policy will be carried out. The government, however, actually does lower the inflation rate to 10 percent. In the figure draw any new Phillips curve you need and indicate the new inflation rate and unemployment rate by labeling it *A*.
   b. Returning to the initial situation of 5 percent unemployment and 20 percent inflation, suppose that when the government announces that the inflation rate will be lowered to 10 percent everyone believes this policy will be carried out. The government then follows through by lowering the inflation rate to 10 percent. In the figure draw any new Phillips curve you need and indicate the new inflation rate and unemployment rate by labeling it *B*.
   c. Returning to the initial situation of 5 percent unemployment and 20 percent inflation, suppose that when the government

announces that the inflation rate will be lowered to 10 percent one half of the people believe the announcement and the other half do not. The government follows through by lowering the inflation rate to 10 percent. In the figure draw any new Phillips curve you need and indicate the new inflation rate and unemployment rate by labeling it C.

d. How does the number of people that believe the government's announcement affect the unemployment rate that results?

2. What short-run effects does a surprise inflation reduction have on the short-run and long-run Phillips curves and the unemployment rate? What long-run effects does it have?

3. What short-run effects does a credible announced inflation reduction have on the short-run and long-run Phillips curves and the unemployment rate? What long-run effects does it have?

4. How do the long-run effects of a surprise inflation reduction compare to the effects of a credible announced inflation reduction?

# YOUR AP SELF TEST ANSWERS

## ■ CHECKPOINT 32.1

### True or false
1. False;  page 810
2. True;  page 810
3. False;  page 811
4. True;  page 812
5. True;  page 813

### Multiple choice
1. d; page 810
2. c; page 810
3. a; page 810
4. c; page 811
5. c; page 811
6. e; page 811
7. b; page 812
8. a; page 813

### Short Response Question

**■ FIGURE 32.6**

Inflation rate (percent per year)

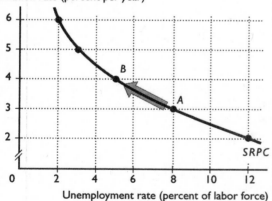

Unemployment rate (percent of labor force)

1. a. Figure 32.6 plots the short-run Phillips curve, labeled *SRPC*;  page 810.
   b. The decrease in the unemployment rate brings a rise in the inflation rate. There is a movement along the short-run Phillips curve, as indicated by the movement from point *A* to point *B*;  page 810.
   c. The movement indicates a tradeoff because a decrease in the unemployment

rate has a rise in the inflation rate as the price; page 810.

### Long Response Questions
1. The slope of the short-run Phillips curve is negative, which indicates that as the unemployment rate decreases, the inflation rate increases. So the price of a lower unemployment rate is a higher inflation rate. Conversely, the cost of a lower inflation rate is a higher unemployment rate;  page 810.

2. a. Okun's Law states that for each percentage point that the unemployment rate is above the natural unemployment rate, there is a 2 percent gap between real GDP and potential GDP;  page 811.

| Unemployment rate (percentage) | Real GDP (trillions of 2000 dollars) |
|---|---|
| 4 | 8.16 |
| 5 | 8.00 |
| 6 | 7.84 |
| 7 | 7.68 |

   b. The completed table is above. When the unemployment rate is 7 percent, it is 2 percentage points above the natural unemployment rate. According to Okun's Law, real GDP is (2) × (2 percent) or 4 percent below potential GDP. So real GDP is (4 percent) × ($8 trillion) or $0.32 trillion below potential GDP. Real GDP is $8 trillion minus $0.32 trillion, which is $7.68 trillion; page 807.

3. When aggregate demand increases, the aggregate demand curve shifts rightward and there is a movement up along the aggregate supply curve. The price level rises and real GDP increases. As the price level rises the inflation rate rises and as real GDP increases the unemployment rate decreases. There is a movement up along the short-run Phillips curve; page 813.

## ■ CHECKPOINT 32.2

### True or false

1. False; page 816
2. False; page 818
3. True; page 818
4. True; page 819
5. True; pages 820-821

### Multiple choice

1. d; page 816
2. d; page 816
3. c; page 818
4. a; page 818
5. b; page 818
6. b; page 818
7. b; page 819
8. b; pages 820-821
9. a; page 821

### Short Response Questions

#### ■ FIGURE 32.7

Inflation rate (percent per year)

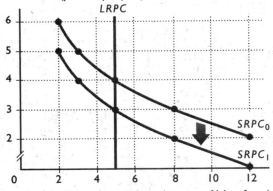

Unemployment rate (percent of labor force)

1. a. Figure 32.7 plots the short-run Phillips curve, labeled $SRPC_0$ and the long-run Phillips curve, labeled $LRPC$; page 816.

   b. The expected inflation rate is 4 percent a year because that is the inflation rate at which the short-run Phillips curve intersects the long-run Phillips curve; page 818.

   c. The new short-run Phillips curve is illustrated as $SRPC_1$; page 818.

2. An increase in the expected inflation rate shifts the short-run Phillips curve upward but does not change the long-run Phillips curve; page 818.

3. An increase in the natural unemployment rate shifts *both* the long-run and short-run Phillips curves rightward; pages 820-821.

### Long Response Questions

#### ■ FIGURE 32.8

Inflation rate (percent per year)

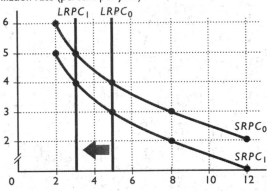

Unemployment rate (percent of labor force)

1. The initial short-run Phillips curve is labeled $SRPC_0$ and the initial long-run Phillips curve is labeled $LRPC_0$ in Figure 32.8. The decrease in the natural unemployment rate by 2 percentage points shifts both the long-run Phillips curve leftward from $LRPC_0$ to $LRPC_1$ and the short-run Phillips curve leftward from $SRPC_0$ to $SRPC_1$. The new short-run Phillips curve and the new long-run Phillips curve intersect at the expected inflation rate; pages 820-821.

2. The potential GDP line best corresponds to the long-run Phillips curve. The potential GDP line shows that a change in the price level does not change potential GDP and has no effect on the natural unemployment rate. The long-run Phillips curve shows that a change in the inflation rate does not change the natural unemployment rate; page 816.

3. There are several key points: First, the long-run Phillips curve is vertical at the natural unemployment rate. Next, the short-run Phil-

lips curve intersects the long-run Phillips curve at the expected inflation rate. Finally, changes in the expected inflation rate shift only the short-run Phillips curve, and changes in the natural unemployment rate shift both the short-run and long-run Phillips curves; pages 816, 818, 820.

4. The natural rate hypothesis is the proposition that when the money supply growth rate changes (so that the growth rate of aggregate demand changes), the unemployment rate changes temporarily and eventually returns to the natural unemployment rate. An increase in the money supply growth rate increases the inflation rate and temporarily lowers the unemployment rate but eventually the unemployment rate returns to the natural unemployment rate. The fall in the unemployment rate was only temporary; page 819.

## ■ CHECKPOINT 32.3

**True or false**

1. False; page 825
2. True; page 825
3. False; page 826
4. False; page 827
5. True; page 827

**Multiple choice**

1. a; page 825
2. d; page 825
3. d; page 826
4. c; page 826
5. c; pages 826-827
6. b; pages 826-827
7. d; pages 826-827
8. b; page 827

**Short Response Questions**

1. Inflation reduction does not always need to lead to higher unemployment rates. If the Fed can credibly announce a policy of lowering the inflation rate, there will be no effect on the unemployment rate; page 827.

2. In the long run, the economy returns to the natural rate of unemployment. So reducing the inflation rate has no long-run effects on the unemployment rate; page 826.

**Long Response Questions**

■ **FIGURE 32.9**

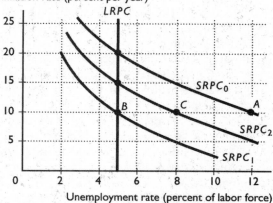

1. a. Because people do not believe the government's announcement, the actual fall in inflation is a surprise. People's expectations about the inflation rate have not changed, so the fall in inflation does not change the short-run Phillips curve. With the surprise fall in inflation, the economy moves along its initial short-run Phillips curve $SRPC_0$ to point $A$ in Figure 32.9. The inflation rate is 10 percent and the unemployment rate is 12 percent; page 826.

   b. Because people believe the government's announcement, the expected inflation rate falls to 10 percent. With the fall in the expected inflation rate, the short-run Phillips curve shifts downward, in the figure to $SRPC_1$. It intersects the long-run Phillips curve at the new expected inflation rate. The credible announcement by the government means that the economy moves down its long-run Phillips curve to point $B$. The inflation rate is 10 percent and the unemployment rate is 5 percent; pages 826-827.

   c. Because one half the people believe the government's announcement, so their expected inflation rate is 10 percent, and the other half do not believe the announcement, so their expected inflation rate remains 20 percent, overall the expected inflation rate is 15 percent. With this fall in the expected inflation rate, the short-run Phillips curve shifts downward in the figure to $SRPC_2$. This Phillips curve intersects the long-run Phillips curve at the expected inflation rate, 15 percent. The inflation rate falls to 10 percent and the economy moves along its short-run Phillips curve $SRPC_2$ to point C. The inflation rate is 10 percent and the unemployment rate is 8 percent; pages 826-827.

d. The more people who believe the government's announcement, the more the expected inflation rate falls and the smaller the resulting increase in unemployment. When no one believes the announcement, the fall in inflation is a surprise and the unemployment rate rises to 12 percent; when half the people believe the announcement, the unemployment rate rises to 8 percent; and when the announcement is credible so that everyone believes it, the unemployment rate remains equal to 5 percent; pages 826-827.

2. In the short run, a surprise inflation reduction does not change the short-run or long-run Phillips curve. The economy moves down along the short-run Phillips curve. The inflation rate falls and the unemployment rate rises. In the long run, the inflation reduction is no longer a surprise. The short-run Phillips curve shifts downward. The long-run Phillips curve does not change. The inflation rate falls and the unemployment rate returns to the natural unemployment rate; pages 826-827.

3. In the short run, a credible announced inflation reduction shifts the short-run Phillips curve downward. It has no effect on the long-run Phillips curve. Because the announcement is credible, the inflation rate falls and the unemployment rate does not change. The long-run effects are identical to the short-run effects; pages 826-827.

4. The long-run effects of a surprise inflation reduction are the same as the short-run effects of a credible announced inflation reduction. In both cases the short-run Phillips curve shifts downward and the inflation rate falls with no change in the unemployment rate. The reason for the similarity is that in both instances people revise the expected inflation rate downward. In the case of the surprise inflation reduction, the expected inflation rate is revised downward because of the actual experience with lower inflation. In the case of the credible announcement, the expected inflation rate is revised downward because people are aware in advance of the Fed's policy; pages 826-827.

# Fiscal and Monetary Policy Debates

# Chapter 33

Chapter 33 discusses the relative strength of fiscal policy and monetary policy, whether they should be used to help stabilize the economy, and if they are used, what they should target.

■ **Discuss whether fiscal policy or monetary policy is the better stabilization tool.**

A change in the quantity of money changes the interest rate, which influences interest-sensitive components of aggregate expenditure. If a change in the quantity of money brings a large change in the interest rate because the demand for money is relatively insensitive to the interest rate and aggregate expenditure is highly sensitive to the interest rate, monetary policy is powerful. The more predictable the demand for money and investment demand, the more predictable is the effect of monetary policy. An increase in government expenditures or a tax cut increases aggregate demand and real GDP, which increases the demand for money and raises the interest rate. The higher interest rate decreases investment, which counteracts the effects of the initial increase in aggregate expenditure. If the interest rate rise is small and a given change in the interest rate has a small effect on aggregate expenditure, the crowding-out effect is small and fiscal policy is powerful. Discretionary fiscal policy actions create policy goal conflicts because it is not clear which of the many spending programs or tax laws should be changed. Monetary policy has fewer policy goal conflicts than fiscal policy and is more flexible.

■ **Explain the rules-versus-discretion debate and compare Keynesian and monetarist policy rules.**

Three broad approaches to the Fed's monetary policy are discretionary policy, which is policy based on the judgments of policymakers, fixed-rule policy, which is policy that is pursued independently of the state of the economy, and feedback-rule policy, which is policy that responds to changes in the economy. For an aggregate demand shock under a fixed-rule policy, in which the quantity of money remains constant, the economy returns to potential GDP when aggregate supply changes. A feedback rule offsets the initial change in aggregate demand. Feedback-rule policies are difficult to use if potential GDP is uncertain, if there are policy lags that exceed forecast horizons, or if the policy creates uncertainty. Aggregate supply shocks, which are changes to aggregate supply, result in larger changes in the price level with a feedback rule that targets real GDP.

■ **Assess whether policy should target the price level rather than real GDP.**

Two possible targets for monetary policy are stabilizing real GDP and the price level. If aggregate demand shocks were the only shocks to affect the economy, then stabilizing aggregate demand would stabilize both the price level and real GDP. But in the face of aggregate supply shocks, stabilizing real GDP means destabilizing the price level and stabilizing the price level means destabilizing real GDP. Inflation targeting is a monetary policy framework that combines an announced target for the inflation rate with publication of the central bank's economic forecasts.

## EXPANDED CHAPTER CHECKLIST

**When you have completed this chapter, you will be able to:**

**1 Discuss whether fiscal policy or monetary policy is the better stabilization tool.**

- Discuss and illustrate the transmission of monetary policy and explain the conditions under which monetary policy is powerful.
- Discuss the transmission of fiscal policy and explain the conditions under which fiscal policy is powerful.
- Describe fiscal policy goal conflicts and monetary policy goal conflicts.
- Discuss why monetary policy is the preferred stabilization tool in normal times.

**2 Explain the rules-versus-discretion debate and compare Keynesian and monetarist policy rules.**

- Describe the policies pursued by a monetarist and by a Keynesian activist.

**3 Assess whether policy should target the price level rather than real GDP.**

- Explain the effects on the economy of real GDP targeting versus targeting the price level.
- Discuss inflation targeting.

## YOUR AP TEST HINTS

### AP Topics

| Topic on your AP test | Corresponding textbook section |
| --- | --- |
| **Inflation, Unemployment, and Stabilization Policies** | |
| Monetary and Fiscal Policies | Chapter 33 |
| • Demand-side effects | Checkpoints 33.1, 33.2, 33.3 |
| • Supply-side effects | Checkpoints 33.1, 33.2, 33.3 |

### Extra AP material

- The AP test does not ask about fixed rules versus feedback rules. But questions about the effects of monetary policy and fiscal policy are a very important component of the test, so be certain to study these effects (covered in this chapter and Chapter 31) thoroughly.

## CHECKPOINT 33.1

**■ Discuss whether fiscal policy or monetary policy is the better stabilization tool.**

### Quick Review

- *Strength of monetary policy* The more insensitive the quantity of money demanded to a change in the interest rate, and the more sensitive investment demand and other components of aggregate expenditure are to a change in the interest rate, the more powerful is monetary policy.
- *Strength of fiscal policy* The power of fiscal policy depends on the strength of the crowding-out effects that counteract it.

### Additional Practice Problems 33.1

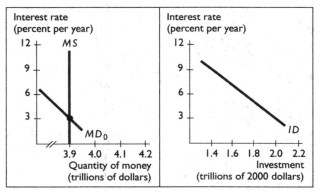

1. The left figure above shows the initial money market equilibrium and the right figure above shows the investment demand curve. Suppose the government increases its expenditures, which increase real GDP, which then, in turn,

increases the demand for money by $0.2 trillion at every interest rate.

   a. Before the government's fiscal policy, in the money market figure show the equilibrium interest rate. Show the effect in the money market from the fiscal policy. What is the new equilibrium interest rate?

   b. Before the government's fiscal policy, using the investment demand curve show the equilibrium quantity of investment? After the fiscal policy, show the new equilibrium quantity of investment? How much investment was crowded out?

2. When is fiscal policy powerful? Why? When is monetary policy powerful? What is the relationship between the conditions that make these policies either stronger or weaker?

### Solutions to Additional Practice Problems 33.1

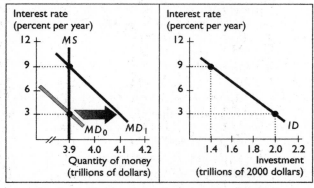

1a. In the left figure, before the fiscal policy the equilibrium interest rate was 3 percent, determined by the intersection of the demand for money curve, $MD_0$ and the supply of money curve, $MS$. The increase in real GDP increases the demand for money and shifts the demand for money curve to $MD_1$. The equilibrium interest rate rises to 9 percent.

1b. Before the fiscal policy, the equilibrium interest rate was 3 percent. The top right figure shows that at this interest rate the equilibrium quantity of investment is $2.0 trillion. When the interest rate rises to 9 percent, the equilibrium quantity of investment decreases to $1.4 trillion. $0.6 trillion of investment is crowded out.

2. Fiscal policy is powerful when the demand for money is sensitive to the interest rate and investment demand is insensitive to the interest rate. In these cases the crowding-out effect is smaller.

Monetary policy is powerful when the demand for money is insensitive to the interest rate and investment demand is sensitive to the interest rate.

Both policy tools affect aggregate demand, but the size of the change in aggregate demand depends on the demand for money and investment demand. Fiscal policy is powerful when monetary policy is weak and monetary policy is powerful when fiscal policy is weak.

### ■ AP Self Test 33.1

**True or false**

1. Monetary policy is more powerful the more sensitive investment demand is to the interest rate.

2. Fiscal policy is more powerful the less sensitive investment demand is to the interest rate.

3. In a liquidity trap, monetary policy is extremely powerful.

4. A major reason fiscal policy suffers from goal conflicts is because there are only a few spending programs and tax laws that can be changed.

5. Monetary policy can be undertaken more rapidly than fiscal policy.

**Multiple choice**

1. When the Fed uses monetary policy, it changes ____ which changes ____ which changes ____.

   a. the supply of money; the interest rate; investment

   b. the supply of money; investment; the interest rate

   c. the interest rate; investment; the supply of money

   d. investment; the supply of money; the interest rate

   e. the interest rate; investment; government expenditure

2. One of the factors that determines the power of monetary policy is the responsiveness of
   a. the supply of money to the interest rate.
   b. the demand for money to the interest rate.
   c. investment to the level of potential GDP.
   d. the unemployment rate to the natural unemployment rate.
   e. inflation to the interest rate.

3. In which case is fiscal policy the strongest?
   a. There is a large crowding-out effect.
   b. The multiplier is large.
   c. Aggregate expenditure is very sensitive to a change in the interest rate.
   d. A change in real GDP results in a large change in money demand.
   e. Real GDP is a fixed amount.

4. If the demand for money is not sensitive to the interest rate and investment is sensitive to the interest rate, fiscal policy is ____ and monetary policy is ____.
   a. powerful; powerful
   b. powerful; weak
   c. weak; powerful
   d. weak; weak
   e. completely ineffective; completely ineffective

5. The term "goal conflicts" refers to the situation in which
   a. fiscal and monetary policy conflict in their goals.
   b. stabilization policy can have side effects that conflict with other goals.
   c. the announcement of policy goals is in conflict with the reality of their actions.
   d. goals are not made clear by either monetary or fiscal policy authorities.
   e. fiscal policy attempts to stabilize the price level and monetary policy attempts to stabilize the inflation rate.

6. The three main goals of monetary policy are
   a. price level stability, real GDP stability, and income redistribution.
   b. price level stability, real GDP stability, and financial market stability.
   c. real GDP stability, financial market stability, and income redistribution.
   d. provision of goods and services, financial market stability, and price level stability.
   e. price level stability, potential GDP stability, and interest rate stability.

7. Discretionary fiscal policy is
   a. volatile, because it responds to rapidly changing political agendas.
   b. flexible, because discretionary fiscal policy is passed quickly through Congress.
   c. coherent, because the Fed dictates it according to its monetary policy.
   d. inflexible, because fiscal policy is political in nature.
   e. completely ineffective because it cannot change real GDP.

8. To deal with normal fluctuations in the economy,
   a. there is no clear winner between monetary policy and fiscal policy.
   b. monetary policy is more flexible and therefore preferred.
   c. fiscal policy is superior with its use of automatic stabilizers and discretionary action.
   d. fiscal policy is better understood by the public and therefore should be used more often than monetary policy.
   e. neither fiscal policy nor monetary policy can do anything to dampen these common occurrences.

## Short Response Questions

**■ FIGURE 33.1**

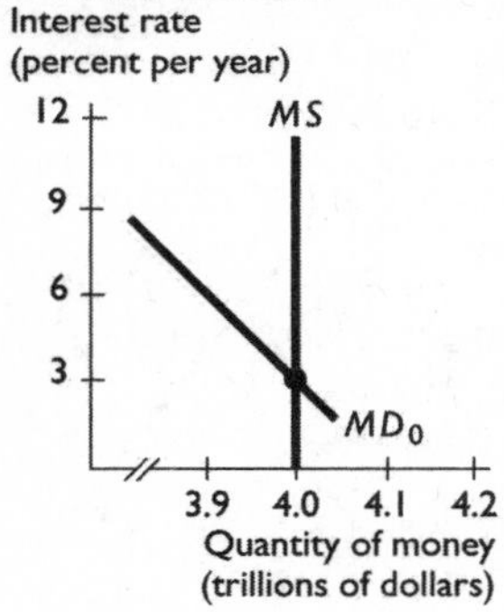

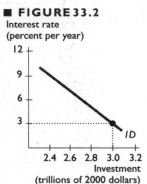

**■ FIGURE 33.2**

1. Figures 33.1 and 33.2 show the money market and the investment demand curve.

   a. The government cuts it taxes. Ignoring any supply-side effects, what is the effect on real GDP and the price level?

   b. What happens to the demand for money when government expenditures are increased? Suppose the change is $0.1 trillion at each interest rate. Use Figure 33.1 to illustrate the effect.

   c. What is the effect of this fiscal policy on investment? Use Figure 33.2 to illustrate the effect.

**■ FIGURE 33.3**

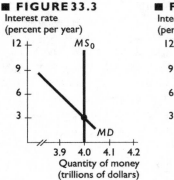

**■ FIGURE 33.4**

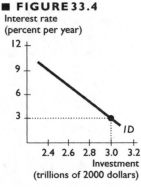

2. Figures 33.3 and 33.4 show the money market and the investment demand curve.

   a. The Fed decreases the quantity of money by $0.1 trillion. Use Figure 33.3 to illustrate the effect of this decrease on the interest rate.

   b. Use Figure 33.4 to illustrate the effect of this monetary policy on investment. Will this policy increase real GDP or decrease real GDP?

## Long Response Questions

1. Explain why monetary policy is more powerful if the quantity of money demanded is insensitive to the interest rate.

2. What is the effect on investment from an increase in government expenditure? Relate this effect to the crowding out effect.

3. What is a liquidity trap? What is the relationship between a liquidity trap and monetary policy?

4. What are the three main fiscal policy goals? How might stabilization lead to a goal conflict?

5. Why is monetary policy considered more flexible than fiscal policy?

## CHECKPOINT 33.2

■ **Explain the rules-versus-discretion debate and compare Keynesian and monetarist policy rules.**

### Quick Review

- *Fixed-rule policy* A fixed-rule policy is a policy that is pursued independently of the state of the economy. A fixed-rule monetary policy is to keep the quantity of money constant.

a. *Flexible-rule policy* A flexible-rule policy is a policy that specifies how policy actions respond to changes in the state of the economy. A flexible-rule monetary policy is to increase the quantity of money when aggregate demand decreases and decrease the quantity of money when aggregate demand increases.

## Additional Practice Problems 33.2

1. The economy shown in the figure is initially on aggregate supply curve $AS_0$ and aggregate demand curve $AD$. Then aggregate supply decreases, and the aggregate supply curve shifts leftward to $AS_1$.

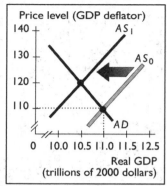

Price level (GDP deflator)

Real GDP (trillions of 2000 dollars)

   a. What are the initial equilibrium real GDP and price level?
   b. If the Fed adopts a fixed-rule policy, over time what happens to real GDP and the price level?
   c. If the Fed adopts a feedback-rule policy that targets real GDP, over time what happens to real GDP and the price level?

2. Can monetary policy offset fluctuations in aggregate supply so that neither the price level nor real GDP changes? Explain your answer.

## Solutions to Additional Practice Problems 33.2

1a. The initial equilibrium is where the aggregate demand curve intersects the aggregate supply curve. As the figure shows, equilibrium real GDP is $11.0 trillion and the equilibrium price level is 110.

1b. In the short run, real GDP and the price level move to the intersection of $AS_1$ and $AD$, so the price level rises to 120 and real GDP decreases to $10.5 trillion. If the Fed is using a

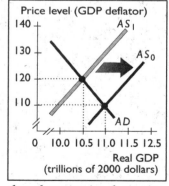

Price level (GDP deflator)

Real GDP (trillions of 2000 dollars)

fixed-rule policy, the changes in the price level and real GDP do not bring any change in policy. With real GDP equal to only $10.5 trillion, there is a recessionary gap so that

eventually the money wage rate falls. When this occurs aggregate supply increases and the aggregate supply curve shifts back to $AS_0$. The price level and real GDP return to their original values of 110 and $11.0 trillion.

1c. In the short run, the price level rises to 120 and real GDP decreases to $10.5 trillion. The Fed increases the quantity of money to restore real GDP back to $11.0 trillion. As a result aggregate demand increases and the $AD$ curve shifts to $AD_1$. Real GDP increases to $11.0 trillion and the price level rises to 130. The feedback rule has restored real GDP but the price level is permanently higher.

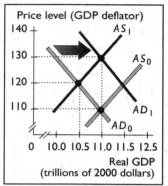

Price level (GDP deflator)

Real GDP (trillions of 2000 dollars)

2. It is not possible for monetary policy to offset fluctuations in aggregate supply so that neither the price level nor real GDP changes. A negative aggregate supply shock raises the price level and decreases real GDP. Monetary policy changes aggregate demand. If monetary policy aims to restore real GDP to potential GDP, it increases aggregate demand. Real GDP increases, as desired, but the price level rises more than otherwise. Similarly, if monetary policy aims to offset the initial increase in the price level, it decreases aggregate demand. The price level falls, as desired, but real GDP decreases more than otherwise.

## ■ AP Self Test 33.2

### True or false

1. An example of a feedback-rule policy is to keep the quantity of money growing at a constant rate to make the average inflation rate equal to zero.

2. A feedback-rule policy attempts to pull the economy out of a recessionary gap by using a policy action.

### Multiple choice

1. Monetary policy that is based on the judgments of the policymakers about current needs of the economy is called ____ monetary policy.
   a. fixed-rule
   b. sure-thing
   c. feedback-rule
   d. discretionary
   e. judgemental

2. A fixed-rule policy is policy
   a. determined by policymakers who use their own judgment to decide what is needed.
   b. that is determined by a preset list of rules.
   c. that is followed regardless of the state of the economy.
   d. determined by the unemployment rate.
   e. that responds to the state of the economy in a fixed way.

3. Economists who believe fluctuations in the quantity of money are the main source of economic fluctuations are
   a. Keynesians.
   b. monetarists.
   c. feedback advocates.
   d. fiscalists.
   e. quantists.

4. To eliminate a recessionary gap that is the result of a supply shock, a feedback-rule monetary policy that targets real GDP will
   a. decrease the quantity of money.
   b. increase the quantity of money.
   c. increase government expenditures.
   d. decrease government expenditures.
   e. decrease taxes.

### Long Response Questions

■ **FIGURE 33.5**

Price level (GDP deflator, 2000 = 100)

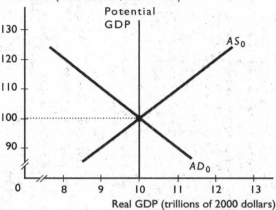

Real GDP (trillions of 2000 dollars)

1. Figure 33.5 shows the economy in its initial equilibrium with real GDP equal to potential GDP of $10 trillion and the price level equal to 100.
   a. Suppose a negative aggregate demand shock hits so that in the short run, the new equilibrium price level is 90. In Figure 33.5, illustrate the effect of this aggregate demand shock. What is equilibrium real GDP?
   b. Suppose that monetary policy follows a feedback-rule policy that moves real GDP back to potential GDP. In Figure 33.5, illustrate the effect of the monetary policy. What is the equilibrium price level?

2. Figure 33.6 (at the top of the next page) shows the economy in its initial equilibrium with real GDP equal to potential GDP of $10 trillion and the price level equal to 100.
   a. Suppose a negative aggregate supply shock hits so that in the short run, the new equilibrium price level is 110. In Figure 33.6, illustrate the effect of this aggregate supply shock. What is equilibrium real GDP?
   b. Suppose that monetary policy follows a feedback-rule policy that moves real GDP back to potential GDP. In Figure 33.6, illustrate the effect of the monetary policy. What is the equilibrium price level?

■ **FIGURE 33.6**

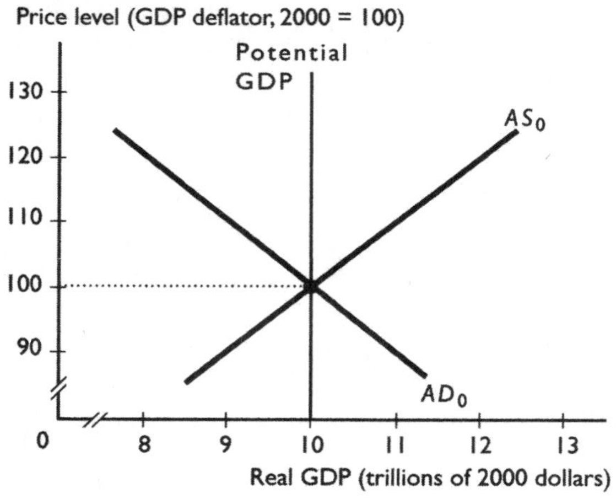

Price level (GDP deflator, 2000 = 100)

Real GDP (trillions of 2000 dollars)

# CHECKPOINT 33.3

■ **Assess whether policy should target the price level rather than real GDP.**

## Quick Review

- *Real GDP target* If monetary policy targets real GDP, an increase in aggregate supply is met with a decrease in aggregate demand and the price level falls; and a decrease in aggregate supply is met with an increase in aggregate demand and the price level rises.

- *Price level target* If monetary policy targets the price level, an increase in aggregate supply is met with an in increase in aggregate demand and the real GDP increases; and a decrease in aggregate supply is met with a decrease in aggregate demand and real GDP decreases.

## Additional Practice Problem 33.3

1. Suppose that in 2007, the inflation rate is 4 percent a year and potential GDP is $13 trillion. Oil prices then increase so that aggregate supply decreases. If the Fed decides that it wants to keep the inflation rate between 1 percent and 7 percent a year and to keep real GDP within the range $12.9 trillion to $13.1 trillion.

a. Is the Fed placing more weight on inflation or on real GDP?
b. What actions will the Fed take?

## Solution to Additional Practice Problem 33.3

1a. The Fed is placing more weight on real GDP. The Fed will accept a decrease in real GDP of $0.1 trillion from potential GDP, which is less than 1 percent. The Fed is willing to accept a 3 percentage point deviation from the midpoint of 4 percent a year, which is a deviation of 75 percent.

1b. The decrease in aggregate supply raises the price level and decreases real GDP. The Fed is more concerned with the decrease in real GDP, so it increases the supply of money. Aggregate demand increases. The price level rises and real GDP moves to its target range.

■ **AP Self Test 33.3**

### True or false

1. The only possible target for stabilization policy is real GDP.

2. Aggregate supply shocks mean that the Fed can simultaneously stabilize real GDP and the price level.

3. Inflation targeting aims to keep the inflation rate within an announced target range.

### Multiple choice

1. Targeting real GDP is equivalent to targeting
a. inflation.
b. unemployment.
c. labor supply.
d. the tax rate.
e. the price level.

2. Two possible targets for monetary policy are
a. real GDP and the price level.
b. real GDP and potential GDP.
c. low taxes and low inflation.
d. low taxes and zero inflation.
e. the unemployment rate and real GDP.

3. Targeting real GDP works best when the source of shocks to the economy come from
   a. the aggregate demand side.
   b. the aggregate supply side.
   c. changes in the natural rate of unemployment.
   d. changes in potential GDP.
   e. changes in the price of oil.

4. If monetary policy targets real GDP, an increase in aggregate supply is met by ____ in the quantity of money and ____ in aggregate demand.
   a. an increase; an increase
   b. an increase; a decrease
   c. a decrease; an increase
   d. a decrease; a decrease
   e. no change; no change

5. If the Fed targets real GDP and the economy experiences an aggregate supply shock, then
   a. monetary policy will not move the economy toward potential GDP.
   b. the price level will fluctuate.
   c. the price level will be effectively stabilized.
   d. both real GDP and the price level will be stabilized.
   e. there is nothing the Fed can do to move the economy back to potential GDP.

6. If the Fed targets the price level, an increase in aggregate supply means that the Fed takes actions to
   a. increase aggregate demand but not aggregate supply.
   b. decrease aggregate demand but not aggregate supply.
   c. increase aggregate supply but not aggregate demand.
   d. decrease both aggregate demand and aggregate supply.
   e. increase both aggregate demand and aggregate supply.

7. If monetary policy targets the price level, then a decrease in aggregate supply is countered with an action by the Fed that
   a. decreases aggregate supply.
   b. increases potential GDP.
   c. decreases aggregate demand.
   d. increases aggregate demand.
   e. decreases potential GDP.

**Long Response Questions**

1. Does it matter whether the Fed targets real GDP or the price level when faced with a decrease in aggregate demand? Does it matter which the Fed targets if it is faced with a decrease in aggregate supply?

2. What is inflation targeting? Why does the central bank announce its inflation rate targets?

## YOUR AP SELF TEST ANSWERS

### ■ CHECKPOINT 33.1

**True or false**

1. True;  pages 834-835
2. True;  page 836
3. False;  page 837
4. False;  page 837
5. True;  page 838

**Multiple choice**

1. a;  page 834
2. b;  pages 834-835
3. b;  page 836
4. c;  pages 834-836
5. b;  page 837
6. b;  page 838
7. d;  page 838
8. b;  page 838

**Short Response Questions**

**■ FIGURE 33.7**

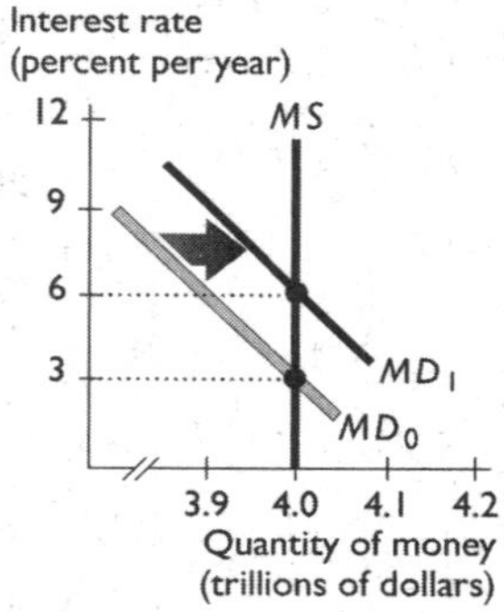

Interest rate
(percent per year)

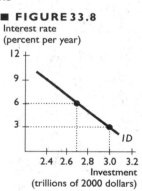

**■ FIGURE 33.8**

Interest rate
(percent per year)

1. a. The cut in taxes increases real GDP and raises the price level;  page 836.
   b. The increase in real GDP increases the demand for money and the demand for money curve shifts rightward. Figure 33.7 illustrates a rightward shift in the demand for money curve. The interest rate rises; page 836.
   c. The rise in the interest rate decreases investment. In Figure 33.8 there is a movement up along the investment demand curve;  page 836.

**■ FIGURE 33.9**

Interest rate
(percent per year)

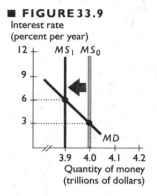

Quantity of money
(trillions of dollars)

**■ FIGURE 33.10**

Interest rate
(percent per year)

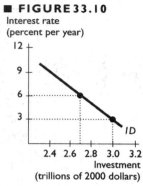

Investment
(trillions of 2000 dollars)

2. a. The decrease in the quantity of money raises the interest rate to 6 percent, as illustrated in Figure 33.9;  page 835.
   b. As Figure 33.10 shows, the increase in the interest rate decreases investment to $2.6 trillion. Real GDP will decrease because investment decreases (as well as other interest-sensitive components) so aggregate demand decreases;  pages 834-835.

**Long Response Questions**

1. When the quantity of money demanded is relatively insensitive to the interest rate, a change in the interest rate brings a small change in the quantity of money demanded. Then, when the quantity of money increases by a given amount, the decrease in the interest rate is large. The larger the decrease in the interest rate, the larger is the change in investment and aggregate expenditure, and the more powerful the monetary policy; pages 834-835.

2. An increase in government expenditure raises the interest rate, which decreases investment. The decrease in investment is the crowding-out effect. The larger the crowding-out effect, that is, the greater the decrease in investment, the weaker the effect of the fiscal policy. So the more the interest rate rises and the more sensitive investment is to the rise in the interest rate, the weaker is fiscal policy;  page 836.

3. A liquidity trap is an interest rate at which people are willing to hold any quantity of money. In a liquidity trap, a change in the quantity of money has no effect on the interest rate. So a change in the quantity of money has no effect on aggregate expenditure. Monetary policy has no effect; page 837.

4. The three fiscal policy goals are to provide public goods and services, to redistribute income, and to stabilize aggregate demand. The main source of conflict that arises from stabilization is the very large number of spending programs and tax laws in place and the difficulty of changing all of them to balance the costs and benefits of one against the costs and benefits of others; page 837.

5. Monetary policy is more flexible than fiscal policy. The Fed and its policy committee, the FOMC, can quickly take policy actions. Every day, the Fed monitors the financial markets and watches for signs that its policy needs to be tweaked to keep the economy on course; page 838.

## ■ CHECKPOINT 33.2

**True or false**

1. False;  page 840
3. True;  page 843

**Multiple choice**

1. d; page 840
2. c; page 840
3. b; page 842
4. b; page 846

**Long Response Questions**

1. a. The negative aggregate demand shock decreases aggregate demand and shifts the aggregate demand curve leftward from $AD_0$ to $AD_1$. Figure 33.11 shows that the price level falls to 90 and real GDP decreases to $9 trillion; page 841.

■ **FIGURE 33.11**

Price level (GDP deflator, 2000 = 100)

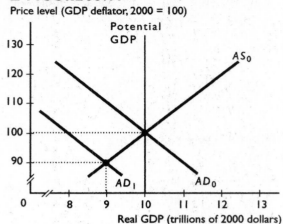

b. If the Fed follows a feedback-rule policy that restores real GDP back to potential GDP, it increases the quantity of money, which increases aggregate demand. In Figure 33.11, the aggregate demand curve shifts rightward, from $AD_1$ back to $AD_0$. Real GDP returns to equal potential GDP of $10 trillion and the price level rises to return to 100; pages 842-843.

■ **FIGURE 33.12**

Price level (GDP deflator, 2000 = 100)

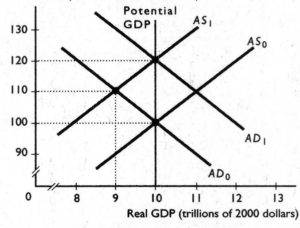

2. a. The negative aggregate supply shock decreases aggregate supply and shifts the aggregate supply curve leftward from $AS_0$ to $AS_1$. Figure 33.12 shows that the price level rises to 110 and real GDP decreases to $9 trillion; page 845.

b. If the Fed follows a feedback-rule policy that restores real GDP back to potential GDP, it increases the quantity of money, which increases aggregate demand. In Figure 33.12, the aggregate demand curve shifts rightward, from $AD_0$ to $AD_1$. Real GDP equals potential GDP of $10 trillion and the price level rises to 120; page 846.

# ■ CHECKPOINT 33.3

**True or false**

1. False; page 848
2. False; page 849
3. True; page 850

**Multiple choice**

1. b; page 848
2. a; page 848
3. a; page 848
4. d; page 848
5. b; pages 848-849
6. a; page 849
7. e; page 849

**Long Response Questions**

1. A decrease in aggregate demand lowers the price level and decreases real GDP. Regardless of the Fed's target, the appropriate feedback monetary policy is to increase the quantity of money, which increases aggregate demand. An increase in aggregate demand can return real GDP and the price level back to their original levels.

   If the Fed is faced with a decrease in aggregate supply and is using a feedback policy, the choice of target is important. If the Fed is targeting real GDP, the appropriate monetary policy is to increase the quantity of money, which can return real GDP to its original level but with a rise in the price level. Or if the Fed is targeting the price level, the appropriate monetary policy is to decrease the quantity of money, which can return the price level to its original level but with a decrease in real GDP; pages 848-849.

2. Inflation targeting is a monetary policy framework in which the central bank announces a target range for the inflation rate and publicizes its economic forecasts and analysis. The central bank attempts to stabilize real GDP and unemployment while keeping the inflation rate within its target zone. The target is announced because the announcement gives the people and businesses an anchor for their inflation expectations, which can help stabilize aggregate supply; page 850.

# International Trade

# *Chapter*

# 34

In Chapter 34 we see that all countries can benefit from free trade but, despite this fact, countries nevertheless restrict trade.

■ **Describe the patterns and trends in international trade.**

The goods and services that we buy from people in other countries are called imports. The goods and services that we sell to people in other countries are called exports. In 2004 manufactured goods were 54 percent of U.S. exports and 66 percent of U.S. imports. Goods comprise 70 percent of U.S. exports and 83 percent of U.S. imports. The rest of U.S. international trade is in services. Trade has grown over time. Between 1960 and 2005 exports grew from 5 percent of total output to 10.5 percent, and imports grew from 4 percent to 16 percent. The biggest U.S. trading partner is Canada. The balance of trade is the value of exports minus the value of imports. In 2005, the United States had a trade deficit.

■ **Explain why nations engage in international trade and why trade benefits all nations.**

Comparative advantage enables countries to gain from trade. A nation has a comparative advantage in producing a good if it can produce that good at a lower opportunity cost than another country. In this case, the domestic no-trade price is lower than the world price. To achieve the gains from trade, a nation specializes in the production of the goods and services in which it has a comparative advantage and then trades with other nations. By specializing and trading, a nation can consume at a point beyond its production possibilities frontier, which is the gains from trade. Offshoring occurs when a U.S. firm either produces in another country or buys finished goods or services from firms in other countries. Offshoring increased in the 1990s because telecommunication prices fell.

■ **Explain how trade barriers reduce international trade.**

A tariff is a tax on a good that is imposed by the importing country when an imported good crosses its international boundary. A tariff on a good reduces imports of that good, increases domestic production of the good, yields revenue for the government, and reduces the gains from trade. A quota is a specified maximum amount of a good that may be imported in a given period of time.

■ **Explain the arguments used to justify trade barriers and show why these arguments are incorrect but also why some barriers are hard to remove.**

The three main arguments for protection and restriction of trade are the national security argument, the infant-industry argument, and the dumping argument. Each of these arguments is flawed. Other flawed arguments for protection are that protection saves jobs, allows us to compete with cheap foreign labor, brings diversity and stability, penalizes lax environmental standards, and protects national culture. Tariffs are imposed in some nations to gain revenue for the government. In addition, trade is restricted is because of rent seeking from those who benefit from trade restrictions.

## EXPANDED CHAPTER CHECKLIST

**When you have completed this chapter, you will be able to:**

### 1 Describe the patterns and trends in international trade.

- Discuss U.S. international trade in goods and services and describe the trends in the volume of trade.
- Discuss the United States' major trading partners and the trading blocs in which the United States is a member.
- Define balance of trade.

### 2 Explain why nations engage in international trade and why trade benefits all nations.

- Discuss the relationship between comparative advantage and opportunity cost.
- Explain how the production possibilities frontier can be used to determine the opportunity cost of producing a good.
- Use the production possibilities frontier to demonstrate the gains from trade.

### 3 Explain how trade barriers reduce international trade.

- Define tariff and quota.
- Explain the effects of a tariff and a quota on domestic consumers, domestic producers, and the domestic government.

### 4 Explain the arguments used to justify trade barriers and show why they are incorrect but also why some barriers are hard to remove.

- Discuss the three main arguments for protection and explain why each argument is invalid.
- Discuss the other arguments (saving jobs, competing with cheap foreign labor, bringing diversity and stability, penalizing lax environmental standards, and protecting

national culture) for protection and explain their weaknesses and errors.

- Explain why governments and rent seekers are in favor of protection.

## YOUR AP TEST HINTS

### AP Topics

| Topic on your AP test | Corresponding textbook section |
| --- | --- |
| **Open economy, international trade and finance** | |
| Comparative Advantage | Chapter 34 |
| • Comparative advantage, specialization, and exchange | Checkpoints 34.2, 34.3, 34.4 |

### Extra AP material

- The textbook shows the effect of a tariff as raising the world price that the domestic country must pay. The AP test often shows the effect of a tariff as a leftward shift of the supply curve. The difference results from different assumptions about the size of the country. The textbook assumes that the country is a small player in the world market, so it can import whatever quantity it wants at the going world price plus the tariff. The AP test assumes that the country is a large player in the world market so that its tariff affects not only the price within the country but also the world price. With this assumption, a tariff is similar to a cost increase insofar as it decreases the supply of the good or service and thereby shifts the supply curve leftward.

- The textbook illustrates the effect of a quota by adding the quota amount to the domestic supply curve. This procedure gives the "total" supply curve as the domestic supply curve, S, plus the quota. (See Figure 34.6 in the textbook.) In this case, because the domestic supply curve is upward sloping, the total—domestic plus quota—supply curve also is upward sloping. The AP test often illustrates a quota using an upward sloping supply curve that becomes vertical at the quota quantity. The AP test assumes that none of the good or service is produced domestically so there is no domestic supply curve. In this case, the supply curve to the country is the supply curve from foreign producers. This supply curve is upward sloping until it reaches the quota quantity. Once at this quantity, no further amount may be imported and so the supply curve becomes vertical.

- On the AP test, be sure you can identify the major trade agreements, such as NAFTA and WTO, discussed in Checkpoint 34.1

## CHECKPOINT 34.1

### ■ Describe the patterns and trends in international trade.

#### Quick Review
- *Imports* The goods and services that we buy from people in other countries are called imports.
- *Exports* The goods and services that we sell to people in other countries are called exports.

#### Additional Practice Problems 34.1
1. The London School of Economics in the United Kingdom buys 100 copies of Windows that were produced in the United States. Describe how the United States and the United Kingdom categorize these goods.
2. A U.S. contractor in Seattle buys 1 ton of lumber from Canada in order to build homes in the state of Washington.
3. Citibank, an American firm, provides financial services to firms in France. Describe how the United States and France categorize these financial services.

#### Solutions to Additional Practice Problems 34.1
1. For the United States, the copies of Windows are exports to the United Kingdom. For the United Kingdom, the copies of Windows are imports from the United States.

2. For the United States, the lumber is an import from Canada. For Canada, the lumber is an export to the United States.
3. For the United States, the services rendered by Citibank are exports to France. For France, the services rendered by Citibank are imports from the United States.

### ■ AP Self Test 34.1
#### True or false
1. The United States exports more services than goods.
2. In 2005, 1 percent of total U.S. output was exported.
3. Canada, Mexico, and Japan are the biggest U.S. trading partners.
4. In 2005, the United States imported a larger value of goods and services than it exported.

#### Multiple choice
1. Goods and services that we buy from people in other countries are called our
   a. imports.
   b. exports.
   c. inputs.
   d. raw materials.
   e. obligations.

2. The largest fraction of U.S. imports is ____ and the largest fraction of U.S. exports ____.
   a. industrial materials; industrial materials
   b. industrial materials; manufactured goods
   c. manufactured goods; industrial materials
   d. manufactured goods; manufactured goods
   e. raw materials; food

3. Goods account for about ____ percent of U.S. exports and services account for about ____ percent of U.S. exports.
   a. 51; 49
   b. 70; 30
   c. 30; 70
   d. 100; 0
   e. 85; 15

4. The largest U.S. trading partner is
   a. Canada.
   b. Mexico.
   c. Japan.
   d. Spain.
   e. Korea.

5. If a college student from North Carolina State University travels to Germany, the money spent on hotels and sight-seeing in Germany is counted as services ____ America and ____ Germany.
   a. exported to; imported from
   b. imported from; imported from
   c. imported from; exported to
   d. exported to; exported to
   e. neither exported to nor imported from; imported from

6. The balance of trade equals
   a. the value of imports minus the value of exports.
   b. the value of exports minus the value of imports.
   c. the value of imports.
   d. the value of exports.
   e. the value of exports divided by the value of imports.

**Short answer and numeric questions**

1. French cheese is flown to the United States abroad a United Airlines plane. Classify these transactions from the vantage point of the United States and from the vantage point of France.

2. What is NAFTA? What is its goal?

## CHECKPOINT 34.2

■ **Explain why nations engage in international trade and why trade benefits all nations.**

*Quick Review*
   • *Comparative advantage* A nation has a comparative advantage in a good when its opportunity cost of producing the good is lower than another nation's opportunity cost of producing the good.

**Additional Practice Problems 34.2**

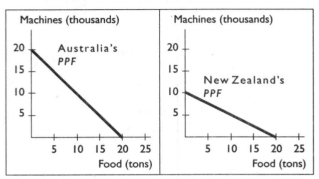

1. Suppose that Australia and New Zealand do not trade with each other. The figure above to the left shows Australia's production possibilities frontier and the figure to the right shows New Zealand's production possibilities frontier.
   a. What was the opportunity cost of 1 ton of food in Australia?
   b. What was the opportunity cost of 1 ton of food in New Zealand?
   c. What was the opportunity cost of 1 machine Australia?
   d. What was the opportunity cost of 1 machine in New Zealand?
   e. Which country has a comparative advantage in producing food? In machines? Why?
   f. If trade between the two countries opens, which good does Australia import from New Zealand? Which good does New Zealand import from Australia?
   g. Does Australia gain from this trade? Explain why or why not.
   h. Does New Zealand gain from this trade? Explain why or why not.

2. In Practice Problem 34.1, suppose that new technology becomes available so that the production of machines doubles in Australia and New Zealand. Now which good does Australia import from New Zealand?

### Solution to Additional Practice Problem 34.2a

1a. In Australia, when 20 tons of food are produced, 20,000 machines are forgone. The opportunity cost of 1 ton of food is (20,000 machines) ÷ (20 tons of food), which is 1,000 machines per ton of food.

1b. In New Zealand, when 20 tons of food are produced, 10,000 machines are forgone. The opportunity cost of 1 ton of food is (10,000 machines) ÷ (20 tons of food), which is 500 machines per ton of food.

1c. In Australia, when 20,000 machines are produced, 20 tons of food are forgone. The opportunity cost of 1 machine is (20 tons of food) ÷ (20,000 machines), which is 1/1,000 of a ton of food per machine.

1d. In New Zealand, when 10,000 machines are produced, 20 tons of food are forgone. The opportunity cost of 1 machine is (20 tons of food) ÷ (10,000 machines), which is 1/500 of a ton of food per machine.

1e. New Zealand has the comparative advantage in producing food because its opportunity cost, 500 machines per ton of food, is less than the opportunity cost in Australia. Australia has the comparative advantage in producing machines because its opportunity cost, 1/1,000 of a ton of food per machine, is less than the opportunity cost in New Zealand.

1f. Australia will import food from New Zealand because the cost of imported food is only 500 machines per ton whereas the cost of domestically produced food is 1,000 machines per ton. New Zealand will import machines from Australia because the cost of imported machines is only 1/1,000 of a ton of food per machine whereas the cost of domestically produced machines is 1/500 of a ton of food per machine.

1g. Yes, Australia gains from this trade. Australia can buy food cheaper from New Zealand than Australia can produce.

1h. New Zealand also gains from this trade. New Zealand can buy machines from Australia at a lower cost than New Zealand can produce. When the opportunity costs between countries diverge, comparative advantage enables countries to gain from international trade.

2. Australia still has the comparative advantage in machines. New Zealand still has the comparative advantage in food. So Australia continues to import food from New Zealand.

### ■ AP Self Test 34.2

**True or false**

1. The United States has a comparative advantage in the production of a good if the opportunity cost of producing that good is higher in the United States than in most other countries.

2. Only the exporting country gains from free international trade because it has a comparative advantage.

3. If Intel produces chips in Taiwan rather than California, Intel has offshored its production of chips.

4. There are no gains from trade when services are offshored.

**Multiple choice**

1. The fundamental force that drives trade between nations is
   a. the government.
   b. NAFTA.
   c. absolute advantage.
   d. comparative advantage.
   e. legal treaties.

2. A nation will import a good if its
   a. no-trade, domestic price is equal to the world price.
   b. no-trade, domestic price is less than the world price.
   c. no-trade, domestic price is greater than the world price.
   d. no-trade, domestic quantity is less than the world quantity.
   e. no-trade, domestic quantity is greater than the world quantity.

3. When Italy buys Boeing jets, the price Italy pays is ____ if it produced their own jets and the price Boeing receives is ____ than it could receive from an additional U.S. buyer.
   a. lower than; lower
   b. higher than; higher
   c. lower than; higher
   d. higher than; lower
   e. the same as; higher

4. When a good is imported, the domestic production ____ and the domestic consumption ____.
   a. increases; increases
   b. increases; decreases
   c. decreases; increases
   d. decreases; decreases
   e. increases; does not change

5. The United States can use all its resources to produce 250 DVDs or 500 shoes. China can use all of its resources to produce 30 DVDs or 300 shoes. The opportunity cost of producing a DVD in the United States is
   a. 2 shoes.
   b. 1/2 of a shoe.
   c. 20 shoes.
   d. 500 shoes.
   e. 1 DVD.

6. The United States can use all its resources to produce 250 DVDs or 500 shoes. China can use all of its resources to produce 30 DVDs or 300 shoes. In this example,
   a. China has a comparative advantage in DVDs.
   b. China has a comparative advantage in shoes.
   c. China has a comparative advantage in the production of both goods.
   d. China has a comparative advantage in neither good.
   e. The United States has a comparative advantage in the production of both goods.

7. Specialization and trade make a country better off because with trade the country can consume at a point
   a. outside its production possibilities frontier.
   b. inside its production possibilities frontier.
   c. on its production possibilities frontier.
   d. on its trading partner's production possibilities frontier.
   e. inside its trading partner's production possibilities frontier.

8. Which of the following is correct?
   i. Offshoring moves an estimated 1.2 million jobs per year away from the United States and into other countries.
   ii. A U.S. firm is offshoring if it hires foreign labor and produces in another country.
   iii. Offshoring of services increased in the last decade.
   a. i only.
   b. iii only.
   c. i and ii.
   d. ii and iii.
   e. i, ii, and iii.

**Short Response Questions**

1. What does it mean for a nation to have the comparative advantage in the production of a good or service?

2. Does specializing according to comparative advantage and then trading allow a nation to produce at a point beyond its production possibilities frontier? Does it allow a nation to consume at a point beyond its production possibilities frontier?

**Long Response Questions**

| Price (dollars per ton) | Quantity supplied (tons per year) | Quantity demanded (tons per year) |
|---|---|---|
| 400 | 38 | 58 |
| 500 | 42 | 52 |
| 600 | 46 | 46 |
| 700 | 50 | 40 |
| 800 | 54 | 34 |
| 900 | 58 | 28 |

1. The table above has the U.S. demand and

supply schedules for potatoes.

a. If there is no international trade, what is the equilibrium price and quantity?

b. If the world price of potatoes is $800 a ton, what is the quantity supplied and the quantity demanded in the United States? Does the United States import or export potatoes? What quantity?

c. If the world price of potatoes rises to $900 a ton, what is the quantity supplied and the quantity demanded in the United States? Does the United States import or export potatoes? What quantity?

d. Would the United States ever import potatoes?

### ■ FIGURE 34.1

Price (dollars per bushel)

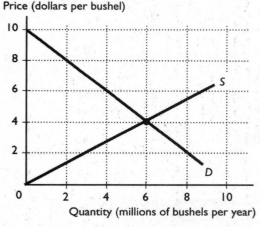

Quantity (millions of bushels per year)

2. Figure 34.1 shows the U.S. demand and supply curves for wheat.

a. In the absence of international trade, what is the price of a bushel of wheat in the United States?

b. If the world price of a bushel of wheat is $6 a bushel, will the United States import or export wheat? Above what world price for wheat will the United States export wheat? Below what world price for wheat will the United States import wheat?

### ■ FIGURE 34.2

Computer chips (thousands per year)

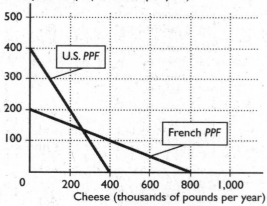

Cheese (thousands of pounds per year)

3. Figure 34.2 has the U.S. and French *PPFs*.

a. What is the opportunity cost of a computer chip in the United States? In France? Who has the comparative advantage in producing computer chips?

b. What is the opportunity cost of a pound of cheese in the United States? In France? Who has the comparative advantage in producing cheese?

c. When the United States and France trade, who exports chips and who exports cheese?

d. The United States produced 200,000 computer chips and 200,000 pounds of cheese before trade. France produced 100,000 computer chips and 400,000 pounds of cheese. Label as point *A* the point that shows the total chip and cheese production before trade.

e. The United States and France both specialize according to comparative advantage after trade. Label as point *B* the point that shows the total chip and cheese production after trade. How does point *B* compare to point *A*?

4. Suppose the United States and France produce only ice cream and cheese. The United States can produce 50 tons of ice cream or 100 tons of cheese and France can produce 20 tons of ice cream or 120 tons of cheese.

a. What is the opportunity cost of a ton of ice cream in France? In the United States? Which nation has the comparative advantage in producing ice cream?

b. What is the opportunity cost of a ton of cheese in France? In the United States? Which nation has the comparative advantage in producing cheese?

c. If France and the United States trade, what does the United States import? What does it export?

d. Before trade the United States produced 25 tons of ice cream and 50 tons of cheese and France produced 10 tons of ice cream and 60 tons of cheese. What is the total production of ice cream? Of cheese?

e. After trade, France and the United States specialize according to comparative advantage. What is the total amount of ice cream produced? Of cheese?

f. Compare your answers to (d) and (e).

5. What are the gains from trade? How do countries obtain the gains from trade?

6. What is offshoring? Why is it controversial? Are there any gains from trade with offshoring?

## CHECKPOINT 34.3

■ **Explain how trade barriers reduce international trade.**

*Quick Review*

- *Tariff* A tariff is a tax on a good that is imposed by the importing country when an imported good crosses its international boundary.

- *Quota* A quota is a specified maximum amount of a good that may be imported in a given period of time.

**Additional Practice Problems 34.3**

| Price (dollars per ton of plywood) | U.S. quantity supplied (tons per month) | U.S. quantity demanded (tons per month) |
|---|---|---|
| 1,000 | 600 | 1,400 |
| 750 | 500 | 1,600 |
| 500 | 300 | 1,800 |
| 250 | 100 | 2,000 |

1. The table above shows the U.S. supply and demand schedules for plywood. The United States also can buy plywood from Canada at the world price of $500 per ton.

a. If there are no tariffs or nontariff barriers, what is the price of a ton of plywood in the United States? How much plywood is produced in the United States and how much is consumed? How much plywood is imported from Canada?

b. Suppose that the United States imposes a $250 per ton tariff on all plywood imported into the country. What now is the price of a ton of plywood in the United States? How much plywood is produced in the United States and how much is consumed? How much plywood is imported from Canada?

c. Who has gained from the tariff and who has lost?

2. For many years Japan conducted extremely slow, detailed, and costly safety inspections of *all* U.S. cars imported into Japan. In terms of trade, what was the effect of this inspection? How did the inspection affect the price and quantity of cars in Japan?

**Solutions to Additional Practice Problems 34.3**

1a. With no tariffs or nontariff barriers, the price of a ton of plywood is equal to the world price, $500 per ton. At this price, 300 tons per month are produced in the United States and 1,800 tons per month are consumed. The difference between the quantity consumed and the quantity produced, which is 1,500 tons per month, is imported from Canada.

1b. If a $250 per ton tariff is imposed, the price in the United States rises to $750 per ton. At this price, 500 tons per month are produced in the United States and 1,600 tons per month are consumed. The difference between the quantity consumed and the quantity produced, which is 1,100 tons per month, is imported from Canada.

1c. Gainers from the tariff are U.S. producers of plywood, who have a higher price for plywood and therefore increase their production, and the U.S. government, which gains tariff revenue. Losers are U.S. consumers, who consume less plywood because of the higher price with the tariff, and Canadian producers of plywood, who wind up exporting less plywood to the United States.

2. Japan's safety inspection (which has since been eliminated) was an example of a nontariff barrier to trade. It served a role similar to tariffs and quotas. The safety inspection added to the cost of selling cars in Japan. It raised the price of U.S. produced cars in Japan and decreased the quantity of U.S. cars sold. The Japanese government, however, received no tariff revenue.

## ■ AP Self Test 34.3

### True or false

1. If the United States imposes a tariff, the price paid by U.S. consumers does not change.

2. If a country imposes a tariff on rice imports, domestic production of rice will increase and domestic consumption of rice will decrease.

3. A tariff increases the gains from trade for the exporting country.

4. A quota on imports of a particular good specifies the minimum quantity of that good that can be imported in a given period.

### Multiple choice

1. A tax on a good that is imposed by the importing country when an imported good crosses its international boundary is a
   a. quota.
   b. nontariff barrier.
   c. tariff.
   d. sanction.
   e. border tax.

2. The average U.S. tariff was highest in the
   a. 1930s.
   b. 1940s.
   c. 1970s.
   d. 1980s.
   e. 1990s.

3. Suppose the world price of a shirt is $10. If the United States imposes a tariff of $5 a shirt, then the price of a shirt in the
   a. United States falls to $5.
   b. United States rises to $15.
   c. world falls to $5.
   d. world rises to $5.
   e. world rises to $15.

4. When a tariff is imposed on a good, the ____ increases.
   a. domestic quantity purchased
   b. domestic quantity produced
   c. quantity imported
   d. quantity exported
   e. world price

5. When a tariff is imposed on a good, domestic consumers of the good ____ and domestic producers of the good ____.
   a. win; lose
   b. lose; win
   c. win; win
   d. lose; lose
   e. lose; neither win nor lose

6. Which of the following parties benefits from a quota but not from a tariff?
   a. the domestic government
   b. domestic producers
   c. domestic consumers
   d. the person with the right to import the good
   e. the foreign government

### Short Response Questions

1. Suppose the U.S. government imposes a tariff on sugar. How does the tariff affect the price of sugar? How does it affect U.S. sugar consumers? U.S. sugar producers?

2. Suppose the U.S. government imposes a quota on sugar. How does the quota affect

the price of sugar? How does it affect U.S. sugar consumers? U.S. sugar producers?

3. Why do consumers lose from a tariff?

### Long Response Questions

| Price (dollars per ton of steel) | U.S. quantity supplied (tons per month) | U.S. quantity demanded (tons per month) |
|---|---|---|
| 1,000 | 20,000 | 20,000 |
| 750 | 17,000 | 22,000 |
| 500 | 14,000 | 24,000 |
| 250 | 11,000 | 26,000 |

1. The table above gives the U.S. supply and the U.S. demand schedules for steel. Suppose the world price of steel is $500 per ton.

   a. If there are no tariffs or nontariff barriers, what is the price of steel in the United States, the quantity of steel consumed in the United States, the quantity produced in the United States, and the quantity imported into the United States?

   b. If the U.S. government imposes a tariff of $250 per ton of steel, what is the price of steel in the United States, the quantity of steel consumed in the United States, the quantity produced in the United States, and the quantity imported into the United States?

   c. Instead of a tariff, if the U.S. government imposes a quota of 5,000 tons of steel per month, what is the price of steel in the United States, the quantity of steel consumed in the United States, the quantity produced in the United States, and the quantity imported into the United States?

   d. Comparing your answers to parts (b) and (c), are U.S. consumers better off with the tariff or the quota? Are U.S. producers better off with the tariff or the quota? Is the U.S. government better off with the tariff or the quota?

2. Figure 34.3 shows the supply of and demand for sugar in the United States.

   a. If the world price of sugar is 10¢ a pound, draw the world price line in the figure. What is the quantity consumed in the

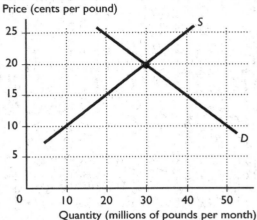

United States, the quantity produced in the United States, and the quantity imported?

   b. Suppose the government imposes a 5¢ a pound tariff on sugar. Show the effect of the tariff in Figure 34.3. After the tariff, what is the quantity consumed in the United States, the quantity produced in the United States, and the quantity imported?

■ FIGURE 34.4

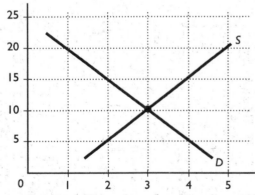

3. Figure 34.4 shows the supply of and demand for memory chips in the United States. The United States is a large producer of these chips, so the supply curve in the figure shows the sum of the supply of chips by U.S. producers and foreign producers.

   a. If there are no tariffs or nontariff barriers,

what is the price of a memory chip and what is the quantity of chips consumed in the United States?

b. If the U.S. government imposes a tariff on chips imported into the United States so that the supply decreases by 2 million chips per month at every price. Show the effect of this tariff in Figure 34.4. What is the effect on the price of a memory chip and the quantity consumed in the United States?

## CHECKPOINT 34.4

■ **Explain the arguments used to justify trade barriers and show why these arguments are incorrect but also why some barriers are hard to remove.**

### Quick Review

- *Rent seeking* Lobbying and other political activity that seeks to capture the gains from trade.

### Additional Practice Problems 34.4

1. Canada has limits on the amount of U.S. television shows that can be broadcast in Canada. What are Canada's arguments for restricting imports of U.S. television shows? Are these arguments correct? Who loses from this restriction of trade?

2. The United States has, from time to time, limited imports of lumber from Canada. What is the argument that the United States has used to justify this quota? Who wins from this restriction? Who loses?

3. In each of the first two Practice Problems, identify who is rent seeking.

### Solutions to Additional Practice Problems 34.4

1. Canada has used a number of arguments, but they are all incorrect. Canada has argued that Canadian television shows are of a higher quality than U.S. shows, but if Canadian consumers can detect a quality difference, they can watch Canadian shows rather than U.S. shows. Canada also has argued that these limitations are necessary to save Canadian culture, but if Canadian consumers want to protect this part of their heritage, they can watch exclusively Canadian shows rather than U.S. shows. The major losers from the Canadian limitations are Canadian consumers who can watch only a limited number of popular U.S. television shows.

2. In past decades, the United States asserted that the lumber industry was needed because it played a major role in national defense. With the use of more exotic materials in defense armaments, the national defense argument has passed into history. More recently, the United States has set quotas and tariffs allegedly for environmental reasons and allegedly because the Canadian government was subsidizing the production of lumber. Both of these arguments are likely not the true reason for the quotas. The quotas and limitations are the result of political lobbying by lumber producers and lumber workers. The winners from the quotas and tariffs are the lumber producers and lumber workers. The losers are all U.S. lumber consumers.

3. Rent seeking is lobbying and other political activity that seeks to capture the gains from trade. In Practice Problem 1, the Canadian producers of television shows are rent seeking. In Practice Problem 2, the U.S. lumber producers and U.S. lumber workers are rent seeking. It is important to keep in mind that free trade promotes prosperity for all countries. Protection reduces the potential gains from trade

## ■ Self Test 34.4

### True or false

1. The national security argument is the only valid argument for protection.

2. Dumping by a foreign producer is easy to detect.

3. Protection saves U.S. jobs at no cost.

4. International trade is an attractive base for tax collection in developing countries

**Multiple choice**

1. The national security argument is used by those who assert they want to
   a. increase imports as a way of strengthening their country.
   b. increase exports as a way of earning money to strengthen their country.
   c. limit imports that compete with domestic producers important for national defense.
   d. limit exports to control the flow of technology to third world nations.
   e. limit all imports.

2. The argument that it is necessary to protect a new industry to enable it to grow into a mature industry that can compete in world markets is the
   a. national security argument.
   b. diversity argument.
   c. infant-industry argument.
   d. environmental protection argument.
   e. national youth protection argument.

3. _____ occurs when a foreign firm sells its exports at a lower price than its cost of production.
   a. Dumping
   b. The trickle-down effect
   c. Rent seeking
   d. Tariff avoidance
   e. Nontariff barrier protection

4. The United States
   a. needs tariffs to allow us to compete with cheap foreign labor.
   b. does not need tariffs to allow us to compete with cheap foreign labor.
   d. should not trade with countries that have cheap labor.
   d. will not benefit from trade with countries that have cheap labor.
   e. avoids trading with countries that have cheap labor.

5. Why do governments in less-developed nations impose tariffs on imported goods and services?
   a. The government gains revenue from the tariff.
   b. The government's low-paid workers are protected from high-paid foreign workers.
   c. The nation's total income is increased.
   d. The national security of the country definitely is improved.
   e. The government protects its national culture.

6. What is a major reason international trade is restricted?
   a. rent seeking
   b. to allow competition with cheap foreign labor
   c. to save jobs
   d. to prevent dumping
   e. to protect national culture

**Long Response Questions**

1. What is the dumping argument for protection? What is its flaw?

2. How do you respond to a speaker who says that we need to limit auto imports from Japan in order to save U.S. jobs?

3. Why is it incorrect to assert that trade with countries that have lax environmental standards needs to be restricted?

## YOUR AP SELF TEST ANSWERS

### ■ CHECKPOINT 34.1

**True or false**
1. False;  page 858
2. False;  page 858
3. True;  page 859
4. True;  page 861

**Multiple choice**
1. a; page 858
2. d; page 858
3. b; page 858
4. a; page 859
5. a; page 858
6. b; page 861

**Short Response Questions**
1. From the U.S. vantage, the cheese is an imported good and the air transportation is an exported service. From the French vantage, the cheese is an exported good and the air transportation is an imported service;  page 858.
2. NAFTA is the North American Free Trade Agreement. It is an agreement among Canada, the United States, and Mexico with the goal of making trade among the three nations easier and freer;  page 859.

### ■ CHECKPOINT 34.2

**True or false**
1. False;  pages 862-863
2. False;  page 868
3. True;  page 869
4. False;  page 870

**Multiple choice**
1. d; page 862
2. c; pages 863-864
3. c; pages 862-865
4. c; page 864
5. a; page 865
6. b; pages 865-867

7. a; page 868
8. d; pages 869-870

**Short Response Questions**
1. A nation has the comparative advantage in the production of a good or service when the nation can produce the good or service at a lower opportunity cost than can other nations;  page 867.
2. Specializing and trading does *not* allow a nation to produce at a point beyond its production possibilities frontier. It does, however, allow a nation to consume at a point beyond its production possibilities frontier and it is this fact that accounts for the gains from international trade;  pages 867-868.

**Long Response Questions**
1. a. In the absence of international trade, the equilibrium price is $600 a ton and the equilibrium quantity is 46 tons;  pages 862-863.
   b. In the United States, the quantity supplied is 54 tons and the quantity demanded is 34 tons. The United States exports 20 tons of potatoes;  pages 862-863.
   c. In the United States, the quantity supplied is 58 tons and the quantity demanded is 28 tons. The United States exports 30 tons of potatoes;  pages 862-863.
   d. The United States would import potatoes if the world price is less than $600 a ton;  pages 864-865.
2. a. In the absence of international trade, the equilibrium price of a bushel of wheat in the United States is $4;  pages 862-863.
   b. If the world price of a bushel of wheat is $6 a bushel, the United States will export wheat because the world price exceeds the no-trade price. If the price of wheat exceeds $4 a bushel, the United States will export wheat. If the price of wheat is less than $4 a bushel, the United States will import wheat;  pages 863-865.

3. a. The opportunity cost of a computer chip in the United States is 1 pound of cheese. In France, the opportunity cost of a computer chip is 4 pounds of cheese. The United States has the comparative advantage in chips; pages 865-866.

   b. The opportunity cost of a pound of cheese in the United States is 1 computer chip. In France, the opportunity cost is of a pound of cheese 1/4 of a computer chip. France has the comparative advantage in cheese; pages 865-866.

   c. The United States has the comparative advantage in chips, so it will specialize in producing chips and export chips to France. France will specialize in cheese and export cheese to the United States; page 867.

**■ FIGURE 34.5**

Computer chips (thousands per year)

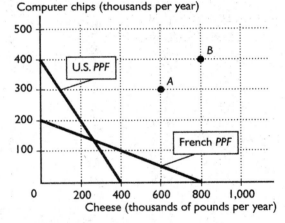

   d. The point is labeled in Figure 34.5; page 868.

   e. The United States produces 400,000 chips and no cheese and France produces 800,000 pounds of cheese and no chips. The total production is 400,000 chips and 800,000 pounds of cheese, labeled as point B in Figure 34.4. More chips *and* more cheese are produced at point B after trade than are produced at point A before trade; page 868.

4. a. In France, the opportunity cost of a ton of ice cream is 6 tons of cheese; in the United States, the opportunity cost of a ton of ice cream is 2 tons of cheese. The United States has the comparative advantage in producing ice cream; pages 865-867.

   b. In France, the opportunity cost of a ton of cheese is 1/6 of a ton of ice cream; in the United States, the opportunity cost of a ton of cheese is 1/2 of a ton of ice cream. France has the comparative advantage in producing cheese; pages 865-867.

   c. The United States imports cheese and exports ice cream; page 867.

   d. 35 tons of ice cream are produced and 110 tons of cheese are produced; page 867.

   e. 50 tons of ice cream are produced in the United States and 120 tons of cheese are produced in France; pages 867-868.

   f. The world production of ice cream *and* cheese increased, which demonstrates the gains from trade; pages 867-868.

5. The gains from trade occur because after specialization and trade, a country can increase its consumption so that it can consume at a point beyond its production possibilities frontier. To obtain the gains from trade a country must specialize and trade; pages 867-868.

6. Offshoring occurs when a U.S. firm either hires labor and produces in other countries or when it buys goods and services produced in other countries. Offshoring is controversial because some observers assert that it is "exporting America." There are gains from offshoring exactly as there are gains from all international trade. In particular, by specializing in producing the goods and services in which it has a comparative advantage (and not producing or "offshoring" the goods in which it does not have a comparative advantage) and trading with other countries, the nation can consume more of all goods and services ; pages 869-870.

## ■ CHECKPOINT 34.3

**True or false**

1. False; pages 873
2. True; pages 874
3. False; pages 874
4. False; page 874

**Multiple choice**

1. c; page 872
2. a; page 872
3. b; page 873
4. b; pages 873-874
5. b; pages 873-874
6. d; pages 874-875

**Short Response Questions**

1. The tariff raises the price of sugar. U.S. sugar consumers decrease the quantity they purchase and U.S. sugar producers increase the quantity they produce; pages 873-874.

2. The quota has the same effects as the tariff in the previous question. The quota raises the price of sugar. U.S. sugar consumers decrease the quantity purchased and U.S. sugar producers increase the quantity produced; pages 874-875.

3. Consumers lose from a tariff because the tariff raises the price they pay and the quantity bought decreases. The tariff makes people pay more than the opportunity cost of the good; page 874.

**Long Response Questions**

1. a. The price is the world price, $500 per ton. At this price, the quantity consumed in the United States is 24,000 tons per month, the quantity produced in the United States is 14,000 tons per month, and the quantity imported is the difference, 10,000 tons per month; page 873.

   b. With a $250 per ton tariff, the price is $750 per ton. At this price, the quantity consumed in the United States is 22,000 tons per month, the quantity produced in the United States is 17,000 tons per month,

and the quantity imported is the difference, 5,000 tons per month; page 873.

   c. With a quota of 5,000 tons per month, the total supply schedule equals the U.S. supply schedule plus 5,000 tons per month. The price of steel is $750 per ton because this is the price that sets the U.S. quantity demanded (22,000 tons) equal to the U.S. quantity supplied (17,000 tons) plus the quantity that can be imported (5,000 tons). At this price, the quantity consumed in the United States is 22,000 tons per month and the quantity produced in the United States is 17,000 tons per month; page 875.

   d. U.S. consumers are no better off or worse off with the tariff or the quota because both raise the price to $750 per ton and decrease the quantity consumed to 22,000 tons. U.S. producers are no better off or worse off with the tariff or the quota because both raise the price to $750 per ton and increase the quantity produced to 17,000 tons. The U.S. government is better off with the tariff because it receives revenue with the tariff and nothing with the quota; pages 873-875.

## ■ FIGURE 34.6

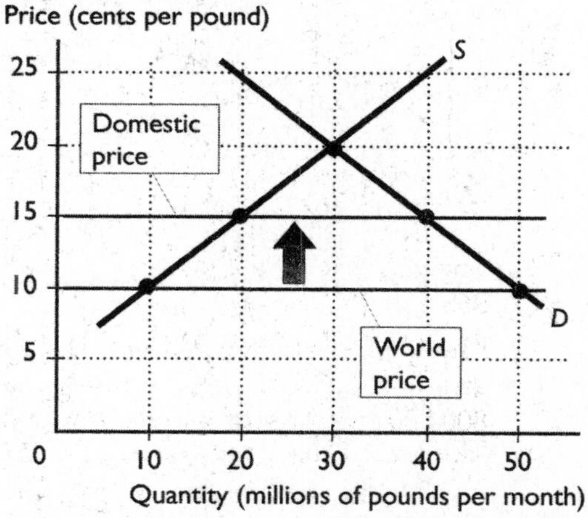

Price (cents per pound)

2. a. The world price line is shown in Figure 34.6. 50 million pounds of sugar are consumed in the United States, 10 million pounds are produced in the United States,

and 40 million pounds are imported into the United States; pages 873-874.

b. The tariff increases the domestic price, as shown in the figure. The quantity consumed in the United States decreases to 40 million pounds, the quantity produced in the United States increases to 20 million pounds, and the amount imported decreases to 20 million pounds; pages 873-874.

**■ FIGURE 34.7**
Price (dollars per memory chip)

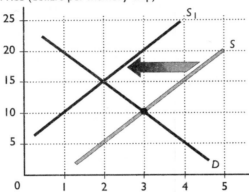

Quantity (millions of memory chips per month)

3. a. The initial equilibrium price and quantity are determined by where the supply curve intersects the demand curve. Figure 34.7 shows that the initial price is $10 per memory chip and that 3 million memory chips per month are consumed in the United States.

b. The tariff decreases the supply of foreign memory chips by 2 million chips per month and thereby decreases the total supply of memory chips to the United States by 2 million chips per month. As a result, the supply curve shifts leftward by 2 million chips. This shift is illustrated in Figure 34.7 by the shift from $S$ to $S_1$. The figure shows that the price of a memory chip rises to $15 per memory chip and the quantity consumed in the United States decreases to 2 million memory chips per month.

## ■ CHECKPOINT 34.4

**True or false**

1. False; page 877
2. False; page 878
3. False; pages 878-879
4. True; page 882

**Multiple choice**

1. c; page 877
2. c; page 877
3. a; page 878
4. b; pages 879-880
5. a; page 882
6. a; page 882

**Long Response Questions**

1. Dumping occurs when a foreign firm sells its exports at a lower price than its cost of production. The dumping argument is flawed for the following reasons. First, it is virtually impossible to detect dumping because it is hard to determine a firm's costs and the fair market price. Second, it is hard to think of a good that is produced by a global natural monopoly. Third, if a firm truly was a global natural monopoly, the best way to deal with it would be by regulation; page 878.

2. Saving jobs is one of the oldest arguments in favor of protection. It is also incorrect. Protecting a particular industry will likely save jobs in that industry but will cost many other jobs in other industries. The cost to consumers of saving a job is many times the wage rate of the job saved; pages 878-879.

3. The assertion that trade with developing countries that have lax environmental standards should be restricted to "punish" the nation for its lower standards is weak. Everyone wants a clean environment, but not every country can afford to devote resources toward this goal. The rich nations can afford this expenditure of resources, but for many poor nations protecting the environment takes second place to more pressing problems such as feeding their people. These na-

tions must develop and grow economically in order to be able to afford to protect their environment. One important way to help these nations grow is by trading with them. Through trade these nations' incomes will increase and with this increase will also increase their ability and willingness to protect the environment; page 880.

# International Finance

## Chapter 35

Chapter 35 studies how nations keep their international accounts, what determines the balance of payments, and how the value of the dollar is determined in the foreign exchange market.

■ **Describe a country's balance of payments accounts and explain what determines the amount of international borrowing and lending.**

There are three balance of payments accounts, which are the current account, the capital account, and the official settlements account. The current account balance equals exports minus imports, plus net interest and transfers received from abroad. The capital account is a record of foreign investment in the United States minus U.S. investment abroad. The official settlements account is a record of the change in U.S. official reserves. The sum of the balances on the three accounts always equals zero. We pay for imports that exceed the value of our exports by borrowing from the rest of the world. A net borrower is a country that is borrowing more from the rest of the world than it is lending to the rest of the world, and a net lender is a country that is lending more to the rest of the world than it is borrowing from the rest of the world. A debtor nation is a country that during its entire history has borrowed more from the rest of the world than it has lent to it, and a creditor nation is a country that during its entire history has invested more in the rest of the world than other countries have invested in it. Net exports equals the sum of the private sector balance and the government sector balance.

■ **Explain how the exchange rate is determined and why it fluctuates.**

Foreign currency is needed to buy goods or invest in another country. The foreign exchange rate is the price at which one currency exchanges for another and is determined by demand and supply in the foreign exchange market. The quantity of dollars demanded increases when the exchange rate falls. The demand for dollars changes and the demand curve for dollars shifts if the U.S. interest rate differential or the expected future exchange rate changes. A rise in either increases the demand for dollars. The quantity of dollars supplied increases when the exchange rate rises. The supply of dollars changes and the supply curve of dollars shifts if the U.S. interest rate differential or the expected future exchange rate changes. A rise in either decreases the supply of dollars. At the equilibrium exchange rate, the quantity of dollars demanded equals the quantity of dollars supplied. The exchange rate is volatile because factors that change the demand also change the supply. Exchange rate expectations are influenced by purchasing power parity, a situation in which money buys the same amount of goods and services in different currencies, and interest rate parity, a situation in which the interest rate in one currency equals the interest rate in another currency once exchange rate changes are taken into account. The Fed and other central banks can intervene directly in the foreign exchange market by pegging the exchange rate. If the peg overvalues the exchange rate, the central bank runs out of foreign reserves; if the peg undervalues the exchange rate, the central bank accumulates foreign reserves.

## EXPANDED CHAPTER CHECKLIST

**When you have completed this chapter, you will be able to:**

**1** **Describe a country's balance of payments accounts and explain what determines the amount of international borrowing and lending.**

- Define the balance of payment accounts, the current account, the capital account, and the official settlements account.
- Define net borrower, net lender, creditor nation, and debtor nation.
- State the relationship between net exports, the private sector balance, and the government sector balance.
- Discuss whether the United States is borrowing for consumption or investment.

**2** **Explain how the exchange rate is determined and why it fluctuates.**

- Explain the role of the foreign exchange market.
- Define currency appreciation and currency depreciation.
- Discuss the relationship between the exchange rate and the quantity of dollars demanded.
- Explain how a change in the U.S. interest rate differential or in the expected future exchange rate changes the demand for dollars.
- Discuss the relationship between the exchange rate and the quantity of dollars supplied.
- Explain how a change in the U.S. interest rate differential or in the expected future exchange rate changes the supply of dollars.
- Illustrate equilibrium in the foreign exchange market and show how a change in the demand for dollars or supply of dollars changes the exchange rate.
- State how the Fed intervenes in the foreign exchange market.

## YOUR AP TEST HINTS

### AP Topics

| Topic on your AP test | Corresponding textbook section |
|---|---|
| **Open economy international trade and finance** | |
| Balance of Payments Accounts | Chapter 35 |
| • Balance of trade | Checkpoint 35.1 |
| • Current account | Checkpoint 35.1 |
| • Capital account | Checkpoint 35.1 |
| Foreign Exchange Market | Chapter 35 |
| • Appreciation and depreciation | Checkpoint 35.2 |
| • Demand and supply of foreign exchange | Checkpoint 35.2 |
| • Determination of exchange rate | Checkpoint 35.2 |

### AP Vocabulary

- On the AP test, exchange rates can be said to be "fixed," "floating," or "flexible." A fixed exchange rate is one for which the central bank (the Federal Reserve for the United States) actively intervenes to keep the exchange rate constant. A floating exchange rate is one that is not influenced by the central bank; that is, the central bank does not intervene in the foreign exchange market. A flexible exchange rate, often called a "managed flexible" exchange rate, is one for which the central bank intervenes to keep the exchange rate within certain bounds and/or from appreciating or depreciating too much or too rapidly.

### Extra AP material

- Fiscal policy influences capital flows and the exchange rate. An expansionary fiscal policy, such as an increase in government expenditure, raises the interest rate. The higher interest rate attracts capital inflows from abroad and raises the exchange rate. Monetary policy also influences capital flows and the exchange rate. An expansionary monetary policy lowers the interest rate. The lower interest rate attracts capital outflows from the nation to abroad and lowers (depreciates) the exchange rate.

## CHECKPOINT 35.1

■ **Describe a country's balance of payments accounts and explain what determines the amount of international borrowing and lending.**

### Quick Review

- *Current account balance* The current account balance equals net exports plus net interest plus net transfers received from abroad.
- *Capital account balance* The capital account balance equals foreign investment in the United States minus U.S. investment abroad.

### Additional Practice Problems 35.1

In 2002 the U.S. economy recorded the following transactions:

Imports of goods and services, $1,418 billion; net interest, –$25 billion; net transfers –$52 billion; increase in U.S. official reserves, $7 billion; exports of goods and services, $975 billion; statistical discrepancy $198 billion; foreign investment in the United States, $885 billion; and, U.S. investment abroad, $556 billion.

    a. Calculate the current account balance.
    b. Calculate the capital account balance.
    c. Calculate the official settlements account balance.
    d. To what do these balances sum?
    e. Was the United States a debtor or a creditor nation in 2002?

2. Suppose the official settlements account equals zero. In this case, what is the relationship between the current account and the capital account? Why does this relationship exist?

### Solutions to Additional Practice Problems 35.1

1a. The current account balance equals exports plus net interest plus net transfers minus imports. So the current account balance equals $975 billion + (–$25 billion) +(–$52 billion) – $1,418 billion = –$520 billion.

1b. The capital account balance equals foreign investment in the United States minus U.S. investment abroad plus any statistical discrepancy. So the capital account balance equals $885 billion – $556 billion + $198 billion = $527 billion.

1c. The official settlements account balance is the negative of the change in U.S. official reserves. When reserves increase by $7 billion, the official settlements account balance is –$7 billion.

1d. Keep in mind that the sum of the current account, capital account, and official settlements account is zero. So, if the previous answers are correct, they will sum to zero. Fortunately, they do: –$520 billion + $527 billion –$7 billion = $0.

1e. Interest payments reflect the value of outstanding debts. The United States is a debtor nation because the value of interest payments received from the rest of the world is less than the value of interest payments made to the rest of the world.

2. If the official settlements account equals zero, then the deficit in the current account equals the surplus in the capital account. Or, if the official settlements account equals zero, then the surplus in the current account equals the deficit in the capital account. This relationship exists because the sum of the current account, capital account, and the official settlements account equals zero. If the official settlements account equals zero, the current account balance must equal the negative of the capital account balance.

## ■ AP Self Test 35.1

### True or false

1. If foreign investment in the United States increases, and U.S. investment in the rest of the world decreases, the current account shows an increase in exports and a decrease in imports.

2. The official settlements account balance is negative if U.S. official reserves increase.

3. The United States has a current account deficit.

4. If the United States has a surplus in its capital account and a deficit in its current account, the balance in its official settlements account is zero.

5. The United States is a net lender and a debtor nation.

6. If the United States started to run a current account surplus that continued indefinitely, it would immediately become a net lender and would eventually become a creditor nation.

7. Net exports equals the private sector balance minus the government sector balance.

8. In 2004, U.S. borrowing from abroad financed investment.

### Multiple choice

1. A country's balance of payments accounts records its
   a. tax receipts and expenditures.
   b. tariffs and nontariff revenue and government purchases.
   c. international trading, borrowing, and lending.
   d. its tariff receipts and what it pays in tariffs to other nations.
   e. international exports and imports and nothing else.

2. Which of the following are balance of payments accounts?
   i.   capital account.
   ii.  tariff account.
   iii. current account.
   a. i only.
   b. ii only.
   c. iii only.
   d. i and iii.
   e. ii and iii.

3. Which balance of payments account records payments for imports and receipts from exports?
   a. current account
   b. capital account
   c. official settlements account
   d. reserves account
   e. trade account

4. The current account balance is equal to
   a. imports − exports + net interest + net transfers.
   b. imports − exports + net interest − net transfers.
   c. exports − imports − net interest + net transfers.
   d. exports − imports + net interest + net transfers.
   e. exports − imports − net interest − net transfers.

5. If an investment of $100 million from the United Kingdom is made in the United States, the $100 million is listed as a ____ entry in the ____ account.
   a. positive; current
   b. negative; capital
   c. positive; capital
   d. negative; current
   e. positive; official settlements

6. If the United States receives $200 billion of foreign investment and at the same time invests a total of $160 billion abroad, then the U.S.
   a. capital account balance increases by $40 billion.
   b. current account must be in surplus.
   c. balance of payments must be negative.
   d. capital account balance decreases by $40 billion.
   e. official settlements account balance increases by $40 billion.

7. In the balance of payments accounts, changes in U.S. official reserves are recorded in the
   a. current account.
   b. capital account.
   c. official settlements account.
   d. international currency account.
   e. international reserves account.

8. If a country has a current account balance of $100 billion and the official settlements account balance is zero, then the country's capital account balance must be
   a. equal to $100 billion.
   b. positive but not necessarily equal to $100 billion.
   c. equal to –$100 billion.
   d. negative but not necessarily equal to –$100 billion.
   e. zero.

9. A country that is borrowing more from the rest of the world than it is lending is called a
   a. net lender.
   b. net borrower.
   c. net debtor.
   d. net creditor.
   e. net loaner country.

10. A debtor nation is a country that
    a. borrows more from the rest of the world than it lends to it.
    b. lends more to the rest of the world than it borrows from it.
    c. during its entire history has invested more in the rest of the world than other countries have invested in it.
    d. during its entire history has borrowed more from the rest of the world than it has lent to it.
    e. during its entire history has consistently run a capital account deficit.

## Short Response Question

1. If its official settlements account equals zero, what will a country's capital account equal if it has a $350 billion current account deficit?

## Long Response Questions

1. What is recorded in the U.S. current account? In its capital account? In its official settlements account?

| Item | (billions of dollars) |
|---|---|
| U.S. investment abroad | 400 |
| Exports of goods and services | 1,000 |
| Net transfers | 0 |
| Change in official reserves | 10 |
| Net interest | 0 |
| Foreign investment in the United States | 800 |

2. The table above has balance of payment data for the United States.
   a. What is the capital account balance?
   b. What is the official settlements balance?
   c. What is the current account balance?
   d. What is the value of imports of goods and services?

3. What is a net borrower? A debtor nation? Is it possible for a nation to be net borrower and yet not be a debtor nation?

| Item | (billions of dollars) |
|---|---|
| Saving | 1,600 |
| Investment | 1,900 |
| Government expenditures | 1,300 |
| Net taxes | 1,400 |

4. The table above has data for the United States.
   a. What is the private sector balance?
   b. What is the government sector balance?
   c. What is net exports?

## CHECKPOINT 35.2

■ **Explain how the exchange rate is determined and why it fluctuates.**

### Quick Review

- *U.S. interest rate differential* On the foreign exchange market, an increase in the U.S. interest rate differential increases the demand for dollars and decreases the supply of dollars.
- *Expected future exchange rate* On the foreign exchange market, a rise in the ex-

pected future exchange rate increases the demand for dollars and decreases the supply of dollars.

## Additional Practice Problems 35.2

1. The figure shows the supply and demand curves for dollars in the foreign exchange market.

   Exchange rate (yen per dollar)

   120

   110

   100

   $S_0$

   $D_0$

   Q
   Quantity (trillions of dollars)

   a. What is the equilibrium exchange rate?

   b. Suppose the U.S. interest rate rises so that the U.S. interest rate differential increases. Assume that the effect on the supply is the same as the effect on the demand. In the figure, show the effect of this change. Does the equilibrium exchange rate rise or fall? Does the equilibrium quantity of dollars exchanged increase or decrease?

2. How and why does an increase in the expected future exchange rate change the demand for U.S. dollars and the demand curve for dollars? How and why does an increase in the expected future exchange rate change the supply of U.S. dollars and the supply curve of dollars? What is the effect on the equilibrium exchange rate?

## Solutions to Additional Practice Problems 35.2

1a. The figure shows that the initial equilibrium exchange rate is 110 yen per dollar.

1b. The increase in the U.S. interest rate differential increases the demand for U.S.

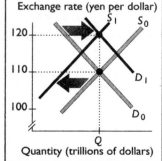

Exchange rate (yen per dollar)

120

110

100

$S_1$   $S_0$

$D_1$

$D_0$

Q
Quantity (trillions of dollars)

dollars and simultaneously decreases the supply of U.S. dollars. As a result the demand curve for dollars shifts rightward, from $D_0$ to $D_1$ and the supply curve of dol-

lars shifts leftward, from $S_0$ to $S_1$. The exchange rate rises. In the figure the exchange rate rises to 120 yen per dollar. Because the effect on the demand is the same as the effect on the supply, the curves shift by the same amount, so the equilibrium quantity of dollars exchanged does not change.

2. An increase in the expected future exchange rate increases the demand for U.S. dollars and shifts the demand curve rightward. The demand for U.S. dollars increases because at the current exchange rate people want to buy U.S. dollars now and sell them in the future at the higher expected exchange rate. An increase in the expected future exchange rate decreases the supply of U.S. dollars and shifts the supply curve leftward. The supply of U.S. dollars decreases because people would rather keep the dollars until they can sell them in the future at the higher expected exchange rate. Because the demand for dollars increases and the supply of dollars decreases, the current equilibrium exchange rate rises.

## ■ AP Self Test 35.2

### True or false

1. The U.S. foreign exchange rate changes infrequently.

2. If the exchange rate increases from 90 yen per dollar to 110 yen per dollar, the dollar has appreciated.

3. The larger the value of U.S. exports, the larger is the quantity of U.S. dollars demanded.

4. An increase in the U.S. exchange rate increases the supply of U.S. dollars and shifts the supply curve of dollars rightward.

5. A rise in the expected future exchange rate increases the demand for dollars and also the supply of dollars and might raise or lower the exchange rate.

6. The equilibrium U.S. exchange rate is the exchange rate that sets the quantity of dollars demanded equal to the quantity of dollars supplied.

7. An increase in the U.S. interest rate differential raises the U.S. exchange rate.

8. To prevent the price of the euro from falling, the European Central Bank might sell euros on the foreign exchange market.

**Multiple choice**

1. The foreign exchange market is the market in which
   a. all international transactions occur.
   b. currencies are exchanged solely by governments.
   c. goods and services are exchanged between governments.
   d. the currency of one country is exchanged for the currency of another.
   e. the world's governments collect their tariff revenue.

2. When Del Monte, an American company, purchases Mexican tomatoes, Del Monte pays for the tomatoes with
   a. Canadian dollars.
   b. Mexican pesos.
   c. gold.
   d. Mexican goods and services.
   e. yen.

3. If today the exchange rate is 100 yen per dollar and tomorrow the exchange rate is 98 yen per dollar, then the dollar ____ and the yen ____.
   a. appreciated; appreciated
   b. appreciated; depreciated
   c. depreciated; appreciated
   d. depreciated; depreciated
   e. depreciated; did not change

4. In the foreign exchange market, as the U.S. exchange rate rises, other things remaining the same, the
   a. quantity of dollars demanded increases.
   b. demand curve for dollars shifts rightward.
   c. demand curve for dollars shifts leftward.
   d. quantity of dollars demanded decreases.
   e. supply curve of dollars shifts rightward.

5. In the foreign exchange market, the demand for dollars increases and the demand curve for dollars shifts rightward if the
   a. U.S. interest rate differential increases.
   b. expected future exchange rate falls.
   c. foreign interest rate rises.
   d. U.S. interest rate falls.
   e. exchange rate falls.

6. As the exchange rate ____, the quantity supplied of U.S. dollars ____.
   a. rises; increases
   b. falls; increases
   c. falls; remains the same
   d. rises; decreases
   e. rises; remains the same

7. In the foreign exchange market, the supply curve of dollars is
   a. upward sloping.
   b. downward sloping.
   c. vertical.
   d. horizontal.
   e. identical to the demand curve for dollars.

8. Everything else remaining the same, in the foreign exchange market which of the following will increase the supply of U.S. dollars?
   a. The Japanese interest rate rises.
   b. The expected future exchange rate rises.
   c. The U.S. interest rate rises.
   d. The U.S. interest rate differential increases.
   e. The exchange rate falls.

9. When there is a shortage of dollars in the foreign exchange market, the
   a. demand curve for dollars shifts leftward to restore the equilibrium.
   b. U.S. exchange rate will appreciate.
   c. U.S. exchange rate will depreciate.
   d. supply curve of dollars shifts leftward to restore the equilibrium.
   e. supply curve of dollars shifts rightward to restore the equilibrium.

10. In the foreign exchange market, when the U.S. interest rate rises, the supply of dollars ____ and the foreign exchange rate ____.
    a. increases; rises
    b. increases; falls
    c. decreases; rises
    d. decreases; falls
    e. increases; does not change

11. A situation in which money buys the same amount of goods and services in different currencies is called
    a. exchange rate equilibrium.
    b. purchasing power parity.
    c. exchange rate surplus.
    d. exchange rate balance.
    e. a fixed exchange rate.

12. Interest rate parity occurs when
    a. the interest rate in one currency equals the interest rate in another currency when exchange rate changes are taken into account.
    b. interest rate differentials are always maintained across nations.
    c. interest rates are equal across nations.
    d. prices are equal across nations when exchange rates are taken into account.
    e. interest rates no longer affect the exchange rate.

**Short Response Questions**
1. Define "currency depreciation."
2. Define "currency appreciation."
3. If the U.S. interest rate rises, in the foreign exchange market what is the effect on the demand for U.S. dollars and the supply of U.S. dollars? On the U.S. exchange rate?
4. If the foreign interest rate rises, in the foreign exchange market what is the effect on the demand for U.S. dollars and the supply of U.S. dollars? On the U.S. exchange rate?
5. If people come to expect that the U.S. dollar exchange rate will rise in the future, in the foreign exchange market what is the effect on the demand for U.S. dollars and the supply of U.S. dollars? On the U.S. exchange rate?

**Long Response Questions**
1. If the exchange rate rises from 90 yen per dollar to 100 yen per dollar, has the dollar appreciated or depreciated? Has the yen appreciated or depreciated?
2. What is the relationship between the value of U.S. exports and the quantity of U.S. dollars demanded? Why does this relationship exist?
3. What is the relationship between the value of U.S. imports and the quantity of U.S. dollars supplied? Why does this relationship exist?
4. Everything else remaining the same, how will a rise in the Japanese interest rate affect the demand for dollars, the supply of dollars, and the U.S. exchange rate?

■ **FIGURE 35.1**

Exchange rate (yen per dollar)

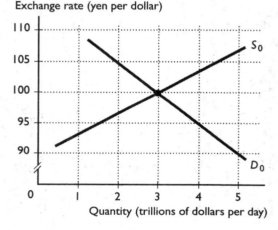

Quantity (trillions of dollars per day)

5. Figure 35.1 shows the foreign exchange market for U.S. dollars.
    a. What is the equilibrium exchange rate?
    b. The U.S. interest rate differential rises. In Figure 35.1, illustrate the effect of this change. What happens to the exchange rate?

**■ FIGURE 35.2**

Exchange rate (yen per dollar)

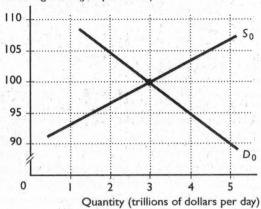

Quantity (trillions of dollars per day)

6. Figure 35.2 shows the foreign exchange market for U.S. dollars. Suppose people expect that the future exchange rate will be lower. In Figure 35.2, illustrate the effect of this change. What happens to the exchange rate? Has the exchange rate appreciated or depreciated?

7. If the Fed believes the exchange rate is too low and wants to raise it, what action does the Fed undertake in the foreign exchange market? What limits the extent to which the Fed can undertake this action?

# YOUR AP SELF TEST ANSWERS

## ■ CHECKPOINT 35.1

### True or false

1. False; page 890
2. True; page 890
3. True; page 890
4. False; page 890
5. False; page 892
6. True; page 893
7. False; page 894
8. True; page 895

### Multiple choice

1. c; page 890
2. d; page 890
3. a; page 890
4. d; page 890
5. c; page 890
6. a; page 890
7. c; page 890
8. c; page 890
9. b; page 892
10. d; page 892

### Short Response Question

1. The current account balance plus the capital account balance plus official settlements account balance sums to zero. So if the official settlements account equals zero, a $350 billion current account deficit means there is a $350 billion capital account surplus; page 890.

### Long Response Questions

1. The current account records payments for imports, receipts from exports, net interest and net transfers received from abroad. The capital account records foreign investment in the United States minus U.S. investments abroad. The official settlements account records changes in U.S. official reserves, the government's holding of foreign currency; page 890.

2. a. The capital account balance equals foreign investment in the United States minus U.S. investment abroad, which is $400 billion; page 890.

   b. The official settlements balance is the negative of the change in official reserves, or –$10 billion; page 890.

   c. The sum of the current account balance, the capital account balance, and the official settlements account balance is zero. The capital account balance is $400 billion and the official settlements account balance is –$10 billion, so the current account balance is –$390 billion; page 890.

   d. The current account balance equals exports minus imports plus net interest plus net transfers received from abroad. Net interest and net transfers are given as zero. The current account balance is –$390 billion and exports are $1,000 billion, so imports equal $1,390 billion; page 890.

3. A net borrower is a country that is borrowing more from the rest of the world than it is lending to the rest of the world. A debtor nation is a country that during its entire history has borrowed more from the rest of the world than it has lent to it. It is possible for a nation to be a net borrower but not be a debtor nation. A country can be a creditor nation and a net borrower. This situation occurs if a creditor nation is, during a particular year, borrowing more from the rest of the world than it is lending to the rest of the world; page 892.

4. a. The private sector balance equals saving minus investment, so the private sector balance is –$300 billion; page 894.

   b. The government sector balance equals net taxes minus government expenditures on goods and services, so the government sector balance is $100 billion; page 894.

   c. The sum of the private sector balance plus the government sector balance equals net exports, so net exports equals –$200 billion; page 894.

## ■ CHECKPOINT 35.2

**True or false**

1. False; page 897
2. True; page 898
3. True; page 898
4. False; page 902
5. False; pages 900, 903
6. True; page 904
7. True; page 905
8. False; page 908

**Multiple choice**

1. d; page 897
2. b; page 897
3. c; pages 897-898
4. d; page 898
5. a; page 900
6. a; page 901
7. a; page 902
8. a; page 903
9. b; page 904
10. c; pages 903, 905
11. b; page 906
12. a; page 908

**Short Response Questions**

1. Currency depreciation is the fall in value of the currency on the foreign exchange market. For instance, if the U.S. dollar falls from 120 yen per dollar to 110 yen per dollar, the U.S. dollar has depreciated; page 897.

2. Currency appreciation is the rise in value of the currency on the foreign exchange market. For instance, if the U.S. dollar rises from 120 yen per dollar to 130 yen per dollar, the U.S. dollar has appreciated; page 897.

3. The demand for U.S. dollars increases and the supply of U.S. dollars decreases. The U.S. exchange rate rises (appreciates); pages 900, 903, 905.

4. The demand for U.S. dollars decreases and the supply of U.S. dollars increases. The U.S. exchange rate falls (depreciates); pages 900, 903, 905.

5. The demand for U.S. dollars increases and the supply of U.S. dollars decreases. The U.S. exchange rate rises (appreciates); pages 900, 903, 905.

**Long Response Questions**

1. When the exchange rate rises from 90 yen per dollar to 100 yen per dollar, the dollar appreciates because the dollar buys more yen. The yen depreciates because it now takes 100 yen to buy a dollar instead of 90 yen to buy a dollar; pages 897-898.

2. The larger the value of U.S. exports, the larger is the quantity of U.S. dollars demanded. This relationship exists because U.S. firms want to be paid for their goods and services in dollars; page 898.

3. The larger the value of U.S. imports, the larger the quantity of U.S. dollars supplied. This relationship exists because U.S. consumers must pay for their imports in foreign currency. To obtain foreign currency, U.S. consumers supply dollars; page 901.

4. An increase in the Japanese interest rate decreases the U.S. interest rate differential. The smaller the U.S. interest rate differential, the smaller is the demand for U.S. assets and the smaller the demand for dollars. And the smaller the U.S. interest rate differential, the greater is the demand for foreign assets and the greater is the supply of dollars. So when the Japanese interest rate rises, the demand for dollars decreases, the supply of dollars increases, and the equilibrium exchange rate falls; page 906.

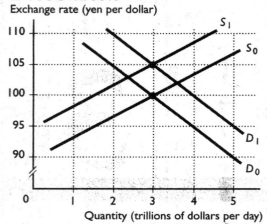

■ **FIGURE 35.3**

Exchange rate (yen per dollar)

Quantity (trillions of dollars per day)

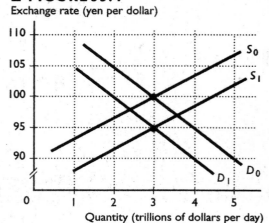

■ **FIGURE 35.4**

Exchange rate (yen per dollar)

Quantity (trillions of dollars per day)

5. a. The equilibrium exchange rate is 100 yen per dollar; page 904.

   b. The increase in the U.S. interest rate differential increases the demand for dollars and shifts the demand curve from $D_0$ to $D_1$ in Figure 35.3. The increase in the U.S. interest rate differential also decreases the supply of dollars and shifts the supply curve from $S_0$ to $S_1$. The exchange rate rises. In the figure, the exchange rate rises to 105 yen per dollar; page 905.

6. The fall in the expected future exchange rate decreases the demand for dollars and increases the supply of dollars. The demand curve shifts leftward from $D_0$ to $D_1$ and the supply curve shifts rightward from $S_0$ to $S_1$. The exchange falls from 100 yen per dollar to 95 yen per dollar in Figure 35.4. The exchange rate depreciates; page 905.

7. If the Fed wants to raise the exchange rate, it will buy dollars. The Fed would have to sell U.S. official reserves to buy dollars. The Fed is limited by its quantity of official reserves. If the Fed persisted in this action, eventually it would run out of reserves and would be forced to stop buying dollars; page 908.

# AP Graphing Questions

## QUESTIONS

### ■ MICROECONOMICS

1. Shoes are a normal good and people's incomes increase. Using an appropriate diagram, determine the effect on the equilibrium price and quantity of a pair of shoes.

2. The price of cheese used to produce pizza rises. Using an appropriate diagram, determine the effect on the equilibrium price and quantity of pizza.

3. Define consumer surplus and producer surplus. Illustrate the consumer surplus and producer surplus in a competitive market that is producing the allocatively efficient quantity of output.

4. Using an appropriate diagram, illustrate the result when the government imposes a $1 per cup tax on coffee paid by the suppliers. Define tax incidence and explain how the elasticity of demand affects tax incidence.

5. Using an appropriate diagram, explain the deadweight loss that results from a negative externality in an unregulated competitive market.

6. Illustrate the case of a perfectly competitive firm that is earning an economic profit. Indicate the amount of the economic profit.

7. Compare the price and quantity set by a single-price monopoly to the price and quantity set by a perfectly competitive market with the same costs as the monopoly.

### ■ MACROECONOMICS

1. Golf balls and golf clubs are complements. The price of golf clubs falls. Using an appropriate diagram, determine the effect on the equilibrium price and quantity of golf balls.

2. New technology for producing memory chips is developed. Using an appropriate diagram, determine the effect on the equilibrium price and quantity of memory chips.

3. The nation's population increases. Using a diagram of the labor market, determine the effect on the full-employment amount of employment.

4. The economy emerges from a recession so investment by business firms is more profitable. Using an appropriate diagram, determine the effect on the real interest rate and quantity of investment.

5. The Federal Reserve increases the quantity of money. Using an appropriate diagram, explain the effect on the interest rate. What will be the short effect on real GDP and the price level?

6. Using an aggregate demand/aggregate supply model, determine the short-run effect on the price level and real GDP from an increase in government expenditures.

7. If the price of oil rises, using an aggregate demand/aggregate supply model, determine the short-run effect on the price level and real GDP.

**NOMICS**

(...hoes)

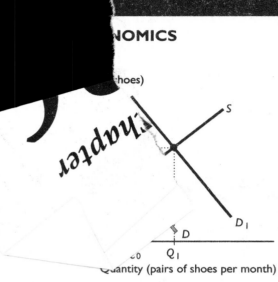

Quantity (pairs of shoes per month)

1. The increase in income increases the demand for a normal good. The demand curve shifts rightward and, as illustrated in Figure 36.1, the equilibrium price of a pair of shoes rises from $P_0$ to $P_1$ and the equilibrium quantity increases from $Q_0$ to $Q_1$; chapter 4.

### ■ FIGURE 36.2
Price (dollars per pizza)

2. The rise in the price of the cheese used to produce pizza increases the cost of producing pizza. The supply curve shifts leftward and, as illustrated in Figure 36.2, the equilibrium price of a pizza rises from $P_0$ to $P_1$ and the equilibrium quantity decreases from $Q_0$ to $Q_1$; chapter 4.

### ■ FIGURE 36.3
Price (dollars per unit)

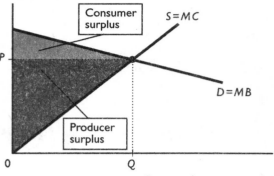

Quantity (units per month)

3. Consumer surplus is the marginal benefit of a good minus the price paid for it, summed over the quantity consumed. Producer surplus is the price of a good minus the marginal cost of producing it, summed over the quantity produced. The demand curve shows the marginal benefit and the supply curve shows the marginal cost. So, as illustrated above, the consumer surplus is the area below the demand curve and above the price and the producer surplus is the area below the price and above the supply curve; chapter 6.

### ■ FIGURE 36.4
Price (dollars per cup of coffee)

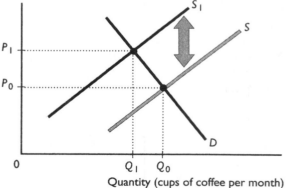

Quantity (cups of coffee per month)

4. The one dollar per cup tax on a cup of coffee paid by suppliers is like an increase in cost to the suppliers. The supply decreases and, as

illustrated in Figure 36.4, the supply curve shifts leftward. The vertical distance between the initial supply curve, $S$, and the supply curve with the tax, $S_1$, indicated by the length of the grey arrow, equals the amount of the tax, \$1 in this case. The price rises but not by the full amount of the tax. Tax incidence refers to the division of the burden of a tax between the buyers and the sellers. For a given elasticity of supply, the more inelastic the demand, the larger the share of a tax paid by the buyers; chapter 8.

■ **FIGURE 36.5**

Price (dollars per unit)

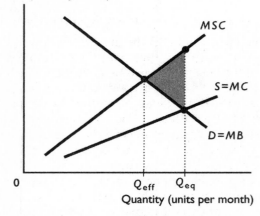

5. The quantity produced in an unregulated, competitive market is the equilibrium quantity, where the supply and demand curves intersect. In Figure 36.5, the quantity produced is $Q_{eq}$. If there is a negative externality, the marginal social cost curve, $MSC$, lies above the marginal private cost curve, $MC$, because the marginal social cost includes costs omitted (the external costs) from the marginal private cost. The allocatively efficient quantity is the quantity that sets the marginal social benefit equal to the marginal (social) cost, which is $Q_{eff}$ in the figure. As a result, an unregulated competitive market over-produces compared to the efficient quantity and there is a deadweight loss, equal to the area of the darkened triangle in the figure; chapter 9

■ **FIGURE 36.6**

Price and cost (dollars per unit)

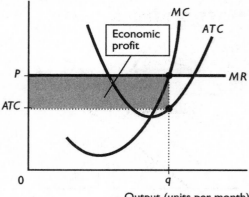

Output (units per month)

6. Figure 36.6 illustrates a perfectly competitive firm. To maximize its profit, the firm produces where $MR$ equals $MC$, which means that the firm produces $q$. The price is $P$. The firm is earning an economic profit because $P > ATC$. The amount of the economic profit equals the amount of the gray area; chapter 13.

■ **FIGURE 36.7**

Price and cost (dollars per unit)

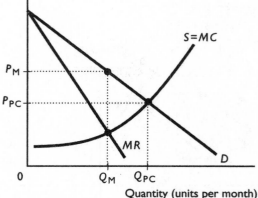

Quantity (units per month)

7. A perfectly competitive market produces where the demand and supply curves intersect, which is $Q_{PC}$ in Figure 36.7. The equilibrium price is $P_{PC}$. A monopoly produces where its marginal revenue and marginal cost curves intersect, which is $Q_M$ in the figure. The price is set from the demand curve as $P_M$. The monopoly produces less and sets a higher price; chapter 14.

# ■ MACROECONOMICS

## ■ FIGURE 36.8

Price (dollars per golf ball)

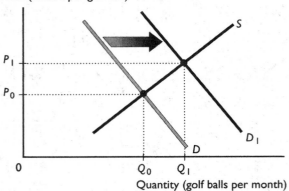

Quantity (golf balls per month)

1. The fall in the price of a complement increases the demand for golf balls. The demand curve shifts rightward and, as illustrated in Figure 36.8, the equilibrium price of a golf ball rises from $P_0$ to $P_1$ and the equilibrium quantity increases from $Q_0$ to $Q_1$; chapter 4.

## ■ FIGURE 36.9

Price (dollars per memory chip)

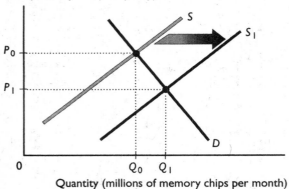

Quantity (millions of memory chips per month)

2. The new technology increases the supply of memory chips. The supply curve shifts rightward and, as illustrated in Figure 36.9, the equilibrium price of a memory chip falls from $P_0$ to $P_1$ and the equilibrium quantity increases from $Q_0$ to $Q_1$; chapter 4.

## ■ FIGURE 36.10

Real wage rate (2000 dollars per hour)

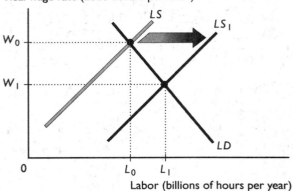

Labor (billions of hours per year)

3. The increase in population increases the supply of labor. The labor supply curve shifts rightward and, as illustrated in Figure 36.10, the equilibrium quantity of employment increases from $L_0$ to $L_1$. The equilibrium quantity of employment *is* the full-employment level of employment, so the full-employment level of employment increases from $L_0$ to $L_1$; chapter 23.

## ■ FIGURE 36.11

Real interest rate (percent per year)

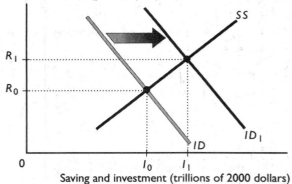

Saving and investment (trillions of 2000 dollars)

4. Because investment is more profitable, investment demand increases. The investment demand curve shifts rightward and, as illustrated in Figure 36.11, the equilibrium real interest rate rises from $R_0$ to $R_1$ and the equilibrium quantity of investment increases from $I_0$ to $I_1$; chapter 24.

■ **FIGURE 36.12**

Nominal interest rate (percent per year)

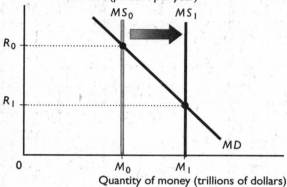

Quantity of money (trillions of dollars)

5. The increase in the quantity of money shifts the supply of money curve rightward from $MS_0$ to $MS_1$. As illustrated in Figure 36.12, the equilibrium (nominal) interest rate falls from $R_0$ to $R_1$. In the short run, the fall in the nominal interest rate lowers the real interest rate so that investment increases. In turn, the increase in investment increases aggregate demand so that in the short run, the price level rises and real GDP increases; chapters 28, 29, and 31.

■ **FIGURE 36.13**

Price level (GDP deflator, 2000 = 100)

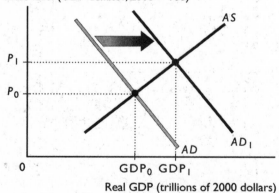

Real GDP (trillions of 2000 dollars)

6. An increase in government expenditures increases aggregate demand because government expenditures are a part of aggregate demand. The aggregate demand curve shifts rightward, as illustrated in Figure 36.13. In the short run, the price level rises, from $P_0$ to $P_1$ in the figure and real GDP increases, from $GDP_0$ to $GDP_1$ in the figure; chapters 29 and 31.

■ **FIGURE 36.14**

Price level (GDP deflator, 2000 = 100)

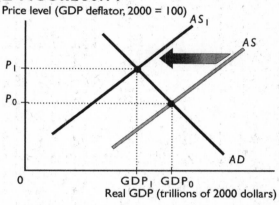

Real GDP (trillions of 2000 dollars)

7. An increase in the price of oil increases firms' costs and thereby decreases aggregate supply. The aggregate supply curve shifts leftward, as illustrated in Figure 36.14. In the short run, the price level rises, from $P_0$ to $P_1$ in the figure and real GDP decreases, from $GDP_0$ to $GDP_1$ in the figure; chapter 29.